Crossroads of War

Crossroads of War

A HISTORICAL ATLAS OF THE MIDDLE EAST

IAN BARNES

with

Malise Ruthven

THE BELKNAP PRESS *of* HARVARD UNIVERSITY PRESS

Cambridge, Massachusetts, and London, England

2014

Cambridge, Massachusetts
London, England
2014

Printed in the United States of America

Library of Congress Cataloging-in-Publication Data

Barnes, Ian, 1946– author.
Crossroads of war : a historical atlas of the Middle East / Ian Barnes with Malise Ruthven.
pages cm
Includes bibliography references and index.
ISBN 978-0-674-59849-2 (alk. paper)
1. Middle East—Historical geography—Maps. 2. Middle East—History—Maps.
I. Ruthven, Malise, author. II. Title.

G2206.S1B3 2014
911'.56—dc23
2014014159

Contents

INTRODUCTION 6
Geography of the Middle East 14

ANCIENT TIMES 18
First Towns, Cities, and Armies 20
Mesopotamia and Sargon the Great c. 2279 BCE 24
Babylonian Empire c. 2000–1500 BCE 26
Hittite Empire 30
Egypt's New Kingdom c. 1550–1077 BCE 34
The Sea Peoples 36
Battle of Megiddo 1457 BCE 38
Battle of Kadesh 1275 BCE 39
States and Kingdoms 1500–c. 700 BCE 40
The Assyrian Empire 42
The Assyrian Empire under Tiglath-Pileser and the Struggle for Egypt 674–663 BCE 44
Nebuchadnezzar and New Babylon 625–539 BCE 46
Darius I and the Persian Empire c. 520 BCE 48
Xenophon and the Ten Thousand 50
Alexander of Macedon 356–323 BCE 52
Diadochi—Alexander's Warring Successors 56
Pompey and the Arrival of Rome 58
Battle of Carrhae 53 BCE 60
First Jewish Revolt 66–74 CE 62
Siege of Jerusalem 70 CE 64
The Parthian Wars 66
Rome's Eastern Borders 114–627 CE 68
Bar Kokhba Revolt 132–136 CE 70
The Sassanian Empire 224–651 CE 72
Palmyra and the East 260–273 CE 74
Trade Routes and their Protectors 76

BIBLICAL INTERLUDE 78
Hebrew Assault on Canaan 80
Struggles of the Judges 82
Saul, King of Israel c. 1021–1000 BCE 84
King David 86
Solomon's Empire 88
Shoshenk's Campaign in Palestine c. 925 BCE 90
Omri's Dynasty 92
Jewish Renaissance 94
Assyrian Attacks 96
Maccabean Revolt 167–160 BCE 98
Hasmonean Expansion 100
Herod 102

CLASH OF FAITHS 104
Armenia and the Battle of Avarayr 451 CE 106
The Middle East at the Dawn of Islam 108
Islam and Arab Conquests 632–718 110
Battle of Yarmuk 636 112
The Saljuq Turks 114
Battle of Manzikert 1071 116
Christian Crusades and Crusader Kingdoms 1095–1270 118
Saladin's Campaigns 1173–85 120
Horns of Hattin 1187 122
Battle of Arsuf 1191 124
Sunnis, Shi'ites, and Khariji 660–c. 1000 126
The Mongols and Ayn Jalut 1260 128
Mamluk Power 130
Timur the Lame's Dominions 1370–1405 132
Spoils of War—the Command of Trade Routes 712–1300 134
Ottoman Expansion 1328–1672 136
Struggle for Persia 1501–1785 138
Ottoman Decline 140
Rise of the Saudi State 1902–1929 142

EUROPEAN INTERVENTION 144
Napoleon's Egyptian Adventures 1798–1801 146
Muhammad Ali Pasha's Wars—Egyptian Expansion 1805–47 150
Arabi Pasha and British Intervention in Egypt 1882 152
The Dream of Israel 154
World War I—The Gallipoli Campaign 1915–1916 156
Palestine Front 1914–17 158
Mesopotamian Front 1914–18 160
Sykes-Picot Plan—Dividing the Ottoman Empire May 1916 162
T. E. Lawrence and the Arab Revolt 1916–18 164
The Road to Damascus 1917–18 166
Treaty of Lausanne and League of Nation Mandates 1923 168
The Arab Rising 1936–37 172
Iraq, Syria, and Persia April–September, 1941 174
El Alamein II 1942 176

TECHNOLOGY AND SOCIETY 178
Aliyah 1945–48 180
The First Arab-Israeli War 1948 182
The Fate of the Palestinians 1948 184
Suez—War of Collusion 188
Six-Day War—Israel and the Arabs 1967 192
Oil Power 194
The October War 1973 196
Israel in Lebanon and Gaza 1982–2012 198
Regional Fault Lines 200
Iran-Iraq War 1980–88 204
Gulf War 1990–91 (Operation Desert Storm) 206
Second Gulf War 2003–11 208
Arab Spring 210

Bibliography 212
Glossary 218
Index 220
Acknowledgements 224

INTRODUCTION

THE PORTION OF THE EARTH'S LANDMASS we now call the Middle East, consisting largely of arid steppelands framed by great river systems, saw a trickle of early humans coming out of Africa. Some of these pioneers created the first agricultural settlements that would eventually grow into towns and cities. These in turn developed military forces intent on controlling their districts, neighboring cities and, on occasion, entire regions.

These lands of the Fertile Crescent, extending from the Upper Nile through the Levant and into Mesopotamia, succored the early civilizations that sought to impose their power by force, leading to successive wars as rival empires sought control of the land-bridge linking Africa, Asia, and Europe. Throughout recorded history the Levantine Corridor has seen the movement of armed forces, as those who controlled this vital strip commanded the whole Near Eastern region.

The region was also the birthplace of four religions that competed with each other for political and cultural dominance. Zoroastrianism, Judaism, Christianity, and Islam all played their part in transforming existing states and constructing new ones, including Sassanian Persia, Biblical Israel, Byzantine Rome, and the empires of Islam. The prophecies of doom and messianic hopes proclaimed by these religions spawned the name of 'Armageddon' with its chilling connotations of global destruction—(though its origin in the Battle of Megiddo was doubtless more prosaic).

Unlike other historical conflicts, the wars that took place in this arc of territory acquired universal, even theological, resonances. Conflicts originating in local disputes or rivalries were etched, by religious propaganda, into the consciousness of peoples far removed, in time and space, from the places where they actually occurred. This cultural feedback, in turn, added symbolic, even transcendental, significance to the local conflicts in which they originated.

Such feedback poses a problem for historians. The texts originating in this area—most notably the Bible and the Koran—have had a more profound impact on the region's history than actual historical occurrences, such as the battles described in this atlas. Far from being reliable guides to history, the texts that have come down to us are for the most part partisan and tendentious accounts of events whose actual occurrence cannot be determined with any degree of certainty. As the famous African-American spiritual goes, "Joshua fit (fought) the Battle of Jericho and the walls came tumbling down". But the remains of that city, one of the world's most ancient, provide no unambiguous evidence that such an event ever happened. As Ian Barnes points out (p. 80), extensive archaeological work has shown that the destruction of the ancient walled city occurred some 300 years before the putative Hebrew invasion.

The narratives enshrined in religious literature are creative embellishments on living traditions: they tell us much about human psychology and motivation, and may perhaps connect us with remote ancestral figures from a past that cannot otherwise be recovered. But they are very far from being authentic or verifiable accounts of what actually happened.

The Biblical accounts of ancient Israel had long periods of oral gestation before being written down. Bible critics since Baruch Spinoza (1632–77) have dissected the various narratives that make up the text of the Bible, posing serious challenges to their historicity and relationship to actual people and events. The story of King David, regarded as the greatest ruler of ancient Israel conventionally described as living between c. 1040 and 970 BCE, is a case in point. Apart from some archaeological fragments found in Northern Israel in the 1990s that may refer to a King of the House of David, there are no references to him outside of the Bible. As the *Encyclopedia of Religion* states in its 2005 edition:

> "Excavations in Jerusalem itself, the great capital of David and Solomon in the Bible... have produced an almost total lack of evidence for significant tenth-century occupation... [It] is unlikely that Jerusalem in the tenth century was the capital of a large kingdom, or a city of any particular importance whatsoever, let alone the center of an empire stretching from Egypt to the Euphrates, as described in *1 Kings* 4:21 for Solomon's reign."

Similar considerations apply to the vexed and highly controversial question of Islamic origins. Until recently it was generally assumed that Islam—the youngest of the three Abrahamic religions—was born "not amidst the mystery which cradles the origin of other religions, but rather in the full light of history," as the orientalist Ernest Renan put it in 1883. The majority of textbooks and popular biographies still take Renan's line: Islam originated among the tribal Arabs of the Hejaz in western Arabia who heeded the divine messages of Muhammad their prophet. Fired by religious enthusiasm they conquered much of the world of late antiquity—from Spain to the Indus Valley and beyond —in the decades that followed his death in 632.

Some modern scholars, however, have challenged this view, which is based exclusively on Muslim sources dating from some two centuries after the events they purport to describe. The Koran makes allusions to battles, but there are no actual descriptions. The commentators who got to work on the Koran in the centuries after Muhammad's death supplied most of the details from the corpus of *hadiths,* 'traditions' or reports passed down orally from his contemporaries before being committed to writing. Like those of other religious founders, his biographies contain numerous allusions to miraculous events and supernatural forces.

According to the revisionist views advanced by a number of scholars since the 1970s, the events described in Muhammad's biographies, which were first written around two centuries after his death, may have occurred in Syria-Palestine rather than Arabia; and while this is both controversial and highly speculative, there can be no doubt that Jerusalem—Islam's second most holy place after Mecca—retained its pre-eminence as a religious center after the Arab conquest. The Dome of the Rock is the first great Islamic structure, built on the site of the Temple destroyed by the Romans in 70 CE. The magnificent octagonal building completed by the Umayyad caliph Abd al-Malik in 691 is constructed around a passage evidently designed for circumambulation. The usual explanation that it was built to commemorate Muhammad's miraculous 'ascension' (*miraj*), when he was miraculously transported from Mecca to Jerusalem, is problematic. There is no reference to this in the

Koranic inscriptions that embellish its magnificent tiled walls, though there are several references to Muhammad and to Jesus, son of Mary.

For medieval, as for modern, Palestinians and Israelis, the walled city exercises a symbolic power far in excess of its strategic location poised at the edge of the great rift valley above the Dead Sea (the lowest spot on Earth). No other city has ever produced such a cacophonous 'hum.' Its actual identity—a smallish city, with a fine covered souq, some beautiful churches, and mosques, and burgeoning suburbs—seems to drown in rhetorical feedback, the hum of divine salvation.

For medieval Christians, Jerusalem was the center of the world. So when Pope Urban II, a ruthless and ambitious Frenchman, launched the First Crusade in 1096 on the back of a populist campaign led by a charismatic preacher, Peter the Hermit, he struck a phenomenal chord. At that time European society was saturated with religious fear, while ordinary living was fraught with eternal hazards. Churches everywhere contained frescos or sculptures depicting the horrors of hell—devils gouging out the eyes of screaming sinners, living humans skinned and eternally roasted, nightmare visions carefully juxtaposed with images of the peace, tranquillity, and safety of heaven for the saved. Salvation depended as much on the strict observance of rituals and sacraments as on good deeds, such as being kind to the poor. As the 'mystical body of Christ' the Church alone had the keys to heaven, the realm of salvation that everyone sought.

Pope Urban's formula was simple. There was no avoiding the consequences of sin, but the slate could be wiped clean by going on the crusade. He judged that the experience would be sufficiently arduous to make the bargain meaningful. Vicious and violent misdeeds, the killings and other brutalities that were occupational hazards for medieval warriors and their thuggish entourages, would be canceled. The knightly classes, a disruptive element in society, could continue doing what they knew best, which was fighting and killing. Only now their energies would be directed towards the 'enemies of God' instead of their fellow Catholics.

And who were these enemies of God? The most obvious ones were bands of Turkish tribes from Central Asia, who were gradually moving into Byzantine territories. In 1071 they defeated the Imperial Army at Manzikert, opening the rich Anatolian pastures to migration. The ostensible excuse for Urban's appeal to arms was a request by the Emperor Alexius in Constantinople, whose territories were being taken over by these semi-nomadic invaders. These encroachments, however, had been going on for many decades without much bothering the papacy. The holy city of Jerusalem, scene of Christ's passion, and site of his crucifixion and tomb, had been under Muslim rule for four centuries without scandal, with Christians pilgrims generally free to travel there. The initial crusades had less to do with the Holy Land than with the consolidation and extension of papal power in the anarchic and faction-ridden lands of Western Europe.

Religious fervor added heroism to the conflict, but also cruelty: the heads of prisoners were paraded on spikes to humiliate and enrage the enemy; there were battlefields where dead horses are described as resembling hedgehogs because of the quantity of arrows sticking into them. Yet in its earlier phases the religious fervor unleashed by the Crusades was asymmetrical. The Muslim idea of the crusade embodied in the Arabic term *al-hurub al-salabiyya* ('the wars of the cross') only appeared in the course of the nationalist struggles in the nineteenth century. The crusaders' Muslim contemporaries employed less emotive, more secular language: 'the wars of the Franks.' Thomas Asbridge, a leading historian of the Crusades, has no doubt that the conflict was between the Franks and Levantines, rather than Christians and Muslims. "One fact is clear: in the Latin East, the primary division was not between Christians and Muslims but between Franks (that is to say, Latin Christians) and non-Franks (be they eastern Christian, Jewish or Muslim)."

The papacy's real agenda was revealed in the Fourth Crusade, when the crusaders sacked Constantinople in a campaign to install a short-lived puppet regime intended to extend papal rule over the eastern branches of Christendom. In the words of a Byzantine witness, the Franks thought nothing of violating nuns, "tearing children from mothers and mothers from children, treating the virgin with wanton shame in holy chapels, viewing with fear neither the wrath of God nor the vengeance of men." Another Greek writer contrasted the brutality of the westerners with the humane treatment the Muslim hero Saladin accorded to the people of Jerusalem, which he reconquered in 1187 (before it was again lost to Islam, briefly, in 1229). Asbridge suggests, however, that for all his energy in uniting Islam (which he achieved by destroying the brilliant civilization that had flowered in Egypt under the Shi'ite Fatimids) Saladin had "neither the will nor resources to complete the conquest of the Palestinian coastline." It would be left to the more ruthless and fanatical Mamluk Sultan Baibars, who held back the Mongol invaders at Ayn Jalut in 1260, to create the conditions leading to the exit of the Franks from Palestine in 1291. Yet, paradoxically, Muslim triumph in the Levant also marked the beginning of a much longer Islamic decline.

The relationship between the rise of the West and Muslim decline—a process that forms the background to many of the events shown in this atlas—has long been the subject of debate among historians. One important issue concerns the role of external factors such as the effects of the Mongol invasions, culminating in the destruction of Baghdad in 1258, contrasted with the plundering of the Americas, which vastly increased the wealth of Europe. But internal factors also played their part, with scholars contrasting the relative autonomy of European cities and corporations with their absence in the lands of Islam including the Levant. As an entity that exceeded the sum of its parts, the western city corporation, and the vast trading companies sustained by it, transcended generational mortality, facilitating the accumulation of wealth and its productive reinvestment. Islamic law, by contrast, mandated the distribution of wealth through rules of inheritance that impeded capital accumulation. And unlike the Roman legal system adopted in western Europe, Islamic law had no provision for corporate groups as legal persons. The scientific and philosophical advances that produced the industrial revolution in Europe led to profound changes in relations between church and state, with the secular knowledge obtained by scientific inquiry outgunning the religious thought. The latter eventually adjusted itself, willingly or otherwise, accepting a reduced status in the hierarchy of cultural forms. Yet at the time of the Crusades this was far from appearing inevitable: there was every possibility that the 'take-off' of the scientific revolution would happen in the east rather than the west. As

Amin Maalouf, Arab writer and historian of the crusades puts it, at that juncture "the Arab world, from Spain to Iraq, was still the intellectual and material repository of the planet's most advanced civilization. Afterwards the centre of world history shifted decisively to the West."

A milestone in this seismic cultural shift was the replacement of the Isma'ili Shi'ite Fatimids—the most sophisticated and scientifically-minded of Egypt's dynasties—with the Sunni Ayyubids and their Mamluk successors. As Max Rodenbeck, historian of Cairo explains, the re-imposition of Islam's majority tradition under Saladin and his successors "came at the cost of restricting free inquiry." The great Isma'ili centers of learning that engaged in scientific and philosophical speculation were abolished or made into Sunni establishments. Al-Azhar, the university founded by the Fatimid Caliph al-Mu'iz in 970 became the bastion of Sunni orthodoxy it remains to this day. Well into the twentieth century the al-Azhar establishment resisted attempts at reform. As Rodenbeck puts it:

> "When it came about that the only education Cairo had to offer was religious, intellectual life withered. Plato was forgotten. The hereafter came to outweigh the here and now. Those scholars who did not succumb to Sufi mysticism sought perfection of form, of comportment, not perfection of mind. Debate about the correct Islamic manner of washing or eating, or over questions like whether a woman need perform ritual ablutions after a visitation by jinns, replaced philosophical conjecture and scientific invention."

It might well be argued that Egypt, the Middle East's most populous country and most influential cultural center, has yet to fully recover from Saladin's rule.

From 1517 Egypt and the Levant came under formal Ottoman control. It was not, however, until the nineteenth century—following Bonaparte's brief incursion—that Levantine societies really began to transform themselves under the impact of European power. Napoleon's conquest was far from being an unqualified success. Though he defeated the Mamluks at the Battle of the Pyramids before capturing Cairo, his efforts to introduce a new system of government by convening a 'General Divan,' composed of notables, lawyers, and Islamic scholars, and to win over the population by using Islamic rhetoric and sponsoring popular festivals, met with decidedly mixed responses. Following Napoleon's departure on board a frigate that had survived Nelson's attack on Abu Qir Bay, the marooned French army faced a series of popular revolts before being forced to leave by a combined force of British, Ottomans, and Mamluks. Nevertheless the French invasion sowed the seeds of the new Enlightenment thinking in Egypt and the Levant, fatally weakening Mamluk power and opening the way for the modernizing autocracy of Muhammad Ali and his successors.

Ottoman Sultans had governed mainly through local leaders known as 'ayan, notables. Many of these became wealthy by keeping the profits of trade or farming for themselves, sending only a little to the Sultan or Emperor's government. By 1800 most of the Ottoman Empire was under the sway of independent officials, with councils of 'ayan controlling the appointment of deputy governors and judges, and engaging in vital tasks such as preventing food shortages and maintaining public buildings.

The weakness of central government was one reason why the Ottomans lost so many of their European provinces to European rivals such as Austria and Russia. The national movements that threatened the Empire, starting with the Greeks in the 1820s, were all supported by outside powers, as was the emergence of Egypt as a virtually independent state under Muhammad Ali. Indeed it was mainly rivalry between Britain, France, and Russia that allowed the Ottoman Empire to survive at all. In the Crimean War (1853–56), Britain and France backed the Ottoman Empire against Russia, which was claiming rights over Christian holy places in Palestine: Jerusalem, as ever, was exerting its formidable symbolic power. Although the treaty that ended the war officially recognized the Ottomans as a European power on terms of formal equality, it limited Ottoman sovereignty by ending its control over shipping in the Black Sea and Danube River. European controls over customs due were imposed in Romania and Serbia. By the 1860s the Ottoman Empire was widely considered the 'Sick Man of Europe.'

The Ottoman rulers understood that reform was necessary if the Empire was to survive. In the 1770s they started hiring European advisors to teach mathematics—vital to artillery and naval operations—to their army and navy officers. From the 1830s they introduced a series of far-reaching administrative reforms—known as the Tanzimat—that increased the power of the state at the expense of the semi-autonomous civil society institutions, such as the *waqfs* (religious trusts) and mystical Sufi orders that had existed under the overall authority of the Sultans. Despite these reforms the Ottomans continued to lose territory with the loss of Libya, Albania, and most of their European possessions in a series of Balkan wars. The Empire's final collapse came with the First World War (1914–18). Having joined the Central Powers (Austria and Germany) against Britain, France, and Russia, the Empire lost its remaining Arab provinces to the three-pronged attack launched by Britain in Iraq and Palestine, and by the Arabian tribes led by Faisal ibn Hussain, son of the ruler of the Hijaz, with the help of the British adventurer T. E. Lawrence.

Although the Ottoman reforms failed to preserve the Empire they created the basis for the constitutional, secular order out of which Mustafa Kemal (known as Atatürk, 'father of the Turks') would create the Turkish Republic after the First World War.

Egypt fared worse than Turkey, losing its effective sovereignty to Britain under the 'veiled protectorate' from the 1880s and a series of one-sided treaties giving Britain rights of military occupation and control over the Suez Canal until the disastrous Suez adventure of 1956. There is no doubt that geopolitical and commercial interests—control over sea routes, colonial rivalries in Africa and substantial European investments—were instrumental in denying Egypt full autonomy before the abolition of the monarchy in 1952.

The discovery of oil, before World War I, added further levels of complexity to the region, as European countries grew increasingly dependent on oil. The oil nexus enabled tribal families in the Gulf and Saudi Arabia to monopolize political power, by controlling their countries' main source of wealth, without the need for a basic political contract between rulers and taxpaying citizens.

Oil has been both a blessing and a curse. Saudi Arabia, once one of the world's poorest countries, is now one of the world's most enigmatically powerful states, a land of contradictory polarities where the pre-modern codes of desert and oasis—puritanical, patriarchal, frugal, and austere—coexist and frequently clash with lavish displays of wealth and such emblems of modernity as air-conditioned shopping malls, designer boutiques, and four-lane highways flashing with super-charged vehicles driven exclusively by males. Thanks to oil, citizens of Saudi Arabia and the Gulf citizens can enjoy European standards of social welfare, health care, and free education. Yet intellectual and political freedoms are absent, and religious intolerance is rife. As the veteran scholar of Islam Bernard Lewis has commented, the absence of viable democratic institutions extends beyond the wealthy oil-bearing states:

> "What is entirely lacking in the Middle Eastern political tradition is representation and what goes with it—the idea that people elect others to represent them, that these others meet in some sort of corporate body, and that that corporate body deliberates, conducts discussions, and, most important of all, reaches decisions that have binding force ... In Roman law and in most of the European systems derived from it or influenced by it, there is such a thing as a legal person, a corporation, an abstraction that nevertheless functions as a legal person."

This absence of representation may be overstated, given the Ottoman experience of constitutional government, briefly in the 1870s and after 1908, which contributed to the vibrant electoral scene that followed the Second World War (despite a succession of military interventions and coups). More generally, however, the region has been characterized by the absence of viable systems of representation. This is partly explicable by the 'rentier system,' whereby governments dependent on revenues from foreign aid, tourism, and the extraction of oil and other minerals tend to foster a culture of dependency, with citizens relying on their rulers for jobs, services and favors without supplying the productivity necessary for viable economic development. As Marwan Muasher, a former Foreign Minister of Jordan has argued, the 'rentier system' makes authoritarianism difficult to challenge, with the political culture becoming one of 'no taxation, no representation.'

This democratic deficit is compounded, in my view, by a feature of the Islamic Sharia law, which has no concept of legal personality or the fictional personhood of groups, allowing organic clusters such as family, tribe, coterie, or sect to subvert the authority of public institutions at the expense of civil society. Under these conditions, real power tends to accrue to the armed forces, whose command and control systems, and institutional boundaries are determined by the exigencies of military logic rather than by structures responsive to the ebb and flow of political ideas and social needs.

In the long term, the participants in mass demonstrations that brought down the regime in Egypt in 2011, while responsible for a hugely impressive expression of public feeling, will need to overcome the inertia of military governance, with its networks of properties and other vested interests, in a country where the institutions of civil society have been weakened by decades of top-down, kleptocratic rule by the *mukhabarat* ('intelligence') state. Egypt's experiment with democracy lasted barely one year, after Muhammad Morsi, its first elected president, was overthrown in what amounted to a military coup. Where the armed forces have met a real challenge, as in Syria, the result has been a bitter civil war, where the 'default identities' of tribe and sect have come to the surface, with brutally savage consequences.

For all the innovations of modernity—from paved highways to radio, television, and social media—the birth lands of the world's three great monotheist religions continue to be plagued by their troublesome Abrahamic legacy. The symbolism of Jerusalem, and the aspirations surrounding it, continues to exercise its psychic hegemony. From the nineteenth century Jews from Eastern Europe began to join their co-religionists in Palestine, gradually translating the spiritual yearning for messianic redemption into the practical program of building a modern state in the land once occupied by their putative ancestors. The project was reinforced by a raft of contradictory ideas: Christian fundamentalists (including the British Foreign Secretary, Arthur Balfour, who wrote an all-important letter to Lord Rothschild favoring a Jewish homeland in Palestine); believers in national self-determination, in the tradition of US President Woodrow Wilson, who considered that Jews, as a nation without a territory must be entitled to one; imperialists who argued that a European state or presence in an otherwise hostile Levant would be a strategic asset for the West; the Zionists themselves—enlightened Jewish radicals who departed from rabbinical orthodoxy by arguing that redemption could be enacted, on earth, in the here and now, rather than in an ever-receding messianic, mystical future; and, most paradoxically and, tragically, by anti-Semites in Russia, Eastern Europe, and Nazi Germany, who considered Jews to be aliens deserving of death, making the Zionist project of a militarily powerful state into the necessary response to the all-too-palpable threat of genocide.

Given the recent struggles between the Middle East's protesting citizens and their governments on lands once occupied by the crusading *faranj* (Franks), and between indigenous people and a new group of settlers whose project for an occidental state in the Levant carries numerous echoes of Outremer, it is clear that despite the appearances of modernity, the tortuous conflicts affecting today's Levantines are strikingly similar to those that afflicted the region almost a millennium ago. Most of the indigenous people lack rights and suffer the burden of untrammeled arbitrary rule. The incomers who arrived in search of a solution to Europe's problem—its failure to accommodate its most vigorous and talented minority—now have full civil rights and a system of accountable government which, for reasons of religious identity, they seem unable, or unwilling, to extend beyond their fortified garrison state. Nourished from afar, the Crusader states proved unsustainable once the impulse for settlement had abated. Today a new Outremer, remains all-powerful, like its medieval predecessors. But there is no guarantee that in an increasingly hostile environment it can maintain this pre-eminence indefinitely.

Malise Ruthven
London, April 2014

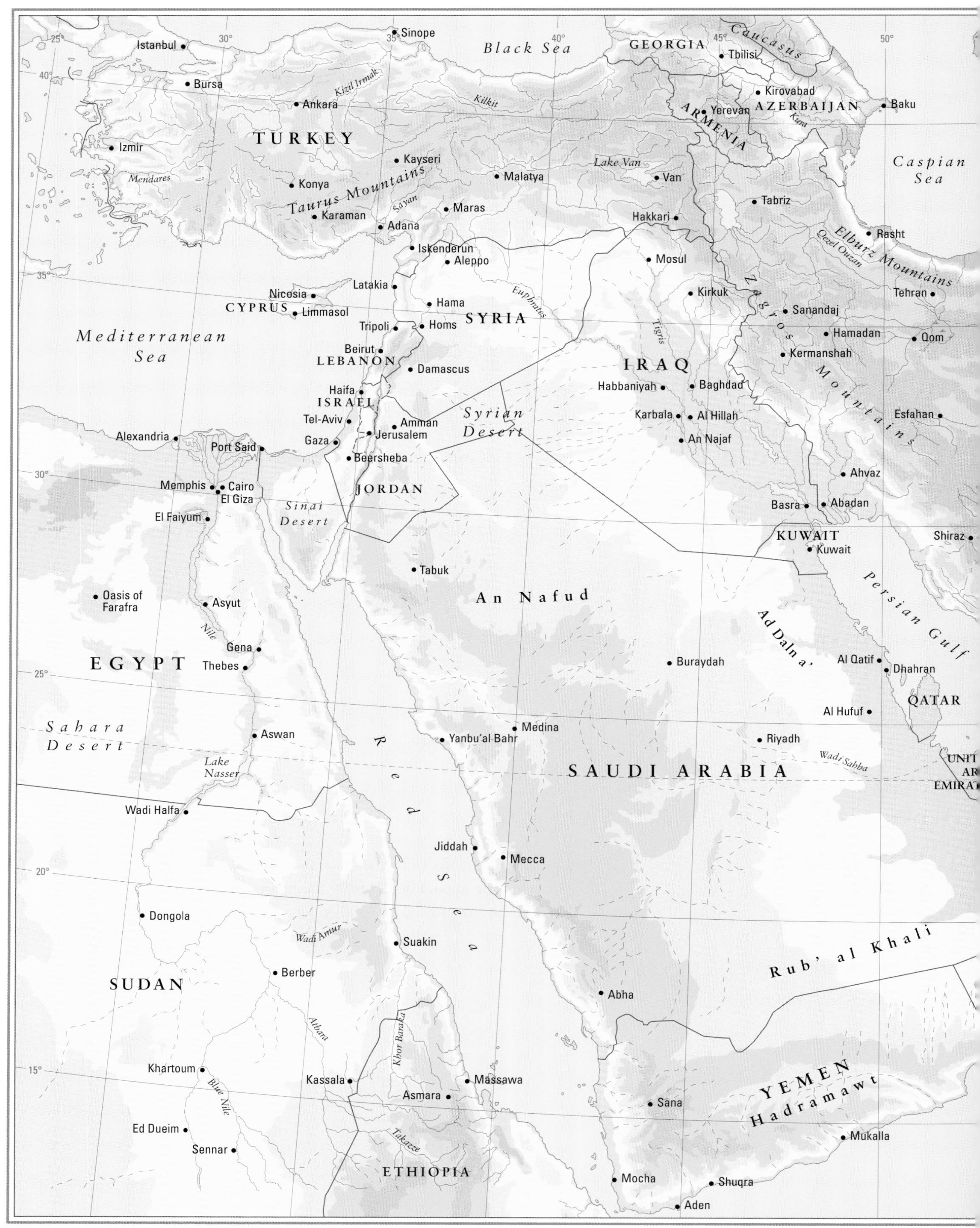

Istanbul
Sinope
Black Sea
GEORGIA
Caucasus
Tbilisi
Bursa
Kizil Irmak
Kilkit
Kirovabad
Ankara
Yerevan
AZERBAIJAN
Baku
ARMENIA
Kura
TURKEY
Izmir
Kayseri
Lake Van
Caspian Sea
Mendares
Konya
Taurus Mountains
Malatya
Van
Sayan
Tabriz
Karaman
Maras
Adana
Hakkari
Rasht
Iskenderun
Elburz Mountains
Aleppo
Mosul
Qezel Ouzan
Latakia
Nicosia
Euphrates
Kirkuk
Tehran
CYPRUS
Limmasol
Hama
Zagros Mountains
Sanandaj
Tripoli
Homs
SYRIA
Tigris
Mediterranean Sea
Hamadan
Qom
Beirut
LEBANON
Kermanshah
Damascus
IRAQ
Haifa
ISRAEL
Habbaniyah
Baghdad
Syrian Desert
Tel-Aviv
Amman
Karbala
Al Hillah
Esfahan
Alexandria
Jerusalem
Gaza
An Najaf
Port Said
Beersheba
Memphis
Cairo
El Giza
JORDAN
Ahvaz
Sinai Desert
Basra
Abadan
El Faiyum
KUWAIT
Kuwait
Shiraz
Tabuk
Oasis of Farafra
Asyut
An Nafud
Persian Gulf
Ad Dalna'
Nile
Gena
EGYPT
Thebes
Buraydah
Al Qatif
Dhahran
QATAR
Al Hufuf
Medina
Sahara Desert
Aswan
Yanbu'al Bahr
Riyadh
Wadi Sahba
Lake Nasser
SAUDI ARABIA
UNIT
AR
EMIRA
Red Sea
Wadi Halfa
Jiddah
Mecca
Dongola
Wadi Amur
Suakin
Rub' al Khali
Berber
SUDAN
Abha
Atbara
Khor Baraka
Khartoum
Kassala
Massawa
Blue Nile
Asmara
YEMEN
Sana
Hadramawt
Ed Dueim
Mukalla
Takazze
Sennar
ETHIOPIA
Mocha
Shuqra
Aden
25°
30°
35°
40°
45°
50°
40°
35°
30°
25°
20°
15°

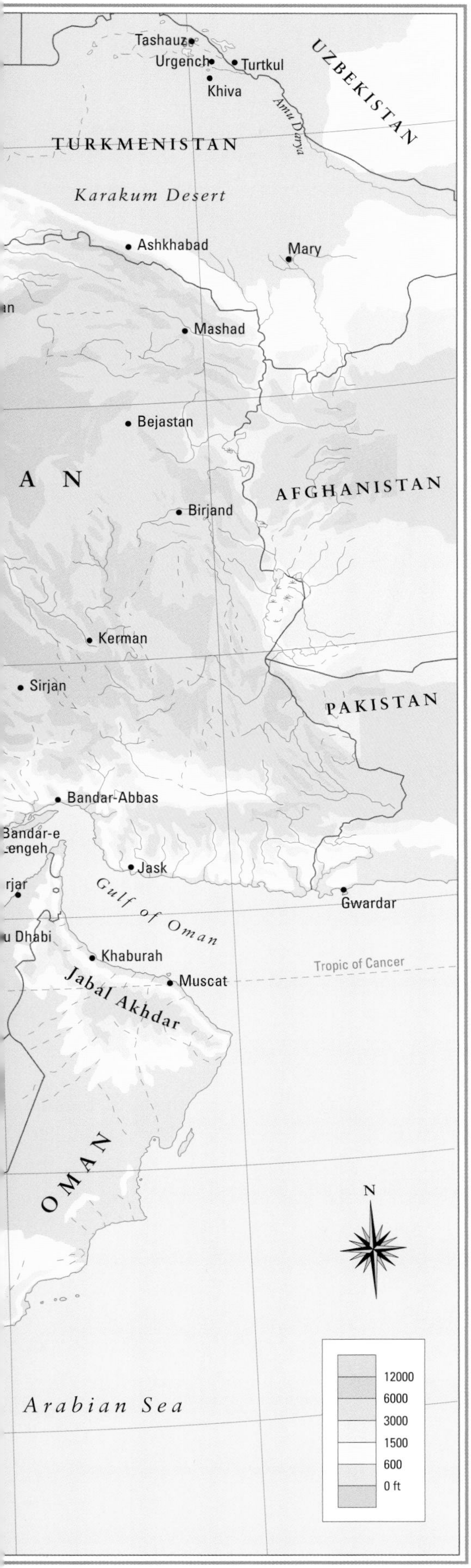

Geography of the Middle East

The Middle East, in ancient times, gave rise to great civilizations which evolved along two major river systems. The Nile supported the Egyptians and the Mesopotamians lived on the banks of the Tigris and Euphrates rivers. Between the two is a parched desert, the Dead Sea, and Palestine, a narrow corridor of land providing the only fertile strip from the Persian Gulf to the Nile Valley. This Levantine conduit was a choke point between Africa and Eurasia, a route through which armies, seeking conquest, were forced to travel. Command over such a small link territory was important in order to control trade from the East to the Mediterranean.

Rising in the complex of great African lakes which span the Equator and the Ethiopian Highlands, the White and Blue Nile unite to form the River Nile, which winds through the Sudan and the eastern end of the Sahara Desert until it unfolds into the fan-shaped swamp of river mouths and marshes which make up its delta. For most of its journey, the river flows through desert, with minimal rainfall and no tributaries to augment it. The people who drained the marshes around the delta and learned to make use of the river formed one of the oldest civilizations of the ancient world. The river was the unifying force for the peoples who lived along it. Its waters and the silt it left behind after the annual floods from the mountains of Ethiopia turned its banks into rich agricultural lands and made Egypt the most dependable source of food in the eastern Mediterranean. Power shifted between the cities of the Nile delta—Memphis in Lower Egypt, and Thebes, the capital of Upper Egypt, which ended where the First Cataract interrupted navigation from the coast. Beyond the First Cataract lay Nubia, the Kingdom of Kush, and, eventually, tropical Africa.

Beyond the desert to the east of Palestine was Mesopotamia, drained by both the Tigris and Euphrates, which in ancient times entered the Persian Gulf separately, some 125 miles northwest of the present coastline. To the east, the region is bordered by a long mountainous area stretching from India to Turkey. Between the mountains and the desert, Mesopotamia was inhabited, like Egypt, by civilizations that had learned to control the waters of the Euphrates and Tigris rivers for their agriculture. Political power was located at various centers—Sumer and Babylonia near the Persian Gulf, straddling the River Euphrates, and Assyria about 435 miles to the north on the River Tigris. Beyond Assyria was the land of the Mitanni. For all its apparent vitality and the growth of dynamic states, Mesopotamia was frequently threatened by raids from eastern tribes from the Zagros Mountains, and no single power managed to dominate all Mesopotamia for long.

To the north of Syria, the main political power was the Hittite Empire, which comprised most of central Anatolia. Around its western borders were states like Ahhiyawa, Arzawa, and Lukka. The Hittites briefly extended their power into the 'fertile crescent,' but their less fertile land had nothing comparable to the great rivers to give it continuity, and they were overrun by migrants from the west. Throughout the 'fertile crescent,' from the Persian Gulf to the borders of Egypt, independent nomadic shepherds roamed the sparse areas of pasture between the desert and the fertile land. When pasture ran out owing to climatic variations, people often moved to reliably fertile Egypt. The Hebrews were one such group and some of them became forced labor in Egypt.

The name Palestine is derived from Philistine, one of the Sea Peoples who came, perhaps, from the Aegean or western Anatolia at the end of the second millennium BCE and briefly dominated the southern part of the land bridge from the Jordan Valley to the Mediterranean. We come to Canaan, that vital conduit of fertile territory that will often appear in our narrative. The Canaanites were urban dwellers and their coastal cities were renowned for mercantile shipping of goods along international trade routes. Canaan's long desert frontier to the east exposed it to penetration from nomadic desert peoples, including the Hebrews themselves, while its strategic position between Egypt to the south and the Mesopotamian and Hittite peoples of the north and east made it a politically sensitive area. It seldom enjoyed peace, however its peoples profited from the trade routes that passed through it.

Traveling north, the route from Egypt passed into the coastal area. The route turned northeast, inland to pass through the town of Aphek and then further northwards to the ridge of Mount Carmel. The Philistines had settled in this coastal plain, establishing themselves at Gaza, Ashkelon, and Ashdod near the coast, and at Gath and Ekron further inland to the south of Aphek. Minor roads led eastwards from the plain, ascending the lowland hills of the Shephelah, which was densely populated, to the hill country of Judah and the deep rift valley of the Salt Sea, now known as the Dead Sea, 1,285 feet below sea level. Beyond the sea lie mountain ridges, with steep gullies running down into the rift valley, and beyond these mountains is desert.

The Judean hills run northwards, parallel with the Jordan Valley, until they turn northwest to meet the Great Sea, as the Mediterranean was called, at Mount Carmel and form the northern limits of the coastal plain. The major coastal route crossed the Carmel ridge to enter the Plain of Jezreel at the ancient fortress of Megiddo, where it split. A western branch hugged the coast and an eastern branch led to Hazor and Damascus. This valley is especially fertile and it runs from the Mediterranean to the Jordan Valley, which is still more than 600 feet below sea level where the River Jordan leaves the Sea of Galilee. This lake was also called the Sea of Chinnereth in the Bible's Old Testament, and variously the Sea of Galilee, Lake of Genneraret, and Sea of Tiberias in the New Testament.

Further northwards, between the upper Jordan Valley and the sea, the land rises steeply into Upper Galilee. Above the Sea of Galilee was Lake Huleh, a small expanse of water now only marshland, just about at sea level, and the site of a crushing defeat of the Crusader army led by King Baldwin III of Jerusalem in 1157. At the eastern side of the very top of the Jordan Valley is Mount Hermon with its snow-covered peak, which marked the northern limits of Palestine or Canaan. The road to Damascus and Mesopotamia passed south of Hermon. The King's Highway, a route used mainly by nomads, ran from Damascus south to Elath, situated on the Red Sea.

The lands which marked the traditional limits of the ancient land of Israel were Beersheba in the south, and Dan in the north. The area contains extreme contrasts including mountain ridges and the lowest point on earth, with extremely fertile land and near desert. Such conditions led to occupation by many kinds of peoples with widely varied ways of life. The land supported settled farming communities, often living in fortified settlements while farming surrounding agricultural lands and engaging in livestock farming. Nomadic shepherds traveled through marginal lands and semi-desert areas without any close association with fixed settlements. Sheep and goats were important for nomads, providing fleeces, skins, and milk, while being able to travel long distances. The nomads needed to ensure they did not compete with each others' routes lest they arrive at some marginal land that had just been grazed by others' herds. This explains why, in the Bible's *Genesis* 13, Abraham and his nephew, Lot, agreed to graze herds in different parts of Palestine because their herdsmen were quarreling over land. However, it was the international trading routes through the region that remained its most important feature.

International commerce was rich and varied in ancient times, with seagoing ships traveling vast distances. Goods from the Spice Islands of Indonesia made their way to the Middle East via both the Red Sea and the Persian Gulf. Chinese silks became very fashionable in the Middle East and they were traded onwards to Rome. Egypt and the Levant were also tied into Mediterranean trade, with special emphasis on Cyprus (Alashiya), noted for its copper, a vital ingredient in making bronze for tools and weaponry. Egypt was linked with Africa via Nubia and the land of Punt, the source of exotic animals and fragrant resins, used in perfumes and religious rituals. Contacts were made with civilizations of Crete and Mycenae. Pots containing perfumed oils from both Mycenae and Minoan Crete were items of trade and have been found in Cyprus, Egypt, the Sudan, and Carchemish. From the Levant, goods exported included glass beads, lapis lazuli, ivory, gold, alabaster, amethyst, ostrich eggs, and faience vases.

Geography has had a powerful impact upon military activity. Moving armies over vast distances has always required prodigious logistical effort. Traveling through wilderness and desert areas requires attention, especially to water supplies. Egyptian pharaohs often campaigned with a fleet supplying an army on the march. During the First World War, British General Allenby organized water pipelines to his front line divisions before he dared to advance towards Jerusalem from Egypt. Likewise, the United States army piped water to its own and allied armies deployed against Iraq after the invasion of Kuwait. Even the most capable of generals could fall foul of geographic conditions. Alexander the Great returned to Susa from the Indus Valley by marching through the Baluchi Gedrosian Desert, where his troops suffered badly with 12,000 dying of thirst during the 60-day march as well as losing many camp followers, livestock, and most of his baggage train.

ANCIENT TIMES

As settlements grew along the river valleys of the Tigris, Euphrates, and Nile, warfare between settled peoples and nomads was often no more than ritualized threat with few casualties, but this could dissolve into bloody hand-to-hand combat with much higher rates of loss. At its cruelest, groups could wipe out others, killing men, women, and children.

As humanity grew in numbers, strong political authority developed to manage agriculture and irrigation, and to defend food supplies from potential enemies.

The emerging elite made decisions about how best to organize the 'state'; in so doing they developed military, political, and diplomatic techniques. This expression of political will was backed by the threat of military action—either for the defense of core territory or to expand the state's area of control, and therefore increase its potenial. Assassination and the deployment of terror tactics were techniques that were developed millennia ago, and are still in use in the modern world, as familiar then as they are now.

As to the nature of war itself, as states emerged ruled by what we might call Kings, their initial military investments were almost all defensive in nature. Offensive action by groups of infantry seemed to have been limited in scope and effect.

This changed after 1700 BCE, organized states now took the offensive and deployed chariots for the first time with the infantry playing a supporting role. Finally, sometime after 1000 BCE, truly disciplined infantry formations deployed on the battlefield alongside the infantry-trained cavalry appeared—the art of war that would hold sway over the battlefields of the Middle East, until the arrival of gunpowder, had evolved.

On the battlefield, equipment deployed falls into two categories—shock and missile. The original shock weapon was the prehistoric club, which evolved into the stone mace. In time, the shock weapon developed into the axe and the sword. Shock weapons constantly developed; in time, the javelin, spear, and pike (for thrusting) evolved. The latter was used to great effect by Philip of Macedon with his discipined phalanx, and was also used by his son, Alexander the Great, in his conquest of one of the greatest empires of antiquity. Missile weapons developed from the thrown stone to the use of a sling, which could deliver a killing blow at relatively long range. The development of bronze, then iron and steel, gave weapons added effectiveness and this occasioned new military tactics.

Alongside offensive weapons, defensive systems were developed. Shields were constructed out of wicker, leather, or wood, while leather and quilted cloth armor was designed, to be superseded by metal plates sewn on to cloth, and finally true body armor whether scale, lamellar, or mail. As metallurgy developed, breastplates, helmets, and other elements of body armor were manufactured. Thus equipped, soldiers marched towards the enemy to conquer or defend their lands. Tactics employed were the deployment of infantry, normally drawn from the poorest groups of society, while an aristocratic or warrior elite would operate around them. Additionally, there would be skirmishing troops armed with slings, bows, and javelins, seeking to disrupt the enemy ranks with these missiles.

In time, alongside the infantry, slow unmanageable chariots appeared, which were developed into very maneuverable weapons platforms. Guided by a driver, the chariot would contain an archer, and masses of chariots could rain down arrows on enemy infantry or run down retreating troops. Chariots were a main strike force until replaced by cavalry.

The task of these early armies was to fight a pitched battle and overwhelm the enemy before they could do the same. Over time, objectives changed and became broader than just defeating a neighboring city. Battles turned into large-scale campaigns to overwhelm the enemy, to exact tribute, and to seize booty. Many early armies were not professional and troops were encouraged by the prospect of loot to make them fight, as well as the fear or charisma of their leaders. When armies engaged on the battlefield, the mass, usually spearmen, stayed together in groups. The warrior elite in their chariots, or on horseback, who were on the flanks or in front with groups of archers or slingers, formed a forward skirmish line, seeking to disrupt the enemy before the infantry battle began. Harassing fire was usually laid down before a cavalry or infantry charge. The skirmishers, meanwhile, had moved to the flanks, or retreated through gaps created in their own force. Sometimes the charge would drive the enemy, terror-stricken, from the battlefield, but more usually the opposing forces would converge and engage in hand-to-hand butchery, this only ending when one side sensed defeat, or their leader was killed. Fear communicated itself quickly through the ranks. In disorganized retreat many of the defeated army would be slaughtered by the victors.

Seige craft remained an important element in making war. Evidence for this is depicted on Pharaoh Ramesses II's mortuary walls showing the Siege of Dapur, in Syria, in 1269 BCE and Assyrian palace reliefs from Nineveh, many of which are in the British Museum, in London. The latter shows the Siege of Lachish in 701 BCE. The town had a double line of walls with towers, a double gate, and was protected by a deep ditch and glacis. The Assyrians constructed ramps up which battering rams were hauled. A breach was made and the Assyrians entered the town.

Naval warfare occurred less often until the wars between the Greeks and Persians, but the first recorded sea battle took place around 1210 BCE, when the Hittite King, Suppiliuma II, defeated a Cypriot fleet, burning their ships at sea. Normally ships were used to transport troops and supplies, however the Greek city states developed warships, while the Persians used Egyptian and Phoenician vessels in the Graeco-Persian Wars. Ships fought by ramming or boarding. In 480 BCE, at the great naval battle of Salamis, in Greece, the Persians were ambushed and badly defeated. The Romans, famed for fighting on land, invented new techniques of naval warfare during the Punic Wars against Carthage. The *corvus* was a boarding bridge which could be lowered on to an enemy vessel, with its spiked end driving into the enemy's deck. The bridge allowed legionnaires to use infantry tactics on deck. Also deployed was the *harpax*, a grapnel fired by a ballista, to become entangled in the opposing ships' rigging, or other fittings, which could then be reeled in and boarded.

Towards the end of the Ancient period the main armies were those of the Persians, Greeks, Macedonians, and Romans. The Greeks were renowned for their hoplite phalanx, where each man protected his comrades, creating a cohesive group bond that allowed them to defeat a Persian army at Marathon, in 490 BCE.

The Persians tended to rely on their archers and cavalry, but their advantage in missile attack was not used effectively against Alexander the Great, and their horse archers were effectively countered by Alexander's Companion Cavalry. An inability to modify battle tactics cost the Persians their entire Empire.

The Romans created the most powerful army during the Ancient period, created around their heavily-armed infantry but also using specialized auxiliary forces, such as heavy cavalry and skirmishers, which were recruited from various parts of the Empire. They also developed different methods of fighting, by which the three infantry lines would allow the engaged front rank to pass back through the second line to the rear, so they could rest and refresh while the second line engaged. This could be carried out multiple times to prevent exhaustion and required intense discipline and training. The commands to implement this maneuver would be made by signal trumpet. Military efficiency made Rome the dominant power in the Middle East and a rival to Parthia.

First Towns, Cities, and Armies

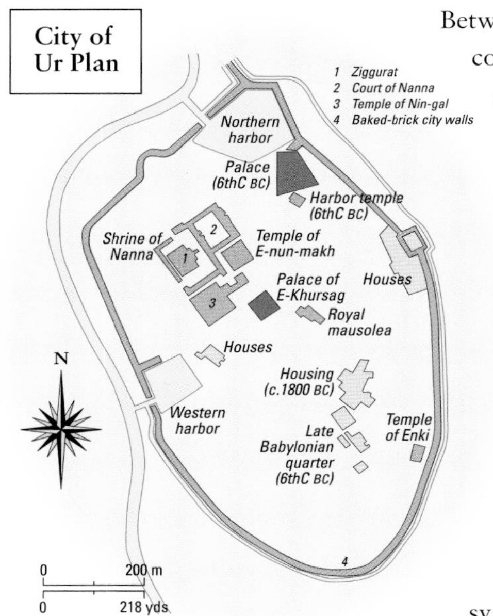

Between 8000 BCE and 6000 BCE, large communities arose in the two major river valleys of the Nile, the Tigris, and the Euphrates. Their growth and development was predicated upon the development of agriculture and the establishment of small settlements, some of which grew into large urban communities. The key to the development of urban settlements lay in the cultivation of cereals, made possible by extensive irrigation and the use of the flood plains adjacent to the river systems and deltas. Wheat and barley were grown extensively in Mesopotamia, while emmer and barley flourished in Egypt.

During the ninth and eighth millennia BCE, large and permanent communities developed for the first time, employing mud, brick, and stone as building materials. The oldest and most developed of these cities was Jericho (Tell es-Sultan) in the Jordan valley. Although largely an agricultural settlement in its origins, Jericho evolved into a major fortified regional center. As effective irrigation systems and agricultural techniques developed, settlements spread out geographically as once arid, semi-desert areas were brought under cultivation and villages were constructed on the edge of the riverine plains of Mesopotamia.

The importance of irrigation systems and of river systems cannot be overemphasized, since the control over them meant not only richer agricultural yields and growth, but also domination over rival communities. For example, one of the major strategic issues that rose in Mesopotamia in the second millennium was the control of the rivers Tigris and Euphrates, and the struggle over water rights, which led rival city-states, some thirty in number, to go to war over a few fields.

By the fourth millennium in Mesopotamia and pre-pharaonic Egypt, the ancient communities had moved away from subsistence farming, and more individuals could engage in other specializations, such as metalwork and building, along with other crafts. The rise of true civilizations was built upon the development of city-states, which was connected to, and stimulated by, a growth in commerce between Mesopotamia, Asia Minor, Greece, and Egypt. A single polity was formed when Upper and Lower Egypt were joined. These regions traded amongst themselves, with overland routes reaching the Indus Valley, Persia, and Afghanistan, which allowed the transport of gold, silver, copper, turquoise, and lapis lazuli.

As the states developed, the cities and governments became bureaucratic and manufacturing societies administered by a ruler and literate elites. These political entities differed greatly from earlier cities like Jericho, which had simply served as an agglomeration of population, since they demanded a high degree of social and economic organization. This necessitated the development of written languages, cuneiform in the Levant and Mesopotamia and hieroglyphics in Egypt. Writing allowed a greater sophistication in communication, and bestowed a degree of centralized control to a ruling class, which supervised the bureaucracies for the administrative functioning of societies, and organized a standing army for external, and sometimes internal, security. Increased literacy allowed the development of law codes, tax records, and accounts recording commercial transactions and, later, works of a religious, literary, and scientific nature. One such work was the *Epic of Gilgamesh*, which tells much about the belief systems of Sumerian society.

The Sumerian city of Ur was highly developed. Its center was dominated by a sacred enclosure containing temples and other religious buildings. One was a three-storey ziggurat, with its base storey alone being forty-nine feet high. A burial area lay to the south of the sacred area containing the deceased kings of Ur. One death pit contained Queen Puabi with 52 attendants to serve her in the afterlife. The grave goods included: a heavy gold headdress made of golden leaves, rings, and plates; a lyre encrusted with gold and lapis lazuli; gold, carnelian, and lapis lazuli beads; a chariot; necklaces; and belts. Further south was a residential area of private houses, mainly constructed of mud-brick, although the foundations were made of baked bricks. The ground floors of these houses contained the kitchen, guest room, store-rooms, and servants' quarters while the first floor included the living rooms.

By 2500 BCE, Ur was a major center of trade and manufacturing, situated on the coast with harbors connected to the sea by canal. The city was enclosed by a large sloping, mud-brick rampart surmounted by walls of baked brick. The city enclosed 148 acres with a population of some 20,000, and beyond the walls were substantial suburbs extending up to a mile. Between and beyond the suburbs lay the irrigated fields which supplied the city with agricul-

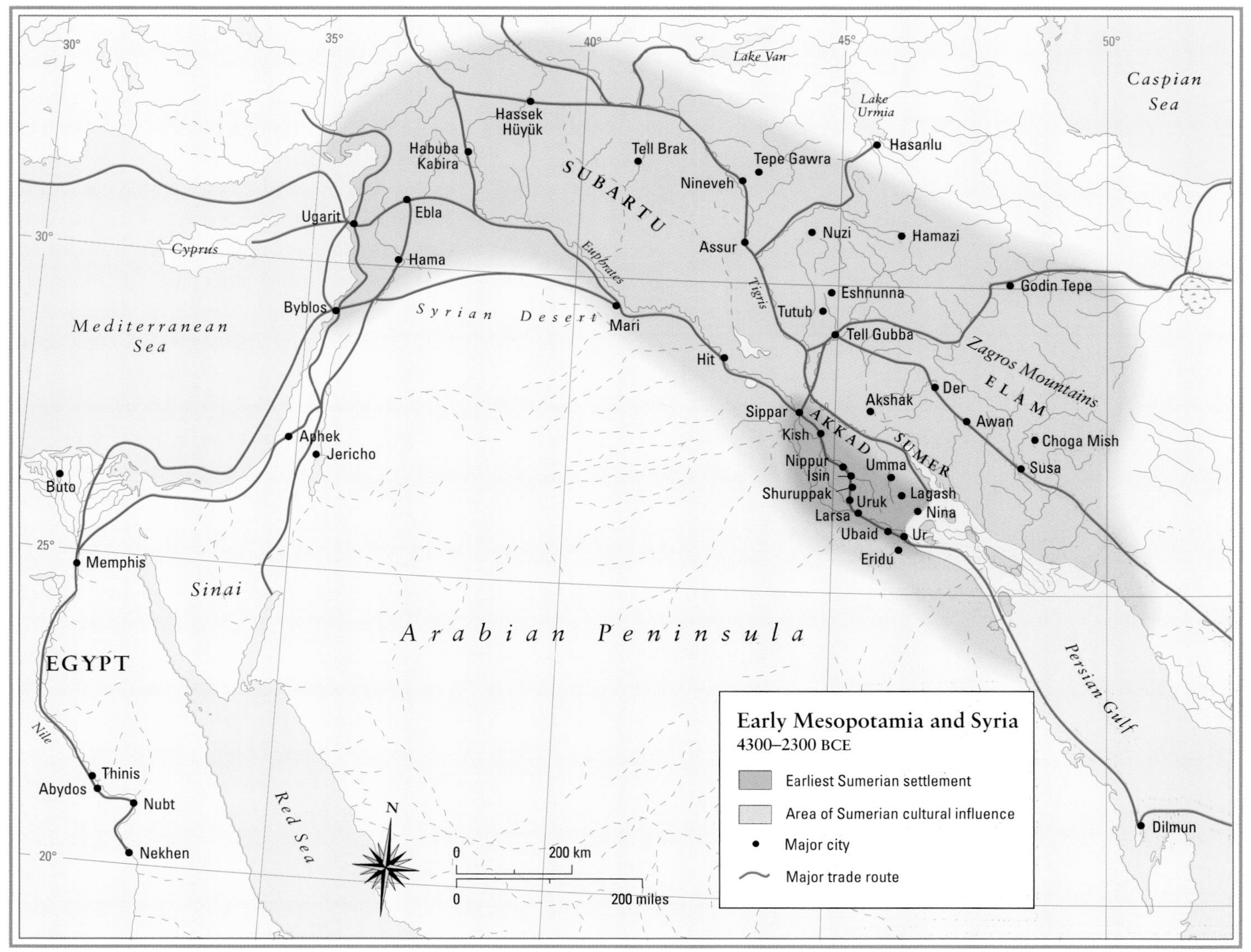

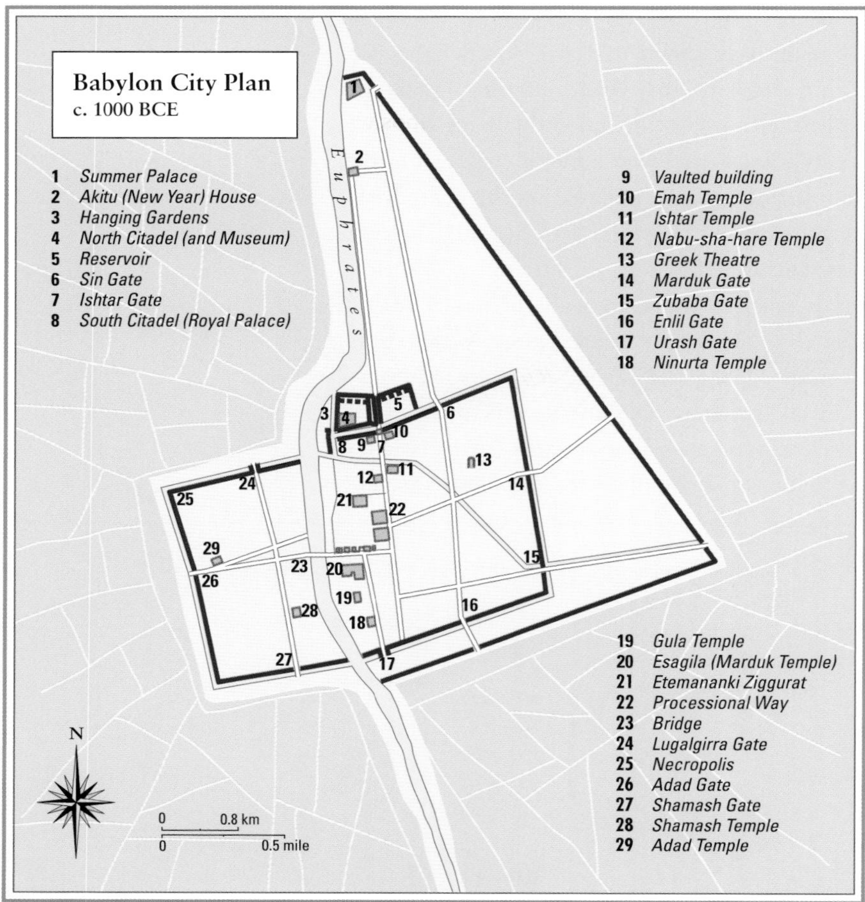

tural produce. In the eighteenth century BCE, Ur declined in trade and prosperity as political power shifted to Babylon. This can be partially explained by the collapse of the Indus civilization in India, which ended a major trade route by sea to Ur. Babylon was in a better position to collect trade from the Iranian plateau and channel it to the Syrian cities of Aleppo, Qatna, and Ebla, and onwards to Egypt.

Two developments of immense importance were the growth of religion and metallurgy. Organized religion played an important role in society, both in spreading belief systems and in carrying out of administration from the temples and the farming of temple lands. With abundant copper supplies, bronze could also be made, allowing the production of tools and weapons.

Warfare for the first armies comprised two activities, that of the infantry and that of siege warfare. The infantry carried wooden shields, little or no metal body armor, maybe a light metal helmet, and possibly a leather corselet. They were organized into ranks but few, if any, could be compared to Greek hoplites or a Macedonian phalanx. The standard infantry weapon was the spear, but other weapons have been observed on limestone reliefs. Long-handled axes and bows were used by Egyptians against Canaanites, and javelins were in common use.

Fortifications were widespread in Mesopotamia and the Levant, with mud-brick walls in the former and sometimes stone in the latter. The walls at Ur had foundations 100 feet thick at the base and walls could be 60 feet high with towers and bastions from which enfilading fire could be used against besiegers. Such defences could be stormed if the walls could be undermined and a breach created. An escalade would be virtually impossible if walls were more than 30 feet high because scaling ladders of sufficient size could probably not be built or transported.

Before the formation of tightly disciplined military units, combat would presumably have been a mêlée with hand-to-hand fighting in small numbers. No one knows the size of the first armies but they were small and it was much safer to fight from behind a city's walls. Because Mesopotamia and the Levant contained so many cities, any military action would require conscript soldiers who were organized by their local King. The tenantry of the temple and the elite could be conscripted and sometimes large numbers could be gathered. A temple at Lagash once provided 500 soldiers for the King. Normally, numbers raised would not run into thousands; the method of raising more troops was to create alliances with other cities.

Whereas Mesopotamia was subject to intense warfare, the inhabitants of the Nile Valley enjoyed a relatively peaceful period from 5000 BCE to 3000 BCE. Evidence for some violence comes from inscriptions on the Narmer Palette, left in a temple in 3100 BCE. It depicts a pharaoh about to club a man with a mace, maybe an enemy captured during the process of unification. The Egyptian military were able to contend with brigands, Berber nomads from the Libyan Desert, or Nubian tribesmen—grave inscriptions give details of defeated enemies. Eventually Egyptian raids were made into Palestine and cities there were besieged. Those at Beni Hasan depict siege-craft, the composite bow, the sickle sword, and eye axes.

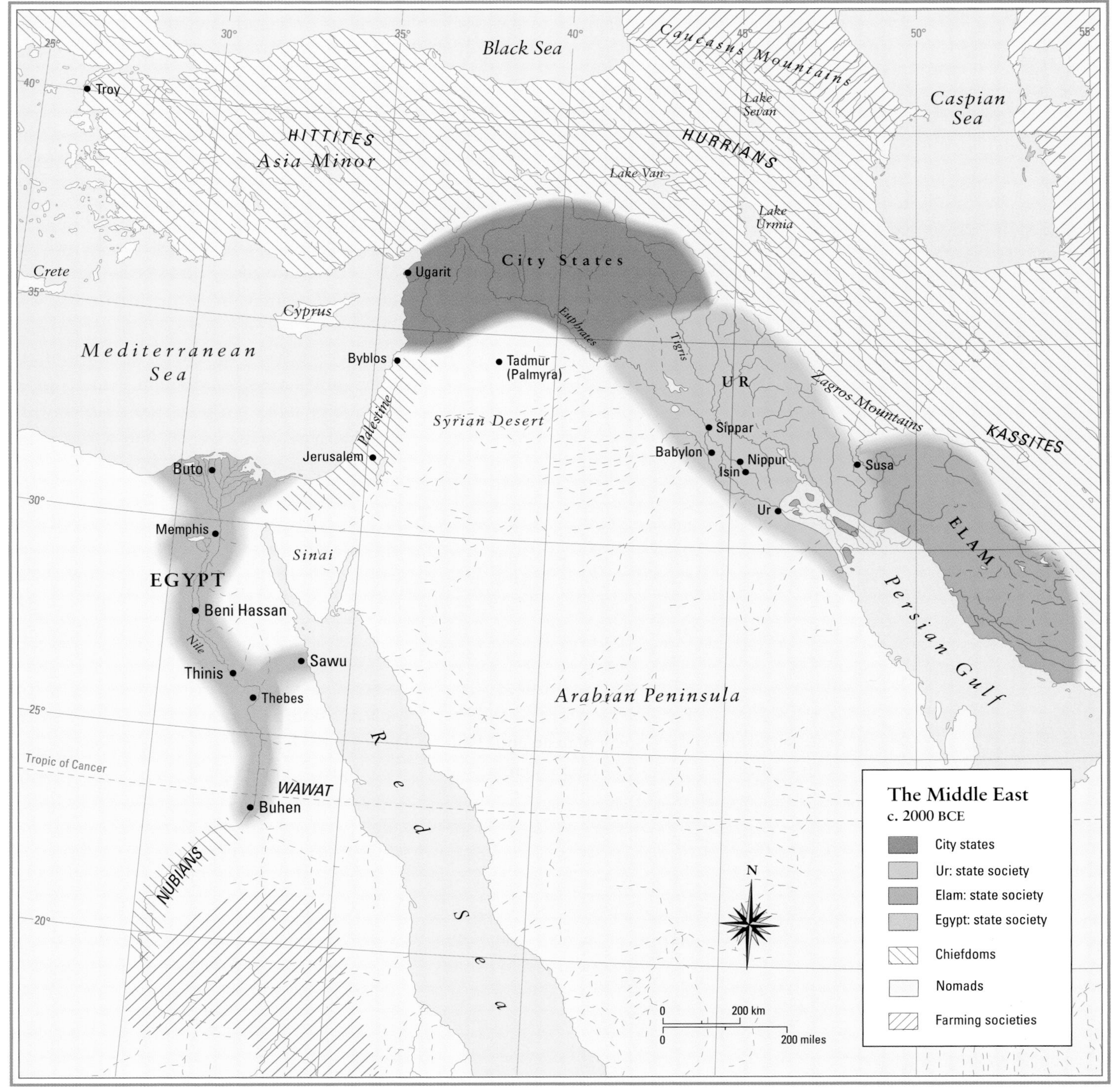

Mesopotamia and Sargon the Great c. 2279 BCE

In this detail, taken from the Stele of the Vultures, which celebrates the victory of Lagash over its neighbor Umma, a group of soldiers march in close formation.

Situated in western Asia, Mesopotamia was one of the cradles of human civilization. A flat and hot landscape comprising marshes and plains, Mesopotamia stretched from Nineveh in the north to the Persian Gulf in the south and between the rivers Tigris in the west and the Euphrates, spreading farther east to the Zagros Mountains. Whereas in Egypt the annual flood of the Nile was sufficient to water the land, with a surplus held back by dikes and basins, in Mesopotamia the annual flood of the Tigris and Euphrates was insufficient to irrigate the land. Instead, major and radial canals were used to allow irrigation to the fields. The earliest known system was that constructed at Choga Mami, in southern Iraq, in about 6000 BCE. These canals required continual maintenance, manpower had to be organized to keep them in repair. The early cities had sufficient population to achieve this. Irrigation could create large agricultural surpluses; the rulers of city-states used the profits for defensive walls, monumental buildings, and other architectural projects.

The various city-states vied with each other for power and hegemony. Hence Kish, Ur, Uruk, and Lagash all achieved supremacy at some stage. There were major religious centers at Eridu, Nippur, and Girsu. South of the city of Akkad were a number of Sumerian city-states where regional power shifted over time from one to another. Important expansionist Sumerian Kings were: Lugal-Anne-Mundu of Adab; Enshakushanna of Uruk, who conquered all Sumer, Akkad, and Hamazi; Eannatum of Lagash; and Lugal-Zage-Si, who had made Uruk his capital and who subjugated Ur, Nippur, Larsa, Lagash, and Kish. This Sumerian Empire was in turn conquered by the most famous monarch from the region, though not the first ruler of a Mesopotamian Empire, the Akkadian Sargon the Great (c. 2334–2279 BCE), after many campaigns.

A legend concerning Sargon has him, as a baby, placed in a basket, sealed with bitumen, and placed on the surface of a river, just like the Biblical tale of Moses. Known to be a cup-bearer to the King of Kish, Sargon usurped the throne and united the Akkadian-speaking cities before overthrowing the Sumerian hegemon, Uruk. One key aim of the Akkadian ruler was to ensure favorable trading terms with the rest of the known world, even if this meant conquering all states and peoples along the major trade routes. Conquest did not necessarily mean use of violence. The knowledge that a city-state could be besieged was often enough to secure submission and impose vassal status on the targeted city, which then paid annual tribute. The growth of a centralized administration with Akkadian lieutenants in all subject cities ensured political control. Records show that Sargon had 5,400 court officials; historians think that this was his standing army. There is evidence to suggest that there was a recruitment system, whereby landholdings were granted for military service. Additionally, Sargon could levy conscripts from royal and temple lands and use this mass labor force to support military operations. Estimates suggest that 10,000 men could build a ramp to the top of a wall 60 feet high in five days. Then attackers could storm the wall being protected by siege towers which would give a more effective field of fire. Even if a ramp was not fully completed it would help sappers to pick holes through higher and thinner parts of a wall to create a breach.

A *Chronicle of Ancient Kings*, written in Babylon, states: "[Sargon] had neither rival nor equal. His splendor, over the land is diffused. He crossed the sea in the east. In the eleventh year he conquered the western land to its farthest point. He brought it under one authority. He set up his statues there and ferried the west's booty across on barges. He stationed his court officials at intervals of five double hours and ruled in unity the tribes of the lands. He marched to Kazallu and turned Kazallu into a ruin heap, so that there was not even a perch for a bird left."

Sargon developed a program of foreign conquest, invading Syria and Canaan four times. Three years were spent subjugating these areas, which were taken into the Akkadian Empire. Amurru was attacked, leading to hegemony over the Amorites. Campaigns were conducted against Elam and the Elamites' capital city of Susa fell. Akkadian forces moved down the Persian Gulf to take Dilmun (Bahrain, Falaika Island in Kuwait, and the eastern Arabia coast), and Magan (Oman) on the Musandam Peninsula, a strategically important location where navies could control the entrance to the Persian Gulf. Sargon also marched into Anatolia and reputedly captured Cyprus. While expanding the Empire, Sargon also had to quash rebellions in some Sumerian cities.

Sargon's military genius and organizational skills, together with the groundwork laid by the Sumerian cities and the already existing

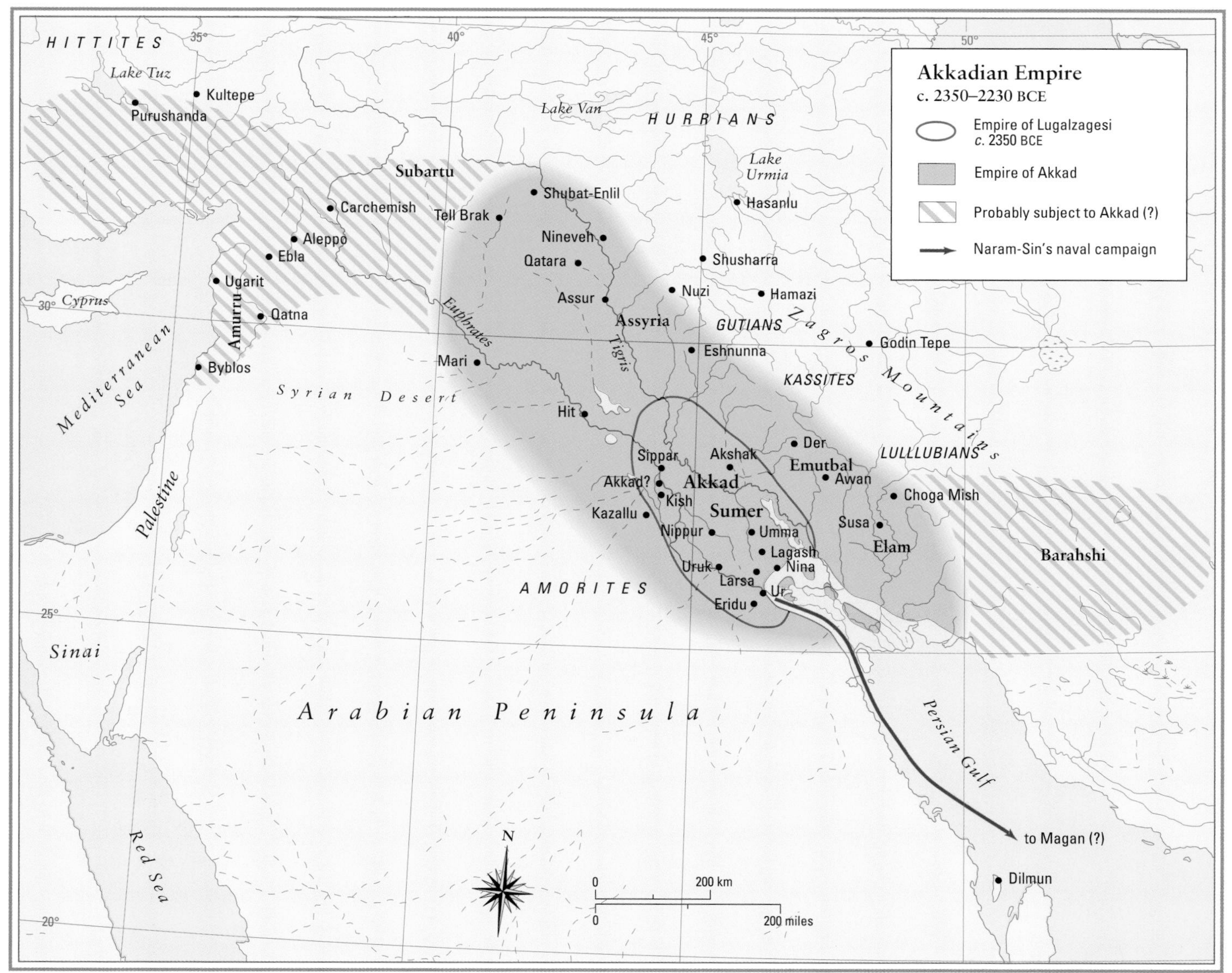

The bronze head of Sargon, the first ruler to unite Sumer and its surrounding Mesopotamian cities and states. The head is all that remains of a full body sculpture.

trade links of Sumer, allowed commercial links to flourish. Trade flowed from the silver mines of the Anatolian Taurus Mountains to the lapis lazuli mines of Badakhshan in Afghanistan. Lapis was carried to Lothal, a port in Gujarat and then transhipped up the Persian Gulf. The cedars of Lebanon were commercially exploited. Cappadocia and Crete were tied in to the trading network, and it is not impossible that relay trading went farther, to Greece. Towards the East, commerce reached Meluhha. The precise location of this site has caused scholarly controversy but the Indus Valley is a likely spot since many Harappan civilization seals have been found in Mesopotamian urban sites. Evidence suggests that ivory, gold, carnelian, and glazed stone beads, pearls from the Persian Gulf, and shell and bone inlays were the goods sent to Mesopotamia, as well as timber and precious woods. These were exchanged for silver, tin, woollen textiles, copper ingots, and bitumen.

During Sargon's rule, the Akkadians took over the Sumerian script and this is seen upon clay tablets from the dynasty and on contemporary cylinder seals. Inscriptions and trade agreements from Nuzi, Nineveh, Chagar Bazar, and Tell Ibraq confirm the rule of the Akkadian Dynasty. Not only did the Akkadians adopt the cuneiform script but they spread their Semitic language throughout Mesopotamia, reducing Sumerian to a temple ritual language.

The last years of Sargon's reign were bedevilled by rebellions, probably because the Empire was dependent on one man and his new administration. However skilled and vigorous Sargon might have been, for its day his Empire was vast and needed consolidation. Rebellions continued during the reigns of Sargon's sons. Rimush (2278–2270 BCE) fought for his legacy but was assassinated by his own people while Manishtushu (2269–2255 BCE) reigned for fifteen years and is reputed to have fought a naval engagement with a coalition of 32 kings from Arab lands. He too was murdered and succeeded by his son, Naram-Sin.

Naram-Sin expanded the Empire after crushing early revolts. He conquered Ebla and Armani, location uncertain. However,

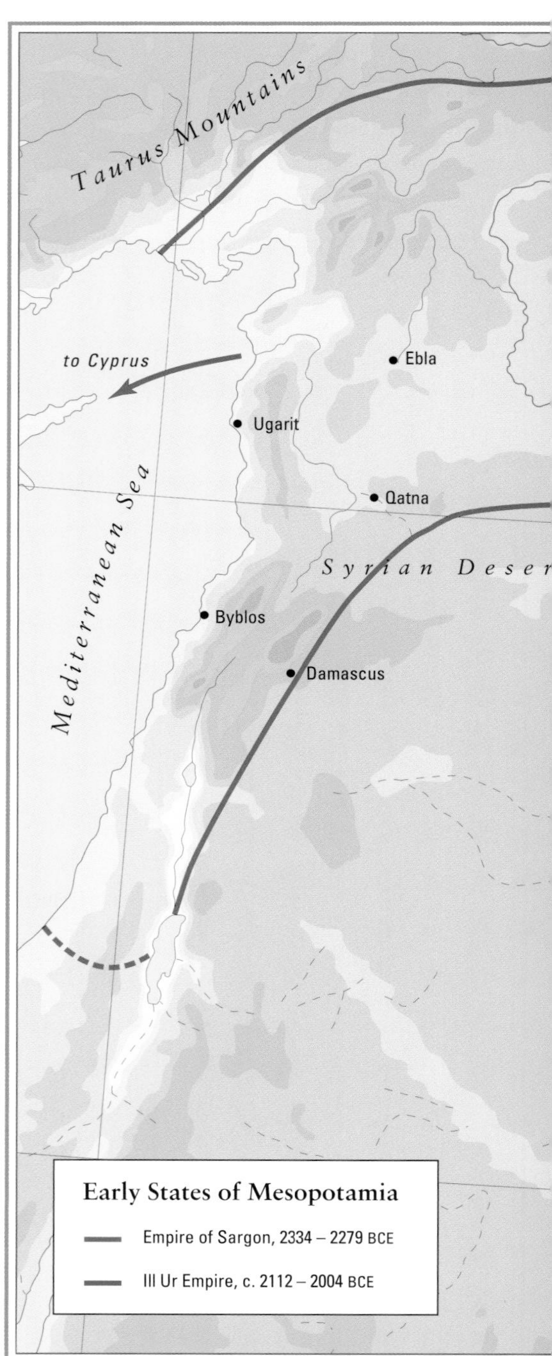

the main threat came from the Zagros Mountains, from the Lullubi and Gutians who raided into Mesopotamia. He defeated the Lullubi, confirmed on the Victory Stele of Naram-Sin, now housed in the Louvre, Paris, France. Hittite evidence states that he fought the Hittites and Hurrians, Zipani of Kanesh, and fifteen other Anatolian rulers. Eventually, the Akkadians fell to the Gutians, who retained control for a century before a new Sumerian dynasty rose in Ur, which established a well-organized and highly-developed Empire in the last century of the second millennium BCE.

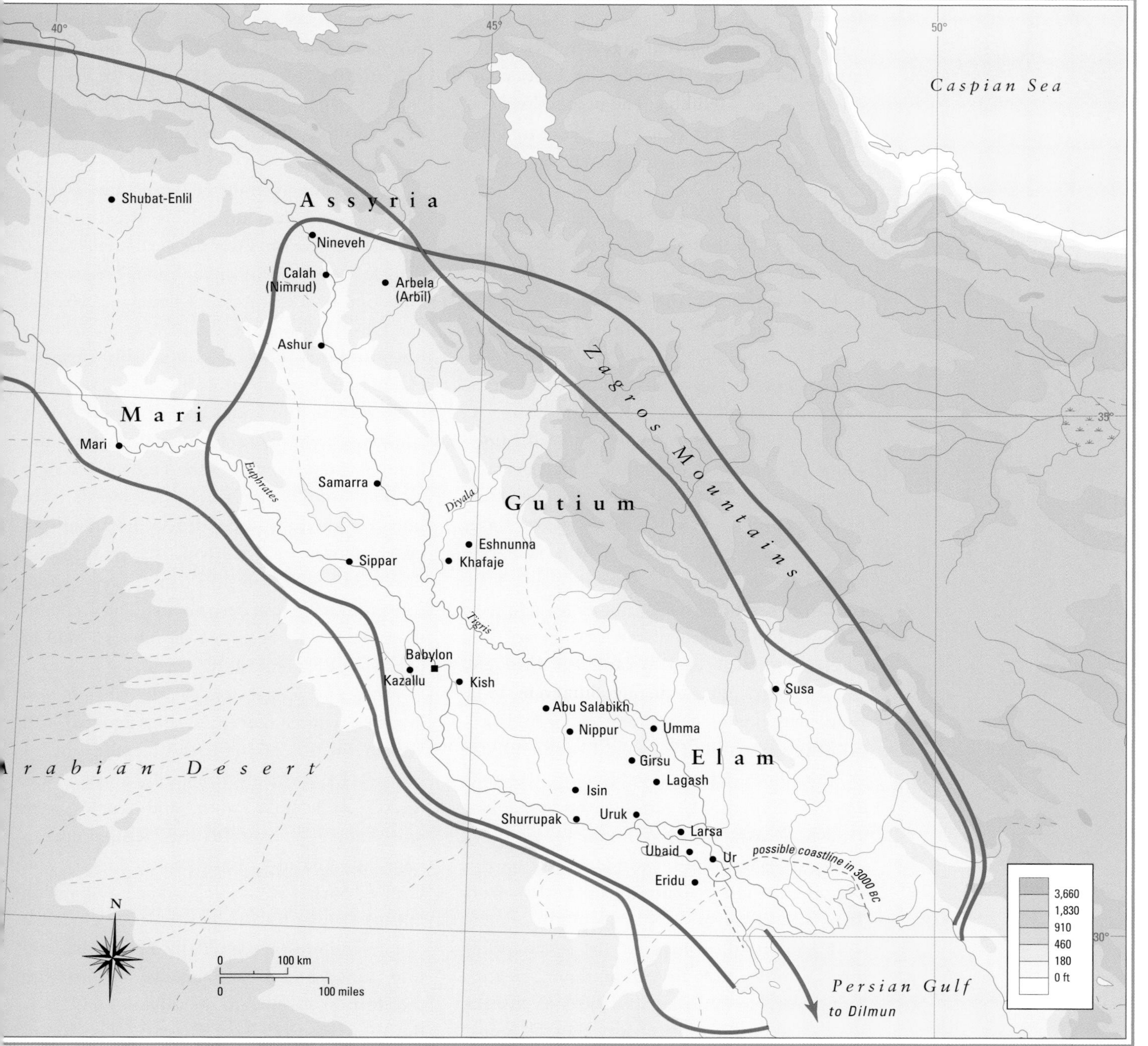

Babylonian Empire c. 2000–1500 BCE

Akkadian and Sumerian culture ended when the final dynasty in the city-state of Ur succumbed to attacks by the King of Elam. More importantly, the semi-nomadic Amorite people were filtering in to Mesopotamia; this became a flood after Ur fell. By the eighteenth century BCE, every city-state in the region was ruled by an Amorite Dynasty, which tended to adopt the culture of Sumer and Akkad and assimilate their religion. These Amorite states became rivals, with Isin and Larsa becoming predominant. The latter was conquered by Kudurmabuk of Elam, who established his son Waradsin as ruler there; he was succeeded by Rim-sin.

During this political ferment, the city of Babylon established itself as a small kingdom in 1894 BCE, during the reign of the Amorite King Sumuabum. It grew into an Empire that would eventually unify the whole of Mesopotamia. The most notable ruler of the Amorite dynasty was Hammurabi (c. 1792–1750 BCE) whose reign witnessed a flowering of cultural and intellectual achievements, including a code of laws that were recorded upon a stele in the cuneiform script of Akkadian, the successor to the Sumerian language. This code was drawn from a legal tradition reaching back to the Kingdom of Eshnunna in the nineteenth century BCE and the laws promulgated by Lipit-Ishtar of Isin (c. 1865 BCE). These were influenced by the previous Code of Ur-nammu of Ur and they all bear a resemblance to the Covenant Code of the Bible, described in *Exodus* Chapters 21–23. Hammurabi's reign is one of the best known periods of Mesopotamian antiquity, owing to many thousands of texts from this period, including some 20,000 tablets from Mari alone.

Hammurabi conquered the surrounding city-states of southern Mesopotamia, creating an Empire that extended into parts of Assyria, while maintaining its heartland around Babylon and Kish. Once Hammurabi had brought Mesopotamia under single rule, the supremacy of Babylon would last for two centuries. One of the key economic and strategic issues of the day was the control of the waters of the River Euphrates and a struggle over water rights. Not only did this involve the building of canals and irrigation systems for agriculture, but it also led to a conflict between neighboring city-states. Hammurabi's main rival was Rim-sin of Larsa, downstream from Babylon.

Hammurabi conquered Uruk and Isin in 1787 BCE and then turned his attention in a northerly direction. Over the next twenty years, there followed a series of coalitions between the kingdoms of Mari, Ashur, Eshnunna, Babylon, and Larsa, followed by almost continuous warfare between 1764 BCE and the time of Hammurabi's death in 1750 BCE. During this time, Hammurabi found himself at war with a coalition comprising Eshnunna, Ashur and Elam, the main powers of the Tigris which were blocking off Babylon's access to metals from Iran. Hammurabi responded by damming the waters above Larsa, depriving the city of water, then suddenly releasing the dam to create widespread flooding and destruction. The events of these times were recorded on tablets found in palaces at Ebla and Mari.

The commercial wealth of Babylon was immense, with Syrian cities being supplied with Persian tin, essential for the manufacture of bronze. Lapis lazuli from Afghanistan was traded, while gold, silver, and textiles were moved along the rivers linking Mesopotamia to cities in Anatolia, the Levant, Egypt, and Cyprus. Such was the importance of Babylon that its Empire became particularly vulnerable to foreign invasion. Gradually, Babylonian culture waned under continuous invasions from the Hittites, who sacked the capital in 1595 BCE, thus bringing the First Dynasty of Babylon to an end. Babylon was then invaded by the Kassites, the Hurrians, and the Mitanni.

By the end of the fifteenth century BCE, the Assyrians, originating from the city of Ashur in northern Mesopotamia, rose in prominence, and had established an Empire by the mid-fourteenth century that had conquered large areas from the Mitanni, Kassites, and the Hittites, ultimately affording the Assyrians control of much of former Babylonia.

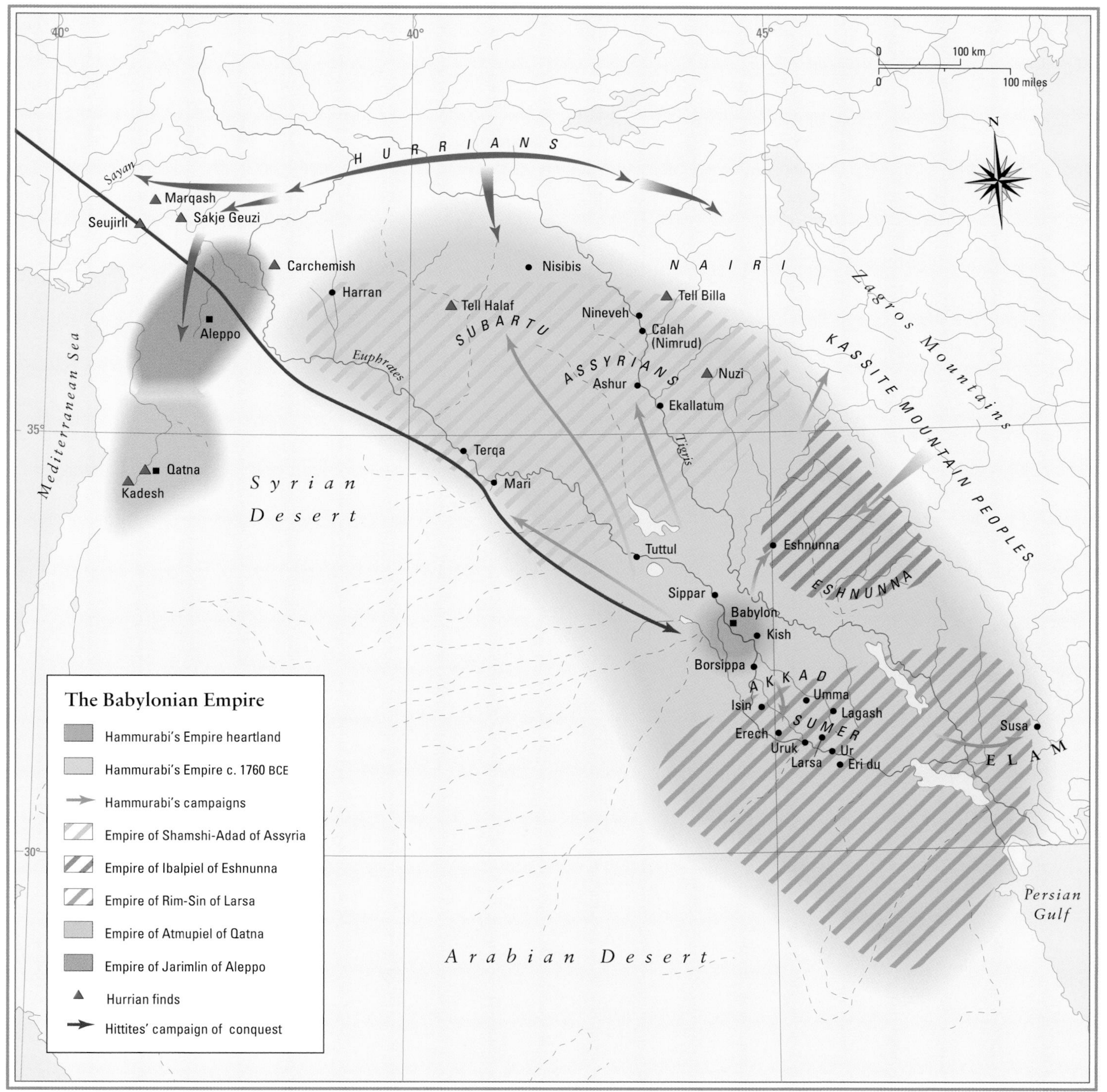

Hittite Empire

The Hittites were an Indo-European people originating in lands beyond the Black Sea, they ruled an Empire that expanded and contracted repeatedly, sometimes being reduced to their heartland in central Anatolia. Early Hittite and Anatolian history has no documentary sources between c. 1800 BCE and the emergence of a fully fledged Hittite state in 1650 BCE. During the period between 1650 and 1200 BCE, the Hittites controlled much of Anatolia and, at the height of their power, contested dominion of the Levant with Egypt. The earliest real historical knowledge we have of the Anatolian plateau comes from the Assyrian merchant colonies in central Anatolia. Further knowledge of the Hittites is derived from Egyptian records and from Hittite royal archives discovered at Hattusas. The clay tablets used a cuneiform system and also hieroglyphs and contain historical information and stories. Seemingly, the King acted as supreme priest, military commander, and chief judge. He always led his armies personally so that victories showed not only the power of the King, but also the support of the gods of the Hatti. The nobility were

A rare representation of a winged god from among the Hittite pantheon of gods, Anatolia, 13th century BC.

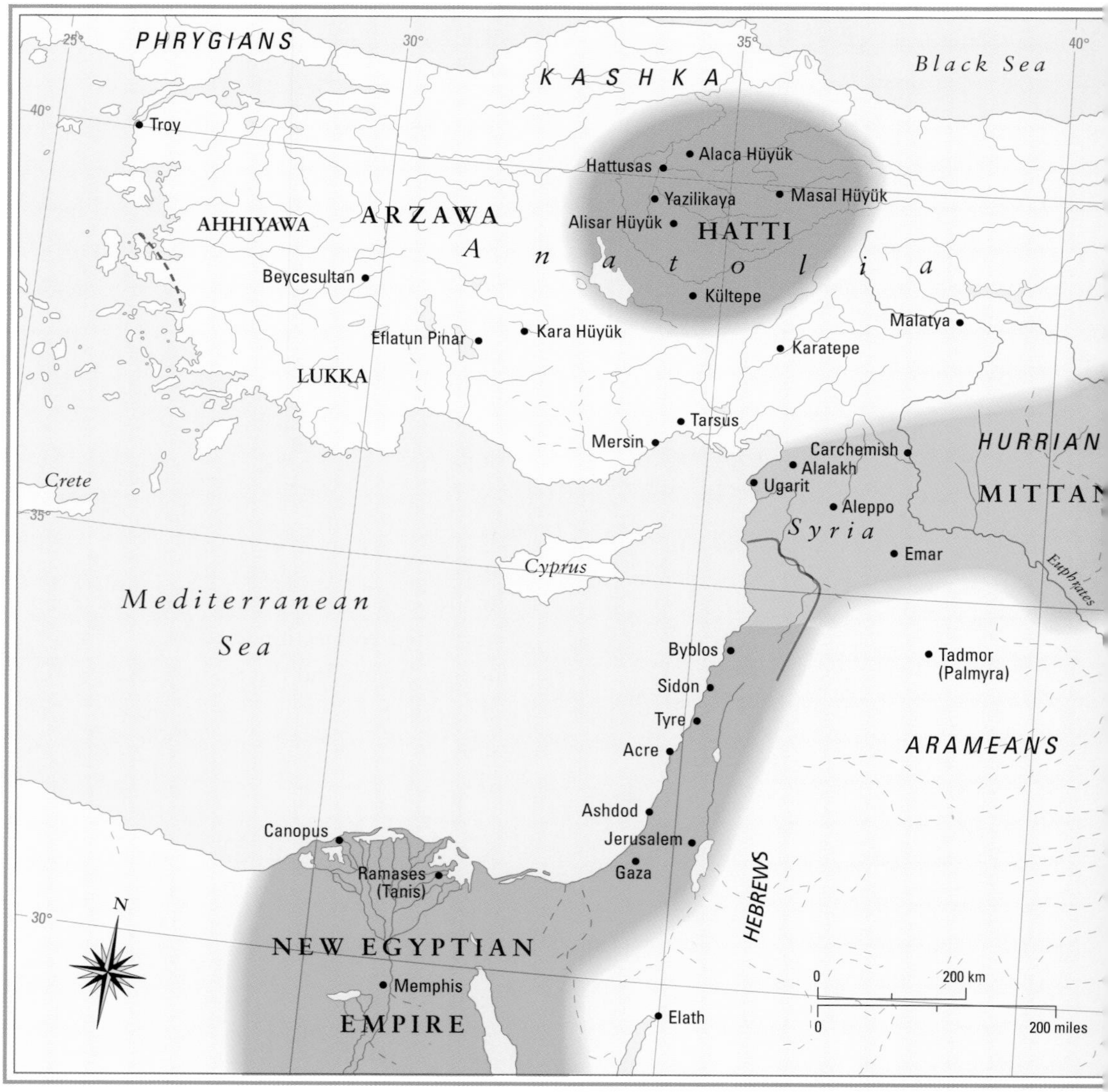

replaced as advisors to the King by a bureaucracy. The Empire was ruled by provincial governors and some client-kings were tied to the Hittite royal family by marriage. Client-kings were expected to raise troops to campaign with the King, and provide labor and goods. At the time, unusual features of Hittite life were that war was conducted in a relatively humane fashion and the administration of justice was lenient, seldom imposing the death penalty or physical punishment. Justice rested on the concept of restitution by restoring stolen property or financial recompense. The Hittites worshiped a storm god, Tarkhunt, who fought with the dragon Illuyankas annually, and a sun goddess, Arinna. The King was their earthly representative, and the Hittites were tolerant of other Anatolian, Hurrian, and Syrian deities. In fact, their pantheon included Akkado-Sumerian gods and myths intermingled with Luwian and Hittite counterparts. Later developments can be found written in the Hittite Indo-European language in an adopted form of cuneiform script. Two early Hittite rulers were Tudkhaliyas I and Pusarma, who lived in the late seventeenth century BCE, however, we know little of them.

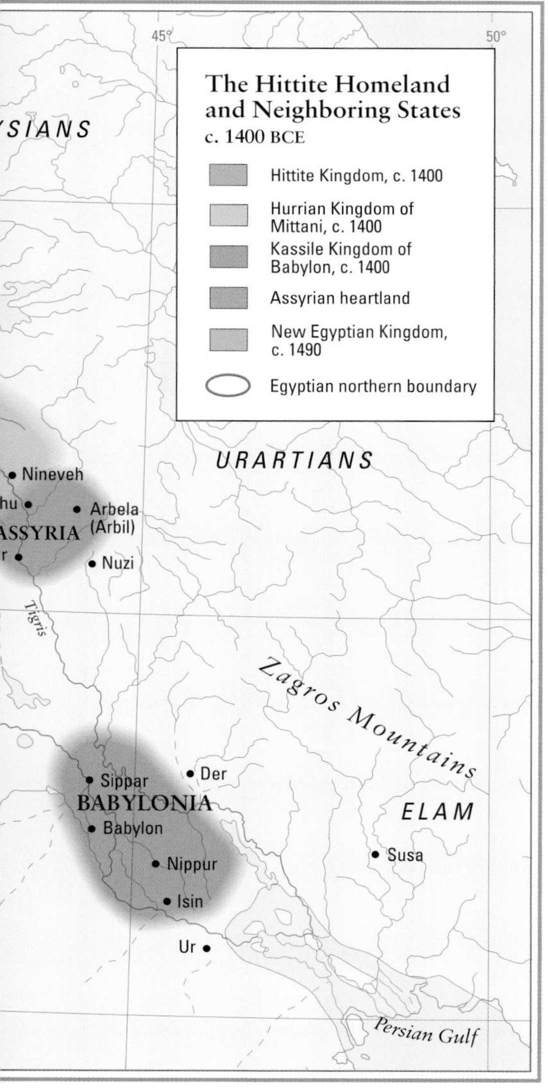

After battles with the native population, the Hittites, under Labarna I, extended control over much of Anatolia and parts of northern Syria. Hattusili I (1586–1556 BCE) shifted the capital to Hattusas, from Nesa, modern Kültepe, and continued Hittite expansion, conquering Alalakh and attacking Arzawa. His successor, Mursilis I, defeated and destroyed Aleppo, an important trading center, and sacked Babylon (c. 1590 BCE) bringing down its First Dynasty. This last onslaught was a mere raid, the Hittites withdrew to Anatolia where they became weakened by a series of disputed successions, fought out with murder and violence.

The desire to control the Levant was fueled by the fact that ports, such as Ugarit, Byblos, Sidon, Tyre, Acre, and Ashdod, were the hubs of a rich and varied maritime trade, as evidenced by the contents of shipwrecks found at Cape Gelidonya and at the headland of Uluburun. The ports, with their Canaanite traders, had connections to Greece, along the Nile into Africa and the trading land of Punt, and through relay trading, overland through Mesopotamia to Afghanistan, and from the Red Sea to India and China.

Hittite armies were adept at deploying a fast, two-wheeled, light-weight chariot, carrying a driver and an archer, both armored in bronze, with the latter using a recurved bow. Their infantry was protected by rectangular shields and was well armed with daggers, spears, sickle-shaped swords, and battle-axes. Their military skills included siege-craft and the construction of strong fortifications, like those discovered at Hattusas.

Mursilis, famous for his conquest of Babylon, was assassinated in 1526 BCE, inaugurating a period of internal strife and weakness with petty king following petty king, such as Khantilis, Zidantas, Ammunas, and Khuzzias. Order was restored by Telepinus in 1530 BCE. His Edict of Telepinus issued firm laws governing royal succession to end lawlessness and designated the nobility as a high court to try constitutional crimes. The Hittite law code was constructed at this time. King Tudkhaliyas II established a new dynasty and he paved the way to build an Empire. However, the early kings of this dynasty gave no hint of the Empire to come. The reigns of Hatusilis II, Tudhkaliyas III, and Arnuwandas I faced great danger. The Kingdom of Mitanni threatened the Hittites in the east, while Arzawa in the west and the Kashka in the north did likewise.

The most powerful Hittite King was Suppilulinmas I (1380–1346 BCE). He fortified and rebuilt his capital, reorganized his lands, and then marched into Syria. His first encounter with Tuishrata of Mitanni resulted in defeat. He found allies and the Mitanni Kingdom was partly overrun, with Ugarit, Aleppo, and Carchemish becoming Hittite dependencies. The Assyrians, ruled by the Mitanni, achieved independence and established their own state based on the capital at Ashur, but a Mitanni rump state remained as a buffer between the two Empires.

Through constant hostilities, Hittite power was projected towards the Aegean Sea, and southward into the Lebanon, wresting most of Syria and northern Phoenicia from Egyptian control. In southwest Anatolia Mursilis II, son of Suppilulinmas I, crushed a revolt in Arzawa and killed its King. He fought annual campaigns against the Kashka and quelled a revolt in Carchemish.

After a period of Egyptian decline a new Nineteenth Dynasty sought to extend its power in Asia with Seti I (c. 1294–1279 BCE) moving back into Palestine and gaining control as far as north Palestine at Beth-shan. Conflict with the Hittites now seemed likely. Both sides raised their forces and both hired numerous mercenaries as well as arming native troops. The Egyptians employed contingents of Sherden while the Hittites engaged the services of Lukka, Dardana, and others. In the struggle for Syria and the Levant, the Hittite King Muwatallis fought Pharaoh Ramesses II at Kadesh in 1275 BCE. Ramesses claimed victory; it was a Pyrrhic one, since the Hittites retained Syria. The war continued for more than ten years and peace finally emerged when Hattusilis III (c. 1275–1250 BCE), brother of Muwatallis, overthrew the latter's son, seizing the throne. A treaty in 1275 BCE concluded a mutual defense agreement and a dynastic marriage. Both sides were exhausted. Now the Hittites looked east towards the emergent power of Assyria, ruled by Shalmaneser I, who had eyes on the Hittite vassal, Mittani.

Other dangers emerged to threaten the Hittites. Hostile coalitions of Aegean peoples, the Acheans (Ahhiyawa), in western Anatolia were barely contained. By 1200 BCE, the Hittite Kingdom collapsed under attack from the migrating Sea Peoples and central Anatolia was swamped by Phrygians, originating in the southern Balkans and crossing into Anatolia via the Hellespont, all this occurring during the brief reign of Suppiluliumas II. Furthermore, the Kashka, inhabiting the mountains of northern Anatolia, were becoming a menace again. Political disruption followed the fragmentation of the Mycenaean confederacy, just before or during the Trojan War, events reflected in the words of the *Iliad* and *Odyssey*. Some city-states emerged that retained a Hittite identity, Carchemish being the most noteworthy. The southernmost area of the region eventually became Aramaean. Hattusas was burned, as was Ugarit in Syria. The Hittites, as with Bronze Age civilization in Mycenaean Greece, and Crete, were swept away in a deluge of fire.

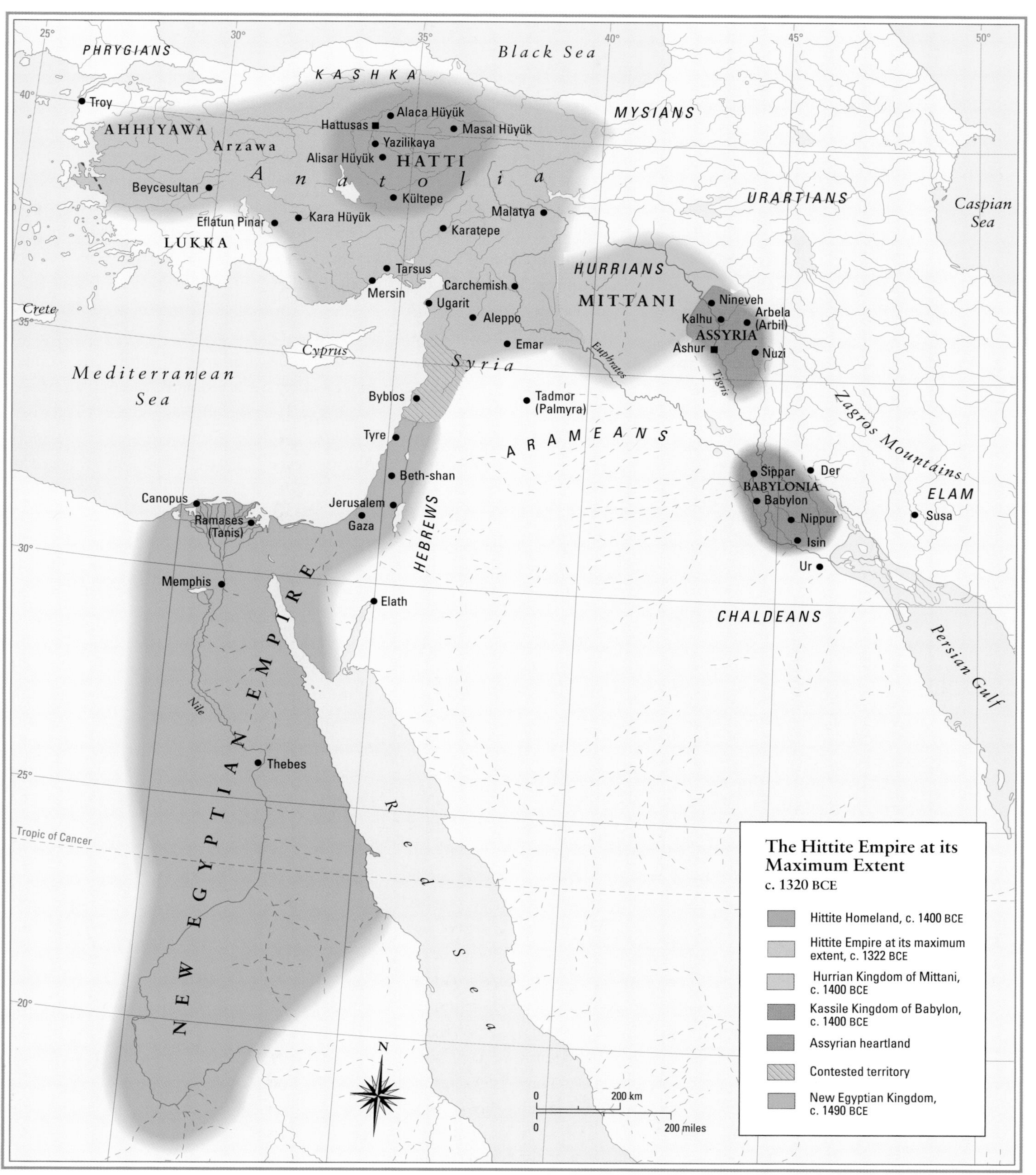
The Hittite Empire at its Maximum Extent
c. 1320 BCE
Hittite Homeland, c. 1400 BCE
Hittite Empire at its maximum extent, c. 1322 BCE
Hurrian Kingdom of Mittani, c. 1400 BCE
Kassile Kingdom of Babylon, c. 1400 BCE
Assyrian heartland
Contested territory
New Egyptian Kingdom, c. 1490 BCE
PHRYGIANS
Black Sea
KASHKA
MYSIANS
Troy
AHHIYAWA
Arzawa
Hattusas
Alaca Hüyük
Masal Hüyük
Yazilikaya
Alisar Hüyük
HATTI
Anatolia
Beycesultan
Kültepe
URARTIANS
Caspian Sea
Eflatun Pinar
Kara Hüyük
Malatya
Karatepe
LUKKA
HURRIANS
Tarsus
Mersin
Carchemish
MITTANI
Nineveh
Kalhu
Arbela (Arbil)
ASSYRIA
Ashur
Nuzi
Crete
Ugarit
Aleppo
Emar
Cyprus
Syria
Euphrates
Tigris
Mediterranean Sea
Byblos
Tadmor (Palmyra)
Zagros Mountains
Tyre
ARAMEANS
Sippar
Der
BABYLONIA
Babylon
ELAM
Susa
Nippur
Isin
Ur
Beth-shan
Canopus
Jerusalem
Gaza
Ramases (Tanis)
HEBREWS
Memphis
Elath
CHALDEANS
Persian Gulf
NEW EGYPTIAN EMPIRE
Nile
Thebes
Red Sea
Tropic of Cancer
N
0
200 km
200 miles
25°
30°
35°
40°
45°
50°
20°

Egypt's New Kingdom c. 1550–1077 BCE

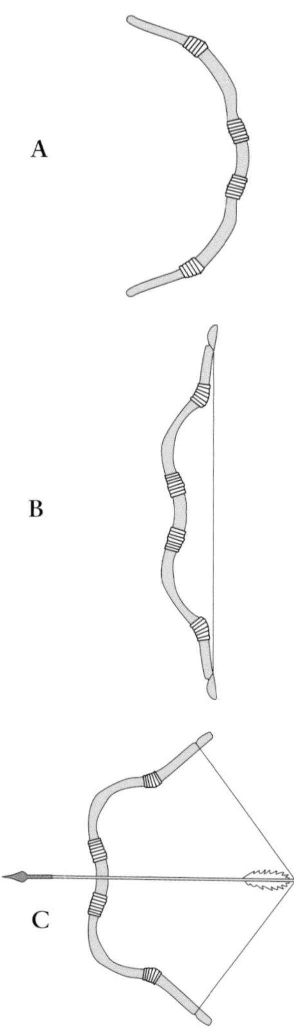

The composite bow, originally developed by horseborne nomads, found favor across the Middle East. Its manufacture might include wood, horn, sinew, or leather. Its construction created a short, powerful bow especially effective when used from horseback or chariot. A. The bow unstrung, curved away from the archer. B. Strung curved toward archer. C. Drawn with arrow, ready to fire.

Egypt had been invaded by the Hyksos from western Asia and was ruled by this foreign power, which introduced horse armor and the composite bow to the Egyptians. About 1530 BCE, Egypt was re-united by Ahmose I (c. 1539–1514 BCE), who drove the Hyksos from their fortress-town at Avaris into Palestine, and then established the Eighteenth Dynasty. This New Kingdom (1550–1077 BCE) became strong, conquering the Nile up to the Third Cataract in Nubia. The Egyptians developed a professional army, which deployed the chariot as an integral part of its army, and the Pharaoh was often depicted as a warrior-king in this vehicle. Military strategies and campaigns, which sought to protect Egypt from enemies in Asia and Kush (a region of present-day Sudan), were planned in a new palace at Memphis. Eventually, the southern border was pushed toward the Fourth Cataract of the Nile and a garrisoned fort was constructed at Napata with its associated temple. Egypt exploited Kushite lands for their gold, copper, ivory, ebony, and animal skins.

Thutmose I (1493–1481 BCE) invaded the Levant and reach the Euphrates, thereby bringing Syria and Palestine into Egypt's orbit. Hegemony over these regions allowed forts to be built containing Egyptian garrisons and the development of a fleet meant that troops could be carried to anywhere on the Canaanite coast, a remarkable projection of power. Queen Hatshepsut (1473–1458 BCE) acted as if she were a male sovereign and maintained control of the recent acquisitions. She used improved maritime skills to make contact with Punt, thought to be eastern Ethiopia and Eritrea, to trade for incense and ebony. Ships could also sail to Eilat at the head of the Gulf of Aqaba where Arabian frankincense and myrrh were available, having been carried overland from the Yemen.

Hatshepsut's nephew, Thutmose III (1479–1425 BCE), campaigned seventeen times in the Levant, suggesting that tributary areas were rebelling or the Mitanni were encroaching. Resistance was stubborn and, despite the aggressive nature of the Egyptian war machine, they lacked effective logistical support, which meant that some operations needed to be repeated. One view is that remnants of the Hyksos settled near Kadesh on the Orontes and constructed an anti-Egyptian confederacy which had to be destroyed. Another rebellion in Palestine occurred in 1416 BCE, which was crushed with remarkable ruthlessness. Farther north, Hittite expansion from Anatolia proved so dangerous to both the Mitanni and Egypt that these powers made peace through dynastic marriages, ensuring no conflict broke out for 50 years, until Mitanni lands were divided between the Hittites and the Assyrians.

Historians have generally misread the reign of Amenhotep IV (c. 1344–1328 BCE), who changed his name to Akhenaten, attacked the priesthood of the Egyptian deities, and worshiped the sun god with the cult of Aten, an attempt at monotheism. Concentrating on his religious policies did not mean he neglected his foreign policies. The *Amarna Letters* show that Akhenaten was fully aware of local power struggles between vassal states in the northern borders of his territories and dealt with them in the face of growing Hittite strength. Ultimately, Egypt only lost the Syrian province of Amurru near the Orontes River. The Pharaoh also campaigned in Nubia, which was increasingly Egyptianized during the New Kingdom.

Later rulers such as Seti I (c. 1294–1279 BCE) and Ramesses II (c. 1279–1213 BCE) attempted to expand Egypt's territories in Syria, which led to further hostilities with the Hittites. This power struggle erupted in the Battle of Kadesh in 1275 BCE, which neither side won. Peace was made and this was sealed by a dynastic marriage. Ramesses III (c. 1184–1153 BCE) was forced to protect Egypt from Libyan attacks and those of the Sea Peoples. One of these gained lands in the Levant. Egypt was gradually weakened by civil unrest and droughts, allowing the country to fall into the hands of the Libyan Meshwesh and Libu peoples, who founded their own dynasties in the country.

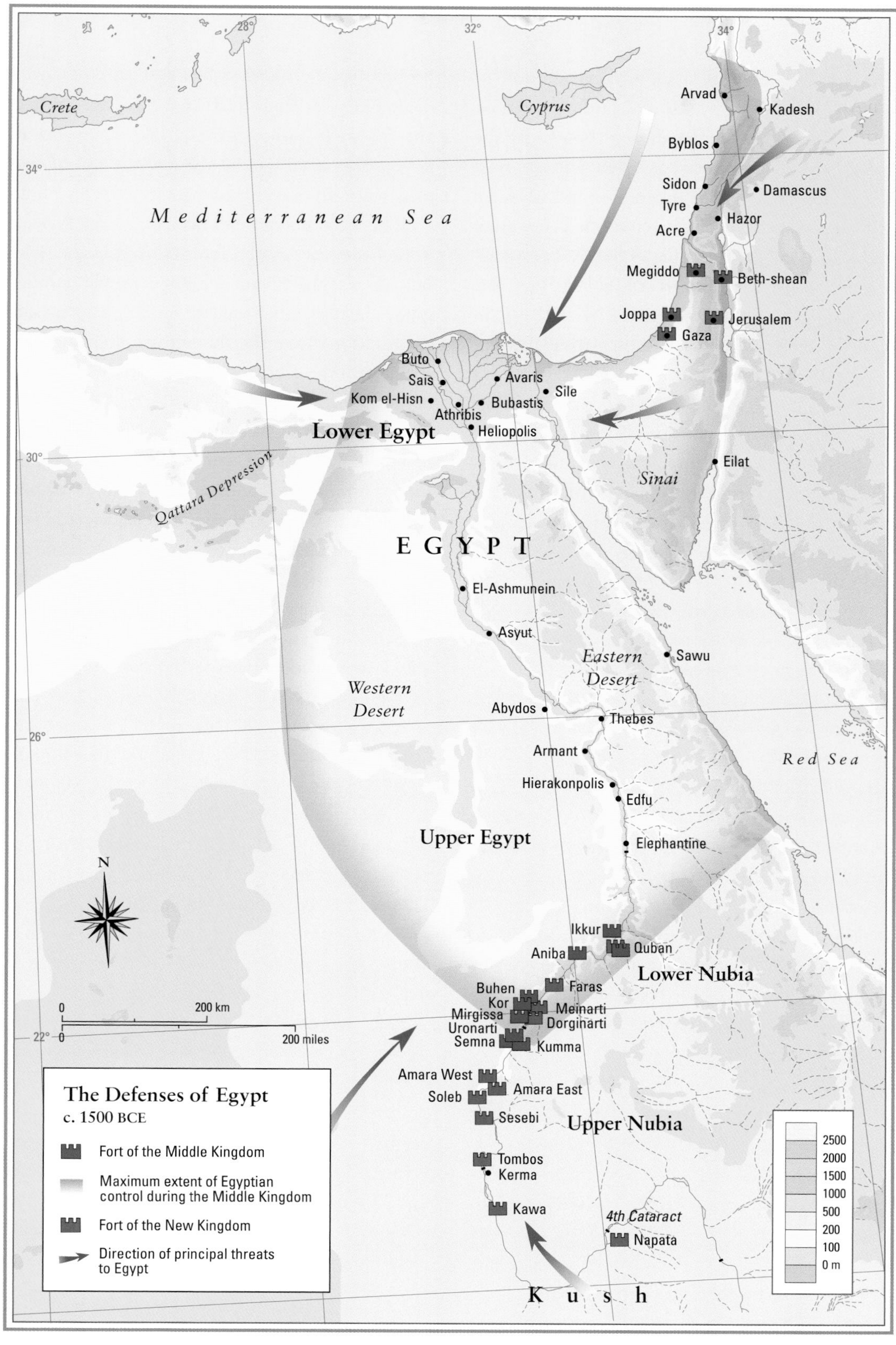
The Defenses of Egypt
c. 1500 BCE
Fort of the Middle Kingdom
Maximum extent of Egyptian control during the Middle Kingdom
Fort of the New Kingdom
Direction of principal threats to Egypt
Mediterranean Sea
Crete
Cyprus
Arvad
Kadesh
Byblos
Sidon
Damascus
Tyre
Hazor
Acre
Megiddo
Beth-shean
Joppa
Jerusalem
Gaza
Buto
Sais
Avaris
Sile
Kom el-Hisn
Athribis
Bubastis
Heliopolis
Lower Egypt
Qattara Depression
Eilat
Sinai
EGYPT
El-Ashmunein
Asyut
Sawu
Eastern Desert
Western Desert
Abydos
Thebes
Armant
Red Sea
Hierakonpolis
Edfu
Upper Egypt
Elephantine
Ikkur
Quban
Aniba
Lower Nubia
Buhen
Faras
Kor
Mirgissa
Meinarti
Uronarti
Dorginarti
Semna
Kumma
Amara West
Soleb
Amara East
Sesebi
Upper Nubia
Tombos
Kerma
Kawa
4th Cataract
Napata
Kush
N
0
200 km
200 miles
2500
2000
1500
1000
500
200
100
0 m
34°
32°
28°
30°
26°
22°

The Sea Peoples

Image of the Sea Peoples based on an Egyptian original; warriors equipped with long, tapering swords and defended by round shields move into the attack.

The Sea Peoples were a loose confederation of peoples who raided by sea and land throughout the Near East and Egypt during the end of the Bronze Age. Their arrival coincided with the mass destruction of Bronze Age cities around 1200 BCE and the two events may be connected. Egyptian sources are the main records of Sea People activity, especially the inscriptions at Medinet Habu, the mortuary temples of Ramesses III (c. 1184–1153 BCE), the Amarna Letters, and the Athribis Stele.

In the fifth year of Pharaoh Merenptah's (1213–1203 BCE) reign, several groups of different Sea Peoples made an alliance with the Libyans (Libu) in a campaign to invade Egypt. The peoples recorded were the Sherden, Lukka, Teresh, and Eqwesh (Achaeans). Merenptah's army met the invaders at Perire and killed 6,000 and captured 9,000.

Further evidence of the Sea People can be found in the *Tale of Wen-amon* c. 1080 BCE, which reports this priest's mission to Byblos to buy timber to construct a sacred barge. He stayed at Dor and was robbed by its Tjekker inhabitants, who were notionally under Egyptian control. Wen-amon fled by sea and was chased by eleven Tjekker ships to Cyprus. The Tjekker have been identified possibly as the Teucri people from the Troad region of Anatolia, and their presence in Palestine shows them to be a migrant people.

The Mednet Habu reliefs and inscriptions are the best information about the arrival of the Sea Peoples. The inscriptions tell how the Hittite Empire was destroyed and describe the attempts of the Sea Peoples to invade Egypt. The reliefs depict two great battles, one on land fought in Phoenicia or Syria, the other at sea, and maybe taking place in the Nile Delta. The land battle shows the Sea Peoples fighting in chariots, their families accompanying them in ox-drawn carts with solid wheels, reminiscent of a cart still used in parts of Anatolia. The Sea People warriors are carefully differentiated in their appearance, dress, and weapons. Three groups can be identified by their helmets: the Peleset, Tjekker, and Denyen (Danuna) wear high 'feathered' headdresses; the Sherden wear horned helmets, and the Shekelesh have a fillet head band similar to the rim of helmets worn in western Anatolia.

The naval battle relief depicts the Sea Peoples in duck-shaped prow and stern vessels, powered by sail alone. The Sherden are shown with other groups using round shields and a long broadsword. This weapon has been identified as Achaean Type B. They wear paneled kilts with tassels and corselets, with layered armor plates, fitted like lobster shells and these are similar to the design of Mycenaean armor. Other Sea Peoples were the Karkiska, Lukka, Teresh, and Washesh. Ramesses III defeated the Sea Peoples on land and sea but some were allowed to settle in Palestine. These were the Tjekker, Denyen, and Peleset, the latter gave their name to Philistine and later Palestine. It is interesting that the pottery of these people is obviously derived from the Aegean, mainly Mycenaean types. Ramesses' strategy in facing the Sea Peoples was to set up ambushes along the coast and Nile Delta so that he could defend his shores with archers. They were hidden and would emerge to shower enemy ships, killing the crew and then setting them alight with fire arrows. His victory at Xois, in the Nile Delta, in 1178 BCE left the enemy with many dead and those captured were forced into the Egyptian navy and army. After defeats at the hands of the Egyptians the Sea People vanished from history.

Where did the Sea People go? Some scholars suggest that the Sherden went to Sardinia, owing to the name similarity. One mooted possibility is that those fleeing from the Trojan War, sometimes deemed to be Teresh, traveled to Italy to form the Etruscan civilization. Long established families in Tuscany have helped researchers by giving them DNA samples which are the same as some inhabitants of the western Anatolian coast. Other Sea Peoples reputedly sailed to Sicily and Corsica but all these theories are just that—no one knows.

After the Philistines (the Peleset) were defeated by Ramesses III, it seems likely that they resided in Egypt before being sent to re-occupy fortified towns destroyed in the invasion. These towns became the military outworks of Egypt defense against any possible enemy. As Egyptian power waned the Philistines expanded their settlements into the Yarkon area where Philistine farmsteads have been discovered at Tel Gerissa and Aphek, with a larger settlement at Tel Qasile. The latter contained a temple similar to sanctuaries excavated at Mycenae, Cyprus, and the island of Melos.

Historians have suggested the expansion was also made possible by the Philistine monopoly of iron, as chronicled in the Bible, which gave them a military edge against Canaanites and Hebrews.

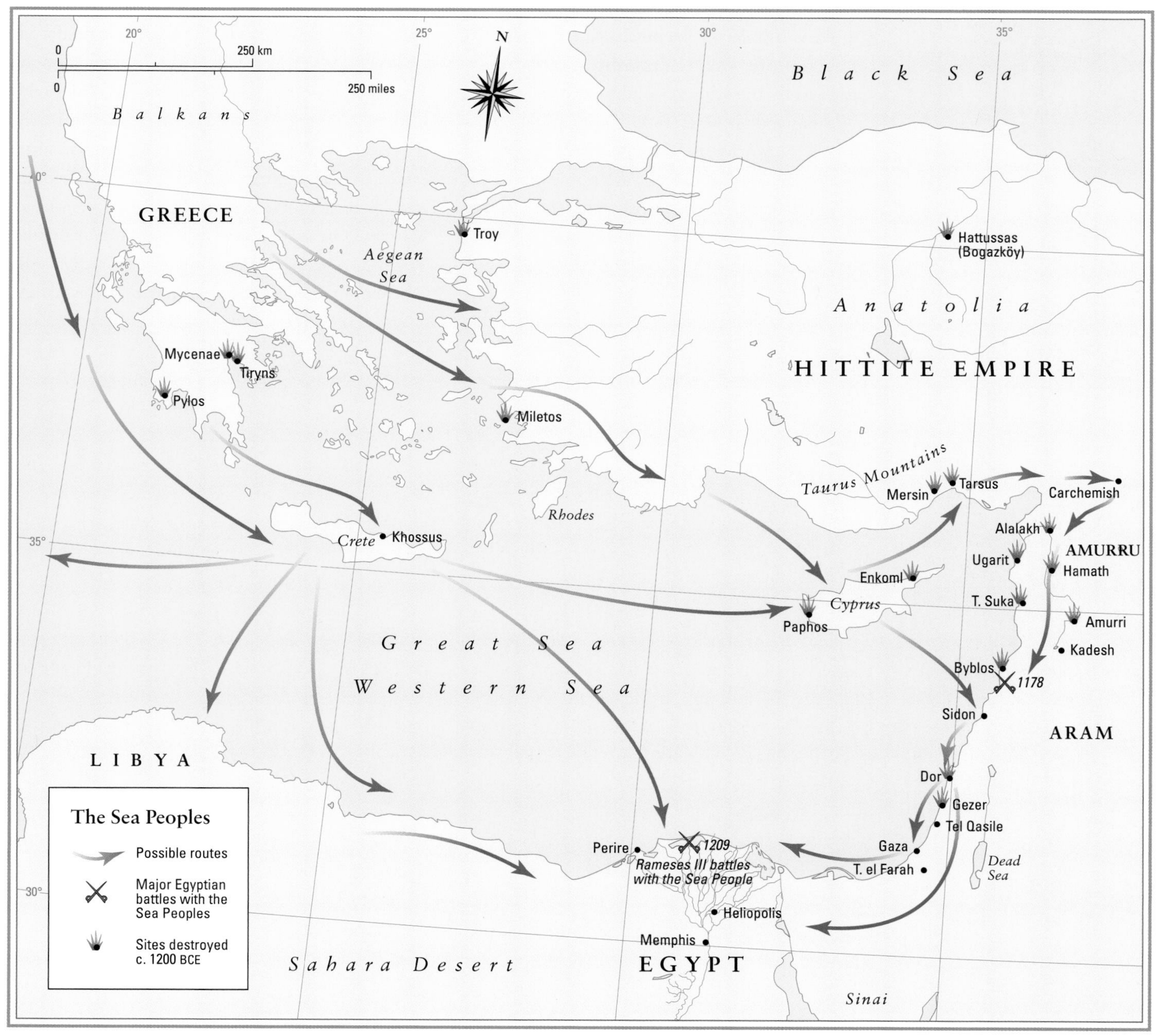

Battle of Megiddo 1457 BCE

Pharaoh Thutmose III wished to continue his ancestors' attempts to control the international trade routes in the Levant and prevent the Mitanni from spreading their influence southward, especially to Byblos, which had strong commercial ties with Egypt. To achieve these goals, Thutmose undertook seventeen campaigns in Palestine on an annual basis. In 1457 BCE, he marched his army to Gaza and then Joppa and prepared to confront a coalition of states led by the King of Kadesh.

Preparations were made by the Canaanites to place their army before the city of Megiddo, on the edge of the Jezreel Valley, an important site guarding trade routes through the Carmel range, especially the 'Way of the Sea.' Ignoring his counsellors' advice, Thutmose advanced through the very narrow Aruna Pass with his vanguard, then deployed on to the Plain of Megiddo to guard the advance of his remaining troops as they trickled through the wadi. The coalition troops had been placed along the edge of the plateau guarding approaches to the city.

Thutmose split his troops into three divisions which attacked the coalition forces with chariots armed with composite bows. He routed his foes and if his troops had not engaged in plundering the enemy encampments, he might have fought his way into Megiddo. He remained to besiege the city into which some of the enemy fled. The booty gained from the battle and the city, which eventually surrendered after a long siege, was enormous and later detailed on reliefs at the temple at Karnak. On subsequent campaigns in northern Palestine, he eventually reached Carchemish, where he erected a stele proclaiming his victories.

Battle of Megiddo
1457 BCE

1. *Thutmose camps by Qina Brook, then despatches his chariots to the low hills around the plain of Megiddo, leaving his infantry to guard his camp.*
2. *The King of Kadesh orders his troops to face Thutmose's forces.*
3. *Thutmose orders his troops to advance on the opposition.*
4. *The two sides clash, the Egyptians taking the advantage. The King of Kadesh orders his remaining forces to retreat back to within the city walls.*

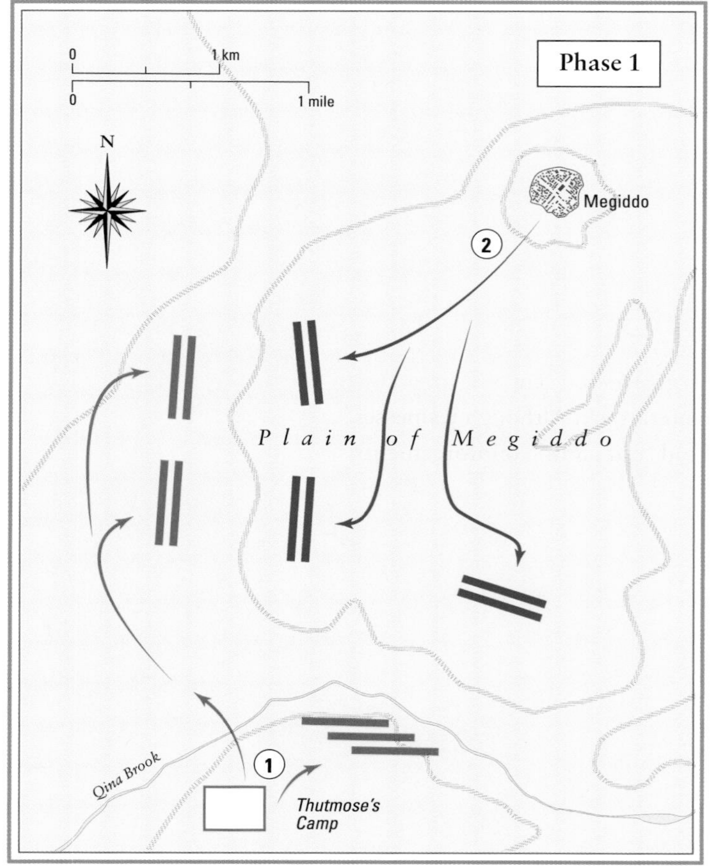

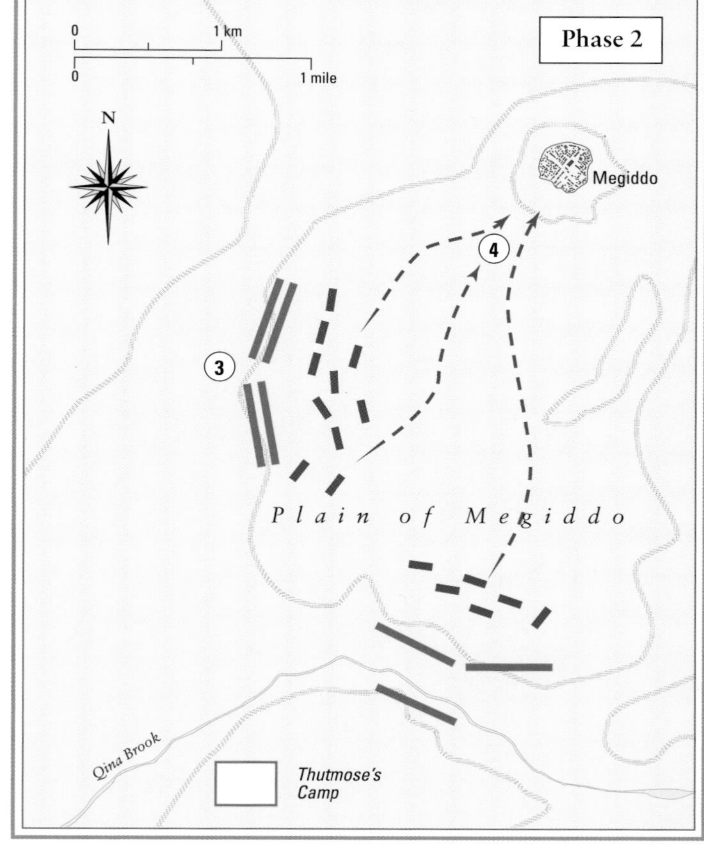

Battle of Kadesh 1275 BCE

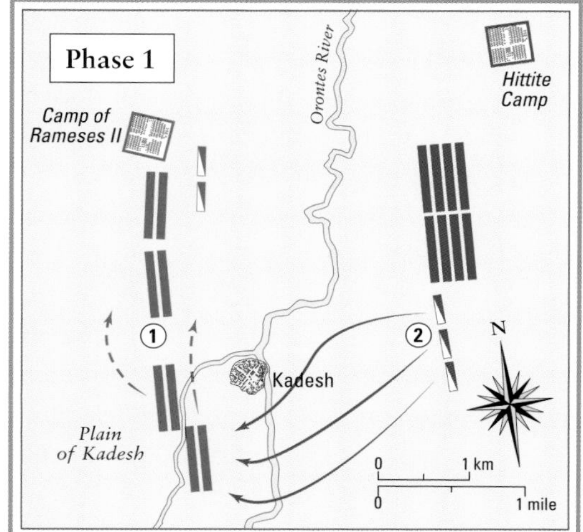

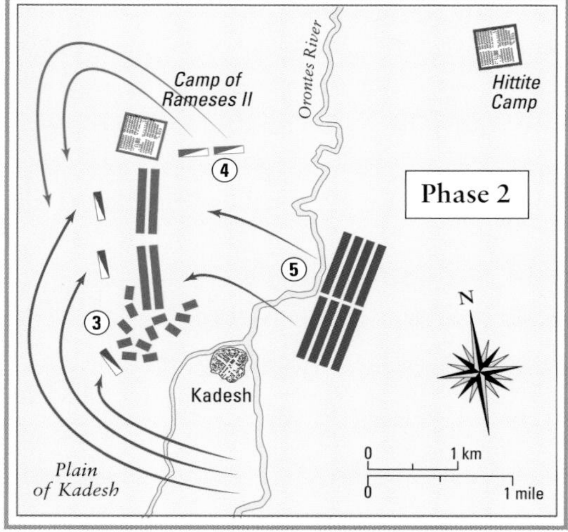

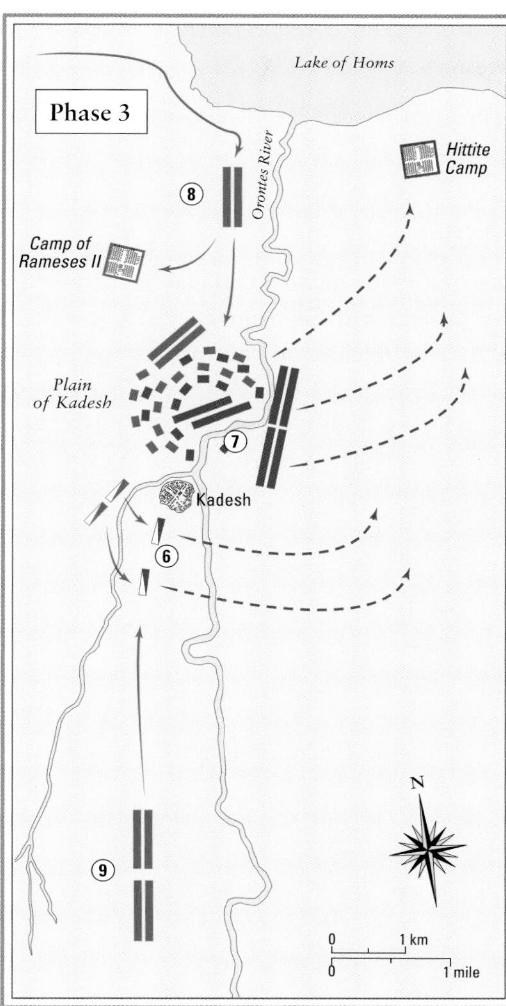

Battle of Kadesh
1275 BCE

1. *Egyptian corps of Amun and Re advance west of Kadesh*
2. *Hittite chariots dash to attack the corps of Re, south of Kadesh, dispersing them north*
3. *The Hittite chariots continue to pursue the Egyptians*
4. *Rameses leads a chariot attack around to the rear of the Hittite chariots*
5. *A second Hittite attack approaches the Egyptians*
6. *The Hittite chariots are slowly beaten back and retreat across the river*
7. *The main Hittite force makes contact with the Egyptians*
8. *The Ne'arin arrive from the north, strengthening the Egyptian's position*
9. *Egyptian Ptah corps arrive from the south, the increased opposing force compels the Hittites to retreat*

After several weak pharaohs had lost hegemony over the Levantine city-states, more aggressive pharaohs sought to regain their power in the region. Rameses II led an Egyptian army comprising many Nubian and Sherden mercenaries in an assault on Kadesh, the Hittite stronghold overlooking the Orontes River. The Hittites had been expanding into a fully-fledged empire from their Anatolian heartland, and by the time of Rameses II their land bordered Egyptian spheres of influence, prompting Rameses to act. Eager to capture Kadesh before the main Hittite army could be deployed, Rameses rashly approached the city without the precaution of careful reconnaissance. This had terrible consequences when he and his advance guard were cut off by a surprise Hittite counterattack. Although Rameses managed to hold out until reinforcements arrived, he was unable to capture Kadesh and was therefore forced into making peace with the Hittites. The outcome of the battle might have been influenced by the Hittites' iron weapons against the Egyptians' bronze. The battle was inconclusive, allowing Hittite power to move south toward Damascus, and Rameses failed in this campaign. The battle is significant because it was the largest chariot battle ever fought. Around 5,000 chariots were involved, as well as 9,000 foot soldiers.

States and Kingdoms 1500–c. 700 BCE

Most historians concentrate their attention on the states of the Middle East that existed in the river valleys of the Tigris, Euphrates, Nile, and the coastal Levant. This approach ignores neighboring states that fought them or became part of the cultures of the Middle East, even borrowing languages and scripts. Hence, the countries of Kush, Elam, and Urartu must receive some treatment.

Kush existed in today's northern Sudan and was the gateway into the heart of Africa, through which passed timber, slaves, and the gold mined in the region. Also known as Nubia, the polity was invaded by Egypt around 1500 BCE, and forts were built to maintain control over the aggressive Kushites. The occupation lasted some 400 years, until the collapse of the New Kingdom, and introduced Egyptian architectural styles, hieroglyphs, and deities into Kush. Kush gradually became powerful enough to invade Egypt, conquering Thebes and Memphis, and establishing a Twenty-fifth Dynasty led by Pharaoh Pianky (Piy), which lasted sixty years until overthrown by the expanding Assyrians.

The Kushite capital at Napata, south of the Fourth Cataract, was a major religious center for the worship of Amonre. In 592 BCE, Pharaoh Psammuthis invaded Kush, seizing Kerma and Napata, which was thoroughly sacked; Greek mercenaries left graffiti there. In response, the Kushites moved their capital to Meroë. Kush retreated into comparative isolation until the Persians, who conquered Egypt in 525 BCE, made an unsuccessful foray into Kush.

Elam was situated in the west and southwest of today's Iran. Its kingdoms were centered on the Iranian plateau, with capitals variously at Anshan and Susa. Developing an urban civilization in the Copper Age, Elam drew much inspiration from Sumeria. Elam became increasingly important when the dynasties at Anshan were established in around 1500 BCE. Before that time, Elamites had invaded Ur and carried off its King, and this destruction of the Third Dynasty of Ur is portrayed in the words of the *Lamentations over the Destruction of Ur*. Elam was attacked by the Kassite King of Babylon who occupied the country briefly in c. 1320 BCE.

The Elamite Empire reached its height under King Shutruk-Nakhante and his three sons. They ravaged Kassite Babylonia and their resulting loot allowed them to restore and expand the temple complexes at Susa. The King made one very destructive raid and his booty included statues of the gods Marduk and Manishtushu. The Elamites also stole the Manishtushu Obelisk, the Stele of Hammurabi on which his law code was engraved, and the Stele of Naram-Sin, which depicts his power and supposed divinity. In 1158, a campaign killed the Kassite King, who was replaced by Shuruk-Nakhante's son, who was, in turn, ousted by the Babylonians three years later. Nebuchadnezzar I of Babylon defeated the Elamite King and seized back the Babylonian treasures, and Elam vanished from history for several hundred years, being overwhelmed by encroaching Persian-speaking peoples.

Urartu was first mentioned in Assyrian inscriptions c. 1274 BCE as being one of a series of small states in the mountainous lands north of Assyria. The country is mentioned again in the ninth century BCE as a state that had absorbed a number of neighboring kingdoms under King Aramu and posed a threat to Assyria. The kingdom suffered defeat at the hands of Tiglath Pileser III in 745 BCE and was raided by Cimmerians and the Assyrian Sargon II in 714 BCE. It grew to its militarily most powerful under King Argishti I (685–660 BCE), who frustrated Assyrian campaigns against him. Eventually, Urartu paid tribute to the Medes under Astages and then to Cyrus II the Great, the King of Fars, the founder of the Achaemenid Persian Empire. By the late sixth century BCE, Urartu ceased to exist except as the Persian satrapy of Armenia.

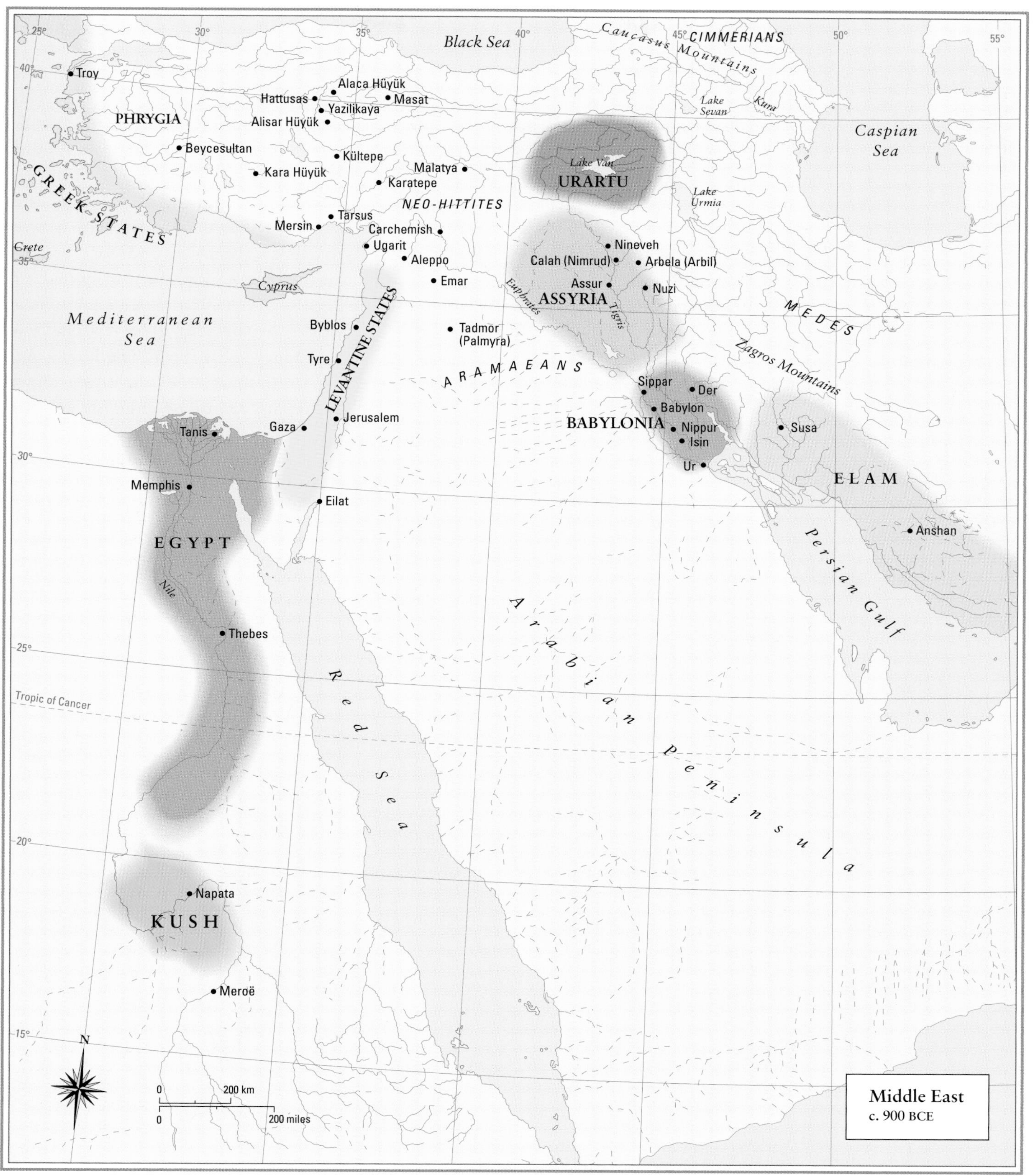

Black Sea
Caucasus Mountains
CIMMERIANS
Lake Sevan
Kura
Caspian Sea
Troy
Alaca Hüyük
Hattusas
Masat
Yazilikaya
Alisar Hüyük
PHRYGIA
Beycesultan
Kültepe
Malatya
Kara Hüyük
Karatepe
Lake Van
URARTU
Lake Urmia
GREEK STATES
NEO-HITTITES
Tarsus
Mersin
Carchemish
Crete
Ugarit
Aleppo
Nineveh
Calah (Nimrud)
Arbela (Arbil)
Cyprus
Emar
Assur
Nuzi
Euphrates
ASSYRIA
Tigris
MEDES
Mediterranean Sea
Byblos
LEVANTINE STATES
Tadmor (Palmyra)
Tyre
Zagros Mountains
ARAMAEANS
Sippar
Der
Babylon
Jerusalem
Gaza
Tanis
BABYLONIA
Nippur
Isin
Susa
Ur
ELAM
Memphis
Eilat
Anshan
EGYPT
Persian Gulf
Nile
Arabian Peninsula
Thebes
Red Sea
Tropic of Cancer
Napata
KUSH
Meroë
N
0
200 km
200 miles
Middle East
c. 900 BCE
25°
30°
35°
40°
45°
50°
55°
40°
35°
30°
25°
20°
15°

The Assyrian Empire

Assyria arose in northern Mesopotamia around the cities of Assur and Nineveh, sometimes known as Subartu, developing into an important Semitic Kingdom, on occasion dominating its neighbors, in turn being dominated. The state's long existence can be divided into three periods: Middle Bronze Age, Late Bronze Age, and Early Iron Age, spanning a little less than two millennia.

At around 2200 BCE there seems to have been a worldwide crisis that affected all the great civilizations of the Early Bronze Age to some degree. It has been suggested that some kind of persistent environmental deterioration may have been responsible. Early states, though not incapable of change, must have been vulnerable, their capacity to cope diminished. Semi-nomadic societies, with little infrastructure, could adapt and change. This may have been Assyria's opportunity. Around 2154 BCE the Akkadian Empire fell and Assyria achieved independent status.

The earliest recorded King was Tudiya, he is described as 'in tents', indicating a nomadic or at least semi-nomadic lifestyle. The Old Assyrian Kingdom of the Middle Bronze Age first appears in around 2100 BCE, having thrown off Sumerian control. King Ushpia, who

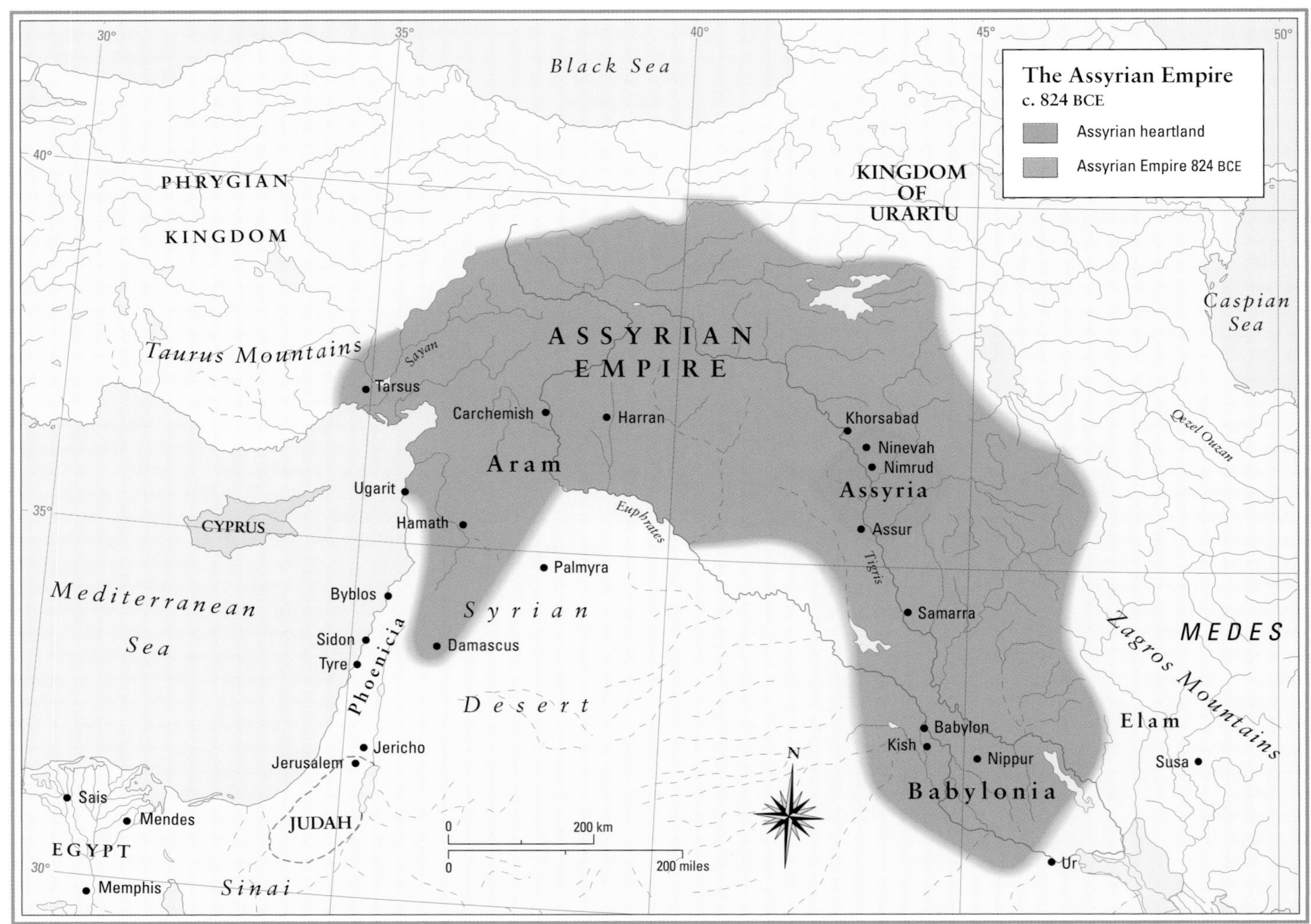

reigned c. 2050 BCE, probably gathered together independent cities and localities, creating an effective monarchy over an Assyrian Kingdom that was now, in part at least, urbanized.

Over the centuries that followed, Assyrian Dynasties campaigned into neighboring states, colonies were founded, particularly in Asia Minor, and Assyrian protectorates were established. These were largely at the expense of Hurrians and Hattians to the north, and Akkadians to the southeast, though the latter were described as being 'liberated' from invading Elamites and Amorites. The freedom of the Akkadians now belonged to Assyria, at least for a time.

The Assyrians established trading relations via their colonies in Asia Minor, which gave Assyria access to valuable metals in exchange for textiles. This process was expanded during the rule of Erishum I c. 1974–1935 BCE. Assyria continued to expand, conquering the Kingdom of Mari in today's Syria. The Empire now stretched in an arc from central Mesopotamia, in the east, across Asia Minor, down into Syria and touching the Mediterranean coast.

By 1750 BCE this era of Assyrian power was eclipsed by the rise of Babylon, under Hammurabi. Assyria's trade faded, taken over probably by Babylonians. However, on the death of Hammurabi Babylonian power rapidly declined and Assyria regained its independence. This led to a period of disunity ended by King Adasi, 1726–1701 BCE, who re-established order. Not much is known of his successor; however, Assyria maintained its defenses and economic stability, surviving attacks by Hittites and Kassites. Assyria was also able to withstand a period of Mitanni influence from 1450 BCE, which was finally cast off by King Eriba-Adad I 1392–1366 BCE. Now followed another period of Assyrian ascendency and new ambitious rulers attacked the Mitanni state, which was also under pressure from the Hittites.

By the reign of Shalamaneser I, 1274–1244 BCE, the powerful Kingdom of Urartu was overrun and Assyrian control reached into the Zagros Mountains. The Mitanni state was destroyed, increasing the pressure on the Hittites and their allies. There were, of course, periods of fluctuating fortune, and revolts and murders all played a part in the protracted story of Assyria. The embattled Hittite Empire finally collapsed around 1180 BCE.

Into the vacuum marched Babylon and Assyria, both bent on expansion and profit. Their ambitions were met by Tiglath-Pileser I, 1115–1177 BCE, one of the Middle East's great conquerors. He campaigned and conquered the Phrygians, Commagene, Cilicia, and Cappadocia, and held on to the province of Subartu. After Tiglath-Pileser's death, without a clear accession, his Empire proved incapable of coping with the changes emerging from the west. Smaller states and societies could, and did, innovate. The Aramaeans were one such people, nomadic, located around the upper Euphrates. The Aramaeans were probably the first to domesticate the camel, the beast most suited for the arid conditions of this region. This animal provided these people with a fast-moving force which, when dismounted, would form into a disciplined infantry unit, not to be compared with later Greek phalanx or the Roman Legion, but fully capable of overawing less disciplined enemies. Now they could infiltrate settled societies and control trade routes. They founded dynasties across the northern arc of the fertile crescent and, for a time, constricted Assyria, taking areas in Syria previously conquered by Tiglath-Pileser I.

As the Assyrian 'Dark Age' cleared, so began the Iron-Age Neo-Assyrian Empire. The campaigns of King Adad-nirari, 911–892 BCE, set the state to become not just a great power, but the greatest Empire the world had seen so far. Successive rulers extended the state that, by 823–824 BCE, included Babylonia and Urartu across an arc down to Damascus, facing lands Egypt considered its own.

In this detail, from a relief from the Palace of Nimrud, an Assryrian wheeled battering ram, manned by archers, attacks the walled defenses of an enemy city.

The Assyrian Empire under Tiglath-Pileser and the Struggle for Egypt 674–663 BCE

In 745 BCE, Tiglath-Pileser III, a regional governor, usurped the Assyrian throne and determined to revitalize the state. Until his reign, Assyria had expanded and contracted in size several times and its client-states and vassals constantly rebelled, meaning that Assyria had to discipline its minions in attempts to keep tribute flowing in. Additionally, Assyria faced

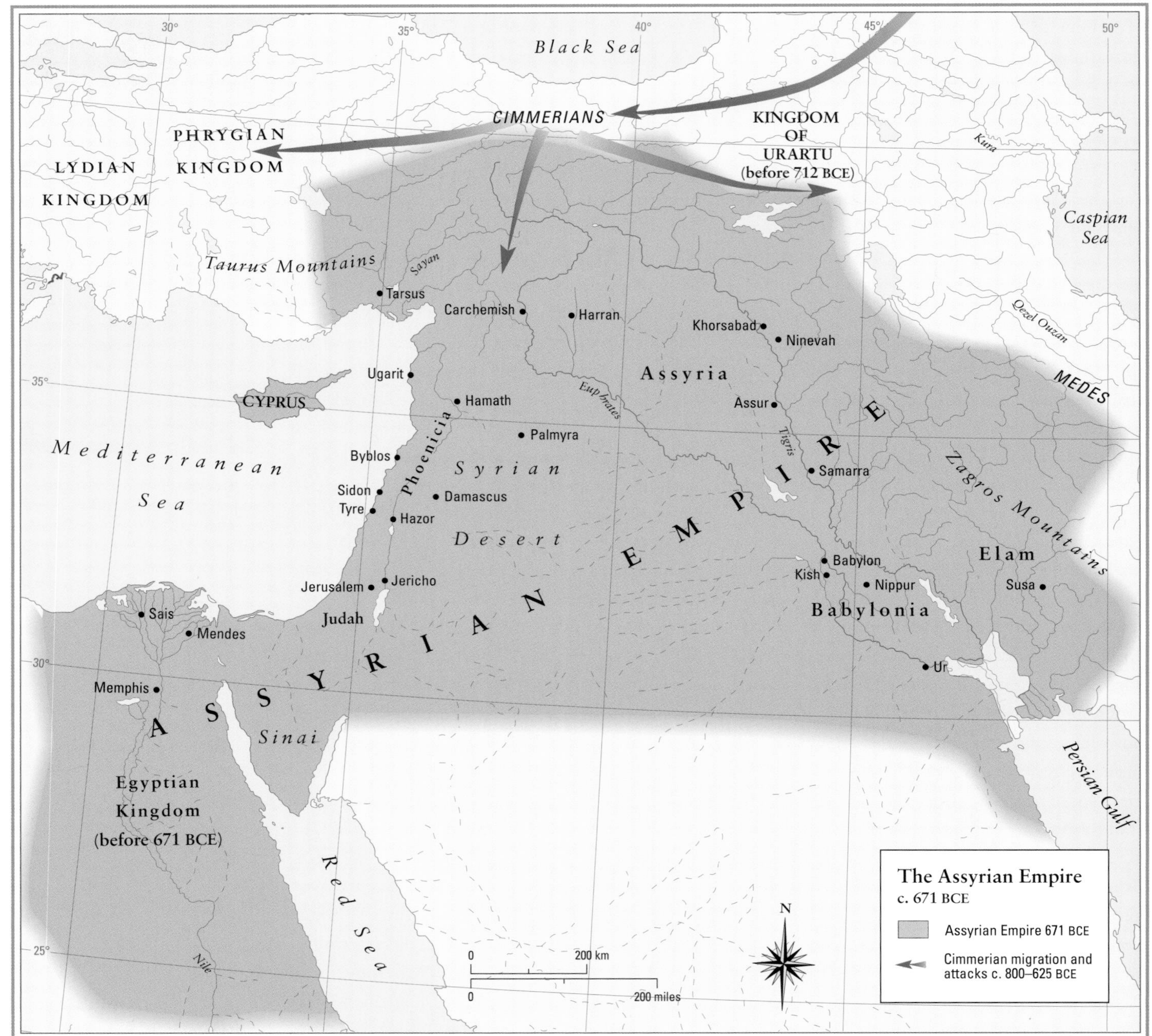

determined enemies and the state required reform to maintain its great power status. Tiglath-Pileser planned to expand beyond the Euphrates to acquire lands rich in timber and minerals, and to use these new territories as springboards into southwestern Asia Minor and Egypt, which would enable him to access the trade of the Mediterranean. To achieve such aims, he expanded the size of the army by recruiting subject peoples as infantry, leaving native Assyrians to provide the cavalry and charioteers. His standing army became the first fully-professional force in the world—a model for future Empires.

Assyria had to assert its power over the Aramean Chaldees of Babylon to the south and over the Kingdom of Urartu, a country around Lake Van in the Armenian Highlands stretching to the Caucasus. Babylon was pacified and Urartu badly defeated, losing some of its territory. Campaigns were also undertaken against the Medes in northern Iran and Assyrian power reached the regions just south of the Caspian Sea. Tiglath-Pileser next launched his armies into Syria where he mopped up the city-states including Hamath, Tyre, Byblos, and Damascus, and Israel. Assyrian victims included Judah, Moab, Edom, Cyprus, the neo-Hittite states, and Arabia.

The campaigns in the Levant saw Assyrian troops reaching the Brook of Egypt, Wadi el-Arish, but it would be Tiglath-Pileser's successors who would finally conquer Egypt, a country that constantly fostered rebellion in Palestine. A base was established at the Wadi, thereby cutting off any Levantine coalition from Egyptian help. He overran Trans-Jordan, deporting part of their populations and destroying numerous cities such as Megiddo and Hazor. Tiglath-Pileser designed a new policy regarding those he subjugated. Instead of receiving tribute from the defeated, he would take their lands and annex them as provinces within his Empire to be administered by governors. He hoped this would reduce any local loyalties and thus eradicate future resistance. Occupied territory was divided into the provinces of Gilead, Megiddo, and Dor. When Damascus was ravaged, that region was divided into four Assyrian provinces.

Tiglath-Pileser's son ruled as Shalamaneser V (726–723 BCE) and drove off forces of the resurgent Pharaoh Piy, a Nubian Kushite King who established the Twenty-fifth Egyptian Dynasty and who also sought to encroach upon Assyrian territory. Sargon II (725–715 BCE) faced rebellion in Babylonia, fought Midas of Phrygia, destroyed the neo-Hittite states in the Taurus Mountains, and finally broke Urartu, a tactical error since it was a bastion against nomads. Piy hoped to advance again while these campaigns were fought but he was pushed back across Sinai. Sennacherib (705–681 BCE) also faced a Babylonian revolt and was confronted by an encroachment into Palestine by Nubian Pharaoh Taharqa. Again, the Egyptians were turned back leaving the Assyrians to crush the revolt the Pharaoh had been supporting.

A portrait of Tiglath-Pileser II, who ruled from 745 to 727 BCE.

In 671 BCE, Esarhaddon (681–669 BCE), having crossed the Sinai Desert, waged war against Taharqa, routed him, and occupied Memphis, managing to seize the royal family except the Pharaoh. As the Assyrians were leaving, Taharqa raised a rebellion resulting in a second Assyrian campaign. Esarhaddon died en route and was succeeded by Ashurbanipal (669–627 BCE), a brutal character and the last great King of Assyria. He crushed the rebellion and took captive all the Egyptian princes save Necho I, the native Egyptian Prince of Sais who managed to convince the Assyrians of his loyalty. He became the Assyrian puppet Pharaoh. Taharqa died in 664 BCE and was succeeded by his nephew, Tantamani, who invaded Upper Egypt, making Thebes his capital. An Assyrian army was sent south, defeating the Nubians and leaving Tantamani to flee into Nubia where he remained.

Assyria was now the largest Empire the world had ever seen, stretching from the Caucasus to Nubia and from Cyprus to Persia.

Nebuchadnezzar and New Babylon 625–539 BCE

The Chaldaeans, a southern Babylonian people, had constantly rebelled against Assyrian rule, and, around 630 BCE, one of their leaders, Nabopolassar, crowned himself King of Babylon and threw the Assyrians out of Uruk. He was aided by his able son, Nebuchadnezzar. Elsewhere, the Medes were making a break for freedom, raiding Assyria and even attacking Nineveh. In 615 BCE, they conquered Arrapha (Kirkuk) and destroyed Assur in the following year. Cyaxares, the Median King, allied with Nabopolassar, aiming to break up and divide the Assyrian Empire between them. The remnants of the Assyrian forces were cornered and defeated at Harran in 609 BCE.

In 605 BCE, Nebuchadnezzar II led his armies to a bloody victory over the Egyptians under Pharaoh Necho II at the Battle of Carchemish. Hot pursuit continued as the Babylonians stormed through Syria and the Levant, inflicting another defeat on the Egyptians at Hamath. In 605 BCE, he became King and now had the task of pacifying his newly-acquired territories. In 604 BCE, he took Ashkelon, deporting part of its population to Babylon, and attempted to invade Egypt but was stopped in a drawn campaign. Jehoiakim, King of Judah, was so terrified of the Babylonians that he became their vassal. When Nebuchadnezzar failed to campaign the following year, Jehoiakim rebelled but soon faced raids from Babylonians working with guerrilla bands of Aramaeans, Moabites, and Ammonites. In 598 BCE, Jehoiakim died and was succeeded by his son, Jehoiachin. The Babylonians returned and destroyed Jerusalem in three months. The King, the Queen Mother, leading officials, and loot were despatched to Babylon and the King's uncle, Zedekiah, was installed in his place. Jehoiakim had inflicted great losses on Judah. Lachish and Debir had been stormed and devastated while the Negev was removed from its control, Judah's economy was damaged and the population reduced. The country's leaders were deported, leaving those behind incapable of husbanding Judah's declining resources.

A carved representation of Nebuchadnezzar.

In 595/594 BCE, rebellion broke out in Babylon. The Levantine peoples plotted together to discuss plans for the possible revolt of Judah, Tyre, Edom, Moab, Ammon, and Sidon. The revolt occurred, but only Tyre and Ammon joined in with Edom supporting Nebuchadnezzar. By January 588 BCE, Jerusalem was besieged and outlying strong points were reduced until only Lachish and Azekah remained. Azekah finally fell and Jerusalem's food ran out as the Babylonians breached the walls. The King and his family were captured while attempting an escape towards the River Jordan. Zedekiah was forced to watch the execution of his sons, then blinded and deported to Babylon, where he later died. More executions and deportations ensued, while Jerusalem was burned and its wall levelled. Judah was no more. Tyre was besieged for thirteen years before agreeing to vassal status.

The Babylonians and Medes remained at peace after their alliance had succeeded in its aim, Median ambitions focussed on Lydia and consolidating their gains in Armenia and northern Iran. This Neo-Babylonian Empire was remarkably short-lived, ending in 539 BCE. Over its brief life-span, an efficient civil service was established, as well as a taxation system to sustain Nebuchadnezzar's armies, which had to be rebuilt after an exhausting war against the Egyptians. Babylonia was redeveloped and lifted out of the poverty it had endured under harsh Assyrian rule. Trade routes were redirected through Babylon and the city turned into a veritable boom town, becoming a large, well-built, and well-designed center. The construction of the Hanging Gardens of Babylon has been attributed to Nebuchadnezzar though historians think that the Assyrian Sennacherib built them in Nineveh.

The Babylonian Empire began its decline with the death of Nebuchadnezzar in 562 BCE, the throne eventually being usurped by an Aramaean, Nabonidus, in 556 BCE. This enigmatic figure was a devotee of the gods, especially the moon-goddess, Sin; his mother was a high priestess of this goddess. The priests of Marduk were concerned by this allegiance. In foreign adventures, Nabonidus commanded a raid into Cilicia and captured Haran, his mother's city. He allied with Astyages of the Medes against the Persians who were becoming powerful under their leader, King Cyrus II.

Much evidence exists that gives Nabonidus a bad name. Exiled Jews in Babylon attacked him and he was the target of negative propaganda by Cyrus. Despite his critics, Nabonidus can be praised as the world's first archaeologist who excavated sites, especially of Naram-Sin's tomb. For some obscure reason Nabonidus decided to reside in the oasis of Tema in Arabia, a major trade hub where he built a palace complex. He stayed there for ten years, leaving his son, Belaharusur, in charge. Known as Belshazzar in the Biblical Book of Daniel, this prince ruled well but he could not carry out the King's ritual task of performing New Year rites associated with Marduk. The priests of Marduk promised Cyrus that they would give him Babylon without a fight if he maintained their privileges. In 539 BCE, Cyrus of Persia attacked northern Babylon, fighting a battle at Opis, whose inhabitants he slaughtered. Other cities then opened their gates, as did Babylon. Nabonidus surrendered and was pensioned off with a parcel of territory in Iran. The rapid and peaceful submission of Babylonia ensured its survival as a cultural center in the new Persian Empire, which was built on tolerance, and negotiation.

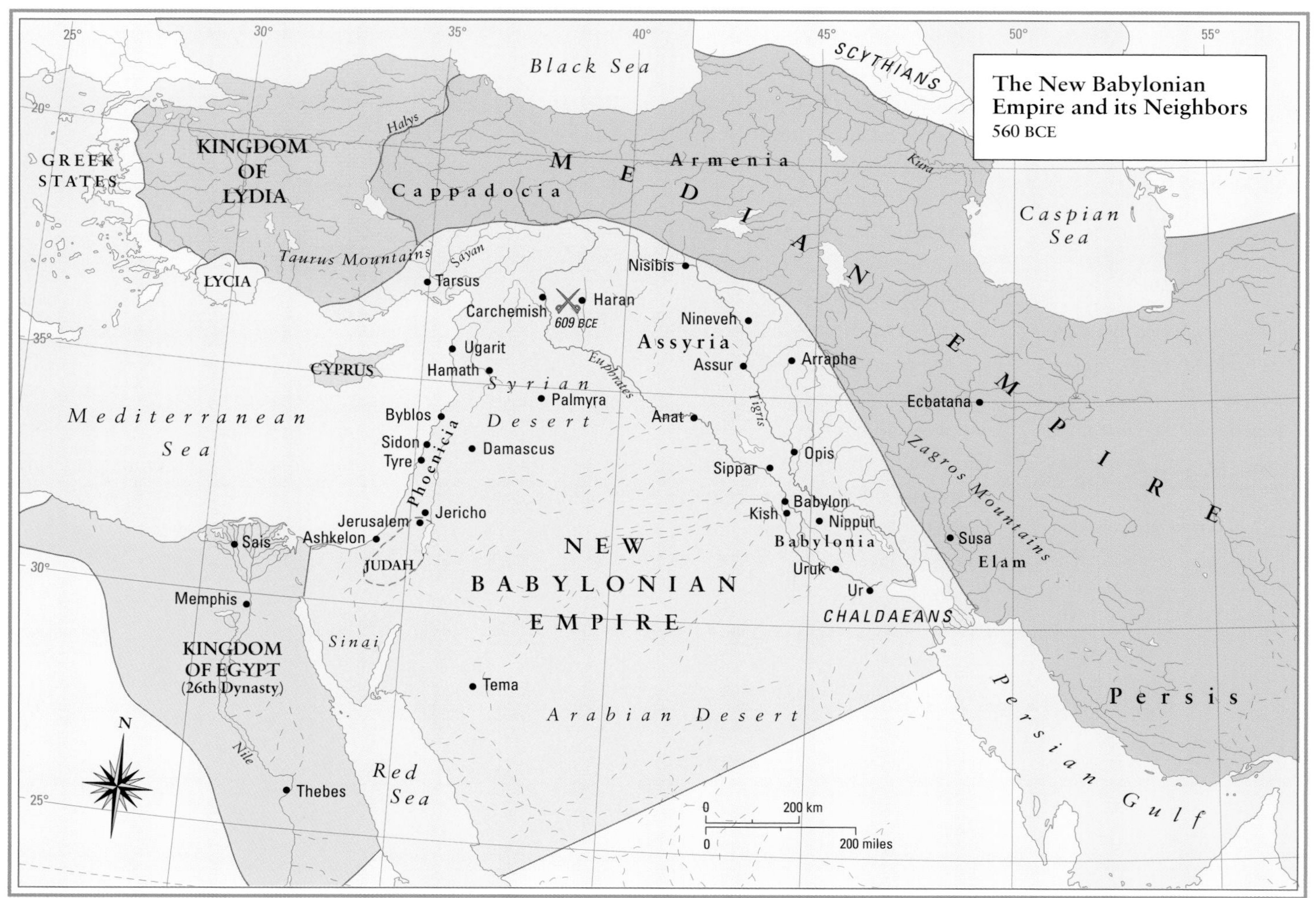

Darius I and the Persian Empire c. 520 BCE

The Persian Empire emerged when Cyrus II, King of Anshan, overthrew the last Median King, Astyages. Cyrus led the Iranian Medes and Persians in various campaigns, defeating Lydia in 546 BCE and Babylonia in 539 BCE. Within a decade, his realm extended from Central Asia to the Ionian coast. His son and heir, Cambyses, increased his domains by seizing Egypt and Libya.

When Darius succeeded to the throne in 522 BCE, he faced rebellion throughout the Empire and spent a year crushing these revolts. He led a campaign to secure the Indus valley, from Gandhara in the northeast to the coast by today's Karachi. He then launched a maritime expedition into the Indian Ocean, which eventually reached the Egyptian end of the Red Sea. His interest in communications led him to construct a canal linking the Red Sea to the Nile and another to connect the Red Sea with the Mediterranean. He also built a vast network of roads linking the regions of the Empire and communications were so enhanced that a royal messenger could ride, using staging posts and fresh horses, from Susa to Sardis, some 1,678 miles, in a week.

A gold Daric coin, minted around 490 BCE and issued exclusively by Darius I. The gold used for these coins was of 95.83 percent purity.

Darius projected Persian power to the north of the Empire where he campaigned against the Scythians, reducing their raids upon the Empire. The vast territories were carefully administered from the capital at Susa with the Empire being divided into satrapies, normally governed by Persian noblemen who were personally loyal to Darius. Each satrapy was required to pay tribute to Darius and to supply troops for his army. His military forces were based around his personal guard of 10,000 'Immortals' who were the most professional and well-equipped force in the army. The rest of the army comprised provincial levies all carrying their regional weapons. His navy was Egyptian and Phoenician.

Darius advanced into Europe on his campaigns against the Greeks. This conflict began when the Greek Ionian cities rebelled and were supported by troops and ships from Athens and Eretria. The cities were eventually retaken after an allied Greek fleet, seeking to relieve Miletus, was destroyed at the Battle of Lade in 494 BCE. Darius then sent his armies across the

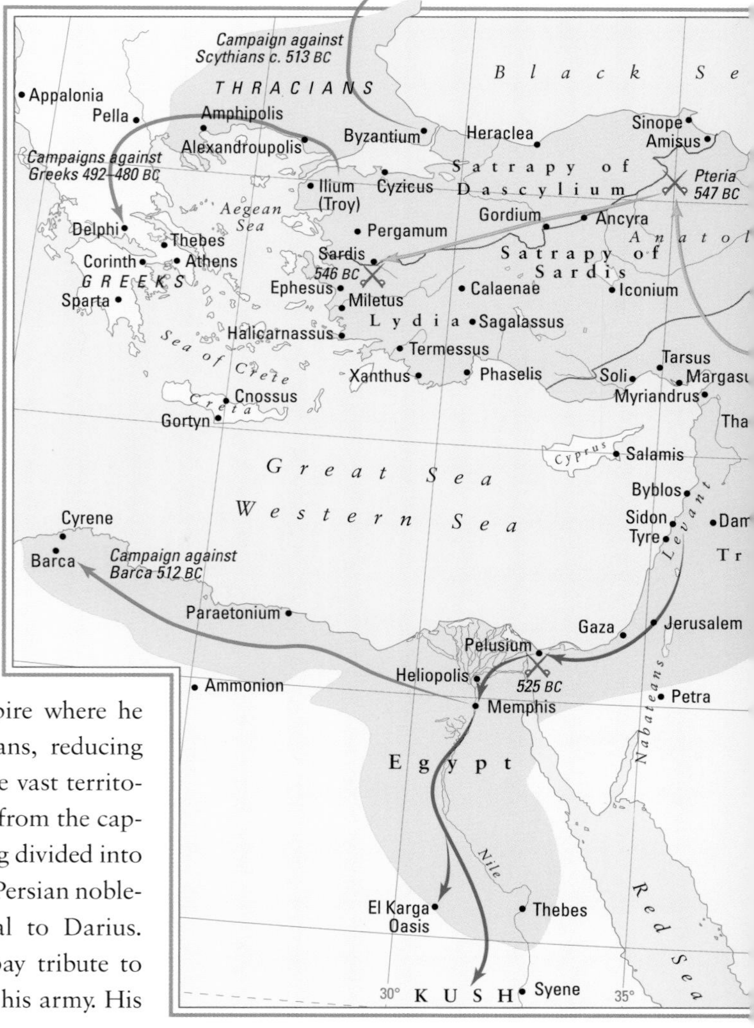

Hellespont into Thrace over a bridge of boats. He conquered Thrace, and Macedonia became a tributary state, while much of Greece remained neutral in the war against Persia. His fleets secured many of the Aegean islands, although a fleet was destroyed by a storm near Mount Athos in 492 BCE. The Persian army was finally defeated by the Athenian army, with support from several other Greek states under the command of Athenian General Miltiades, at the Battle of Marathon in 490 BCE.

The Persian Achaemenid Empire reached its greatest extent by 520 BCE under the rule of Darius I (521–486 BCE). Darius died in 486 BCE and his son Xerxes (485–465 BCE), after crushing rebellions in Egypt and Babylonia, assembled an enormous fleet and again crossed the Hellespont. He forced the pass at Thermopylae, defeating Leonidas, King of Sparta, in 480 BCE, and marching to Athens, which was occupied for a while. His fleet was defeated at Salamis and his army at Plataea, thus ending his enterprises in Greece.

Despite these setbacks in Greece, the Empire continued to flourish under the Achaemenid kings, although their reigns often ended in murder because of disputed successions. Intermittent conflict with Greece continued, but the Empire remained a cohesive entity. The last Persian King, Darius III (336–330 BCE) was defeated by Alexander the Great, who added the Persian Empire to his conquests.

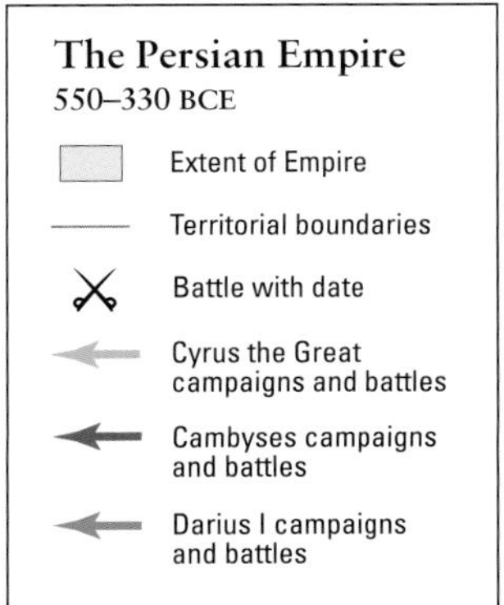

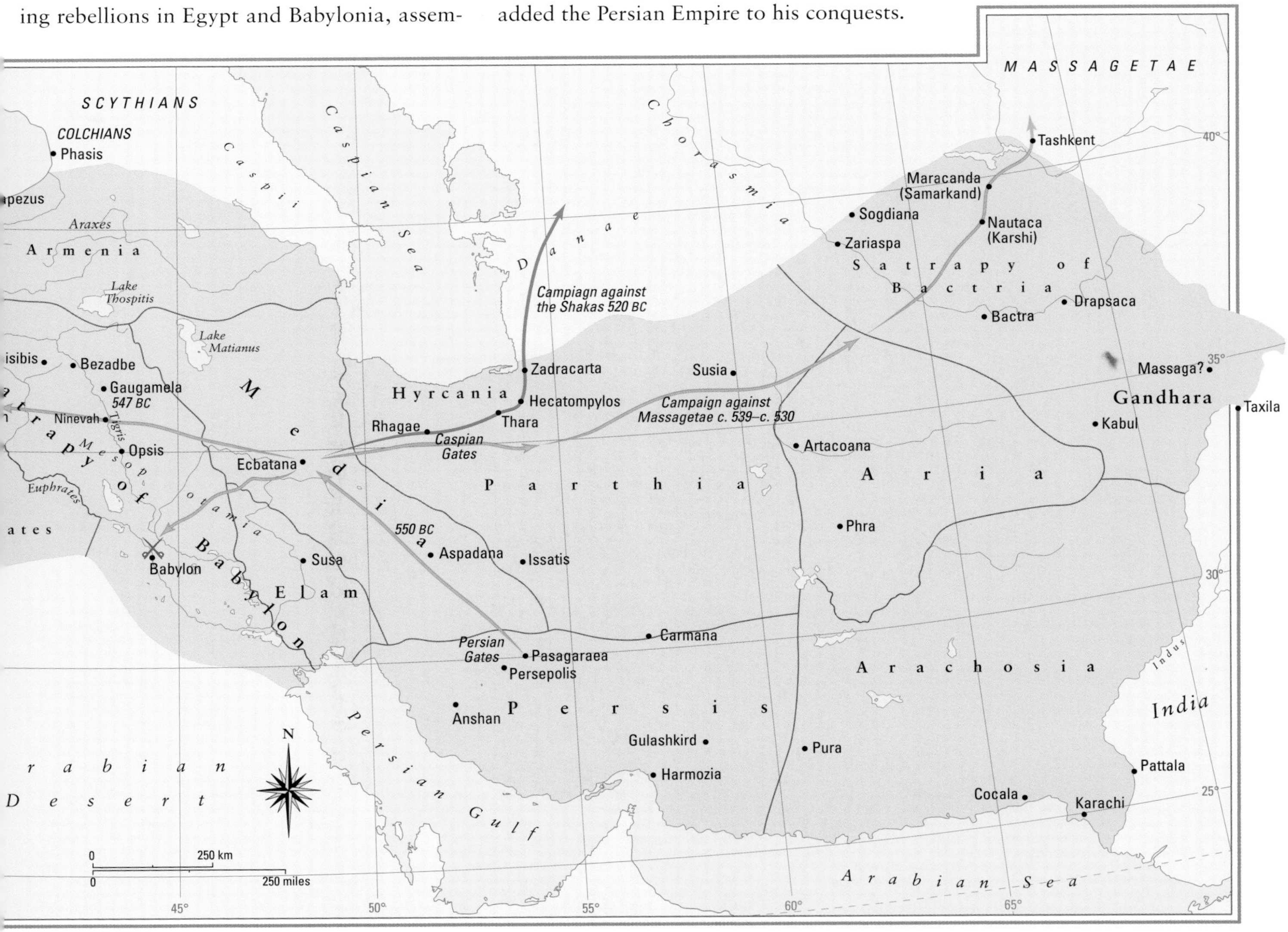

Xenophon and the Ten Thousand

After Athens was defeated in the Peloponnesian War, Sparta became the dominant force amongst the Greek states and then sought to influence politics in neighboring Persia. The Spartans wanted to manipulate the succession to the Persian throne by backing Cyrus the Younger, who was Governor of Sardis and the younger son of King Darius I, against his brother, the newly crowned Artaxerxes II. The resulting Greek expedition was recorded by the author and soldier Xenophon in his *Anabasis*, the Expedition of Cyrus. A force of some 13,000 Greek mercenaries was recruited by Clearchos, the Spartan General, and marched to Sardis to join Cyrus. The Greek forces thought it was to fight the Pisidians who inhabited part of southern Anatolia rather than become engaged with a vast Persian army in a dynastic dispute.

When the Greeks discovered they had been

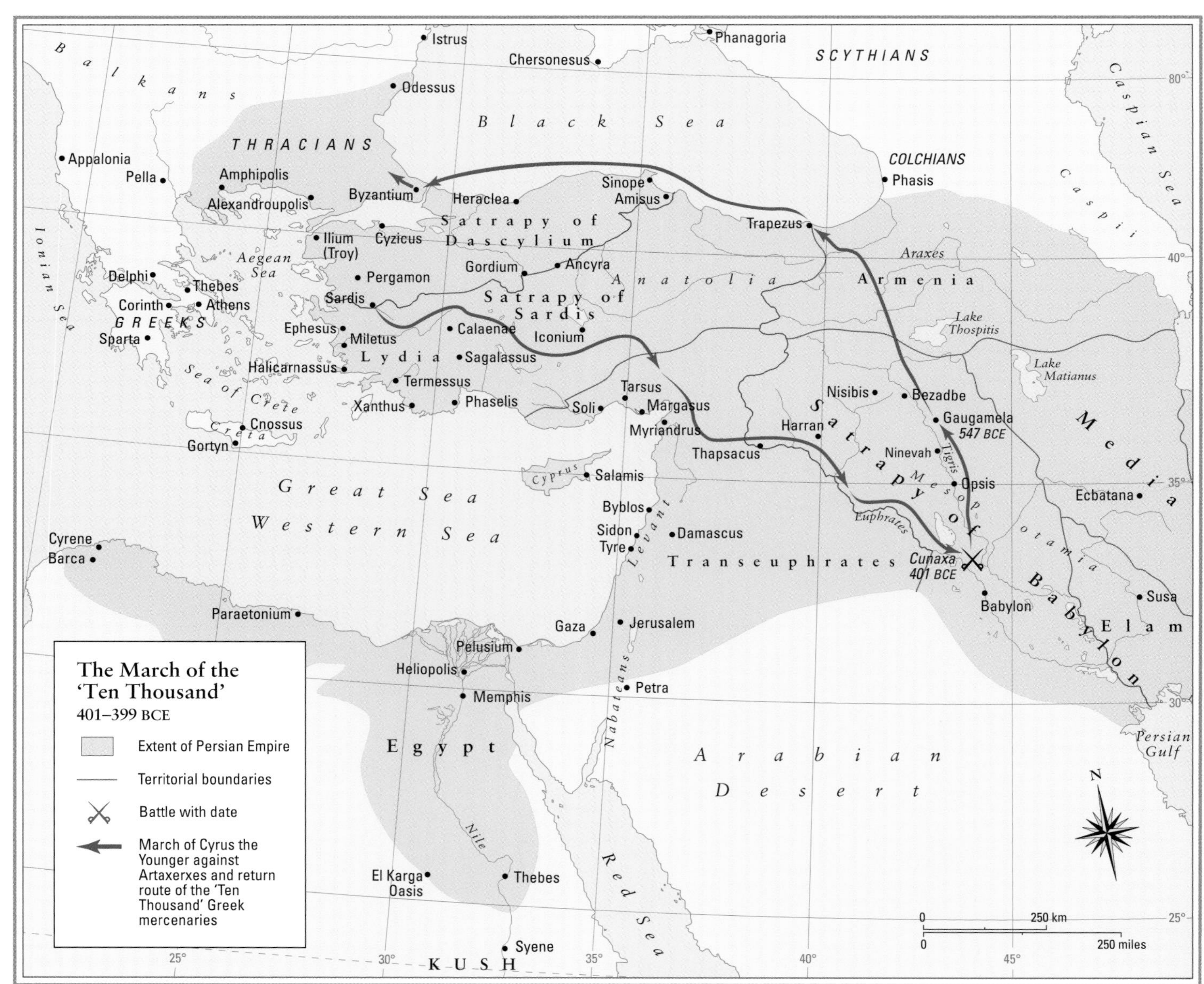

duped by Cyrus, they wished to return home but Clearchos persuaded them to go on. The expedition marched to Mesopotamia, where they engaged the Persians in battle at Cunaxa. The Greeks were placed on the right of Cyrus and his Persians and when the battle began, although outnumbered, they charged the left flank of Artaxerxes' army, which broke ranks and fled without even engaging the Greeks. On the Persian right, the engagement was difficult and hard fought. Cyrus personally charged his brother's bodyguard but was killed by a javelin, which so demoralized his men that they retreated. The Greek hoplites, not knowing that Cyrus was dead, stood firm against the more lightly-armed Persians. Led by Clearchos, they advanced against Artaxerxes' army's right wing and caused it to retreat. However, the Persians captured the Greek camp and destroyed their food supplies.

The Greeks were now stranded. They faced a limited choice: to surrender to Artaxerxes or to march out of the country. The Greek leaders were invited to negotiate with the Persians but were murdered, leaving the mercenaries to elect new leaders, including Xenophon. The remaining 10,400 men then set out to travel north through 1,500 miles of harsh terrain, through winter snow drifts, defending themselves against fierce Kurds and Armenians.

Artaxerxes was happy to see the Greeks leave since he did not wish to face them in battle and risk suffering more casualties. He provided the Greeks with provisions but was keen for the Greeks to be assaulted en route. Xenophon's account is written in the third person but the *Anabasis* was designed to promote Xenophon as the savior of the mercenary force. He recounted how many men experienced sickness and how, when the provisions had been expended, the soldiers were forced to forage in any villages they might find. He described how the cold killed some men while they slept and others suffered snow blindness. Negotiating rivers and mountains, the force stumbled on, with bands of the enemy seizing baggage animals and harassing the rearguard. In some villages they were entertained lavishly and Xenophon lists breakfasts of lamb, kid, pork, veal, and chicken with wheat and barley loaves. Eventually, the 6,000 survivors reached Trapezus, a Greek colony on the Black Sea from where they were taken by ship to the Greek mainland. Xenophon had become famous and saw further military exploits after fighting in Thrace, with Seuthes II of the Odrysian tribe. He later joined a Spartan force in Anatolia under King Agesilaos II.

The exploits of the Ten Thousand were not the only example of Sparta meddling in others' affairs. Help was given to the tyrant Dionysius I of Syracuse, who was paramount in Sicily except over lands ruled by Carthage. Spartan aid was important in his victory over the Carthaginians at the Battle of Motya in 337 BCE. The Spartans assisted the Egyptians in their struggle against their Persian overlords. Sparta also went to war with Persia's ally Corinth. Corinth was allied with Athens, Argos, and Boeotia. Persia, which supported Athens and its allies against an expansionist Sparta, changed sides to back Sparta in the Corinthian War after learning that Persia had been betrayed by Athens, which had allied with Pharaoh Hakor of Egypt against Artaxerxes. The Athenian General, Chabrias, fought a three-year-long war (385–383 BCE) against the Persians to prevent the reoccupation of Egypt. Artaxerxes, now supporting Sparta, then brokered a peace between the two sides. By this 'King's Peace,' Sparta was not to interfere in Anatolia again and Persia regained control over the Ionian cities that had previously been liberated from Persian rule by King Agesilaos of Sparta.

The events initiated by Sparta displayed the growing connection between the Greek world and the Near East. All political players were intent on controlling valuable trade routes. Such were the complex international politics of the day.

This illustration shows an attack on a poorly armored Persian light infantryman by an armored Greek hoplite.

Alexander of Macedon 356–323 BCE

Alexander of Macedon, known as Alexander the Great. He captured many lands during his campaigns and ruled over one of the largest empires known. He died of fever in 323 BCE at the age of only 32 years.

When Alexander's father, Philip II of Macedon, was assassinated, he inherited not just his country, but the leadership of the Greek world and a large and capable army with which he intended to invade Persia to avenge invasions of the Greek homeland. His father had built a well-disciplined and drilled infantry, using an eighteen-foot pike in a phalanx formation, fully capable of resisting a hoplite or cavalry charge. Additionally *peltasts*, or skirmishers, armed with multiple javelins, could be used as a flank guard or to harass the enemy. The elite unit of the army was the Companion heavy cavalry, which would charge in a wedge formation into enemy cavalry, or into infantry if the enemy ranks were in disorder. They were never used against well-armed or disciplined infantry. The importance of the various different units was the way in which Philip and Alexander mixed and deployed them in mutually supporting tactics.

In 334 BCE, Alexander crossed the Hellespont with 35,000 men. At the River Granicus, he gave battle to a Persian army commanded by the Greek mercenary Memnon of Rhodes. Alexander led a charge across a riverbed forcing his way up the river bank to crash into the enemy, which included a substantial number of Greek hoplites. The Persians and Greek mercenaries were destroyed. Alexander followed his victory by occupying or reducing all the Greek Ionian cities, ensuring that the Persian fleet had no bases in Asia Minor. He defeated the Lycian and Pisidian hill tribes in western Anatolia and advanced towards Darius III, meeting the main Persian army in northeastern Syria at Issus in 333 BCE. Alexander was victorious against a more numerous enemy. When his pike men breached the Persian ranks, Alexander exploited the situation by charging in with his heavy cavalry, resulting in a complete rout of the Persian forces. Darius' family was captured. Alexander marched south to Syria, Phoenicia, and Egypt, thereby capturing the ports of the eastern Mediterranean. The sieges of Tyre and Gaza were arduous, but their capture gave him strategic control of the sea.

Alexander now decided to seek Darius again, and crossed the Euphrates and Tigris rivers, finding the Persian monarch at Gaugamela in 331 BCE. Darius was completely defeated and after fleeing the field was murdered by his own generals. Alexander reached the Persian capital at Persepolis and burned the royal palace, arguably in revenge for the burning of the Acropolis in 480 BCE. Alexander had to win the loyalty of the Persian satraps and enforce his rule, which now stretched beyond the Caspian Sea to today's Afghanistan and Baluchistan, northward to Bactria and Sogdiana. The Macedonian army was led through the ice and frost of the Hindu Kush and the arid Uzbek deserts. In 326 BCE Alexander crossed the River Indus and fought his final battle on the banks of the Hydaspes against the Kingdom of Porus in the Punjab. The Indian army was slaughtered and Alexander's plans became even more grandiose as he dreamed of marching along the plains of the Ganges to seize the north of India. His troops refused to travel farther and Alexander fought his way down the Indus valley to the Arabian Sea and then westward through the Makran Desert, where thousands of his men died. After reaching Babylon, new campaigns were planned: the capture of Arabia and a march along the southern shores of the Mediterranean to Carthage, while his navy was to circumnavigate Africa. However, Alexander died of fever in 323 BCE, probably having little stamina to fight off the infection after suffering terrible wounds while on campaign. His Empire had not been fully organized and upon his death it began to disintegrate.

Alexander founded many cities named after himself but the most important was Alexandria on the Nile delta, soon to become a center for science, philosophy, and commerce.

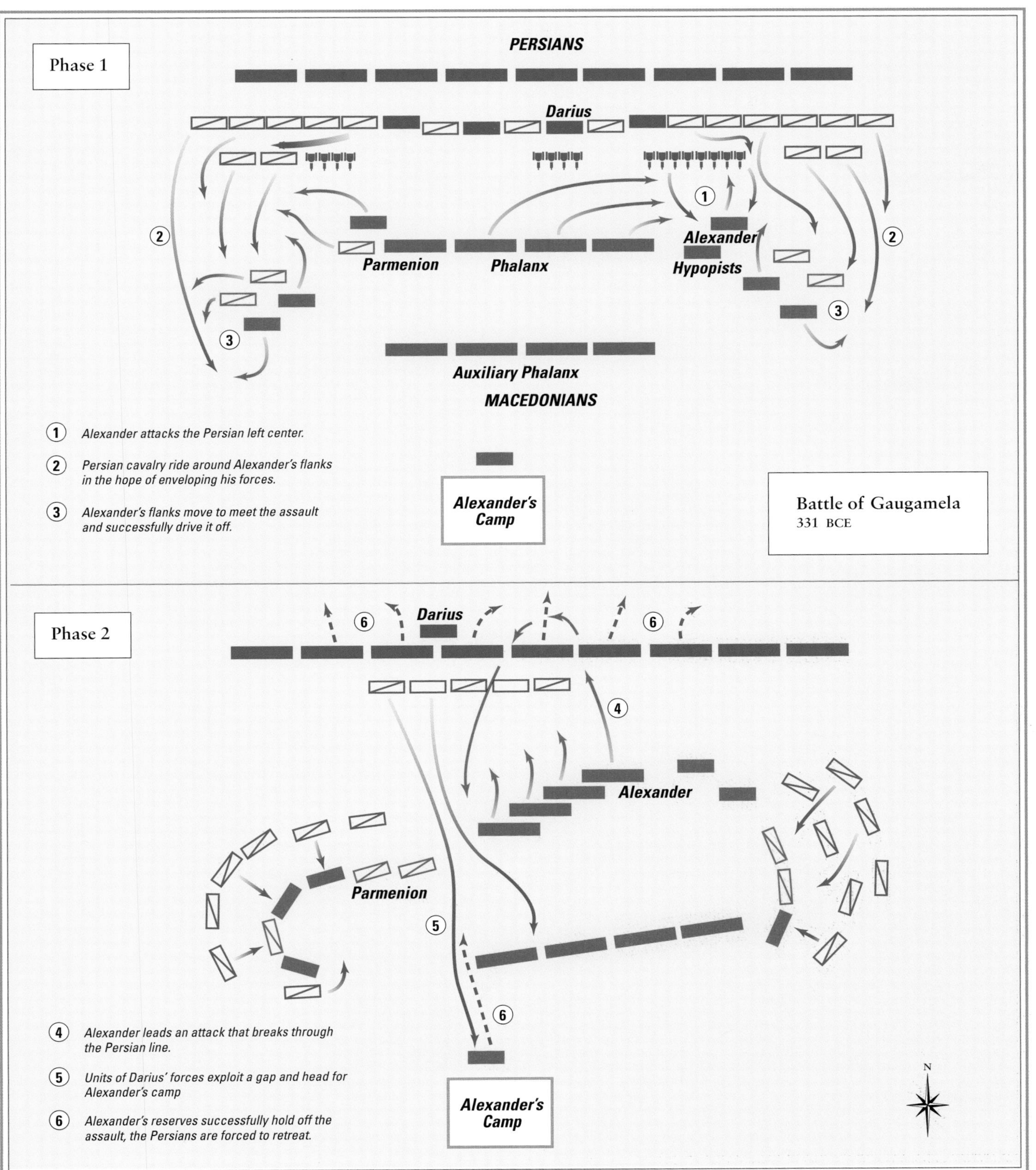
Phase 1
PERSIANS
Darius
Alexander
Hypopists
Parmenion
Phalanx
Auxiliary Phalanx
MACEDONIANS
1 Alexander attacks the Persian left center.
2 Persian cavalry ride around Alexander's flanks in the hope of enveloping his forces.
3 Alexander's flanks move to meet the assault and successfully drive it off.
Alexander's Camp
Battle of Gaugamela
331 BCE
Phase 2
Darius
Alexander
Parmenion
4 Alexander leads an attack that breaks through the Persian line.
5 Units of Darius' forces exploit a gap and head for Alexander's camp
6 Alexander's reserves successfully hold off the assault, the Persians are forced to retreat.
Alexander's Camp
N

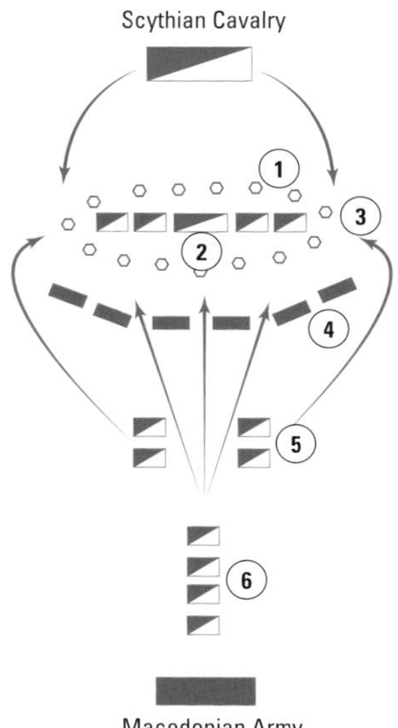

1. *Scythians circling Alexander's cavalry*
2. *Position to which Scythians are to be driven*
3. *Alexander's advance cavalry*
4. *Alexander's light troops*
5. *Alexander's cavalry to block flanks*
6. *Alexander's cavalry to advance and destroy Scythians*

Most military analysts concentrate on Alexander's big battles but it would be wise to examine his innovations, which had little to do with his father's tactics and experiences. He faced Scythians at his new frontier town of Alexandria Eschate (Khojend). The horsemen gathered across the River Jaxartes and Alexander determined to cross the river in the face of these hostile horse-archers. During his career, he had developed field artillery which shot bolts. His prefabricated light catapults only weighed 85 pounds and his larger ones could be carried disassembled in wagons. These weapons gave him covering fire while he and his soldiers crossed the Jaxartes on rafts.

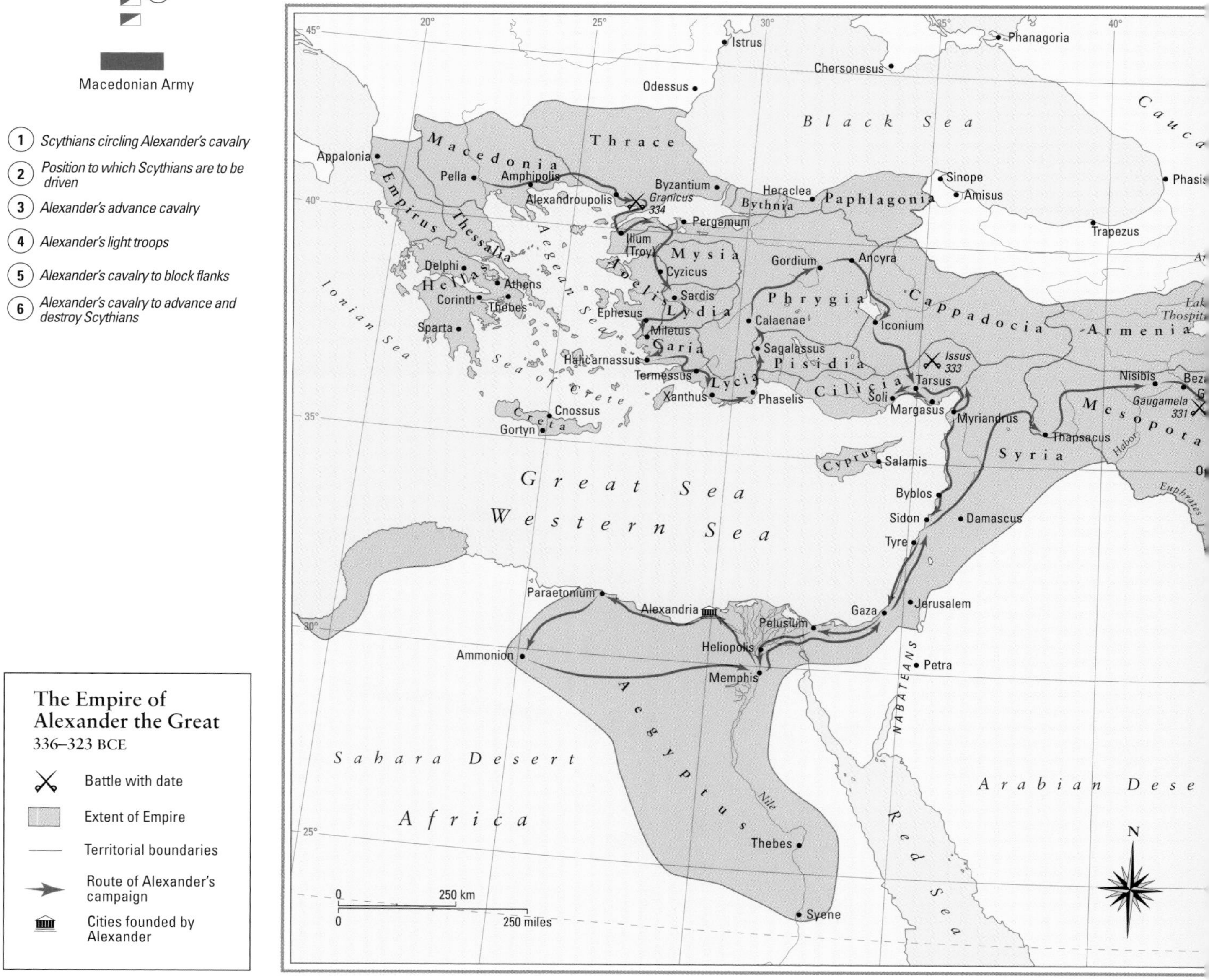

Alexander knew of Darius' defeat at the hands of the Scythians and how they could use feigned-retreat tactics and could fire arrows backwards as they circled their prey. He sent forward a unit of Greek mercenary cavalry and four squadrons of lancers as bait. He deployed his archers, Agrianian *peltasts*, and sling-men in front of him to act as a screen. While this was happening, the Scythians were circling his bait

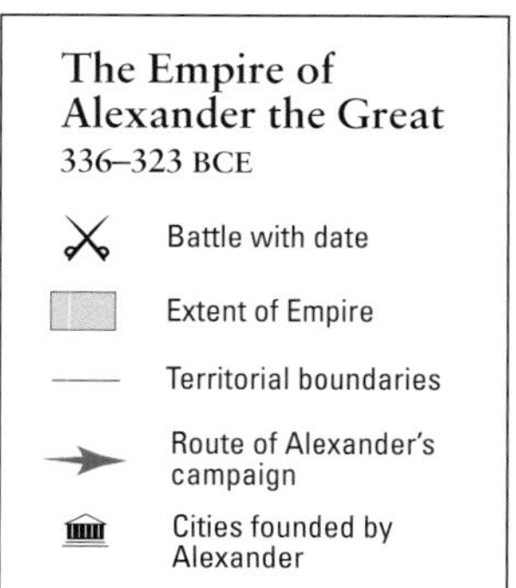

force trying to shoot them down. The screen of light troops moved forward in a crescent disposition. Next, Alexander launched three squadrons of Companion cavalry and his mounted javelin-men at the enemy, who were being pinned down between the light troops and the initial cavalry force. As the Scythians' control fell apart, Alexander's main force passed through the light infantry and charged the concentrated horse-archers. Reports say his force killed slightly less than a thousand men, far fewer than the total Scythian force deployed.

The Scythians were astonished at this defeat and sent envoys to Alexander, who apologized that the defeated force were freebooters and not official soldiers. His victory was a moral one, since he had demonstrated that he could defeat Scythian tactics. The Scythians had always been difficult to defeat; their mobility meant they had no base to capture and no communication system to cut. Alexander could turn to the works of Xenophon to learn how to fight mountain men, but it was his own fertile imagination which devised how to defeat these nomads.

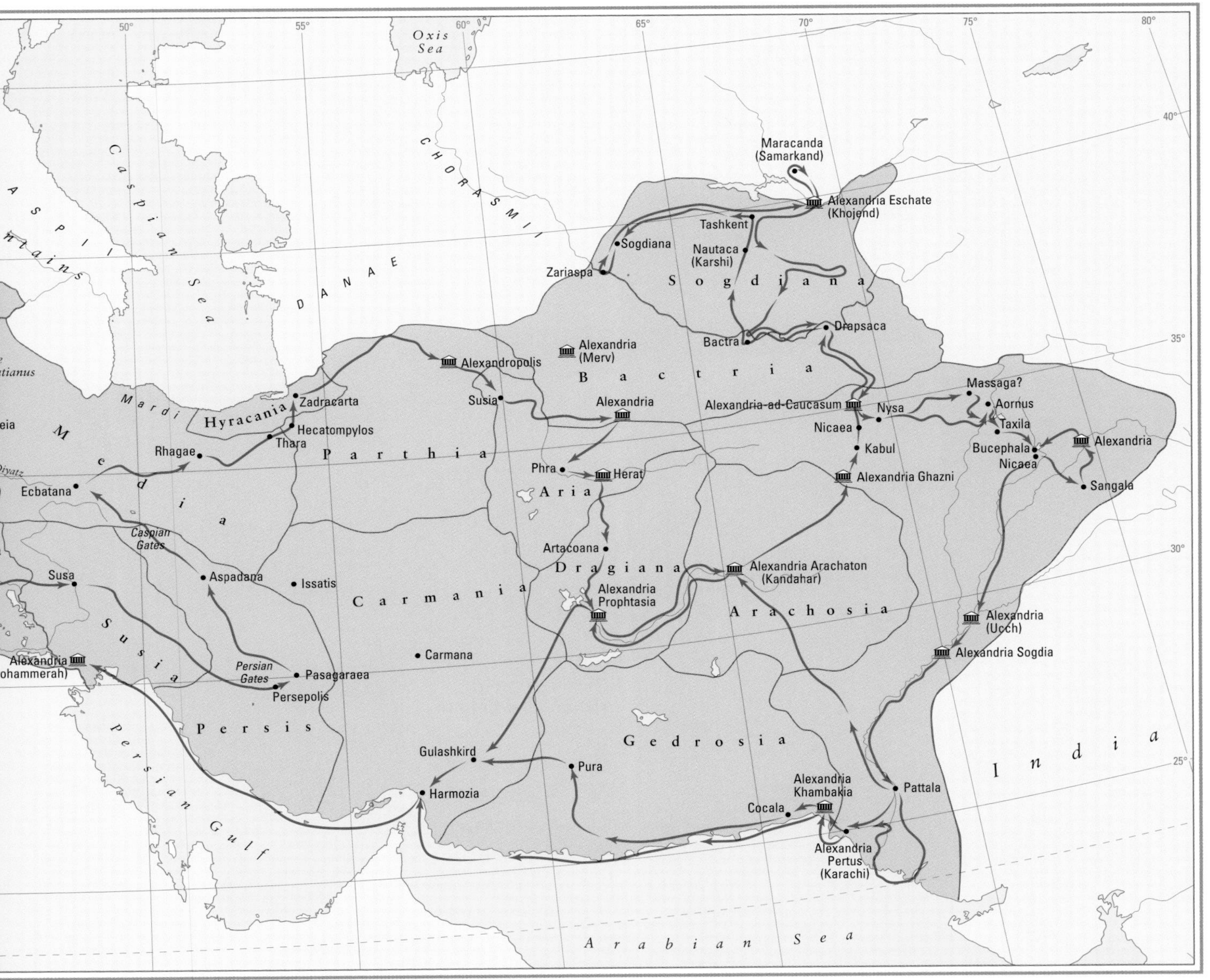

Diadochi—Alexander's Warring Successors

When Alexander the Great died in 323 BCE, his Empire immediately began to unravel. The Macedonian generals seized control of their satrapies and engaged in internecine strife lasting until 311 BCE when the surviving generals, the 'Diadochi', divided Alexander's Empire between themselves. Lysimachos held Thrace, Ptolemy ruled Egypt and Cyprus, Antigonus controled Phrygia and Persia, while Seleukos held sway in the east.

Peace failed to endure and violence broke out again. The Bactrian Princess Roxana, Alexander's wife, his mother Olympias, and his posthumous son were murdered, and these events promoted a further round of campaigning. The final battle of the Diadochi took place at Corupedium in 281 BCE and victory left Seleukos in control of Alexander's Empire in Asia except for the Ptolemaic Kingdom of Egypt. His success was short-lived. Seleukos returned to Macedonia to take personal possession, leaving Asia to his son, Antiochus I. However, on his arrival he was murdered by Ptolemy Keraunos, who proclaimed himself King of an independent Macedonia.

Antiochus inherited a realm with constantly shifting borders that was hard to hold. In Asia Minor, the Greek state of Pergamon broke away, followed by Galatia and the regions of Cappadocia and Pontus. In the east, the provinces of Sogdiana and Parthia became independent, as did Bactria, the latter being a Hellenized state that grew into an empire itself, expanding into

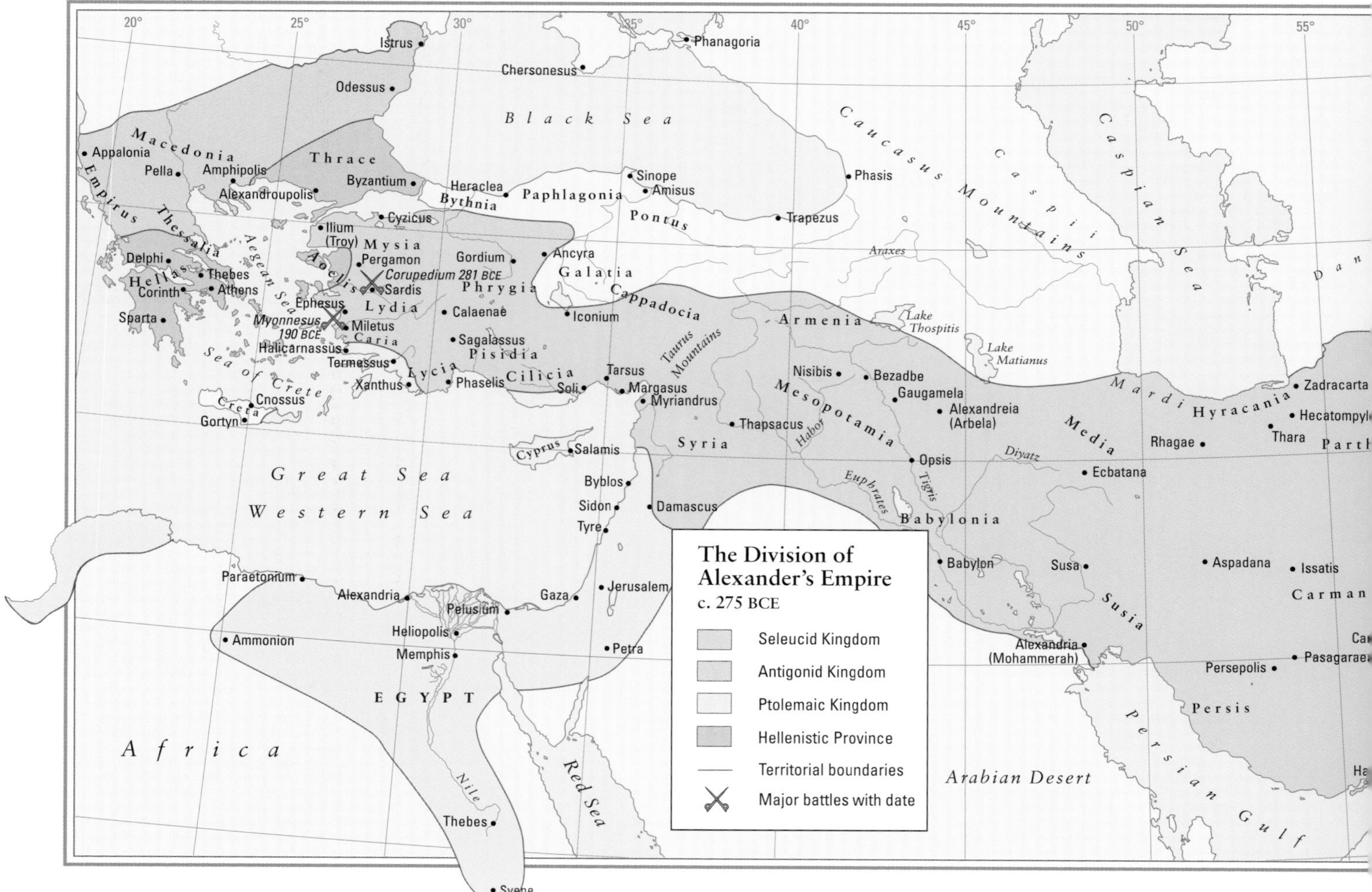

Sogdiana and the Indus Valley. The Seleucid Empire achieved its greatest successes under Antiochus III. He defeated the Bactrian state but gave it honorable peace terms, invaded Parthia, and seized Armenia. Negotiations with Macedon concluded that Antiochus could seize Egypt and Ptolemaic Cyprus while Macedon could acquire Egyptian territories in the Aegean Sea and southern Anatolia. Eventually, attacks on Egypt allowed the Seleucid Empire to acquire Palestine and parts of Syria. Antiochus meddled in Macedonian affairs, invading Greece in 192 BCE, but came up against Rome, intent on expanding its possessions, and was driven back to Asia Minor. The Romans defeated the Seleucid fleet at Myonnesus in 190 BCE, and Antiochus was beaten at Magnesia the same year. He was forced to surrender Asia Minor west of the Taurus Mountains by the Peace of Apameia 188 BCE and these territories were shared between Rhodes and Pergamon. Armenia took advantage of this situation to reassert its independence and Seleucid territories contracted to northern Syria and eastern Asia Minor. After Antiochus' death in 187 BCE, his son became the new ruler and persecuted the traditionalist Jews in Palestine, which precipitated a revolt led by Judas Maccabeus and the creation of the Hasmonean state, which was eventually annexed by Rome. Between 95–64 BCE, the Seleucid family was torn apart by murder and treachery and the remnants of the state were turned into a Roman province by Pompey.

In Egypt, the descendants of Ptolemy ruled for two centuries. With relatively secure frontiers and a strong navy, Egypt developed its economy and Alexandria became an important international commercial center. The Greeks adopted Egyptian customs, with royal brothers and sisters marrying each other to produce a new Pharaoh.

Rome gradually expanded in the Mediterranean until Egypt was bordered by Roman Cyrenaica and Syria. Egypt became involved in the Roman civil war waged after Julius Caesar was assassinated. Prior to that event Cleopatra, ruler of Egypt, had a son by Caesar, Caesarion, and he became joint ruler under the auspices of Mark Antony. Shortly afterwards, Octavian, Caesar's legal heir, declared war on Cleopatra, and she and Mark Antony were defeated at the Battle of Actium in 31 BCE. Mark Antony committed suicide, followed by Cleopatra, who was believed to have committed suicide by snake bite. The Romans captured Alexandria, and Caesarion was killed on Octavian's orders. Egypt now became the Roman province of Aegyptus. The once vast Empire of Alexander the Great had now been partitioned between Roman and Parthia.

Pompey and the Arrival of Rome

Shown in middle age, a marble bust of Gneaus Pompeius Magnus, Pompey the Great. He was consul three times and celebrated three major victories.

The relationship between Rome and Pergamum was unusual. This Hellenized kingdom was a powerful state, with cities and bustling ports. Its King died in 133 BCE and his will bequeathed his state to Rome together with his treasury. Elsewhere, Rome was turning the Mediterranean into a Roman lake. Southern Gaul was acquired, providing a land bridge between Italy and Spain. In 118 BCE, the first Roman colony was founded at Narbo Martius (Narbonne). In North Africa, Jugurtha of Numidia was defeated in 105 BCE, while Mauretania became a protected kingdom and friendly Leptis Magna in contemporary Libya hosted a Roman garrison

In 101 BCE, Roman forces invaded Cilicia, burning out its pirates' nests and making the area a province. In 96 BCE, Ptolemaeus Physkon, King of Cyrene, willed his state to the people of Rome, thereby allowing Rome to penetrate further into Libya. Geopolitically, Rome was projecting its power eastward along both the Mediterranean's southern and northern shores. Wars with Mithridates of Pontus ended in 63 BCE and the campaigns displayed the skill of a young general, Gnaeus Pompeius Magnus (Pompey the Great), whose reputation as a brilliant general thrust him firmly into Near Eastern affairs.

Pompey's career in the East (67–61 BCE) began with a campaign against Aegean pirates, ably helped by young senator Julius Caesar. Between March and May 67 BCE piracy in the east Mediterranean was eliminated. Pompey was backed by an army of twenty legions and 500 ships, Roman law, the *lex Gabinia*, granting him three years' command over all seas and coastal areas as far as 50 miles inland from the Straits of Gibraltar to the Bosphorus. Rome and Italy were placed under his sole military authority. His powers were given unlimited duration by the *lex Manilia*, which also awarded him the power to make treaties and alliances.

Pompey continued the Roman policy of attempting to weaken major regional powers in the east while bolstering small states. At this time, Asia Minor comprised kingdoms such as Bithynia, Pontus, and Cappadocia, which were still ruled by Iranian princes, the remnants of the satraps holding power under the old Persian Achaemenids. After Mithridates was defeated, his relation, Tigranes of Armenia, surrendered to Rome in 66 BCE, was shorn of his recent conquests and was fined an indemnity of 6,000 talents. Pompey felt free to consolidate Rome's eastern territories and establish a series of buffer client-states. He created four provinces: Asia remained intact; Bithynia-Pontus (excluding eastern Pontus); Cilicia, including Pamphylia and Isauria; and Syria, the area around Antioch. The client-kingdoms comprised: eastern Pontus, Cappadocia, Galatia (under King Deitarus), Lycia, and Judea. The buffer states, friends (*amici*) or allies (*socii*) of Rome, were a barrier against Parthia. In northern Mesopotamia, some lands were given to Tigranes. In the south, Jewish Judea remained, as did Arab Chalcis (Ituraea) and Nabatea. This was the scenario when Pompey was accosted by various Jewish embassies who were involved in the struggle for the Judean kingship.

The Jerusalem delegations were mutually hostile: Hyrcanus II and Antipater were supported by the Pharisees, whereas the Sadducees maintained that Aristobulos was the more effective of the two Hasmonean brothers and should be King. Pompey supported Hyrcanus, and he returned to Jerusalem as King in 64 BCE. The Nabataeans who had backed Hyrcanus were ordered to quit Judea. When Aristobulos tried to seize the Judean kingship, Pompey quickly returned to Jerusalem and besieged the Temple precinct where the usurper's supporters sought refuge. The three-month siege ended with the walls being breached and the rebels killed. Hyrcanus was established as High Priest.

Jewish spirits were dashed further when Pompey decided to diminish the area of the Judean state and eradicate the status of king in Hasmonean lands. The expanded Judean state of Alexander Jannaeus was pruned. The Greek city-states in the northeast were placed outside Jewish control in a league known as the Decapolis. The coastal cities from Dor southward to Gaza were given limited autonomy. Some northern territories were ceded to Ituraea and Ptolemais. These two areas were placed under the loose jurisdiction of the new Roman province of Syria. A statelet was created for the Samaritans around Shechem and Mount Gezerim. Hyrcanus II retained the title of High Priest but received the low status title of Ethnarch rather than King, demonstrating to the Jews that they were now a client-state, and their leader only existed at the whim of the Senate in Rome.

Battle of Carrhae 53 BCE

Roman politics were complex and replete with patronage, nepotism, bribery, and the pursuit of personal power and prestige. In 56 BCE, meetings were held between Julius Caesar, Crassus, and Pompeius Magnus to create the First Triumvirate. This entailed Crassus and Pompeius seeking a dual consulship, with Pompeius being given the Spanish provinces, Caesar having his term of office in Gaul increased by another five years, and Crassus being given the rule of Syria. Crassus planned to wage war on Parthia hoping a victory would give him a military reputation similar to that held by Caesar and Pompeius. Caesar endorsed his dreams.

Crassus raised a large army comprising seven legions, or 35,000 heavy infantry, 4,000 light infantry, and 4,000 cavalry including 1,000 Gallic horsemen commanded by his son, Publius. He was joined by 6,000 cavalry provided by Armenian King Artasvades. The latter suggested that Crassus take a route to Parthia via Armenia in order to avoid the waterless Mesopotamian deserts. If he did this, Artasvades would provide reinforcements of 16,000 cavalry and 30,000 infantry. Crassus refused and was led through the most desolate stretches of the desert by Ariamnes, an Arab chieftain secretly working for the Parthians. Meanwhile, the Parthian King, Orodes II, divided his army, leading his foot archers and some cavalry to attack the Armenians while his General, Surena, led 9,000 horse archers and 1,000 heavily armored cavalry cataphracts to harass and delay Crassus. When Artasvades informed Crassus that the bulk of the Parthian army was in Armenia and requested help, Crassus continued on his way until he met Surena's force near the town of Carrhae (or Harran).

Crassus ignored the advice of his senior officers, who urged him to form a marching camp with a view to engage the Parthians on the following day. He advanced toward the enemy in a hollow square. Realizing that a cataphract charge would not break the Romans, Surena ordered his horse archers to attack on all sides. Crassus attempted to disperse the enemy with light troops but these retreated under a hail of arrows. The horse archers returned to the attack and the legionaries were left to defend themselves with shield and armor. Every time the legionaries advanced the horse archers retreated, firing Parthian shots over their horses' rumps. This occurred time and time again.

Using their shields, the legionaries went into testudo formation, which reduces speed and mobility. The Roman historian Cassius Dio said about Carrhae, "For if the (legionaries) decided to lock shields for the purpose of avoiding the arrows by the closeness of their array, the (cataphracts) were upon them with a rush, striking down some, and at least scattering the others, and if they extended their ranks to avoid this, they would be struck down by arrows." The Romans suffered heavy casualties and the arrow storm continued as the Parthians had access to more missiles carried by supply camels. Publius and his Gallic cavalry tried to damage the Parthians but they were cut off and killed. The fighting continued in this fashion until nightfall when Crassus ordered the surviving troops to retreat to Carrhae while leaving their thousands of wounded to be captured.

Surena sent a message to the Romans next morning requesting a truce so that the Roman army could retreat to Syria in exchange for Rome surrendering all territory east of the River Euphrates. At a meeting with the Parthians, Crassus and his generals were killed. The remnants of the Roman army tried to flee but most suffered death or captivity. Approximately, 20,000 Romans were killed and 10,000 captured.

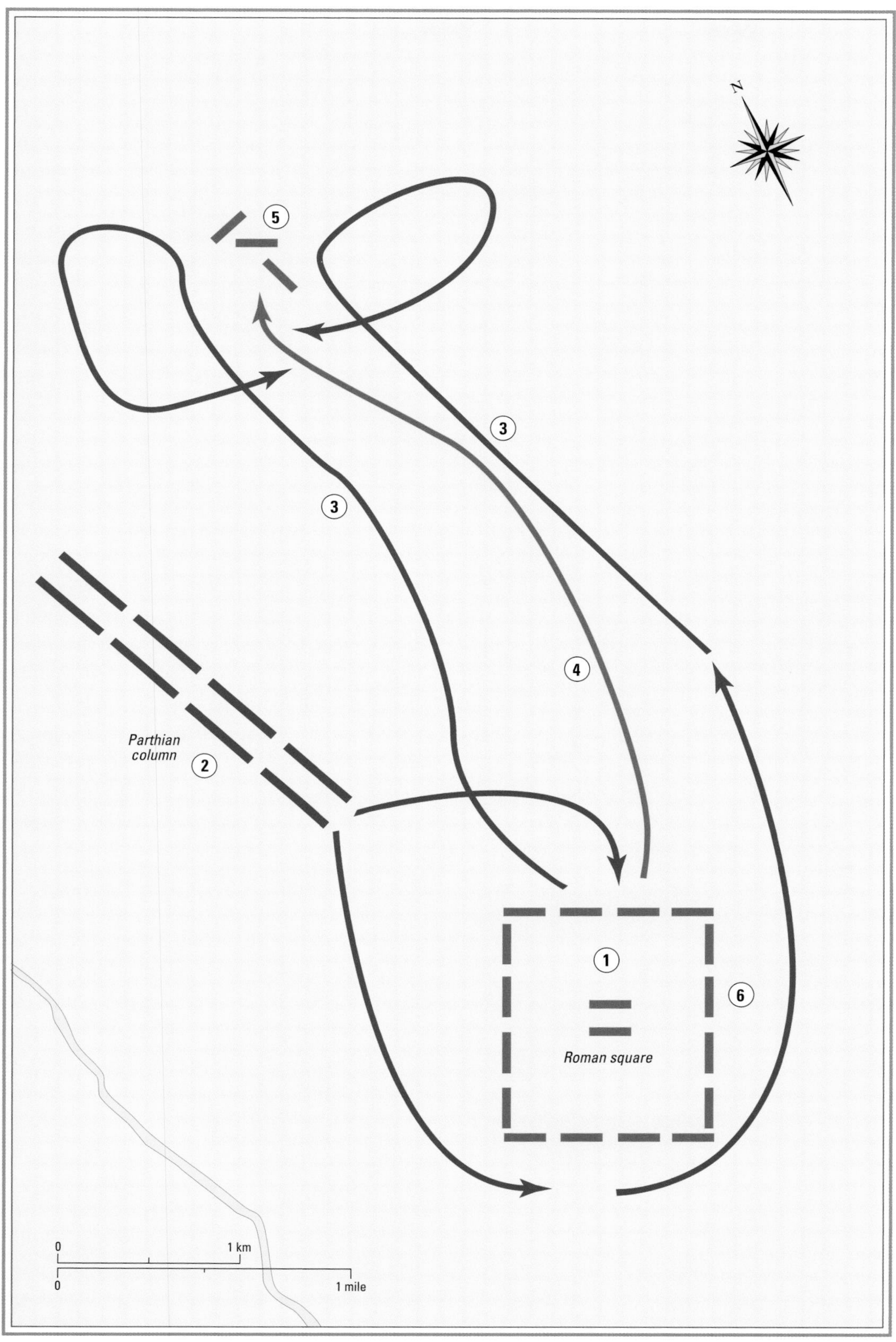

First Battle of Carrhae
53 BCE

1. *The Roman army, commanded by Marcus Licinius Crassus, advances in a square formation, providing defense against attack from any direction.*
2. *The Parthian mounted army harasses the advancing Romans using mounted archers. Their initial attacks fail to inflict significant casualties.*
3. *Most Parthian units withdraw northeastward.*
4. *Encouraged by the Parthian withdrawal, the Roman cavalry and light infantry, commanded by Publius, the son of Crassus, pursue.*
5. *The isolated Roman force, now out of view of the main Roman force, are attacked in detail and destroyed.*
6. *The Parthians return to attack the Roman main force. With them they bring the severed head of Publius, which they exhibit to the Romans and Crassus. Disheartened, the Romans begin to withdraw, under increasing pressure from mounted archers and cataphracts (heavy cavalry).*

First Jewish Revolt 66–74 CE

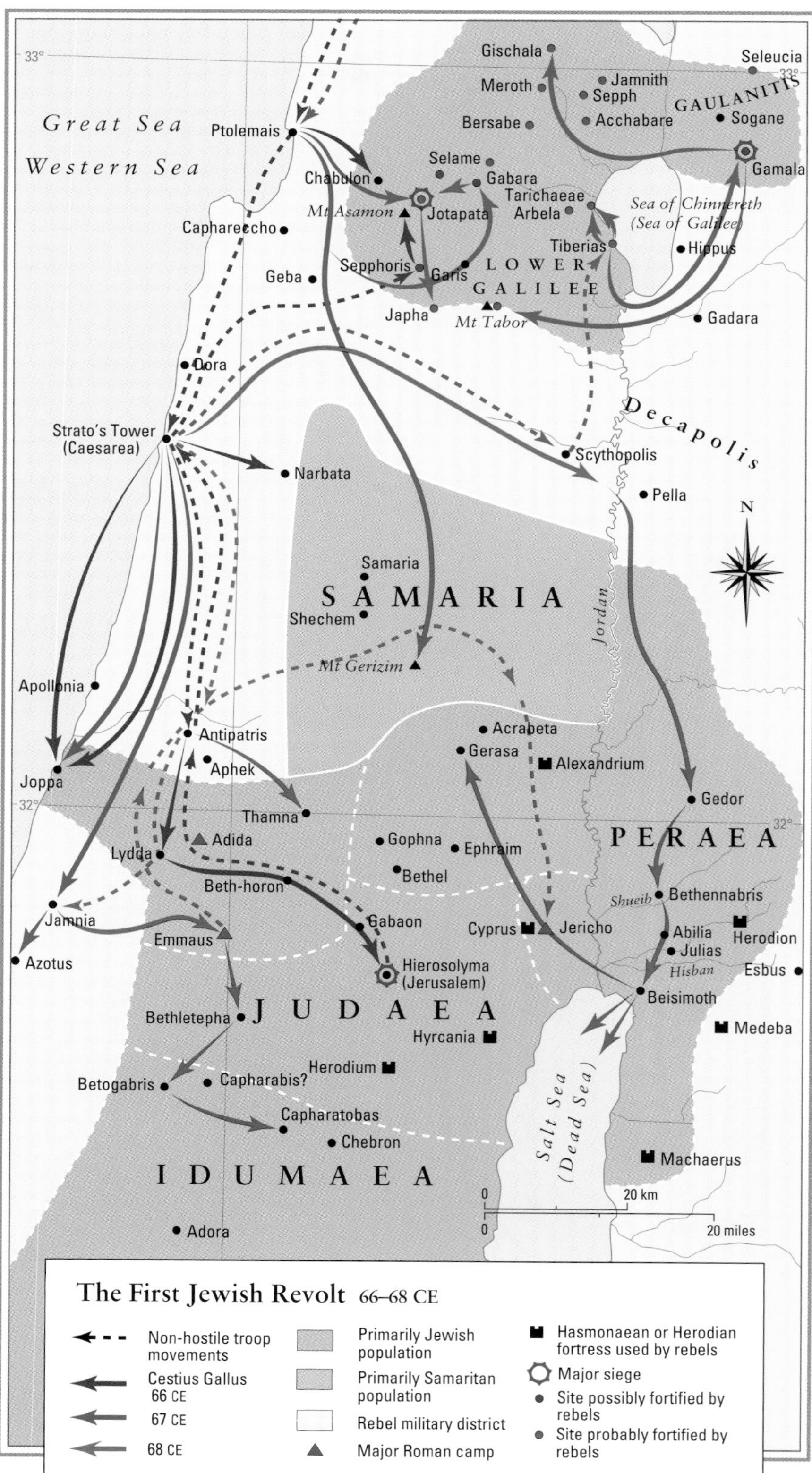

Roman rule in Judaea was harsh and suppressed nationalist aspirations, which were kept alive by Zealot resistance. Procurators Albinus (62–64 CE) and Gessius Florus (64–66 CE) added insult to injury exercising power via their corrupt and cruel regimes. The latter seized a large amount of money from the Temple, and the Jews, led by Eleazar, the son of the High Priest, refused to make offerings to the Emperor, considered by Rome to be treason. Other important incidents were the capture of Masada by dissidents and the failure of Herod Agrippa II to control his state by either persuasion or force. Gentile-Jew communal massacres added to the state's disintegration, with violence in Caesarea, Ptolemais, Gabe, Samaria, Ascalon, and in the Decapolis. Similar eruptions occurred in Syria and Egypt.

Cestius Gallus, the Syrian legate (63–66 CE) failed to break the rebellion in Jerusalem and his second attempt was prevented by a Jewish victory at Beth-horon in October 66 CE, led by Pharisees and Sadducees. Josephus's *The Jewish War* provides key evidence about the division of the country into military districts under designated leaders, with Galilee and the area around Gamala in Gaulantis being handed to Josephus himself. He repaired the walls of Gamala and fortified Seleucia in Upper Galilee while Meroth, Jamnith, and Acchabare were circumvallated (surrounded by ramparts) and cities and villages fortified. A few of these fortifications were intended to be obstacles blocking the roads from Roman bases at Ptolemais and Scythopolis, or from Phoenicia and from Agrippa's base at Caesarea Philippi. Others defended large population centers or became major strongholds.

In December 66 CE Emperor Nero sent Vespasian to pacify Judaea. He mustered his troops in Syria while his son, Titus, was sent to Egypt to seek reinforcements. In spring, 67 CE, Vespasian advanced into Galilee from Antioch via Ptolemais, where Titus and his Egyptian force joined him. The generals commanded some

60,000 legionaries and auxiliaries. Galilean resistance fell apart under this pressure, the city of Sephoris joining the Romans immediately. Jotapata was besieged for two months before its garrison was annihilated. Josephus's force at Garis fled, leaving Lower Galilee open to the Romans. Josephus had retreated to Tiberias and took refuge in a cave system where he was surrounded before surrendering. Only Gamala continued to resist but was captured at the end of 67 CE. The Romans cleared resistance in northern Palestine; the legions then went into winter camps at Caesaria and Scythopolis, thereby keeping Galilee isolated from other rebel areas.

Vespasian chose to ignore Jerusalem for a while, knowing that the conflicts between the different leadership factions would undermine its defense. Instead, he marched on the Peraea, where he rapidly subjugated the population as far south as Machaerus. By late spring, he had taken Antipatris, Lydda, and Jamnia. A legion was emplaced outside Emmaeus, and after marching through Samaria, the Romans entered Jericho. Nero's suicide was announced while Vespasian was traveling to Caesaria to plan the siege of Jerusalem, causing him to delay operations until the Roman political situation quietened. In summer, 69 CE, the armies of the eastern portion of the Empire declared Vespasian Emperor.

Vespasian completed his conquest of Judaea, controlling Acrabeta, Bethel, and Ephraim, together with Hebron in the south. Only Jerusalem, Macherus, Herodium, and Masada remained at bay against Rome. Jerusalem was besieged from March to September in 70 CE, ending with the incineration of the city and the deaths of the defenders. The fortress at Masada remained an outpost of resistance. Situated on a spur of rock overlooking the Dead Sea, sheer cliffs fell away on three sides making it practically impregnable. The Zealot defenders held out against the Romans for three years until a ramp was built during 73–74 BC and the walls were breached. Inside 960 defenders and their families had committed suicide.

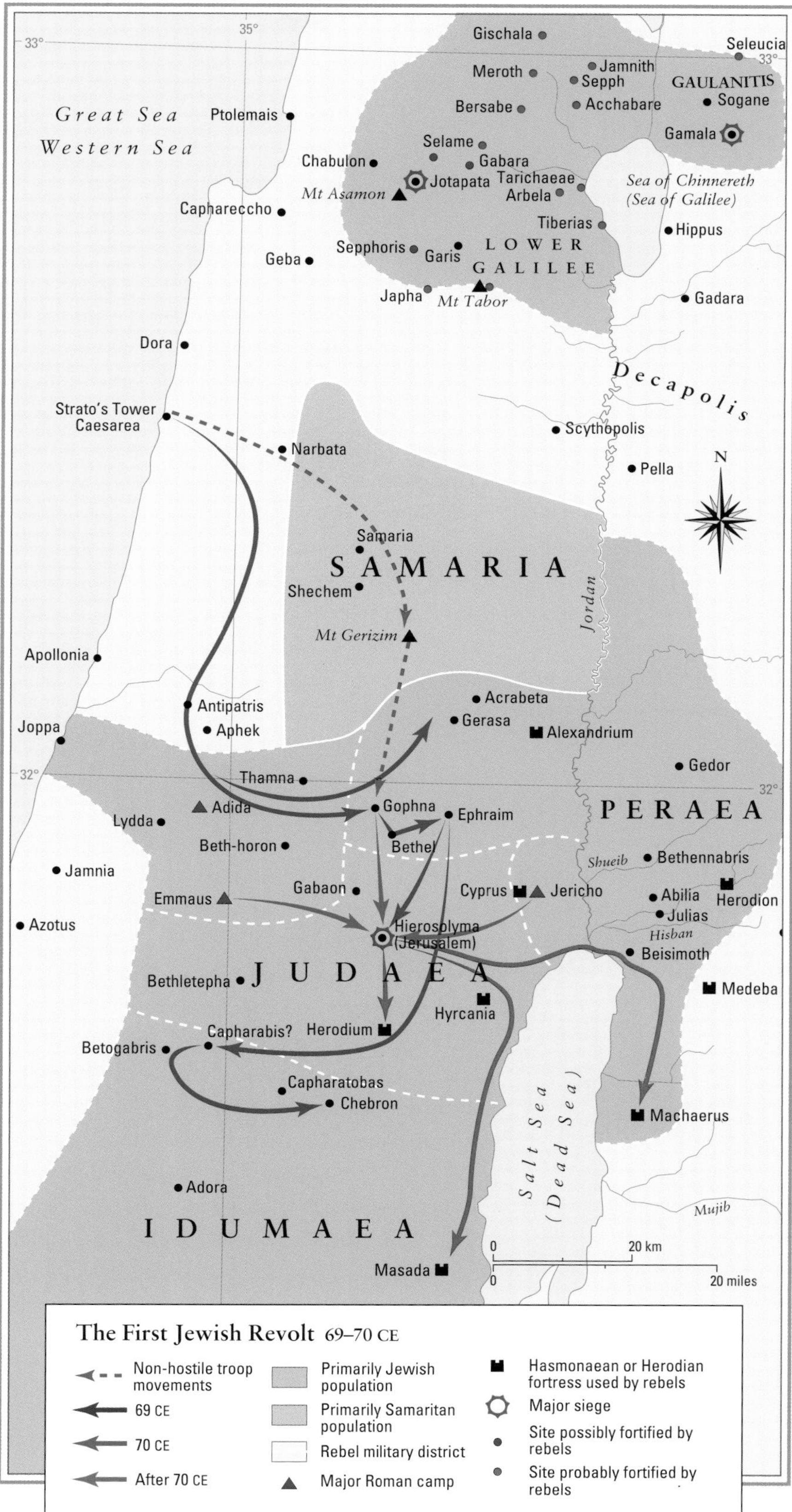

Siege of Jerusalem 70 CE

The Roman legionary, the backbone of the field army, was well trained, well equipped, and signed up for 25 years service. The soldier, above, wears an iron Gallic helmet and the lorica sedmentata body armor. He would have been armed with two pila (throwing spears), a gladus (short stabbing sword) and a large rectangular shield of wood and leather with a metal central boss. The Roman army went out of its way to reward bravery in combat and punish weakness.

In Jerusalem a state of civil war existed, with a hill in the southwest of the city held by aristocratic patriots, while the Zealots under John of Gischala held the eastern city and a major area of the Temple court. The aristocrats asked Simon bar Giora, leader of a revolutionary faction, for help but instead he began killing those amongst them who proposed surrender. In the spring, 70 CE, Titus Flavius marched on Jerusalem and planned to attack the north wall, one of three defense lines. Titus carried out a personal reconnaissance, but he and his party were attacked. Titus was without armor and most of his bodyguards were elsewhere. He charged through his enemies and escaped, pursued by a volley of arrows. Even while pitching camp the Romans were attacked twice by sorties from the city and fought them off with difficulty. The Roman general had four legions plus supporting troops, totaling some 35,000 men. Amongst these was the 12th Legion, which had been heavily defeated earlier and now sought revenge.

Jerusalem held a garrison of some 24,000 men and was a natural fortress. Situated on high ground, it was constructed around two hills, which were natural strong points. The Temple was a fortress within the walls and the city's defenders had been strengthening the fortifications. Simon bar Giora commanded the main fighting force but the entire population could help the defense and their numbers were large, estimated at 600,000 by Tacitus and a million by Josephus. Above the Kidron Valley were the Upper and Lower halves of the old city, dominated by towers and Herod's Palace. Dividing the old city from the new was the First Wall, which was joined to the Temple. The Second Wall surrounded part of the new city and all of it lay within the First Wall, which was the weakest part of the city's defenses.

The Jews initiated attacks against Roman siege towers but battering rams were finally put in place, despite the defenders using catapults they had captured from the Romans years earlier. On 25 May, a breach was made and Roman soldiers entered and took Bezetha, the new part of the city. Five days later, the second wall was breached. The legionaries engaged in street fighting but they were thrown back. The second wall was breached again, leaving the Romans to face the walls enclosing the Temple and the upper and lower parts of the city. The city was circumvallated, which sealed off Jerusalem from the rest of the world. Anybody fleeing the city was caught and crucified, sometimes as many as 500 daily. Starvation killed inhabitants, with the dead stacked in houses and thousands thrown over the walls into the ravines below.

The Antonia fort was the next target, with battering rams employed until a breach was made on 24 July, followed by close-quarter combat. The Temple gates were set alight and soon the Temple was no more than burnt-out embers. Rebel survivors made a final stand in Herod's Palace but as the rams continued their work everyone was massacred. Jerusalem was then incinerated, leaving a city of the dead. Simon bar Giora and John of Gischala were taken prisoner and formed part of Titus' triumphal procession in Rome in 71 CE, the event commemorated on the triumphal Arch of Titus, which remains standing in Rome. Simon bar Giora was thrown to his death from the Tarpeian Rock by his captors.

The Jewish historian Josephus estimated that over a million people died in the siege through violence, starvation, or disease. Those captured were enslaved and Cornish legend claims that some were sent to the mines in Cornwall, Britain. Some people escaped and fled around the Mediterranean; they may have been the cause of the Kitos War (115–117 CE) when tens of thousands of Roman citizens were slaughtered, especially in Cyrene and Cyprus. Titus succeeded his father as Emperor and was followed by his brother Domitian. Later, Hadrian re-founded Jerusalem as a Roman colony named Aelia Capitolina and renamed Judaea as Syria Palaestina.

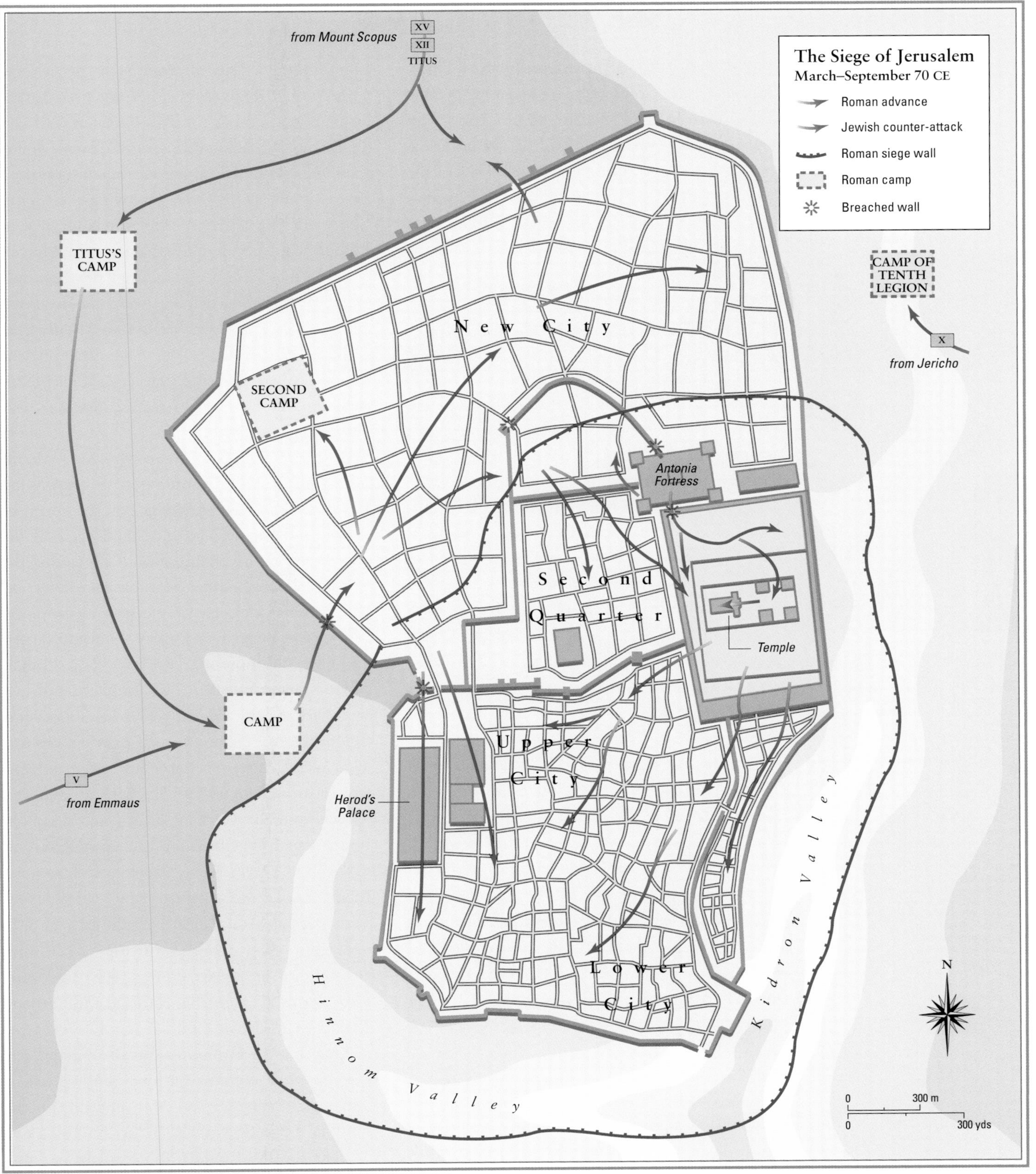

The Siege of Jerusalem
March–September 70 CE
Roman advance
Jewish counter-attack
Roman siege wall
Roman camp
Breached wall
from Mount Scopus
XV
XII
TITUS
TITUS'S CAMP
CAMP OF TENTH LEGION
X
from Jericho
New City
SECOND CAMP
Antonia Fortress
Second Quarter
Temple
CAMP
V
from Emmaus
Upper City
Herod's Palace
Lower City
Hinnom Valley
Kidron Valley
N
0
300 m
300 yds

The Parthian Wars

The Emperor Trajan. Under his rule the Roman Empire attained its maximum extent. In 113 Trajan began his last campaign against the Parthian Empire. By 116 the campaign was over, with Parthia under the rule of a puppet, Parthamaspates.

The origins of the Parthians are obscure but they appear to be one of the Iranian-speaking peoples living beyond the Seleucid dominions. These 'Parni' settled in the Province of Parthava and eventually turned upon their Seleucid rulers and seized control of the province and nearby Hyrcania, southeast of the Caspian Sea. Antiochus III was forced to recognize Parthian independence and that of Bactria as well. The accession of Mithridates I (171–138 BCE) led to a series of campaigns capturing the Iranian Plateau, Media, and Mesopotamia. Although extensive, Parthian land holdings were not as vast as the Achaemenids' nor was there a sound administration, merely a collection of noblemen and sundry vassal kings. Political chaos riddled Parthia; many kings are only identified by the coins in circulation. King Phraates III was murdered by two rival sons in 58 BCE; Orodes II (57–38 BCE) prevailed in this contest.

Elsewhere, Tigranes II united Lesser and Greater Armenia and formed an alliance with Pontus. Together these Hellenized states spread their power and Armenia ruled from the Caucasus to the Mediterranean, coming into conflict with Rome's eastward advance under Pompey.

The Romans were already in conflict with Pontus, and Armenia was drawn into war and defeat, forcing it to become an ally of Rome. This new power in the East next sought to meddle in Parthia's unstable politics. Marcus Licinius Crassus, one of the Roman triumvirs with Pompey and Julius Caesar, longed for military glory and loot for the Roman treasury. Accordingly, he raised a large army which advanced through inhospitable lands to reach Carrhae, where he died with a large part of his army in 53 BCE. Roman forces were no match for the Parthian horse archers whose maneuvers outwitted Rome's infantry tactics allowing the heavily armored cataphract cavalry elite, where both man and horse wore scaled armor, to charge home. The aftermath of battle saw numerous Parthian raids into Roman territories, instigating a series of Roman-Parthian wars.

During the Roman civil war following Julius Caesar's assassination, the Parthians supported Brutus and Cassius, even supplying them with troops for the Battle of Philippi in 42 BCE in Macedonia. They then occupied Syria, taking all coastal cities except Tyre. They next invaded Hasmonean Judea, helping Antigonus to usurp its throne. For a while the Roman Middle East became Parthian-controled. The situation was reversed when the civil war ended. However, Rome and Parthia fought many wars over who should rule in Armenia.

In 115 CE, Emperor Trajan (98–117 CE) decided to attack Parthia, ostensibly because King Osroes I had placed his nephew on the throne of Armenia. Rome held political influence over the state and had the final authority in naming the Armenian King. Other reasons may exist: to acquire more defensible frontiers; or an aspiration to re-create Alexander's Empire. Trajan advanced through Mesopotamia, making it a Roman Province. He conquered the Parthian vassal state of Adiabene and the city of Adenystrae while sending another column to seize Babylon. His war ships sailed down the Euphrates, were dragged across a portage to the Tigris, and captured Seleucia and the Parthian capital at Ctesiphon. Trajan compelled Charax to be a client-state and created the provinces of Babylon and Assyria. Trajan placed the Parthian King's exiled son, Parthamaspates, on the Parthian throne

Trajan died while returning to Rome. Rome, however, persisted in eastern campaigns and invaded Armenia three more times. Hadrian (117–138 CE), Trajan's successor, decided that the Euphrates was the real defense line of the Roman Empire and returned Adiabene, Armenia, and Mesopotamia to the previous Parthian vassals. In 161 CE Vologases IV defeated the Romans in Armenia but was beaten in turn in 163 CE. Roman armies invaded Mesopotamia in 165 CE, defeating the Parthians at Dura-Europos and Seleucia. Emperor Septimus Severus (193–211 CE) seized northern Mesopotamia and sacked the Parthian capital while Caracalla (198–211 CE) sacked Arbela in 216 CE.

The last Parthian King, Artabanus V, drove Roman forces back but was killed at the Battle of Hormizdagan while fighting a federation of nobles led by the future Sassanian King Ardashir. The conflict between Rome and Parthia, partially explained by the desire to control the Silk Road, as expanding trade along this major route was benefited Palmyra. Palmyrene merchants lived at both Charax and Alexandria, but Rome only really benefited from the trade when Palmyra was taken in 270 CE.

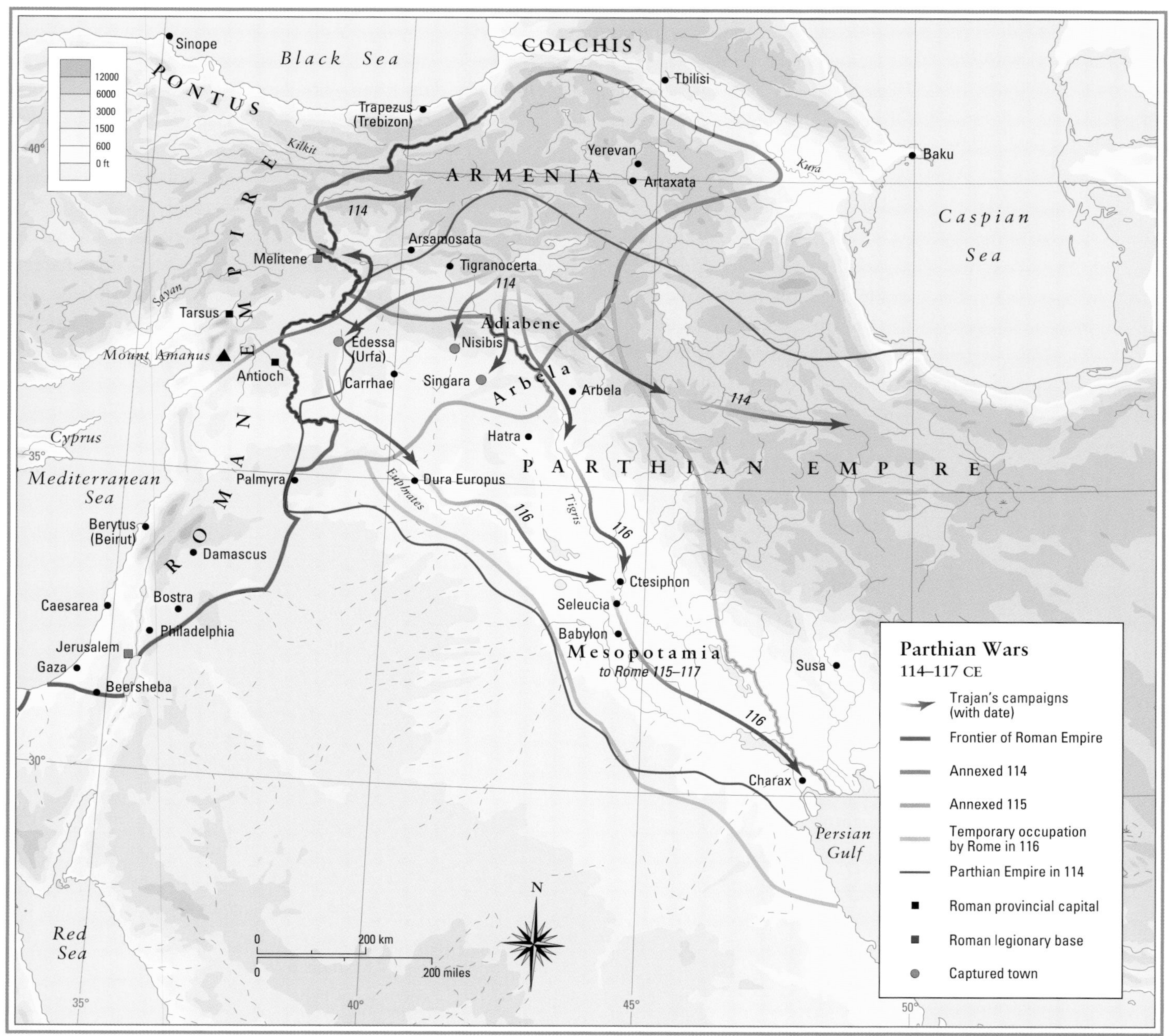

Rome's Eastern Borders 114–627 CE

Rome's eastern provinces were exceptionally important to its Empire. Syria, like Cappadocia, faced Persia, and was defended by legions at Cyrrhus, Laodicea, Raphaneae, and Emesa. These bases were the springboard for the conquests of Emperor Septimus Severus (193–211 CE), who extended Roman possessions to the Tigris to create the new provinces of Osrhoene and Mesopotamia. The provinces sustained a caravan trade bringing wealth to the Empire through rich commercial centers like Antioch, fed by caravan cities in the east, such as Dura-Europus and Palmyra. Other centers were Apamea, Seleucia, and Emesa. Phoenicia had been created as a new province by Septimus Severus; on its mountains grew cedars of Lebanon and other valuable species used in shipbuilding. While Palestine was a poor and overpopulated region, Arabia produced wheat and olive oil and benefited from livestock breeding. It also exported perfumes and incense; the caravan trade provided income for Bostra and Petra. Egypt, too, was an important grain producer feeding the city of Rome itself.

After the death of Septimus Severus, the Roman Empire suffered some two centuries of political chaos when a series of military figures contended for the throne of the Caesars. The Empire sank into crisis; Emperors were chosen by their troops, and the government of the state was generally located in a military camp somewhere near the borders. The traditional Roman aristocracy was marginalized and was no longer capable of acting as political cement. To add to the chaos, Franks and Alemanni raided Gaul and Spain, before returning to their homeland in 253 CE. Gaul then broke away and, under Postumus, linked with Germania, Britannia, and Hispania to constitute a rival Gallic Empire.

In the east, Persian invasions occurred between 256–263 CE and Emperor Valerian was defeated and captured in the Battle of Edessa by King Shapur I of Sassanid Persia in 260 CE. Palmyra broke away and established an Empire encompassing Egypt, Syria, Judea, and Arabia Petraea. This situation was restored by Aurelian (270–275 CE), who reconquered the east as well as obtaining the surrender of the last Emperor of breakaway Gaul. His successor was Probus (276–282 CE), who defended Egypt from attacks by the nomadic Nubian Blemmyes. This people, together with the Nobatae, forced Diocletian (284–305 CE) to make peace with them, move the Roman border northward to Philae, and pay them an annual gold stipend.

Diocletian's co-Caesar Galerius (305–311 CE) fought the Sassanid King Narseh. After initial failure, Galerius invaded Armenia and defeated Narseh twice. During the Battle of Satala in 298 CE, the Romans captured Narseh's wife, harem, and treasury. Galerius marched into Media and Adiabene, engaging the Persians several times, seizing the city of Nisibis. He advanced down the Tigris and sacked Ctesiphon, returning to Roman territory via the Euphrates. The war was ended by the Peace of Nisibis in 299 CE, and the Tigris was established as the new frontier between Rome and Persia. Armenia continued as a Roman client-state, and the five satrapies of Ingilene, Sophanene, Arzanene, Corduene, and Zabdicene, all beyond the Tigris, became part of the Roman Empire.

Intermittent warfare recommenced in the 330s. Early Persian victories achieved little but in 359 they gained Amida. Rome retaliated when Julian (361–363 CE) won the Battle of Ctesiphon in 363 CE but was killed in combat. His successor Jovian (363–364 CE) made peace with the Persians, returning their possessions east of the Tigris as well as Nisibis and Singara. In the 380s, the Persian ruler Shapur III made peace with Theodosius I (379–395 CE) and they divided Armenia between them. Both Rome and Persia faced barbarian incursions, and concern about them meant that they existed together peacefully until the 420s.

Violence broke out again when the Persian King Chosroes invaded Byzantine Armenia, Mesopotamia and northern Syria in 540 CE. In the reign of Justinian (527–565 CE), General Belisarius was summoned to confront the Sassanids and campaigning lasted until 562 CE. Neither side had achieved much, so a Fifty Years' Peace was signed. The Persians returned Lazica (western Georgia) to the Romans but Justinian was required to pay an annual tribute of 500 pounds weight of gold. Emperor Heraclius (610–641 CE) suffered a major Persian invasion, which swept through Asia Minor to Constantinople. The Emperor drove them back and defeated the enemy at the Battle of Nineveh in 627 CE; however, he soon faced a new enemy when Arabs surged out of the desert, defeating the Byzantine army at Yarmuk in 636 CE.

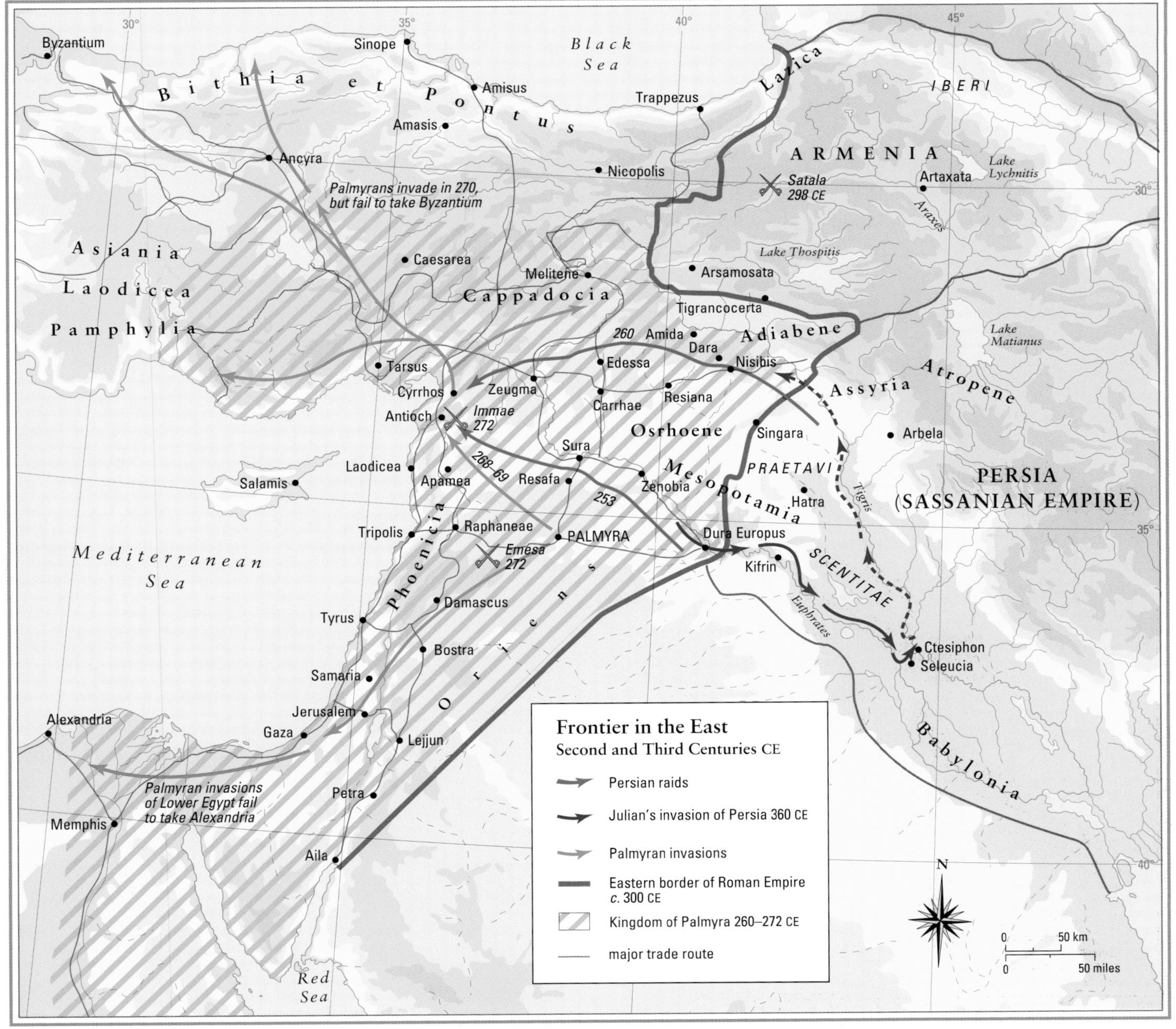

Bar Kokhba Revolt 132–136 CE

The second Jewish revolt began around 132 CE during Emperor Trajan's reign. Two main reasons underpinned the event: Hadrian had attempted to ban circumcision amongst all subject peoples in the Empire, irrespective of their faith. Secondly, he planned to construct a new city on Jerusalem's ruins. This city was to be the pagan Aelia Capitolina with a temple to Jupiter. Hadrian happened to be present in Syria and Egypt between 129–131 CE and the revolt began upon his departure.

The rebel leader was known as Simeon bar Kokhba, to his friends, and Simeon bar Kosiba ('son of the lie' = false messiah) to his enemies. His name and title as found in the caves of Wadi Murabba'at and Nahal Hever in the Judaean desert, are recorded as Simeon bar Kosiba, Prince of Israel. Bar Kokhba means 'son of the star' and this comes from rabbi Akiba ben Joseph (40–c. 135 CE), who honed the school of Biblical interpretation known as Midrash. After he met Simeon bar Kokhba, Akiba was fascinated with his power and perceived a sense of destiny, visualizing him as the promised messiah. Akiba was criticized for his misjudgment; there is no record of him taking part in the revolt.

Jerusalem was taken swiftly from the Roman Governor Quintus Tineius Rufus and held out for two years. The rebels minted coins in the initial year of the rebellion with words on them such as 'liberation of Israel', 'liberation of Jerusalem' and 'the priest Eleazar', the latter suggesting the renaissance of the Temple cult. Hadrian then recalled the skilful General Julius Severus from Britain to command the Roman forces against the rebels. Severus had extensive experience of guerrilla warfare against the Celts in Britain and this proved valuable in future engagements in Judaea. He gathered a huge force, with troops arriving even from the Danube frontier. Eventually Severus deployed twelve legions.

Rebel forces were mainly concentrated in the Judaean desert around Herodium, Tekoa, Qiryat Arabayya, En-gedi, and the unidentified Beth Mashko, the final three being centers of rebel administration. Guerrilla warfare ensued, with the Roman cohorts inching their way into enemy territory with heavy losses on both sides. The rebels were flushed out of caves and Roman patrols cut supply routes, so many insurgents starved to death. The final battle of the rebellion took place in 135 CE, when the mountain fortress of Bether was captured and Simeon bar Kokhba killed. That siege lasted a year, and the whole war three and a half years. Roman losses had been severe but the war was a disaster for the Jews. Cassius Dio, the Roman historian, states that 50 important outposts and 985 villages were burned down. Some 580,000 men were killed and numerous others died from famine and disease. The market place was swamped by Jewish slaves and the price of a Jew in the Hebron market was lower than the cost of a horse. Surplus slaves were moved on to Gaza and Egypt. Hadrian celebrated with a Roman coin depicting an enslaved woman with the words 'Judaea Capta.' Rabbi Akiba, the spiritual leader of the rebellion, was flayed alive.

Archaeological and manuscript evidence concerning the revolt has been excavated in numerous caves in Wadi Murabba'at, Nahal Hever, Nahal Mishmar, and Nahal Ze'elim. Papyri fragments in Hebrew, Aramaic, Greek, and Latin have been found, alongside many domestic items. The Cave of Horrors contained the bodies of 40 men, women, and children who had starved to death. The Cave of Letters also contained human remains.

Jerusalem was next rebuilt as Colonia Aelia Capitolina, a Roman provincial city, inhabited by gentiles, Romans, Greeks, and other peoples from the Empire. Jews were forbidden to go there on pain of death. Only on the anniversary of the destruction of the Temple were Jews allowed to grieve for its loss. The southern gate of the city facing toward Bethlehem depicted the carved image of a pig. On the Temple hill, a sanctuary was built to Jupiter Capitolinus and the Province of Judaea was renamed Syria Palaestina. In Judaea, Jews were apparently liquidated but some survived in Galilee, which, like Samaria, seemed not to have been involved in the rebellion. The law proscribing the practice of Judaism in the area was rescinded in 138 CE. Tiberias in Galilee became the home of Jewish elders who completed the Mishnah there, as well as the Jerusalem Talmud, compiled during the second to fourth centuries, with other early rabbinical texts. Scholars such as rabbis Simeon ben Gamaliel II, Simeon bar Yohai, and Meir provided a focal point for Jewish religious life. The religion was also kept alive in the synagogues, and in the religious center at Babylon, where scholars compiled the Babylonian Talmud.

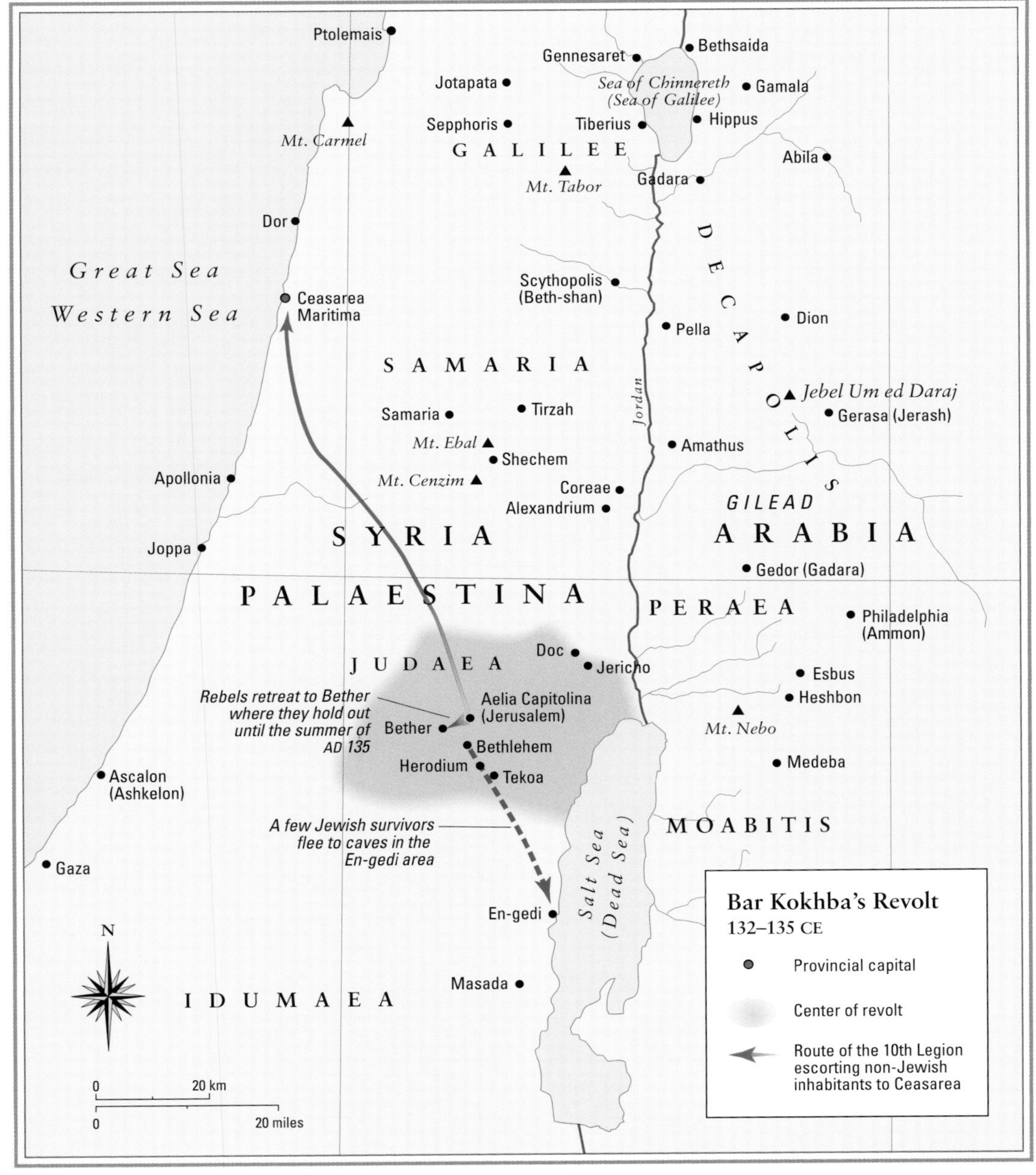

The Sassanian Empire 224–651 CE

In this rockface carving from Nagsh-I Rustam, Emperor Shapur I, on horseback, looks down on the Roman Emperor, Valerian (standing). Next to Valerian is Philip the Arab (kneeling), both suing for peace.

The Sassanian revolution against their fellow Persians, the Parthians, began in Fars (originally Parsa) Province. It was led by Ardashir I, who won a decisive victory over the Parthian Artabanus V and was crowned at Ctesiphon in 226 CE. He then campaigned against the eastern provinces that border modern Afghanistan and then through the northeast frontier region of Central Asia. His son, Shapur I, attacked eastern Roman provinces and won the Battle of Edessa, in 260 CE, where he captured the Roman Emperor Valerian. However, the Sassanians failed to incorporate Syria, the province becoming part of the breakaway Palmyrene Empire. Emperor Aurelian reconquered the Palmyrene Empire in 273, thereby regaining Roman possessions in the Near East. Shapur's conquests were extensive. In the Tigris-Euphrates area, he acquired the territories of Khuzistan, Maishan, Asuristan, Adiabene, and Arabistan. In the Zagros Mountains of western Iran, he gained Fars, Elymais, and Media; in the Caucasus area, he won Balasgan, Albania, Machelonia, Georgia, and Armenia. Taking the areas of northern Iran flanking both sides of the northern Zagros Mountains, he acquired Patishkhwagar, Gorgan, Abarshahr, and Parthia. North and west of the Hindu Kush, the Sassanians won Aria, Merv, and Kushanshahr, while in the territories flanking the lower reaches of the Indus, they seized Seistan, Turan, Makran, and part of today's Pakistan. Possession was also taken of part of Oman and Arabia. At its greatest extent, the Sassanian Empire spread through today's Syria, Lebanon, Israel, Jordan, Palestine, Egypt, Dagestan, and the Yemen.

The Sassanid Dynasty achieved its territorial successes through a well-developed military force. At its heart were the heavily-armored cataphractarii, armed with bow, sword, and lance. These were supported by light cavalry, including horse archers, who were drawn from subject peoples and mercenaries such as Khazars, Kushans, and White Huns. These were supplemented by a corps of war elephants and infantry. The latter were mainly local militias armed with their customary weapons and of no great worth except providing labor in sieges. However, there were some heavy infantry from the Medes and there were mercenaries from Deylem (Gilan Province) who were capable of fighting Roman and Byzantine heavy infantry on equal terms. Sassanid archers, who fought from behind mantlets, were also an important element. Various Kurdish and Arab troops were used as skirmishers. The Persians possessed well-designed and efficient siege engines: battering rams, catapults, and siege towers. The Sassanids also had a fleet which was deployed in 570 in an expedition to seize Yemen. All of these were deployed in a long series of wars with the Roman Empire where the fortunes of war swung backward and forward.

The constant wars and the victories of Heraclius, who thrust into Sassania from two directions, sapped Sassanian morale. In 622, a seaborne expedition struck at Armenia through the Black Sea and in 627, a southern incursion almost reached Ctesiphon. Yazdegerd III was the last Sassanid monarch and he felt the force of an Arab invasion. The Sassanians were defeated at Qadisiya, Ctesiphon, Jalula in 637, and finally at Nahavend in 642. The Sassanid Empire was no more, although there was resistance in some remote provinces for a few years.

The impact of Sassanian culture was substantial. The Byzantine army copied and raised their own cataphractarii while the Arabs adopted a part of Sassanian culture in terms of dress, architecture, and art. Further east, at the Chinese Tang capital of Xian, several thousand Persians were said to have inhabited a settlement there in the mid-eighth century. A Persian gnostic religion, Manichaeanism, spread across the trade routes of central Asia. Under Sassanian rule, hammering and chasing of gold and silver was introduced. Glassware of great beauty was created. Sassanian influences can be found in Tang music; further afield, a Sassanian cut-glass bowl found its way to Japan and is now in the Tenri Museum in Nara Prefecture.

There are few primary sources recounting the Sassanians but Shapur I left inscriptions in Greek, Parthian, and Pahlavi on the Ka'bah-I Zardusht at Naqsh-I Rustam. Further historical sources are provided by Syriac Church records, the Babylonian Talmud, Islamic authors, as well as Sassanian literature.

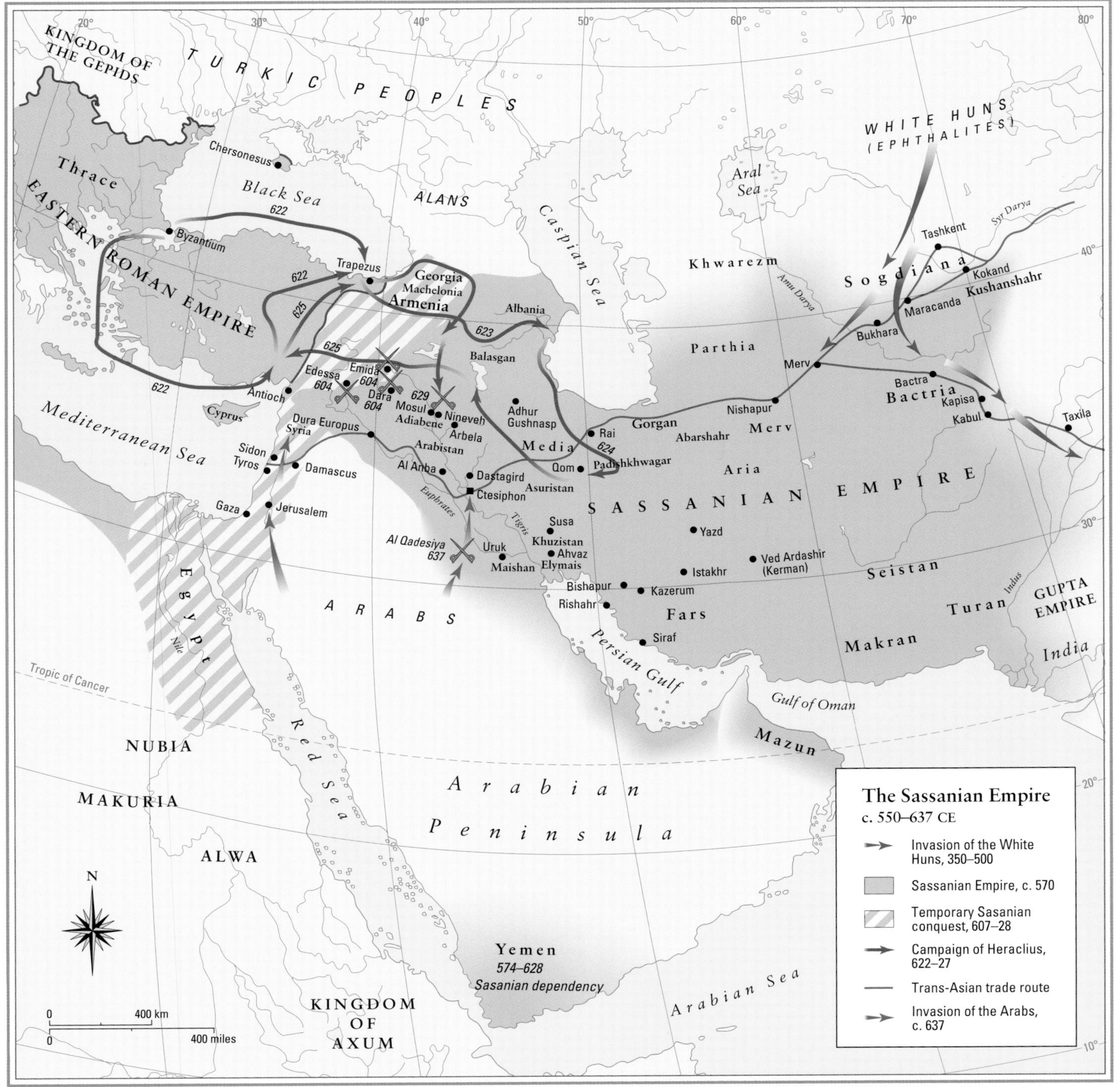

Palmyra and the East 260–273 CE

Rome's Rebellious Empires c. 265 CE

- Loyal to Rome
- Client state
- Gallic Empire
- Palmyrene Empire

Palmyra was an ancient trading city which is mentioned in the Bible (*Chronicles II*, 8:4) as Tadmor, a desert city built or fortified by King Solomon of Israel. It certainly existed some 2,000 years before the Romans first saw it. Situated in Syria, it comprised part of a vast trade network connecting Dura-Europus on the Euphrates to Antioch. The city became an important caravan station that funneled goods from China and India to the Roman Empire. Virtually independent under Seleucid rule, the city came under Roman control in the first century CE. Rich merchants from Palmyra had colonies in Alexandria and Charax, at the head of the Persian Gulf, and owned vessels which navigated westward to Italian waters.

The Romans annexed the city in 217 CE and incorporated it into Syria. When the Sassanians defeated the Parthians, their control of the river mouths of the Tigris and Euphrates cut the trade routes between India and Rome. Between 235 CE and 284 CE Rome's concern with international threats had a severe impact on Palmyra. Franks were invading Gaul, the Alemanni northern Italy, the Quadi and Marcomanni into Pannonia, the Goths into the Balkans and Asia Minor, and the Sassanians also raided Asia Minor and Syria. The Roman troops guarding

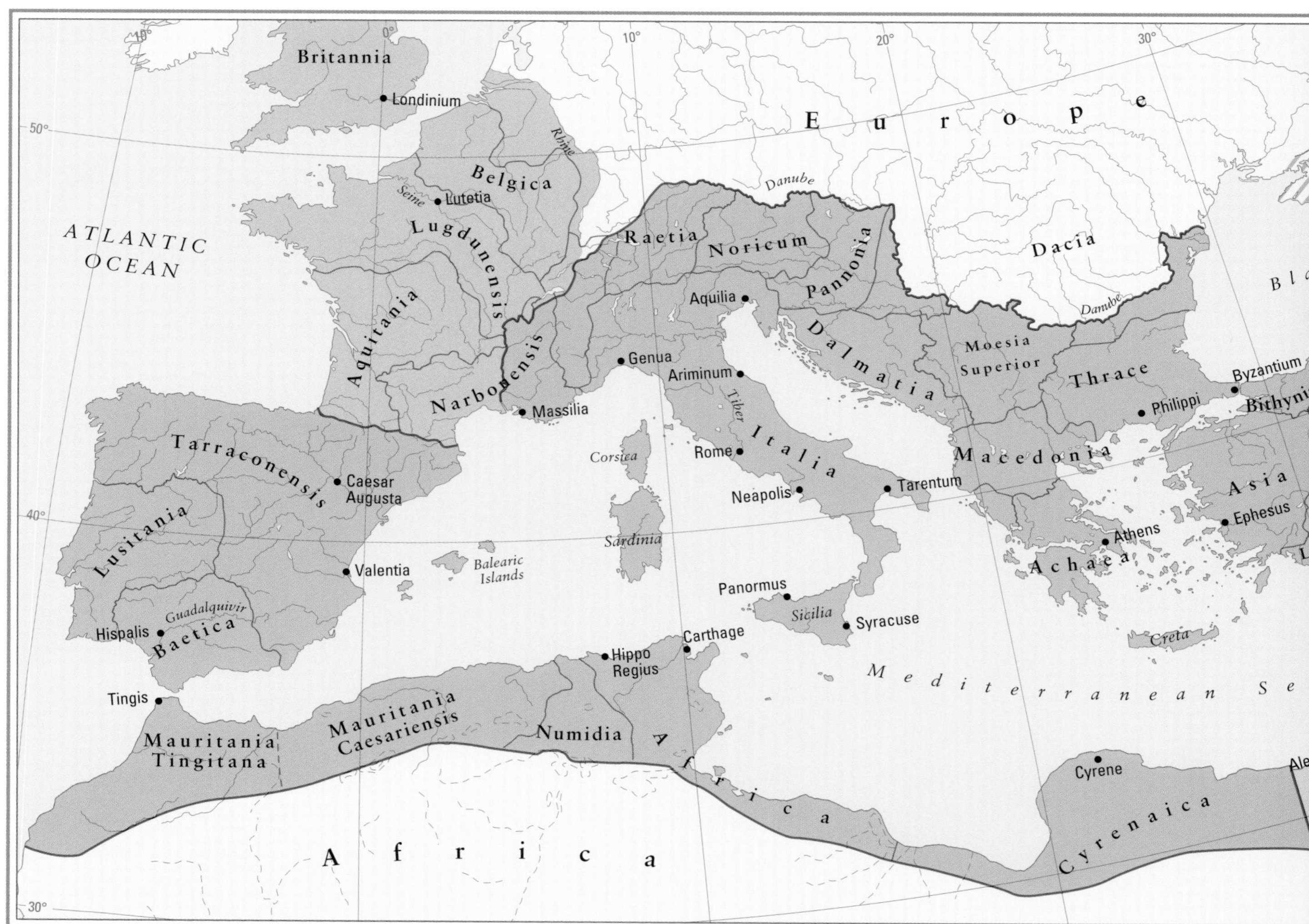

the borders were static in nature and found it almost impossible to defend the vast stretches of the Empire's frontier. Military and adminstrative failure led to changes of Emperor, more than twenty in 50 years, the Empire collapsed into three parts: Gallia, the rest of the Empire, and, eventually, the Palmyrene Empire.

In 260 CE, the Persians overran several Roman provinces and captured Emperor Valerian. In response, the Emperor Gallienus asked the King of Palmyra, Septimius Odaenathus, for assistance in defending the eastern frontier against the Persians. He managed to drive the occupying Sassanians from the Roman lands but was assassinated in 267 CE. His son, Vaballathus was made King but the real power was his mother, Zenobia,

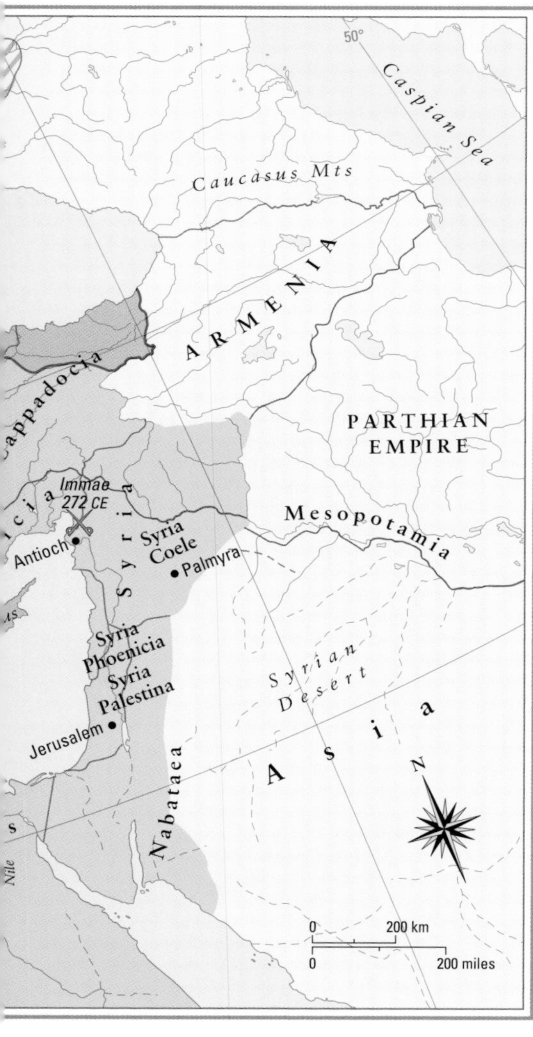

who claimed Cleopatra, the last Egyptian Pharaoh, as an ancestor.

Zenobia used her forces to conquer Syria, Egypt, Lebanon, and much of Asia Minor and cut the grain supplies to Rome. In 270 CE, Aurelian became Emperor, immediately campaigning against the barbarian invaders along the Imperial frontiers. He defeated the Alemanni, Goths, Vandals, Juthingi, Sarmatians, and the Carpi in Europe, before concentrating on eastern affairs. He advanced into Asia Minor, destroying every resisting city, although most surrendered readily. Near Antioch at Immae in 272 CE, the Roman and Palmyrene armies met. The Palmyrene general, Zabdas, believed that his armored cataphracts were the key to victory and charged the Roman cavalry, which countercharged and then broke as in a rout. In fact, Aurelian had planned this feigned retreat to tire out the enemy heavy cavalry in intense heat. At a given moment, the light Roman cavalry wheeled and slaughtered the unprepared Palmyrenes. Zenobia realized her infantry would be incapable of facing the disciplined heavy infantry of the Romans and retreated to Antioch, fleeing under cover of night to Emesa. The two armies clashed again with a similar result for the cavalry and the legionnaires slaughtered their opponents. The Byzantine historian Zozimus stated that the Palestinian contingent in Aurelian's army were adept at killing armored soldiers with their heavy-duty clubs.

Zenobia escaped to Palmyra, which was placed under siege by Aurelian. The whole campaign had only taken six months. This campaign was helped by the Emperor's clemency: he did not execute dignitaries in captured cities and consequently most cities just opened their gates. Zenobia fled the city, hoping to gain Sassanian help against the Romans, but was captured. Aurelian returned to Palmyra when it rebelled in 273 CE and sacked the city. Later, Aurelian advanced on the Gallic Empire in 274 CE and defeated it. Thus, the Emperor reunited the entire Roman Empire except for Dacia, lost and never regained.

Trade Routes and their Protectors

Archaeological evidence from Sumeria (c. 2400 BCE) suggests that cloves, which could only be found in the Moluccas, were popular there. The Egyptian medical papyrus, the *Ebers Papyrus* (c. 1550 BCE), states how embalming a body required the body cavities to be rinsed out with a variety of spices, including cassia and cinnamon, which were native to Southeast Asia. There are numerous records that recount the use of spices, as does archaeology, which attests to a rich trade in goods from the Indonesian islands to the Near East. Pharaoh Ramesses II, who died c. 1213 BCE, had peppercorns inserted into his nostrils when he was embalmed.

The lands comprising the Fertile Crescent provided entrepôt trading centers connecting the Silk Road to the Roman Empire. The road ran from Linzi and Changsha in China, through central Asia, the Kushan Empire, and Parthian Empire, and on to Rome. The route was aided by Han Chinese expansion between 140 and 87 BCE when Xinjiang was conquered, ensuring that the Chinese part of this caravan trading road reached Kokand. The route then journeyed through the Kushan and Parthian Empires to reach the Mediterranean and Roman commercial system.

The Silk Road was a cobweb of caravan routes that crossed Asia into Asia Minor and the Mediterranean littoral. Some 4,000 miles long, it bypassed the Takla-Makan Desert: one branch passed north via Karashahr and Aksu, another went south via Cherchen and Yarkand. The Road then ascended the Pamirs into Afghanistan and traveled across Persia/Parthia to Antioch in Syria, with offshoots from Bactria to Turkestan and India. Goods were moved along the road by Sogdian or Uighur middlemen engaged

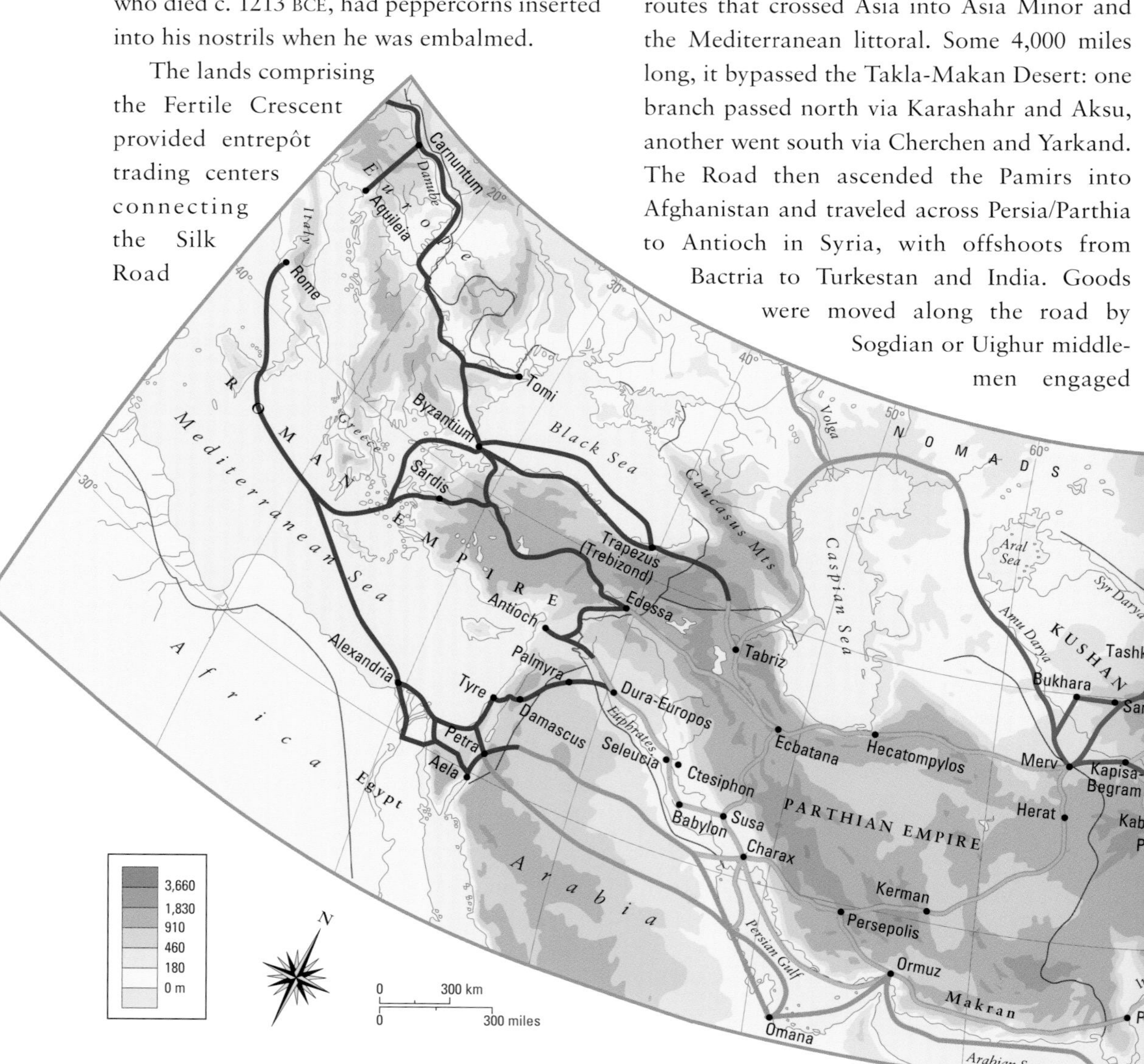

in relay trading. Chinese silk, lacquer, and spices traveled to the West, while wool, gold, silver, glass, medicines, and gems went East.

Chinese maritime links with India were extremely important when Parthia sought to control East-West trade. The Sino-Indian silk trade was mentioned in the navigational manual *Periplus Maris Erethryaei* (c. 90 CE), many years after sailors in the Indian Ocean, Persian Gulf, and Red Sea had learned how to use the monsoon winds in coastal and oceanic voyages. The maritime version of the Silk Road left India and sailed up the Persian Gulf with ports at Ormuz, Dilmun, and Charax, a Babylonian commercial center.

The Roman poet Lucan described Cleopatra as wearing silks, and the wealthy enjoyed silk clothing and cushions. Pliny claimed that silk drained Rome of gold and accused China of greed. In reality, most of the cost went to middlemen en route and to the dyeing trade at Tyre and the weavers at Sidon, Tyre, and Berytus, where Chinese silk was often rewoven. Evidence, therefore, exists of a silk industry in the Roman Near East.

Over time, with the rise of Byzantium and the decline of the Western Roman Empire, Constantinople became the terminus and entrepôt of the commerce between Europe and Asia. Greek and Syrian merchants facilitated Byzantine trade with China and India despite trade being occasionally suspended when Byzantium was at war with the Sassanian Empire in Persia.

The immense wealth that trade generated in the Near East in ancient times partially explains why different civilizations wanted to control trade routes. The trade routes were also important for the exchange of ideas, religions, and philosophies between East and West. Buddhism spread from the Kushan Empire to China, Christianity spread everywhere, and Islam proselytized from Arabia to North Africa and Spain in the west, and as far east as the Indonesian islands.

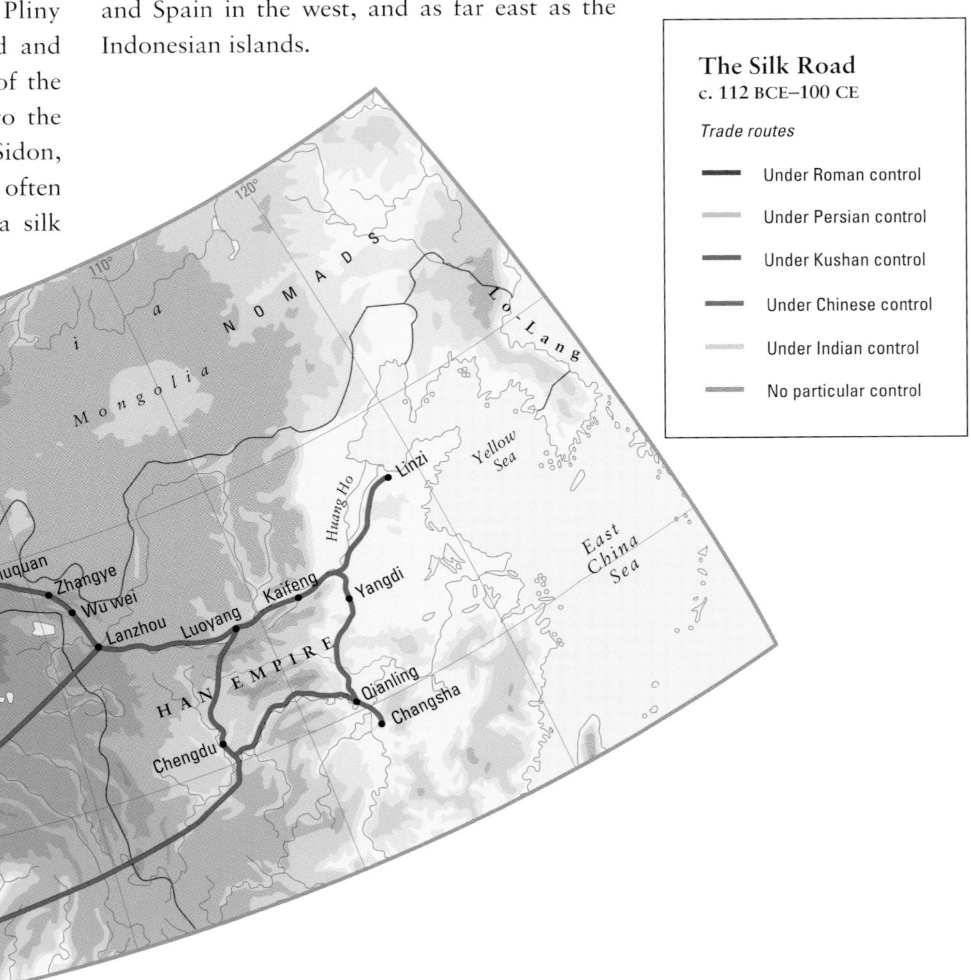

Biblical Interlude

At the time of the Hebrew move into Palestine, the Ancient World had been dislocated by the attacks of the Sea Peoples. The Hittite Empire was destroyed and Egypt had been weakened. Many Canaanite cities had been devastated and overall a power vacuum existed in Palestine. The Hebrews were ethnically and linguistically linked to the Canaanites and might have been joined by Hebrew clans who had not sojourned in Egypt. These nomadic peoples drifted into the hill country of Palestine, leaving the Canaanites and Philistines in their coastal cities.

The Hebrews did not have an elite strike force nor were they well armed. The sling was a common weapon amongst shepherds who could drive off predators with stones. The Hebrew tribal forces comprised mainly unarmored spearmen with shields. Some swords or helmets might have existed but would not be the norm. Under the Judges or inspired leaders, the tribes sometimes cooperated but they fought amongst themselves and it was difficult to rally them to fight a common foe. Initially, they did not have iron weapons and this was a disadvantage when fighting the Philistines, who did. The Hebrews did not understand siege warfare but could take towns by stratagems, such as the capture of Ai. Nor did the Hebrews have chariots, so combating Canaanite chariots was difficult and dangerous. However, when Deborah and Barak faced Sisera at the Battle of Megiddo, the Hebrews waited until the enemy chariots became bogged down in ground just saturated by rain; then the lightly armed Hebrew infantrymen could advance across the ground and kill the charioteers.

The major danger facing the Hebrews was the Philistines based in their five cities with their use of chariots, body armor, and iron. By approximately 1020 BCE, the now sedentary Hebrews faced Philistine encroachment and even lost the Ark of the Covenant. In this situation, the tribes united under a single war leader, King Saul. He raised an army of some 3,000 men who were motivated by religious unity at a time of national crisis. Despite some success, Saul and his son were killed at Mount Gilboa and it was left to the leader, described in the Bible as King David, to pick up the pieces. He turned Israel into a militarized state with an elite strike force based upon the bandits he had led. He also used mercenaries, many coming from Philistia after its subjugation by David. He brought Canaanite towns into his kingdom and was now capable of raising both taxes and men. Interestingly, little direct evidence exists for the reigns of David or Solomon and David has been considered as a bandit folk-hero by some. Nevertheless, some form of Israelite state must have existed to organize and manage a descent into the plains to capture or receive tribute from the Philistines and Canaanites.

After Solomon died the state separated into Israel in the north and Judah in the south. The two states fought each other, and the northern kingdom constructed a number of fortresses amongst which was Samaria. After Pharaoh Shoshenk invaded Israel, Judah saw the dangers and built its own fortified cities, including Lachish. The strength of the two small countries was such that they could defend themselves against their neighbors, especially Damascus and Edom. Alliances with other states helped build security and Omri of Israel managed to secure the marriage of his son Ahab to Jezebel, the King of Tyre's daughter. When Ahab came to the throne, he is credited with possessing 2,000 chariots and a force of 10,000 infantry.

Then Assyria turned its eyes on Palestine. The kings of Israel and Judah engaged in diplomatic maneuvers to retain their independence. Walls of fortifications were rebuilt and Hezekiah constructed the Siloam Tunnel, some 566.5 yards long, to secure a water supply in Jerusalem. The Assyrian advance brought the independence of Israel to an end and later the Babylonian Empire eradicated Judah as a state.

In time, the Babylonian Empire gave way to the Persian, which in turn was superseded by the Macedonian regime of Alexander the Great. His demise ushered in a series of wars between his generals who were all vying to take his Empire. Six wars were fought over Syria and Palestine, with the Seleucid Empire finally taking the region. Greek rule grew harsh, with a decision to force all subjects to worship Greek gods. The Temple in Jerusalem was desecrated and the Maccabean revolt ensued, led by Mattathias and his five sons. Years of warfare followed, with the Jews employing hit and run guerrilla warfare. The Macedonian phalanx proved to be too inflexible a unit when fighting over the broken terrain that characterized Judah. The Jews only lost when they adopted conventional military tactics. The Hasmonean Dynasty followed, which lasted until 37 BCE. However, Judea became a client kingdom of Rome; Pompey the Great intervened in a Judean civil war and eventually the last Hasmonean King was replaced on Roman orders by Herod the Great.

Palestine was finally divided into provinces and placed under procurators or governors. The Romans found the Jews a difficult people to control and faced three revolts: the Great Revolt of 66–73 CE; the Kitos War of 115–117 CE; and the Bar Kokhba Revolt of 132–135 CE. The First Revolt was initially very successful but was overwhelmed by the greatest military power in the world and Jerusalem was destroyed with great loss of life and enslavement for many.

In 115 CE, Emperor Trajan conducted a campaign against Parthia. While he was advancing through Mesopotamia, the second revolt broke out. Jewish rebels began attacking the small Roman garrisons remaining behind. The revolt spread to Cyrenaica, Cyprus, and Egypt, with Roman citizens and soldiers alike being killed. Towns elsewhere with substantial Jewish populations also rebelled.

The third revolt was more successful than the first as the Jews had developed guerrilla tactics of ambush and raid to keep the Romans guessing rather than allowing themselves to be trapped in fortresses where Roman siege skills made their defeat inevitable. In 131 CE, the revolutionaries established their own government in Jerusalem, declaring 'Year One of the Redemption of Israel.' Inevitably, Roman power eventually defeated the revolt and a terrible price was paid by the Jews. Those who did not, or could not, flee the land were killed or enslaved; the Jewish religion was proscribed; Jerusalem was Romanized and resettled by non-Jews and a temple to Jupiter was built on the site of the Holy of Holies. The surviving Jews joined Jewish communities abroad and became a people without a homeland.

Although not in the Biblical period there were other revolts later. In Judaea, the Jews were virtually exterminated but they survived in Galilee, which, like Samaria, does not appear to have been involved in the revolt. Tiberias in Galilee became the residence of Jewish patriarchs who there completed the Mishnah, the first major work of rabbinical literature, the Talmud, and other early rabbinical texts. In 484 and 495, the Samaritans rebelled against Christian Byzantine rule and slaughtered Christians and burned churches. They were suppressed with great brutality and loss of life. During the Byzantine-Sassanian War of 602–628, the Sassanian King made an alliance with the exiled Jewish population in his lands and recruited a 20,000-strong Jewish army, which marched to Palestine. Joined by Jewish recruits from Tiberias, Nazareth, and the Galilee they seized Jerusalem and established a Jewish-Sassanian Commonwealth within the Sassanian Empire. Eventually, Byzantine troops re-conquered Palestine and retribution was taken against the Jews; many died or were exiled, while large numbers fled to Egypt. Byzantine control was short-lived as Arab armies swept into Palestine and captured Jerusalem in 638, while other Arab armies swept away the Sassanian Empire.

Hebrew Assault on Canaan

The saga of the invasion of Canaan can be found in the Bible books of *Joshua* and *Judges* and probably displays the combined experience of several invading groups over decades. There is no doubt that the Hebrews fought to gain control of Canaan, but the epic campaigns are undoubtedly heavily embellished. It is recounted that, when the Hebrews approached Canaan, Moses sent spies in advance, including Joshua of Ephraim. Having gathered intelligence about possible invasion routes, Joshua and Moses moved the Hebrews from Abel-shittem in Moab to Gilgal.

Extensive archaeological work on Jericho shows the walled city had been destroyed some 300 years before the Hebrew invasion. Tales of such an occasion may be merged into the Biblical account. Ai, a settlement of some 1,000 people, was captured and destroyed. Identified as el-Tell near Bethel, archaeological digs show that it was not inhabited during the Hebrew conquest. However, Kirjath-Sepher and Lachish were vanquished, the former by fire, followed by Israelite occupation. Eglon (Tell el-Hesi?) and Hazor (Tell el-Qedah) were destroyed in the late thirteenth century and therefore demonstrate the accuracy of parts of the Biblical invasion epic.

An interesting development in the invasion was the treaty made with the mixed-origin inhabitants of Shechem, a city dominating part of the hill country. The inhabitants may have been part of the folk movement that brought Abraham to Canaan in earlier times and this 'kinship' fostered a mutual covenant. The Hebrews traversed Shechemite land peacefully.

Joshua's campaign in central Canaan eventually split the land in two when his forces defeated and routed a coalition of kingdoms which comprised Jerusalem, Hebron, Jarmuth, Lachish, and Eglon. This success was followed by a swift advance to the south of Azekah. Joshua marched to attack Libnah, Lachish, Eglon, Hebron, and Debir, but was not necessarily solely responsible for their destruction. Caleb of Judah was campaigning in the region after Joshua's death. Possibly, in other years, raiding Philistines or Egyptians were responsible for their destruction, but events were all compounded into one heroic epic.

Upper Galilee's fertile hills and forests were next to receive the Hebrew onslaught. Hazor, which had existed for some 1,500 years, was the major Canaanite population center. As the Hebrews encroached, maybe over years, gradually constricting Hazorite control, its King, Jabin, called out his allies from Canaanite communities in Upper and Lower Galilee. The Canaanites were convinced that the Hebrews could not confront their armored charioteers and cavalry. The Canaanites gathered at the Waters of Meron while the Hebrews camped in broken land and forests nearby. Chariots were totally unsuitable for this terrain and lightly armed, mobile Hebrew soldiers hamstrung horses, used fire, and routed their enemy. They ensured that the Canaanites could not retreat to Hazor but were forced to Sidon or the Valley of Mizpeh. Hazor's inhabitants were then butchered and the city torched. The Hebrew pastoralists did not rebuild this remarkable city; that was left to Solomon.

The *Book of Joshua* describes a Holy War of Yahweh, which gave the Hebrews a land of milk and honey. The military process did not destroy the Canaanite population and skirmishing continued, with sporadic outbursts of ethnic cleansing. Small groups inhabiting conquered land were often absorbed while *Joshua* 24 suggests that other people gave up their gods to join the Hebrews in a covenant with Yahweh. Women were acquired and assimilated, and peoples such as the Kenites were already believers in Yahweh and merged with Judah. Israel was therefore born of many strands.

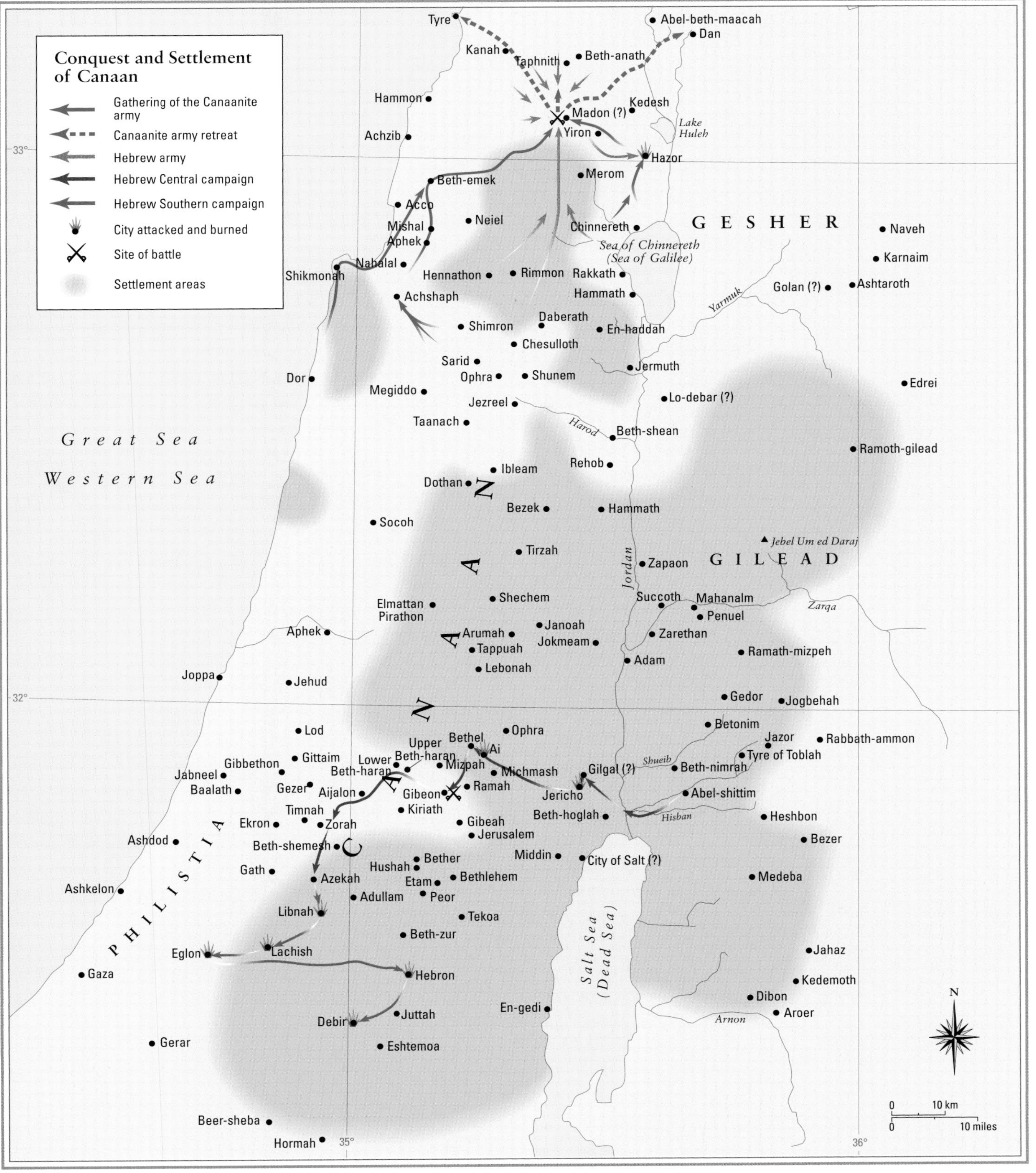
Conquest and Settlement of Canaan
Gathering of the Canaanite army
Canaanite army retreat
Hebrew army
Hebrew Central campaign
Hebrew Southern campaign
City attacked and burned
Site of battle
Settlement areas
Tyre
Abel-beth-maacah
Dan
Kanah
Taphnith
Beth-anath
Hammon
Kedesh
Madon (?)
Lake Huleh
Achzib
Yiron
Hazor
Merom
Beth-emek
Acco
Neiel
Mishal
Aphek
Chinnereth
Sea of Chinnereth (Sea of Galilee)
GESHER
Naveh
Karnaim
Nahalal
Shikmonah
Hennathon
Rimmon
Rakkath
Golan (?)
Ashtaroth
Achshaph
Hammath
Yarmuk
Daberath
Shimron
En-haddah
Chesulloth
Sarid
Jermuth
Dor
Ophra
Shunem
Megiddo
Edrei
Jezreel
Lo-debar (?)
Taanach
Harod
Beth-shean
Great Sea
Western Sea
Rehob
Ramoth-gilead
Ibleam
Dothan
Bezek
Hammath
Socoh
Jebel Um ed Daraj
Tirzah
Zapaon
GILEAD
Jordan
Shechem
Elmattan Pirathon
Succoth
Mahanalm
Penuel
Zarqa
Janoah
Aphek
Arumah
Zarethan
Tappuah
Jokmeam
Ramath-mizpeh
Lebonah
Adam
Joppa
Jehud
CANAAN
Gedor
Jogbehah
32°
33°
Betonim
Lod
Ophra
Jazor
Rabbath-ammon
Upper Beth-haran
Bethel
Ai
Tyre of Toblah
Gibbethon
Gittaim
Lower Beth-haran
Mizpah
Shueib
Beth-nimrah
Jabneel
Michmash
Gilgal (?)
Baalath
Gezer
Aijalon
Gibeon
Ramah
Jericho
Abel-shittim
Timnah
Kiriath
Beth-hoglah
Hisban
Heshbon
Ekron
Zorah
Gibeah
Jerusalem
Bezer
Ashdod
Beth-shemesh
Bether
Middin
City of Salt (?)
Gath
Hushah
Etam
Bethlehem
Medeba
Azekah
Ashkelon
Adullam
Peor
PHILISTIA
Libnah
Tekoa
Beth-zur
Salt Sea (Dead Sea)
Jahaz
Eglon
Lachish
Hebron
Gaza
Kedemoth
Dibon
Juttah
En-gedi
Debir
Arnon
Aroer
Eshtemoa
Gerar
N
0 10 km
0 10 miles
Beer-sheba
Hormah
35°
36°

Struggles of the Judges

Israel had been forced to adapt from a semi-nomadic to an agricultural economy. As Hebrews were transformed into small peasant farmers they became more affluent. Hebrew towns were not sophisticated, but under the influence of trade, tribes benefited and prosperity improved.

Although the Israelite league had covenanted with Yahweh, pagan cults continued. Some worshipped fertility cults. Others worshipped Baal as well as Yahweh. In the *Book of Judges* there is criticism of Israel for accepting this theological chaos.

According to the Bible, twelve judges emerged to deliver Israel from danger and apostasy—they cannot be exactly located in time, but the Bible probably places them in chronological order. The Judges were various in character and seem to be the champions of local tribes in different locations. The charismatic Judges were able to incite the tribes to rally and repulse Israel's enemies.

Othniel, the first of the Biblical judges, is supposed to have repelled the invasion of Cushan-rishathaim of Aram-naharaim. This figure has a manuafctured name meaning Cushan of Double Wickedness, and since Othniel was an inhabitant of the south courty, speculation says the threat was from Edom; also, Aram and Edom was readily confused in Hebrew. However, a district of Qusana-ruma is known in northern Aram and the invasion may have come from this region.

The Judge Ehud's success was against Moab. Previously, Sihon, the Amorite, had seized Moabite land north of the River Arnon. Israel, in turn, seized this territory, and the tribe of Reuben settled there. Apparently, Moab regained this region and threatened the tribe of Benjamin. The Moabites were repulsed; the Bible does not say whether the Moabites were ejected. Whatever the case, after eighteen years of paying tribute to the Moabite King, Ehud killed him and 80 years of peace ensued.

Shamgar is a mysterious individual, who was not even an Israelite. Existing before Deborah, he defended Hebrew territory from a Sea People attack. Allegedly, he was King of Beth-anath city in Galilee. He repelled the Philistines, killing 600 of them, and saving himself and Israel.

Deborah and Barak of Naphtali can be placed in history at approximately 1125 BCE or a little before. Israel was nearly cut in two by the Valley of Jezreel, and Canaanite leagues dominated neighboring Israelite clans. Deborah and Barak rallied six tribes from Benjamin to Galilee. After severe rainfall the land was so saturated that Canaanite chariots were bogged down, enabling Israelite light infantry to massacre their crews. This success did not make the Israelites masters of Jezreel but gave them a long breathing space, allowing them to move to, and settle in, the valley.

Gideon of Manasseh was called to action when Jezreel and the neighboring hill country were attacked by camel-riding desert nomads. These raiders were Midianites, Amelkites, and Bene Qedem. This is the first historical reference to domesticated camels, used here as a mobile, deadly strike force, which raided annually. Gideon rallied his tribe and his neighbors and drove the raiders from the land. His victories gave him tremendous prestige and authority. His tribe wanted him to assume the mantle of kingship but he absolutely refused.

The story of Jephthah, who was a Gileadite leader of an outlaw band, tragically shows that human sacrifice still persisted in Israel despite its incompatibility with religious beliefs. When the Ammonites, wealthy from the caravan trade, threatened to expand territorially into Israelite Trans-jordan, Jephthah was promised Yahweh's help if he sacrificed the next living thing that he saw; unfortunately, this was his virgin daughter. The Ammonites were repelled but Jephthah had to kill his daughter as his side of the bargain with Yahweh.

Samson's career is depicted in *Judges* 13–16, which recounts his marital and raiding adventures, an accurate reflection of the hostile situation on the borders of Philistia before full-scale war broke out.

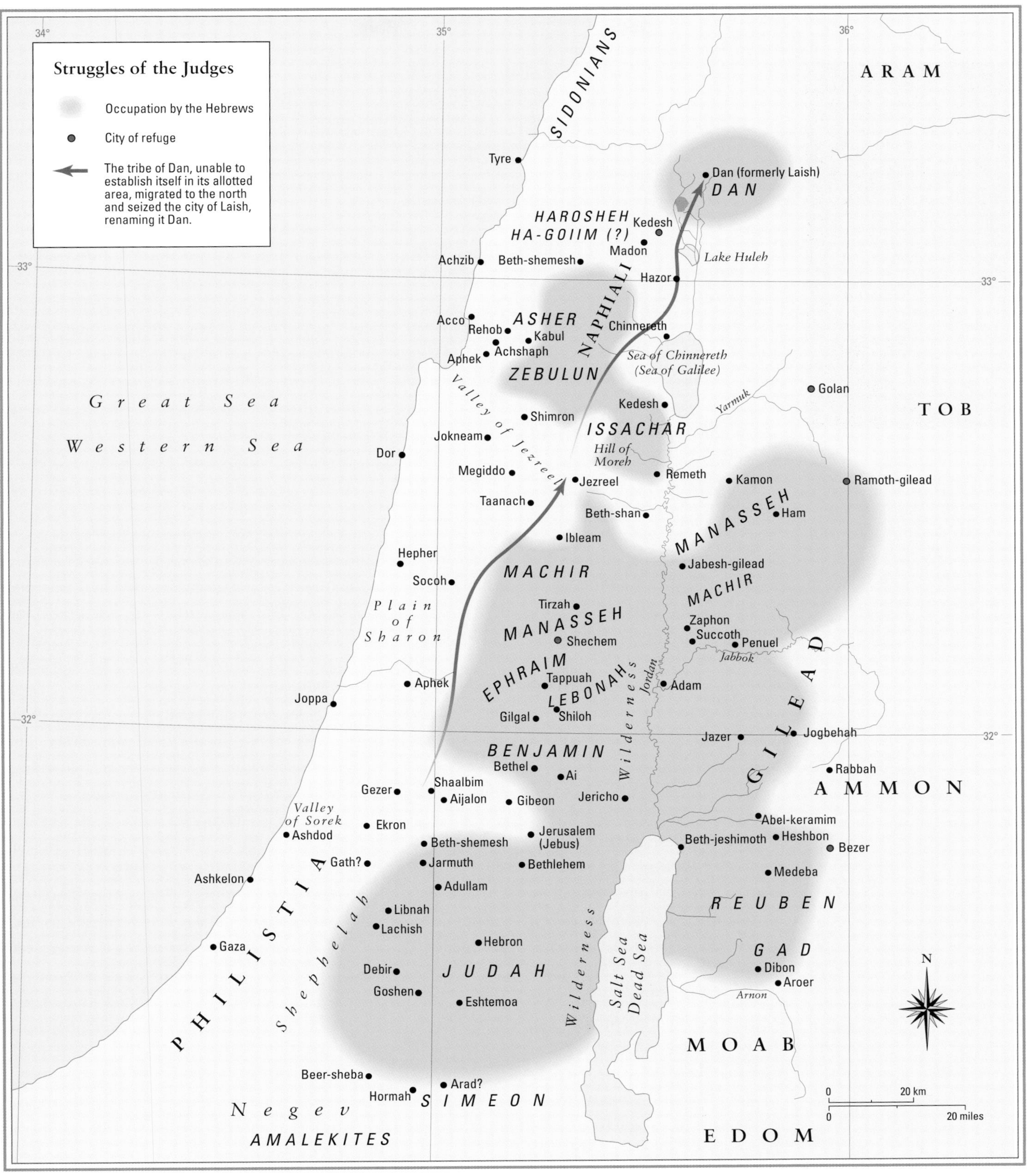
Struggles of the Judges
Occupation by the Hebrews
City of refuge
The tribe of Dan, unable to establish itself in its allotted area, migrated to the north and seized the city of Laish, renaming it Dan.
34°
35°
36°
33°
32°
ARAM
SIDONIANS
Tyre
Dan (formerly Laish)
DAN
HAROSHEH HA-GOIIM (?)
Kedesh
Madon
Lake Huleh
Achzib
Beth-shemesh
Hazor
NAPHTALI
Acco
ASHER
Rehob
Kabul
Chinnereth
Achshaph
Aphek
Sea of Chinnereth (Sea of Galilee)
ZEBULUN
Valley of Jezreel
Golan
Great Sea
Western Sea
Kedesh
Yarmuk
TOB
Shimron
ISSACHAR
Jokneam
Hill of Moreh
Dor
Megiddo
Remeth
Kamon
Ramoth-gilead
Jezreel
Taanach
Beth-shan
MANASSEH
Ham
Ibleam
Hepher
Jabesh-gilead
Socoh
MACHIR
MACHIR
Plain of Sharon
Tirzah
MANASSEH
Zaphon
Shechem
Succoth
Penuel
Jabbok
EPHRAIM
Tappuah
Aphek
LEBONAH
Wilderness
Jordan
Adam
GILEAD
Joppa
Gilgal
Shiloh
Jazer
Jogbehah
BENJAMIN
Bethel
Ai
Rabbah
Shaalbim
Gezer
Aijalon
Gibeon
Jericho
AMMON
Valley of Sorek
Ekron
Ashdod
Abel-keramim
Jerusalem (Jebus)
Heshbon
Beth-shemesh
Beth-jeshimoth
Bezer
Gath?
Jarmuth
Bethlehem
Ashkelon
Adullam
Medeba
Libnah
REUBEN
Lachish
Hebron
Gaza
GAD
Debir
JUDAH
Dibon
Aroer
Goshen
Eshtemoa
Arnon
Salt Sea
Dead Sea
Wilderness
Shephelah
PHILISTIA
N
MOAB
Beer-sheba
Arad?
Hormah
SIMEON
Negev
AMALEKITES
EDOM
0
20 km
0
20 miles

Saul, King of Israel c. 1021–1000 BCE

In this painting, attributed to the studio of Rembrandt, King Saul listens to the harp played by the hero David. Aware of the threat to his kingship posed by the young hero, he decides to promote David to the rank of Captain of One Thousand, in the hope that he would die in battle.

The Philistine occupation of parts of Israel, especially the Saddle of Benjamin, northeast of Gibeah, caused such a furor that the Hebrew tribal elders united in their demands for a King. At a meeting at Mizpah, summoned by Samuel, the judge and prophet, the famed warrior Saul was anointed King.

Saul's objective was to unite the tribes, keeping them bonded by their religious faith and covenant with God. Saul had the huge task of defining a strategy to outwit the better armed and disciplined Philistines, who possessed iron weapons and chariots. However, it was not to be the powerful Sea People who tested Saul's determination, but the Ammonites. The Ammonite, with a capital at Rabbath-ammon, wished to reassert control over Gilead, from which they had been expelled.

The Ammonite leader, Nahash, invaded Gilead and besieged the Hebrew town of Jabesh-gilead. The inhabitants promised to make a treaty accepting Nahash's sovereignty but he laid down a cruel condition of peace: taking the right eye of every male in the city. As was normal under siege conditions, the town elders agreed that if they were not relieved within a given time, in this case seven days, they would concur.

The Jabeshites despatched messengers requesting aid. Saul heard the news and summoned Israelite warriors to muster at Bezek, between Shechem and Beth-shan. Saul led his men in a forced night-march across the Jordan through the Wadi Yabis below Jabesh-gilead. At dawn, Saul sent three columns into the sleepy Ammonite camp, achieving total surprise. The slaughter began, continuing into the day with the destruction and rout of the Ammonite army. Reputedly, Nahash was killed. After the victory, Samuel led the Israelite army to Gilgal and Saul was re-affirmed as King.

Meanwhile, some fourteen miles to the west at Geba and Michmash, Philistine troops occupied the strategically important pass at the Saddle of Benjamin, which controlled the Way of Beth-horon into the Hebrew highlands. Saul raised a force of 3,000 men, retaining 2,000 as he marched on Michmash and leaving the balance as a reserve with his son, Jonathan. However, that reckless prince assaulted Gibeah, surprising the Philistines in a victorious attack.

Saul broadcast news of the victory while the furious Philistines gathered their chariots, cavalry, and infantry in large numbers and camped at Michmash, east of Beth-aven. The Israelites fled in dismay, hiding in caves, woods, and hills, while some crossed the Jordan River to reach Gad and Gilead.

Saul led his remaining 600 men to Gibeah, carefully avoiding three large companies of raiders despatched from Michmash. Elsewhere, Jonathan and his armor-bearer surprised a Philistine outpost on a rocky promontory and killed its twenty-man garrison. The Philistines at Michmash were shocked by this event and became panic-stricken. Seeing their confusion, Saul attacked and created more alarm, leading to a Philistine rout, inflicting heavy losses. Israelite deserters materialized out of their hiding places and joined in the slaughter. The Hebrew heartland was now secure, providing Saul with a base for future campaigns.

Saul then campaigned against all his surrounding enemies: Moab, Ammon, Edom, Zobah, and Philistia. The Prophet Samuel returned to Saul, stating that God required the total destruction of the Amalekites who had abused the Hebrews when they first entered Canaan. Although required to kill every living thing, Saul captured the Amalekite King, Agag. While he butchered Agag's followers, he chose to send his best flocks and oxen to Gilgal. Samuel condemned Saul for not killing everything as God had demanded, claiming that God had rejected him. Despite Saul's remorse, Samuel hacked Agag to death with a sword.

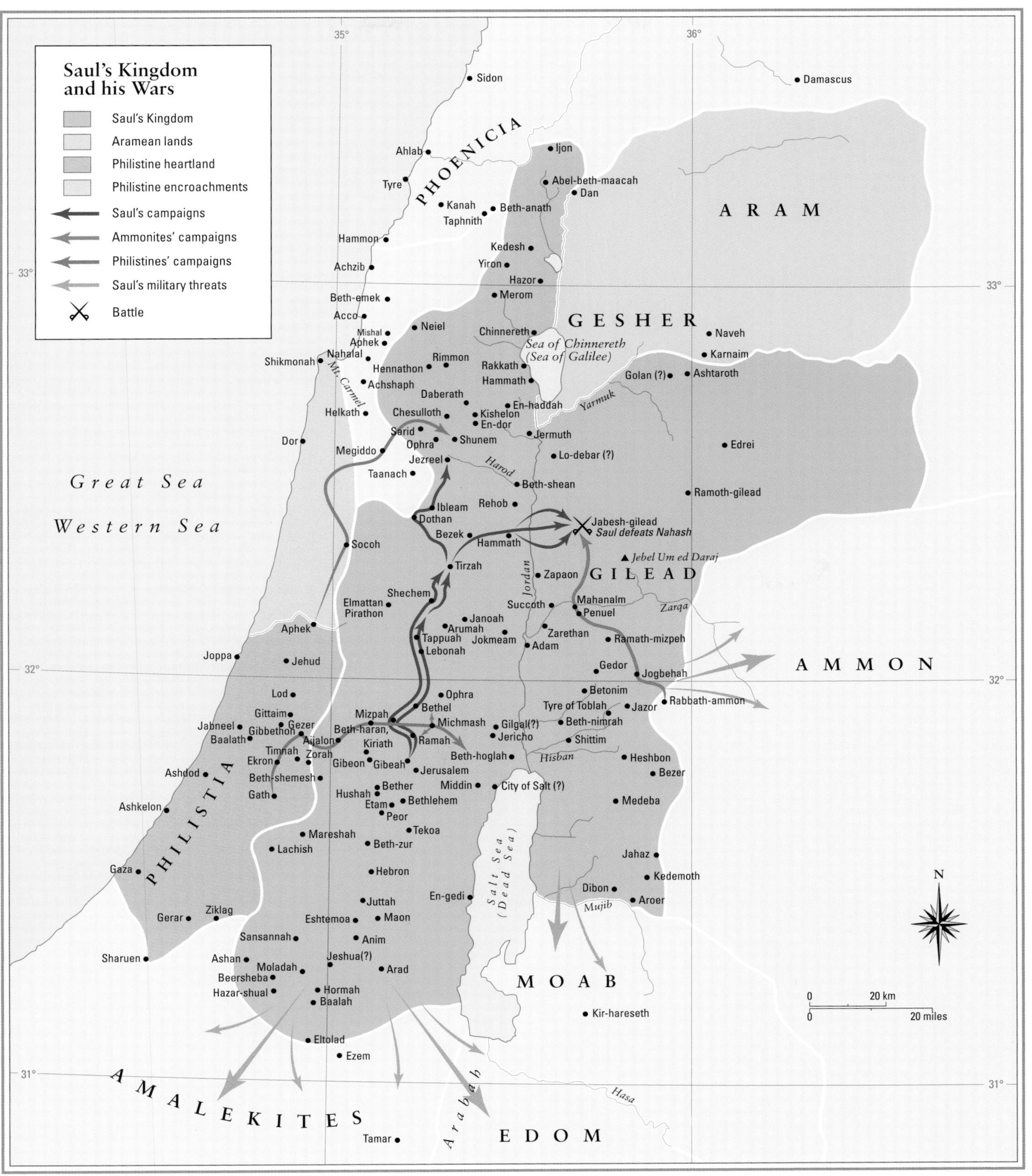
Saul's Kingdom and his Wars
Saul's Kingdom
Aramean lands
Philistine heartland
Philistine encroachments
Saul's campaigns
Ammonites' campaigns
Philistines' campaigns
Saul's military threats
Battle
35°
36°
33°
32°
31°
Sidon
Damascus
PHOENICIA
Ahlab
Tyre
Ijon
Abel-beth-maacah
Dan
Kanah
Beth-anath
Taphnith
ARAM
Hammon
Kedesh
Achzib
Yiron
Hazor
Beth-emek
Merom
Acco
Neiel
GESHER
Mishal
Aphek
Chinnereth
Naveh
Sea of Chinnereth (Sea of Galilee)
Karnaim
Shikmonah
Nahalal
Rimmon
Hennathon
Rakkath
Mt. Carmel
Achshaph
Hammath
Golan (?)
Ashtaroth
Daberath
Yarmuk
En-haddah
Chesulloth
Kishelon
Helkath
En-dor
Sarid
Shunem
Jermuth
Dor
Ophra
Edrei
Megiddo
Jezreel
Lo-debar (?)
Harod
Taanach
Beth-shean
Great Sea
Ramoth-gilead
Western Sea
Ibleam
Rehob
Dothan
Jabesh-gilead
Saul defeats Nahash
Bezek
Hammath
Socoh
Jebel Um ed Daraj
Tirzah
Jordan
Zapaon
GILEAD
Shechem
Mahanalm
Elmattan
Succoth
Zarqa
Pirathon
Penuel
Janoah
Aphek
Arumah
Zarethan
Tappuah
Jokmeam
Ramath-mizpeh
Lebonah
Adam
Joppa
Jehud
AMMON
Gedor
Jogbehah
Ophra
Betonim
Lod
Bethel
Rabbath-ammon
Tyre of Toblah
Jazor
Gittaim
Mizpah
Gezer
Michmash
Gilgal(?)
Beth-nimrah
Jabneel
Gibbethon
Beth-haran,
Baalath
Aijalon
Kiriath
Ramah
Jericho
Shittim
Timnah
Zorah
Ekron
Beth-hoglah
Hisban
Heshbon
Gibeon
Gibeah
Ashdod
Jerusalem
Bezer
Beth-shemesh
Bether
Middin
City of Salt (?)
Gath
Hushah
Etam
Bethlehem
Medeba
Ashkelon
Peor
PHILISTIA
Tekoa
Mareshah
Beth-zur
Lachish
Salt Sea (Dead Sea)
Jahaz
Gaza
Hebron
Kedemoth
N
Dibon
Juttah
En-gedi
Aroer
Mujib
Gerar
Ziklag
Eshtemoa
Maon
Sansannah
Anim
Sharuen
Jeshua(?)
Ashan
Arad
Moladah
MOAB
Beersheba
Hazar-shual
Hormah
Baalah
0
20 km
0
20 miles
Kir-hareseth
Eltolad
Ezem
AMALEKITES
Hasa
Arabah
Tamar
EDOM

King David

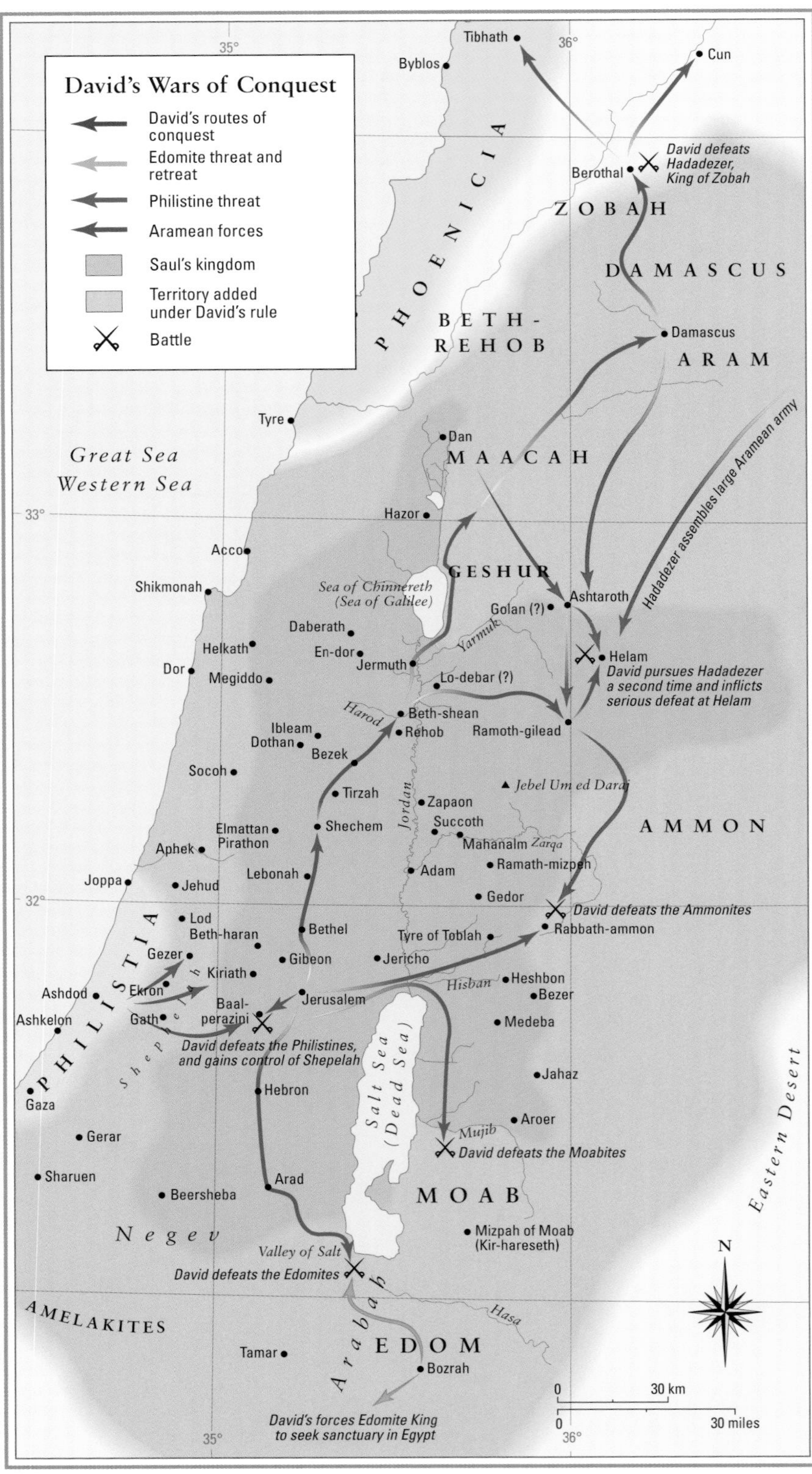

According to Biblical accounts, David came to Saul's notice either because of his soothing harp music or his slaughter of the giant Philistine warrior, Goliath. The morale of the Philistine army that faced Saul's forces in the Valley of Elah was so damaged that its soldiers fled back to Gath and Ekron. After David became a famous warrior, Saul became jealous of David's success, thinking he planned to usurp his throne, and David was forced to flee Gibeah. He gathered his brothers, clan, and those unhappy with Saul around him, creating an outlaw band of 600 men who moved to the Forest of Hereth. Meanwhile David's parents were sent for safety to the Moabite King. David was hunted by Saul's forces through the Wilderness of Ziph and that of Maon. Next he moved to Philistia and saw King Achish of Gath who gave him command of the town of Ziklag in the Negev.

Elsewhere, the Philistines marched from Aphek and attacked Saul at Mount Gilboa, where the Israelites were defeated and Saul died. David took over the task of leading an Israelite resurgence, defeating the Philistines and liberating occupied lands. He was anointed King in Judah and was eventually accepted by the northern tribes, thereby ruling a united people.

David defeated two Philistine onslaughts and made their five cities tributaries, using their inhabitants as mercenary soldiers. King David then consolidated his internal borders by capturing the remaining Canaanite city-states north and south of Mount Carmel in Jezreel and Galilee. Although some had partially Israelite residents, they had never been under Hebrew control. They were annexed directly into the state and became the King's subjects. The kingdom had grown from a collection of tribes into a truly multi-cultural state with a new capital at Jerusalem, which housed the Ark, thus becoming the religious cult center of the people.

David next set about securing Israel's borders by creating an Empire. War was waged against Ammon and its allies, the Aramaean kingdoms such as Maachah, Beth-Rehob, and Aram-Zobah. Aramaean intervention was ended when the Ammonites were beaten at the Battle of Ramah. It is written that during the siege there, David remained in Jerusalem, dallying with Bathsheba, thereby earning a sharp admonition from the prophet Nathan. The conquest of Moab and Edom took place with extreme brutality and mass executions of captured Moabite soldiers. The Edomite royal family was virtually eradicated, after which Edom was ruled as a conquered province. Syria faced David and Hadadezer of Aram-Zobah was defeated, endowing Israel with copper mines and booty. Gifts were then received from the King of Hamath, a state north of Aram-Zobah on the Orontes River. Later, David negotiated a treaty with Hiram, King of Tyre, an alliance which was of great financial benefit.

This consolidated, small, but complex Empire was focused upon the personality of David of Judah and his Canaanite subjects, but not the Israelites. Hence, power was concentrated in the Crown and was only threatened by the failed rebellion of David's son, Absalom, and a northern rebellion. This dissent was ultimately resolved by the choice of Solomon as David's heir.

David's ambitions were made possible by his use of personal troops based upon his bandit band, which included professional mercenaries. His men were well armed with spears and javelins, and swords became increasingly used. Armor was worn, including helmets, shields, and bronze, or iron scale armor. Lead pellets have been found showing that the sling was a common missile weapon. This professional elite became a nucleus around which David deployed the tribal levies who were forced to learn military efficiency and discipline. Once in place, David's kingdom could collect tribute and men to swell his forces. Financial levies could be used to fortify towns or strengthen them, testified by the construction of casement walls. Having subjected regions where chariots were in use, David saw their worth and commenced building a chariot force.

David's Empire was potentially very wealthy. He controlled Palestine, through which goods traveled from the east and from the trading cities of Phoenicia, whose ships roamed the Mediterranean. He also controlled the great international trade and invasion routes that ran through Palestine between Damascus and the Egyptian frontier, the coastal Way of the Sea and the inland King's Highway.

Solomon's Empire

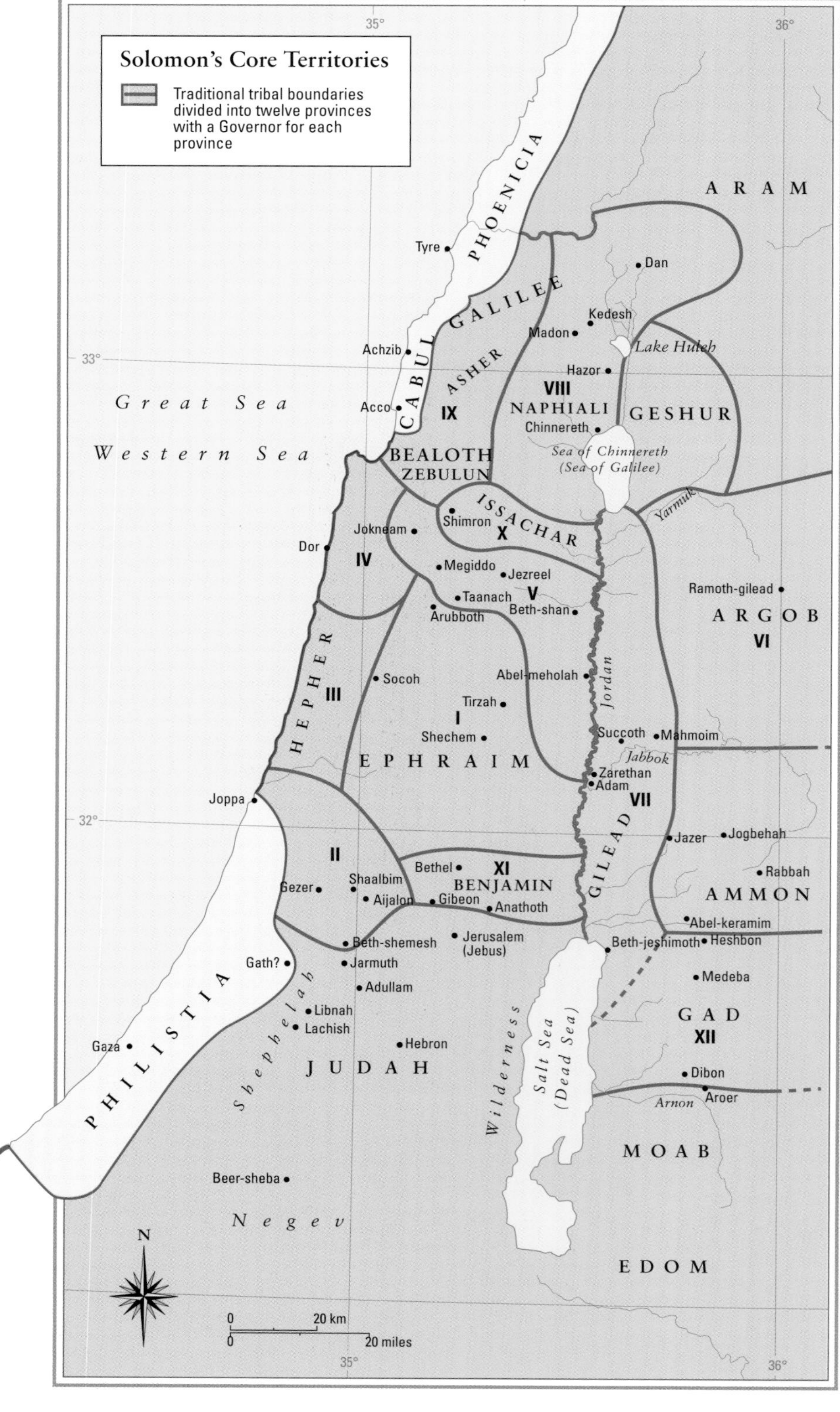

Solomon, David's successor, engaged in considerable diplomatic activity on his accession, developing a series of alliance systems that were a basis for Israel's commerce. The most important treaty was with Tyre, a link established by David. The Phoenicians held the Levantine coastline from Acre (Acco) northward. Under King Hiram I (c. 969–936 BCE), Tyre expanded its maritime interests into Cyprus, Sicily, Sardinia, Spain and, possibly, North Africa. The Sardinian copper mines were particularly important. Solomon himself controlled the Arabah, south of the Dead Sea, where copper deposits were numerous. Ezion-geber, at the head of the Gulf of Aqaba, was home to the largest copper refinery known in the ancient Near East. Solomon's fleet was supplied with vessels designed to transport smelted metal such as copper ingots. They copied Phoenician teechnology, with the mining industry and fleet staffed and aided by Phoenicians. Thus, Solomon's copper supply was adequate for domestic use, with a surplus for export. Trade with Phoenicia led to export of wheat and olive oil in return for Lebanese hardwoods used in Solomon's building projects.

The Bible recounts that Solomon was inspired by the Phoenician experience and wished to expand Israel's trade through the Red Sea to the south. Accordingly his fleet made regular journeys to Ophir. This fabled land of wealth may have been located in the city of Zimbabwe; gold from its mines possibly found a way to Sofala on the coast. More likely, Ophir was found on the African coast of the Red Sea or in the Yemen part of the Arabian Peninsula, the purported home of the Queen of Sheba. The Bible reports imports to Israel from Ophir of gold, silver, almug wood, jewels, ivory, peacocks, and monkeys.

Sheba, if located in the Hadhramaut, lay across the caravan routes leading to Mesopotamia and the Levant. This Arabian kingdom dominated the spice and incense trade and may have traded into Ethiopia and Somalia after Egyptian influence weakened in these regions. It is possible that Solomon's control of Ezion-geber brought him into competition with Shebean camel caravans. It is also possible that the Queen of Sheba visited Solomon to take gifts and negotiate a trade treaty. Solomon apparently treated her with great respect, suggesting a successful agreement. Consequently, if *I Kings* 10: 15 is understood correctly, taxes and excise duties poured into the Israelite treasury as a result.

The Bible suggests that Solomon traded in horses from Cilicia and chariots from Egypt. He may have sought these products as essential items for his armed forces. Indeed the Bible reports that he owned thousands of horses and chariots. This trade shows Solomon's fortunate geographical position. The Way of the Sea originated in Egypt and traversed the coastal plain through the Megiddo Pass in the Jezreel Valley, where it met the main routes to Phoenicia and the Aramean cities of Damascus and Hamath. Israel's ownership of fortified cities, like Megiddo, Gezer, and Hazor provided strategic protection of trade and of Jerusalem. Hazor was placed at the junction of the roads to Hamath and Damascus and the point where the road to Damascus crossed the River Jordan. Megiddo guarded the pass where the Way of the Sea crossed from the Sharon plain into the Jezreel Valley, while Gezer controlled the direct road to Jerusalem from the west.

Most of Soloman's reign appeared to be peaceful, and only two enemies posed a threat. Hadad, an Edomite, had fled to Egypt when David slaughtered his family. He returned and probably raided caravans from Ezion-geber. King Rezon of Damascus exploited his geographical position to threaten the caravan trade.

There was a disadvantage in the Phoenician connection. Hiram seems to have been the senior partner in the Tyrian-Israel

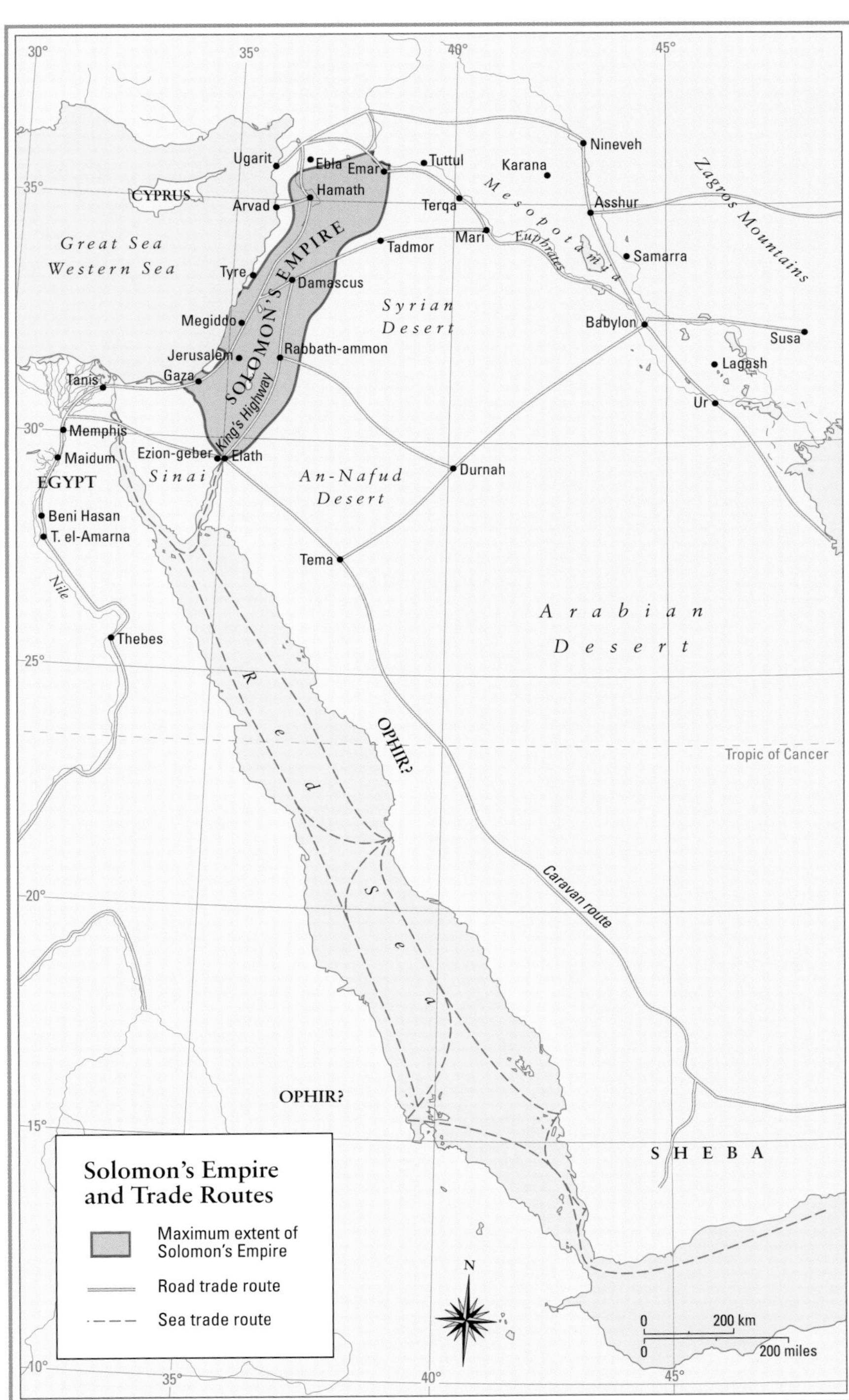

relationship by virtue of his provision of wood, craftsmen, and sailors. Solomon owed Hiram so much money that he handed over some twenty cities in the Jezreel Valley as either collateral or compensation.

Shoshenk's Campaign in Palestine c. 925 BCE

Shoshenk I was a strong leader who reunited a divided Egypt and restored Egypt's influence, both by diplomatic and military means.

Shoshenk (Shishak I), first Pharaoh of the Twenty-second Dynasty, became Egypt's monarch during Solomon's reign. Diplomatic relations were cordial, but the Solomonic state was an obstacle to Egyptian commercial and territorial ambitions, since Israel controlled traffic on major trade routes. When Israel split into two, Shoshenk saw an opportunity to exploit the power vacuum that was created.

The Bible mentions an Egyptian invasion during which the Pharaoh is reported to have captured fifteen Judaean fortresses and stolen the gold from Solomon's Temple and palace as compensation for sparing Jerusalem. The Bible states that the Egyptian invasion force comprised 1,200 chariots and 60,000 cavalry, suggesting that the campaign was a very serious attempt to destroy the Hebrew successor states. Shoshenk had the story of his war inscribed into the Theban Temple of Amon at Karnak, proclaiming that settlements in Judah, Israel, trans-Jordan, and the Negev were all attacked. The Karnak carvings show the god Amon holding ropes tied to captured kings while other captives kneel before him. Archaeological evidence is plentiful and backs up the Egyptian version of the invasion.

The Egyptian army advanced along the Way of the Sea, establishing its base at Gaza, where the force divided. One raiding force attacked Sharuen in the Negev, and inscriptions identified at Karnak list the captured settlements of Beersheba, Arad-jerahmeel, Arad-rabbah, Ramat Matred, and Ezion-geber. The Egyptians purged the entire Negev and archaeology shows that agricultural settlements established by Solomon were destroyed, suggesting that the Pharaoh wished to end Judaean control of the area and its influence over Edom rather than settle the area with Egyptians. Karnak lists seventy place names from the Negev.

The Egyptian northern force moved to Ashdod and Ekron in Philistia, where a two-pronged attack was launched into Judah. One division of Shoshenk's army marched north, veering eastward along the Way of Beth-horon, while a second division ripped into the central hill country eight miles south along the Way of Beth-shemesh through Kijath-jearim. The two forces met at Gibeon, near Jerusalem.

The Pharaoh's force traveled along the central ridge road to enter the Kingdom of Israel. There were no defensive border fortifications because Judah was not considered to be a threat; Jereboam, King of Israel, regarded his exile in Egypt and former Egyptian friendship as a guarantee against attack, but Shoshenk ignored the past and proved no friend. The strong invasion force fought its way through all obstacles and Davidic and Solomonic fortifications posed little resistance to Egyptian might and military technology. The casement walls designed to resist battering ram attacks were the latest inventions but were soon smashed and the new gates houses were also destroyed, as archaeological evidence at Gezer, Hazor, and Megiddo shows. Shechem was probably destroyed, and the Egyptians assaulted and damaged the new capital of Israel at Tirzah. The Wadi Farah provided a road to the fords of Adam on the Jordan, which were crossed. The Egyptians turned north to Succoth and through the Jabbok Valley to Mahanaim and Penuel. It is possible that Shoshenk planned to destroy Israelite power across the Jordan.

Shoshenk retraced his steps down the Jabbok Valley and then moved north, annihilating Zaphon before re-crossing the Jordan and taking the route through the Jezreel Valley at Beth-shan, capturing the cities of Rehob, Beth-shan, and Shunem. Taanach was burned and, five miles away, Megiddo was attacked, destroyed and then rebuilt as an Egyptian outpost, guarding the Way of the Sea as it passed the Carmel ridge.

The campaign was now over and Shoshenk returned toward Egypt, following the Way of the Sea and capturing towns along this route.

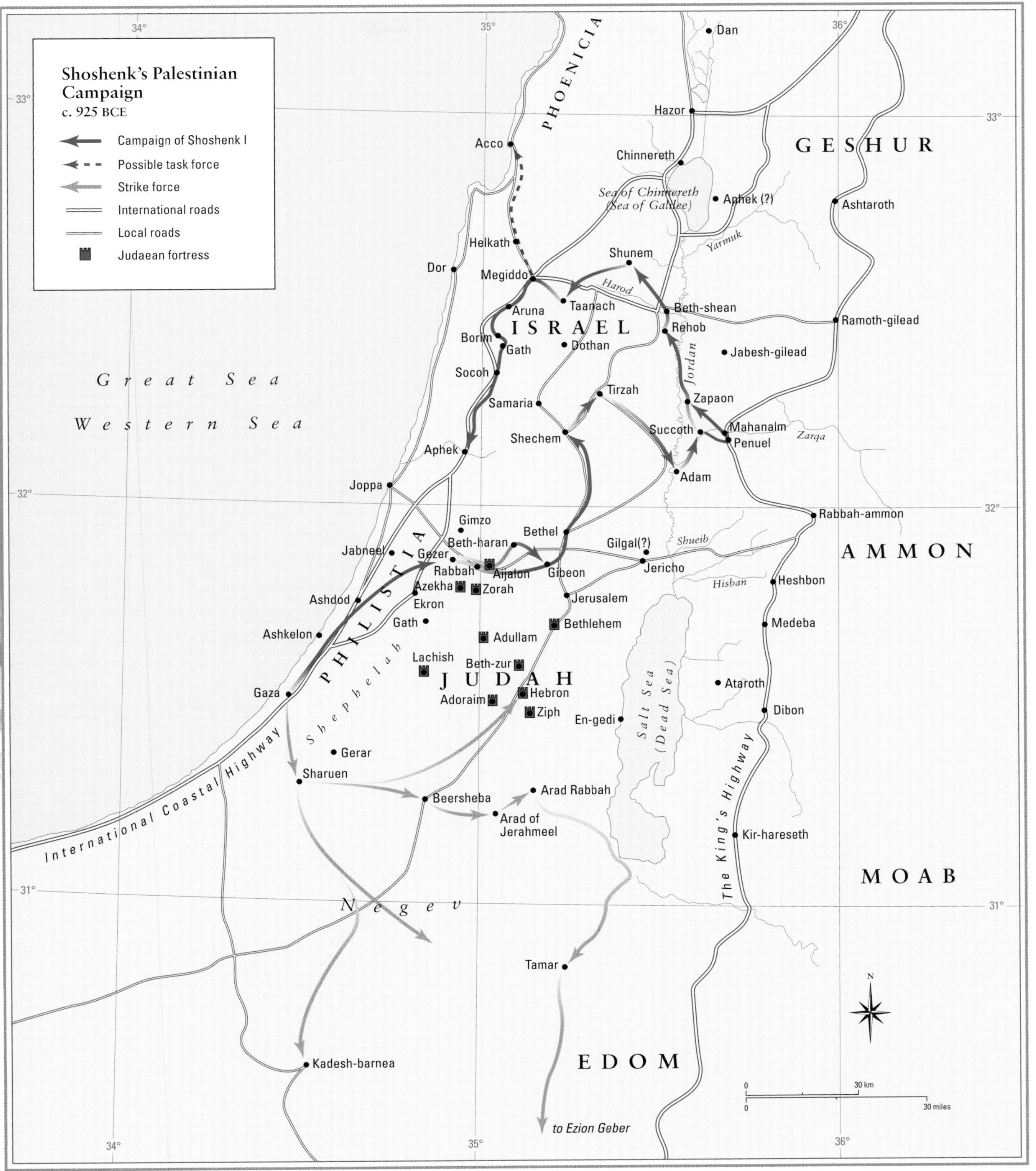

Shoshenk's Palestinian Campaign
c. 925 BCE
Campaign of Shoshenk I
Possible task force
Strike force
International roads
Local roads
Judaean fortress
PHOENICIA
GESHUR
ISRAEL
PHILISTIA
JUDAH
AMMON
MOAB
EDOM
Great Sea
Western Sea
Sea of Chinnereth (Sea of Galilee)
Salt Sea (Dead Sea)
Shephelah
Negev
International Coastal Highway
The King's Highway
Yarmuk
Harod
Jordan
Zarqa
Shueib
Hisban
Dan
Hazor
Acco
Chinnereth
Aphek (?)
Ashtaroth
Helkath
Shunem
Dor
Megiddo
Taanach
Aruna
Beth-shean
Rehob
Ramoth-gilead
Borim
Gath
Dothan
Jabesh-gilead
Socoh
Tirzah
Zapaon
Samaria
Succoth
Mahanaim
Penuel
Shechem
Aphek
Adam
Joppa
Rabbah-ammon
Gimzo
Bethel
Beth-haran
Gilgal(?)
Jabneel
Gezer
Rabbah
Aijalon
Gibeon
Jericho
Azekha
Zorah
Heshbon
Ashdod
Ekron
Jerusalem
Gath
Bethlehem
Medeba
Ashkelon
Adullam
Lachish
Beth-zur
Ataroth
Hebron
Gaza
Adoraim
Ziph
Dibon
En-gedi
Gerar
Sharuen
Arad Rabbah
Beersheba
Arad of Jerahmeel
Kir-hareseth
Tamar
Kadesh-barnea
to Ezion Geber
N
0
30 km
0
30 miles
33°
32°
31°
34°
35°
36°

Omri's Dynasty

There were constant hostilities during the first forty years of the successor states of the divided Israelite Kingdom, with border disputes occurring in Benjamite territory. Judah fought to secure buffer areas as a defensive bastion for Jerusalem and succeeded. Reheboam also built fifteen defensive cities and dispersed his sons amongst them to secure his territory. After Shoshenk's invasion, both Israel and Judah needed to reorganize and redevelop defenses.

Jeroboam's son, Nadab, first King of northern Israel, was assassinated and the throne was usurped by Baasha, who left his son Elah to reign after him. He was murdered by the chariot commander, Zimri, who wiped out Baasha's entire family. Meanwhile, the Israelite army was fighting Philistines near Gibbethon. The troops proclaimed their leader, Omri, as King and he moved on Zimri in the capital, Tirzah. The city fell and Zimri sacrificed himself in the palace's citadel.

Omri founded a dynasty and introduced political and religious changes to Israel in his attempt to re-create a Solomonic state with Judah as a junior partner. Omri wanted peace and trade expansion, making an alliance with the Phoenicians. His crown prince, Ahab, married Jezebel of Tyre and Sidon to seal the deal. Omri bought land and built Samaria as his capital, using Phoenician architects. The Omride state grew in wealth and rivaled that of Solomon.

Omri's son, Ahab, succeeded his father in 869 BCE, ensuring the continuation of existing policies. However, he made the mistake of isolating his Samaritan palace from the city, in effect removing the ruler from the people who had anointed him King. Jezebel, Ahab's wife, introduced the Baal cult, causing consternation in traditional quarters. Ahab rebuilt Megiddo and Hazor, the former becoming a base for the Israelite chariot force, as shown by its large stable block. Hazor became a strong fortress with a water source reached by a huge tunnel, a miracle of contemporary engineering.

These fortifications might have been in response to invasions by the Damascus Arameans. Ben-hadad, King of Aram, was defeated in a siege at Samaria and was driven off next year on the Jordan. Each side wanted to command Aphek, a strategic point east of the Sea of Chinnereth, where an important route led up to the Bashan plateau on the road to Damascus. Ben-hadad was defeated and surrendered. Terms returned some Israelite cities and allowed Israelite commerce into Damascus. Ben-hadad was freed. Ahab's trans-Jordan interests included keeping Gilead and controlling Ammon and Moab. Ammon retained its independence, but Mesha, Moab's King, temporarily became a tributary, with Israelite colonists placed in Moabite lands north of the River Arnon.

Elsewhere, Judah, under King Asa and his son Jehoshaphat, regained control of Edom along with lands lost in Shoshenk's military campaign and rebuilt Ezion-geber. A merchant fleet was built on the Red Sea but proved incapable of revisiting Ophir. The Wilderness of Judah was colonized in places such as the City of Salt, and agriculture was encouraged, though in harsh conditions.

International threats now faced the two kingdoms. In 859 BCE Shalamaneser III succeeding to the Assyrian throne. He crossed the Euphrates, and Syria and Israel formed an alliance to resist this threat. They fought, and halted, the Assyrian advance at Qarqar, with Ahab supplying 2,000 chariots. Ahab, with Judaean help, then assaulted Syria to improve his border security. Seeking to hold Gilead and take the Bashan plateau, the hostile forces met at Ramoth-gilead. Ahab was fatally wounded during the battle. Ahab was succeeded by his son Ahaziah, then his brother Jehoram in 849 BCE.

Meanwhile, Mesha of Moab rebelled. Confused fighting followed, with Mesha defeated but surviving, while the Edomites, who had changed sides, managed to take and hold the copper mines of the Arabah and Ezion-geber.

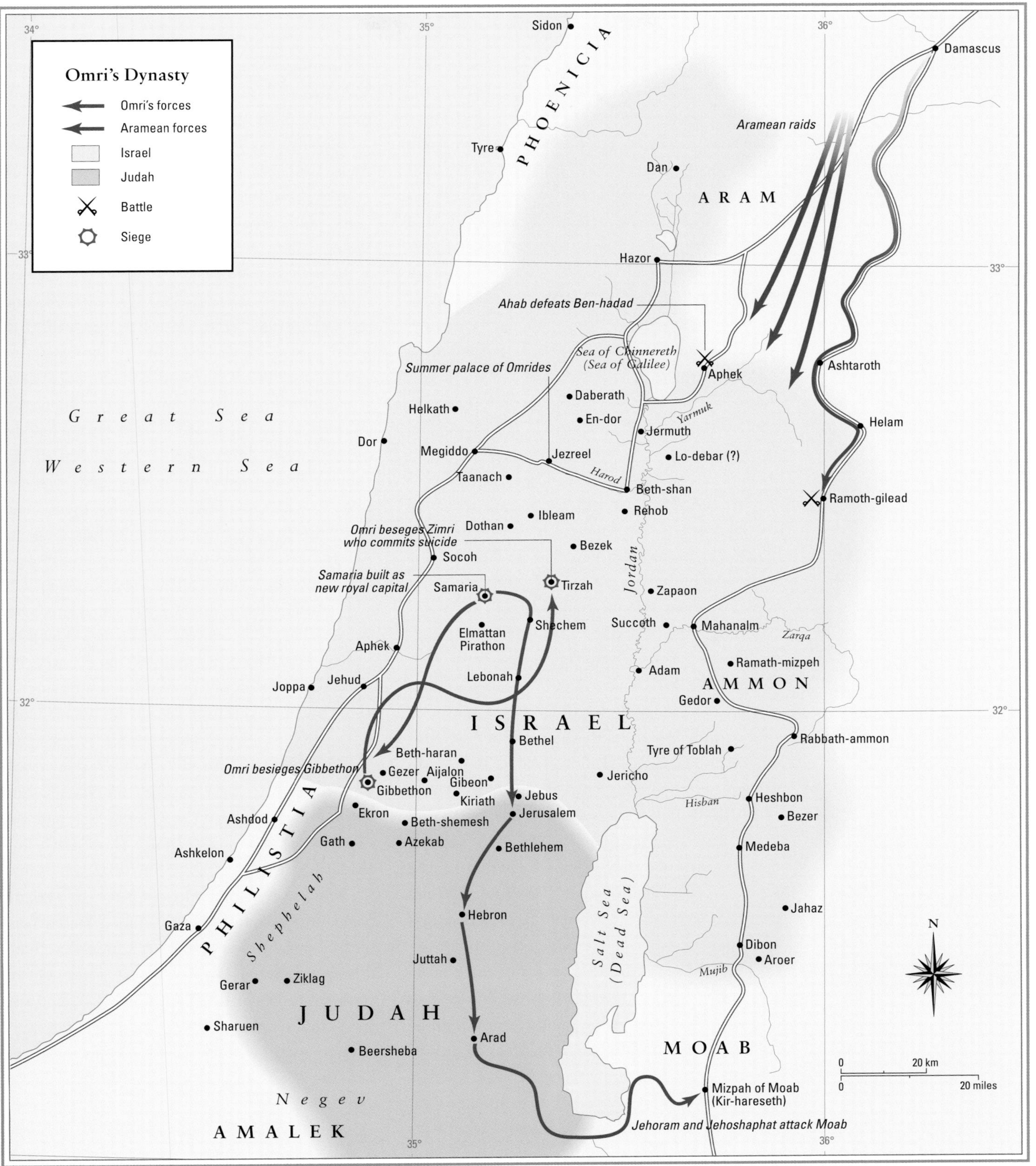

Omri's Dynasty
Omri's forces
Aramean forces
Israel
Judah
Battle
Siege
Great Sea
Western Sea
PHOENICIA
ARAM
ISRAEL
AMMON
PHILISTIA
JUDAH
MOAB
AMALEK
Negev
Shephelah
Aramean raids
Ahab defeats Ben-hadad
Summer palace of Omrides
Omri beseges Zimri who commits suicide
Samaria built as new royal capital
Omri besieges Gibbethon
Jehoram and Jehoshaphat attack Moab
Sea of Chinnereth (Sea of Galilee)
Salt Sea (Dead Sea)
Jordan
Yarmuk
Harod
Zarqa
Hisban
Mujib
Sidon
Tyre
Dan
Damascus
Hazor
Aphek
Ashtaroth
Helam
Ramoth-gilead
Helkath
Daberath
En-dor
Jermuth
Lo-debar (?)
Dor
Megiddo
Jezreel
Taanach
Beth-shan
Rehob
Ibleam
Dothan
Bezek
Socoh
Samaria
Tirzah
Zapaon
Shechem
Succoth
Mahanalm
Elmattan Pirathon
Aphek
Ramath-mizpeh
Lebonah
Adam
Joppa
Jehud
Gedor
Bethel
Rabbath-ammon
Beth-haran
Tyre of Toblah
Gezer
Aijalon
Gibeon
Jericho
Gibbethon
Kiriath
Jebus
Jerusalem
Heshbon
Ekron
Beth-shemesh
Bezer
Ashdod
Gath
Azekab
Bethlehem
Medeba
Ashkelon
Hebron
Jahaz
Gaza
Dibon
Aroer
Juttah
Ziklag
Gerar
Sharuen
Arad
Beersheba
Mizpah of Moab (Kir-hareseth)
N
0 20 km
0 20 miles
34°
35°
36°
33°
32°

Jewish Renaissance

When Joash became King of Judah (c. 837 BCE), he ensured his state's survival by sending the invading Hazael of Damascus some Temple treasure as tribute. In 800 BCE, upon Joash's assassination, his son, Amaziah, used an Assyrian threat to Damascus to divert his forces and defeat the Edomites in the Valley of Salt, thus gaining the copper deposits there. Amaziah had used some Israelite mercenaries who were sent home, unpaid, before his victory was achieved. With no booty, these men looted some cities of Judah and this event became a *casus belli* between the two Hebrew states. A battle took place at Beth-shemesh, where Amaziah was captured. Jerusalem fell; the city and Temple were plundered and a section of the city wall was torn down.

Jehoash, King of Israel, continued victorious elsewhere. The prophet Elisha urged him to wage war against Damascus and the strategic area of Aphek was captured, which Jehoash's son, Jereboam II, used as a jumping-off point to invade Aramean Syria and seize Damascus. Meanwhile, Amaziah was murdered, leaving his throne to Uzziah in 783 BCE.

International events consolidated the position of the Hebrew kingdoms. The Assyrians were troubled by a rebellious Babylonian vassal and pressure from Urartu. Nevertheless, Adad-nirari III (811–784 BCE) captured Damascus and exacted a heavy tribute. Syria then became embroiled in conflict with Hamath. To the south, Egypt was quiescent. This international power vacuum left Jereboam II of Israel and Uzziah of Judah in a favorable position.

Uzziah wanted to develop his country in an efficient, integrated manner. New wells were dug and cisterns built, and agricultural innovations took place that allowed large flocks and herds to flourish. He built military-agricultural settlements in the Negev in order to command and police Arabian trade routes. Standard fortifications were constructed with casement walls and a minimum of eight towers to guard crossroads and strategic points. Agricultural settlements were created at many of these forts.

Uzziah also improved Jerusalem's fortifications, using wooden mantlets on the walls to protect defenders. He built war engines to fire bolts and throw large projectiles. The Bible claims he had over 300,000 soldiers with an elite strike force that was reminiscent of David's personal guard. War was waged against Edom and the land down to Ezion-geber was captured. Judah's position along the trade routes was further secured by its dominance of the northwestern Arab tribes in the Edom desert. The northern stretches of the King's Highway were held by the tributary Ammonites. Uzziah secured the Shephelah, invaded Philistia, then destroyed fortifications at Azekah and built a fort there. Gath and Jabneh were assimilated, as was some of Ashdod's territory. Judaean cities were constructed amongst the Philistine population.

In Israel, Jereboam II established the basic conditions for economic prosperity. He used Aphek as a base for the invasion of Syria. He seized control of the plateau around Lodebar and captured Ramoth-gilead. Some evidence claims that he attacked Karnaim. His campaign was a 'blitzkrieg' through Aram, which took him to the farthest extent of David's and Solomon's holdings. Thus, Jereboam had the capacity to command both Damascus and Hamath.

Israel now benefited from the rich agriculture of Gilead and tribute from defeated peoples. Shops, workshops, and houses were built during this renaissance. Excavations at Hazor show examples of the finest houses dating from Jereboam's reign. The walls at Hazor were strengthened, with projecting parts allowing flanking fire from the ramparts. A new bastion measuring 33 by 23 feet was added to the northwestern corner of the city, possibly an extra defense against a future Assyrian attack.

Israel and Judah at the Time of Jeroboam II
Israel
Judah
Byblos
Lebo-hamath
Hamath
Sidon
SIDONIANS
Damascus
Tyre
Dan
Aram
Hazor
Acco
Lake Gennesaret
Karnaim
Aphek
Ashtaroth
Great Sea
Western Sea
Dor
Zebulun
Yarmuk
Megiddo
Lodebar
Ramoth-gilead
Salchah
ISRAEL
Abel-meholah (Elisha)
Samaria
Samaria
Shechem
Aphek
Joppa
Jordon
Rabbah-ammon
Jabneh
Bethel
Jericho
AMMON
Ashdod
Ekron
Jerusalem
Ascalon
Gath
Mamte
Hebron
Gaza
PHILISTIA
PHILISTINES
Moresheth-gath (Micah)
Gerar
Salt Sea (Dead Sea)
Kiriathalm
Dibon
MOAB
Syro-Arabian Desert
Beersheba
Bab edh-Dhra
JUDAH
Negev
Zoar (Bela)
Tamar
Beer-lahal-rol
Arabah
Punon
Wilderness of Shur
Kadesh-barnea (En-Mishpat)
Edom
MEUNITES
N
Sinai
Ezion-geber
Eilat
0
50 km
0
50 miles
34°
33°
32°
31°
30°
35°
36°

Assyrian Attacks

Assyrian kings preserved their history on clay tablets, including records of military campaigns. Many tablets piece together the tale of Assyrian expansion westward, resulting in the ultimate collapse of Israel. King Ashurnasirpal II (883–859 BCE) consolidated the conquests of his father, Tukulti-Ninurta II. He put down rebellions and re-organized his provinces. He devastated Armenia, pacified the Arameans, and exacted tribute. He crossed the Euphrates and campaigned onward to the Mediterranean via Carchemish and the Orontes, where he won tribute from coastal cities such as Tyre, Sidon, Byblos, and Arvad.

In this detail from a contemporary obelisk, Jehu, King of Israel, pays tribute to Shalamaneser III, King of Assyria.

Shalamaneser III (858–824 BCE) also reached the Mediterranean in his first year of rule. Every state of northern Syria was forced to pay him tribute. In response, the small states of old Canaan, led by Hamath and Damascus, allied to resist Assyrian incursions. In 853 BCE, Shalamaneser returned westward and found a coalition of twelve states confronting him at the Battle of Qarqar, including Hadadezer of Damascus and Ahab of Israel. The Assyrians claimed victory in the battle but were prevented from acquiring Aramaea and the Levant.

In 841 BCE, Shalamaneser campaigned westward for the sixteenth time and failed in his siege of Damascus against King Hazael. Nevertheless, Tyre, Sidon, and Jehu of Israel paid tribute. In 837 BCE, the Assyrian King made his last, and 21st, expedition to the west. He received tribute from Damascus, Tyre, Sidon, and Byblos. Thereafter, Assyria was forced to defend its eastern and northern borders. Campaigns acquired Cilicia and expeditions were mounted against Sardur I, King of Urartu (Van). During this period, Damascus found the time to prosecute war against Israel and Judah.

Shalamaneser's grandson, Adad-nirari III (811–783 BCE) also led campaigns westward, receiving tribute from Tyre, Sidon, Damascus, Israel, Edom, and the Philistines. In 802 BCE, he nearly wiped out the Damascan state, but rebellions, plague, epidemics, and Armenian incursions caused the loss of most Syrian lands. This allowed a breathing space for Israel and Judah to rebuild and prosper.

Weak Assyrian kings were replaced after a civil war by Tiglath-Pileser III (744–727 BCE). He reduced the independence of governors and campaigned in Azerbaijan to split the Medes and Urartu. The latter formed an alliance with the Syrian city of Arpad, but Urartu was defeated and Arpad wiped out. A northern Syrian alliance was crushed, leaving all the rulers from Damascus to eastern Anatolia paying tribute. In 735 BCE, an expedition to Urartu was partially successful. These achievements, as well as improved military equipment, restored Assyria's strength.

In 743 BCE, Tiglath-Pileser marched to the Lebanese mountains while King Azariah of Judah paid tribute. From this time, his annual western campaigns changed; he no longer just received tribute but moved the elites of conquered peoples to other parts of his Empire. In 734 BCE, an Assyrian expedition took him to the Brook of Egypt. The next year, Israel was devastated and Megiddo and Hazor were flattened. Israel's territories beyond the Jordan, Galilee, and the coastal region were turned into the Assyrian Provinces of Gal'aza (Gilead), Magidu (Megiddo), and Du'ru (Dor).

In 732 BCE, King Ahaz of Judea asked Tiglath-Pileser for help against Damascus. This city was taken and destroyed and the country divided into four Assyrian provinces. Samaria received mercy since its people had killed their rebellious King Pekah. In 724 BCE, Shalamaneser V (727–722 BCE) campaigned against Hoshea, King of Israel. Hoshea was captured and Samaria besieged. In 721 BCE, Israel was annihilated and Sargon II (722–705 BCE) captured Samaria and exiled the population's elite to Assyria and Media.

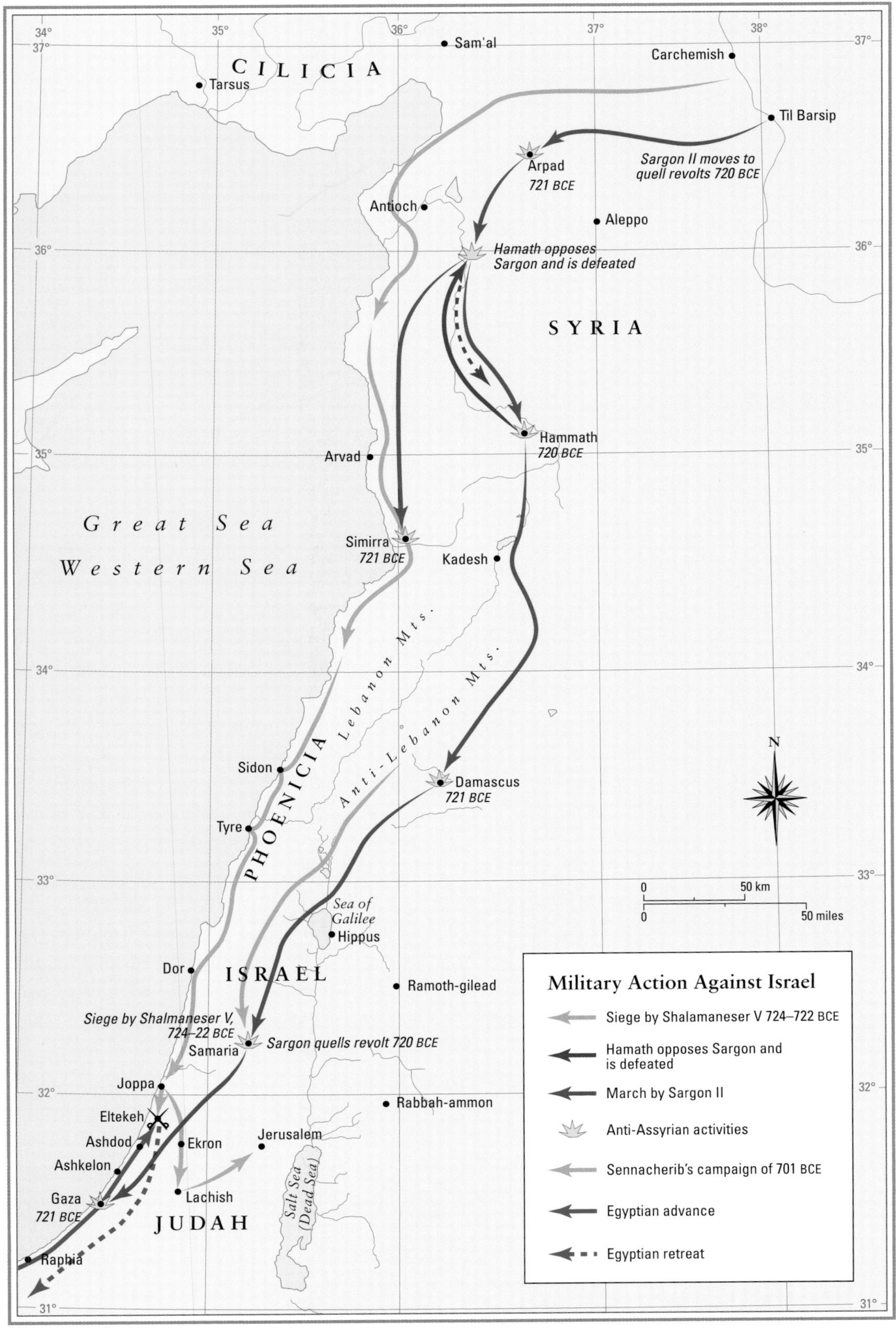
CILICIA
Tarsus
Sam'al
Carchemish
Til Barsip
Sargon II moves to quell revolts 720 BCE
Arpad 721 BCE
Antioch
Aleppo
Hamath opposes Sargon and is defeated
SYRIA
Hammath 720 BCE
Arvad
Great Sea
Western Sea
Simirra 721 BCE
Kadesh
Lebanon Mts.
Anti-Lebanon Mts.
Sidon
PHOENICIA
Damascus 721 BCE
Tyre
Sea of Galilee
Hippus
Dor
ISRAEL
Ramoth-gilead
Siege by Shalmaneser V, 724–22 BCE
Samaria
Sargon quells revolt 720 BCE
Joppa
Rabbah-ammon
Eltekeh
Ashdod
Ekron
Jerusalem
Ashkelon
Lachish
Salt Sea (Dead Sea)
Gaza 721 BCE
JUDAH
Raphia
0 50 km
0 50 miles
N
Military Action Against Israel
Siege by Shalamaneser V 724–722 BCE
Hamath opposes Sargon and is defeated
March by Sargon II
Anti-Assyrian activities
Sennacherib's campaign of 701 BCE
Egyptian advance
Egyptian retreat

Maccabean Revolt 167–160 BCE

During the period of Seleucid rule over Palestine, rebellion broke out when a Syrian official and a Jew tried to offer a sacrifice on a pagan altar. This apostasy so incensed Mattathias of Modin that he killed the Syrian and the apostate and fled with his five sons into the Judean wilderness of hills, wadis, and caves. Here they could survive any attacks mounted by Seleucid forces occupying the urban centers on the plains, and engage in guerrilla warfare against Syrians and Hellenized Jews.

In 166 BCE, Mattathias died and his son, Judas (Judea), known as Maccabeus ('the hammer') assumed the leadership of the revolt, his family becoming known as the Maccabees. Judas' military campaigns lasted for six years, and shocked and damaged the Syrian military establishment. His successes boosted his aura of greatness, his band of guerrillas grew into a small army.

Appollonius, the Syrian governor in Samaria, launched an assault againtst Judas with his militias but they were trapped in the valley of Nahal el-Haramih where he and his men were slaughtered. Victory brought loot, captured weapons, and recruits and Judas was lauded as a military and political leader.

This pushed Seron, the governor of Coele-Syria, to march against Judas with an army that included many Hellenized Jews. He intended to unite with the Seleucid garrison at Jerusalem, but Judas trapped him in a narrow gorge at Beth-horon, and attacked the flanks of Seron's army, killing him and 800 of his men.

The Seleucid King Antiochus IV Epiphanes (175–164 BCE) divided his army into two divisions, taking one part to attack Persia and giving the other portion to his chief minister Lycias, who acted as regent while the King was absent. Lysias was ordered to pacify Judea and he despatched the generals Ptolemy, Nicanor, and Gorgias with some 40.000, 7,000 cavalry and war elephants into Judea where they pitched camp near Emmaus.

Judas and his brothers grouped their forces at Mizpah, prayed, and marched against the Syrians (165 BCE) at Emmaus. Meanwhile, Gorgias led a night column of 5,000 infantry and 1,000 cavalry hoping to surprise the Jewish camp, which he found abandoned. Judas launched a surprise attack on Seleucid forces and defeated them. The road to Jerusalem was now clear, allowing Judas to find priests to purify and rededicate the Temple in 164 BCE. Mount Zion was fortified as was Beth-zur but the Syrian fortress in Jerusalem remained untaken.

Judea was now blessed with a two-year period of peace and Judas used this respite from attack to combat those tribes that were persecuting Jewish minorities as a response to the rededication of the Temple. The Idumeans were attacked at Acrabatene, as were the Ammonites in trans-Jordan. Simon, Judas' brother, forayed into Galilee, while Judas and brother Jonathan campaigned in Gilead. The Jewish minorities were transported to Judea, thereby increasing its population and the size of the Maccabean army.

Judas confronted and defeated a large Syrian army, led by Nicanor, at Beth-horon near Adasa. Judas managed to put the enemy right wing to flight but fell fighting and was buried secretly at the family sepulchre at Modin. Meanwhile, the Seleucid kingship was being fought over by two factions, with both claimants seeking support from Judas' successor, Jonathan Maccabee.

Antiochus IV died in 164 BCE, leaving a minor, Antiochus V, under the vice-regency of Lysias. The latter invaded Judea, stormed Beth-zur, defeated Judas at Beth-zechariah, and forced the Jews back to Jerusalem. The Jews sued for peace, which Lysias was forced to grant owing to murderous strife amongst the Seleucid royal family. The Jews were granted religious freedom, but the Temple fortifications were destroyed. This hiatus allowed the Maccabees to garrison cities and fortify Jerusalem but Jonathan and his sons were murdered by Seleucid agents.

Simon, Jonathan's brother, succeeded him and started constructing a theocratic state. The Jews were now sovereign in both religion and politics.

Seleucid Palestine on the Eve of the Maccabean Revolt
Boundaries of the Jewish state
Other boundaries
Greek city
Sidon
SIDON
CHALCIS
ABILENE
Damascus
ITURAEAN ARABS
Tyre
PANEAS
Paneas
TYRE
ULATHA
Kedesh/Kudisos
TRACHON
Asor/Hazor
Seleucia
Maked
Ptolemais (Acre)
Great Sea
Western Sea
Arbela
Sea of Chinnereth (Sea of Galilee)
Casphor
Carnaim
Raphon
Dathema
Bo(s)or
Alema
GALILEE
Hippos
Dium
Nazareth
Philoteria
Abila
AURANITIS (HAURAN)
Great Plain
Gadara
Dora
Arbatta
GALAADITIS (GILEAD)
Scythopolis (Bethshan)
Strato's Tower
Ephron
Bosor(r)a
Pella
SAMARITIS
ARABS
Jebel Um ed Daraj
Gerasa
Samaria
Amathus
Jordan
Apollonia
Sichem
Pharathon
Mt. Gerizim
Zarqa
Tephon
Acrabatha
Alexandrium
Joppa
Ramathaim (Arimathaea)
Jazer
Thamnatha
AMMANITIS
Adida
Lydda
Philadelphia (Rabbatamana)
Modin
Beerzeth
Port of the Jamnites
Lower Beth-horon
Bethel
Aphaerema
Berea (Beeroth)
Jamnia
Gazara
Michmas
Dok
Jericho
LAND OF TUBIAS
Elasa
Maspha (Mizpeh)
Accaron
Adesa
Caphor
Emmaus
Salama
JUDAEA
Ashdod
Cedron
Jerusalem
PARALIA
Hyrcania
Desert of Judah/ Wilderness of Tekoa
Medaba
Nadabath
Bethbassi
Adullam
Bethzacharia
Ascalon
Marisa
Bathzeth
Tekoa
Bethsura
Asphar
Macherus
Arabian Desert
Anthedon
Hebron
Gaza
Adora
Salt Sea (Dead Sea)
IDUMAEA
Engaddi
Masada
Raphia
Border with Ptolemaic Kingdom
Negev
Alusa
NABATAEA
ARABS
N
0
20 km
0
20 miles
35°
36°
33°
32°
31°

Hasmonean Expansion

The ruling family springing from the Maccabee line were known as the Hasmoneans. When Simon Maccabee (140–135 BCE), was murdered along with two of his sons, his third son, John Hyrcanus (134–104 BCE), moved to Jerusalem, where he was acknowledged as Simon's successor.

John attacked his weaker neighbours in order to augment his territories. Samaria and Shechem were key targets and both cities were destroyed. Galilee, inhabited by Aramaic-speaking gentiles, was captured and Hyrcanus forcibly Judaized the inhabitants, including circumcision of all males. The same brutal fate was meted out to the inhabitants of occupied Idumaea (Edom). The Idumaeans were integrated into Judaea and one of their number, Antipas, grandfather of Herod the Great, became the regional governor. Hyrcanus went on to conquer the settlement at Medeba, east of the Dead Sea. The northern frontier was home to cities such as Pella, Dion, Gadera, and Hippos, all east of the Jordan, which formed a league with other cities, such as Philadelphia and Gerasa, to constitute the Decapolis. These Greek cities remained un-Judaized, but paid tribute. As trading connections expanded, the Hasmoneans began to adopt a religious view that Judaism was compatible with Hellenism; John's sons had Greek names.

Hyrcanus died in 104 BCE and was succeeded by his son Aristobulos (104–103 BCE); he suffered from insanity and died young. A brother, Alexander Jannaeus (103–76 BCE) became King. Alexander's attack on Ptolemais failed, but he succeeded in capturing all the other port cities of the Levant, Gaza being seized with extreme brutality. Other Hasmonean successes were the seizure of towns in Galaditis, Gaulantis, and Syria. The southern and eastern borders were secured by the forts at Hyrcania, Masada, and Macherus, which were linked to other fortifications at Beth-zur, Gezer, Alexandrium, and Dok.

Alexander died from a war wound and his wife, Alexandra Salome (76–67 BCE) became Queen rather than allowing a son to succeed. The older son, Hyrcanus II, was passed over, possibly because he was mentally impaired. The next son, Aristobulos II (66–63 BCE), was not put forward lest there be strife or even civil war. Instead, the malleable, weak-minded Hyrcanus was appointed High Priest by Alexandra Salome, which pleased the Pharisees who had been critical of her monarchy. As a woman the Queen could not preside over the Sanhedrin, the Jewish high council, and placed her brother in this position. Alexandra Salome's reign, based upon the power of the Pharisees, was eventually regarded as a golden age of peace.

Disaster occurred when the Queen died in 67 BCE and the Jewish state was eventually destroyed by an ensuing conflict. The Pharisees backed Hyrcanus II as King and High Priest while the Sadducees supported Salome's second son, Aristobulos, who already controlled some parts of Judaea. The latter usurped the monarchy after defeating his brother. At this point a new key figure, Antipater, son of Antipas, entered the arena. He became an adviser to Hyrcanus and persuaded him to regain his crown. The two escaped to Petra, capital of Nabatea. The Nabataeans, ruled by Aretas, wanted to expand their power northward and were easily persuaded to help Hyrcanus return to Jerusalem and regain his kingship. Aristobulos sealed himself inside Jerusalem because he was not strong enough to face the three besieging forces of Hyrcanus, Antipater, and the Nabataeans. Meanwhile Aristobulos, seeking allies to assist him in outlasting the siege, went to Damascus, which had just been occupied by a Roman army under Pompey. Roman power had emerged from the central and western Mediterranean and was now colliding with the Asian and Near Eastern world. It was this power that would mediate the Jewish civil war.

Jewish Expansion Under the Hasmonean Dynasty
Judea before the Maccabean revolt
Conquests of Jonathan
Conquests of Simon
Conquests of Hyrcanus I
Conquests of Aristobulus I
Conquests of Alexander Jannaeus
Aristobulus completes the conquest of Upper Galilee by defeating the Itureans (104 BCE)
Jannaeus subdues the attack of Demetrius III and executes 800 in reprisal (88 BCE)
Simon is murdered in a palace coup (135 BCE)
John Hyrcanus attacks and conquers Medeba in 129 BCE
Syrian Desert
Arabian Desert
Great Sea
Western Sea
PHOENICIA
ITUREA
GALILEE
SAMARIA
JUDEA
PEREA
IDUMEA
NABATAEA
Negev
Arabah
Jordan
Yarmuk
Hisban
Lake Huleh
Sea of Chinnereth (Sea of Galilee)
Salt Sea (Dead Sea)
Tyre
Pantas
Kedesh
Gischaia
Asor (Hazor)
Seleucia
Ptolemais (Acco)
Gennesaret
Bethsaida
Dathema
Jotapata
Asochis (Hannathon)
Taricheae
Cana
Arbela
Sepphoris
Hippos
Geba
Philoteria (Beth-yerah)
Abila
Gadara
Dor
Legio
Scythopolis (Beth-shean)
Strato's Tower
Narbata
Pella
Dion
Samaria
Gerasa
Shechem
Amathus
Appollonia
Aphek
Pharathon
Acrabeta
Coreae
Arimathea
Zeredah
Lebonah
Alexandrium
Joppa
Gedor
Jazer
Adida
Lydda
Modein
Ber-zetha
Gophna
Apherema
Bethel
Tyrus
Abila
Rabbath-ammon
Beth-horon
Mizpah
Adasa
Michmash
Doc
Jericho
Jamina
Gezer
Emmaus
Kidron
Ekron
Beth-ramatha
Esbus (Heshbon)
Samaga
Ashdod
Jerusalem
Beth-haccherem
Hyrcania
Bethlehem
Medeba
Ashkelon
Adullam
Nezib
Asphar
Lemba
Machaergs
Lachish
Marisa (Mareshah)
Beth-zur
Anthedon
Gaza
Adora (Adoraim)
Hebron
En-gedi
Orda
Gerar
Masada
Eglaim
Raphia
Beersheba
Malatha
Kit-Moab
Elusa
Gabalis
Zoar
N
0
20 km
20 miles
34°
35°
36°
33°
32°
31°

Herod

Herod I, or Herod the Great, was certainly ruthless and ambitious. According to Josephus, he ruled for 37 years.

Herod the Great ruled Palestine on behalf of Rome from 40 BCE and his family remained important for the next 150 years. He was not afraid to use force to stabilize his disorderly Kingdom but is mainly remembered for his building program. Herod constructed new cities and provided buildings for every type of public use, from baths, theaters, and gymnasia, to a temple for emperor worship, a port, and the rebuilding of the Temple on a magnificent and grandiose scale.

Jerusalem was restored, with improved walls, and four great towers in a huge new fortress, the Antonia. The city had slopes on three sides faced with smooth stones to deter attackers. In 27 BCE, Herod rebuilt an enlarged Samaria as another military bastion surrounded by a two-mile-long wall. This served to intimidate the surrounding countryside, while also being a refuge in times of disturbance and war. The city was renamed Sebaste. A new port was built at Caesarea. A 200-foot wide breakwater protected the harbor and a large anchorage was enclosed by a semicircular sea wall.

Elsewhere, Herod overhauled the fortresses at Alexandrium, Hyrcania, and Masada, the latter also being endowed with some remarkable palaces. New fortresses were raised at Herodium and Jericho. A new city was built north of Jericho and named Phasaelis, after Herod's murdered brother. A shrine was built to cover the cave of Machpelah where the Patriarchs were interred. Herod's Temple, which took 84 years to complete, is his best remembered project. An extravagant building, it incorporated 162 Corinthian columns, the tallest being 100 feet high.

Herod's will divided the kingdom into three parts, the tetrarchies. Archelaus was to be King over Judea, Idumaea, and Samaria, a region incorporating the Hellenized cities of Sebaste and Caesarea. Herod Antipas was created tetrarch of Galilee and Peraea, territories separated by the Decapolis. Their half-brother, Philip, was made tetrarch of the mainly gentile areas north and east of the Sea of Galilee, the poorest of the three tetrarchies. Salome, Herod's sister, was given Azotus, Jamnia, Phasaelis, and Herod's palace in the free city of Ascalon. The Greek cities of Gaza, Gadara, and Hippus were placed under the authority of the Governor of Syria. This patchwork of states was then subsumed under the overrule of Rome.

The tetrarchs argued over their prizes, even going to Rome to plead their cases for territorial augmentation at the expense of the others. In the tetrarchies, violence broke out against Archelaus, and Herodian troops slaughtered rioters and drove others, led by Herod's cousin, Achiab, into the hills. Varus, the Governor of Syria, led Roman troops to pacify the area but several palaces were burned at Jericho, Beth-ramatha, and Amathus. Varus returned again from Syria with two legions and a cavalry force loaned by Aretas IV of Nabataea. The Romans and their allies pacified the region leaving the brothers, Herod Antipas, Archelaus, and Philip I, to rule.

Emperor Augustus reduced Archelaus' rank from King to ethnarch. He reigned for ten years until both Jews and Samaritans complained about his harshness. He was summoned to Rome, deposed, and exiled to Gaul. Samaria, Judaea, and Idumaea became the Roman Province of Judaea (6 CE). In Galilee and Peraea, Antipas ruled for 43 years, bringing peace and prosperity to his holdings. He rebuilt destroyed cities and founded Tiberias, but was ultimately deposed by Emperor Caligula. Antipas is the Herod to whom Pontius Pilate, procurator of Judaea, sent Jesus (*Luke* 23: 7–15). Philip ruled with moderation living quietly with Salome, the instigator of John the Baptist's death. He established Paneas as his capital and renamed it Caesarea Philippi. Antipas and Philip established a peace lasting through the first three Roman governors. Caesarea Maritima became the capital, and Jerusalem lost rank.

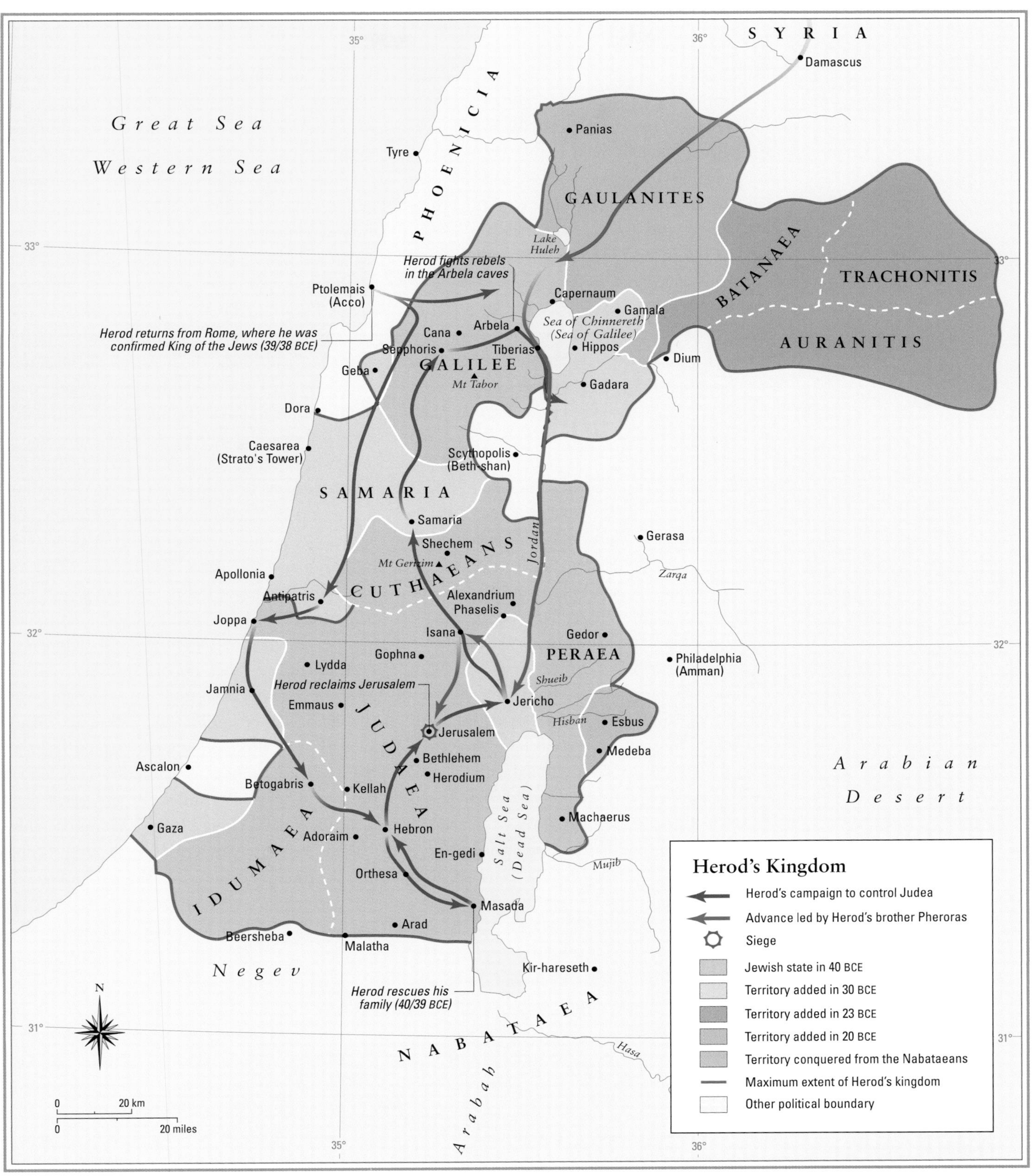

SYRIA
Damascus
Great Sea
Western Sea
PHOENICIA
Tyre
Panias
GAULANITES
Lake Huleh
Herod fights rebels in the Arbela caves
Ptolemais (Acco)
Capernaum
Gamala
BATANAEA
TRACHONITIS
AURANITIS
Herod returns from Rome, where he was confirmed King of the Jews (39/38 BCE)
Cana
Arbela
Sea of Chinnereth (Sea of Galilee)
Sepphoris
Tiberias
Hippos
Dium
Geba
GALILEE
Mt Tabor
Gadara
Dora
Caesarea (Strato's Tower)
Scythopolis (Beth-shan)
SAMARIA
Samaria
Gerasa
Shechem
Mt Gerizim
CUTHAEANS
Jordan
Apollonia
Zarqa
Antipatris
Alexandrium
Phaselis
Joppa
Isana
Gedor
Gophna
PERAEA
Philadelphia (Amman)
Lydda
Shueib
Herod reclaims Jerusalem
Jamnia
Jericho
Emmaus
JUDAEA
Hisban
Esbus
Jerusalem
Bethlehem
Medeba
Herodium
Arabian Desert
Ascalon
Betogabris
Kellah
Salt Sea (Dead Sea)
Machaerus
Gaza
Hebron
Adoraim
IDUMAEA
En-gedi
Mujib
Orthesa
Masada
Arad
Beersheba
Malatha
Negev
Kir-hareseth
Herod rescues his family (40/39 BCE)
NABATAEA
Hasa
Arabah
N
0 20 km
0 20 miles
35°
36°
33°
32°
31°
Herod's Kingdom
Herod's campaign to control Judea
Advance led by Herod's brother Pheroras
Siege
Jewish state in 40 BCE
Territory added in 30 BCE
Territory added in 23 BCE
Territory added in 20 BCE
Territory conquered from the Nabataeans
Maximum extent of Herod's kingdom
Other political boundary

Clash of Faiths

The Arabs who broke out of the Arabian Peninsula became a formidable military and ideological force. They conquered half the provinces of the Byzantine Empire as well as defeating the armies of Sassanian Persia. By 646, Egypt had come under Muslim control. Acquiring ships from Egypt and Syria, the Arabs conducted seaborne raids, conquering Cyprus in 649 and pillaging Rhodes in 654. The Arabs were motivated by a desire for plunder, as well as religious faith, but in the process these nomadic people changed their behavior. Caliph Umar encouraged the tribes to settle with a system of stipends paid from the common treasury of the caliphate, and these tribes were used to control the conquered lands. The Arabs were kept apart from the conquered population in armed camps that evolved into garrison cities such as Basra and Kufa in Iraq. Despite the tensions over the distribution of booty that would erupt into open civil war, the overall control exercised by the fledgling Islamic government remained under dynastic rule.

Under the Umayyads and their Abbasid successors the remarkable expansion continued with the Arab armies reaching as far as France and the Indus Valley. Southern France suffered raids until 1000 CE. Al-Andalus was a Muslim state established in Spain, and raids continued with the capture of Crete in 824. Crete was held from 827 to 861 while the control of Cyprus was shared. Attacks were launched at Byzantine Sicily, where an Arab base was established at Palermo. The Byzantine capital in Sicily, Syracusa, on the eastern coast, held out until 878. In 840, Bari in Italy was taken, but was retaken by the Byzantines in 876. Even Thessalonica in northern Greece was raided in 904. Muslim shipping raided Christian shipping, looted coastal cities, and penetrated river valleys to attack inland communities. Bases were built on the southern coast of France, then attacks were launched up the River Rhône to Upper and Lower Burgundy and from there into the Kingdom of Italy.

The Aghlabids, hereditary governors of the Abbasids, were responsible for the conquest of Byzantine Sicily, and the Balearics, assaulting Sardinia and Corsica, where they established colonies. They robbed, ransomed or raided monasteries and towns, including Rome, desecrating churches and stealing treasures. The Aghlabid fleet reigned supreme in the central Mediterranean. Further expansion was held back by the Byzantine Empire, which revived its fleet and reduced the Muslim bases, while the Muslim states in Spain and North Africa disintegrated into civil war. The fear of Muslims was prevalent in most Christian countries well before the call for the First Crusade; the clash of faiths had a long history.

Western and central European monarchs underestimated Muslim military strength and strategy, equating the so-called infidels with other raiders such as the Vikings and Magyars. However, Byzantine forces came to know and respect them. The Arabs were great horsemen but they also deployed infantry. Arab light cavalry would torment their opponents using composite bows and press home a charge with heavy cavalry if the opportunity arose. When the enemy appeared too strong, the cavalry would retire to their infantry support. The infantry were drawn up into blocks with aisles for the cavalry to retreat through. These blocks constituted ranks of kneeling spearmen with their spear butts dug into the ground. Behind were archers and javelin men loosing their missiles overhead. The heavier javelins could damage armored cavalry. The infantry were disciplined to receive an attack and remain immovable. Once enemy cavalry were bested, their retreating forces would be hit by Arab cavalry passing back through the infantry. Sometimes Arab bowmen would advance in skirmish order, accompanied by javelin men to protect the infantry from enemy archers.

The Muslim conquests drove a wedge between Sicily, Constantinople and the Italian mainland. Muslim Sicily became increasingly independent from Africa, and the island passed from the Aghlabids to the Fatimids in 909. Arabs immigrated to Sicily and Christians were converted to Islam, making Sicily politically and culturally part of the Arab world, while allowing existing Christian communities to exist across the island.

In the east the unity of the Abbasid Empire did not last long. Its great achievement was the gradual fusion of Arab and Persian cultures, with the movement of the empire's center from Syria to Iraq. The caliphs sought to offset the power of hereditary governors by recruiting war-like tribes from peripheral regions. By the late 10th century they were virtual prisoners of the Buyids, a warrior clan of Shi'ites from south of the Caspian Sea. In time the Buyids gave way to Saljuq Turks from central Asia, who occupied Persia, and attacked Byzantine provinces in Anatolia and Fatimid possessions in Syria and Palestine. The Saljuq conquest of the Levant ushered in new changing alliance systems. The Saljuqs soon quarreled amongst themselves and factionalism was prevalent. It was caused by the Saljuq practice of dividing up provinces equally among the male successors of each deceased ruler. For example, in 1094, when Malik Shah died, a civil war in Mesopotamia broke out.

When the First Crusade began, Syria and north Palestine were occupied by Sunni Saljuq emirs, acknowledging the Caliph in Baghdad and the authority of their Sultan. In reality, however, they acted unilaterally and received little assistance from the Sultan. South Palestine and Jerusalem were controlled by Shi'ite Fatimid forces, under the authority of their Caliph in Cairo. The two Muslim groups hated each other, just as they hated the Crusaders.

The First Crusade (1096–99) defeated the Saljuqs in battles at Nicaea and Dorylaeum, and then besieged Antioch before marching to Jerusalem and defeating a Fatimid army at Ascalon. The Crusaders established these states: the Counties of Edessa and Tripoli, the Principality of Antioch, and the Kingdom of Jerusalem. Crusader control was aided by the construction of some three dozen castles and the military might of the Knights Templar and the Knights Hospitaller. One castle at Krak des Chevaliers, garrisoned by the Knights Hospitaller, housed 2,000 troops. The Crusaders were aided by the disunity of the Saljuq emirs but this was ended by Saladin, who became Sultan of Egypt after ending the Fatimid Dynasty, as well as Syria, Yemen, and Palestine. In 1187, he destroyed a Crusader army at the Horns of Hattin, killing and capturing most of its 20,000 men. The garrisons of Crusader castles were now so weak that Saladin could capture them with ease. Within three months Saladin took Acre, Toron, Beirut, Sidon, Nazareth, Caesarea, Nablus, Jaffa, and Ascalon.

When King Richard I of England arrived in Palestine with the Third Crusade he needed to find some answer to Saladin's horse archers and Mamluks. There was a growing need for infantry to keep the mobile and swift-moving horse archers at bay. The crossbow had a greater range than the composite bow of the Arabs and could bring down a man or a horse, whereas Muslims' arrows could not always penetrate Crusader armor. Spearmen were also important; they used pikes or long spears to screen the flanks of Crusader forces until a charge by heavy cavalry knights and sergeants-at-arms could be driven home. This occurred at the Battle of Arsuf. When Richard faced Saladin in 1192, he drew up a line of spearmen, kneeling on the ground with a spear held butt to the ground to create a hedge of steel against possible cavalry charges. Behind that line were crossbow men with assistants to help in reloading and to keep up a good rate of fire. The enemy attacked but the line held and when Richard ordered his armored knights forward, Saladin withdrew. Eventually, Richard and Saladin signed the Treaty of Jaffa in 1192, which gave the Crusaders control of the coast from Acre to Jaffa and allowed access to Jerusalem for pilgrims and freedom of movement between Christian and Muslim lands.

Armenia and the Battle of Avarayr 451 CE

When discussing a clash of faiths, most people think of conflicts between Christianity and Islam. However, in the case of Armenia the clash was between Christianity and Zoroastrianism, the religion of the Sassanian Dynasty in Persia. Armenia was a Christian country, ruled since 64 CE by the native Arsacid Dynasty. It was a buffer zone between the Romans and Parthians, and Armenian independence and resistance lay in the hands of the nobility, the *nakharars*, who inhabited virtually impregnable mountain fortresses. The Armenians were the first people to be converted to Christianity. After King Tiridates III was converted by Gregory the Illuminator, the King proclaimed Christianity as the religion of the state in 301 CE. This occurred twelve years before the Roman Emperor Constantine's Edict of Milan granted tolerance toward Christians in the Roman Empire. Gregory became the Catholicos, the head of the new Armenian Church.

Armenian independence was lost when the Armenian nobility asked Shah Bahram to depose Artashir IV in 428 CE because of his bad behavior and incompetence. This was achieved but Armenia became a Sassanid satrapy complete with a Persian Governor, although the Armenians were told that they could practice their faith. However, Shah Yazdegerd II viewed matters differently and felt that all his subjects should become Zoroastrians. In particular, he felt they at least should change from the Romanrite to the Syriacrite of the native Nestorian Christians, or convert to his religion. Armenian nobles were summoned to court under coercion. Persians were sent in to close and seal churches, and several hundred Magi were sent to convert the Armenians. They were attacked by Christians and plans to build Zoroastrian fire-temples were disrupted.

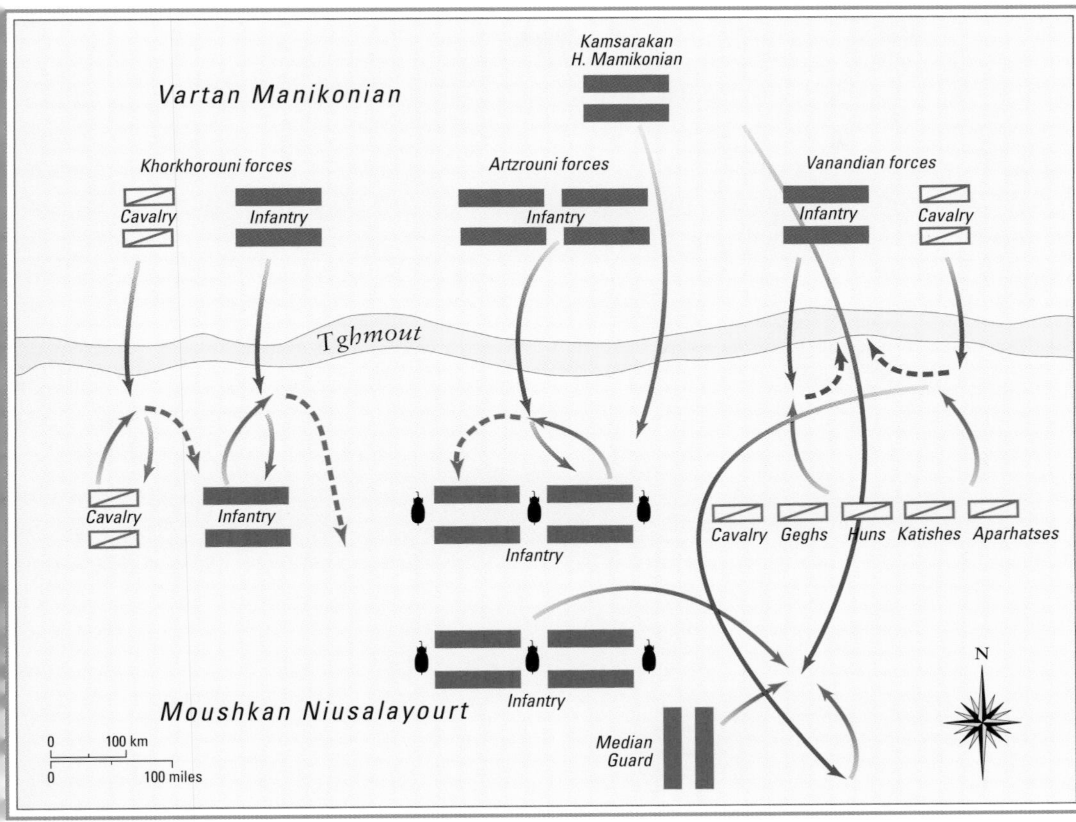

The Persians retaliated by raising a vast army, while the Armenians raised 66,000 troops including their highly-regarded armored cavalry. Even some women were armed and armored. No-one knows how many Persian troops there were, but estimates vary from 160,000 to well over 200,000, including 20,000 Armenians, led by certain renegade nobles led by Vassak Siuni. Amongst the army were 10,000 Immortal cavalry. The Persian army also included contingents from the Caucasus, Caspian, and Central Asia and a corps of elephants mounted with towers containing archers.

Led by Vartan Mamikonian, the Armenians crossed a river running across the Persian front and the Armenian cavalry collided with the Persians at the Battle of Avarayr in 451. As the battle raged, Vartan noticed that his advancing left wing was being pushed back. He attacked the victorious Persian wing and forced it back on to the elephants. The elephants were killed and the Immortals fled the field. The battle became very confused and Vartan and many notable soldiers were killed. The death toll is unknown, but there was great slaughter, with the Persians losing more soldiers than the Armenians. The surviving Armenians retired to their mountain strongholds and continued a guerrilla campaign. The Persian losses were so great that they did not pursue the Christians immediately. Their problems were compounded by a disastrous campaign against the Kushans.

The Shah punished some Armenian priests and *nakharars* and put a new Governor in place in Armenia. Armenian resistance continued for decades after the battle, under the leadership of Vahan Mamikonian, Vartan's nephew. Christian feeling was so strong in Armenia that Shah Peroz I signed the Nvarsak Treaty in 484 CE that guaranteed religious freedom to the Armenians and allowed them to build new churches. Thus, Avarayr can be seen as a moral victory for the Armenians and its day is still celebrated each year.

The Middle East at the Dawn of Islam

The home of Islam, Arabia, was ringed by old civilizations and empires and subject to the influences of the ancient Mesopotamian and Egyptian cultures. The major powers of the day exerted influence all over the region, imbuing the Middle East with Graeco-Roman values that often conflicted with those emerging from the Sassanian state in Persia. Thus, the Orthodox-rite Eastern Roman Empire of Byzantium confronted the Zoroastrians of Persia in long drawn-out wars, competing for control of the land bridge connecting the Middle East to Africa. Both sides of this conflict sought allies amongst the Arabian tribes. Byzantium's ally was a Christian Arab tribe from the borders of the Syrian desert, known as the Ghassanids. The Sassanians' ally was the Lakhmids, also Christian Arabs from Iraq. The first alliance eventually broke down in a disagreement over religion. The Christian Orthodox Byzantines believed that Jesus Christ and God were two natures within one being, while the Ghassanids were Monophysite Christians who opined that God and Jesus were only one entity.

The power struggle for the Middle East had an impact upon trade and relationships with the many kingdoms within the Arabian Peninsula. In northern Arabia, two kingdoms have left their remains. Firstly, Nabataea, with its capital at Petra, controlled the incense trade from the Yemen and held the important port of Elath in the Gulf of Aqaba. Secondly, Palmyra held sway over trade traveling up the Tigris and Euphrates rivers from India, Afghanistan, and China, and the spice trade from Indonesia. For a short period under Zenobia, while Rome was in chaos, it became a powerful empire. In central Arabia, the greatest city along the trade routes was Mecca, an important commercial center that sent its own caravans northward and southward, growing wealthy from the profits.

In the regions of southern Arabia, like Yemen, that enjoyed some rainfall, or the monsoon on the Omani coasts, agriculture was possible, as was the collection of fragrant resins such as frankincense and myrrh. The area had been the home of the ancient states of Ma'in, Saba, and Qataban. The southern kingdoms fought amongst themselves in ever-shifting patterns of alliances until the Yemeni Kingdom of Himyar emerged in the second century BCE. One Himyarite King, Dhu Nuwas, changed the state religion to Judaism and started to persecute Christians. Kaleb, the Christian King (Negus) of Axum, situated in northern Ethiopia and Eritrea, invaded Himyar, with the approval of Byzantine Emperor Justin I, and annexed it. Himyar became a springboard for an Axumite attack on Mecca in 570. The eastern part of the Yemen was tied to the Lakhmids, and hence the Sassanian Empire, by alliances. When a Persian army descended upon Himyar, the Yemen became a Sassanian vassal and then a province with a Persian satrap.

It may be that the polytheistic Arabian peoples were subjected to a rich and varied diet of cultures and as a young man Muhammad encountered Judaism, Christianity, and Zoroastrianism. He would have observed the fissures and disharmony within the differing Christian rites, and would be familiar with the history of Judaism in the Yemen and known the Jewish community in Medina. Out of this mélange of experiences would be forged the new faith of Islam. This new faith and culture brought new irrigation techniques, new crops, and new ideas to Western Europe. In Baghdad, the scholars of the Arab world translated philosophical and scientific works from Greek, Syriac, Persian, and Sanskrit. Hunayn Ibn Ishaq translated the works of Galen, and some of Ptolemy and Hippocrates. Al-Razi wrote about gynaecology, obstetrics, and ophthalmic surgery, while Ibn Sina (Avicenna) wrote on medicine, his textbooks being used at the universities of Montpellier and Leuven in the seventeenth century. His other writings covered philosophy, astronomy, alchemy, geology, psychology, Islamic theology, logic, mathematics, and physics.

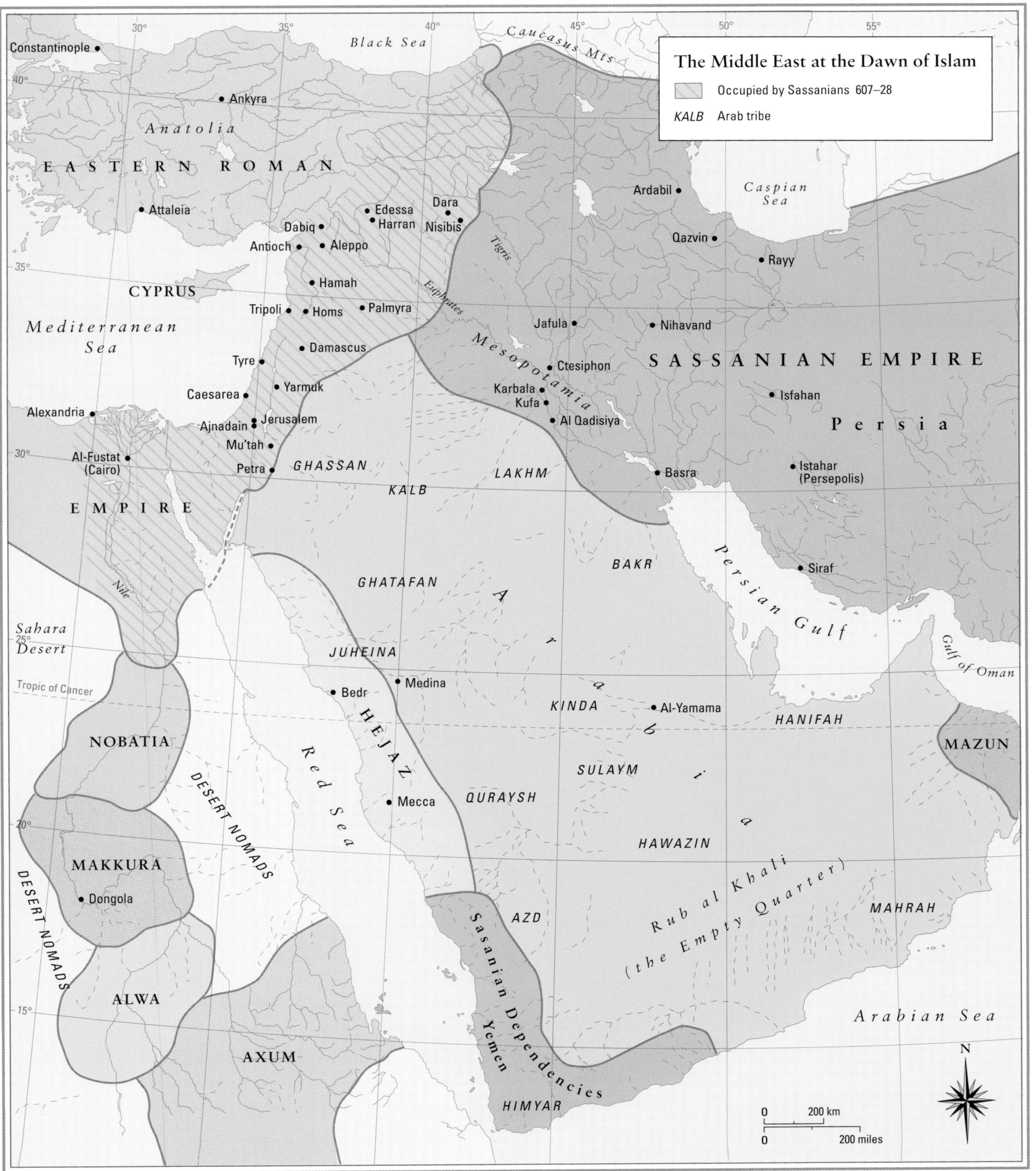

The Middle East at the Dawn of Islam
Occupied by Sassanians 607–28
KALB Arab tribe
EASTERN ROMAN EMPIRE
SASSANIAN EMPIRE
Anatolia
Persia
Arabia
Mesopotamia
Black Sea
Caucasus Mts
Caspian Sea
Mediterranean Sea
Red Sea
Persian Gulf
Gulf of Oman
Arabian Sea
Sahara Desert
Tropic of Cancer
Rub al Khali (the Empty Quarter)
Sasanian Dependencies
Yemen
CYPRUS
NOBATIA
MAKKURA
ALWA
AXUM
MAZUN
HEJAZ
DESERT NOMADS
Constantinople
Ankyra
Attaleia
Edessa
Harran
Dara
Nisibis
Dabiq
Antioch
Aleppo
Hamah
Tripoli
Homs
Palmyra
Damascus
Tyre
Yarmuk
Caesarea
Alexandria
Jerusalem
Ajnadain
Mu'tah
Petra
Al-Fustat (Cairo)
Dongola
Bedr
Medina
Mecca
Al-Yamama
Ardabil
Qazvin
Rayy
Jafula
Nihavand
Ctesiphon
Karbala
Kufa
Al Qadisiya
Isfahan
Basra
Istahar (Persepolis)
Siraf
Tigris
Euphrates
Nile
GHASSAN
LAKHM
KALB
GHATAFAN
BAKR
JUHEINA
KINDA
HANIFAH
SULAYM
QURAYSH
HAWAZIN
AZD
MAHRAH
HIMYAR
30°
35°
40°
45°
50°
55°
25°
20°
15°
0 200 km
0 200 miles
N

Islam and Arab Conquests 632–718

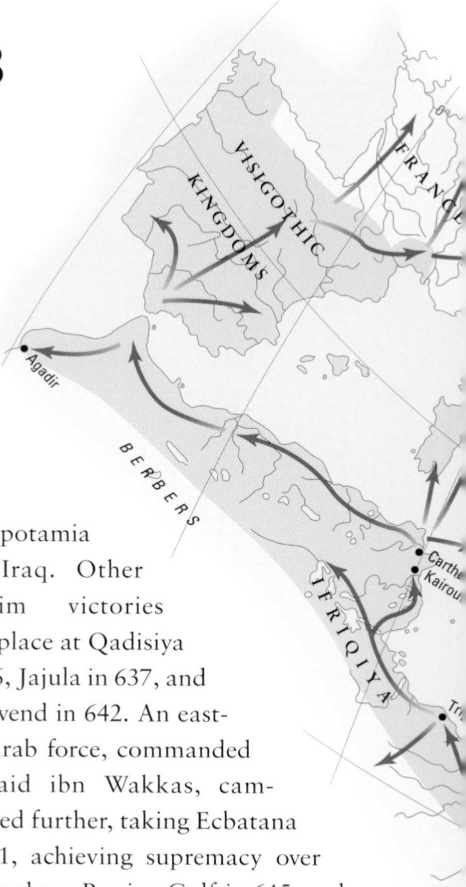

The birth and spread of Islam was a pivotal Asian, and eventually worldwide, event. Islam is predicated upon Muhammad's prophetic teachings—the verses of his revelations being known as the Koran and compiled from 610 in Mecca when Muhammad was 40. He emphasized social reform and sought to replace old tribal loyalties with an Islamic community. Arousing the enmity of rich conservative merchants, protective of their local cults, Muhammad fled to Medina, where he was given supreme authority to arbitrate local disputes and to establish Islam. He sought to isolate Mecca by cutting its trade routes with Syria and, in 630, the Meccans submitted. Many Arabian tribes converted to Islam and Muhammad became the most important and powerful leader in Arabia, enforcing the principles of Islam and laying the foundations of an Islamic Empire.

When Muhammad died in 632, at a time when some tribes were falling away from the faith, Abu Bakr became the caliph (632–34), or successor to the Prophet. He turned the tribes into a powerful military force capable of spreading the faith far and wide. He realized that the Arabs required external enemies to loot and plunder lest they began fighting each other again. The Byzantine Empire became a target when Abu Bakr despatched his General, Khalid, with raiding parties into Palestine. These eventually unified and defeated a larger Byzantine force at Ajnadain in 634. Under the next Caliph, Umar (634–44), Arab armies invaded Syria, defeating the Byzantines at Yarmuk in 636 and captured Jerusalem in 638. Soon the Arabs had taken major cities, including Damascus, advancing into northern Syria as far as the region of Tarsus. Many of the captured territories passed readily into Arab hands, as their inhabitants were indifferent or detested Byzantine tax gatherers. Arab armies broke into the Sassanian Empire, seized the capital Ctesiphon in 637, and acquired Mesopotamia and Iraq. Other Muslim victories took place at Qadisiya in 636, Jajula in 637, and Nehavend in 642. An eastern Arab force, commanded by Said ibn Wakkas, campaigned further, taking Ecbatana in 641, achieving supremacy over the northern Persian Gulf in 645, and capturing Khorasan in 652.

The Arab invasion of Egypt, led by Amr ibn al-As, defeated the Byzantines at Heliopolis in 640, while Alexandria and Egypt capitulated in 642 after the surrender was arranged by Cyrus, the patriarch of Alexandria. Islamic forces entered Cyrenaica, acquiring Tripoli in 647, and Carthage in 695, and retook it in 698, thereby destroying the Exarchate of Africa. The expansion was also based upon the zeal of the caliphs and a feeling of righteousness on the part of the conquerors. Large-scale population movement led to the eviction of the Persian ruling classes in Bahrain and Oman. The Arabs were helped by the fact that they normally adhered to Muhammad's dictum to respect the faiths of other peoples. However, they levied a tax on non-believers and this led to the poorer class converting to Islam across the Near East.

A new venture for the Arabs was a response to Byzantine naval power. The Arabs constructed their own fleet, which saw action in the captures of Cyprus and Rhodes. In Asia, Arab power conquered Kabul, Bukhara, and Samarkand, finally acquiring Transoxiana and the Indus region by 711. In North Africa, Tariq crossed the Straits of Gibraltar, defeated the Visigoths in 711, and acquired most of Spain. The final thrust in this initial burst of territorial acquisition was a failed attempt to capture the Byzantine capital at Constantinople in 718.

The Arab conquests resulted in an influx of wealth into Medina, which became a center for Koranic study. The later removal of the capital to Damascus in 658, and the restoration of administration and taxation, created a consolidation of the conquests and led to the spread of Arabic, which supplanted Greek or Aramaic as the major common language.

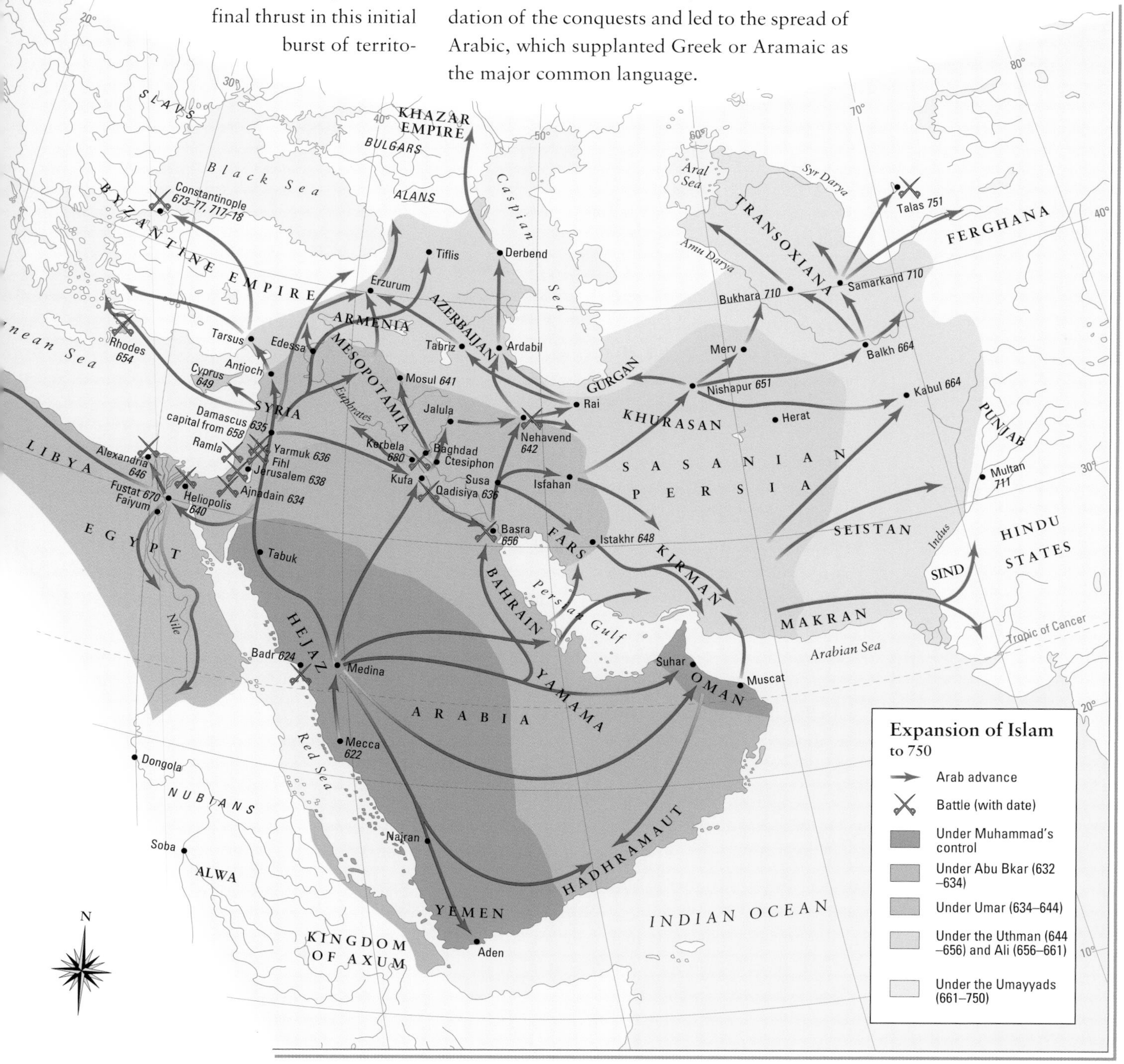

Expansion of Islam
to 750

- Arab advance
- Battle (with date)
- Under Muhammad's control
- Under Abu Bkar (632–634)
- Under Umar (634–644)
- Under the Uthman (644–656) and Ali (656–661)
- Under the Umayyads (661–750)

Battle of Yarmuk 636

The tomb of Khalid ibn al-Walid (592–642) lies in the mosque in Homs, Syria. He was a noted hero and commander, and was a companion of the prophet Muhammad. He is reputed to have been victorious in over 100 battles with the Byzantine and Sassanian empires.

After Caliph Abu Bakr had united the Arabian tribes and defeated all rebels, he decided on a policy of expansion. Iraq was conquered and then a campaign was mounted against Byzantine Syria in 634. The Byzantine presence was so strong that Arab reinforcements were soon called for and the campaign was led by General Khalid ibn al-Walid. The Byzantines were defeated both at Ajnadayn, in 634, and Fahl, in 635, with Damascus falling in September 634. When Abu Bakr died that year, Umar became the next Caliph and continued his predecessor's policies. Southern Palestine was captured, followed by Tiberias and Baalbek, with Emessa being taken in 636. Next, an advance was made toward Aleppo.

Byzantine Emperor Heraclius responded by raising a large army of Franks, Slavs, Georgians, Armenians, Christian Arabs, as well as Byzantines. He knew that the Arab invaders were divided into four small armies: one in Palestine, another in Jordan, a further force near Damascus, and a final one at Emessa. Heraclius hoped that he could advance and defeat these separate forces in detail rather than risk a large-scale pitched battle against a combined force. The Arabs decided to retreat in the face of the Byzantine armies and pulled back from northern Syria, concentrating their forces on a plain at Jabiya. Here, they could readily receive reinforcements from Arabia or, if they wished, could retreat into the Arabian Peninsula. The Arabs were subjected to raids by the Byzantine's Christian Arabs and decided to pull back even further to Dara and camped on the plain at Yarmuk.

The two forces which confronted each other were entirely different in character. The Byzantine army was the most professional force in the region. It was partially a standing army and partially a mercenary force. In time of war, more mercenaries were incorporated, whether Christian Arabs, Persian heavy cataphracts, or Gothic heavy cavalry. The Byzantine infantry comprised two types. One category, the *skutatoi*, were armed with spear, sword, and axe, carried an oval shield, wore chain-mail shirts or padded leather, and had a segmented helm. The other class, the *psiloi*, carried javelins and a composite short bow, and wore similar armor to the *skutatoi*. Offensively, bows would be used to weaken an enemy before the spearmen charged. Defensively, a shield wall could be formed while the archers stood to the rear to fire arrows over their comrades. The cataphracts were heavily armored cavalry and carried lance, sword, and composite bow. They could harass with arrows or charge home. In overall command of the Byzantine forces was Vahan the Armenian.

The Arabs, ethnically united and driven by religious fervor, were extremely mobile on horse or camel-back. They could attack out of the desert without warning. The majority of Arab troops were infantrymen; they would deploy archers to weaken the enemy ranks and then charge with spear and sword to pin the enemy for a cavalry charge from the flanks. Arab cavalry was light and armed with lance and sword. Its task was to harry the enemy flanks and rear. The overall commander of the Arabs at Yarkuk was Khalid.

The Battle of Yarmuk began on 15 August 635. The armies lined up across a front of several miles, stretching between the Wadi al Yarmuk gorge on one side, and the Wadi Ruqqad on the other. The first day was spent with champions from each army dueling, then the Byzantine infantry probed the Muslim lines, only to be driven back. On the second day there was a Byzantine attack across the Muslim front, which nearly collapsed in places and only held when the cavalry reserve entered the fray. Both sides had suffered casualties on this day, but neither side had gained an advantage. On the third day there was a combined cataphract and infantry attack on the Muslim right flank which only held when helped by the cavalry reserve. Day four saw Vahan attacking the Arab right flank and Khalid countered with an assault on the Byzantine center and right. The Byzantine left flank was exposed, and its Christian Arab cavalry support fled. However, the Muslim infantry on the left flank suffered heavy casualties while holding the Byzantine attack. On the fifth day Vahan sent emissaries to Khalid to negotiate a truce. The latter considered this a sign of Byzantine weakness, refused, and both sides regrouped. The sixth and final day initiated the last attack with the Byzantine left collapsing and then the center and right; Byzantine troops fled and the Arabs pursued them with no quarter given.

Some 50,000 Byzantine troops were thought to have been killed and just 4,000 Arab soldiers. This crushing defeat left a few Byzantine garrisons scattered here and there to be mopped up. By 639, Byzantine Armenia fell and by 640, all of today's Israel, Lebanon, Syria, and Jordan were captured, with Egypt being invaded and captured by 642. The battle displayed how a weaker Arab units could concentrate their forces in different locations on a battlefield and prevent any breakthrough. The Byzantine cavalry were not used to good effect and were never concentrated in force during any part of the battle. Arab mobility and Khalid's experience and skill won the battle.

Yarmuk was incredibly important. The Byzantines were wrong footed and pushed back into Anatolia, transforming the Middle East from a Christian to a Muslim territory until some parts were re-gained centuries later during the Crusades.

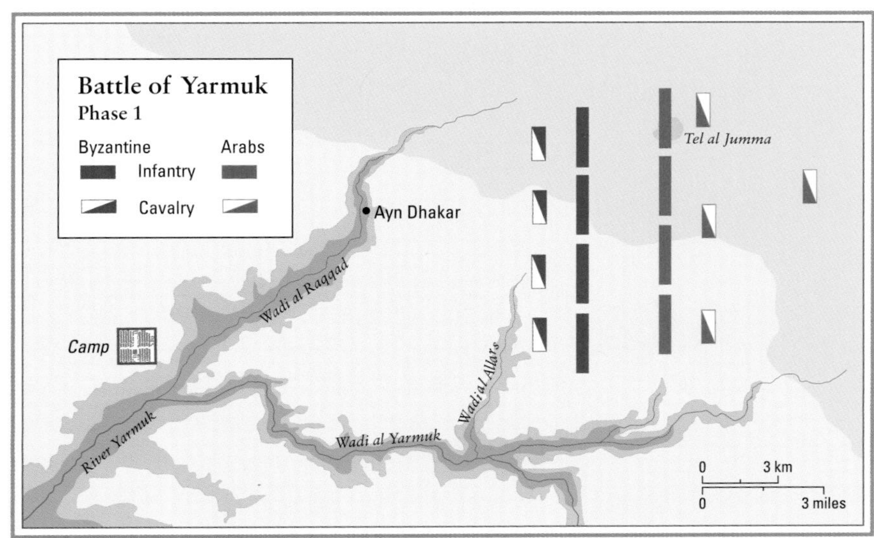

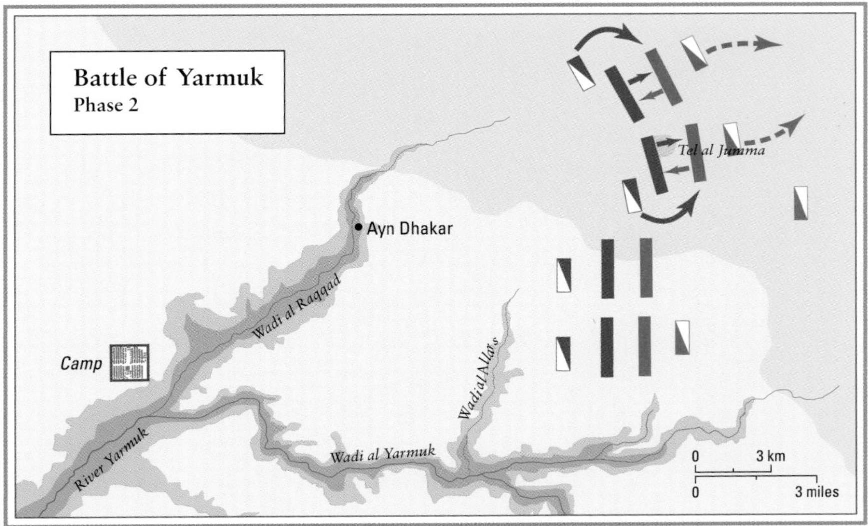

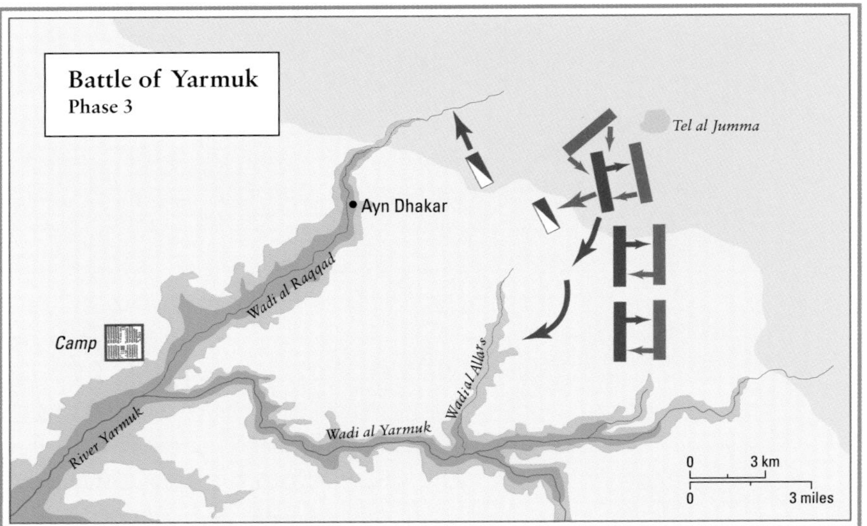

The Saljuq Turks

Amongst great Saljuq architectural achievements is the Toghrol Tower; built in the twelfth century, it is located south of Tehran in Iran.

The Saljuq Turks, originally a nomadic tribe of Oghuz Turkmen that had converted to the Sunni branch of Islam, migrated from central Asia and southeast Russia into the Middle East, where they settled in the lands of the failing Abbasid caliphate. The successor Buyid Dynasty grew even weaker and the rival Ghaznavids looked toward India, allowing the Saljuq conquest of Persia. The Saljuqs then defeated the Ghaznavids in 1040 at the Battle of Dandanqan, seized their western lands, and reduced them to tributary status. The Saljuqs imposed a military sultanate over the caliphate and occupied Baghdad in 1055. They then attacked the eastern Anatolian provinces of the Byzantine Empire and then turned south against the Fatimids in Egypt.

In 1043, Basil II, Byzantine Emperor, took Armenia by force after it had fragmented into several small kingdoms. However, within two decades the region was conquered by the Saljuq leaders Alp-Arslan and Malik-Shah, and Mesopotamia, Syria, and Palestine were also annexed. Systematic raids into Asia Minor resulted in conquest, seriously threatening the Byzantine Empire. In 1071, the Saljuqs defeated the Byzantines at the Battle of Manzikert, capturing Emperor Romanus IV Diogenes in the process and then established themselves in Nicea. The Emperor had been betrayed on the battlefield and his Cuman mercenaries defected to the Turks while the Varangian Guard of Scandinavians and Anglo-Saxons fought to the last man.

This first blow against Byzantine hegemony was alleviated by the diplomacy of Emperor Alexius Comnenus, who, on his coronation in April 1081, negotiated with the Saljuqs, and recognized their claims in Asia Minor, so that he could turn his attention elsewhere. In 1091, the Byzantines defeated a combined Saljuq/Pecheneg invasion and later destroyed a Saljuq fleet.

In the aftermath Comnenus communicated with Western monarchs and asked for help against the Turks. To his consternation, mercenaries failed to materialize, although his territories were crossed by the hosts of the First Crusade, which helped the Byzantines recapture western Anatolia. In 1099, the Crusaders captured Jerusalem and Palestine and established the first Crusader states. Once created, these Christian states would frequently be allied with local Muslim rulers against other Muslims. However, Imad ad-Din Zengi reunited the petty rulers of Syria and captured the Crusader County of Edessa, which triggered the Second Crusade. Zengi's son, Nur ad-Din, succeeded Zengi in Aleppo and negotiated an alliance to fight this new Crusade, which landed in 1147. The new Crusade foolishly tried to attack Damascus but was pushed away and harried by Turkish horse-archers. The Crusaders retreated to the coast, leaving the Zengids to expand their territories.

At its height, under Malik Shah, the Saljuq Empire was larger than the Sassanid Empire and its power was bolstered by the vassalage of the Turkic Qarakhanids, who ruled Transoxiana, and the Ghaznavids, whose lands included contemporary Afghanistan, western Punjab, and much of Baluchistan. The Saljuqs were keen promoters of Sunni Islam and hoped to root out Shi'ites. They made a strong impression on Islam in both a political and a religious sense, demonstrated by the building of mosques and Madrassahs in which religious scholars and state administrators were educated and trained. Religious tolerance toward Christians and Jews followed the teachings of Muhammad, despite the militant Christianity of the Crusaders. The Saljuqs became heavily Persianized and they were influenced by Persian and Arab learning. Their capital at Konya became a center for learning and the arts. The Turks also exchanged teachers and religious leaders with Constantinople.

The fundamental weakness of the Saljuqs was revealed by the death of Malik Shah. His lands were split between his brother and sons, and contested by other members of the family in a whirlwind of internecine strife. War was waged by different factions as male successors carved out domains for themselves.

As well as the various competitive heirs, the Artuqid's Turkmen Dynasty ruled in northeastern Syria and northern Mesopotamia, the Danishmends grabbed part of northern Asia Minor, the Sultanate of Rûm, established 1077, controlled Anatolia, while the atabeg of Mosul held substantial power. This political chaos weakened the Saljuqs, who were keener on fighting each other than on attacking Crusaders. Further fragmentation took place as more atabegs became independent and far-flung regions of the Empire rebelled in Afghanistan and Central Asia. Bordering states grew stronger and encroached on Saljuq lands, notably the Kingdom of Georgia and the Armenian Kingdom of Cilicia in Anatolia. Even the Abbasid Caliph An-Nasr showed his authority by forming an alliance with Shah Takash of the growing Khwarizm Empire, who had defeated the notional Saljuq sultan, Togrul III and caused the collapse of the Saljuq Empire. Only the Anatolian Sultanate of Rûm remained within the Saljuq state. Eventually, the Mongols arrived in the thirteenth century and conquered the region, only being turned back by the Battle of Ayn Jalut in 1260, which the Mongols were never able to avenge. Most of the Saljuq Empire was taken over by one inheritor of Ghenghis Khan to become the Ilkhanate.

The Saljuq Turks

- Major Saljuq campaign
- Saljuq Sultinate at its maximum extent, c. 1090
- Byzantine Empire, c. 1095
- Territory lost to Byzantine Empire and crusader states, 1097–99
- Extent of the Khwarizm Shahdom, c. 1220

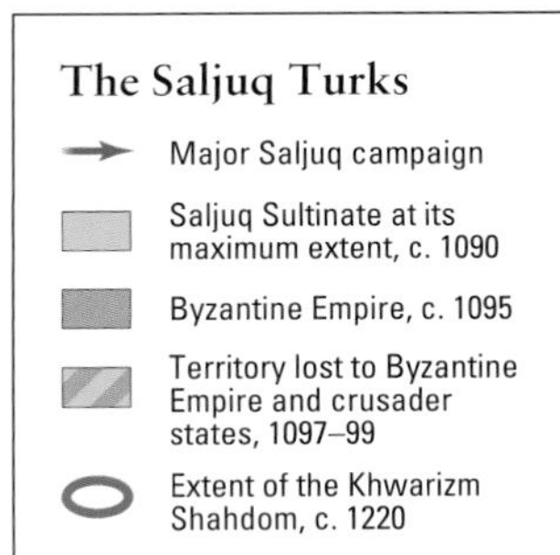

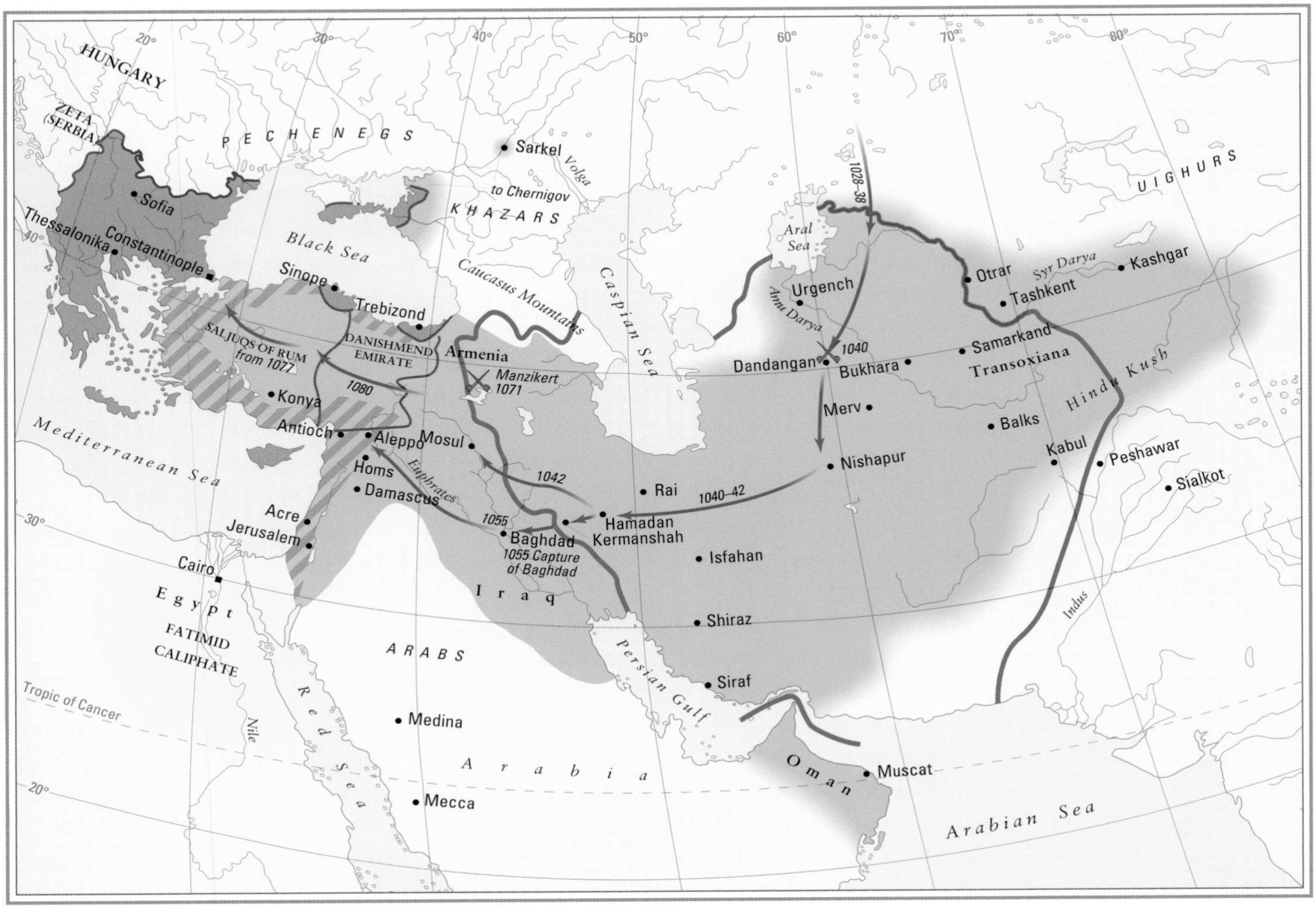

Battle of Manzikert 1071

When the Saljuq Turks began to take Byzantine territory, they captured Armenia in 1067, followed by Caesarea. In 1068, Romanos IV ascended the Byzantine throne and was eager to regain lost lands. He made a series of peace treaties with Sultan Alp Arslan, who was ready to sign, as he was launching a campaign against Fatimid Egypt by attacking Aleppo. This encouraged Romanos to break the resulting treaty and lead a large army into Anatolia where he intended to retake lost Byzantine fortresses. Substanital forces accompanied Romanos: some 10,000 professional Byzantine soldiers; 500 mercenary Frankish and Norman soldiers under Roussel de Bailleul, who had served with Roger de Hauteville in Sicily; some Oghuz, Pecheneg and Bulgarian mercenaries; infantry commanded by the Byzantine vassal the Duke of Antioch; a group of Georgian and Armenian soldiers and most of the Scandinavian and Anglo-Saxon Varangian Guard. In total, at least 40,000 men, possibly as many as 70,000, traveled with Romanos.

The Byzantines marched across Anatolia, stopping at Sebasteia and Theodosiopolis, then advanced towards Lake Van in Armenia hoping to retake Manzikert before Alp Arslan knew of their presence. Romanos was unaware that Alp Arslan was nearby with some 30,000 cavalry and made the mistake of despatching General Joseph Tarchaneiotes, with some Varangians, Byzantines, Pechenegs, and Franks, with orders to capture Khliat; this divided his army in half. Romanos continued toward Manzikert, which was swiftly taken.

On 24 August, some foraging units left Manzikert and were attacked by advancing Saljuqs. Romanos ordered General Basilakes to counter with a cavalry attack, but his force was defeated and the General was captured. The Byzantine left wing was sent out, commanded by Bryennios, but this was forced to retreat when it was nearly surrounded by Turkish horse archers. Elsewhere, the Saljuq army disappeared into the nearby hills and Romanos had no intelligence as to their whereabouts. On 25 August, some of Romanos' Turkish mercenaries met their Saljuq kin and deserted.

On 26 August, Romanos deployed his army in the normal fashion, with two wings and a center with a reserve to the rear, commanded by Andronikos Doukas. The Saljuqs faced them in a large crescent formation some two and a half miles away. Horse archers attacked the Byzantines as they moved forward with the center of the crescent retreating while the flanks gradually surrounded their enemies. The Byzantines survived the arrow storm but when they sought to engage the Saljuqs gave ground and continued to harass the Byzantines in hit and run attacks. As night grew closer, Romanos decided to disengage and return to his camp, but the right wing panicked and Doukas, commander of the reserve, marched off the field claiming that the Emperor was dead. Doukas should have covered the retreat, but the hostility between the two men prevailed. As the right wing became disordered the Saljuqs attacked and routed it—the Armenians were the first to run. The center, with Romanos and the Varangian Guard, was then surrounded. Romanos was wounded and captured, while the Varangians fought to the end. The professional soldiers had been wiped out, while the less well-disciplined soldiers fled and were pursued through the night.

Romanos was ransomed and returned to confront the Doukas family, who defeated him in three battles and usurped the throne. Romanos was captured, blinded, and died of his wounds. This treachery ushered in a period of internal political weakness and instability and this factor is key in explaining the eventual decline of Byzantium and a whole series of usurpations which exacerbated this process. Manzikert was a Byzantine disaster; although many leaders and troops survived to fight another day, their defeat demonstrated the

Saljuq forces could beat the Byzantine professional army, who lost their reputation for invincibility.

Further Byzantine weaknesses developed. Roussel de Bailleul, with his 3,000 Frankish and German mercenaries, attempted to create an independent principality in Galatia and defeated the Doukid family. Ultimately, and ironically, the Byzantines asked the Saljuqs to deal with this issue, which they did successfully. Byzantium faced other difficulties. In Italy, its territories were being whittled away by Normans, under the leadership of Roger Guiscard. He defeated the Byzantines in Albania at Dyrrhachium in 1082 and then captured most of Macedonia and Thessaly. There were also Byzantine campaigns against the Pechenegs. In sum, there were not enough Byzantine troops to regain lost territories in Anatolia. The Saljuqs sensed the problems facing the Byzantines and poured into western Anatolia setting up their capital at Nicae. This meant that the Emperors lost western Anatolia's tax revenues and, as a result, the Byzantines grew weaker and more reliant on mercenaries. They also had to deal with the Crusade which they had invited to help restore their dominance after Manzikert. Manzikert had demonstrated to the western states that Byzantium was too weak to defend Christians in the East and so the Crusaders took on the task.

One hundred years of peace ensued between Byzantium and the Saljuqs, which allowed Byzantium to regain some of its vitality. The Hungarians were defeated and the Byzantines asserted control over the Balkans. Cilicia was regained from an Armenian dynasty and the Crusader Principality of Antioch was reduced to a vassal. However, the Byzantines under Manuel I Komnenos were beaten again by the Saljuqs at the Battle of Myriokephalon in September 1176.

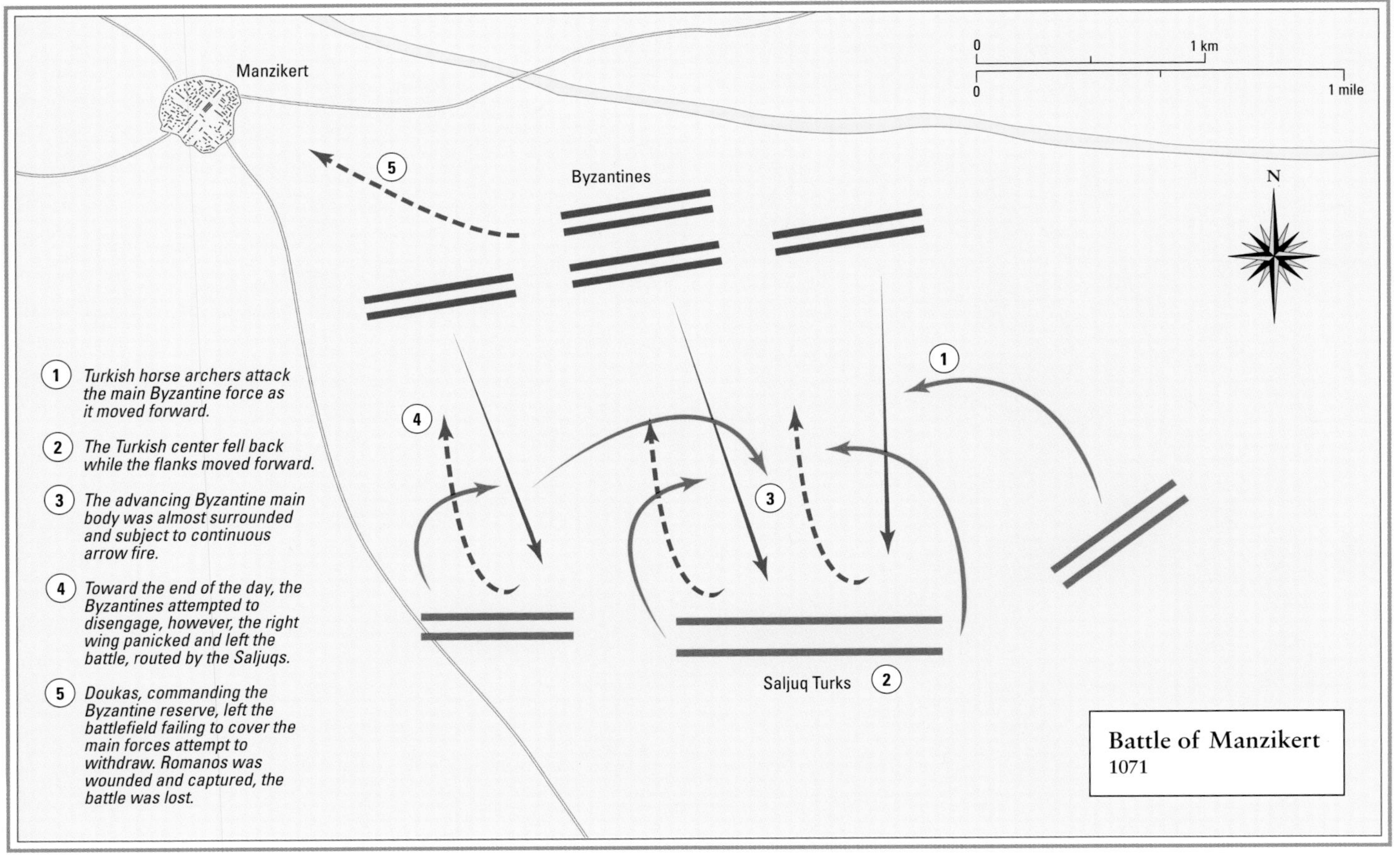

Christian Crusades and Crusader Kingdoms 1095–1270

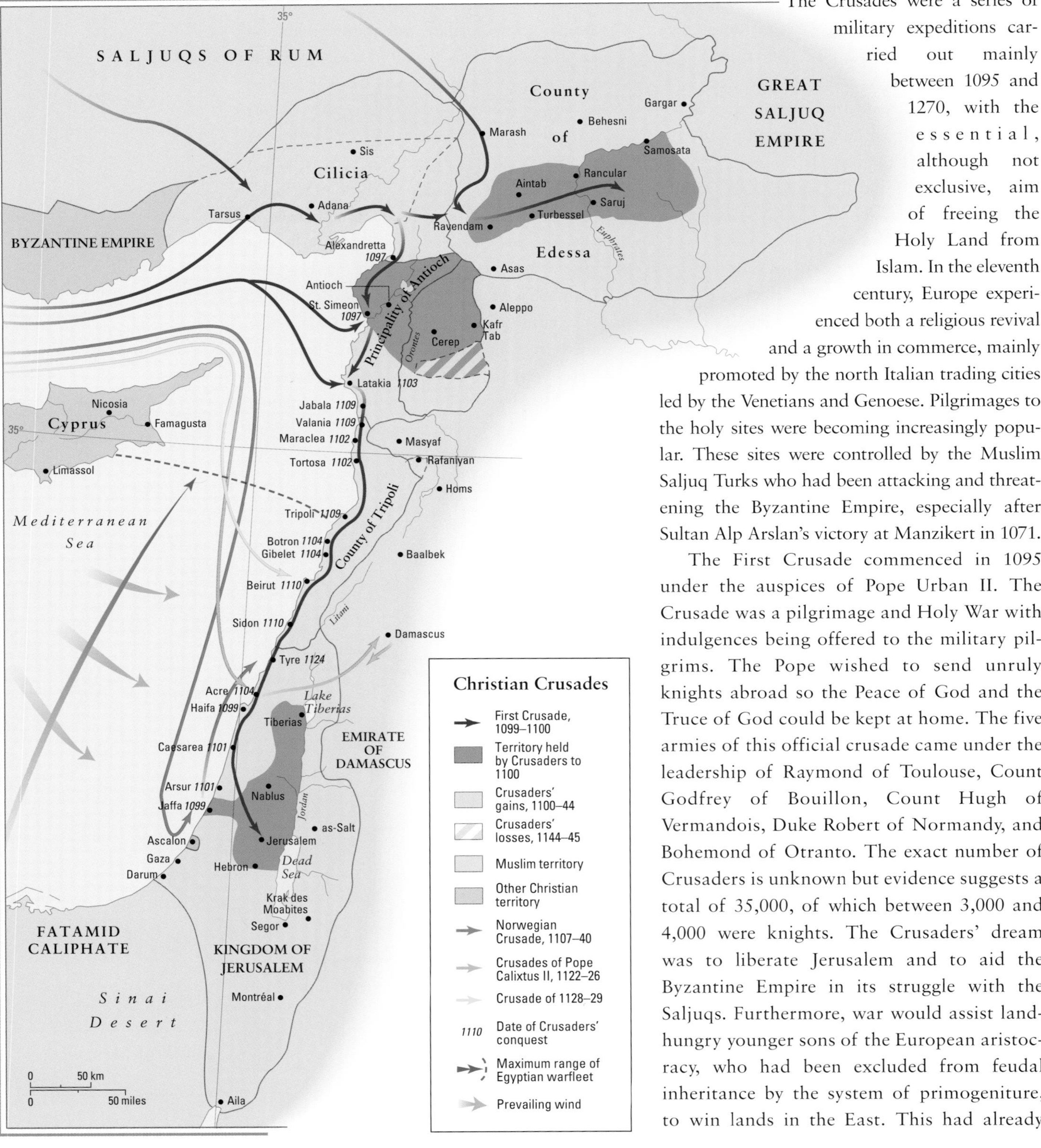

The Crusades were a series of military expeditions carried out mainly between 1095 and 1270, with the essential, although not exclusive, aim of freeing the Holy Land from Islam. In the eleventh century, Europe experienced both a religious revival and a growth in commerce, mainly promoted by the north Italian trading cities led by the Venetians and Genoese. Pilgrimages to the holy sites were becoming increasingly popular. These sites were controlled by the Muslim Saljuq Turks who had been attacking and threatening the Byzantine Empire, especially after Sultan Alp Arslan's victory at Manzikert in 1071.

The First Crusade commenced in 1095 under the auspices of Pope Urban II. The Crusade was a pilgrimage and Holy War with indulgences being offered to the military pilgrims. The Pope wished to send unruly knights abroad so the Peace of God and the Truce of God could be kept at home. The five armies of this official crusade came under the leadership of Raymond of Toulouse, Count Godfrey of Bouillon, Count Hugh of Vermandois, Duke Robert of Normandy, and Bohemond of Otranto. The exact number of Crusaders is unknown but evidence suggests a total of 35,000, of which between 3,000 and 4,000 were knights. The Crusaders' dream was to liberate Jerusalem and to aid the Byzantine Empire in its struggle with the Saljuqs. Furthermore, war would assist land-hungry younger sons of the European aristocracy, who had been excluded from feudal inheritance by the system of primogeniture, to win lands in the East. This had already been achieved by the earlier Norman conquests in Sicily, southern Italy, and Spain.

Crossing Anatolia, the Crusaders entered Saljuq lands where Baldwin of Boulogne established the first Christian state at Edessa (1098–1291). The next target was Antioch, which was besieged for seven grueling months until it was eventually taken. The Crusaders then discovered that a large Turkish army was descending upon them. By now they were exhausted and weakened by illness and starvation, but at this low point in their fortunes their morale was restored by the apparently miraculous discovery of the Holy Lance beneath an altar in the city; the spear was widely considered to have been used by a Roman soldier to pierce Christ's side when he was on the cross. Bishop Aldhemar, who had seen one of these already in Constantinople, remained sceptical about the find but he was sick with the fever which was to end his life and could do nothing to stem the exaltation of the soldiers. Raymond of Toulouse, too, was ill; it was Bohemond who organized a desperate sortie from the city and, carrying the Holy Lance in their midst, the starving Christians defeated and put to flight a much larger Turkish army. This victory seemed little short of miraculous and was wholly attributed to the presence of the Holy Lance; probably without the faith and hope it had inspired the Crusaders would not have succeeded.

Bohemond (1058–1111) became the Prince of Antioch. Bohemond and Baldwin stayed in their new cities, leaving the deliverance of Jerusalem to others. When Jerusalem was captured in 1099, the Crusaders sacked the city and engaged in a killing frenzy, slaughtering almost the entire population, whatever the victim's religion. A Latin Kingdom of Jerusalem was established in 1100, lasting until 1291, while the County of Tripoli existed from 1102 to 1289. This loose confederation of states was defended by the construction of a chain of castles.

The Turks were pushed back from the Crusader bridgeheads in Palestine; between 1100 and 1144 all the Crusader holdings were connected in a long thin territorial block. In 1144, Edessa fell to the Saljuqs, resulting in the Second Crusade, led by Louis VII, King of France, and Emperor Conrad III. With forces numbering some 50,000 men, they arrived in Syria and, instead of recapturing Edessa, laid siege to Damascus. The Crusader army was defeated, leading to a shame-faced return to Europe.

In Egypt, a new unified Muslim state developed, led by Salah al-din Yusuf ibn Ayub, or Saladin. He negotiated a truce with the Crusader states but this was broken in 1187 and a Crusader army was destroyed at Hattin. Saladin then retook much of the Crusader territory and captured Jerusalem after a two-week siege. Europe responded with a Third Crusade (1189–1193), commanded ultimately by King Richard I of England. He defeated Saladin at Arsuf in 1191 but, despite recovering some Crusader lands, failed to take Jerusalem. The Fourth Crusade (1201–1204) fell foul of Venetian duplicity and ended up besieging Constantinople, which was taken by storm. Byzantine lands were then divided between a number of European rulers, leaving the Byzantine Emperor with some small territories.

The remaining three Crusades were noticeable for their failure and the last Crusader stronghold of Acre fell in 1291. The Crusaders had virtually extinguished Byzantium, while Islam had reorganized itself under Mamluk leadership and was accordingly strengthened.

Louis IX of France led the Seventh and Eighth Crusades. In 1249, he captured Damietta in Egypt and took Cairo. After the fall of Antioch, Louis attacked Tunis but died during the siege in 1270. For this, he was made a saint.

The Latin Kingdoms in Greece not only facilitated Western commercial interests in the eastern Mediterranean; the West was also indebted to the East when books lost to the West were discovered in Muslim and Byzantine libraries and translated into Latin.

Saladin's Campaigns 1173–85

The fragmentation of the Saljuq Empire allowed the Crusades to establish Christian states in the Levant. A Muslim response began when the Saljuq governor of Mosul, Zengi, seized Aleppo in 1128. Nur ad-Din, his son, ruled Syria and Mesopotamia from his capital at Damascus from 1154 to 1174. He sent the Kurdish General, Salah al-Din (Saladin), to seize control of Fatimid-ruled Egypt in 1169. This General deposed the last of the Fatimid caliphs, thereby establishing his own Ayyubid Dynasty in its place in 1171.

Saladin learned much of his military craft during campaigns between 1164 and 1169 when he defended Egypt from three Crusader invasions. In 1173, Nur al-Din died, providing Saladin with the opportunity to acquire Nur al-Din's lands. He used his wealthy agricultural possessions in Egypt to finance the construction of a small but extremely well-disciplined army. The elite of Saladin's forces were Mamluks. These soldiers were bought as slaves from the mountains and nomadic steppes or were incorporated from defeated enemies, an admixture of Circassians, Turkic tribesmen (mainly Kipchaks), and Armenians. These forces were well equipped with mail shirts and sometimes lamular armor, and carried composite bows, swords, lances, and shields. These Muslim warriors developed a longer lance than usual allowing them to fight on equal terms with Crusader knights. Additionally, Saladin recruited Turkoman light cavalry from Anatolia who fought as horse-archers, attacking in waves, often feigning retreat and firing backwards in the nomad way, before they turned to attack the flanks of an enemy who had become extended in pursuit.

Saladin's forces advanced along the North African coast to Gabès in today's Tunisia while his brother, Turan Shah, marched south along the Nile into Nubia, crossed the Red Sea, and eventually reached the Yemen. Saladin increased the size of his armies as he seized control over much of the Arab world. He captured Damascus in 1174, Aleppo, Mosul, and parts of Iraq in 1183. During this period, Saladin launched an invasion of the Kingdom of Jerusalem, joining battle with the Crusader forces of King Baldwin IV of Jerusalem, Raynald of Châtillon, Lord of Oultrejordan, and the Knights Templar. The battle at Montgisard, near Ramla, on 25 November 1177, was a crushing defeat for Saladin where he lost nearly his entire army.

Saladin then made sure he fully controlled his domains before again assaulting the Crusader statelets. As Sultan of Egypt and Syria, Saladin's lands enclosed the Crusader positions while his military and diplomatic skills prepared Islam for jihad against the Christian coastal lands, which was proclaimed in 1187. That year saw the Crusaders' field army eradicated at the Horns of Hattin. For the Crusaders this was an irreplaceable loss, even though other smaller forces were raised to break sieges of Crusader settlements and castles.

The Crusader defeat meant that Crusader fortress garrisons were undermanned and incapable of defense. Saladin captured most of the Kingdom of Jerusalem. Within three months, Acre, Toron, Beirut, Sidon, Nazareth, Caesarea, Nablus, Jaffa, and Ascalon had fallen. Jerusalem, Holy City to Christians and Muslims alike, fell to Saladin in October 1187, after being held by the Crusaders for 88 years.

The Muslim forces then emplaced in Acre were besieged by Guy of Lusignan in 1189 but Saladin was unable to lift the siege because Richard I, the Lionheart, arrived in the Levant with Phillip II of France and troops of the Third Crusade. Richard captured Acre in 1191 and killed 2,500 prisoners. He advanced on Jerusalem and, despite defeating Saladin at the Battle of Arsuf the same year, was unable to reach Jerusalem. Saladin died in Damascus on 4 March 1193. His dynasty was not to last long, and in 1250 the last Ayyubid Sultan was assassinated by his Mamluk soldiers, paving the way for the Mamluk Sultanate of Egypt, which lasted until 1517.

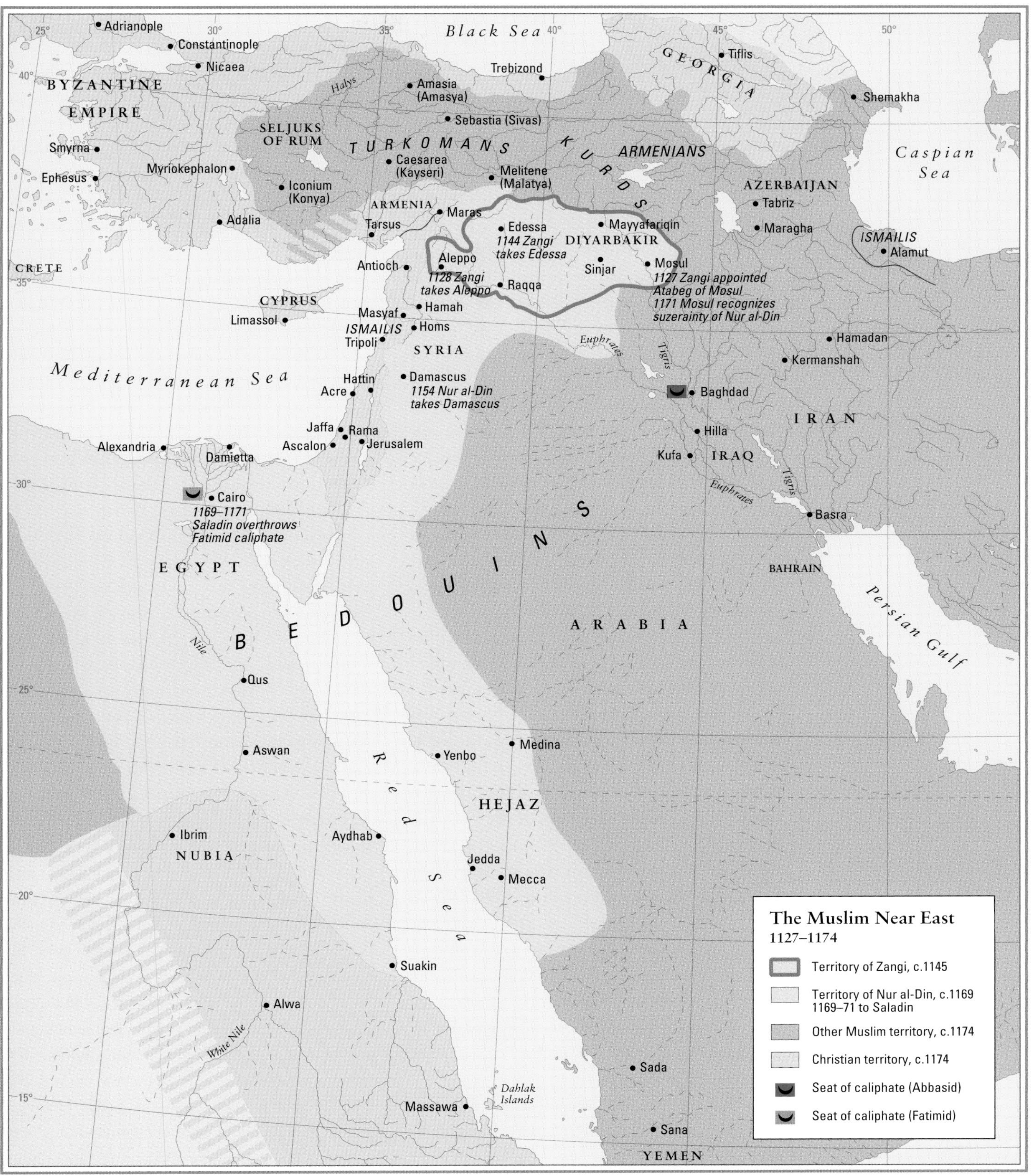
The Muslim Near East
1127–1174
Territory of Zangi, c.1145
Territory of Nur al-Din, c.1169
1169–71 to Saladin
Other Muslim territory, c.1174
Christian territory, c.1174
Seat of caliphate (Abbasid)
Seat of caliphate (Fatimid)
Black Sea
Caspian Sea
Mediterranean Sea
Red Sea
Persian Gulf
BYZANTINE EMPIRE
SELJUKS OF RUM
TURKOMANS
KURDS
ARMENIANS
GEORGIA
AZERBAIJAN
ISMAILIS
ARMENIA
DIYARBAKIR
CYPRUS
CRETE
SYRIA
IRAQ
IRAN
EGYPT
BEDOUINS
ARABIA
HEJAZ
NUBIA
YEMEN
BAHRAIN
Adrianople
Constantinople
Nicaea
Smyrna
Ephesus
Myriokephalon
Iconium (Konya)
Adalia
Amasia (Amasya)
Trebizond
Sebastia (Sivas)
Caesarea (Kayseri)
Melitene (Malatya)
Tiflis
Shemakha
Tabriz
Maragha
Alamut
Maras
Tarsus
Edessa
1144 Zangi takes Edessa
Mayyafariqin
Aleppo
1128 Zangi takes Aleppo
Antioch
Raqqa
Sinjar
Mosul
1127 Zangi appointed Atabeg of Mosul
1171 Mosul recognizes suzerainty of Nur al-Din
Masyaf
Hamah
Homs
Tripoli
Limassol
Hattin
Acre
Damascus
1154 Nur al-Din takes Damascus
Jaffa
Rama
Ascalon
Jerusalem
Alexandria
Damietta
Cairo
1169–1171 Saladin overthrows Fatimid caliphate
Hamadan
Kermanshah
Baghdad
Hilla
Kufa
Basra
Qus
Aswan
Yenbo
Medina
Ibrim
Aydhab
Jedda
Mecca
Suakin
Alwa
Sada
Massawa
Dahlak Islands
Sana
Halys
Euphrates
Tigris
Nile
White Nile

Horns of Hattin 1187

In 1186, Raynald de Châtillon, Lord of Kerak in Oultrejordan, broke a truce by raiding a caravan traveling between Cairo and Damascus, and Saladin declared war stating that he would behead Raynald if he were ever captured. Saladin summoned his troops and sent some 6,500 cavalry on a reconnaissance near Tiberias, which engaged a force of Templar and Hospitaller knights at the Spring of Cresson in 1187. Only three knights escaped the ensuing slaughter. Saladin's force then moved on to Nazareth where they massacred the entire Crusader garrison.

In response, a Crusader army was mustered at Acre. Only 80 of the 2,200 knights were Templars or Hospitallers, the remainder being secular or mercenary knights. Some sources state that there were only 1,200 knights accompanied by 15,000 infantry and 4,000 light cavalry, plus some crossbowmen from Italian merchant vessels. Saladin had raised 30,000 men of which 12,000 were cavalry, both horse archers and Mamluks. The Muslim force marched on Tiberias and laid siege to its castle hoping to entice the Crusaders away from their base at the Springs of La Sephorie. The town was quickly taken, but the citadel held out while Arab sappers began mining under the walls. Raymond of Tripoli advised the Crusaders that their route would take them over the waterless Plain of Toran and it would be more prudent to draw Saladin towards them while the Crusaders' garrison held out in the castle at Tiberias. The Crusaders took up the challenge, despite this advice. Unfortunately, Raynold de Châtillon and Gerard de Ridefort, Grand Master of the Knights Templar, persuaded Guy Lusignan, King of Jerusalem, to advance along the Wadi Hamman hoping to reach the Springs of Tur'an.

Once the Springs were reached at noon, there were still nine miles to Tiberias and sound sense would dictate that the Crusaders should camp and advance next day. Meanwhile, Saladin deployed his troops at the Horns of Hattin to block the Crusaders' advance, while his horse-archers skirmished with the Hospitallers, Templars, and Turcopole infantry and cavalry. The swift, mobile Turcopole cavalry received the brunt of the attacks; they were the greatest danger to Saladin's force, they had the speed to catch his horse-archers. Once they were broken, the Crusaders had to rely on the slow, trudging infantry to shield the knights and hold the Turkish horsemen. After the Crusader army had marched five miles, it ground to a halt and pitched camp near Meskana, despite there being no water available. The Crusaders hoped that a quick dash next morning to the Horns would enable them to find water. Saladin's troops, supplied with water carried by camels from Lake Tiberias, surrounded the Crusaders. The Turks were resupplied with arrows allowing them to continue their hit-and-run tactics.

Next morning clouds of smoke from fires set by Saladin's soldiers swept across the Crusaders, blinding them and increasing their thirst. At about 9:00am Saladin's troops advanced in a crescent formation firing a hail of arrows and as the Crusaders charged the Muslims retreated, while archers fired at vulnerable Crusader horses. The Crusader infantry saw Lake Tiberias in the distance and broke toward it but were gradually herded on to one of the Horns of Hattin where they were killed or captured. A knight's charge by Raymond of Tripoli and his men passed through Saladin's ranks and into the Wadi Hamman. He rode off the field with his men, making for Tyre; they were not pursued. The Crusaders made several charges but could not make contact—the Muslim horsemen simply retired, firing their bows. Some 300 Crusaders managed to escape towards Acre but the rest were driven onto the other Horn of Hattin where they were surrounded and cut down by arrows. In the end, some 150 knights surrendered. Amongst the prisoners were King Guy, his brother Amalric, Raynald de Châtillon, William of Montferrat, Gerard de Ridefort, Humphrey of Toron, and many others. Some 3,000 Christians managed to escape the battle.

Saladin personally beheaded Raynald de Châtillon as a truce breaker and his soldiers beheaded any remaining Templars and Hospitallers, their mortal enemies, all except for the Grand Master who was freed because he had persuaded a Crusader castle to surrender. Saladin had him executed on another occasion, after he was captured again. Raymond of Tripoli's wife, Eschiva, surrendered the citadel of Tiberias to Saladin and was allowed to go free with her family members. The destruction of the large Crusader army was a drain upon the garrisons of Crusader castles and Saladin was able to capture some 30 castles within the year. Another eleven castles were handed over as a ransom for King Guy. Jerusalem was besieged and eventually surrendered, and thousands of Muslim slaves were liberated. Conrad of Montferrat arrived in Tyre and organized the defense of the city with the aid of survivors of Hattin, keeping it in Crusader hands.

Ernoul, a squire of Balian of Ibelin who commanded the Crusader rearguard, claimed that news of the defeat caused Pope Urban III to die of shock. The new Pope, Gregory VIII, issued the Papal bull *Audita tremendi* calling for a Third Crusade, which was rapidly planned and despatched. In England, a special Saladin tithe raised 100,000 silver marks for the Crusade.

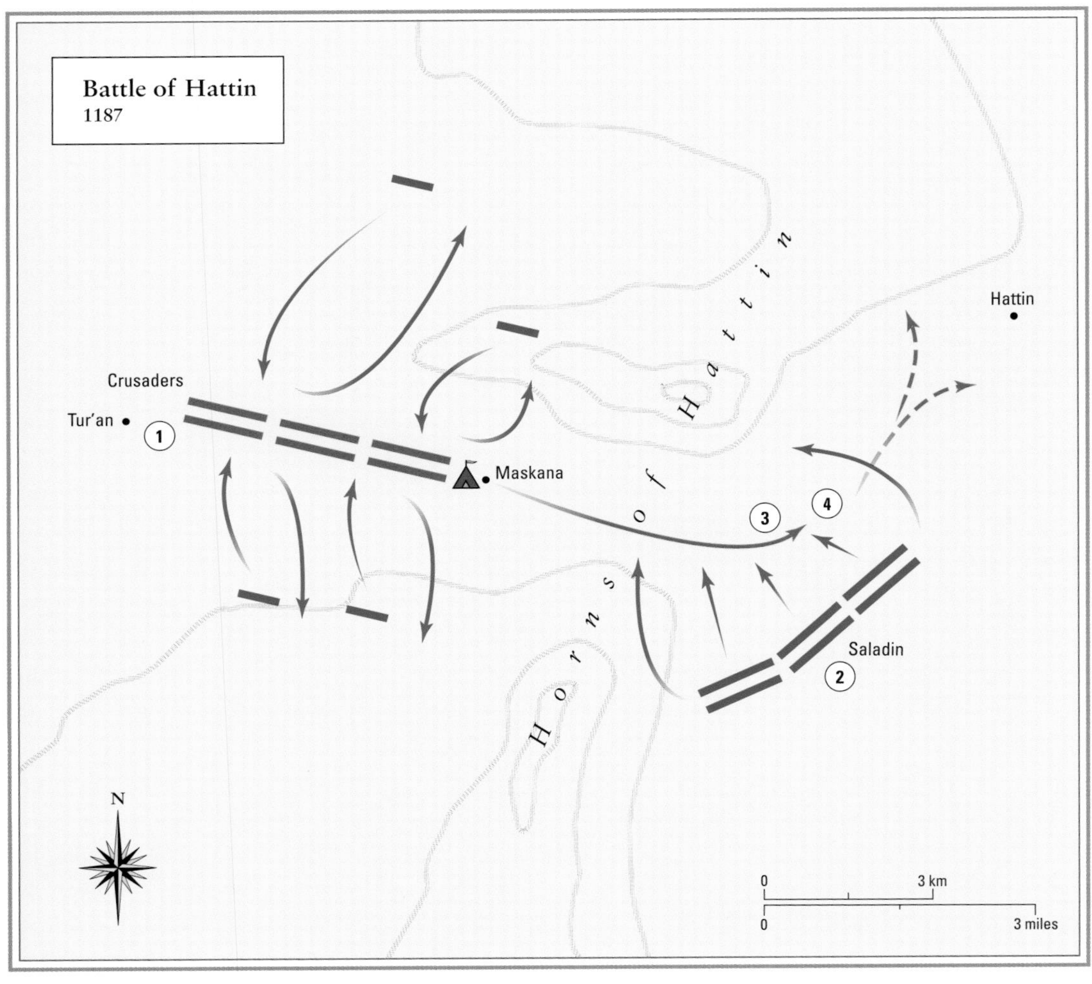

1 The Crusader army leaves Sephoria passing the spring at Tur'an heading via the Horns of Hattin to Tiberias. Almost immediately they come under attack by mounted skirmishers.

2 Arriving to face the Crusaders, Saladin orders a full attack, sending wings of his army around behind the Crusaders and seizes the well at Tur'an.

3 The Crusaders, pushing on, beset on all sides, are forced to a halt on the arid plateau not far from the village of Maskana. Here they made camp, still surrounded.

4 On the morning of 4 July, demoralized, the Crusaders break camp and head from the village of Hattin. Saladin blocks the route to Hattin with his main force, after several charges the Crusader army lose cohesion, the bulk of the infantry flee, some holding high ground around the Horns of Hattin. During the final melee, Count Raymond escapes towards the Sea of Galilee. The rest fall into captivity or are killed on the battlefield.

Battle of Arsuf 1191

The Great Seal of Richard I of England, also commonly known as Richard the Lionheart. He also held the titles of Duke of Normandy, Duke of Aquitaine, Duke of Gascony, Lord of Cyprus, Count of Anjou, Count of Maine, Count of Nantes, and sometime Overlord of Britanny. To his Muslim subjects and enemies, he was simply known as Melek Ric (King Richard) or Malek al-Inkitar (King of England).

During the Third Crusade, the Crusaders landed and captured Acre. From there, they planned to march to Jaffa and use that city as an advance base to march on Jerusalem. Led by King Richard I of England, the Crusader army marched on Jaffa. Richard knew that the Crusader army, that had been annihilated at Hattin had traveled in the heat and without water. Therefore, he only marched in the morning and near the sea where it was cooler, camping where there was a water supply. The fleet sailed down the coast in support carrying supplies and taking on board any wounded.

Richard knew Saladin would be determined to stop him, so deployed his troops carefully. The cavalry marched in twelve groups of 100 knights and men-and-arms each, and a supply train accompanied them. Surrounding them was the infantry, comprising crossbowmen and spearmen. The crossbowmen intended to shoot down any Arab horse-archers while the spearmen protected the bowmen. The troops were rotated, so some infantry were always resting on the coastal side of the column. Richard kept a rigid control over his men, knowing that the knights would like nothing better than to charge the Arab force. He was aware that breaking ranks would allow the Arabs to penetrate any gap created. The Arabs used hit-and-run tactics hoping to tempt the knights into such a rash maneuver. A contemporary Arab account of the event was recorded by Baha' Al-Din Yusuf ibn Shaddad. He said that discipline was tight in the Crusader ranks and that the infantry soaked up the attacks. He mentioned that the infantry gambesons (padded jackets) were not penetrated by Arab arrows and that some marched with up to ten arrows sticking out of their clothing. The crossbows, on the other hand, could bring down a man or horse and at a longer range than the Arab bows.

Saladin realized that his hit-and-run tactics were failing and that he would have to bring his entire force to bear on the Crusaders. He decided that he would launch an attack from the forests of Arsuf where there was space to deploy all his troops. On 7 September 1191, the Arab forces swarmed out of the woods, light skirmishers being sent first, while serried ranks of Mamluk cavalry waited for the final charge home. As the vanguard entered Arsuf, the Hospitaller crossbowmen at the column's rear were walking backward as they fired. They became disorganized and the Arabs swept in. The Hospitaller Master and companion charged the Arabs, followed by his own knights and three companies of Frenchmen. Richard ordered the rest of the knights to follow suit and each unit attacked in echelon from rear to front. The Arabs broke, Richard ordered no pursuit and regrouped. The Arabs returned and the Crusaders made three charges in total, driving the Arabs from the battlefield. Victorious, the Crusaders made camp at Arsuf.

The Crusaders felt that the disaster at Hattin had been avenged. Despite Richard's (the Lionheart) victory, Saladin's army was not destroyed. Its morale dipped as Saladin's reputation had been seriously damaged and the Crusaders gained a respite while Saladin regrouped his forces. In contrast, Richard's reputation soared. He advanced and captured Jaffa as planned, but failed to reached Jerusalem. However, Crusader success on the Levantine coast meant that Saladin had to withdraw into the hinterland after demolishing fortifications at Ascalon, Gaza, Blanche-Garde, Lydda, and Ramleh. Richard besieged and captured Darum, a severe blow since its garrison comprised Saladin's household troops. However, in 1192, Saladin retained Jerusalem by treaty.

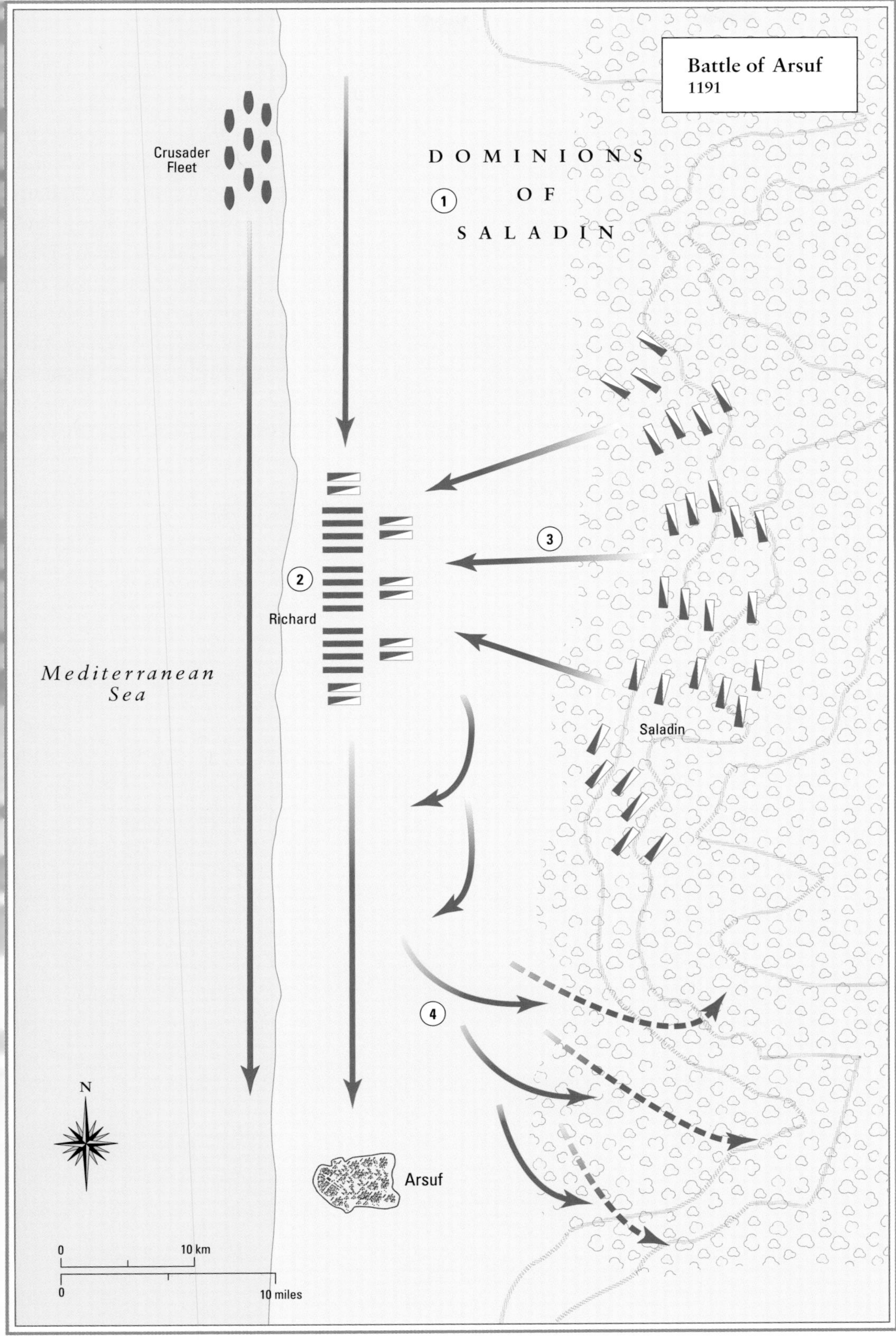

1. Saladin's scouts shadow the Crusader army as it leaves camp.
2. The Crusader army advances. Its most experienced and reliable units are placed at the front, rear, and landward flank. The fleet sails in parallel, thus able to resupply the advancing army.
3. The Ayyubid army launch its first attack, rushing the advancing Crusaders from the nearby cover of woodland. This determined attack fails to disrupt or slow the Crusader's advance towards Arsuf.
4. After suffering continuous harassment during the march, some mounted elements of the Crusader army begin to counterattack. This turns into a full, though unplanned, counterattack which drives off the Ayyubids.

Sunnis, Shi'ites, and Khariji 660–c. 1000

As a monotheistic faith, Islam shares many of the same beliefs as Judaism and Christianity, though it differs on important details. Muslims believe that God's message has been communicated to humanity via a series of prophets, including Abraham, Moses, and Jesus, with the final revelation being given to Muhammad, 'seal' of the Prophets. Muslims are required to surrender themselves to the will of God as revealed in the Koran—the record of divine revelations given to Muhammad—and to act in an ethical manner in emulation of the Prophet's custom, known as the sunna. All Muslims are expected to observe the five 'pillars' of Islam, comprising belief, prayer, fasting in Ramadan, charity, and once-in-a-lifetime pilgrimage to Mecca.

The major cleavages in Islam revolve around the question of leadership, going back to the death of the Prophet in 632. It came to a head in the first civil war (656–661) and its aftermath in the following generation (680–81). On the Prophet's death, leadership passed to Abu Bakr, Muhammad's father-in-law and one of the oldest Companions, with leaders from different groups giving him the oath of allegiance. However, there were some Muslims who thought the caliphate should be vested in Ali ibn Abi Talib, Muhammad's first cousin and husband of his daughter Fatima. Hence there was a division between the elective versus the hereditary principle in the choice of leader. When Abu Bakr died in 644, after reuniting the tribes following a period of disorder, the caliphate passed to Umar (634–44), an early convert to Islam and a born leader, who presided over the first great wave of Arab conquests beyond the Arabian peninsula. Murdered by a Persian slave, he was succeeded by Uthman (644–56), a devout Muslim but with family links to the Meccan clans that had opposed Muhammad before their late conversion to Islam. Uthman's policy of appointing members of his own clan as provincial governors led to accusations that he benefited his clansmen at the expense of Muslims of higher religious standing, and he was assassinated in 656.

Though Ali (656–61) now assumed the caliphate, his rule was contested by the kin of Uthman and others who disputed the validity of his election. Ali's failure to punish Uthman's murder so incensed two of Muhammad's earliest companions, Talha and Zubayr, that they rebelled, being supported by Aisha, Muhammad's young widow. Ali defeated the two in battle, but failed to beat Muawiya, Uthman's kinsman, the Governor of Syria, at the indecisive Battle of Siffin. Ali and Muawiya reached a compromise that provoked a rebel-

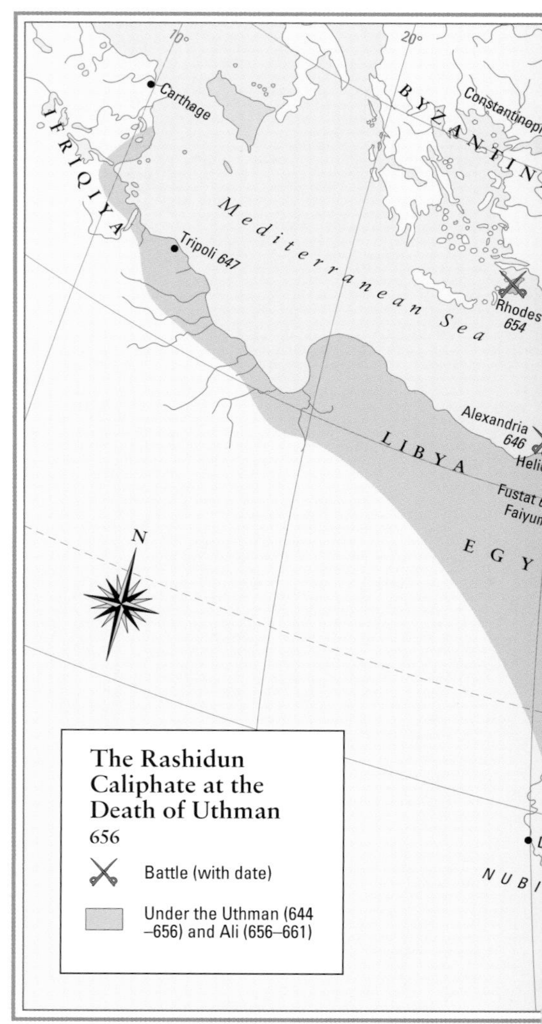

lion amongst his more militant supporters, who came to be known as Kharijis, or Seceders. Although Ali managed to defeat the Kharijis in July 658 at the Battle of Nahrawan, many of them survived to continue the movement which transmuted into Ibadism, a moderate form of Islam. Ibadism is found mainly in Oman and Zanzibar, with small communities at M'zab in Algeria, Jerba in Tunisia, and Jebel Nafusa in Libya.

One of the Khariji leaders, Ibn Muljam, sought revenge and assassinated Ali in the mosque at Kufa in 661. Ali's elder son Hasan negotiated peace with Muawiya who became the first Umayyad caliph. On Muawiya's death in 680, the succession passed to his son, Yazid, but this was contested by Ali's younger son, Hussein, who attempted to regain the caliphate for the Prophet's line of descent. Hussein, his supporters, and several sons were killed by Yazid's soldiers on the Plain of Karbala, south of Baghdad, though one survived to keep his lineage going. In due course, the majority of Muslims who accepted the legitimacy of the Umayyads became known as Sunnis. Those who followed Hussein and his descendants from the Prophet's family became known as Shi'ites, partisans of Ali. The death of Hussein at Karbala is commemorated in passion plays throughout the Shi'ite world, including Iran and Iraq (where Shi'ites form majorities), and Bahrain and Pakistan, where they are minorities living under Sunni majority rule.

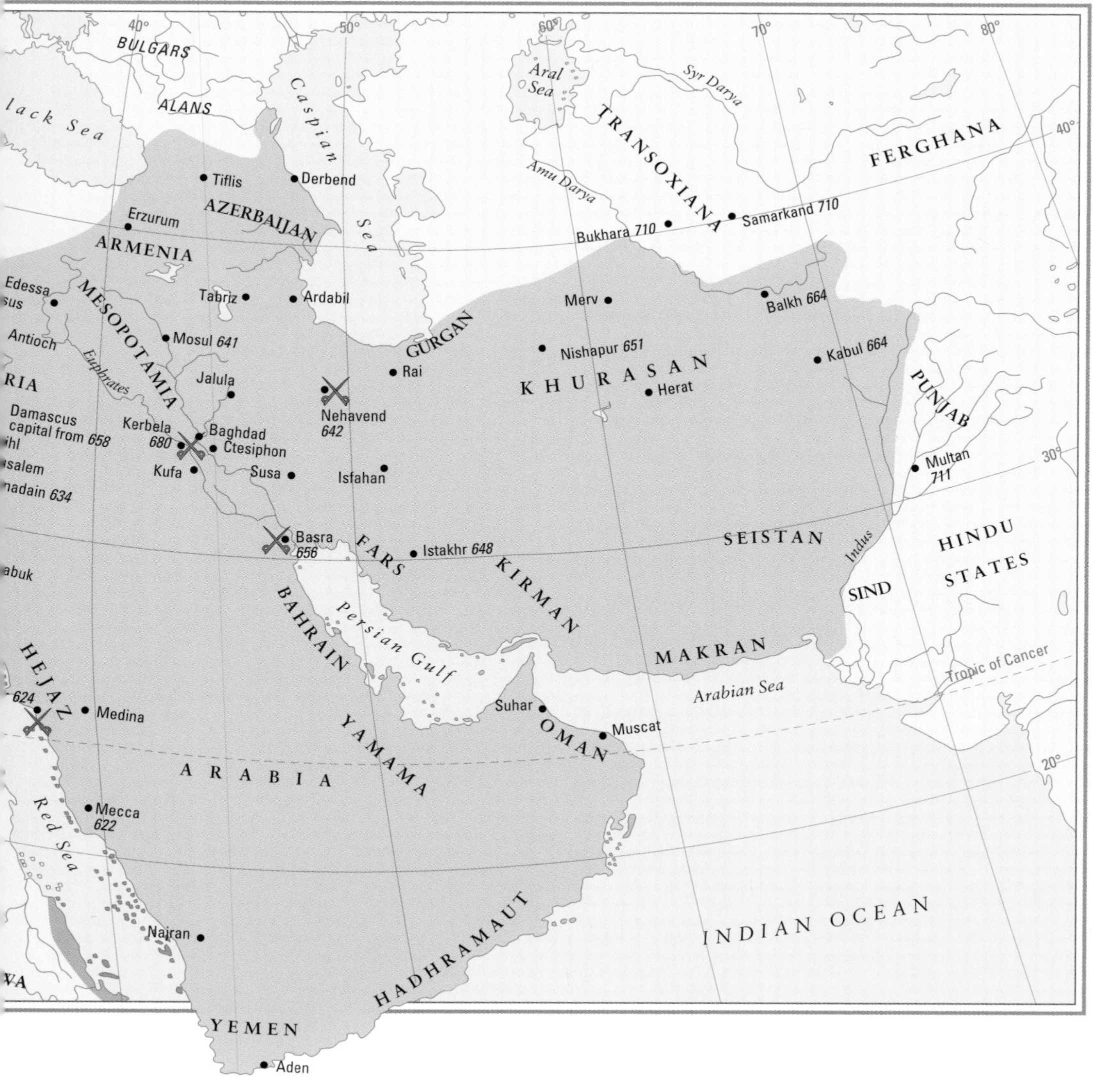

The Mongols and Ayn Jalut 1260

Ghengis Khan's warlike empire-building career extended his rule over the Eurasian steppes. To his west, the Saljuq Sultanate in eastern Persia and Transoxiana had dissolved, giving rise to the Turkish Khwarazmian Dynasty with its capital at Samarkand. In 1219, this new Empire was totally destroyed by the Mongols. Ghengis's successors, Ogedei and Quyuk, went on to conquer southern Russia and defeated the Saljuqs of Anatolia at the Battle of Köse Dagh in 1243, making the region a Mongol protectorate. The Near East became the next target when the Great Khan Mongke sent his brother, Hulegu, on a mission of conquest.

This illustration, from a Persian manuscript, shows Ghengis Khan ascending his throne in the spring of 1206.

Hulegu was given a variety of tasks: destroy the fortresses of the Nizari Ismailis, known as the 'Assassins', who had survived Saladin's destruction of the Fatimid Empire; make the Abbasid Caliph submit; and bring Syria and Egypt into the Mongol realm. In the event, Hulegu established his own Ilkhanate in Iran and Iraq. Hulegu's campaign began in 1253. He attacked the Assassins, then reached Baghdad in 1258. The Caliph's army was defeated by the feigned-retreat tactic. The city itself capitulated and some 200,000 people were slaughtered. Envoys were despatched to the Mongol camp by leaders from Upper Mesopotamia and Syria while Christian Armenia and Georgia allied with the Mongols. The vassal Saljuq Sultans of Anatolia offered their troops to Hulegu. Even Bohemond VI of Antioch made submission to Hulegu. Only Egypt and a few cities in Syria and Arabia were left to the Islamic heartland. Hulegu sent envoys to Egypt demanding that Kutuz, the Mamluk Sultan, surrender to him.

Kutuz refused Mongol demands, possibly because he was reinforced by his commander Baibars and his men, who had been campaigning elsewhere as mercenaries for several years. Another reason for making a stand was the retreat of Hulegu and most of his forces in 1259, caused by the death of Mongke, which meant a Mongol council had to choose a new Great Khan. Hulegu was thought to be a supporter of Kublai, who was opposed by Berke of the Golden Horde to the northwest of his lands. The remainder of the Mongol force was left in the command of Kitbuqa, who was trusted to consolidate Mongol conquests in Syria. He commenced actions by sending troops to Gaza and Nablus while raiding Hebron, Ascalon, and Jerusalem. On 26 July 1260, Kutuz left Cairo with a well-trained Mamluk force, together with soldier refugees of the Khwarazmians, Ayyubids, Kurds, Bedouin, and Turcomen. All told they might have numbered 20,000 men.

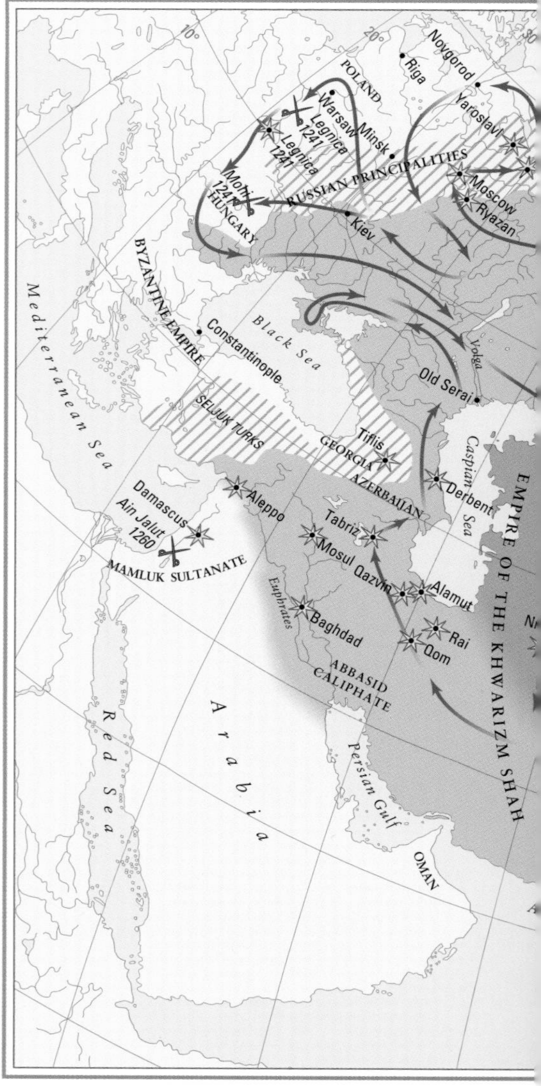

Baibars led the vanguard, managing to push a Mongol detachment forward from Gaza, then northward. The Mamluk force followed, crossing Crusader lands and encamping near Acre. Kutuz learned that Kitbuqa had entered Galilee and pitched camp at Ayn Jalut, the Spring of Goliath, at the foot of Mount Gilboa. The Mongol force numbered some 12,000 men, many of whom were Georgian and Armenian auxiliaries, and some riders from disbanded Ayyubid armies. The battle began on 3 September, with the Mongol right defeating the Mamluk left. The Mamluks, drawn from Kipchak Turks, also used the feigned-retreat tactic. Kutuz fought bravely, leading his bodyguard into the fray, causing the Ayyubids to desert the Mongols. Kitbuqa was killed in combat and the Mamluks defeated the previously unstoppable Mongol horse archers. The Mongols retreated, abandoning Damascus and Aleppo and their run of success was ended.

Mamluk victory can be explained in a number of ways: their horse-archers were an asset; they were better disciplined; their bows were more robust, better made, and could fire heavier arrows farther than the Mongols could. Thus, the Mongols were outshot and outmaneuvered. The Mamluks trained every day and knew how to fight as a unified force. The Mamluk victory gave them Syria, and Upper Mesopotamia was controlled by an ally. Ultimately, Kutuz was not so fortunate; he was murdered by Baibars when out hunting.

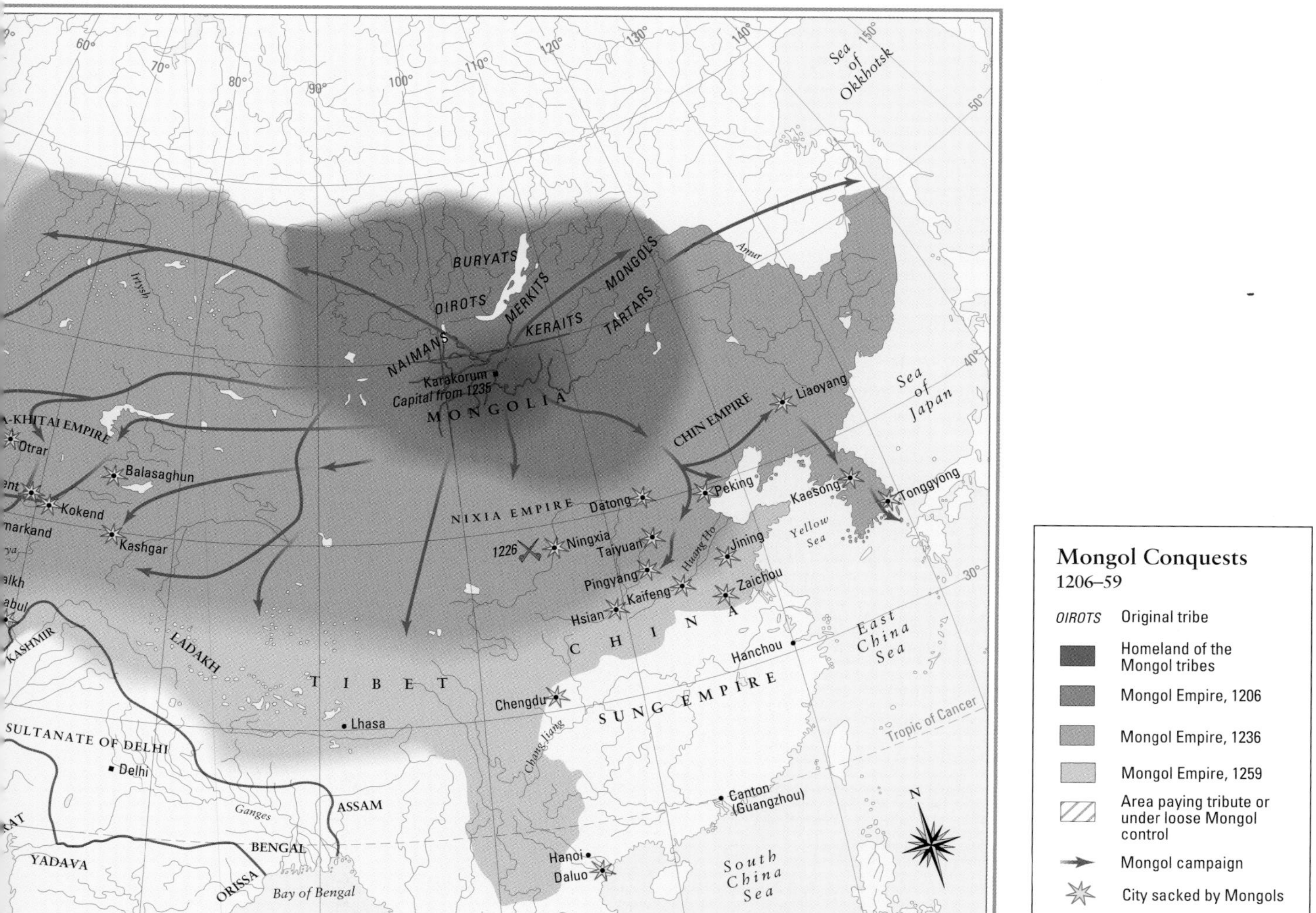

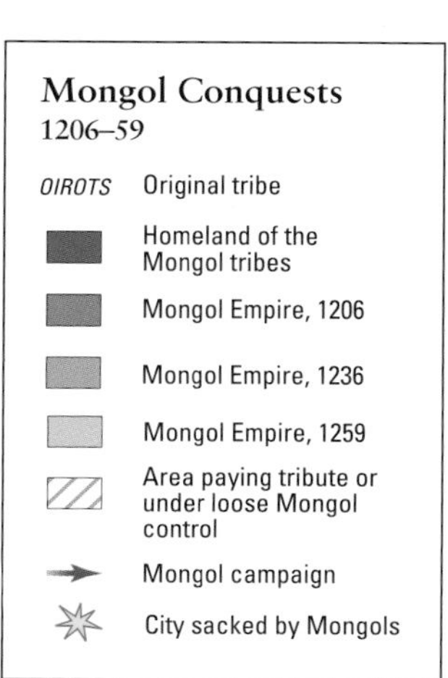

Mamluk Power

After the Battle of Ayn Jalut against the Mongols, Baibars killed Sultan Kutuz, the last Ayyubid Sultan of Egypt, seizing the throne for himself, supported by his Mamluk soldiers thus inaugurating 250 years of Mamluk rule. Over the next few decades, the Mamluks fought off Mongol campaigns of revenge and confronted the Crusader states.

In December 1260, a 6,000-strong Mongol force raided into northern Syria, then faced 1,500 riders of the Mamluk Sultanate at the First Battle of Homs in 1269, where they were decisively defeated. Baibars later decided to attack the Saljuq Sultanate of Rûm. This Mongol protectorate, which fielded an army of Mongols, Georgians, and Rumis, was destroyed by Baibars but he retreated back to Syria, dying shortly thereafter in 1277. A Second Battle of Homs occurred in 1281. This was really a drawn battle, which resulted in the Ilkhanate ruler converting to Islam and negotiating a peace treaty with the Mamluks. A Mongol invasion took place between 1299 and 1300, leading to a Mamluk defeat at the Battle of Wadi al-Khanzandar in 1299, with the Sultan's forces pursued back to Gaza. However, the Mongols withdrew to fight their kin from the Chagatai Khanate, which allowed the Mamluks to retake Palestine and Syria. In 1303, a final battle occurred at Marj al-Saffar; this ended in a Mongol defeat which kept the Mongols away from the Sultanate until 1399.

In the Crusader states, Baibars attacked the Principality of Antioch capturing the city in 1268 with all of northern Syria following. In 1291, Acre was taken, thereby ending the Crusading project in the Near East. By this time, too, the Sultanate had expanded into the upper Euphrates valley and Armenia.

Baibars was a member of the Mamluk Bahri Dynasty, which originated from Roda Island in the Nile. In 1382, the last Bahri Sultan was deposed and replaced by a Circassian dynasty, the Burjis, led by Barakh and Barkuk. In the late fourteenth century Syria became a battleground between the Mamluks, the emerging Ottoman Empire, and the Turkoman Timur the Lame. When Barkuk died in 1399, the Ottoman Bayezid I invaded Syria. This conflicted with Timur's interests, and he took Aleppo and Damascus, only for Egypt to regain these lands after Timur died. Ottoman ruler Bayezid II captured Adana, Tarsus, and other Mamluk lands and, in 1517, after a war the Sultan, Selim I, incorporated Egypt and its dependencies into the Ottoman Empire, but retained the Mamluks as a ruling class.

The Mamluks did not simply concentrate on war. Islam flourished as did scholarship and medicine. Building projects included irrigation works, canals, mosques, seminaries, and inns. However, Mamluk civilization reached its apogee before the Circassian Dynasty came to power and it was the Burjis who presided over Mamluk decline. The population declined, ravaged by a series of plagues, and this hastened economic decay. The tax burden had to be increased to finance military expeditions, such as the conquest of Cyprus in 1426. Another factor depressing the economy was the development of Western naval power, which enabled the Portuguese to attack Arab trade in the Red Sea, which had a negative impact upon the Muslim commercial communities down the east coast of Africa. The Portuguese seized Kilwa and sacked Mombasa in 1505, then established trading stations in Zanzibar and Pemba. In 1509, the Portuguese were victorious over a combined Egyptian-Indian fleet. Aden was occupied in 1513, and Hormuz, on the Persian Gulf, acquired in 1515.

The death blow for the Mamluks was the continued growth of Ottoman military power, which was based not just upon cavalry, but also artillery, a technology not espoused by the Mamluks. The Ottomans used not only siege guns, as in the final assault on Constantinople in 1453, but also developed a variety of new field artillery.

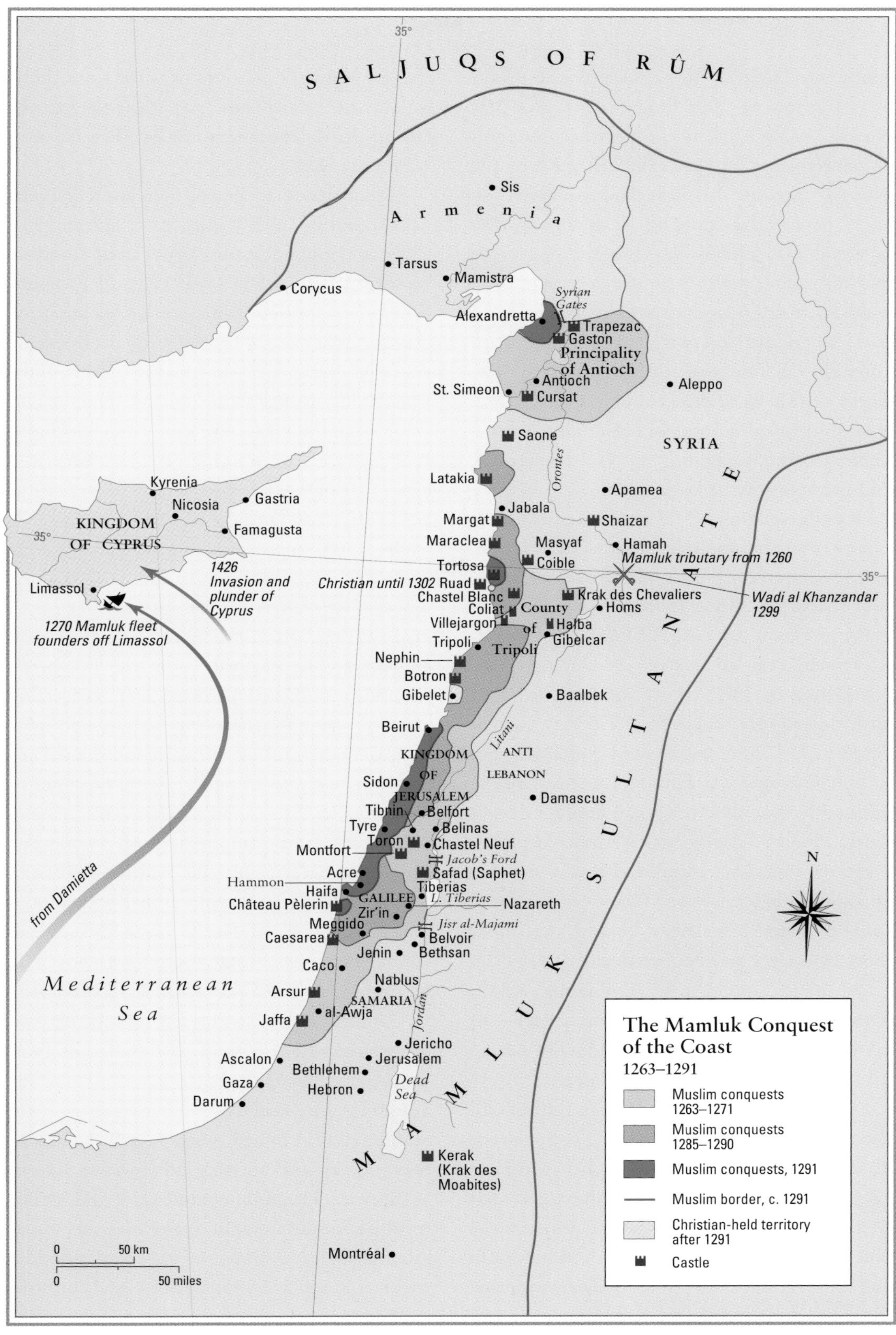
SALJUQS OF RÛM
Sis
Armenia
Tarsus
Mamistra
Corycus
Syrian Gates
Alexandretta
Trapezac
Gaston
Principality of Antioch
Antioch
Aleppo
St. Simeon
Cursat
Saone
SYRIA
Latakia
Orontes
Apamea
Kyrenia
Nicosia
Gastria
KINGDOM OF CYPRUS
Famagusta
Jabala
Margat
Shaizar
Maraclea
Masyaf
Hamah
Mamluk tributary from 1260
Tortosa
Coible
1426 Invasion and plunder of Cyprus
Christian until 1302 Ruad
Limassol
Chastel Blanc
Krak des Chevaliers
Wadi al Khanzandar 1299
Coliat
County of Tripoli
Homs
1270 Mamluk fleet founders off Limassol
Villejargon
Halba
Tripoli
Gibelcar
Nephin
Botron
Gibelet
Baalbek
Beirut
KINGDOM OF JERUSALEM
Litani
ANTI LEBANON
Sidon
Damascus
Tibnin
Belfort
Tyre
Belinas
Toron
Chastel Neuf
Montfort
Jacob's Ford
Acre
Safad (Saphet)
Hammon
Haifa
Tiberias
GALILEE
L. Tiberias
Château Pèlerin
Nazareth
Zir'in
Meggido
Jisr al-Majami
Caesarea
Belvoir
Jenin
Bethsan
from Damietta
Caco
Nablus
Mediterranean Sea
Arsur
SAMARIA
Jaffa
al-Awja
Jordan
Jericho
Ascalon
Jerusalem
Bethlehem
Gaza
Hebron
Dead Sea
Darum
MAMLUK SULTANATE
Kerak (Krak des Moabites)
Montréal
0 50 km
0 50 miles
The Mamluk Conquest of the Coast
1263–1291
Muslim conquests 1263–1271
Muslim conquests 1285–1290
Muslim conquests, 1291
Muslim border, c. 1291
Christian-held territory after 1291
Castle

Timur the Lame's Dominions 1370–1405

Timur the Lame or Tamerlane rose to power by eliminating his brother-in-law, Mir Husein. Being of Turkic origin not Mongol, he nevertheless provided the last gasp of the Mongol appetite for war and conquest. In 1370, he became King of Transoxiana and imposed his rule on his subjects, ensuring that his realm, with its capital at Samarkand, was secure from nomad attack. He believed that he could recreate the domains of Ghenghis Khan and his successors. The world he inhabited was no longer unified but was split into a number of disintegrating khanates: the Chagatai, the Golden Horde, and the fragmented Ilkhanate.

An illustration of Timur's ruthlessness can be found when there was a power vacuum in the Ilkhanid Dynasty in Persia after its ruler died. In 1383, Timur began the conquest of Persia. By 1385, he had seized Herat, Khorasan, and all eastern Persia, with the rest falling by 1387. A key incident occurred with the capture of Isfahan. The city surrendered in 1387 and was treated mercifully, but it rebelled against Timur's tax system by killing his tax collectors and a number of soldiers. Timur's revenge was terrible. The massacre of the city's inhabitants was ordered and somewhere between 100,000 and 200,000 souls perished. One record states that more than 28 towers were constructed from about 1,500 heads each. Like Ghenghis Khan, Timur used terror to control the behavior of his citizens and enemies. By inducing peaceful surrender, he preserved his soldiers' lives.

Timur became involved in the affairs of the Golden Horde. He supported Tokhtamysh against a rival and then turned against him in a series of campaigns that finally brought Tokhtamysh to bay in the Siberian forests in the Battle of Kunduzcha in 1391. Timur then waged war against Georgia, Turkestan, and Armenia, conquering an expanse of empire from southern Russia and southward to Afghanistan, the Hindu Kush, northern India, Persia, and Mesopotamia.

The Timurid army was then launched into Azerbaijan in 1385, and he took Sultaniya in 1390, and Baghdad in 1393. Timur justified his campaigns as those of a good Muslim. When he invaded India in 1398, he proclaimed that the Indian Muslims were excessively tolerant of Hindus and should be punished. He advanced through the Punjab and reached Delhi, where the city was sacked and the population massacred. He returned home, bringing back elephants to create a new kind of heavy cavalry.

In 1402, his forces tore through Asia Minor, defeating the Ottoman Turks. At Ankara, he utilized the feigned-retreat tactic against the Ottomans' Serbian cavalry and captured the Bayezid Sultan. He seized Aleppo and sacked Damascus. However, he ensured that all artists, musicians, and artisans were spared, as at Isfahan, so that they could be taken to Samarkand and Bukhara to embellish the cities and benefit the economy. The rest of Damascus' population was slaughtered. Later on, he assaulted Russian principalities and dukedoms, advancing almost to Moscow. Timur planned to attack China but he died before that was possible, on 19 January 1405, at Otrar in Kazakhstan.

Timur's Empire collapsed rapidly. He had always seemed dedicated to the idea of punishment, rather than the consolidation of his domains. He failed to create the normal attributes of Empire, with a well-developed bureaucracy and creating links with religious authorities. He conquered peoples and if they rebelled, he did it again, rather than trying to attempt any accommodation. The use of fear and terror replaced conciliation and authority. He sought to conquer, not rule. It has been estimated that he was responsible for 17 million deaths and the depopulation of many regions.

Yet the arts and architecture were not ignored during his time. His home cities were beautified and became great centers of commerce. One cherished dream was to monopolize trade by reactivating the Silk Road and controlling its entire length. His campaigning destroyed much of the known world and, in so doing, transformed it. Although he was an ardent Muslim, he destroyed Islamic regimes. The destruction of Delhi ensured that the Sultanate of Delhi would not survive, and it was one of Timur's direct descendants who invaded India and replaced the Sultanate with the Mughal Empire. The defeat of the Ottomans gave the Byzantine Empire a respite for some 50 years. Victory over the Mamluks demonstrated their declining power, while the defeat of the Golden Horde allowed the rise of the Grand Duchy of Moscow. The assaults on the khanates meant that the Chagatai Khanate was destroyed and the Golden Horde so weakened that it disintegrated into the Kazan, Crimean, and Astrakhan Khanates. The weakened Nogai Horde, Kazan, and Astrakhan were conquered by the growing power and confidence of the Grand Duchy of Moscow in 1552 and 1556.

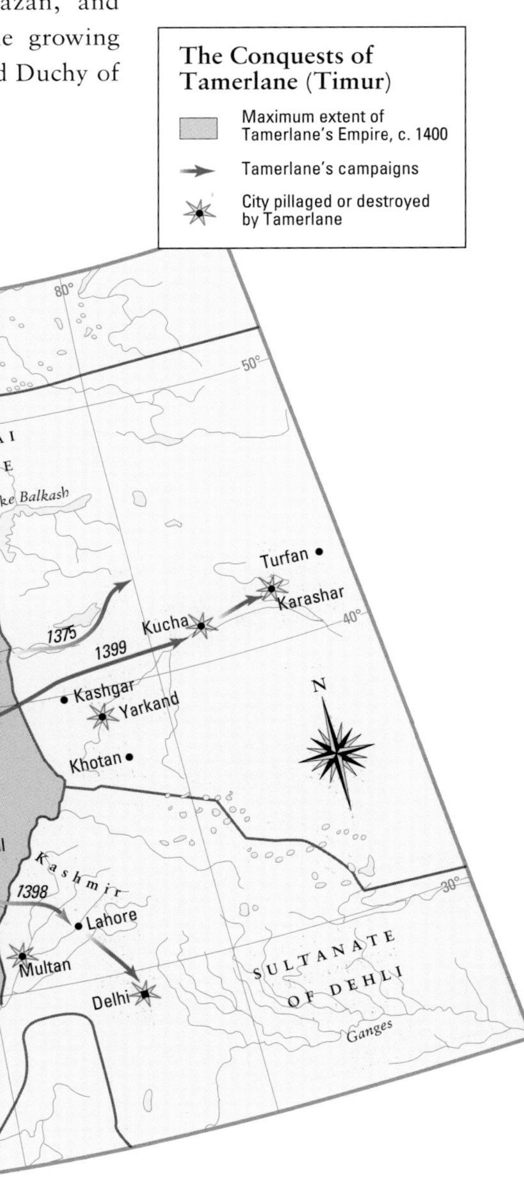

Spoils of War—the Command of Trade Routes 712–1300

The Arab conquests stimulated international trade by joining two sea routes together, one through the Red Sea and the other through the Persian Gulf. Arab expansion also created a vast free trade area of great benefit to both Arab and non-Arab merchants. By the ninth century international commerce was fueled by two powerful economies. The first was the Abbasid Caliphate, with its capital at Baghdad. The Empire's borders stretched along the Mediterranean coast, and reached across the Near East to Central Asia and India. The second powerhouse was the Tang Dynasty in China, which clashed with the Abbasids in Central Asia where Chinese expansion had been stopped by the Arabs at the AD 751 Battle of Talas. Trade routes joined the regions in a symbiotic relationship; the Silk Road was the land route, but a maritime connection also existed, with Arab traders sailing all the way to China and back until 878–79. Then, a Chinese rebel army, led by Huang Zhao, slaughtered some 26,000 Jews, Muslim Arabs, Muslim Persians, Zoroastrians, and Christians, all members of the foreign merchant class in Guangzhou. Afterward, Chinese traders tended to ship goods to the Palembang entrepôt where Arab and Indian vessels relayed the goods onward, using the Arab trading station at Kalah on the Malay Peninsula. The Indian Ocean had been sailed by Chinese junks since before the dawn of Islam; Indian Ocean traffic now came under Arabian control.

The wealthy Chinese desired ivory, incense, copper, black slaves, rhinoceros horn, fabrics, rugs, metal-ware, iron ore, bullion, pearls, coral, and aromatic woods from Persia, East Africa, and India. Chinese merchants traded Chinese ceramics, silks, and spices. Evidence for this trade exists in the writings of Al-Mas'udi (c. 896–956), an Arab historian and geographer whose *Muruj al-Dhabab* describes ships from Basra, Siraf, Oman, and India and their merchandise arriving before 877. The Chinese traveler I-Ching met a Persian ship owner in Hong Kong, in 671, and another in 727. Chinese accounts described Persian voyages to Ceylon and Malaysia, and the use of large vessels to sail to Guangzhou. Evidence of trade is further strengthened by a navigation guide written by Kia Tan (730–835), a Chinese trader, who described the passage from Guangzhou to the Persian Gulf.

The inter-continental trade routes were first reported in the mid-first-century Greek-authored *Periplus of the Erythraean Sea* which depicted trade in the Red Sea and Indian Ocean, including the harbors of Sri Lanka and the west

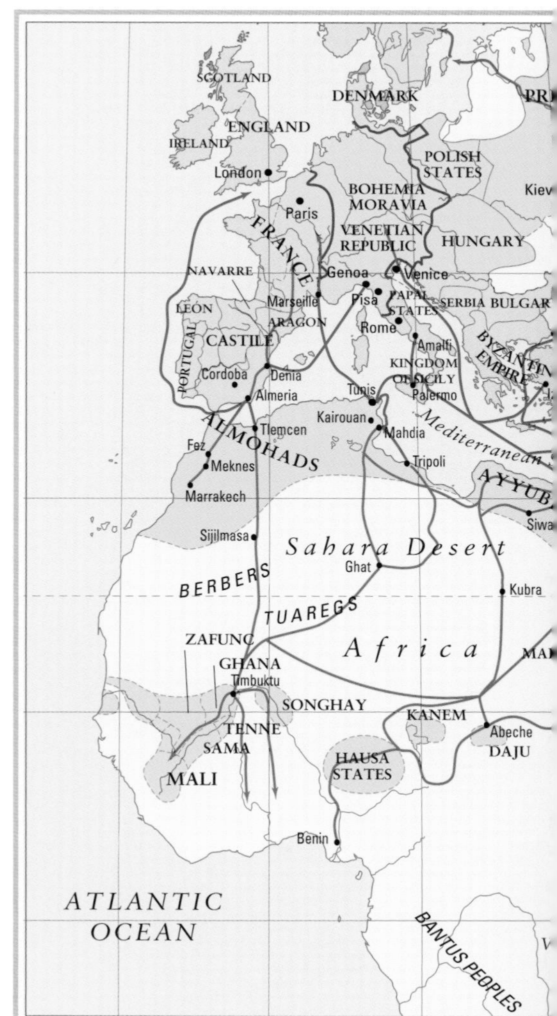

coast of India. The Prophet Muhammad's maternal uncle, Abu Waqqas, sailed from Ethiopia to Guangzhou in 616, and is buried there. In 1154, Al-Idrisi, a Moroccan geographer, published his *Geography,* which showed Chinese ships carrying iron, swords, leather, silk, and velvet to Aden, the Indus, and Euphrates. Marco Polo accompanied a princess sent by sea by Kublai Khan as a bride to the Persian Il-khan Arghun (1291/92) and Ibn Battuta's travels took him to the ports of Calicut and Quilon in India, Sudak in the Crimea, and Alexandria in Egypt, later visiting Fuzhou, Hangzhou, and Guangzhou. The world was becoming a network of global commerce negotiated by seafarers.

Other links in international trade were the Volga and the Dvina-Dnieper routes from northern Europe. The first connected the Caspian Sea to Scandinavia and vessels carried amber, furs, hides, and slaves, which could then be transferred to the Silk Road. The second route stretched between the Baltic and Black Sea, and Constantinople (Miklagarðr). Large silver hoards have been found in Scandinavia containing Arab silver coins. Over 40,000 have been found in Gotland alone. A bronze statuette of the Buddha traveled from northern India to the small island of Helgö in Lake Mälar in Sweden in the sixth or seventh century CE. This demonstrates that far-ranging trade contacts existed before the Viking era.

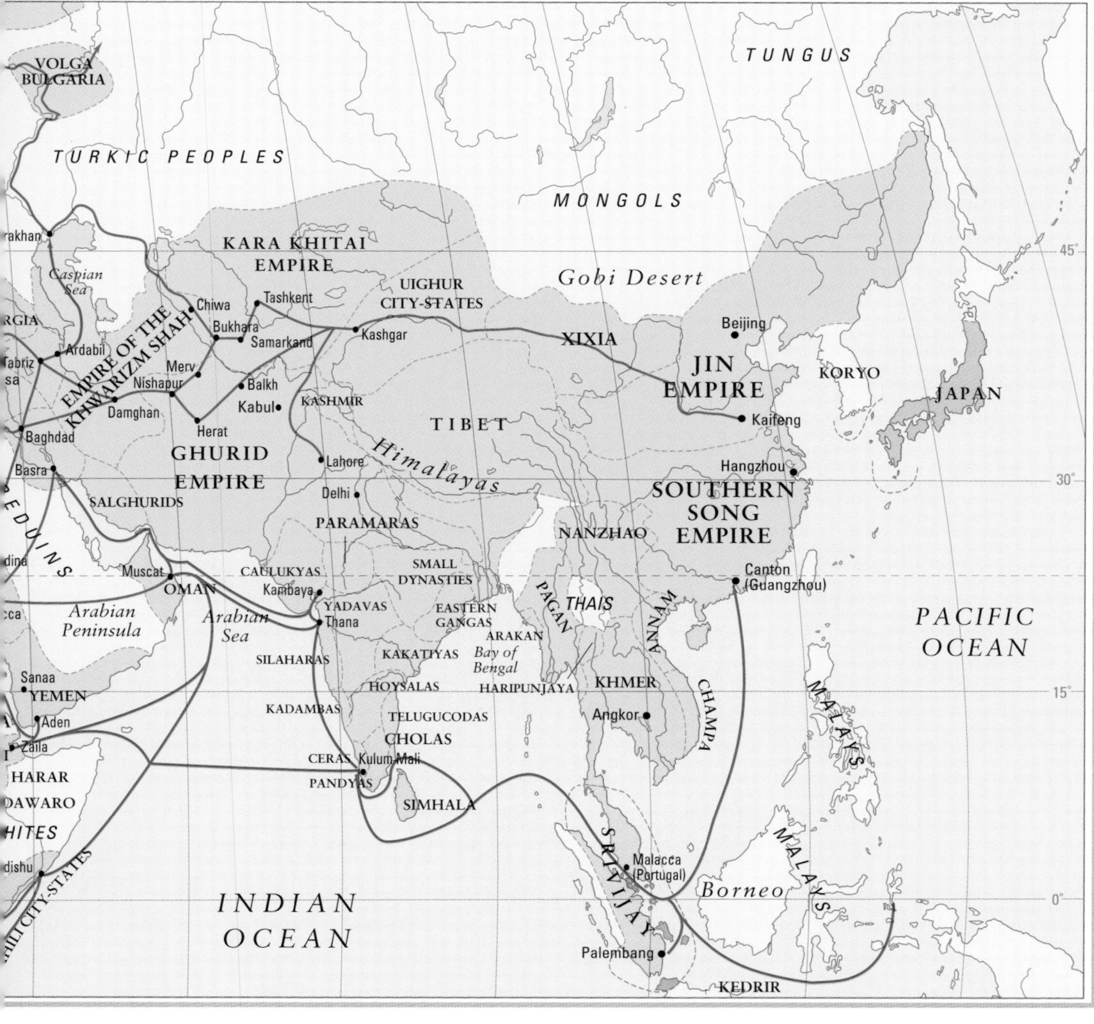

Trade Routes
c. 1200
Major trade routes

Ottoman Expansion 1328–1672

Süleyman bin Selim Khan, known to the west as 'the Magnificent', and in the east, as 'Lawgiver'. He ruled from 1520 to 1566 and this portrait is attributed to the Italian artist Titian.

The destruction of the Saljuqs in Anatolia in 1242–43 by the Mongols led to the political fragmentation of the region and the growth of several petty states, all vassals of the Mongols. One state ruled by the Osmanli dynasty made a bid for power, capturing Bursa, which they made their capital in 1326. When this Ottoman power raided Europe it was taking advantage of the Byzantine weakness that was a result of the damage incurred by the ravages of the Fourth Crusade. The Ottoman state expanded under Orkhan (c. 1324–1362), Sultan Murad (1360–1389), and Bayezid I (1389–1402). During these years continuous Ottoman expansion was achieved by both warfare and alliances.

By 1345, the Ottomans acquired the Karasi emirate and reached the Dardanelles. Led by Osman's son, Orkhan, the Ottomans crossed to Gallipoli in 1355 and gained a toehold in Europe. They soon occupied northern Greece, Macedonia, and Bulgaria, and gained control of the Balkans by decisively defeating the Serbs at the Battle of Kosovo Polje (The Field of Blackbirds) in June 1389. Despite being defeated by Timur the Lame at Ankara in 1402, this minor setback was wiped out by the storming of Constantinople in 1453, with the Byzantine capital falling to Sultan Mehmet II. The Byzantine lands of the Morea were finally overrun from May 1460 to the summer of 1461.

The Ottoman Empire then gradually spread and consolidated throughout the Balkans and into Hungary, defeating the Magyars at the Battle of Mohacs in 1526, and briefly besieging Vienna in 1528. The Ottomans then withdrew into Hungary and Romania while many Serbs and Croats moved into exile north of the rivers Sava and Danube where they acted as frontier troops to protect the Holy Roman Empire. Thus, the Habsburg Dynasty became the major buffer against further incursions. Over the next hundred years the Ottomans were pushed back but charged forward again to attack Vienna in 1683 when they were driven back by combined forces of Polish and German troops.

The Ottomans' European adventure is only part of the picture. During the Golden Age of Ottoman power under Süleyman I the Magnificent (1520–1566), Ottoman power was projected along the southern coast of the Mediterranean turning the sea into a virtual Ottoman lake. Cyprus, Rhodes, and Crete were acquired as defense bastions. Elsewhere, power spread through Mesopotamia to the Persian Gulf and into the Caucasus and Arabia and, with it, the eastern Red Sea coast. The Ottoman Navy roamed the Mediterranean and the Ottomans traded with most Mediterranean peoples, marginalizing the European trading centers of Genoa, Venice, and Marseille.

As lands were acquired by the Ottomans, they were usually occupied by an armed force, though not inevitably. Then, some regions were controlled by a Ottoman administration, while others simply paid tribute. Hence, Dubrovnik (Ragusa), Moldavia, and Wallachia paid tribute while the rest of the Balkans were directly ruled. Moldavia and Wallachia were governed by hospodars (princes) chosen by the Sultan and most of the officials were Christian. Christian princes and nobles such as Vlad Tepes of Wallachia or Marko Kraljevic were employed by the Ottomans. These willing tools of Ottoman command were more afraid of Habsburg power spreading than they were of the Ottomans. Ottoman rule was remarkably tolerant and was often less harsh than under Christian landlords. Christian peasants were left alone, provided they paid their taxes. Much provincial autonomy was retained with the tribesmen of Albania and Montenegro being virtually independent.

The Ottoman Empire became an essential ingredient in the European balance of power, often working with France against Austrian and Russian influence and expansion, thus creating a certain Ottoman stability.

HOLY ROMAN EMPIRE
POLAND
RUSSIA
HUNGARY
Vienna 1529
PODOLIA
Dniester
Dnieper
Donets
Volga
Buda
HUNGARY 1541
TRANSYLVANIA
MOLDAVIA
JEDISAN
KHANATE OF THE CRIMEA
Azof
BUJAK
Mohacs 1526
BOSNIA-HERZEGOVINA
Belgrade
WALLACHIA
Bucharest
Danube
Dobruja
Kaffa
CYRCASSIANS
Terek
Caucasus Mts.
VENETIAN REPUBLIC
Sarajevo
SERBIA
BULGARIA
Varna 1444
Black Sea
Adriatic Sea
Sofia
GEORGIA
NAPLES
RUMELIA
Sinope
Samsun
Trebizond
TREBIZOND
Constantinople 1453
Scutari
Otranto
Salonica
Erzerum
ALBANIA
Bursa
ARMENIA
KARASI
Ankara
Van
Aegean Sea
GERMIYAN
Ionian Sea
KARAMAN (CARAMANIA)
SHAHRZUR
Athens
AYDIN
HAMID
KURDISTAN
MOREA
Konya
MENTESHE
CILICIA
Adana
TEKKE
MESOPOTAMIA
Aleppo
Rhodes
Tigris
Crete
Cyprus
Famagusta
Mediterranean Sea
Baghdad
SYRIA 1516
Benghazi
Arabia
TRIPOLI 1551
Cyrenaica 1521
Alexandria
Jerusalem
Cairo
Aqaba
EGYPT 1517
HEJAZ 1517
Africa
Nile
Red Sea
Medina
Tropic of Cancer
N
0 200 km
0 200 miles
Mecca
20°
30°
40°
50°
Rise of the Ottoman Empire 1328–1566
Ottoman territory, 1328
Ottoman territory, 1355
Ottoman vassal from 1394
Ottoman territory, 1402 (prior to Mongol attack)
Ottoman territory, 1451
Ottoman territory, 1481 (Mehmet II)
Ottoman vassal from 1475
Ottoman territory, 1520 (Selim I)
Ottoman vassal from 1541
Ottoman territory, 1566 (Suleiman I)

Struggle for Persia 1501–1785

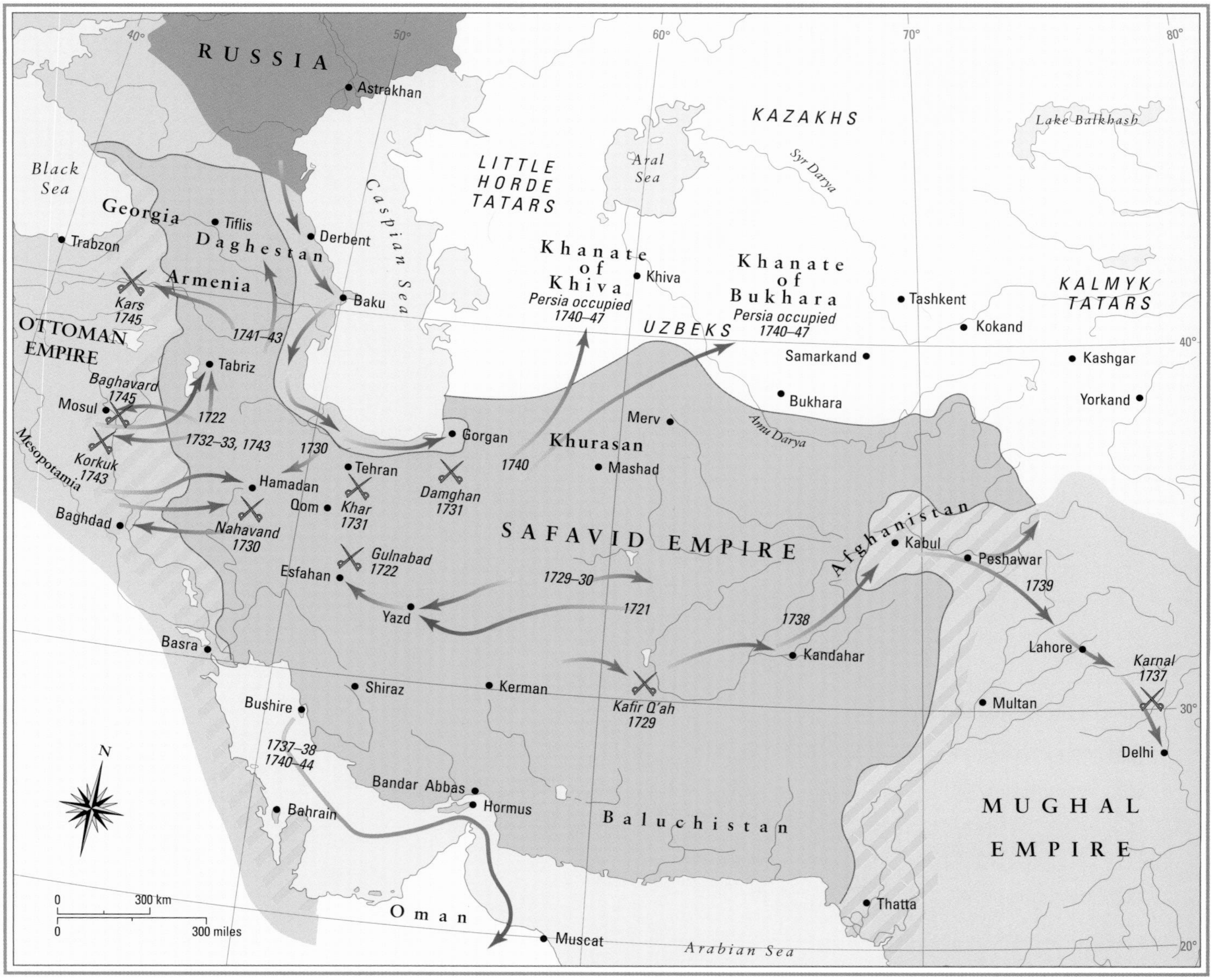

Persia or Iran disintegrated into rival mini-states after the destruction caused by Timur the Lame. Eventually, one militant Sufi brotherhood, the Qizilbash tribal group, backed Ismail, the last in line of the hereditary Grand Master of the Safaviyeh order, to be King. Using their military muscle, he united the various diverse territories in the decade following 1501, when he founded the Safavid Dynasty, becoming Shah. The Turkic-speaking Qizilbash confederation of tribes gained

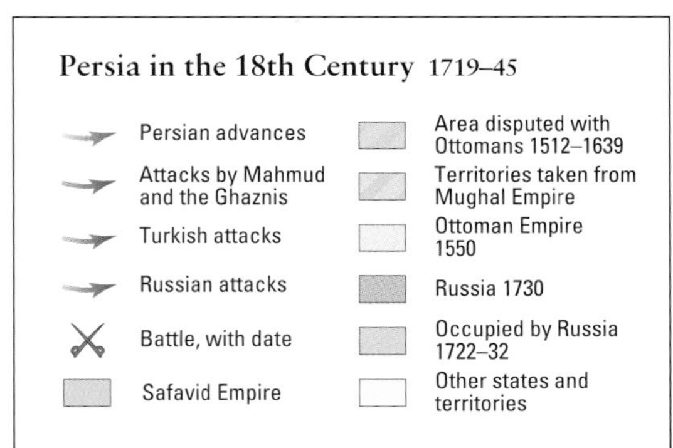

much influence in the realm, but warred amongst themselves, severely weakening the state in a civil war. It was at this point that the Ottomans in the west, and the Uzbeks in the north, encroached upon Persia, seizing territory.

The fifth Safavid Shah, Abbas I, decided to reform the state, diminish Qizilbash influence, and regain lost lands. Abbas gained power when he was just sixteen years old, and reigned from 1587 to 1629. He purged many of the Qizilbash from positions of power, only keeping those imbued with personal loyalty to the Shah. He then promoted people of various ethnic backgrounds, based upon their abilities, to political and military positions, turning the Safavid state into a meritocracy. Abbas employed two mercenaries, the English Shirley brothers, Anthony and Robert, who arrived with 5,000 horses to train the Persians after the English military fashion and also reform and retrain the artillery force.

Abbas knew that the Qizilbash would always constitute a large part of Persian armed forces but he created four Royal formations with personal loyalty to the Shah, a standing army. The first unit was the Shahsevans or Qizilbash, with personal loyalty to Abbas, comprising 12,000. The second type of soldier were the Gulams or Georgian, Armenian, and Circassian slaves from the Caucasus, who were trained into a 15,000-strong cavalry force. Thirdly, a 12,000-strong musketeer corps was trained using contemporary high-quality weaponry. Finally, an Artillery Corps of 12,000 men under French direction was created, which depended on foreign equipment until the Persians became self-sufficient in weapons manufacture.

Abbas began his military campaigns against the Uzbeks in 1597. He fought hard to recapture the city of Mashhad and, in 1598, defeated the Uzbeks at Herat, and pushed them beyond the River Oxus, which led to the re-conquest of eastern Khurasan. Abbas then decided to settle scores with the Ottomans, and the Battle of Sufian took place near Tabriz. Engagements with the Ottomans were successful and Abbas regained lands lost to Turkey: Tabriz, Erivan, Shirvan, and Kars. His next project was to deal with Portuguese encroachments. With English help, the Portuguese were pushed out of Bahrain and from Hormuz on the Persian coast. Abbas then negotiated arrangements with the English East India Company and the Dutch East India Company for mutual commercial gain.

Persia began to decline as the English and Dutch cut it off from commercial sea routes. Enemies crossed the borders from Mughal India, seizing Kandahar. Baloch tribes raided, Tsarist Russia encroached from the north, and the Hotakis Dynasty of Afghans took part of Khurasan. The Safavid Dynasty first fell in 1722 and a military leader named Nadir declared himself Shah in 1736. In 1729, seeking to restore the Safavids, Nadir had defeated the Ghilzai Afghans at the Battle of Damghan, damaging the Afghan Hotaki dynasty beyond repair and ending their seven-year rule over parts of Persia. In the Siege of Kandahar (1737–38), Nadir took the city and razed it to the ground. He captured Kabul, Peshawar, and Lahore. From 1730–35, Nader's forces expelled the Ottomans from western Persia and seized Georgia and Armenia.

In 1739, Nadir invaded India and at the Battle of Karnal defeated the Mughal Emperor. Delhi was sacked, the treasury looted, and the famous Peacock Throne stolen. The value of the booty allowed Nadir to stop collecting taxes for three years. In fact, the indemnity levied upon the Mughals was the equivalent today of almost half a billion dollars. In 1745, Nadir was victorious over the Ottomans at the Battle of Baghavard, which ended with a peace treaty in which the Ottomans recognized Nadir as Shah.

In 1746, the oppression and cruelty of his rule led to his assassination and the disintegration of Persia into civil war as rival military figures vied for power. Khiva and Bukhara regained their independence. The chaos only ended in 1796 when the Qajar dynasty achieved power, which lasted until 1925. Meanwhile, Russia expanded under Tsar Alexander I who seized Derbent, Baku, Shirvan, Shaki, Karabakh, and part of Talish.

Ottoman Decline

Mohammed VI, Sultan of Turkey, the last Caliph of Islam from the Ottoman Dynasty. He was elected by the Turkish National Assembly in November 1922. He was deposed and expelled from Turkey in March 1924.

Flaws and decay began to appear in the Ottoman state as a consequence of administrative weakness, corruption, lack of centralization, religious conservatism, and poor quality leadership. Added to these was disaffection amongst the Janissaries, the loss of Mediterranean trade to Greek, Slav, and Italian merchants, and defeats on the battlefield.

Fratricide was prevalent in the ruling family, with a Sultan, upon succession, killing his brothers so they could not compete for the throne. However, many Sultans were weak, and a properly contested succession might have winnowed out the less able. Instead, many Sultans were unfit for their task and spent time in seclusion unconcerned that reform of the state was necessary. The succession was also susceptible to conspiracy and manipulation by the harem or court eunuchs. Six Sultans were deposed in the 150-year-long period after 1566. Many were controlled by powerful Grand Viziers (Prime Minister).

Originally nomads, the Ottomans inherited a Byzantine administrative system after the fall of Constantinople. The original cavalry army received land for military services and these 'Spahis' fed off plunder and the tax dues from the peasants on their land. However, as larger armies became necessary more land was required and as conquests ceased it became more difficult to increase the numbers of cavalry. The lack of soldiers was solved by a blood-tax, by which every five years one in five male Christian children were taken for religious conversion and training for the administration or the military, becoming Janissaries; this was the *devsirme* which was deeply resented, though offered advancement.

The Empire depended upon a stream of booty, but when expansion slowed then stopped the Sultans found it difficult to run both an administration and an effective army. Offices were bought and sold and corruption was rife. The Janissaries became ill-trained and loss status. Many were allowed to marry and live outside the barracks and some became traders on the side. In 1826, they mutinied and were gunned down by the Sultan's new artillery regiments. Despite these ills, Turkish power was capable of staging occasional comebacks, especially under a dynasty of Viziers supplied by the Köprülü family. This family of Albanian descent produced two effective ministers. The first became a symbol of anti-corruption, executing thousands. His son, Ahmed, spent his rule (1661–76) waging war. He conquered Crete and acquired Polish Podolia.

The first real sign of decline occurred in 1683, when Grand Vizier Kara Mustafa attacked Vienna. Victorious rescuing Poles advanced to Buda and Belgrade, and in 1699 the war ended with the Treaty of Karlowitz. Austria retained conquests in Hungary, Transylvania, Bosnia-Herzegovina, Croatia, and Slavonia; Venice kept Morean Greece and much of Dalmatia; Poland regained Podolia; Russia received Azov. Some lands were ultimately taken back but the Ottomans now faced a menacing Russia. Later European imperial powers threatened the more far-flung Ottoman possessions, while Balkan peoples were inspired to seek freedom through their own individual nationalist aspirations.

In 1768, Russia occupied Moldavia and Wallachia and, after the Napoleonic Wars, France took Algeria in 1830, and created a protectorate in Tunisia (1881). In the Balkans, the Greeks achieved independence in 1829 while a Russo-Turkish War (1877–78) saw the creation of an autonomous Bulgaria, Serbia, Romania, and Montenegro. Britain established a protectorate over Egypt in 1882, having interests in the Suez Canal and the Egyptian cotton crop, and Kuwait in 1899. Italy invaded Tripoli and Cyrenaica in 1911. In 1912, the states of Serbia, Bulgaria, Greece, and Montenegro seized all surviving Ottoman lands in Europe except for Constantinople's small hinterland. This first Balkan War was followed by a second when

Bulgaria attempted to seize territory from its former allies. Romania and the Ottoman Empire joined in attempting to gain from Bulgaria. At the outbreak of the First World War in 1914, Turkey was allied with Austria and Germany against France, Russia, and Britain. With the ultimate defeat of the Central Powers, the Ottoman Empire lost all its Arab-speaking provinces.

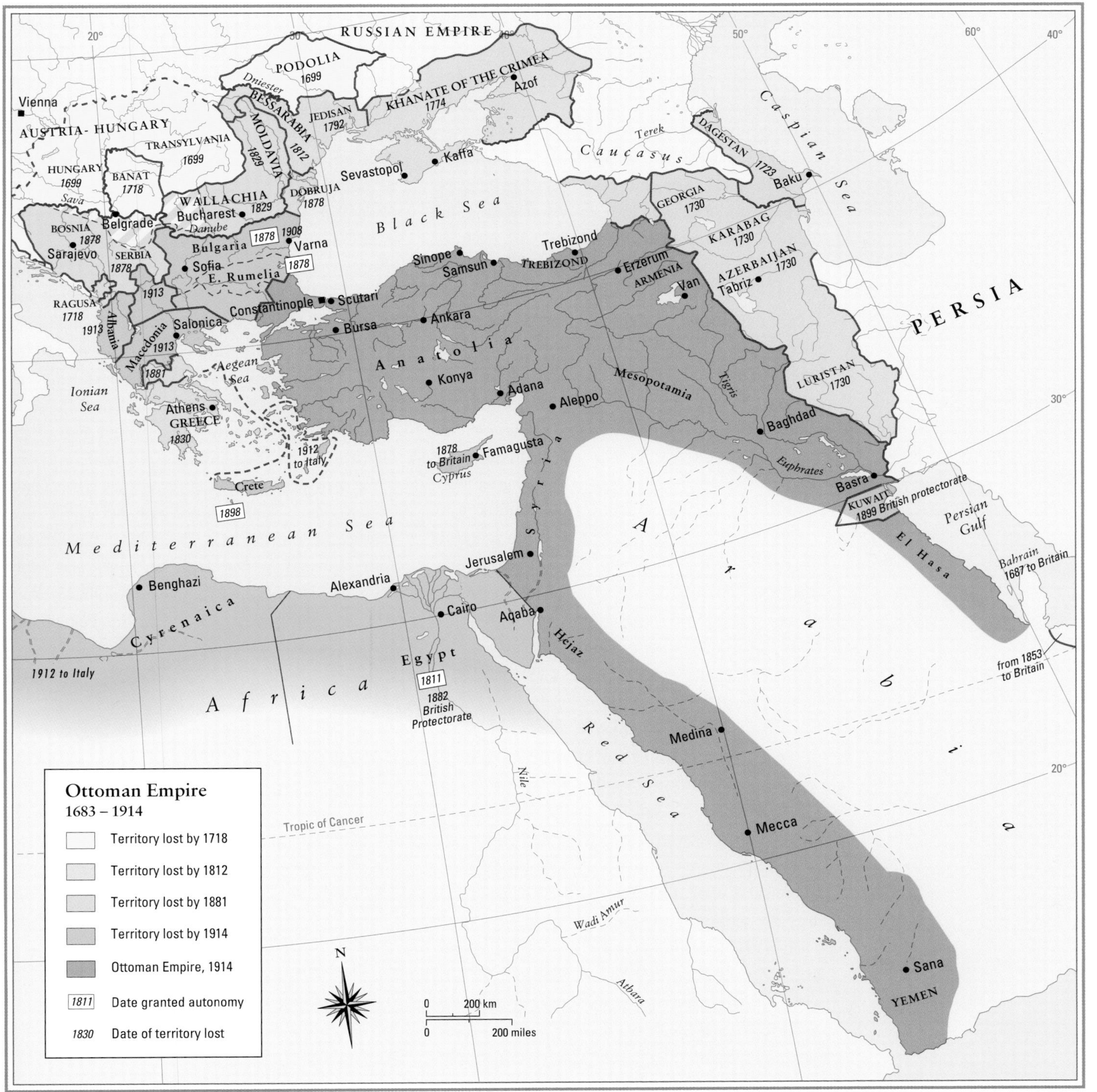

Rise of the Saudi State 1902–1929

The Arabian peninsula had been fought over by the al-Saud family and the pro-Ottoman al-Rashid family during the nineteenth century, with the al-Sauds finally expelled from Nejd after the Battle of Mulayda in 1891. One member of the family, Abd al-Aziz bin Saud (Ibn Saud), was determined to restore the family's fortunes. With supporters and family members, he scaled the walls of Riyadh's Mismak Fort in 1902 and was proclaimed ruler of Riyadh.

In his quest to re-establish his family's rule over the Nejd and to acquire other parts of Arabia, Ibn Saud was confronted by three main enemies. Firstly, there was the al-Rashid family in Ha'il, then the Hashemite Sharifs of Mecca in the Hejaz, and finally the Ottoman Turks in Al Hasa. Ibn Saud's success was achieved with the help of the Ikhwan (brethren), a movement of Beduin inspired by the austere Wahabi creed that underpinned the first Saudi State in the eighteenth century. They believed in persecuting non-believers and abhorred foreigners. The Ikhwan were organized into agricultural communities, called Hijras. The Hijras were spread over the Nejd, located in strategic places where they could be readily mobilized for war, sparing Ibn Saud the cost of creating a standing army. The problem was that the Ikhwan became so powerful that they could force Ibn Saud's hand.

In 1913, Ibn Saud had led 1,500 men from Riyadh, who then scaled the walls of the fort at Al Hufuf under cover of darkness driving the Turks out of Al Hasa and annexing both it, and Al Qatif, into the Nejd. Ibn Saud became the Imam as well as the Emir of Nejd and all tribal sheikhs were instructed in Ikhwan beliefs, directed to join this movement, and pay him taxes, and reside in Riyadh where the Imam could control them. They could not leave without his permission.

In 1921, Ibn Saud captured Ha'il and deposed the al-Rashid family. He was now Sultan of Nejd and its dependencies and controlled central Arabia. By 1922, the Wahabi forces were in control of all the desert oases from the Jordanian and Syrian borders to Oman. The Ikhwan not only threatened the Hejaz, but the territories of Iraq, Syria, and Transjordan, which were protected by Britain under the terms of the mandates it acquired from the League of Nations after the First World War.

In September 1924, the Ikhwan took the town of Taif, which they ransacked for three days, after which the inhabitants succumbed to Saudi rule. The following December Ibn Saud entered Mecca after its ruler, the Sharif Hussein, had abdicated in favour of his son Ali. The citizens were spared, but the Sharif's palaces were looted and the tombs of eminent Muslims destroyed. In January 1925 Ibn Saud's troops appeared before the last Sharifian stronghold of Jeddah and imposed a siege that lasted almost a year. In December 1925, following British mediation, the Sharif Ali left the city and Ibn Saud was proclaimed King of the Hejaz. Although Britain abandoned the Hejaz, it was determined to protect Iraq and Trans-Jordan, where two of the Sharif's sons had been installed as monarchs. Under agreements with Britain Ibn Saud recognized their borders,which Britain policed with its air force, preventing the Ikhwan raids. The Ikhwan rebelled and were defeated at the Battle of Sibila and other engagements in 1929. Their most prominent leader, Faysal al-Duwaysh, died in prison after being handed over by the British.

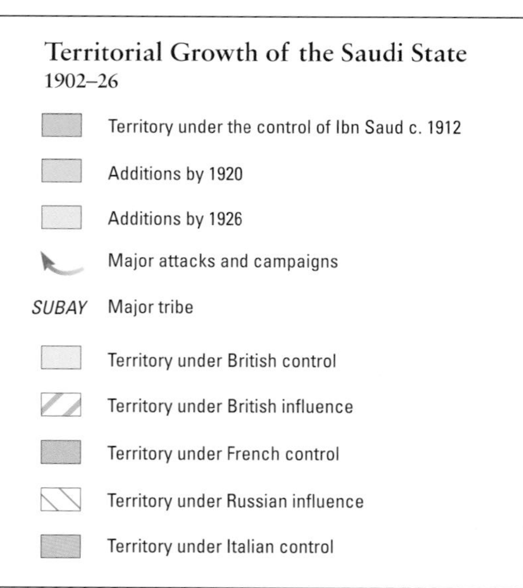

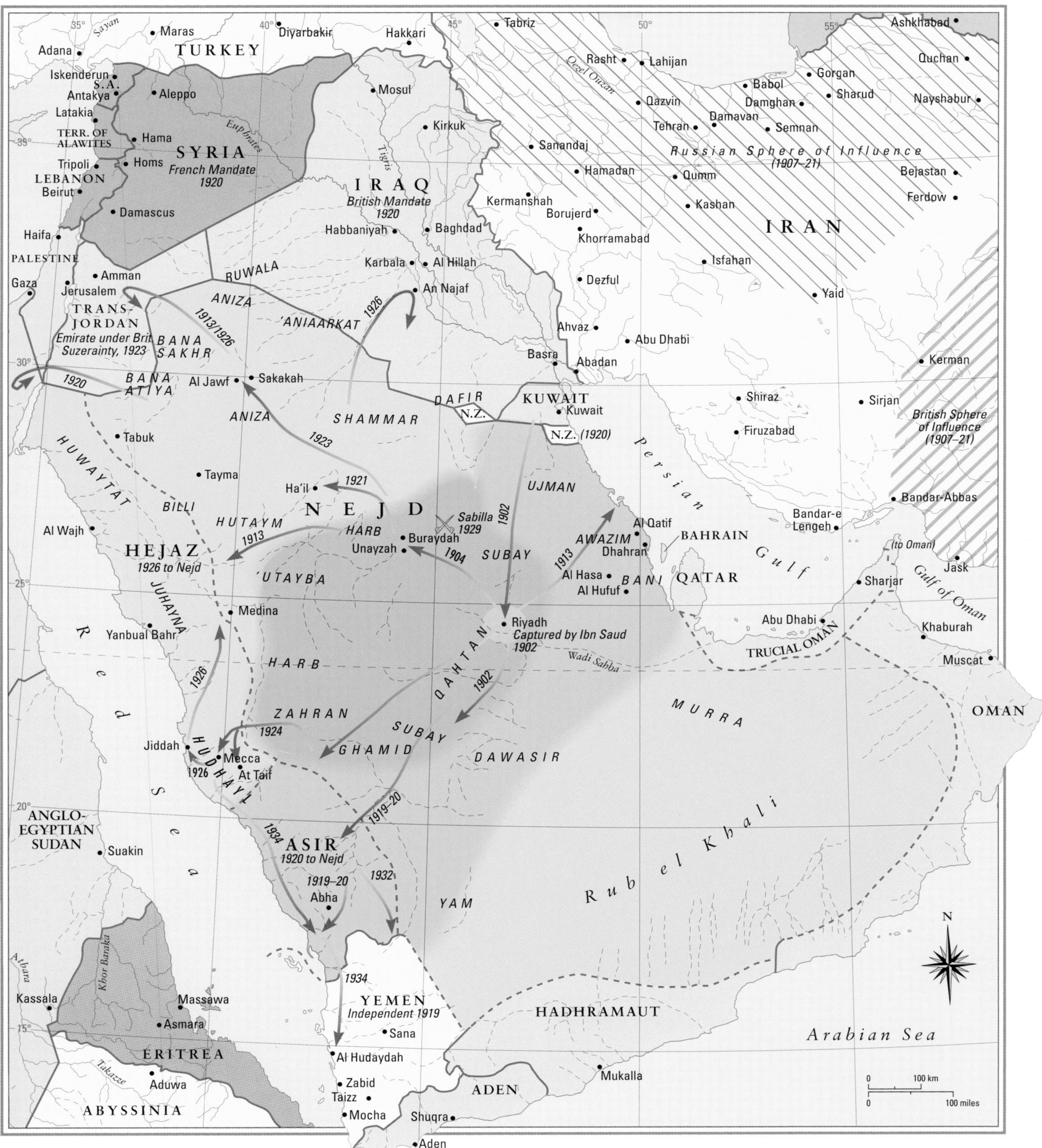
TURKEY
SYRIA
French Mandate 1920
IRAQ
British Mandate 1920
IRAN
LEBANON
PALESTINE
TRANS-JORDAN
Emirate under Brit Suzerainty, 1923
TERR. OF ALAWITES
S.A.
KUWAIT
N.Z.
N.Z. (1920)
NEJD
HEJAZ
1926 to Nejd
ASIR
1920 to Nejd
YEMEN
Independent 1919
HADHRAMAUT
ADEN
OMAN
TRUCIAL OMAN
QATAR
BAHRAIN
ANGLO-EGYPTIAN SUDAN
ERITREA
ABYSSINIA
Russian Sphere of Influence (1907–21)
British Sphere of Influence (1907–21)
Persian Gulf
Gulf of Oman
Red Sea
Arabian Sea
Rub el Khali
Euphrates
Tigris
Qezel Ouzan
Sayan
Wadi Sabba
Khor Baraka
Atbara
Takazze
RUWALA
ANIZA
'ANIAARKAT
BANA SAKHR
BANA ATIYA
ANIZA
SHAMMAR
DAFIR
UJMAN
HUWAYTAT
BILLI
HUTAYM
HARB
'UTAYBA
SUBAY
AWAZIM
BANI
JUHAYNA
HARB
QAHTAN
ZAHRAN
SUBAY
GHAMID
DAWASIR
HUDHAYL
MURRA
YAM
Sabilla 1929
Riyadh
Captured by Ibn Saud 1902
1902
1904
1913
1913/1926
1920
1921
1923
1924
1926
1919–20
1932
1934
Maras
Diyarbakir
Hakkari
Tabriz
Adana
Iskenderun
Antakya
Aleppo
Latakia
Hama
Homs
Tripoli
Beirut
Damascus
Haifa
Gaza
Jerusalem
Amman
Mosul
Kirkuk
Habbaniyah
Baghdad
Karbala
Al Hillah
An Najaf
Basra
Abadan
Ahvaz
Dezful
Kuwait
Rasht
Lahijan
Qazvin
Tehran
Damavan
Semnan
Babol
Gorgan
Damghan
Sharud
Sanandaj
Hamadan
Kermanshah
Borujerd
Khorramabad
Qumm
Kashan
Isfahan
Yaid
Abu Dhabi
Shiraz
Firuzabad
Sirjan
Kerman
Ashkhabad
Quchan
Nayshabur
Bejastan
Ferdow
Bandar-Abbas
Bandar-e Lengeh
(to Oman)
Jask
Sharjar
Khaburah
Muscat
Al Jawf
Sakakah
Tabuk
Tayma
Ha'il
Buraydah
Unayzah
Al Wajh
Al Qatif
Dhahran
Al Hasa
Al Hufuf
Medina
Yanbual Bahr
Jiddah
Mecca
At Taif
Abha
Abu Dhabi
Suakin
Kassala
Massawa
Asmara
Aduwa
Sana
Al Hudaydah
Zabid
Taizz
Mocha
Shuqra
Aden
Mukalla
N
0
100 km
100 miles
35°
40°
45°
50°
55°
30°
25°
20°
15°

European Intervention

During the seventeenth and eighteenth centuries, Europe had emerged as the most powerful region in the world, especially those countries with an Atlantic coastline. Only three major non-European powers still existed: the Ottoman Empire, Mughal India, and Manchu China. None of these states had a transoceanic military reach and all were declining in power. In Europe, Britain, France, Spain, Portugal, and the Netherlands all had intercontinental reach, while Russia had expanded into Asia by land.

Two technological factors helped to drive the rising tide of European power: better sails and improved gunpowder weaponry. The Portuguese ships commanded by Vasco da Gama, which rounded the southern tip of Africa in 1498, were larger and sturdier than the lateen-rigged dhows that previously dominated the Indian Ocean trade. They were soon improved upon by Dutch and British ships. Forged in the stormy waters of the Atlantic, European shipping was able to hold more cargo, to engage in longer journeys, and to carry powerful cannon. With the development of new artillery citadels, fortresses ceased to be impregnable, giving the military advantage to well-organized 'modern' powers, able to make the costly investment in cannon and other firearms. As military technology advanced, a shift took place in the balance of power between the traditional warrior classes, for whom military prowess was vested in notions of high-birth, group solidarity, honour, and courage—classic virtues of the traditional warrior class who formed the cavalry and infantry of Middle Eastern societies. It was these societies that frequently, though not always, lacked economic and technological investment and knowledge necessary to keep up with the latest military developments. Under European pressure the fragmented Muslim states that followed the collapse of the Arab caliphate and the Mongol invasions were consolidated into larger units dominated by the three great 'gunpowder empires' of Ottoman Eurasia, Shi'i Iran, and Mughal India.

An important consequence of the changes wrought by European control of the oceans was the decline of the overland trade route (the Silk Road) between China and the Mediterranean, from which the caliphs had garnered much of their wealth during the Muslim world's Golden Age prior to the Mongol invasions. At the same time the global ascendancy of Europe was driven by competition between European states. Britain and France had fought against each other in India and in North America. The French defeat at the Battle of Quebec in 1759 gave the British control of what would become Canada. In India the British East India Company's defeat of the Muslim ruler of Bengal and his French allies at the Battle of Plassey in 1757, set the scene for the expansion of British power under the vestigial presence of the Mughal Emperor. By the late eighteenth century Britain was the dominant Imperial power, though weakened when the United States won its independence in 1783.

These changes internationally were also facilitated by improved infantry weapons and the growth of professional armies. The matchlock had been transformed into the much lighter musket, which could be fitted with a bayonet, thereby making the pike redundant. The British used its version, nicknamed the Brown Bess, which fired a three-quarter-inch bullet, which had immense destructive effect when it found its mark. Soldiers fought in close-order drill and used volley fire against the enemy. Military structures changed with the French, the dominant power on Continental Europe, deploying a battalion of approximately 500 men with three battalions comprising a regiment. The eighteenth-century British regiment comprised ten companies of about eighty men. The traditional system of using a large number of mercenary troops to augment an already existing force was almost abandoned.

Since power was unevenly distributed, the changes brought about by what we would now call 'globalization' under European auspices were far from uniform. In India the great Mughal Empire was already in terminal decline, having been weakened from the east by British incursions from Bengal, from the south by the rise of the Hindu Marathas, and from the west by Afghan invaders and the Persian ruler Nadir Shah, who sacked Delhi in 1739. Some Muslim rulers, such as the Nizam of Hyderabad, went with the grain of the new forces, backing the British East India Company's increasingly professionalized army against his fellow Muslim ruler Tipu Sultan of Mysore.

Persia, a Shi'ite power since the Safavids made Ithna'shari Shi'ism the official religion from 1501, proved less susceptible to the consolidation of power emanating from Europe. The Qajars, who came to power in 1779, had to compromise with powerful tribal confederations within their own armies, making the dynasty vulnerable to manipulation by the Russians and British based in India. In 1828 Persia lost Erivan and Nakhchivan to Russia, as the Tsars, equipped with armies forged in the Napoleonic wars, pushed their way into Muslim Inner Asia.

In the Middle East, Southeast Europe, and North Africa the consolidation and centralization of Ottoman power, intended to strengthen the Empire's defenses, had the opposite result. The policy of administrative reform (*tanzimat*) weakened the autonomy of both Sufi lineages and local leaderships, provoking rebellions by the Empire's Christian subjects (aided by Russia and Austria), and by Arabs and others abetted by European powers. A significant theme in this period that continues to the present is the gradual—and contested—control by the centralizing state of tribal systems located in 'peripheral regions' such as mountains and deserts. The territorial map demarcating a ruler's possessions acquired a significance it did not have when power flowed through different levels of authority under a suzerain such as the Mughal Emperor or Ottoman Sultan-Caliph. Territorial nationalism, predicated on clearly demarcated geographical frontiers, began to replace ideas of allegiance rooted in tribal or religious ideas.

After the Suez Canal was constructed and opened in 1869, Britain regarded a friendly regime in Egypt as essential to protect the seaway to the Indian Raj. After Egypt was bankrupted by the cost of construction, the rebuilding of Cairo, and its empire-building adventures in the Sudan, Britain became one of the European financial controllers of Egypt, leading it to crush an anti-European nationalist uprising in 1882. The Khedive's son was installed as ruler and Egypt became a 'veiled protectorate' under a regime Britain controlled through financial leverage. In 1914, the protectorate became official and the then Khedive Abbas Hilmi II was deposed, having supported the Central Powers during the First World War, and his uncle, Husein Kamel, became head of state with the new title of Sultan, thereby renouncing any remaining Ottoman claim on the country.

Britain developed other interests in the Middle East, especially in the Arabian Peninsula. By 1892, Bahrain had become a British protectorate as Qatar had done before. The Trucial States became protectorates in 1892, while Kuwait became one in 1899. Elsewhere, Aden had been acquired in 1839, becoming a coaling station, and the hinterland of the Hadramaut became another protectorate. In Persia, Britain and Russia acquired spheres of influence. British geologists discovered oil and established the Anglo-Persian Oil Company in 1909, enabling the British navy to begin the switch from coal to oil in 1913.

During the First World War, new technologies, such as submarines and aircraft, made fighting even more difficult and dangerous. Without air superiority, and the consequent aerial attacks by bomb and machine gun, Allenby's final defeat of the Ottomans in Palestine would not have happened so quickly. When the Ottoman Empire joined the Central Powers in 1914, Britain regarded its defeat as essential in order to defend the Suez Canal and to protect British oil assets in Persia.

Until the early nineteenth century slavery was an infamous part of this emerging global scene. The transportation of slaves between Africa and the Americas was a vital part of the economic order, with Muslims engaged as slavers and victims.

Napoleon's Egyptian Adventures 1798–1801

When Napoleon Bonaparte landed in Egypt on 1 July 1798, the country was a province of the Ottoman Empire, controlled by Mamluk beys or emirs. His ambition was to protect French commerce in the Mediterranean, which was threatened by British shipping, and to use Egypt as a staging post to link up with Tipu Sultan of Mysore, India's last independent Muslim ruler, to drive out the British. After taking Alexandria, Bonaparte issued a proclamation falsely claim-

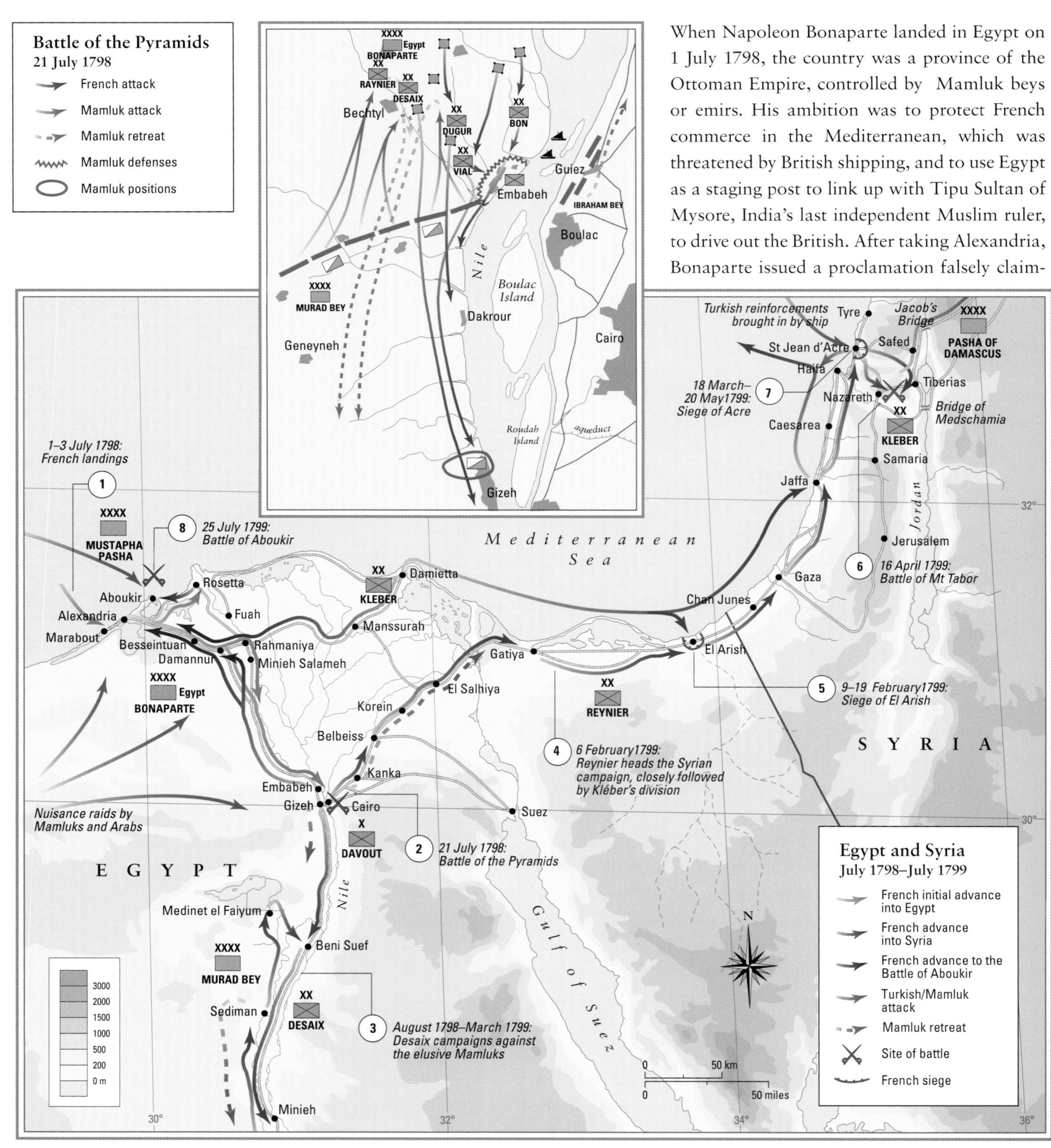

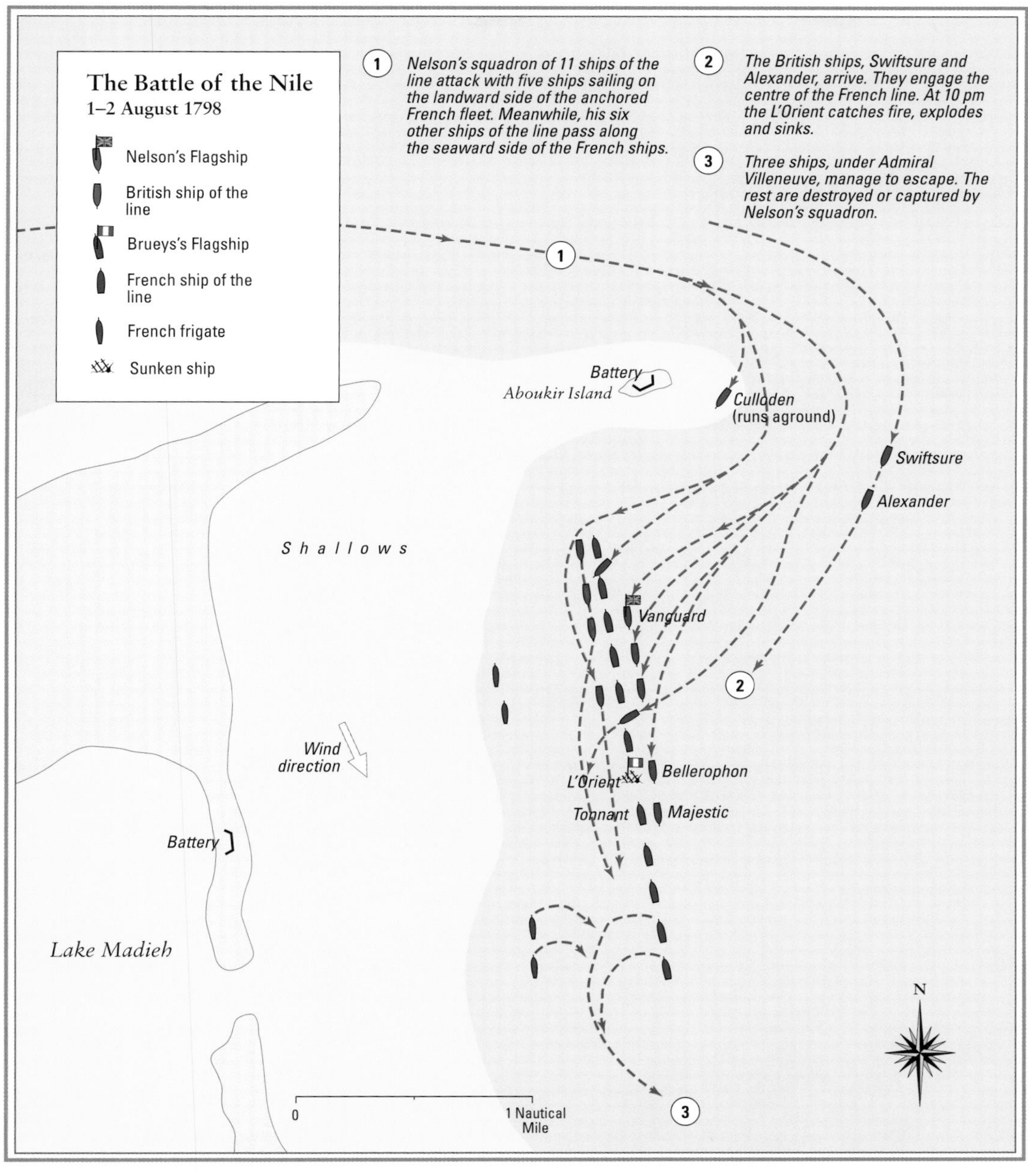

ing that he had been sent by the Ottoman Sultan Selim III to punish the rebellious Mamluk beys who had been cruelly oppressing the Egyptian people with their taxes. The proclamation declared that the French were 'muslims' in the sense that they believed in one God but that God 'has no son'—a clear rejection of Christian teaching. It claimed that, far from being a crusade to abolish Islam, the French had come to save Egypt from the oppressive Mamluk sultans and to restore the rights of the people in the name of liberty and equality. These claims were generally rejected, especially by the scholars of al-Azhar, whom Napoleon tried to win over.

Napoleon's victory at the Battle of Imbaba outside Cairo revealed the stark reality of the new military power coming from Europe. The Mamluk Emirs, with their razor-sharp sabers and jewel-encrusted pistols, headed an Ottoman-Egyptian army of around 8,000 cavalry and 10,000 infantry. In the past they would have easily triumphed over even the best-trained infantry. But they were no match for a larger French army of 28,000 peasants, passionately devoted to their commander, backed by the latest gunpowder weapons forged in the workshops and factories of Europe. The French artillery, having greater range and accuracy than the Ottoman cannon, began firing at a much longer distance than the Mamluk cavalry was used to. The horsemen who penetrated this barrage had to confront a square of disciplined infantry, six lines deep and bristling with bayonets, before being blasted by a hail of musketfire. The Mamluk cavalry charged repeatedly, but without effect. At the end of the day French casualties were few—around 30 killed and 200 wounded; the Ottoman-Egyptians suffered between 800 and 1,600 dead.

Faced with defeat, the Mamluk Emirs fled the city with their families, taking with them all their jewelry and valuables, only to have them stolen by the Bedouin tribesmen outside the city walls. The tribes were loyal to themselves, not to the Ottoman system of government. Before being occupied by French officers the empty Mamluk palaces were ransacked by looters. Cairo became a ghost town. Meanwhile, a British fleet, commanded by Rear Admiral Horatio Nelson, finally tracked down the French fleet.

This painting, by Jean-Leon Gerome, shows Napoleon accompanied by his general staff.

French Admiral Brueys d'Aigalliers, guardian of Napoleon's supply line to France, moved his warships to Aboukir Bay, northeast of Alexandria. His ships comprised nine of 74 guns, three of 80 guns, and the flagship *L'Orient* of 120 guns, plus four frigates. The thirteen ships-of-the-line were anchored near together in a line, and close to the shore. A battery was emplaced on Aboukir Island and another in a promontory fort. British Admiral Nelson sailed into the bay with some of his thirteen 74s sailing around the vanguard of the French line inshore of the French fleet while others kept seaward, meaning that the front of the French line was attacked from two sides simultaneously. The French fleet was refitting and the landward side cannon were cluttered up with stores, which impeded the use of the guns. The French ships were not close enough together and some British ships broke the line and were able to rake the bows and sterns of vessels with devastating effect, with cannon balls cleaving their way the whole length of a deck. The British ships advanced along the French line taking one ship after another. In the initial stages thirteen British ships were taking on eight French giving them superiority in firepower. During these exchanges of fire, the *L'Orient* caught fire and its magazines exploded. Only two French ships escaped. After the battle ended, the French had lost eleven ships: two destroyed and nine captured, of which three were found unseaworthy and burned. Two ships escaped with two frigates.

The Ottomans responded to the French invasion by creating an army on the island of Rhodes designed to mount an amphibious assault in Aboukir Bay, while a second army, under Jazzar Pasha, moved into Palestine with a forward position at al-Arish. Napoleon decided to advance into Syria and defeat Jazzar's forces, before the Rhodes expedition arrived. Al-Arish was quickly taken, followed by Gaza, where 2,000 Turks were massacred. Jaffa was then

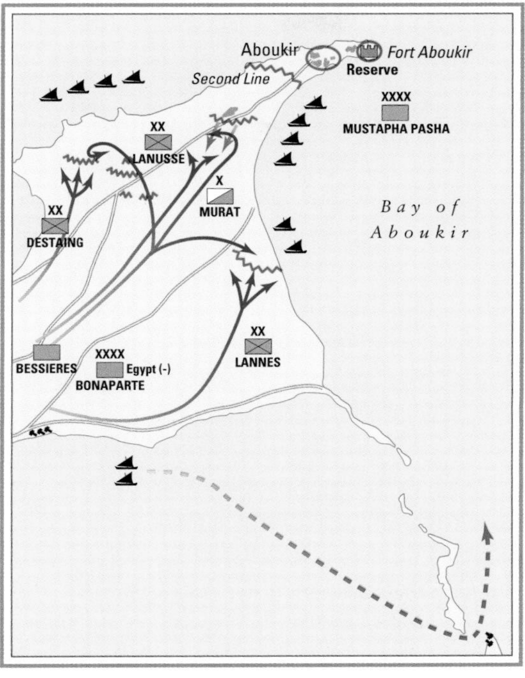

Battle of Aboukir
25 July 1799

French attack
Turkish attack
Turkish retreat
Turkish defences
Turkish positions

attacked in March 1799.

Despite fierce resistance, the French broke in, captured the city, and butchered some 4,000 prisoners-of-war. Napoleon then advanced along the coast capturing Haifa and Tyre, before reaching and besieging Saint-Jean-d'Acre. The port was ably defended by Jazzar and Antoine de Phélippeaux, a French émigré engineering officer and former fellow-student of Bonaparte, while the port was supplied by Commodore Sir Sidney Smith whose HMS *Tigre* and HMS *Theseus* were used as naval support against the French. Repeated assaults on Acre's walls failed and even when a usable breach was made, entry could not be forced. Napoleon also faced a Turkish army sent to relieve Acre, which he defeated at the Battle of Mount Tabor, near Nazareth. The French then retreated from Acre and when they reached Egypt Napoleon marched headlong to Aboukir Bay, where the army from Rhodes had landed, and defeated them. Realizing that his army was shrinking through war and disease, and that his career would be best served in France, Napoleon left Egypt on a frigate that had escaped the destruction at Aboukir Bay, leaving his troops under the command of General Kléber, who defeated a Turkish force near Heliopolis before his assassination by a Syrian fanatic in June 1800.

In March 1801 British troops landed under General Sir Ralph Abercromby, who died of wounds he received in a bloody but indecisive battle outside Alexandria. The British were joined by an Ottoman force that landed at Aboukir and, despite the loss of their commander, they captured Rosetta. With another Ottoman army entering from Syria, Cairo was now under threat—not just from British and Ottoman forces, but from the plague now raging in the area. By the end of June acceptable terms had been agreed and the French left Egypt with the honors of war. A Treaty of Paris secured peace in June 1802 between France and the Ottoman Empire.

Though lasting barely three years, the French occupation had far-reaching consequences. It fatally weakened the power of the Mamluk sultans. The vacuum this left was quickly filled by Muhammad 'Ali, a young Ottoman soldier who had commanded a group of Albanians sent to expel the French. In 1811 Muhammad 'Ali, now confirmed as the Ottoman Sultan's viceroy, destroyed the power of the Mamluks, using his Albanians to massacre nearly 500 of them after a grand reception in Cairo's citadel. Freed from the Mamluk threat, Muhammad 'Ali embarked on an ambitious program of reform, using mainly French advisors, some of whom were converts to Islam.

The seeds of Muhammad 'Ali's reforms had been sown by Napoleon. The French General had introduced a crash program in the form of a council or Diwan comprising sheikhs, notables, and 'ulama (religious scholars). More ambitiously he went on to organize a general Diwan with representatives from different provinces. Engineers cleared canals, built windmills, and improved flood-control works on the Nile. In Cairo new hospitals and libraries were begun, and the streets cleared of garbage. A period of French-inspired modernization had begun.

Muhammad Ali Pasha's Wars—Egyptian Expansion 1805–47

Muhammad Ali Pasha, Governor of Egypt 1805–49.

Muhammad Ali was born at Kavala in Macedonia in 1769. An orphan, he was illiterate until he was 40, but being highly disciplined, intelligent, and physically strong, he rapidly rose to prominence, becoming the commander of a 6,000-strong Albanian force sent by the Ottoman Sultan to fight the French. Although the French army had been expelled from Egypt they still retained some influence. A combination of French backing, popular support mediated through the 'ulama' (religious scholars) and intrigues with some of the Mamluk beys enabled him to become the effective power in Egypt, which the Sultan acknowledged by making him the official Wali or Viceroy in 1805.

After destroying the remaining Mamluks, he set about an ambitious program of modernization. French officers were brought in to train a new army recruited from the Egyptian peasantry in addition to the Turks, Kurds, Circassians, and Albanians of his personal household, while arms factories were founded and a navy built, also with French advisors. He brought all Egypt's agricultural land under state control, confiscating tax farms, awarding estates to members of his family and tax-free lands to village headmen, who took control of taxes and forced recruitment. New irrigation canals extended the cultivation of land, and the production of high-quality, long-staple cotton for the international market added cash to the state coffers. While some Muslims benefited from these changes, many of the members of the new elite of landowners and merchants that prospered under Muhammad Ali's regime belonged to Jewish and Christian minorities—including Egyptians, Syrians, Italians, and Greeks—who had the advantage of international contacts.

Muhammad Ali used his new European-style army to support Ottoman power in the Arabian Peninsula for a time, destroying the rule of the Saudis and Wahabis who had taken over the Hejaz, disrupting the Meccan pilgrimage. The prestige this earned him throughout the Islamic world encouraged him to push south into the Upper Nile region to clear out the remaining Mamluk forces and to incorporate the Sudan into Egypt, which was achieved by 1821. The penetration of this region by 'Turks' that the Sudanese tribes considered to be 'infidels' was one of the triggers for the Mahdist revolt in the 1880s.

In 1821, the Greeks rebelled against Ottoman rule and Sultan Mahmud II's army failed to put an end to the revolt. He offered Muhammad Ali the island of Crete as a reward for defeating the Greeks. An Egyptian force was sent but it failed in its task. The Ottoman and Egyptian fleets were annihilated at the Battle of Navarino in 1827, where the combined squadrons of Britain, France, and Russia destroyed 70 of the 78 Ottoman vessels. The Cretan reward was now withdrawn and Muhammad Ali requested Syria as compensation for his lost fleet and the resources he had used in the Greek campaign, but was refused by the Sultan. A fresh fleet was constructed and a new army raised.

In 1832, Egyptian forces under Muhammad's son, Ibrahim Pasha, invaded Syria, advancing to the Anatolian border while capturing all the important cities including Damascus. The Pasha's motives were aggrandizement for himself and his dynasty, a desire to control the trading cities and trade routes through the Levant, and to obtain the Sultan's mandate to rule in Syria. Also, the Pasha of Syria had refused to return refugees fleeing Egypt. In December 1832, Ibrahim won a famous victory at Konya that left Constantinople open to attack. Further advances were called off as a response to British and French pressure. The 1833 Convention of Kutahya gave Syria and Adana to Egypt with Muhammad Ali becoming their Governor-general while Crete and the Hejaz were given to him as compensation. Muhammad Ali's achievements led to the growth of the idea of an Egyptian nation, but it has never been clear that this was his aim. He thought primarily in terms of personal and dynastic power. Indeed, he may have harbored the idea of replacing the Sultan. Any such ambition, however, was thwarted by the European powers who preferred a weak to a reinvigorated Ottoman Empire.

The Sultan next offered the Pasha hereditary rule in Egypt and Arabia if he left Syria and Crete. Muhammad Ali refused and the Sultan ordered his army to attack Syria. Ottoman forces were crushed at the Battle of Nezib in 1839, leaving the road open to Constantinople, while the Ottoman fleet deserted to the Pasha. Britain, France, Austria, and Russia now intervened and signed the 1840 Convention of London, which offered the Pasha hereditary rule over Egypt while he could hold southern Syria in his lifetime. Egyptian troops did not move, so British naval forces bombarded Beirut and Acre cutting Ibrahim's lines of communication. Ibrahim withdrew and Muhammad Ali agreed to withdraw from his gains. The Pasha now was forced to return Crete and the Hejaz, and leave Syria. In exchange, he, and his issue, would become hereditary rulers of Egypt and the Sudan. The Ottoman fleet was returned and the Egyptian army reduced in size. Egypt now ceased to be a challenge to the Ottoman Empire and the European nations were happy that the balance of power was restored.

Northeast Africa
1805–74

- Ottoman Empire, 1840
- Ottoman Vice-Royalty of Egypt under Muhammad Ali, 1840

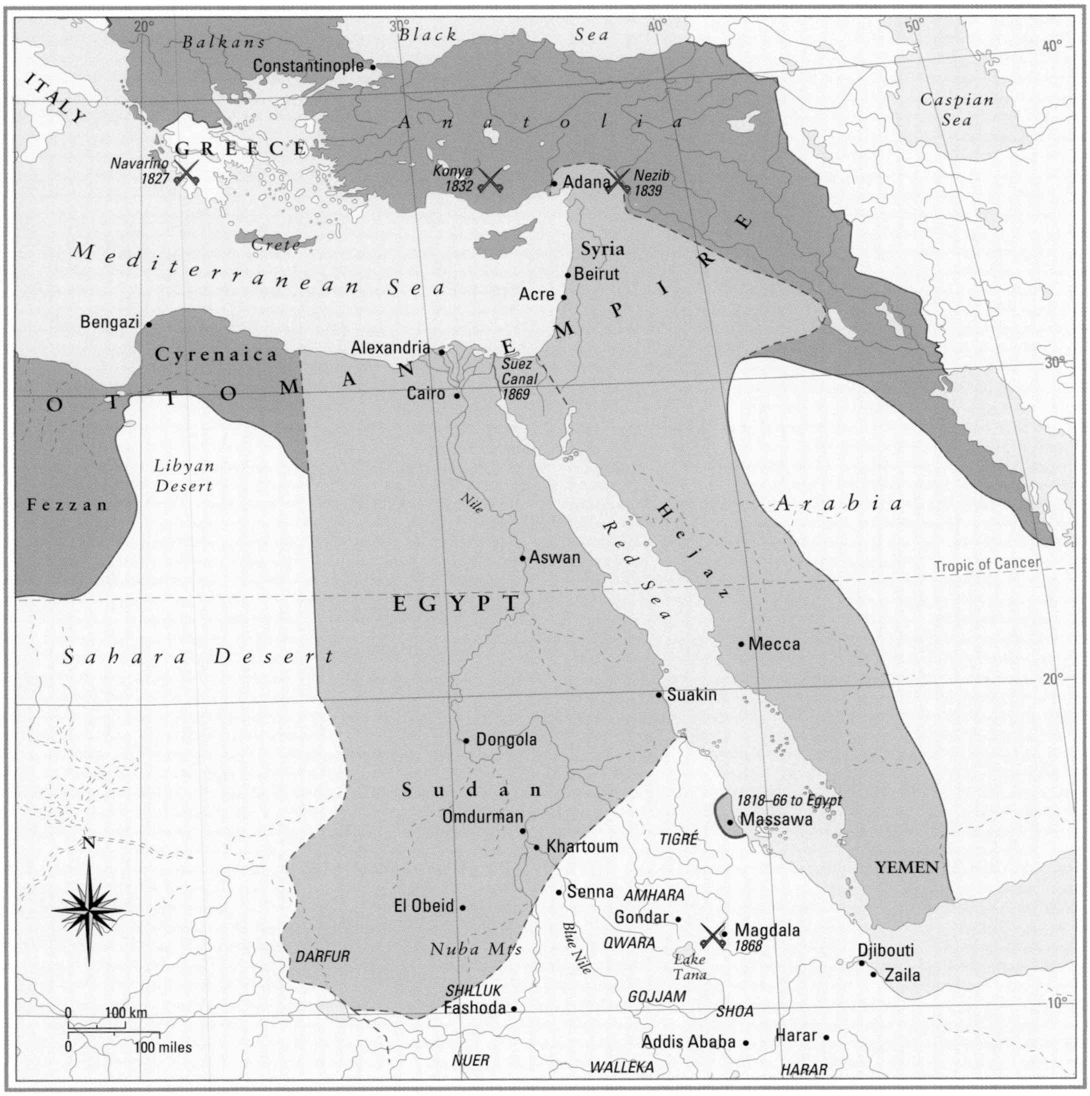

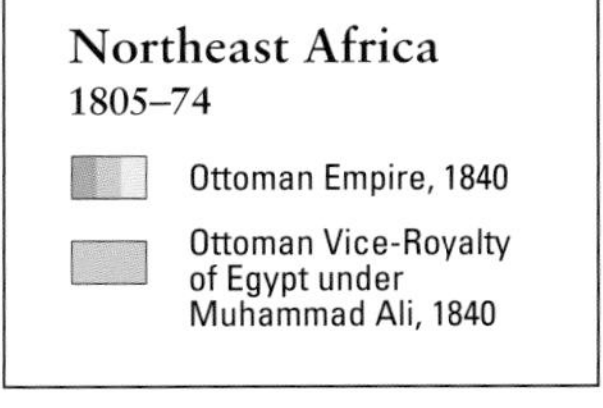

Arabi Pasha and British Intervention in Egypt 1882

Ahmed Urabi, known by his Egyptian followers as El Wahid (the 'Only One'), and in the west as Arabi Pasha. In 1879 he led the revolt against Taufiq Pasha, under whose rule European domination had developed.

Under the rule of Muhammad Ali's grandson, Ismail, whom the Sultan confirmed in the official title of Khedive (viceroy) in 1867, Egypt acquired a massive burden of debt. Ismail was highly extravagant, building flashy royal palaces and a new western-style city, inspired by Paris, on land reclaimed from the Nile. But he also invested in major infrastructure projects, including the Suez Canal, new irrigation canals and ports, and an extensive railway network. Unlike his grandfather, who relied exclusively on government revenues, Ismail financed his projects not just by extorting taxes out of the peasants, but by borrowing heavily from European banks, using his vast holdings of real estate (which included around one-eighth of Egypt's cultivated land) as collateral, and mortgaging the income from cotton. In 1863, when he came to power, the American Civil War was raging, causing the value of Egyptian cotton exports to soar. By 1869 the Civil War was over and the price of cotton collapsed. Ismail was forced by his creditors to accept British and French financial control. When he resisted, supported by what would become the National Assembly, the British and French governments persuaded the new Ottoman Sultan, Abd al-Hamid II, to revoke his appointment and depose him in favor of his more pliable son, Taufiq.

This crude exercise of foreign power encouraged nationalist feelings, especially in the army, where newly-commissioned Egyptians faced discrimination from Turks and Circassians who still held sway in the officer corps. After three young Egyptian officers, led by Ahmed Arabi, presented a petition of complaint to the Prime Minister, they were briefly arrested by Circassian officers. In the ensuing popular demonstrations the weak Taufiq accepted some constitutional demands, while appealing to the Sultan for support. The Sultans' commissioners, however, were sidelined by the British and French consuls, who had been instructed to oppose any Ottoman interference in Egyptian affairs. Faced with growing public pressure, the Khedive brought Arabi into the government, first as under-secretary then as full minister of war. Alarmed at the growing unrest and that the government would renege on its debt (though Arabi had accepted Franco-British control over Egypt's finances in the short term) Britain and France decided to intervene to protect their interests.

On 20 May 1882, an Anglo-French fleet arrived at Alexandria where Arabi and his men were establishing coastal defenses against just such a threat. Nationalist fervor was outraged by the fleet's arrival and 50 Europeans were killed in the city. British Admiral Seymour ordered that the Egyptians dismantle their coastal defenses. Arabi refused, so the British fleet opened fire, killing around 1,000 Egyptians. Two days later, a large naval force landed and drove Egyptian troops out of Alexandria. British General Garnet Wolsey disembarked British soldiers and advanced towards Cairo, but met stiff Egyptian opposition in the Battle of Kafr-el-Dawwar, which held up the British for five weeks. Wolsey redeployed his troops to Alexandria, deciding to take the Suez Canal, capturing it from both ends using his own force and several thousand Indian troops staged through Aden. By early September, the Canal was in British hands. Arabi Pasha attempted to regain the Canal when he attacked the British at Kassassin on 28 August and 9 September. He was eventually repulsed, but the British sustained heavy casualties. Arabi then tried to dig in his troops at Tel el-Kebir, but his trenches were incomplete when the British, led by the Highland Brigade, marched through the night, made a frontal assault at dawn, and charged with fixed bayonets.

The Egyptians were routed, losing some

2,000 dead and wounded, Arabi was arrested and exiled to Ceylon, and British financial control was restored. The British set about restructuring and retraining Egyptian officialdom and finances; Taufiq made several concessions ensuring that European lives would not be placed at risk again. A British military presence began a permanent British military garrison in Egypt and British Army officers were seconded to command and train the Egyptian Army. This force was reformed with the eventual appointment of British-trained Egyptian officers and non-commissioned officers.

The Suez Canal remained under European control until 1952, a vital link with India and for staging troops around the world to defend the British Empire. While Britain was in effective control of Egypt, it also acquired the Sudan, where half a century of Egyptian rule provoked the messianic movement led by Muhammad Ahmed, a pious shaikh of the Sammaniya religious order, who declared himself the Mahdi—the expected savior—and called for the restoration of true Islam. In 1885 the Mahdists defeated General Gordon at Khartoum, inflicting a national humiliation that the British would avenge when they desecrated the Mahdi's tomb after the Battle of Omdurman in 1898.

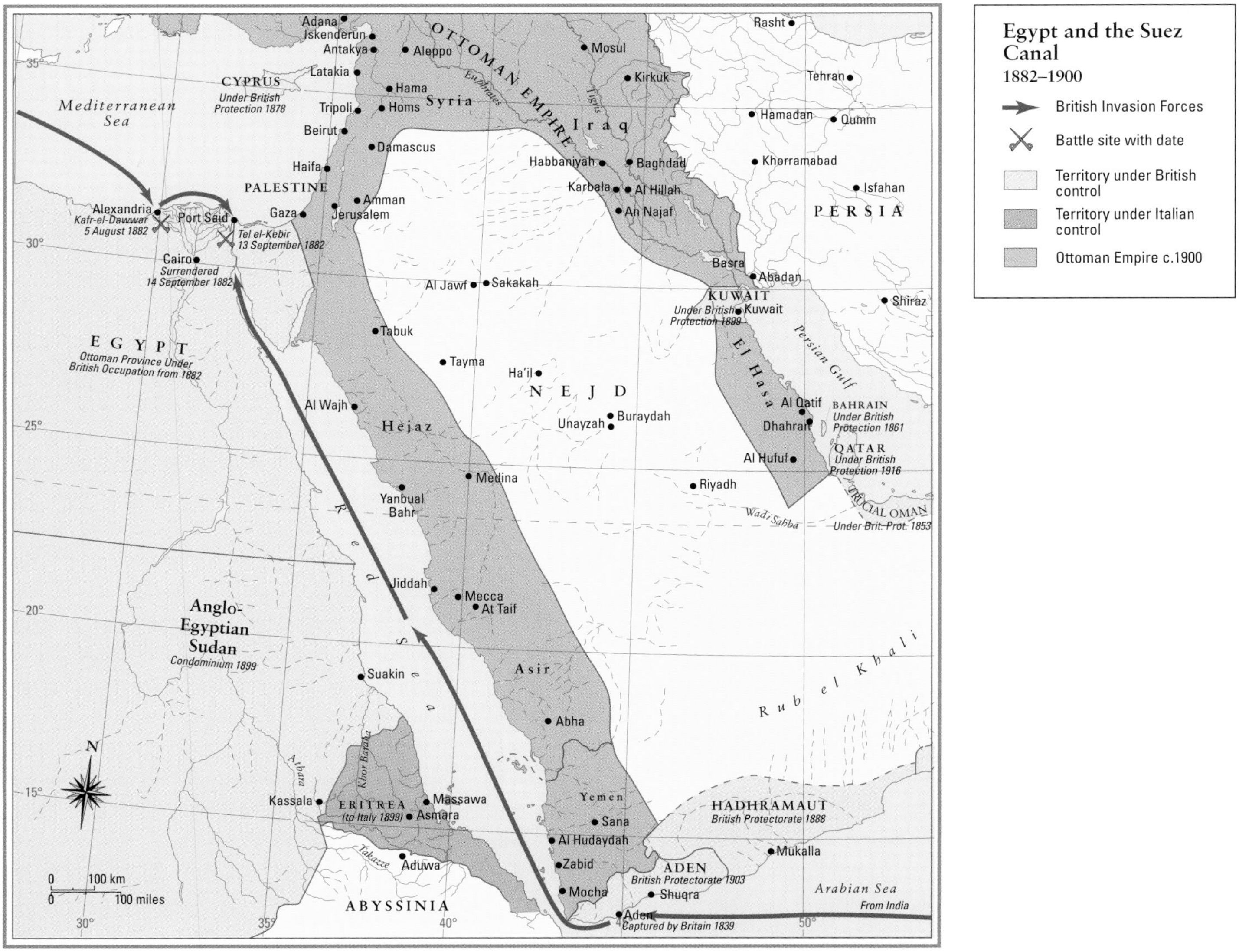

The Dream of Israel

Following the expulsion of the Jews from Spain in 1450, European Jews faced an uncertain, often hostile world. A response that came to be widely discussed in the nineteenth century when nationalist movements were emerging throughout Europe, was that Jews must have a homeland of their own. Although Palestine—the ancient lands of Israel and Judah—where Jewish communities had continued to reside since late antiquity was the main focus of Zionist aspirations, other options were considered. These included Kenya, Uganda, Madagascar, Argentina, and North America. For religious, practical and historical reasons, however, the Zionist movement settled overwhelmingly for Palestine—despite the objections of orthodox rabbis who saw Zionism as pre-empting the commands of God. For example, Yehonathan Eibshutz, a celebrated German rabbi, wrote in the mid-eighteenth century that massive immigration of Jews to Palestine, even with the consent of all the world's nations, was prohibited before the coming of the Messiah. In the early nineteenth century both supporters of the Jewish Enlightenment, such as Moses Mendelsohn, and opponents such as Rabbi Rafael Hirsch, subscribed to this view, with Hirsch writing in 1837 that God had commanded Jews "never to establish a state of their own by their own efforts."

Inevitably support for the Zionist idea grew with the momentum of the pogroms and persecutions in Russia and Eastern Europe. Forerunners of modern Zionism included the Lithuanian Vilna Gaon, the Russian Rabbi Menachem Mendel of Vitebsk, the Bosnian Rabbi Judah Alkalai, the German Rabbi Zvi Hirsch Kalischer, and the British Sir Moses Montefiore. In 1861 Moses Hess, a friend of Karl Marx and Frierich Engels, published *Rome and Jerusalem*, a tract that called for what would come to be known as Labor- Zionism. His ideas were aired at the first Zionist Congress in Basel in 1897. In 1882, Judah Leib (Leon) Pinsker observed the Odessa pogrom and claimed that Jews could only be free in their own land, which he advocated in his *Auto-emancipation*. A start to this project could be the acquisition of land in Palestine.

The most prominent early Zionist, however, was Theodor Herzl, later President of the World Zionist Federaton, who had worked as the Paris correspondent of the Viennese *Neue Freie Presse* and was profoundly influenced by the virulent anti-Semitism during the Dreyfus Affair in France, when many Roman Catholic priests preached anti-Semitism from the pulpit. In *Der Judenstaat*, which he published in 1896, Herzl outlined his plan for a Jewish state based upon the purchase of land, the creation of laws, and productive work in agriculture, industry, and trade. An important influence on Herzl was his friend William Hechler (1845–1931), one time Anglican Chaplain to the British Embassy in Vienna. Like many protestants, Hechler was a 'premillennialist' who believed that the 'restoration' of Jews to Palestine was a necessary prelude to the Second Coming of Christ. His booklet *The Restoration of the Jews to Palestine* (1894) predated *Der Judenstaat* by just two years. Hechler's diplomatic contacts helped Herzl gain access to Kaiser Wilhelm II and the Grand Duke of Baden as well as members of the British political establishment.

By the beginning of the twentieth century premillennial ideas concerning the desirability of the restoration of Jews to Palestine were widespread in evangelical circles in Britain and the United States. The two key figures in persuading the British government to support a Jewish homeland in Palestine were liberal Prime Minister David Lloyd George and his Foreign Secretary, Arthur James Balfour (1848–1930), who drafted the famous Balfour Declaration after discussions with Herzl's successor as leader of the Zionist movement, the chemistry professor Chaim Weizmann. Both Balfour and Lloyd George came from evangelical backgrounds and appear to have been influenced by premillennial teachings.

Under Ottoman rule, the Jewish population

of Palestine grew considerably, with some Palestinian notables, including members of the Ottoman parliament, expressing concern that "the Jews intend to create a state in the area that will include Palestine, Syria, and Iraq." Between 1880 and 1914 more than 60,000 Jews entered Palestine, mainly from Russia, Galicia, Romania, and Poland. Jews and Jewish philanthropists bought whatever land they could, generally paying more than market prices, in some cases to wealthy or absentee landowners prepared to disregard the interests of their tenants. In England, Montefiore was appointed Executor of the will of an American Jew named Judah Touro. His wealth was bequeathed to finance Jewish residential settlements in Palestine. In 1855, he bought an orchard near Jaffa that was used to provide agricultural training to Jews. In 1860, he constructed the first residential settlement outside Jerusalem for the New Yishuv at Mishkenot Sha'ananim. This almshouse was provided with walls and a strong gate to deter bandits. Much money was spent in the promotion of industry, education, and health. The aim was to have the New Yishuv self-supporting should a Jewish homeland be established. Montefiore also built a windmill in Yemin Moshe to provide cheap flour for poor Jews and provided a printing press and a textile factory. He also helped finance Russian Jewish agricultural settlements—part of the Bilu movement. This was helped, as well, by Baron Edmond de Rothschild and Maurice de Hirsch, who established a wine industry and a winery at Rishon le Zion. Another example of Rothschild's generosity occurred after Jewish settlers bought land near the source of the Yarkon River in 1878—this turned out to be a malarial swamp at Petah Tikva, which the Jews evacuated, instead founding a town at Yehud. Rothschild provided funds to drain the swamp and the settlers returned in 1883 and were joined by immigrants escaping the Russian pogroms of 1905.

Other dreams were realized when a group of 65 Zionists laid the foundations of Tel Aviv in 1909 on sand dunes purchased from local Arabs. A school there taught in Hebrew and this was to be the case with a Hebrew University and a Jewish Technical School—the Technion. In 1911 a socialist commune created Kibbutz Degania near the Sea of Galilee, the very first kibbutz in Palestine, which became the driving force for the moshav movement.

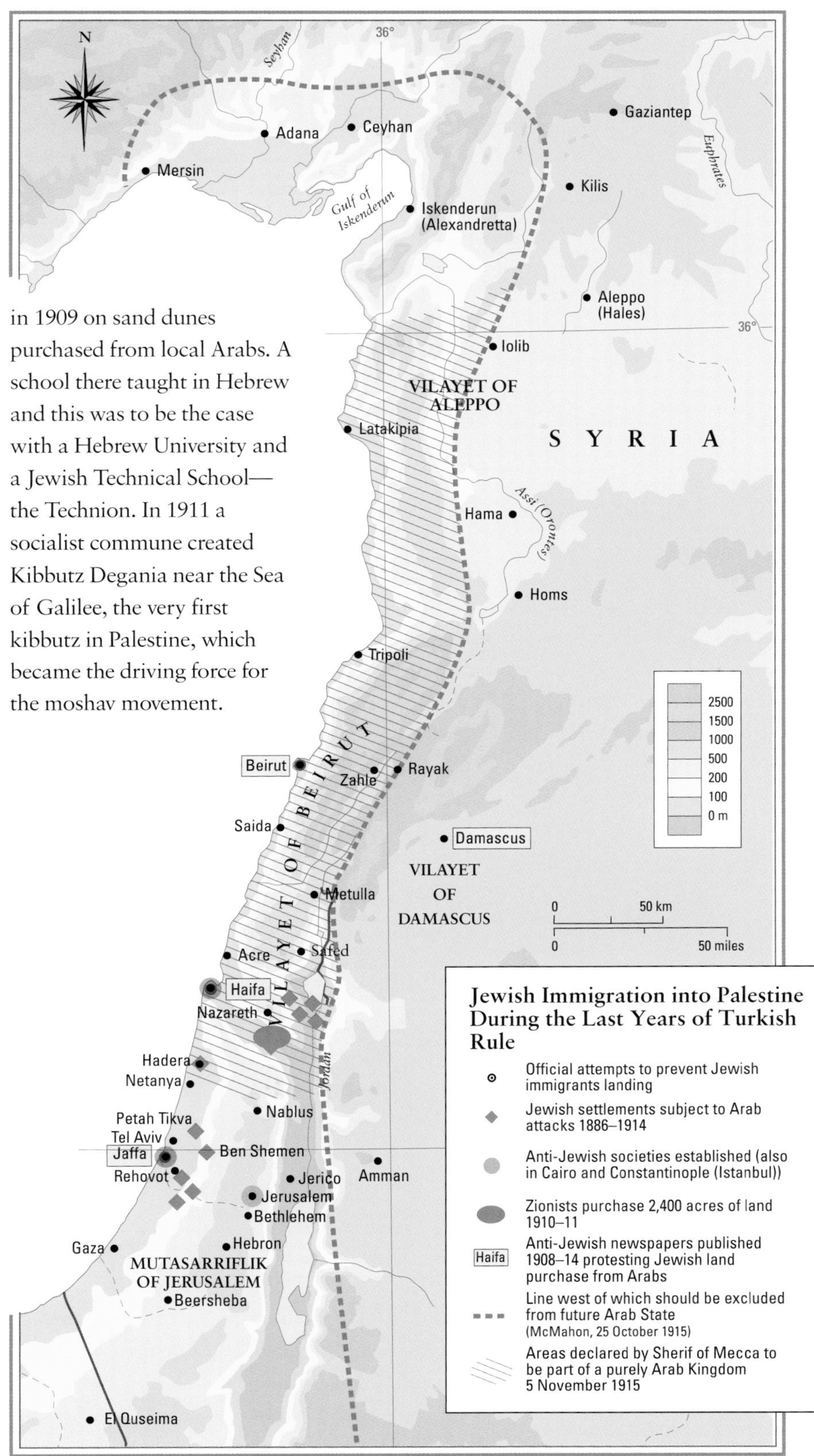

World War I—The Gallipoli Campaign 1915–1916

The landings finally took place on 25 April with the ANZACS landing near Gaba Tepe, in an area that became 'ANZAC Core'. The British 29th Division landed on five beaches. The result was chaos, some beaches suffered withering losses, other met little opposition; nowhere did the landing force cooperate in any planned way. None of the first day's objectives were achieved, Turkish forces counterattacked and largely held their possessions. Mustafa Kemal, perhaps the only capable commander on the battlefield, quickly occupied the commanding position of Sari Bair Ridge with his entire 19th Division. The campaign dissolved into a war of attrition with casualties mounting on both sides. Later attempts with landings in Suvla Bay, incompetently planned and badly led, failed.

By the end of 1914, mobile warfare had ended on the Western Front; on the Eastern Front Russia, defeated in East Prussia and Poland, had lost the initiative to the Central Powers. In the Middle East the Ottoman Empire deployed its forces in the Caucasus, determined to retake territory lost to Russia in 1878. In Mesopotamia, British forces, from India, had landed, taken Basra, and were slowly moving north. At the beginning of January 1915 a German-led Ottoman force had attacked the Suez Canal in Egypt.

Against this background, Allied High Command had to consider their plans for 1915. The 'Westerners,' mostly French, argued that final victory could only be achieved on the Western front. The 'Easterners,' mostly British, viewed the prospect of a new front against the Ottoman Empire as a more economical way to defeat the Central Powers. From these debates the plan to attack the Dardanelles developed, aimed at the nearby prize of Constantinople, thus giving access to the Black Sea, and direct aid to Russia. This strategy would convince Greece, Bulgaria, and Romania to join the Allies, possibly knocking the Ottoman Empire out of the war.

The plan called for a naval force of eighteen battleships, supported by cruisers and destroyers, to 'force' the Dardanelles, enter the Sea of Marmara, and threaten Constantinople.

On 19 February, the fleet commanded by Admiral Sackville Carden began their initial bombardment. By the 25th, the outer forts were largely destroyed and the entrance to the straits cleared of mines. Marines were landed on the Asian shore at Kum Kale and at Sedd el Bahr on the Gallipoli Peninsula. However, by 4 March, the fleet had not made its main attack, frustrated by the Ottoman mobile batteries which evaded the Allied bombardment but still posed a threat to the minesweepers attempting to continue clearing mines. Under pressure from Winston Churchill, First Lord of the Admiralty, Carden proposed a new plan to attack around 17 March. Before the plan was carried out, Carden was relieved, suffering from stress, and was replaced by Admiral John de Robeck.

On 18 March, the main attack began. As the fleet advanced the *Bouvet*, an elderly French battleship, was hit by shells and later struck a mine and sank, losing 660 of her crew. The minesweepers could take no more shellfire from the Turkish batteries, and fled leaving most of the minefields uncleared, but the fleet pressed on. Five more major warships struck mines and two sank, which persuaded the Fleet Commander to issue a general recall: the naval attempt had failed.

Lord Kitchener now agreed to despatch the Mediterranean Expeditionary Force (MEF), which comprised a division of Australians and New Zealanders (ANZACS), one British division and one French, some 78,000-strong commanded by General Sir Ian Hamilton. An ill-organized logistics plan delayed departure and, by the time the MEF was on its way, Ottoman forces were well prepared. General Otto Liman von Sanders, a German officer, commanded the 5th Army of five divisions, including the 19th led by Mustafa Kemal, who knew the area well. The Ottoman forces in the area numbered around 62,000 in all.

The Ottoman army had undergone years of reform, particularly after the Balkan wars, and aided by a German military mission, had evolved into a more capable fighting force. Now, this largely conscript army withstood an ill-planned and chaotically-executed Allied attack. The Ottoman Empire mobilized some 2,800,000 men for the war, mostly drawn from the Muslim millet (confessional community) of around 15 million though Christians, Jews, and Druze were also conscripted. The determination of the Ottoman soldiers came as a shock to the Allies, while the defeat of the Allied naval force gave the Ottoman forces an unquestionable lift in morale.

In western capitals those deemed responsible for the fiasco were relieved of command, including Winston Churchill.

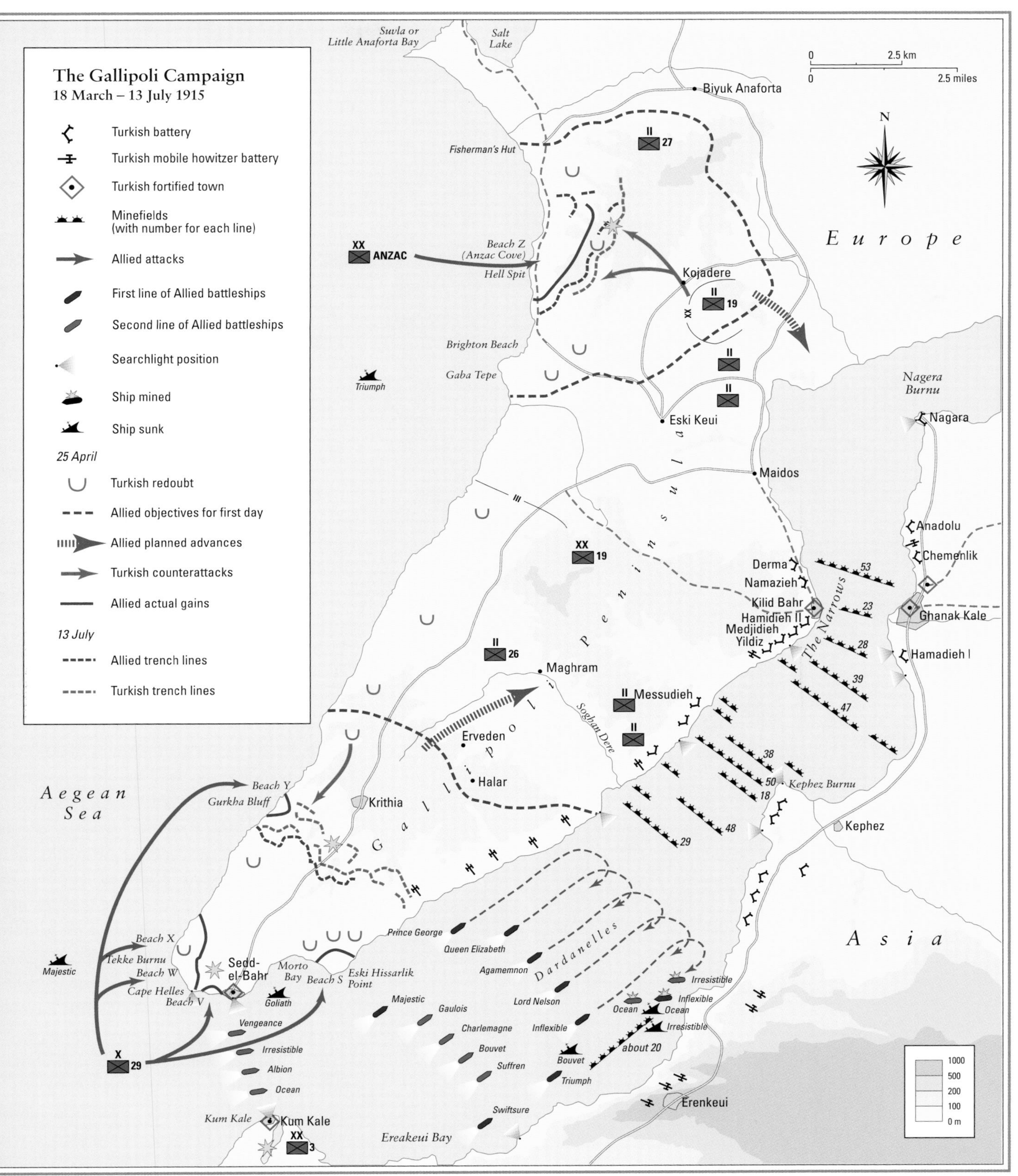
The Gallipoli Campaign
18 March – 13 July 1915
Turkish battery
Turkish mobile howitzer battery
Turkish fortified town
Minefields
(with number for each line)
Allied attacks
First line of Allied battleships
Second line of Allied battleships
Searchlight position
Ship mined
Ship sunk
25 April
Turkish redoubt
Allied objectives for first day
Allied planned advances
Turkish counterattacks
Allied actual gains
13 July
Allied trench lines
Turkish trench lines
Suvla or Little Anaforta Bay
Salt Lake
Biyuk Anaforta
Fisherman's Hut
Beach Z (Anzac Cove)
Hell Spit
ANZAC
Kojadere
Brighton Beach
Gaba Tepe
Triumph
Eski Keui
Maidos
Europe
Nagera Burnu
Nagara
Anadolu
Chemenlik
Derma
Namazieh
Kilid Bahr
Hamidieh II
Medjidieh
Yildiz
The Narrows
Ghanak Kale
Hamadieh I
Maghram
Messudieh
Sogban Dere
Erveden
Halar
Krithia
Gallipoli Peninsula
Kephez Burnu
Kephez
Aegean Sea
Beach Y
Gurkha Bluff
Beach X
Tekke Burnu
Beach W
Cape Helles
Beach V
Sedd-el-Bahr
Morto Bay
Beach S
Eski Hissarlik Point
Majestic
Goliath
Vengeance
Irresistible
Albion
Ocean
Prince George
Queen Elizabeth
Agamemnon
Dardanelles
Lord Nelson
Inflexible
Gaulois
Charlemagne
Bouvet
Suffren
Triumph
Swiftsure
about 20
Asia
Erenkeui
Kum Kale
Ereakeui Bay
0 2.5 km
0 2.5 miles
N
1000
500
200
100
0 m
53
23
28
39
47
38
50
18
48
29

Palestine Front 1914–17

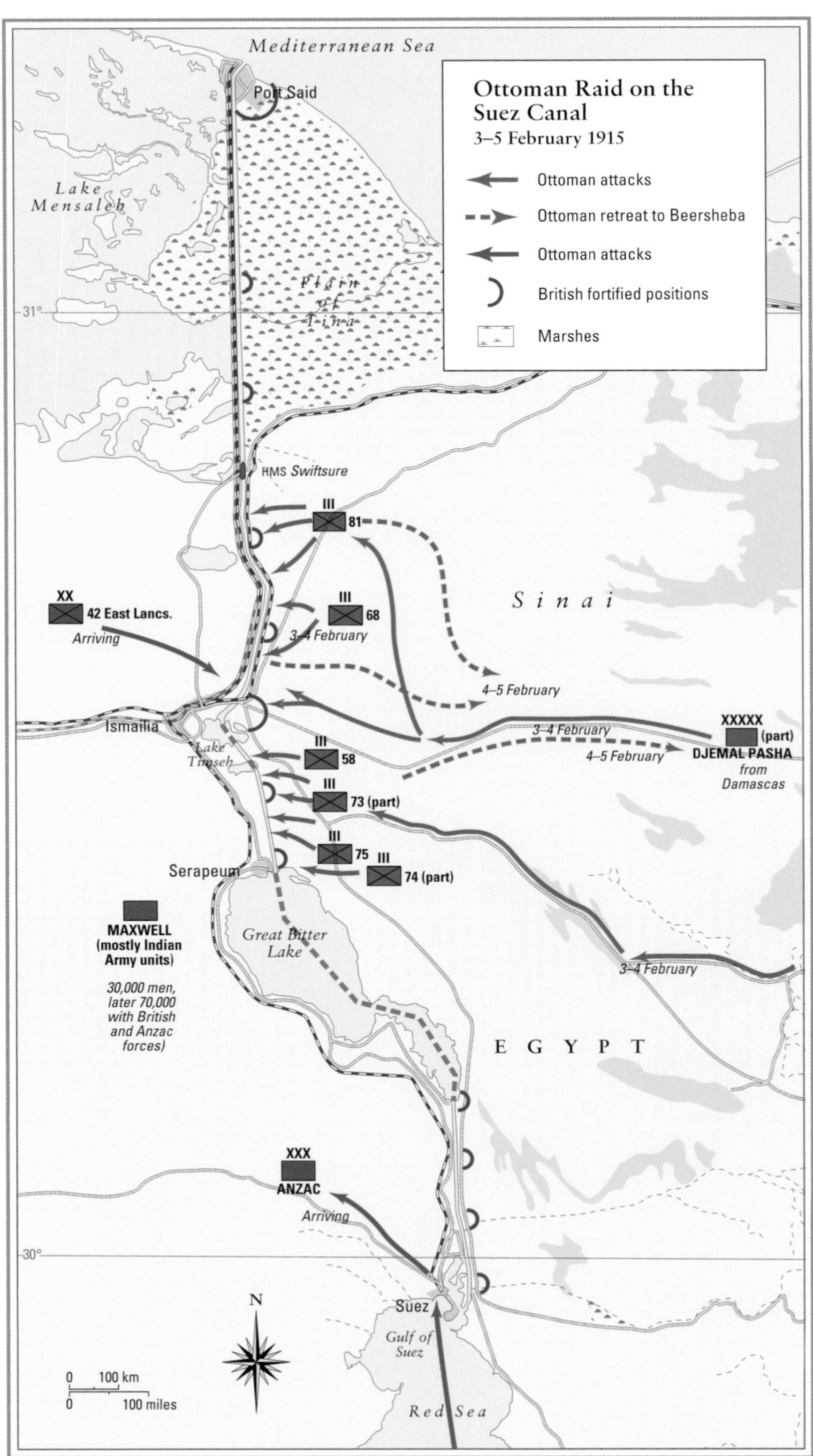

In January 1915 the Ottomans attempted to invade Egypt, despatched 20,000 men from Beersheba across the Sinai Desert, thereby avoiding Allied naval domination of the coast road, to reach the Suez Canal. Air patrols spotted the strike force, whose attacks were broken up by the British Royal Navy and French Navy, shelling from warships on the Canal, and by determined infantry resistance. The Ottomans tried to cross the Canal on pontoons but were repelled by Indian troops and Pioneers supported by Egyptian gunners. A similar attack was driven back by Gurkhas and Indian Rajputs supported by shellfire from the French warships *Requin* and *d'Entrecasteaux*.

After the failed Gallipoli Campaign, an Egyptian Expeditionary Force (EEF) was formed with a plan to re-capture the Egyptian territory in Sinai. To make life difficult for the Ottomans, the British decided to destroy the water wells and cisterns across central Sinai, forcing the Ottomans to use the northern route. Troops of the Indian Bikaner Camel Corps, with other units, destroyed a well-boring plant, water wells, and pumping equipment at Jifjafa. Camel-borne troops, with elements of the Australian 3rd Light Horse Brigade, drained pools and cisterns of 5,000,000 gallons of water in the Wadi Mukhsheib and then sealed the cisterns so they could not refill. Meanwhile, the British were constructing a water pipeline to supply their own troops. Part of the British force was the ANZAC Mounted Division and the Desert Column which, by January 1917, had taken Sinai after the battles of Romani, Magdhaba, and Rafa. During this period a railway and water pipeline were constructed, which reached El Arish by January 1917. Two attempts to take Gaza in March and April 1917 failed.

The British commander, Sir Archibald Murray, was replaced by Sir Edmund Allenby in June 1917. He was provided with reinforcements, raising the EEF to ten divisions with instructions to capture Jerusalem by Christmas.

The British Camel Corps move out of their encampment near Beersheba, December 1917.

Amongst his units were ANZAC and Indian divisions and units from the West Indies with Arab, French, and Italian support. Intelligence was supported by the Jewish Nili Spies operating in Palestine, led by men such as Avshalom Feinberg. The EEF was reorganized into the 20th and 21st Infantry Corps and the Desert Column became the Desert Mounted Corps; Allenby used these units in the Third Battle of Gaza in October 1917. Rather than assault the heavily defended Gaza position, Allenby sent his cavalry to attack Beersheba, which the Australian Light Horse cavalry charge seized on 31 October. Allenby could now roll up the Ottoman position from the east and when Allied infantry pressed home on the town, the Ottomans quit their lines and retreated north to Junction Station on the Beersheba-Jerusalem railroad. This station was captured on 12 November and the Ottoman army left Jerusalem on 9 December, allowing Allenby to walk into the city just two days later.

The war in Palestine then stagnated as troops were moved back to the Western Front to counter Germany's March 1918 offensive. Allenby spent the summer training new troops sent from India while two raids into Trans-Jordan failed. By September 1918, Allenby had raised his troop numbers to eleven divisions, comprising four cavalry and seven infantry. Like Pharaoh Shoshenk, Allenby planned to advance northward along the Way of the Sea, while supplied by an accompanying fleet, although swift cavalry advances often outran supplies and infantry support. Allenby's Australian and New Zealand horse plus British yeomanry were armed with rifle and bayonet, and were mobile infantry. The Indian cavalry were armed with lances and swords, and were an incredibly brave body of men. In the aftermath of Megiddo, the Mysore and Jodhpur Lancers cleared out the machine gun nests on the lower slopes of Mount Carmel at lance point before charging into Haifa.

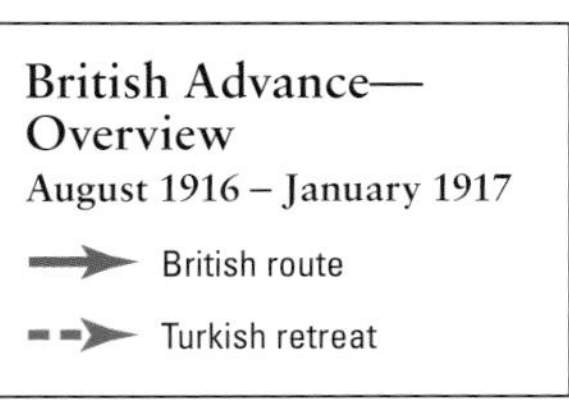

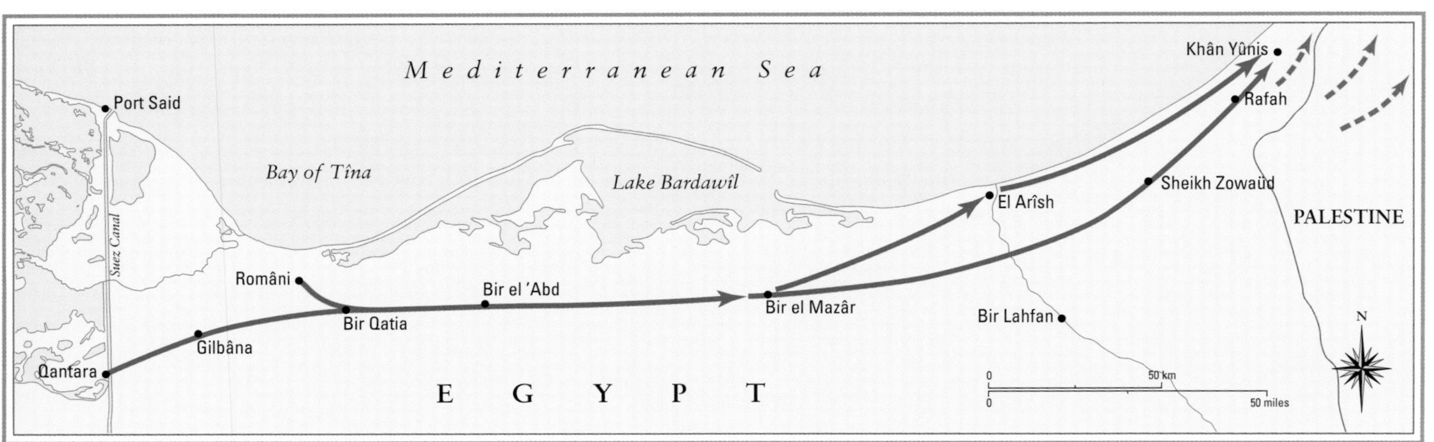

Mesopotamian Front 1914–18

After the Ottoman Empire entered the war allied with the Central Powers in November 1914, an Allied expedition to Mesopotamia was mounted to protect the British-controlled Persian oil wells at Ahwaz. British and Indian forces pushed into southern Mesopotamia, using the Tigris and Euphrates rivers for their advance. Unfortunately, planning for logistics was inadequate as were supplies. Capturing An Nasiriyah and Al 'Amarah by July 1915, the British forces stormed up the Tigris in an over-extended fashion, defeating the Ottomans at Es Sinn just south of Kut al Imara, then pushing on to Baghdad, but were stopped by the defenders at Ctesiphon. The British withdrew to Kut, followed by the Ottomans, who surrounded the British position.

Britain shipped in three new divisions in an attempt to relieve Kut but their deployment was delayed by supply problems, giving the Ottomans time to build defensive positions south of the town to bar any relief force. The relieving divisions reached within seven miles of Kut but suffered 23,000 casualties in the process. In April 1916, Charles Townsend's surrounded Expeditionary Force D surrendered, placing 10,000 into captivity of which 4,000 died.

Eventually, a new commander, Lieutenant-General Frederick Maude, was appointed and he made determined efforts to build a supply infrastructure so that ships could be unloaded quickly at Basra, to construct improved storage facilities, and to improve the quality of the river boats transporting supplies to the troops. Rest camps were established and medical facilities created. Once this had happened more troops and equipment could be sent to the front lines. Maude launched an offensive on 13 December 1916, advancing up the Tigris. The Ottomans were forced out of their positions and again brought to battle at Kut. Maude outflanked the Ottomans, who were forced back in a fighting retreat.

British forces arrived near Baghdad in early March 1917 where the Ottomans tried to stop them on the Diyala River. Maude outmaneuvered the opposition, and entered Baghdad, capturing some 15,000 prisoners. The broken Ottoman 6th Army retreated to Mosul, where some 30,000 soldiers were concentrated. The British advance stopped owing to the heat; Maude died of cholera, and was replaced by General William Marshall. Campaigning began again in February 1918, with the British capturing Hut, Khan al Baghdadi, and Kifri in April 1918. Over the remainder of 1918 troops were being moved from Mesopotamia to join the Sinai and Palestine campaign and to be involved in the Battle of Megiddo in September 1918. Marshall also despatched some troops east to join General Lionel Dunsterville's Dunsterforce in Persia in the summer of 1918. Conflict in Mesopotamia was largely at an end.

When the Allies and the Ottoman Empire began to discuss armistice conditions, Marshall was ordered by the British War Office to seize as much territory as possible to be used as a bargaining chip at the peace table. Accordingly, a new offensive was mounted, with a British force leaving Baghdad on 23 October 1918, commanded by General Cobbe. Two days later 75 miles had been covered, reaching the Little Zab River. The Ottoman 6th Army, under Ismail Hakki Bey, fought the British at the Battle of Sharqat; however, the battle ended when the 13th Hussars captured the Ottoman artillery. Ismail Hakki Bey knew about the peace talks taking place and, wishing to spare his men, surrendered on 30 October. The British 18th Division marched toward Mosul, and even when the Armistice of Mudros was signed on 30 October, continued to advance on the city, despite Ottoman protests. British troops reached Mosul on 14 November, thereby gaining control of Mosul Province and its oilfields and ending the war.

The seizure of Mosul nearly caused an international incident but the Turkish national leader, Mustafa Kemal, was engaged in organizing resistance to the Allied advance into Turkish lands.

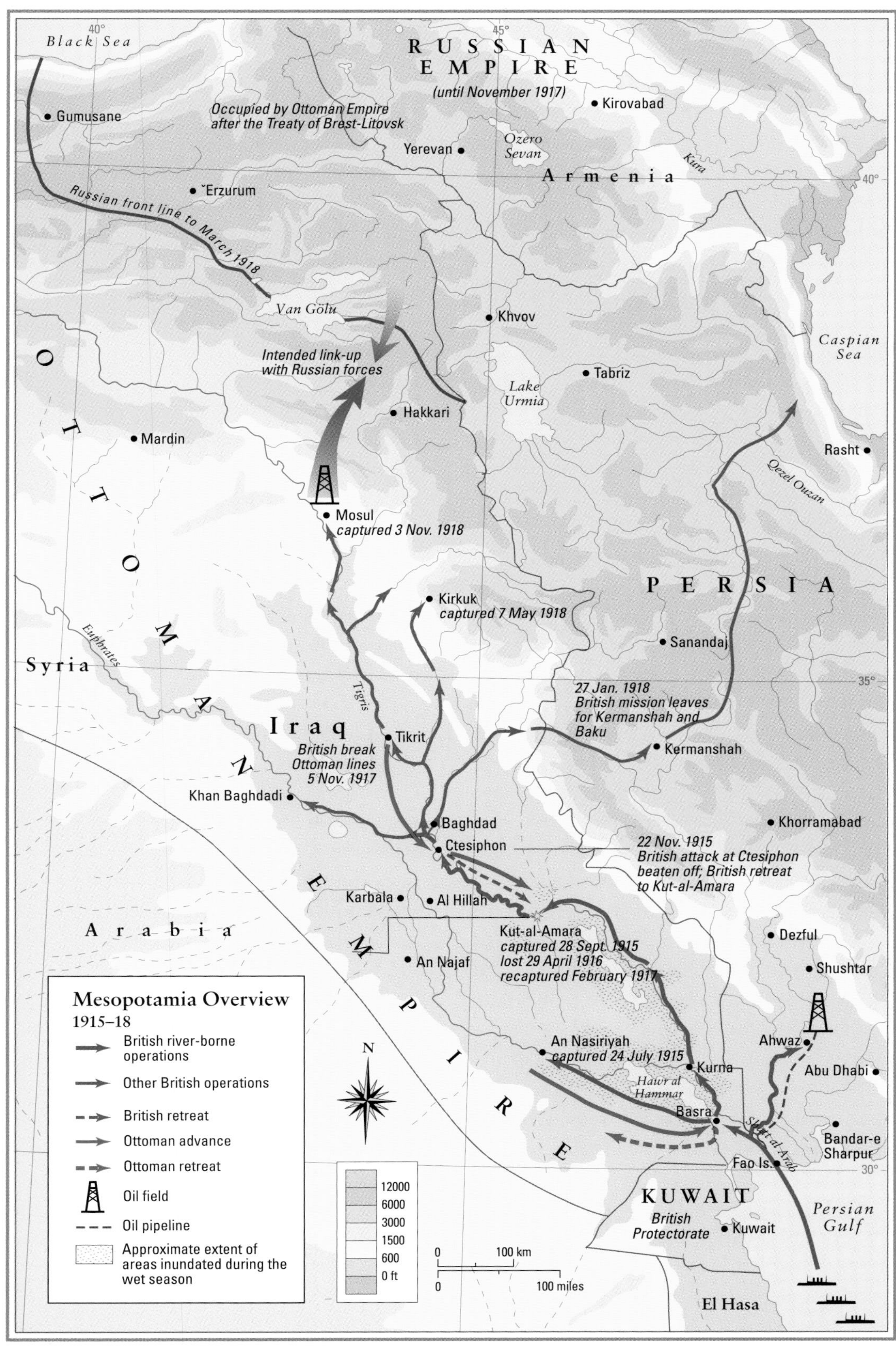
Black Sea
RUSSIAN EMPIRE
(until November 1917)
Kirovabad
Gumusane
Occupied by Ottoman Empire after the Treaty of Brest-Litovsk
Yerevan
Ozero Sevan
Kura
Armenia
Erzurum
Russian front line to March 1918
Van Gölu
Khvov
Caspian Sea
Intended link-up with Russian forces
Tabriz
Lake Urmia
Hakkari
Mardin
Rasht
Qezel Ouzan
OTTOMAN EMPIRE
Mosul captured 3 Nov. 1918
Kirkuk captured 7 May 1918
PERSIA
Sanandaj
Euphrates
Syria
Tigris
27 Jan. 1918 British mission leaves for Kermanshah and Baku
Iraq
Tikrit
British break Ottoman lines 5 Nov. 1917
Kermanshah
Khan Baghdadi
Baghdad
Khorramabad
Ctesiphon
22 Nov. 1915 British attack at Ctesiphon beaten off; British retreat to Kut-al-Amara
Karbala
Al Hillah
Arabia
Kut-al-Amara captured 28 Sept. 1915 lost 29 April 1916 recaptured February 1917
Dezful
An Najaf
Shushtar
Mesopotamia Overview 1915–18
British river-borne operations
Other British operations
British retreat
Ottoman advance
Ottoman retreat
Oil field
Oil pipeline
Approximate extent of areas inundated during the wet season
N
An Nasiriyah captured 24 July 1915
Ahwaz
Kurna
Abu Dhabi
Hawr al Hammar
Basra
Shatt-al-Arab
Bandar-e Sharpur
Fao Is.
KUWAIT
British Protectorate
Kuwait
Persian Gulf
El Hasa
12000
6000
3000
1500
600
0 ft
0
100 km
100 miles
40°
45°
35°
30°

Sykes-Picot Plan—Dividing the Ottoman Empire May 1916

Conflict in the Caucasus, Mesopotamia, the Dardanelles, and Palestine made Britain realize that the fate of the Ottoman Empire needed to be decided. If the Turks lost, the allied powers would want to divide Ottoman territories amongst themselves. Britain could not make unilateral decisions since its allies, France, Russia, and Italy, all had interests in the region. Other interested parties were the Hashemite Arabs from the Hejaz and Zionist politicians, such as Theodore Herzl.

In 1915, the Constantinople Agreement between France, Britain, and Russia stated that, in the event of Entente victory, Constantinople and the Dardanelles would be given to Russia. The failure of the Gallipoli Campaign in 1916, and the Russian Revolution in 1917, destroyed that possibility. However, the Agreement raised the question of further dismemberment of the Ottoman lands. In 1916, Britain and the Hashemite Arabs made an agreement that a Greater Syria would be created after the war if the Arabs supported Britain in the Palestine Campaign. France was afraid that Britain would use the Arab connection to block French interests in Syria and the Lebanon, which France felt should be a French sphere in line with the traditional interest that France had sustained in the region since Napoleon Bonaparte's ill-fated mission to Egypt. Britain had to reach an agreement with France, or France would not agree that its ally should control fighting in the Middle East, rather than concentrating its forces on the Western Front.

An agreement was negotiated by Britain's Sir Mark Sykes and France's François Georges Picot. The Sykes-Picot Plan was a secret plan, only exposed when the Bolsheviks siezed power in 1917. The plan was to divide the Ottoman Empire into four zones: British, French, Russian, and International. The national zones would be further divided into a directly-controlled territory and a semi-autonomous territory which would become a sphere of influence, another display of an imperialist land-grab. Britain would keep its Protectorate of Egypt and would rule Mesopotamia and Acre directly, while having spheres of influence in Persia and through Trans-Jordan. France would rule the Lebanon, coastal Syria and southeast Anatolia directly, and Syria through to Mosul indirectly. Russia would retain its sphere of influence in Persia and would rule northeast Anatolia directly. Italy was drawn into this arrangement by the Treaty of St. Jean de Maurienne, which gave Italy southern Anatolia (Adalia) and a small sphere of influence in adjacent lands. Palestine was to become an International Zone, except for the British presence in Haifa/Acre. The rump of Anatolia would be Turkish.

The Sykes-Picot Agreement contradicted the agreement with the Hashemites and the letters of Sir Henry McMahon, Britain's High Commissioner in Egypt, to Hussein bin Ali, Sharif of Mecca. The political waters were muddied further in November 1917, when the British Foreign Secretary, A. J. Balfour, wrote an ambiguous letter to Lord Rothschild, a leading Zionist. Balfour said that Britain would view with favor the establishment of a national home for the Jews in Palestine. Zionists thought this meant a Jewish state, and that Britain would encourage immigration and settlement. This conflicting policy was intended to win the support of the Jewish lobby in the United States to use the Zionists to control Palestine and to eradicate French and Russian interests there. Confusion was increased by the 1918 Hogarth Message to the Sharif promising the Hashemite Arabs independence in the Hejaz and Palestine.

The 1919 Paris peace talks at the war's end

presented an opportunity to amend the Sykes-Picot proposal and Britain's machinations. Russia could be ignored since it was now largely under Bolshevik control. Britain controlled all the Middle East and was determined to keep Palestine and the oil region of Kurdish Mosul. French diplomacy forced Britain to hand over Syria and the Lebanon, and this meant that British promises to the Hashemites were broken, Feisal was kicked out of Damascus, and Britain's reputation was tarnished. In Turkey Nationalists, led by Mustafa Kemal, fought against the peace treaties and foreign occupation to establish the secular Republic of Turkey after a war with Greece and agreements with France and Italy.

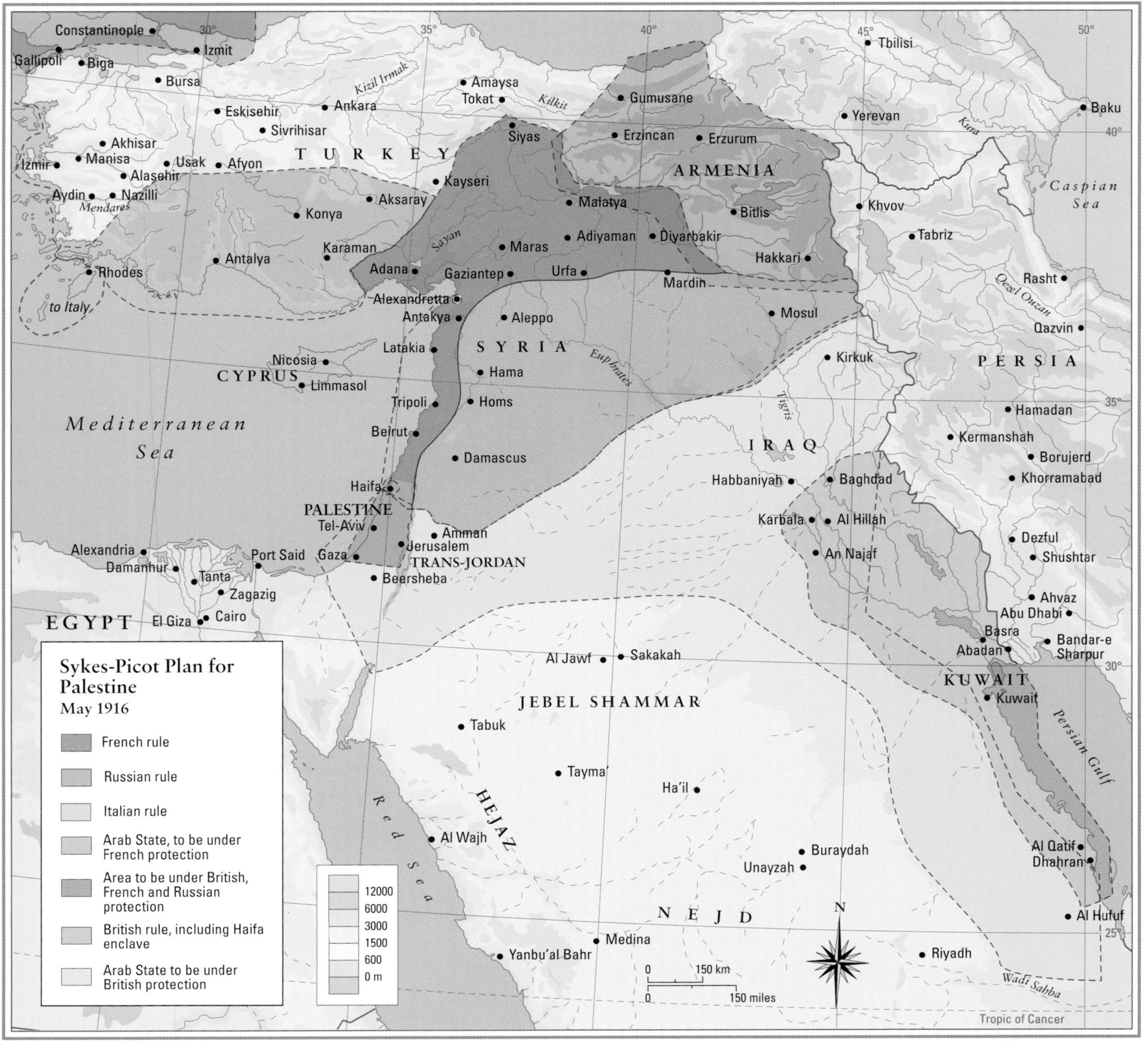

T. E. Lawrence and the Arab Revolt 1916–18

Thomas Edward Lawrence, photographed just north of Aqaba in 1917. After the successful seizure of Aqaba, Lawrence was promoted to Major, and his strategy for the Arab Revolt was supported by his commander, General Sir Edmund Allenby.

During the First World War, Britain made overtures to the Arab subjects of the Ottoman Empire. The most important of these Allies gained were the Hashemite Arabs of the Hejaz region around Medina and Mecca led by Sharif Hussein. In 1916, they rebelled against Ottoman rule and were supplied by the British with allied support, military supplies, advisors, and finance. The Hashemites began operations by successfully attacking the Ottoman garrison in Mecca, but they were unable to defeat enemy forces in Medina, which was the railhead of the line which connected the Hejaz to Damascus. The Medina garrison held out until ordered to surrender on 10 January 1919.

Military tasks included harassing Ottoman troops along the Hejaz railway, attacking the enemy around Amman in Trans-Jordan, and supporting British, Indian, and ANZAC soldiers of the Egyptian Expeditionary Force (EEF) stationed in southern Palestine in their push northward, leading to the Battle of Megiddo in the fall of 1918. The Hejaz railway was important to the Ottomans, helping them to control the western side of Arabia and supplying the Medina garrison. To destroy it became the key task of the Northern Arab Army (NAA), led by Hussein's son, Feisal. The NAA numbered some 5,000 men; with supporting irregulars the force, on occasion, could reach 20,000 men. The NAA was strengthened by Arabs who had served in the Ottoman army but had been made prisoners-of-war. Let out of POW camps, they joined the NAA, becoming a cadre of non-commissioned and commissioned officers. They struck at blockhouses, stations, and trains, but never managed to close the railway. The attacks on the railway were nevertheless important in tying down Ottoman troops and forcing constant repairs to damaged parts of the line.

Into this environment came T. E. Lawrence, an intelligence officer who became the main liaison between Feisal, his brother Abdullah, and the commander of the EEF, General Allenby. He managed to persuade the brothers to co-ordinate their forces and operations, and helped to organize British naval support to turn back an Ottoman attack on the port of Yenbu in December 1916. In July 1917, Lawrence, Feisal, and some Arab irregulars marched on Aqaba, the only Ottoman-controlled port on the Red Sea. The port was rapidly captured and later defended against Ottoman attempts to re-take the city.

By 1918, the Arab campaign reached Trans-Jordan and a battle was fought at Tafilah by the Dead Sea. The NAA were used to guerrilla tactics and a formal battle was normally unthinkable for them, yet they thoroughly routed the Ottomans, and returned to their normal hit-and-run policy. The high point of the Arab Revolt was reached with the Battle of Megiddo in September 1918. The EEF attacked along the coast, encircling the enemy with a cavalry assault, while the NAA harried the Ottoman eastern desert flank, eventually joining up with the EEF at the rail junction at Dera'a, before marching onward and entering Damascus. Ottoman units were attacked by aircraft and the EEF moved to Aleppo at incredible speed.

As soon as Hashemite forces entered Damascus, they began to administer the city, much to the annoyance of the French, who complained that this broke the Sykes-Picot Agreement of 1916. Lawrence entered the city with Feisal, who became ruler of Syria, a fact confirmed by Allenby. Britain hoped to ensure that the Arab leaders received recompense for their losses in men but also to ensure that pro-British leaders ruled as the Middle East with its oil was transformed from an Ottoman Empire to a series of Hashemite Kingdoms. Eventually, Feisal's Greater Syrian regime was crushed by the French after France was awarded a League of Nations' mandate over the country. Feisal was moved on to Iraq, where his family ruled until 1958, while his brother, Abdullah, was given Trans-Jordan.

The Arab Revolt
June 1916 – June 1917
Territory under Allied control
Ottoman Empire c.1900
British advances during 1917
Arab guerrilla attacks on Hejaz railway, disrupting troop movements
Principal towns captured by Arabs
Blockaded towns by Arab and Allied forces
Under Arab control by June 1917
SUBAY Major tribe
RUSSIAN EMPIRE
OTTOMAN EMPIRE
PERSIA
Caspian Sea
Syria
Iraq
NEJD
Hejaz
Asir
Yemen
Red Sea
Persian Gulf
Gulf of Oman
Arabian Sea
Rub el Khali
KUWAIT
Under British Protection 1899
BAHRAIN
Under British Protection 1861
QATAR
Under British Protection 1916
TRUCIAL OMAN Under Brit. Prot. 1853
OMAN
British Protectorate 1891
HADHRAMAUT
British Protectorate 1888
ADEN
British Protectorate 1903
Lahej Under Ottoman occupation
Aden Captured by Britain 1839
ERITREA
(to Italy 1899)
ANGLO-EGYPTIAN SUDAN
ABYSSINIA
PALESTINE
Cyprus
El Hasa
Railway under construction
Euphrates
Tigris
RUWALA
ANIZA
'ANIAARKAT
BANA SAKHR
BANA ATIYA
HUWAYTAT
BILLI
JUHAYNA
HARB
HUTAYM
SHAMMAR
DAFIR
UJMAN
AWAZIM
BANI
SUBAY
'UTAYBA
QAHTAN
MURRA
DAWASIR
ZAHRAN
HUDHAYL
GHAMID
YAM
Maras
Diyarbakir
Hakkari
Tabriz
Adana
Iskenderun
Antakya
Aleppo
Mosul
Rasht
Lahijan
Qazvin
Tehran
Latakia
Limassol
Hama
Homs
Tripoli
Beirut
Damascus
Kirkuk
Sanandaj
Hamadan
Qumm
Kermanshah
Borujerd
Kashan
Khorramabad
Habbaniyah
Baghdad
Haifa
Megiddo
Dera'a
Jerusalem
Gaza
Port Said
Amman
Karbala
Al Hillah
An Najaf
Isfahan
Dezful
Yaid
Tafilah
Ahvaz
Abu Dhabi
Ma'an
Aqaba
Al Jawf
Sakakah
Basra
Abadan
Kerman
Shiraz
Sirjan
Tabuk
Firuzabad
Muwela
Tayma
Ha'il
Bandar-Abbas
Bandar-e Lengeh
(to Oman)
Jask
El Ala
Al Wajh
Buraydah
Unayzah
Al Qatif
Dhahran
Al Hufuf
Sharjar
Medina
Yanbual Bahr
Riyadh
Abu Dhabi
Pirate Coast
Khaburah
Muscat
Wadi Sahba
Jiddah
Mecca
At Taif
Suakin
Kunfida
Abha
Atbara
Khor Baraka
Kassala
Massawa
Asmara
Loheiya
Sana
Al Hudaydah
Mukalla
Takazze
Aduwa
Zabid
Taizz
Mocha
0 100 km
0 100 miles
N
35°
40°
45°
50°
55°
60°
30°
25°
20°
15°

The Road to Damascus 1917–18

Ottoman cavalry moving from Bir-es-Saba to the front, April 1917.

After Allenby captured Jerusalem many of his troops were returned to Europe to combat the German Spring Offensive. He spent the summer of 1918 training new troops, integrating reinforcements from India, and generally reorganizing his forces. His infantry and cavalry raided the Ottoman forces twice during this period. The first assault crossed the Jordan and cut the Hejaz railway near Amman, while the second captured Es Salt on the road to Amman; the troops were forced back, yet they managed to retain two bridgeheads over the Jordan. Further reinforcements arrived from Britain, South Africa, and French North Africa.

Allenby planned to attack the key road and rail center of Ottoman communications. Ottoman reinforcements and supplies traveled along the Hejaz Railway running south from Damascus. The Ottoman 4th Army relied on this line, and a branch running west from Dera'a supplied the 7th and 8th Ottoman Armies. Arab irregulars were to attack the Hejaz Railway while deception plans were carried out to persuade the Ottomans that the Egyptian Expeditionary Force would launch an offensive in the Judaean Hills along the Jordan Valley. In fact, the main attack was to commence on the Mediterranean coast, where troops had been massed to such an extent that they outnumbered the Ottomans five to one. Three cavalry divisions had also been moved from the Jordan Valley to the coast at night. Allenby's deception plans were made possible by air superiority, using British and Australian fighter aircraft to attack any enemy reconnaissance aircraft. On 16 September 1918, the Arabs attacked the rail center at Dera'a and this turned into a large-scale uprising as neighboring Arab villages took up arms spontaneously. British troops attacked in the hills above the Jordan on the 17th and 18th. On the 19th, a bombing raid succeeded against a major Ottoman telephone exchange and railway station at Al-Afuleh. Other bombing raids damaged other communications.

Allenby's main assault began on 19 September when a massive artillery barrage by 385 guns and two warships landed on Ottoman divisions defending Nahr el Faliq. A creeping barrage then preceded an infantry assault, which broke through Ottoman lines allowing the Desert Mounted Corps to pour through. The Ottomans broke and retreated under air attacks. The Desert Mounted Corps swiftly captured the defiles through the Carmel Range and, by the 23rd, had captured Haifa. Ottoman armies were encircled and attempted to retreat, but again were strafed from the air. Waves of aircraft struck the 7th Army with attacks every few minutes, and it was routed in 60 minutes, not the five hours that was expected. All its guns were lost, as were all motor vehicles and 837 wagons. Finally the Ottoman 4th Army began its retreat; harassed by aerial attack, the force disintegrated, leaving its transport and retreating northward on foot. By the 25th, Amman was taken and many Turks surrendered with the rest being forced to surrender near Damascus.

On 26 September, Allenby wrote: "I desire to convey to all ranks and all arms of the Force under my command, my admiration, and thanks for their great deeds of the past week, and my appreciation of their gallantry and determination, which have resulted in the total destruction of the 7th and 8th Ottoman Armies opposed to us. Such a complete victory has seldom been known in all the history of war."

The Egyptian Expeditionary Force had advanced 300 miles, captured 75,000 prisoners, 360 artillery pieces, all Ottoman transport and equipment, and lost 5,720 casualties. Aleppo, Beirut, Damascus, and Homs all fell, and the Ottoman Empire sued for peace.

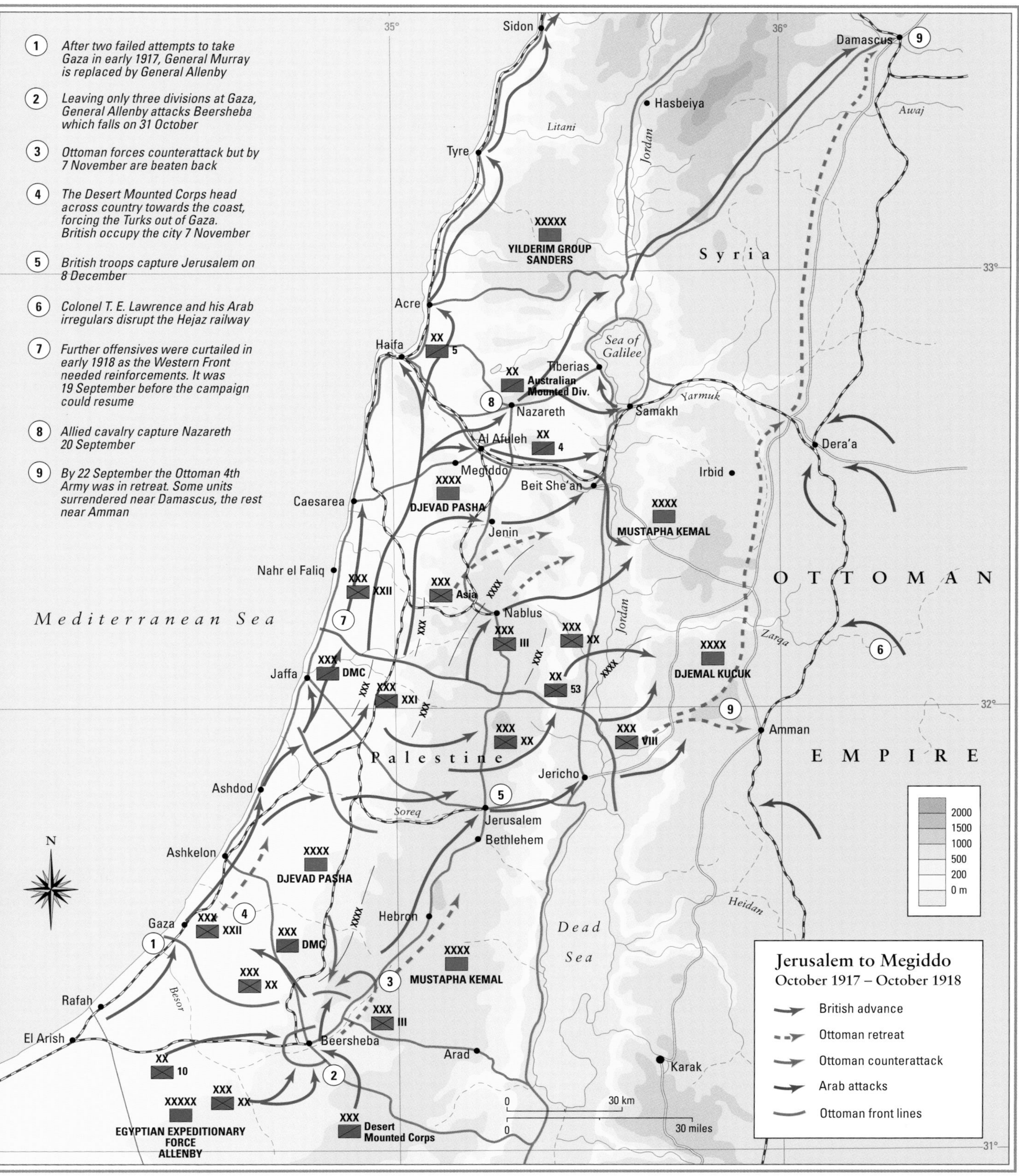

1 After two failed attempts to take Gaza in early 1917, General Murray is replaced by General Allenby
2 Leaving only three divisions at Gaza, General Allenby attacks Beersheba which falls on 31 October
3 Ottoman forces counterattack but by 7 November are beaten back
4 The Desert Mounted Corps head across country towards the coast, forcing the Turks out of Gaza. British occupy the city 7 November
5 British troops capture Jerusalem on 8 December
6 Colonel T. E. Lawrence and his Arab irregulars disrupt the Hejaz railway
7 Further offensives were curtailed in early 1918 as the Western Front needed reinforcements. It was 19 September before the campaign could resume
8 Allied cavalry capture Nazareth 20 September
9 By 22 September the Ottoman 4th Army was in retreat. Some units surrendered near Damascus, the rest near Amman
Jerusalem to Megiddo
October 1917 – October 1918
British advance
Ottoman retreat
Ottoman counterattack
Arab attacks
Ottoman front lines
2000
1500
1000
500
200
0 m
30 km
30 miles
Mediterranean Sea
Syria
OTTOMAN EMPIRE
Palestine
Sidon
Damascus
Hasbeiya
Tyre
Acre
Haifa
Tiberias
Sea of Galilee
Nazareth
Samakh
Al Afuleh
Megiddo
Beit She'an
Dera'a
Irbid
Caesarea
Jenin
Nahr el Faliq
Nablus
Jaffa
Amman
Jericho
Ashdod
Jerusalem
Bethlehem
Ashkelon
Hebron
Gaza
Rafah
El Arish
Beersheba
Arad
Karak
Dead Sea
Litani
Jordan
Yarmuk
Awaj
Zarqa
Soreq
Besor
Heidan
35°
36°
33°
32°
31°
N
YILDERIM GROUP SANDERS
Australian Mounted Div.
DJEVAD PASHA
MUSTAPHA KEMAL
DJEMAL KUCUK
Asia
DMC
Desert Mounted Corps
EGYPTIAN EXPEDITIONARY FORCE ALLENBY

Treaty of Lausanne and League of Nation Mandates 1923

The peace treaty negotiations ending the hostilities with the Ottoman Empire resulted in the Treaty of Sèvres, agreed by Sultan Muhammad VI in August 1920. The terms imposed on the Ottoman Empire were far more severe than those facing the defeated German Empire. Meanwhile, when the Ottoman armies collapsed in 1918, Constantinople became the center of an Allied military administration. Italian soldiers landed at Antalya, Greeks moved into Smyrna, and the French occupied Cilicia. Turkish nationalists, such as Mustafa Kemal, feared the break-up of Anatolia and opposed the Sultan's acceptance of the peace terms.

The Sultan renounced all claims to non-Turkish territory. The Kingdom of the Hejaz was recognized but it was seized by Nejd in 1926. Armenia, too, was deemed to be independent and there was talk of a possible Kurdish state. Mosul, Mesopotamia, and Palestine were mandated to Britain and Syria and Lebanon went to France. The area of Greek settlement at Smyrna and its hinterland were assigned to Greece for five years, after which a plebiscite was to be held to decide its future. The Dodecanese Islands and Rhodes were confirmed Italian, as they had been occupied since 1912. Turkish Thrace, except for the Çatalca strip and the remaining Turkish Aegean islands, went to Greece. France received a large sphere of influence in East-Central Anatolia. Italy's zone of influence was envisaged as a future Italian colony, which would be called Lycia. Military restrictions as to the size of the Turkish army and navy were laid down and an air force forbidden.

In response, Nationalist congresses met at Urzurum and Sivas, and affirmed the unity of Turkish territory, condemning the foundation of Armenia while forming a provisional government at Ankara, with Mustafa Kemal as

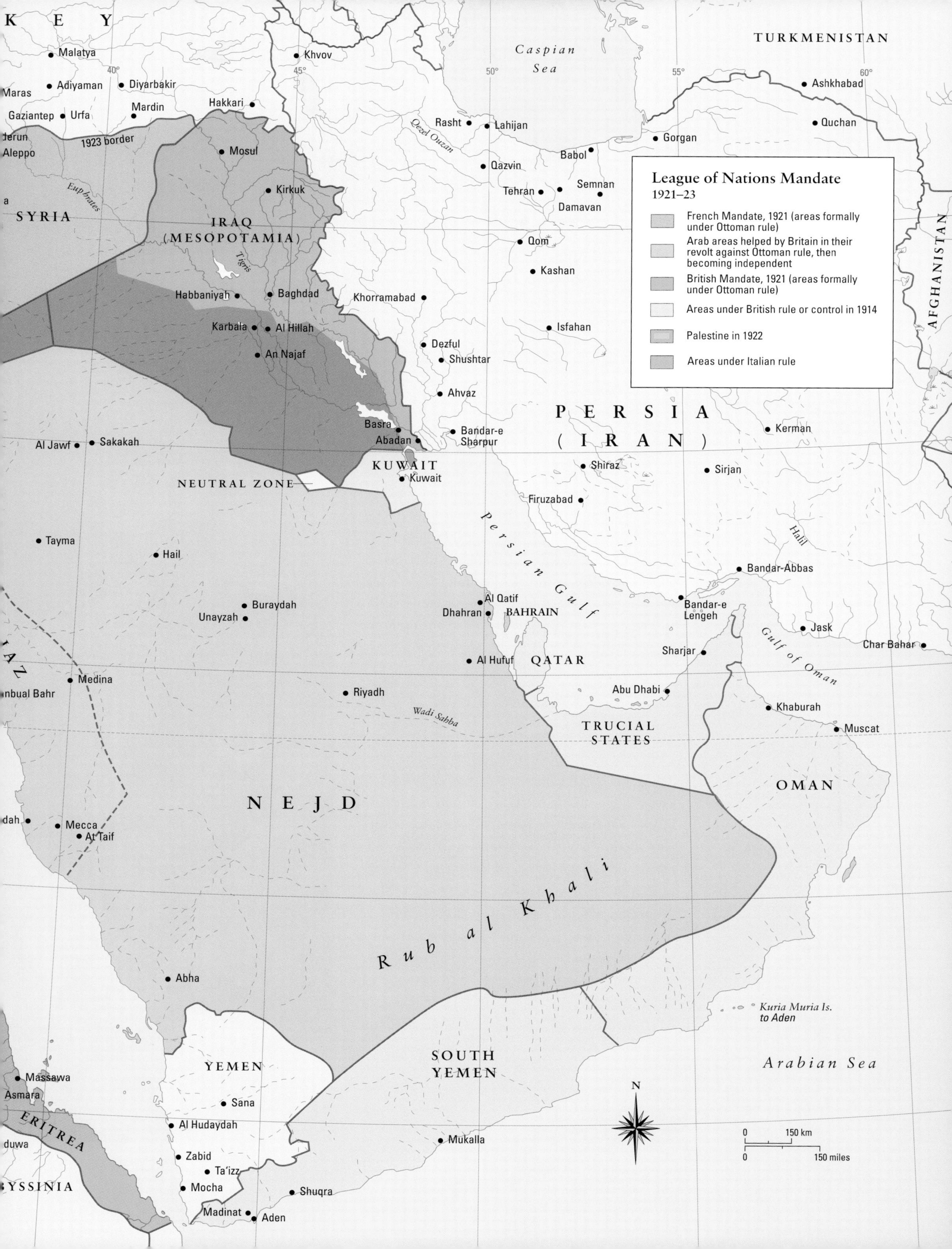

League of Nations Mandate 1921–23
French Mandate, 1921 (areas formally under Ottoman rule)
Arab areas helped by Britain in their revolt against Ottoman rule, then becoming independent
British Mandate, 1921 (areas formally under Ottoman rule)
Areas under British rule or control in 1914
Palestine in 1922
Areas under Italian rule
TURKMENISTAN
Caspian Sea
AFGHANISTAN
SYRIA
IRAQ (MESOPOTAMIA)
PERSIA (IRAN)
KUWAIT
NEUTRAL ZONE
BAHRAIN
QATAR
TRUCIAL STATES
OMAN
NEJD
Rub al Khali
YEMEN
SOUTH YEMEN
ERITREA
Persian Gulf
Gulf of Oman
Arabian Sea
Kuria Muria Is. to Aden
1923 border
Euphrates
Tigris
Qezel Ouzan
Halil
Wadi Sabba
Malatya
Khvov
Adiyaman
Diyarbakir
Maras
Mardin
Hakkari
Gaziantep
Urfa
Aleppo
Mosul
Kirkuk
Rasht
Lahijan
Qazvin
Tehran
Semnan
Damavan
Babol
Gorgan
Ashkhabad
Quchan
Qom
Kashan
Isfahan
Khorramabad
Habbaniyah
Baghdad
Karbala
Al Hillah
An Najaf
Dezful
Shushtar
Ahvaz
Basra
Abadan
Bandar-e Sharpur
Kerman
Shiraz
Sirjan
Firuzabad
Kuwait
Al Jawf
Sakakah
Tayma
Hail
Buraydah
Unayzah
Al Qatif
Dhahran
Al Hufuf
Bandar-Abbas
Bandar-e Lengeh
Jask
Char Bahar
Sharjar
Abu Dhabi
Khaburah
Muscat
Medina
Riyadh
Mecca
At Taif
Abha
Massawa
Asmara
Sana
Al Hudaydah
Zabid
Ta'izz
Mocha
Madinat
Aden
Shuqra
Mukalla
N
0 150 km
0 150 miles
40°
45°
50°
55°
60°

Mustafa Kemal Atatürk, 1881–1938, founder of the Turkish secular state. He sent a telegram to what turned out to be the last meeting of the Ottoman Parliament in Constantinople (Istanbul) on 12 January 1920. In it he declared the rightful government of Turkey was in Ankara, calling itself the Representative Committee. The 600-year history of the Ottoman Empire effectively came to an end.

President. The Greek response was to wage war, defeating the Turkish Nationalists at Alasehir, Bursa, and Adrianople. As well as plans to liberate Turkey and revising Sèvres, the Turkish Nationalists engaged in diplomacy. Firstly, a bloody campaign was launched against Armenia, which coincided with a Soviet pacification of Soviet Armenia. The Turks took Kars and the Red Army seized the rest. A peace treaty with the Soviets in 1920 ended Armenian independence and consolidated Turkey's easternmost frontier. In 1921, an agreement with France provided for the French evacuation of Cilicia in return for economic concessions. A similar compact was made with the Italians. During the summer of 1921, confused fighting between Greeks and Turks continued; the Greek advance on Ankara was contained at the Battle of Sakarya. A Nationalist counterattack broke the Greeks; Smyrna was taken in the fall. An armistice at Mudania, in October 1922, allowed for the restoration of eastern Thrace and Adrianople to Turkey, in return for the Turkish neutralization of the Straits under international control.

Eight months of peace negotiations followed in Lausanne, Switzerland. The Treaty of Lausanne was signed on 24 July 1923. The existing status of the mandates was retained and Turkey renounced its rights in areas such as Egypt, which were *de jure* still Ottoman territory. Any claim to the Dodecanese Islands was renounced but the islands of Imbros and Tenedos were returned to Turkey. Some one million Anatolian Greeks were displaced, mainly to Attica, in Greece, and some half-million Muslims became refugees and moved to Turkey. The remaining piece of Ottoman lands to be regained was Hatay Province, part of the Syrian mandate. In 1938, it became Hatay State and joined Turkey the following year after a referendum.

October 1923 saw the proclamation of the Turkish Republic, with Mustafa Kemal elected President, a post he held until his death in 1938. The President sought to westernize and secularize Turkey by dissolving dervish orders, banning the fez, abolishing the caliphate, making civil marriage compulsory, introducing the Latin alphabet, reforming education, and bringing in Swiss civil and fiscal law, and Italian criminal law. State intervention built up trade and industry. In 1935, Mustafa Kemal was awarded the title Atatürk (Father of the Turks), for his salvation and modernization of the state.

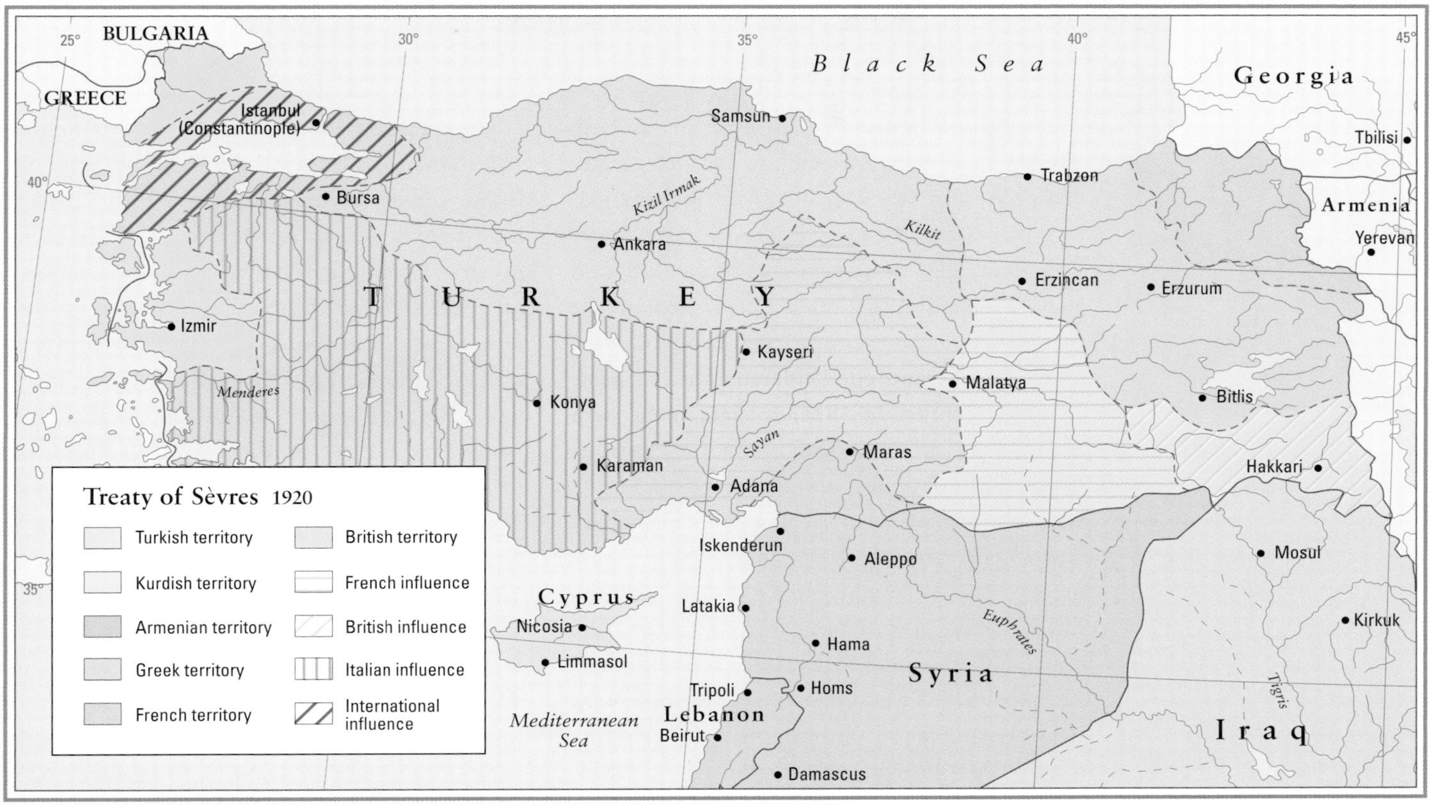

BULGARIA
GREECE
Black Sea
Georgia
Istanbul (Constantinople)
Samsun
Tbilisi
Trabzon
Bursa
Kizil Irmak
Kilkit
Armenia
Yerevan
Ankara
Erzincan
Erzurum
TURKEY
Izmir
Kayseri
Malatya
Menderes
Konya
Bitlis
Sayan
Maras
Karaman
Adana
Hakkari
Iskenderun
Aleppo
Mosul
Cyprus
Latakia
Nicosia
Euphrates
Kirkuk
Hama
Limmasol
Syria
Tigris
Tripoli
Homs
Mediterranean Sea
Lebanon
Beirut
Iraq
Damascus

Treaty of Sèvres 1920

- Turkish territory
- Kurdish territory
- Armenian territory
- Greek territory
- French territory
- British territory
- French influence
- British influence
- Italian influence
- International influence

BULGARIA
Adrianople 25 June 1920
Black Sea
Sea of Marmara
Constantinople (Istanbul)
Sea of Marmara
Inonu 9-11 Jan. and 26-31 March 1921
Bursa
Kizil Irmak
Eskisehir 19 July 1921
Aegean Sea
Kutahya 17 July 1921
Ankara Turkish capital from 1923
Polatli
Sakarya August 1921
Afyon Karahisar 28 March and 11 July 1922
TURKEY
Smyrna (Izmir)
Usak 29 August 1920
Dumlupinar 26–30 August 1922
Aydin 27 June–4 July 1921
Menderes
Konya
ITALIAN ZONE until 1921
Karaman
Cilicia
French occupation ended January 1922
to Italy 1912
Antalya
Mediterranean Sea

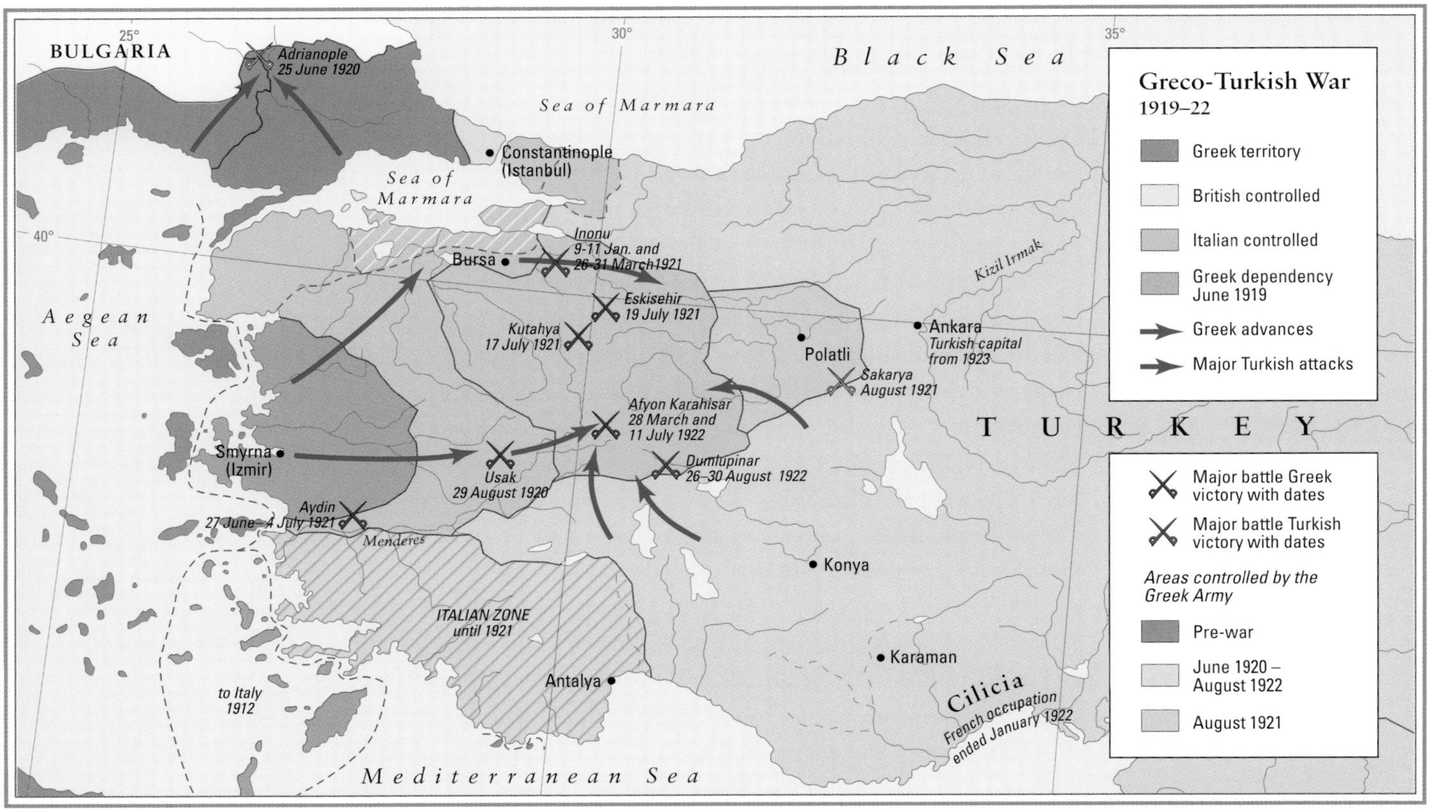

Greco-Turkish War 1919–22

- Greek territory
- British controlled
- Italian controlled
- Greek dependency June 1919
- Greek advances
- Major Turkish attacks

- Major battle Greek victory with dates
- Major battle Turkish victory with dates

Areas controlled by the Greek Army

- Pre-war
- June 1920 – August 1922
- August 1921

The Arab Rising

Lord Peel, Chairman of the Peel Commission, is seen leaving the King David Hotel on his way to the Government House opening ceremony in 1936.

In 1936 in Palestine, a group of recently formed Arab political parties coalesced into the Arab Higher Committee, which orchestrated strikes and political protests against the British mandatory power and the growing Jewish population. This nationalist movement was responding to a rise in Jewish immigration occasioned by the increasingly anti-Semitic policies in Nazi Germany, where Adolf Hitler became Chancellor in 1933. Between 1933 and 1936, more than 164,000 Jewish immigrants arrived in Palestine, more than doubling the Jewish population, which accounted for over a quarter of the inhabitants. Furthermore, land sales to Jews were increasing, driving many Arabs off the land into urban squalor. Jewish businesses and farms were employing fewer and fewer Arabs, leading to rising unemployment. Added to these issues was the Arab resentment of imperial rule and their desire for an Arab government. In October 1935 a large arms shipment was discovered at Jaffa, destined for the Haganah, a Jewish paramilitary organization established, after the 1929 Arab riots, to defend the Jews of the Yishuv, the collective name for the Jewish population in Palestine. Arabs feared the growth of this Jewish 'army,' visualizing it as the first stage in an armed Jewish takeover of Palestine.

The British government was hard-pressed to find a workable strategy: it relied on Arab goodwill for oil, yet it had promised the Jews a homeland in Palestine according to the Balfour Declaration. The Arabs, under the leadership of Haji Amin al-Husseini, would not guarantee the Jewish community citizenship or guarantee its safety if an Arab political entity emerged. Violence began in April 1936 when a Jewish convoy was attacked and two drivers killed. Deaths and beatings escalated, with Jewish buildings and orchards burned. The British Army tried to keep the peace but troops were killed in the effort. In reality, the British had few options: impose a partition, pull out of Palestine and let strife increase, or stay on and muddle through.

A Royal (Peel) Commission on Palestine was sent to the Middle East and it published a report in November 1937. Palestine was to be divided into three: a Jewish state along the coast from north of Gaza to beyond Acre including Galilee; an Arab state in the Negev and what is now termed the West Bank; and a British section around Jerusalem and Bethlehem with a corridor to Jaffa. The Arab state would be linked to Jordan and 225,000 Arabs would be transferred from the Jewish state to the Arab state and Trans-Jordan. The Jews accepted the recommendations but the Arabs refused partition. The insurgency intensified and ultimately the Woodhead Commission reversed Peel and the matter was shelved until after the Second World War. British interests faced other threats at this time. In 1935, the Italians had invaded Ethiopia, which could mean a fascist state was threatening Egypt and the Suez Canal from both Libya and Ethiopia. By 1937, the Spanish Civil War had broken out.

Meanwhile, sniping, bombing, and murder continued. Britain responded by destroying Arab villages in reprisal and the Royal Air Force gathered photographic intelligence, and bombed targets. The British were aided by 20,000 Jewish policemen and the Haganah was armed. Charles Orde Wingate, an officer who was both pro-Zionist and a Christian, later known for fightng the Japanese in Burma, organized Special Night Squads which attacked Arabs, engaging in terror tactics, beatings, torture, and summary executions. The execution of Shaikh Izzedin a-Qassam, a former preacher in the Ottoman army, created a martyr for the Palestinian cause. The revolt, or Arab nationalist uprising, was suppressed but at great human cost. Actual losses are variously calculated. Over 400 Jews and 262 British died while the Arabs lost approximately 5,000 dead, 15,000 wounded, and 5,000 imprisoned. The uprising had lasted for three years.

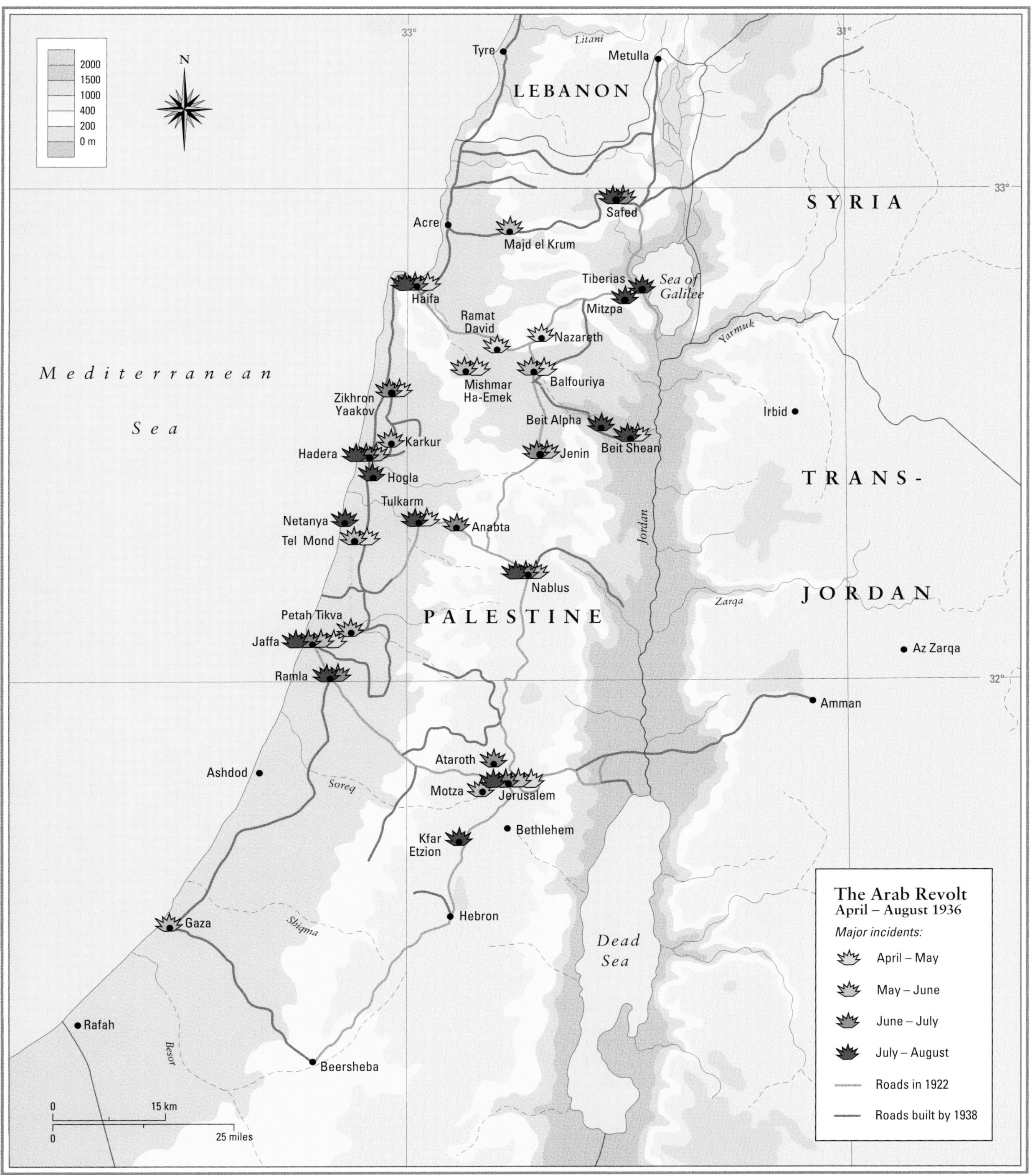

2000
1500
1000
400
200
0 m
N
Tyre
Litani
Metulla
LEBANON
SYRIA
Safed
Acre
Majd el Krum
Haifa
Tiberias
Sea of Galilee
Mitzpa
Ramat David
Nazareth
Yarmuk
Mediterranean
Sea
Mishmar Ha-Emek
Balfouriya
Zikhron Yaakov
Irbid
Beit Alpha
Karkur
Beit Shean
Hadera
Jenin
Hogla
TRANS-
Tulkarm
Netanya
Anabta
Tel Mond
Jordan
Nablus
Zarqa
JORDAN
Petah Tikva
PALESTINE
Jaffa
Az Zarqa
Ramla
Amman
Ataroth
Ashdod
Soreq
Motza
Jerusalem
Bethlehem
Kfar Etzion
Hebron
Gaza
Shiqma
Dead Sea
Rafah
Besor
Beersheba
0
15 km
0
25 miles
The Arab Revolt
April – August 1936
Major incidents:
April – May
May – June
June – July
July – August
Roads in 1922
Roads built by 1938

Iraq, Syria, and Persia April–September 1941

World War II cast its long shadow over the Middle East. By 1940 France had fallen, its middle eastern mandates fell under 'Vichy' pro-Axis control. The British position in the region was precarious. Rommel and his Afrika Corps had advanced from El Agheila in Libya to the western border of Egypt. The British garrison in the Libyan town of Tobruk was besieged by Axis forces.

In April 1941, in addition to all those separate campaigns, a new problem arose with Iraq, a British mandate until 1932 when it gained full independence. The pro-British Regent, Emir Abdul-Illah, and his government wished to declare war on Germany but nationalist activists wanted concessions from the British first. On 3 April the Emir was overthrown in a coup led by General Rashid al-Kilani, a former Prime Minister, known for his Axis sympathies. The General objected to the arrival of the 10th Indian Division to the port of Basra and his objections were ignored, so he ordered his troops to surround the British airbase at Habbaniya, some 50 miles west of Baghdad. On 2 May, British aircraft bombed Iraqi positions and the Iraqis shelled the British base. After intense pressure from London, General Wavell, the area commander, agreed to send a relief force to Habbaniya.

'Habforce' was created mainly out of units of the 1st British Cavalry Division based in Palestine. This force was despatched across the desert on 13 May, reaching Habbaniya on 18 May, but the Iraqis were already withdrawing. Attacked by the Luftwaffe from bases in Vichy Syria and northern Iraq, Habforce still secured the British base, and then took Baghdad. Meanwhile, the 10th Indian Division occupied Basra and pacified the region. Rashid fled, the Emir Abdul-Illah was restored.

Evidence of German involvement in the region caused British Prime Minister Churchill grave concern and he wanted to ensure that a new war front was not opened up from bases in Vichy Syria and Lebanon. Wavell wanted to husband his forces but he was overruled by Churchill and the angst of Charles de Gaulle, the Free French leader. Wavell committed part of the British 1st Cavalry Division and most of the 7th Australian Division and Free French units, totaling some 34,000 men. Operation Exporter began on 8 June, with an advance along the coast road toward Beirut and over the mountains into Syria. Initially, the advance was successful but stalled when the Vichy French counterattacked. Savage fighting followed but British air superiority and Habforce attacks

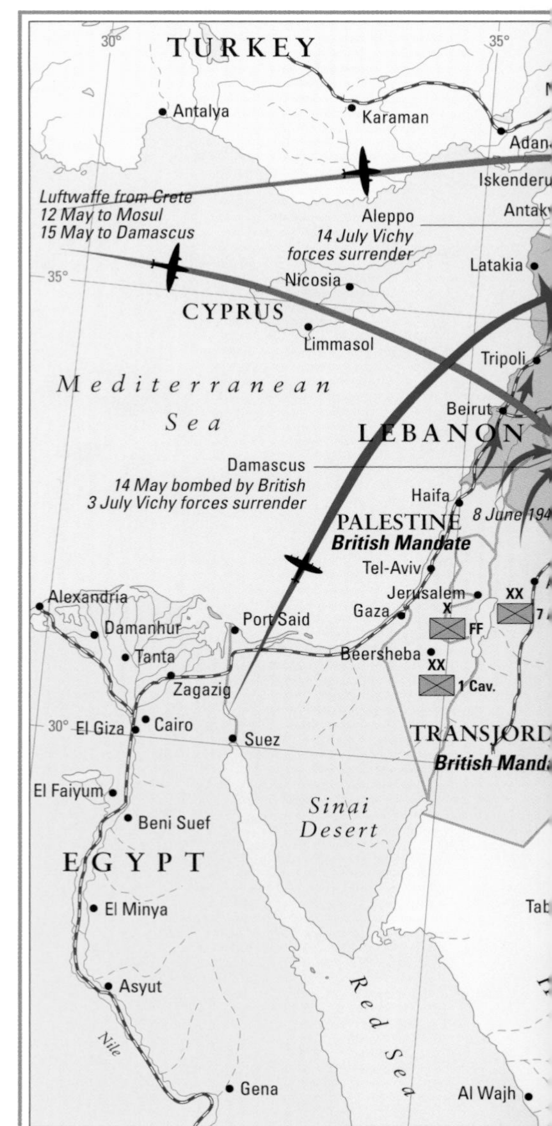

from Iraq ensured the advance toward Aleppo and Homs continued. Two extra British brigades from Palestine broke the Vichy French, allowing the capture of Damascus. Supported by naval gunfire, the Australians broke the defenses of Beirut and, in a fierce five-day battle, captured the city. French forces surrendered in eastern Syria, and the French commander, Dentz, signed an armistice.

On 27 June Germany invaded the USSR. Britain was determined to support its new ally and, in conjunction with the Soviets, entered the neutral country of Persia on the night 24/25 August 1941. Soviet columns advanced southward from the Caucasus Mountains and from Central Asia, east of the Caspian Sea. A British force advanced northward from the Persian Gulf, westward from Iraq, and overland from India. Tehran was occupied on 17 September. Protective of his country's neutrality, the Persian ruler, Shah Reza Pahlavi, had refused to expel German nationals. His army offered little resistance, and a ceasefire was ordered on 28 August. With Iran now an important supply line for the Soviet Union, the Allies needed a more pliable regime, and Britain pressured the Shah to abdicate in favor of his 22-year-old son, Mohammed Reza.

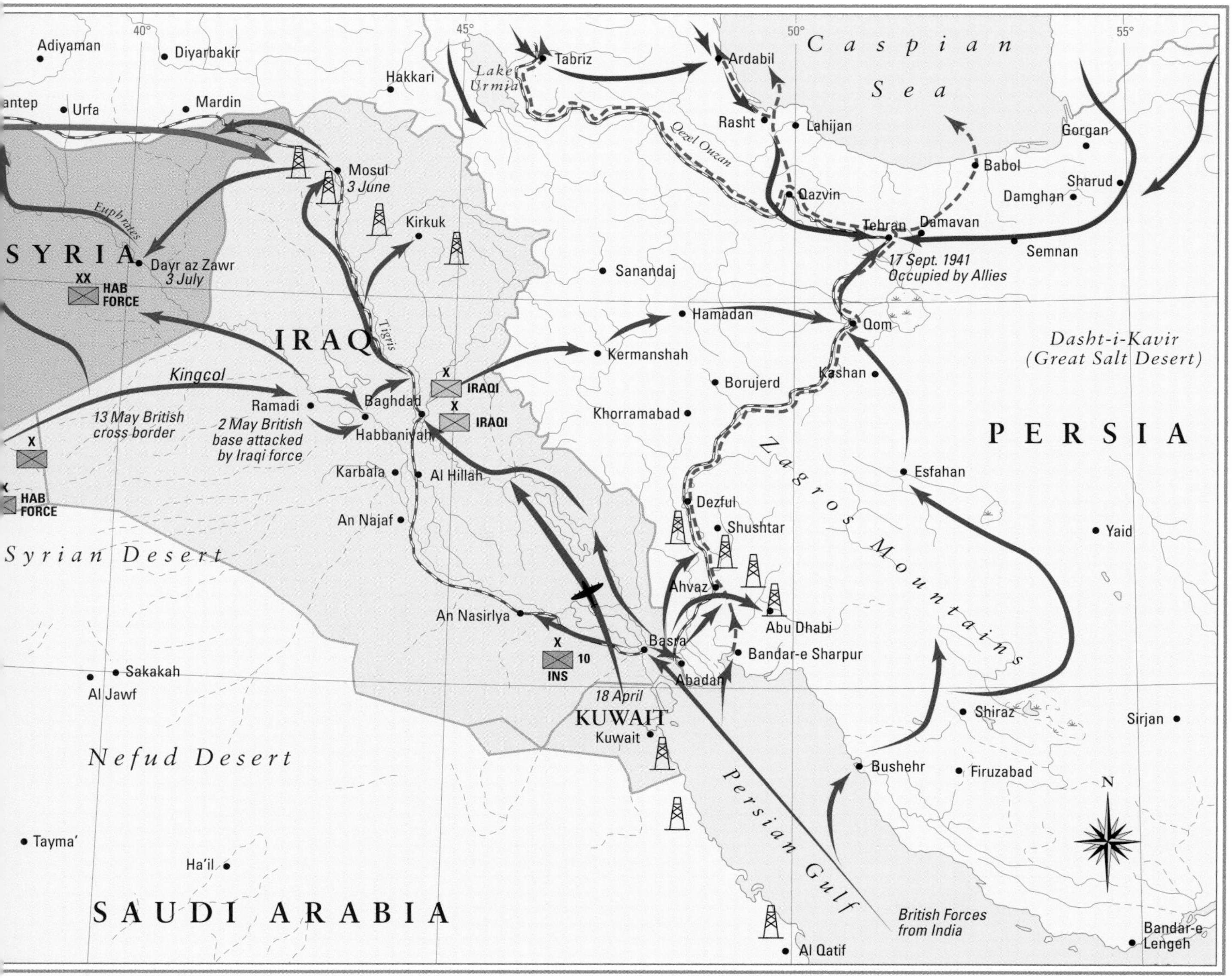

El Alamein II 1942

1942 was initially very disappointing for British armies in North Africa. In January, Rommel made a surprise attack at Adjabiya and he soon captured Benghazi. In early February, the British withdrew to the Gazala Line and May was a disastrous month, when the Afrika Korps swung through the desert outflanking the British defenses and breaking the Gazala Line, which led to the fall of Tobruk. The British withdrew to a new defensive line at El Alamein after losing Mersa Matruh, with 6,000 men made prisoner.

A new commander, Lieutenant-General Montgomery, was certain that Rommel would attack and attempt to break through the defenses but also was sure the Afrika Korps could be stopped. Then the British 8th Army would advance and drive the Germans and Italians from North Africa. Rommel launched an attack on 30 August and was subjected to constant attack from RAF bombers and a barrage of anti-tank and artillery fire laid down by Allied artillery. The British tanks avoided a tank battle and the dangers of powerful German 88mm guns, which were impressive tank-busting weapons, but instead were used as mobile artillery to shore up any weaker part of the Axis defense line. The British barrage continued until 4 September when Rommel ordered a withdrawal from his start lines after suffering heavy losses. His troops had suffered 2,940 casualties, lost 50 tanks, and 50 guns, and 400 trucks. Rommel returned to Germany because of illness, leaving the Afrika Korps in the care of General Stumme. Even though the British lost many more tanks, they had reduced the enemy to numerical inferiority and were able to build up reserves more quickly. The Allied Desert Air Force had proved its worth and gained full air superiority.

On the night of 23 October 1942 nearly 900 guns of all calibers from the British artillery opened fire on the German and Italian rear echelons, seeking to cause maximum disruption to command and supply lines. Once this was achieved, the barrage moved forward, shells falling in front of advancing troops. On the right of the advance was the 9th Australian Division and to their left were the Scots of the 51st Highland Division, then two brigades of New Zealanders with the 9th Armored Brigade. Their main objective was the Miteiraya Ridge. The sappers advanced first to clear paths through the minefields that had been laid down by the enemy, sometimes two miles deep. This was no easy task as a German counter-barrage was being laid down. Through these gaps, marked by white tape, the infantry

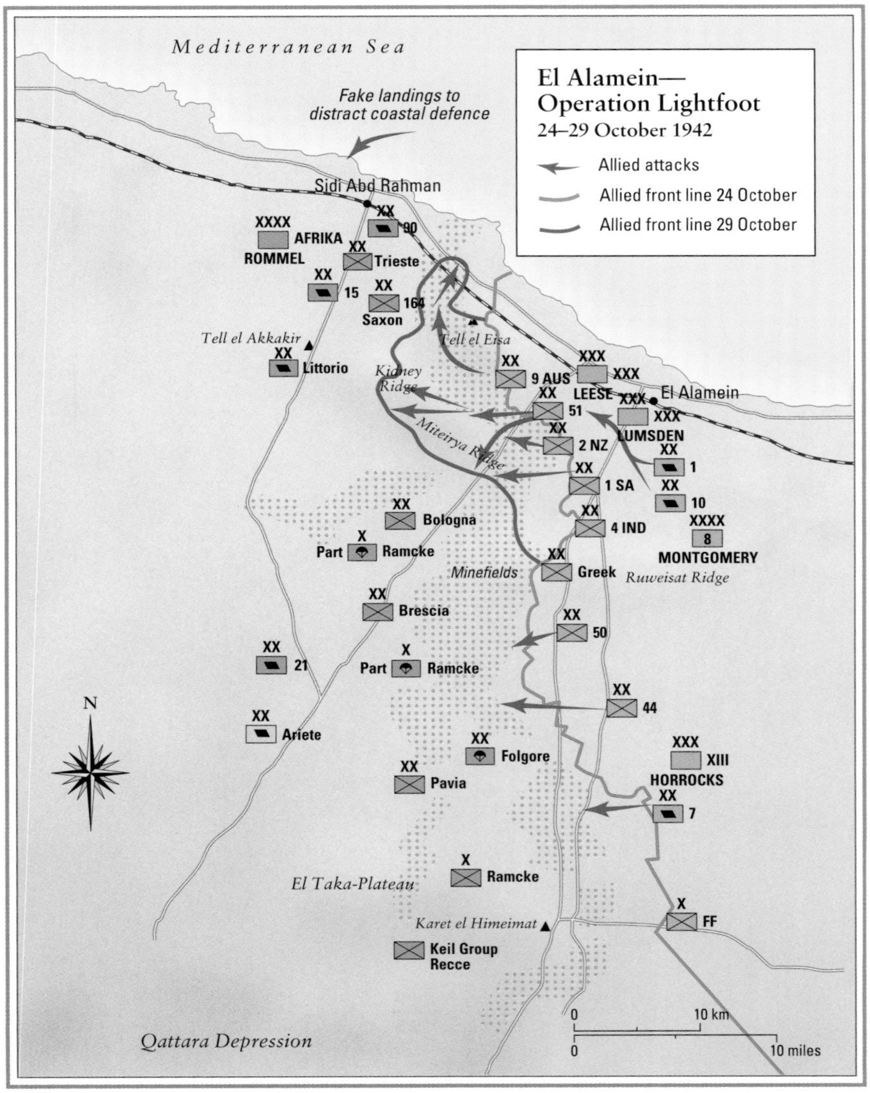

El Alamein—Operation Lightfoot 24–29 October 1942

advanced and started to clear enemy positions. By the morning of 24 October most of the objectives had been taken and the infantry began to dig in and wait for the armor to move up and support them. But behind the infantry there was absolute chaos as the armor tried to advance up the narrow tracks through the minefield. If one was blocked by a destroyed or damaged vehicle then a massive bottleneck would be caused, making a fine target for long-range German artillery. With the armor still unable to reach the infantry in the front, the battle was beginning to stall. However, General Montgomery still wanted his troops to advance to reach more defensible positions in the face of the inevitable Axis counterattack.

Rommel returned from Germany on 25 October and immediately ordered his 21st Panzer to move up north to attempt to hold the Allied advance, but they burned up precious fuel doing so. Montgomery organized the armor he required to draw in as many Axis tanks and infantry as possible, in order to wear them down in a war of attrition where he clearly outnumbered the opposition. He ordered the 9th Australian Division to break out toward Tel el Eisa, and this achieved his aim as it drew many Axis tanks and infantry into that sector.

The 2nd Battalion, the Rifle Brigade, advanced to a forward position, known as 'Snipe', on the night of 28 October with orders to hold a defensive position until relieved by advancing armor. The armor did arrive but attracted so much artillery fire that the tanks were forced to retire. All around the Snipe position was advancing Axis armor and the 2nd Battalion was able to take a vicious toll of the enemy, thanks to the anti-tank guns that were attached to the unit. After a hard engagement that lasted all day, the Snipe position claimed 34 armored vehicles, damaged many more, and caused the counterattack to falter.

Rommel began to prepare to fall back but first had to break his troops out of a salient holding out near Tel el Eisa. For this task, he made an assault group from the 21st and 90th Light Divisions, which were immediately attacked by RAF bombers but still went into the attack. The assault was successful with the troops leaving through a gap made in the salient. Meanwhile, Montgomery was organizing another thrust forward preceded by an immense barrage. The orders were the same as after the first barrage with similar bottlenecks occurring. Enough units got through for the advance to succeed although losses were great on both sides; the battle ended as Rommel withdrew with only 40 serviceable tanks while Montgomery still had huge reserves. By 4 November the battle was over as Tel Aqqaqir was seized by the Argyll and Sutherland Highlanders.

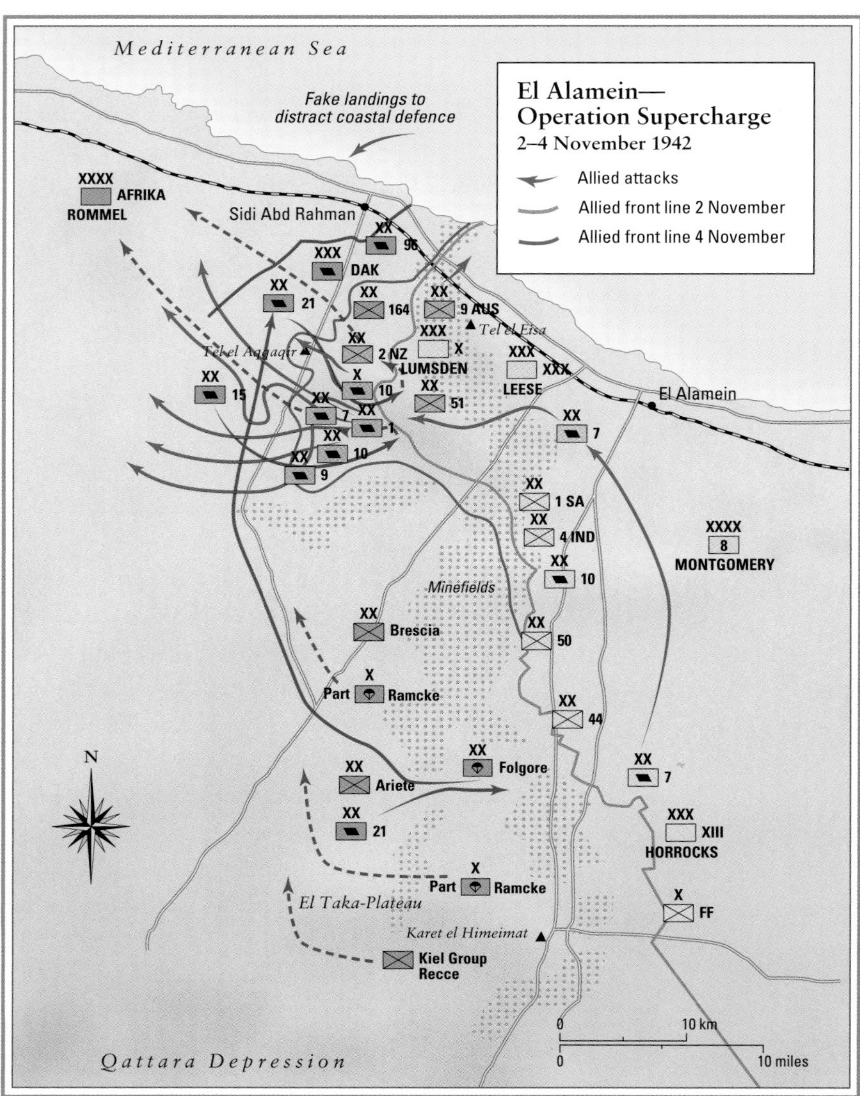

Technology and Society

The Second World War introduced new technologies and tactics to the Middle East, notably mobile armored warfare—'blitzkrieg' or 'lightning war'. This warfare, of rapid movement and maneuver led by an armored spearhead backed by motorized infantry and covered by close air support, was designed to punch through enemy positions. Other developments included the first use of cruise missiles, Germany's vengeance weapons, the V1 and, a little later, the V2 ballistic missile. Personal weapons, the assault rifle and the hand-held rocket launcher completed the military iconography of the modern battlefield that became so familiar in the Middle East.

The Middle East's military and technologial capabilities were developed in the 1940s, supplying the Allied forces, fighting in North Africa, with munitions and maintenance. Aircraft, missiles, tanks, and modern infantry weapons are all now designed and constructed in the Middle East. Israel now holds the technological lead and is the only nuclear power in the region.

During the immediate post-war years most of the equipment used by the armed forces of the Middle East was imported from the USSR and the US, though with Britain and France also playing a significant role.

Since the 1960s, industrial and technical capabilities have dramatically developed in the region, through local design and licenced production, notably the familiar AK47 assault rifle, commonly used throughout the Middle East. These mass-produced weapons have found their way from official government forces into the hands of various illegal groups and local militias.

War always leads to refugee problems and the Middle East has been no exception. In the aftermath of the Second World War people were displaced in Eastern Europe as well as there being many Holocaust survivors. The movement of many people to Palestine, and later the State of Israel, solved some problems for the Jews but, in turn, displaced Palestinian Arabs became refugees, forced to live in camps in other countries where they were not assimilated. The disruption and distress caused by the diaspora of Palestinians partially explains the *intifada*, a Palestinian uprising on the West Bank after Israel captured the region. Israel has generally succeeded in assimilating Jewish immigrants who arrived after Israeli independence in 1948, despite having to accommodate different religious practices and traditions.

Since 1945, a major problem for the Middle East has been superpower involvement, with the projection of Cold War ideologies and conflicts into the Arab-Israeli dispute, and into the region in general. The US post-war strategy to deal with Soviet expansion was containment via alliance systems, without any direct US involvement. The USSR, being adjacent to the Middle East by virtue of its Caucasian and Central Asian republics, found the presence of the US in the region a rationale for Soviet involvement in an anti-neo-imperialist stance. In this situation, after British withdrawal from the area, the US promoted arms sales to Iran and Saudi Arabia. Both the US and USSR saw the value of Middle Eastern oil and, despite the US lack of dependency on Gulf oil, needed to protect the security of oil since it was crucial to US global interests and the economies of its allies.

During the 1967 war, the US backed Israel while the Soviet Union supplied Egypt with missile defense systems including mobile radar stations. British tank laser-guided target systems were battle-tested by being fitted on Israeli tanks. A *quid pro quo* was an Israeli commando team being sent into Egyptian territory to helicopter out a mobile radar system for intelligence evaluation by the US and British military. In 1973, during the Yom Kippur War, both the US and USSR conducted massive resupply operations to their respective allies which almost led to a confrontation. During the war, the Israelis managed to encircle the Egyptian 3rd Army, and the US determined that, by terminating the Israeli resupply operation, they would prevent the Israelis from destroying the 3rd Army, thus persuading the Egyptians to consider making peace with the Israelis. Meanwhile, the Soviets placed its airborne divisions on alert while amphibious warfare vessels with their complements of marine infantry were deployed in the Mediterranean. The world reached the penultimate nuclear alert. However, the situation was defused when the Americans managed to persuade the Egyptians to announce they did not require Soviet help. The US and USSR pulled back from the nuclear brink and together imposed conditions to end hostilities.

Since the Yom Kippur War, contending sides in the Middle East have been supplied with modern weaponry and this has strengthened the autonomy of some Middle Eastern states and has allowed dictatorships to maintain domestic security. In 1985 the *Al-Yamama*, in Arabic, the Dove, arms contract was signed between Britain and Saudi Arabia, reputedly paid for by the delivery of 600,000 barrels of oil per day to the United Kingdom. Through these, and later deals, the weaponization of the Middle East continued apace.

By the 1990s, the armed forces of the Middle East were amongst the most lavishly-equipped in the world. A survey carried out in 1997 revealed that some 20,000 modern battle tanks were available to the region's armies. Syria, alone, deemed it necessary to deploy 4,600 tanks, almost exclusively supplied by the Soviet Union and its successor states.

The unstable nature of the region was displayed in the 1980–88 Iran-Iraq War, which was followed by the Iraqi invasion of Kuwait leading to the first Gulf War. This war exacerbated the region's refugee problem when, after regaining its freedom, Kuwait ensured that 200,000 Palestinians living in Kuwait were expelled.

In recent years, a new 'cold war' between the US and so-called Islamic terrorists has evolved, best understood by the Al-Qaeda attacks on 11 September 2001 in New York City and Washington, D.C. This event was predated, by 7 August 1998 bombings of US Embassies in Nairobi, Kenya, and Dar es Salaam, Tanzania, as well as a suicide bombing that damaged USS *Cole*, a guided missile destroyer, in the Yemeni port of Aden. Such events led to the US-sponsored war on terror with Saddam Hussein of Iraq being accused of aiding Al-Qaeda. This resulted in the March 2003 invasion of Iraq led by US and British forces to destroy so-called weapons of mass destruction.

In 2010 the first instance of cyber attack in the region occurred. The target was Iran's nuclear program where, reportedly, the attack destroyed 20 percent of Iran's nuclear centrifuges; the alleged perpetrator was Israel. Technology is also operated in near space, satellites continually monitor the region, in the high-atmosphere advanced aircraft operate on the same monitoring mission. Below these, the ubiquitous UAV, Unmanned Aerial Vehicles, commonly known as 'drones.' These remotely-controlled aircraft, once again, collect data and, when required, they can deliver a warload—not always with the accuracy their controllers claim.

The entire region continues to be extremely volatile after 2010, with a revolution in Egypt, a civil war in Syria, and severely damaged and politically unpredictable Iraq and Libya. Civil unrest in the region, now collectively known as the 'Arab Spring', a reaction to the post-colonial governments in the region. These governments were largely controlled by selective political or familial elites which, over the last 50 or 60 years, increasingly failed to appeal to the changing aspirations of their populations. The increasing access to mass media, together with the spread of social media, has focussed anti-government attitudes among large sections of the region's national populations. Through social media concerned individuals can spread the word, raise awareness, and face governmental attempts at media management and outright repression.

Aliyah 1945–48

Between 1948 and the late 1960s around 770,000 Jews left Arab states for Israel. Amongst them were 49,000 Yemenite Jews who fled to Israel in Operation Magic Carpet, which airlifted the entire community between June 1949 and September 1950.

The 'Aliyah' continued for years; over 770,000 refugees from Arab lands reached Israel with 260,000 from Morocco alone. Between 1948 and 1970, 80 percent of European Jewish immigrants originated from Communist-run Central Europe and comprised 36 percent of all Jewish immigrants. During this period the population of the new state of Israel increased from 657,000 to over 3,000,000. More Jews reached Israel from Iran, India, and the Soviet Union. Other more surprising origins of migrants were Jewish Argentinians and the Ethiopian Falashas. Arriving in Israel destitute, the immigrants were absorbed and assimilated into society, learning Hebrew in Israel's armed forces.

Aliyah, the Hebrew word for 'ascent', is a term used for the immigration of Jews from the Diaspora to Palestine and Israel. Jews had been returning to Palestine in significant numbers since the 1880s, and the British Mandatory power had put a cap on immigration in order to sustain good relations with the Arabs after the Second World War and to ensure supplies of oil on which Britain was dependent. Even the British Labour Party, which had embraced the notion of a Jewish state in Palestine, continued the restrictions outlined in the 1939 White Paper when they were voted into power in July 1945.

The aftermath of war and the plight of Holocaust survivors created pressure for illegal migration by groups such as the Aliyah Bet, which organized a Bricha, 'flight' movement run by wartime partisans and surviving ghetto fighters. Jewish survivors were smuggled from Eastern Europe to Italy where ships attempted to break the British naval blockade of Palestine. Over half of the ships were stopped and the passengers were deported to Cyprus internment camps or to the Atlit detention camp, south of Haifa. The interception of the SS *Exodus*, and the return of its 4,515 passengers to France, was a famous case. All told, some 50,000 people ended up in detention camps and some 1,600 drowned after accidents at sea. Jews from Arab countries tended to take a more successful overland route to Palestine. The Aliyah Bet managed to insert 110,000 Jews into Palestine.

Zionists waged a limited guerrilla war against British targets, with the aim of forcing Britain into granting Jewish independence. The Jewish militants came from a number of groups including the underground Jewish militia, the Haganah, and the more violent Lehi (also known as the Stern gang) and Irgun Zvi Leumi, with which it formed an alliance to fight the British. Each side engaged in tit-for-tat kidnap, sabotage, beatings, and arrests. Lehi achieve notoriety with the assassination in Cairo of the British government minister Lord Moyne, and later with the killing of the United Nations mediator Count Bernadotte in September 1948. The Irgun bombing of the British Military Headquarters in the King David Hotel in Jerusalem in July 1946 caused 91 deaths and left 42 wounded.

The Mandatory Authorities clamped down on the whole population of Palestine, imposing a

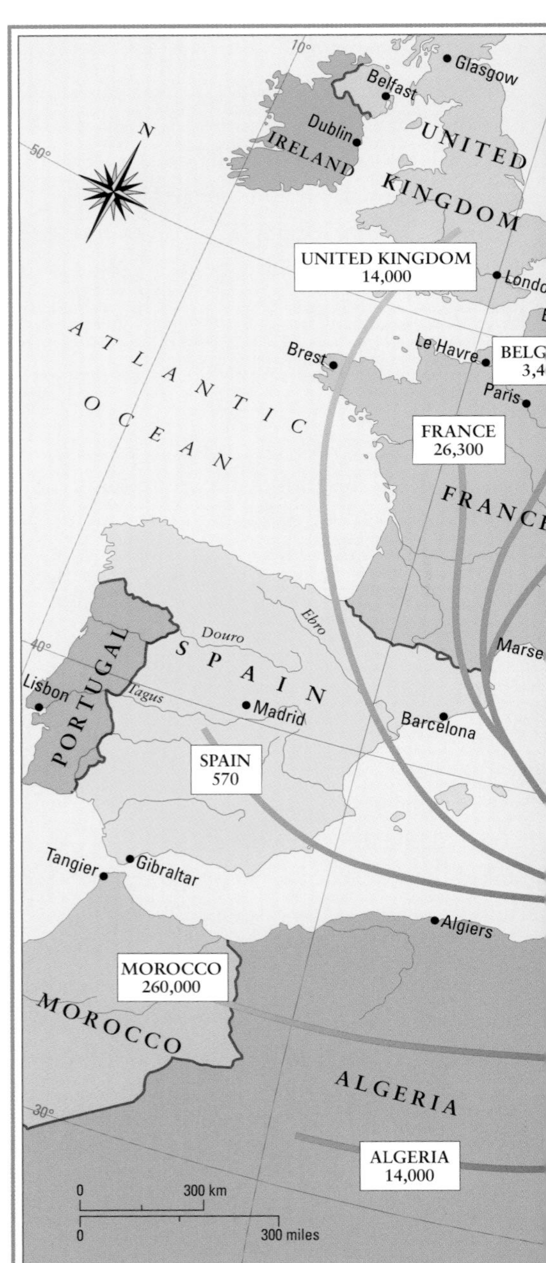

curfew, with 120,000 taken in for questioning. The US Congress criticized the heavy-handed treatment, which placed further pressure upon the British government, thereby vindicating the campaign's success.

The massacre of 40 Jews in Kielce in July 1946 by communist-backed forces contributed to the mass emigration of some 100,000–120,000 Polish Jews. Zionists organized, aided, and planned the departure under the auspices of Berihah, also responsible for the migration of Jews from Romania, Hungary, Czechoslovakia, and Yugoslavia, some 250,000 people including the Poles. World public opinion, increasingly sympathetic to the notion of a Jewish state, condemned the British actions and this became an important factor in Britain's decision to hand over Palestine to the United Nations in 1948.

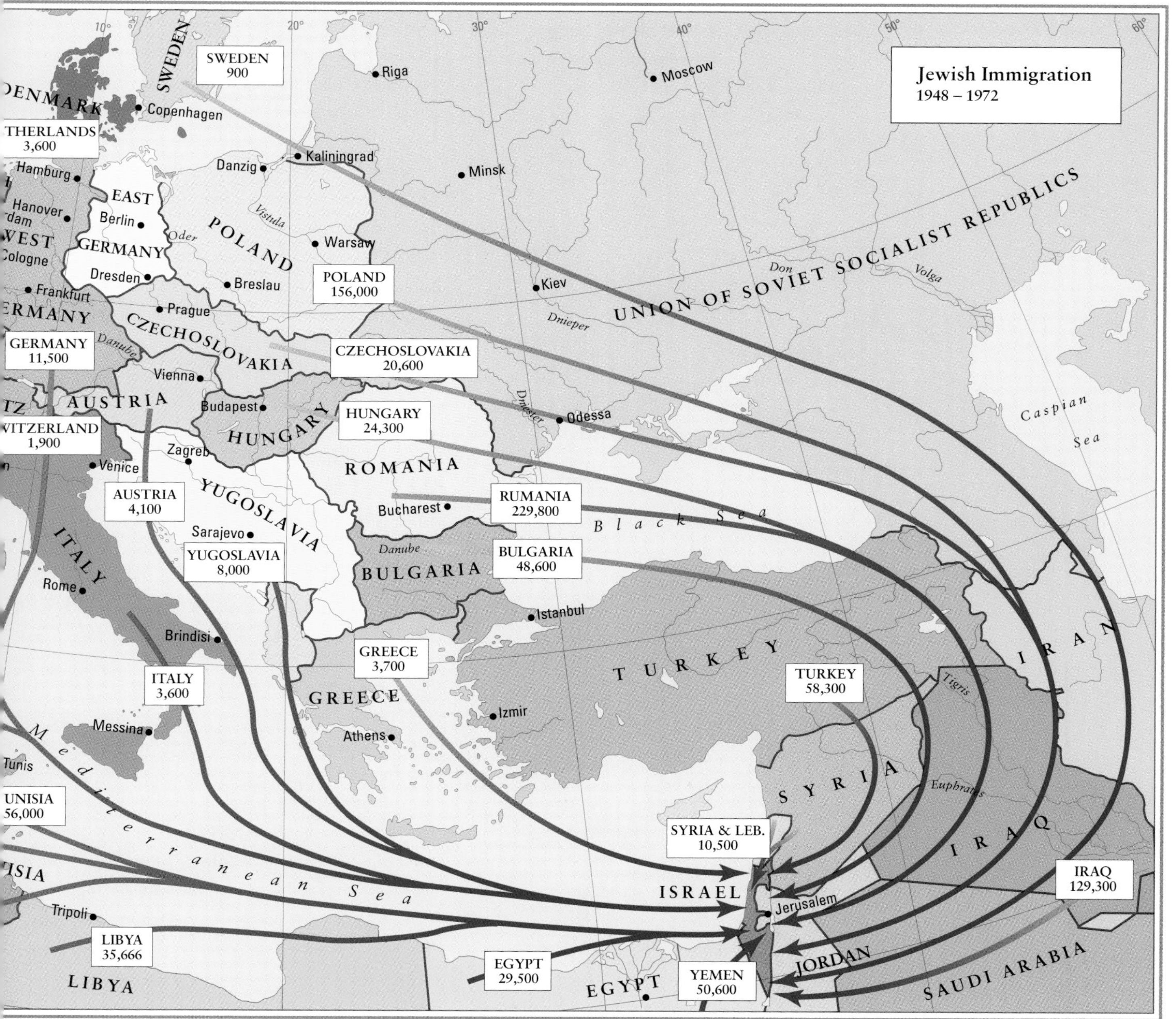

The First Arab-Israeli War 1948

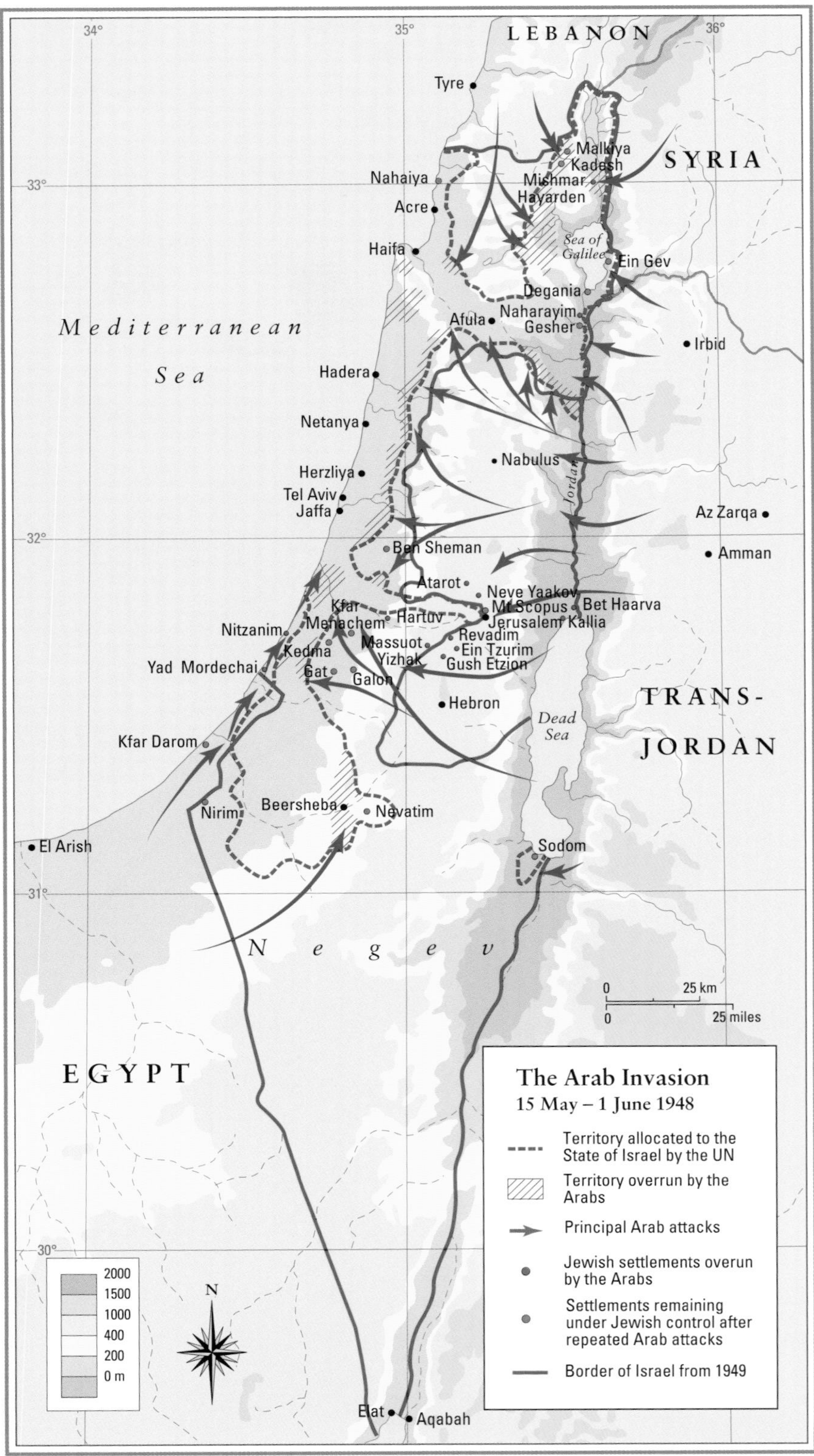

The First Arab-Israeli War—known by Israel as the War of Independence—is separated into two halves. The pre-independence period prior to the British withdrawal was a civil war between Arabs and Jews in Palestine. After the British withdrawal on 14 May 1948 and the Declaration of the State of Israel, it became an international war between Israel and some Arab states (Egypt, Iraq, Transjordan, and Syria). After Britain relinquished its mandate to the UN, the plan was to partition Palestine into a checkerboard of six parts, three Arab and three Jewish, with Jerusalem under international trusteeship. Around 55 percent of Palestine was allocated to the Jewish state, although the Palestine Arabs constituted a two-third majority, compared with 600,000 Jews. Cities such as Haifa and Jaffa, allocated to the Jews under the plan, contained large Arab majorities. The Jews were outnumbered, but were better prepared for the fighting. Many of the Jewish soldiers in the Haganah had gained extensive training and combat experience during the war. They had stockpiles of arms and ammunition that had been smuggled in by the Jewish Agency. Palestinian fighters had little combat experience and access to weapons, relying on the armies of Jordan, Syria, and Egypt. These countries did not commit their national armies, but called on irregular volunteers—such as Arab Nationalists and the Muslim Brotherhood.

Before the British withdrawal, volunteer Arab irregulars blockaded the Jewish quarter of Jerusalem. Villages that blocked the route to Jerusalem were captured or destroyed and a road was constructed to pass a particular choke point on the Tel Aviv to Jerusalem road. By mid-June Jerusalem could be resupplied.

Haifa fell to Jewish forces on 21–23 April as the British army withdrew. When the Haganah launched its final assault on Arab neighborhoods, Jewish aircraft attacked the city, provoking terror among the Arab population. By early May only 3,000–4,000 Arabs from an original population of

70,000 remained. Haifa secured, the Haganah concentrated on the rest of the coastline that had been awarded to the Jewish state under the UN plan. The Irgun, working independently of the Haganah, attacked the major Arab port of Jaffa. Panicked residents left en masse. Jewish forces concentrated on securing the northeastern territories conceded to the Jewish state under the UN plan. With mass evacuations and expulsions, the roads became clogged with refugees.

On 14 May 1948 the State of Israel was proclaimed and the governments of Egypt, Transjordan, Iraq, Syria, and Lebanon declared war on Israel. The Arab armies were ill-equipped, having only recently obtained independence from colonial rule. Their forces did not exceed 25,000 men, whereas the Israeli Defense Force, the Haganah numbered 35,000. In the course of the conflict both Arabs and Israelis increased their numbers, though the Arabs never came near to reaching the Israeli figure of 65,000 in mid-July, which swelled to more than 96,000 by December 1948.

Between UN brokered truces, hostilities continued. In Operation Dani the Israelis targeted Lydda and Ramlah, seizing the towns and driving out some 100,000 Arab Palestinians. In Operation Dekel Nazareth was seized and in Operation Brosh the Israelis took the lower Galilee from Haifa to the Sea of Galilee. By October, the besieged Israeli settlements in the Negev were rescued when an operation broke the Egyptians, forcing them to retreat from the northern Negev. Operation Hiram captured the whole of upper Galilee, an area reserved to the Arab state in the partition plan. Israeli soldiers then advanced to the Litani River in Lebanon. In December, the Israeli Defense Force drove the Egyptian army into the Gaza Strip, where it became encircled. In the following year the Israelis reached the Gulf of Aqaba, thereby clearing the Negev of Arab forces.

In July 1949 armistices were signed between Israel and the four Arab combatant countries; Israel had acquired some 18 percent more land than the partition plan had allocated. Egypt occupied the Gaza Strip and Trans-Jordan gained the West Bank. The casualties suffered were high; over 4,000 Israeli soldiers died and over 2,000 of its citizens.

Estimates of Arab losses vary from 8,000 to 15,000; about 750,000 were forced from their homes or fled in fear. More than 400 Arab villages were depopulated while ten Jewish villages and neighborhoods also lost their inhabitants. After the war, hundreds of thousands of Jews fled or were expelled from Arab countries and arrived in Israel. Soon Israel's Jewish population doubled to 1,700,000. Palestinian *fedayeen* began to launch cross-border operations into Israel from Syria, Egypt, and Jordan. The Israelis retaliated, launching seventeen raids on Egypt, with 400 Israeli deaths between 1951 and 1956.

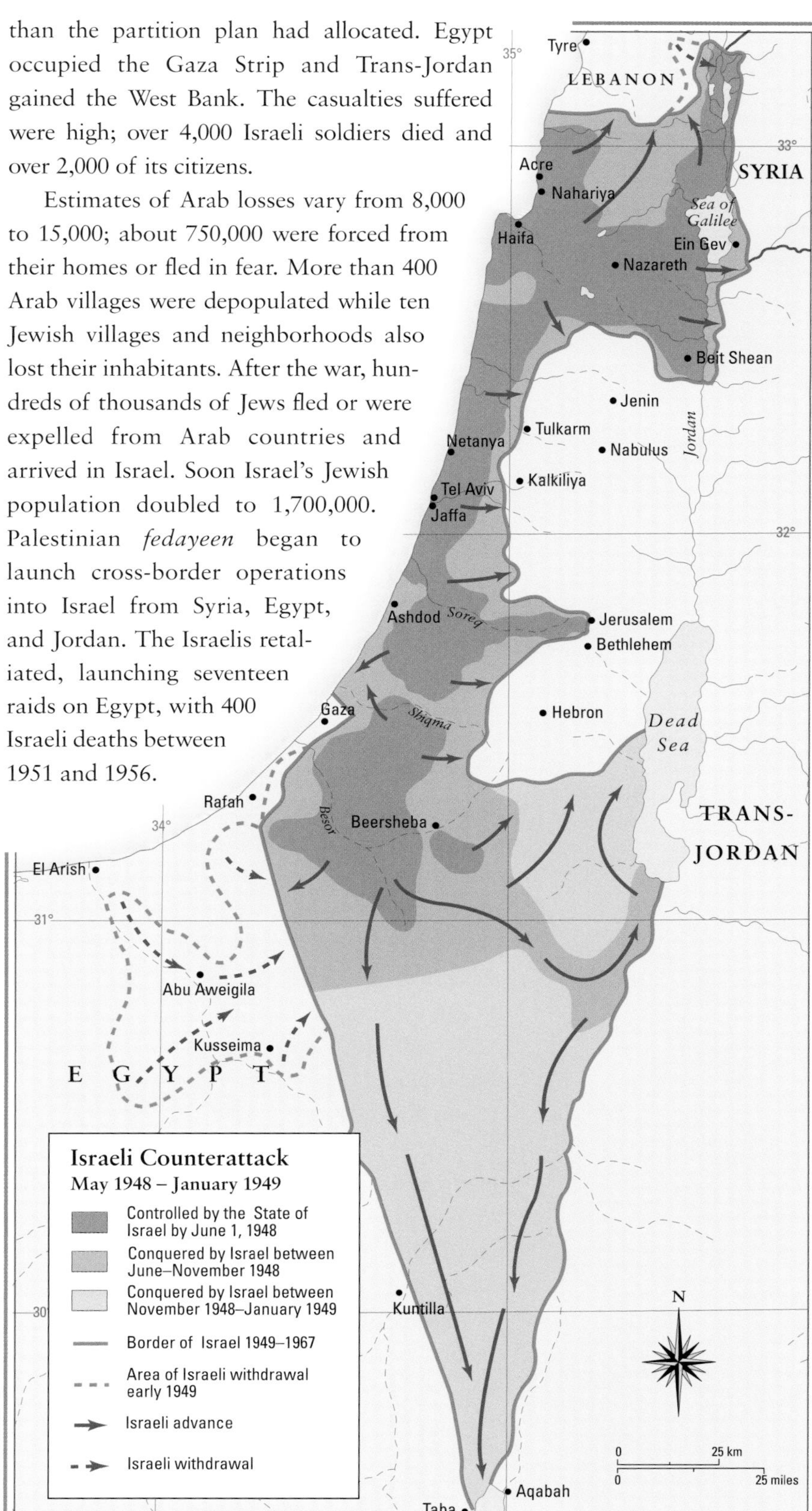

The Fate of the Palestinians

Arab refugees leaving the Galilee area, October–November 1948.

Palestine endured the 1947–48 Civil War in the British Mandate and the 1948 Israeli War of Independence. Both proved an unmitigated disaster for the Palestinian Arabs. This catastrophe or 'Nakba' in Arabic, led to 750,000 or more Arabs fleeing or being forced from their homes and lands, in what has been dubbed as ethnic cleansing. In sum, approximately 80 percent of the Arab inhabitants of the land that became Israel vanished, fleeing elsewhere. Both Israelis and Palestinians have differing explanations of these occurrences and all reflect some form of nationalist rhetoric. To exacerbate matters, many remaining Palestinian Arabs became internal refugees, displaced persons, as they were forced from their homes and told where to live by Israeli authorities and the Israeli Defence Forces.

Several historians have asserted that expulsion by the Haganah and IDF was deliberate. This was not government policy, but local Israeli commanders acting in their own interests. Arab depopulation became rife, with Arabs moving to Arab parts of Palestine such as the Gaza Strip, Beersheba, Nazareth, Bethlehem, Jaffa, and Haifa. Some wealthier Palestinians moved to Jordan, Egypt, and Lebanon. Many of these were middle-class professionals and the natural leaders of the Palestinians. Their migration severely damaged the well-being of those who remained.

Fear spread amongst the Arabs when fighters from armed Jewish groups, Irgun and Lehi, attacked the Arab village of Deir Yassin on 9 April 1948. This village came under attack when Jewish militias sought to lift the Arab blockade of Jerusalem. Some 107 of the 600 inhabitants were killed, including women and children, which induced fear and panic in all the Arab villages facing advances of Jewish forces. There are tales of Jewish loud-speaker vans approaching Arab villages, telling the inhabitants to evacuate their homes lest there be another Deir Yassin. Whatever the truth of the matter, Arabs fled. Deir Yassin was a catalyst in the Arab mass exodus from the city of Haifa. Half the inhabitants apparently fled before the battle for Haifa began, with another 5,000–15,000 leaving during the fighting, while some 15,000–25,000 were ordered to leave by Arab leaders. Some reports claim that the Haganah mortared the city to encourage the Arabs to flee.

Jewish forces armed themselves with home-made weapons, such as the Davidka mortar. This contraption fired a shell carrying 60 pounds of TNT. It was used to capture the town of Safed and against Jaffa. Legend has it that when the first shell exploded there it caused a mushroom cloud while it started to rain, as happened in Japan in the American nuclear bomb attack. Fears were raised that Jewish forces had nuclear weapons, which precipitated flight. Thus, a mixture of force and psychological warfare eroded Arab morale, causing more Arabs to leave. In the fall of 1948, David Ben-Gurion, the Israeli leader during the Arab-Israeli War, and Yitzak Rabin, a deputy commander in Operation Danny, ordered the expulsion of the 60,000 inhabitants of Lydda and Ramlah. The population of Lydda left on foot while citizens of Ramlah were removed using IDF buses and trucks.

The expulsions were accompanied by the destruction of some Arab districts in cities and hundreds of villages. After the war ended, some Palestinians attempted to return home but the Israeli Prevention of Infiltration Law classed these people as infiltrators from surrounding hostile countries, who were illegal. The Israeli government enacted laws that consolidated the nationalization of land and property, which was used to house and fund those Jewish refugees entering Israel during the Aliyah. Absentee property housed one-third of

Israel's Jewish population and, by 1954, a third of new immigrants made homes in urban areas abandoned by Arabs. Between 1948 and 1953, 370 new Jewish settlements were constructed, 350 on absentee property.

Palestinian refugees also included internally displaced people or absentees. These were the people, and their descendants, who had fled, or were expelled from their homes in Palestine by Jewish militias or the IDF before and during the 1948 Israeli War of Independence. This applied to 46,000 of the 156,000 Palestinians who remained in Israel after independence. Some of these Arabs are Christian (ten percent), the majority being Sunni Muslims. Amongst the Palestinian Arabs are the Bedouin, who mainly inhabit the Negev Desert. Originally there were 110,000 Bedouin but many were expelled to Gaza, Egypt, and Jordan, leaving just 11,000 in Israel. Those remaining were moved into closed military dominated zones. Some Bedouin, in declining numbers, have served in elite tracker units in the IDF to contain infiltrators. Military administrative rule limited the movement of Arab citizens in Israel and the internally displaced were not allowed to return to their homes. The villagers of Ghassibiya, Bir'im, and Iqrit applied to the Israeli High Court to have their property recognized and this was granted in the 1950s but the IDF refused to abide by court rulings, claiming the villages were closed military zones.

Other than the Bedouin, Palestinians inhabit some 80 towns and villages in Galilee, such as Nazareth and Umm el Fahm, which are entirely Arab. Fifty percent of the population of these towns comprised internally displaced refugees from neighboring towns and villages destroyed in the 1948 War. Some Israeli towns such as Acre, Haifa, Jaffa, Lod, Ramla, and Jerusalem, have mixed populations of Jews, Palestinians, Circassians, and Greek Orthodox. Palestinians are not required by law to serve in the armed forces, unlike the Druze and Circassians.

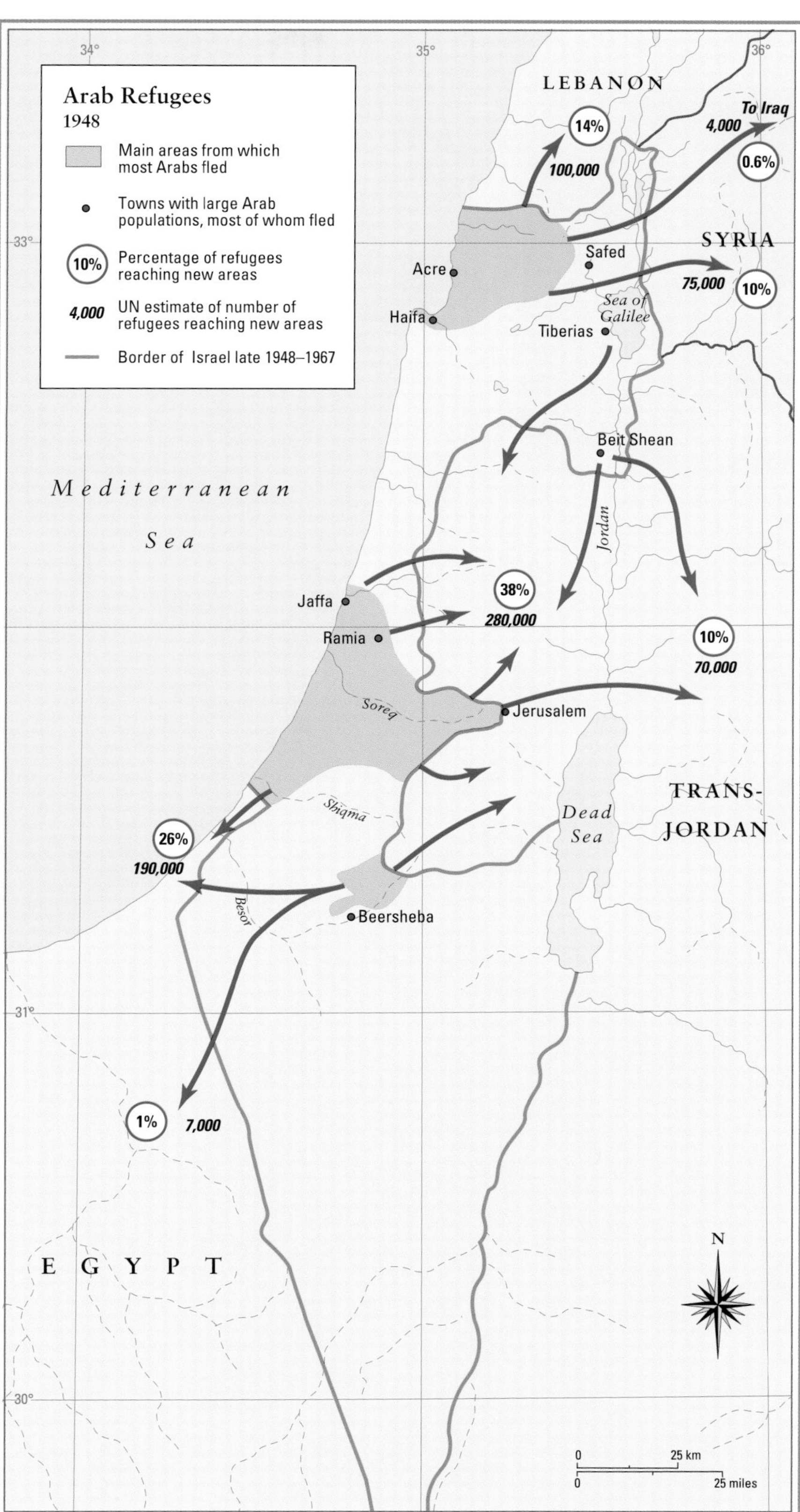

Suez—War of Collusion

Gamal Abd al-Nasser championed the dream of a Pan-Arab union of states.

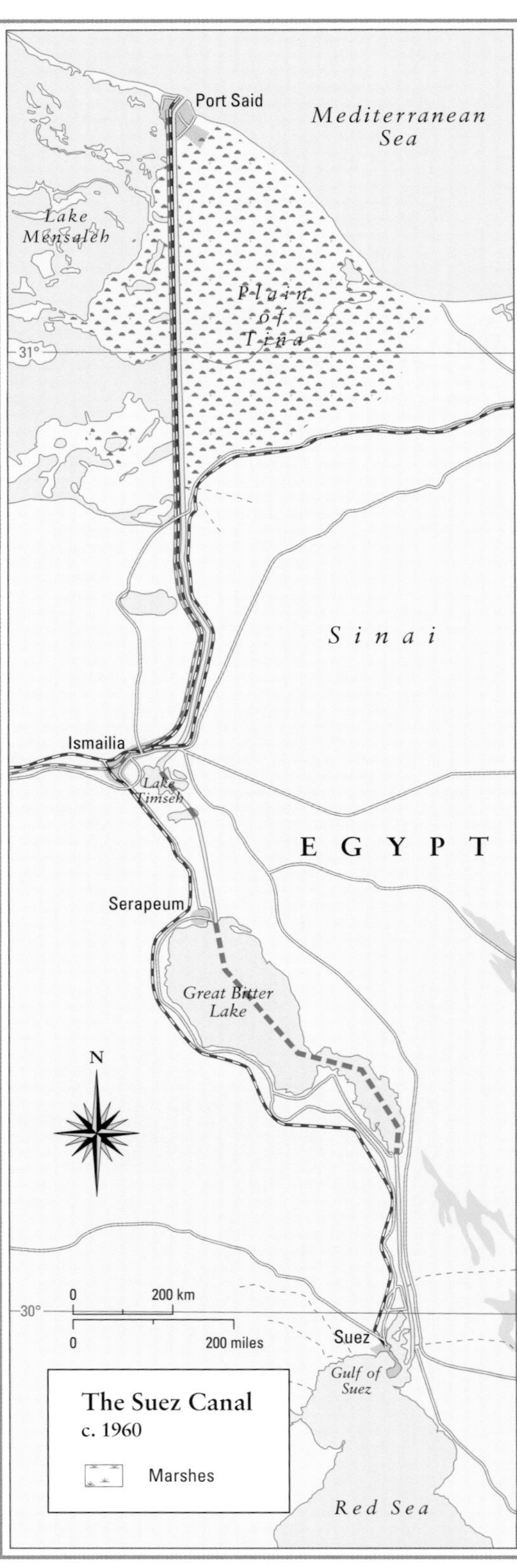

The Egyptian President Gamal Abd al-Nasser, who rose to power in the military coup that overthrew the monarchy in 1952, had ambitious plans to make his country fully independent after seven decades of direct or indirect rule by Britain. A long-discussed project since earlier in the century was the construction of a high dam at Aswan on the upper Nile, which would regulate the flow of the river while providing much-needed electricity and water for irrigation. Nasser also needed to modernize his army, the mainstay of his regime. Though initially well disposed to Nasser, the US made the promise of financial credits and arms and wheat supplies conditional on Egypt joining the Baghdad Pact, an alliance that formed part of an American strategy of 'containment' towards the Soviet Union. Nasser rejected this as being contrary to his policy of 'non-alignment', instead concluding an arms deal with Soviet-dominated Czechoslovakia. Although the US and Britain responded with a promise of a loan for building the dam, they were clearly irritated by Nasser's ability to exploit cold war rivalry. Then the US Secretary of State John Foster Dulles was infuriated by Nasser's recognition of Communist China, while Nasser made a 'deadly enemy' of Anthony Eden, the British Prime Minister, by persuading King Husein of Jordan to dismiss General Glubb, the British commander of his army.

On 19 July 1956 Dulles cancelled the credit agreement. A week later the Egyptian government nationalized the Suez Canal, stating that income from the canal had to make up for the withdrawal of the credits. The British regarded the Egyptian action as illegal theft that was breaking a treaty. British and French interests were also damaged and the two countries expected American backing in any retaliation. However, the Americans were keen to oust Britain and France from the Middle East and replace their influence with its own. President Eisenhower was

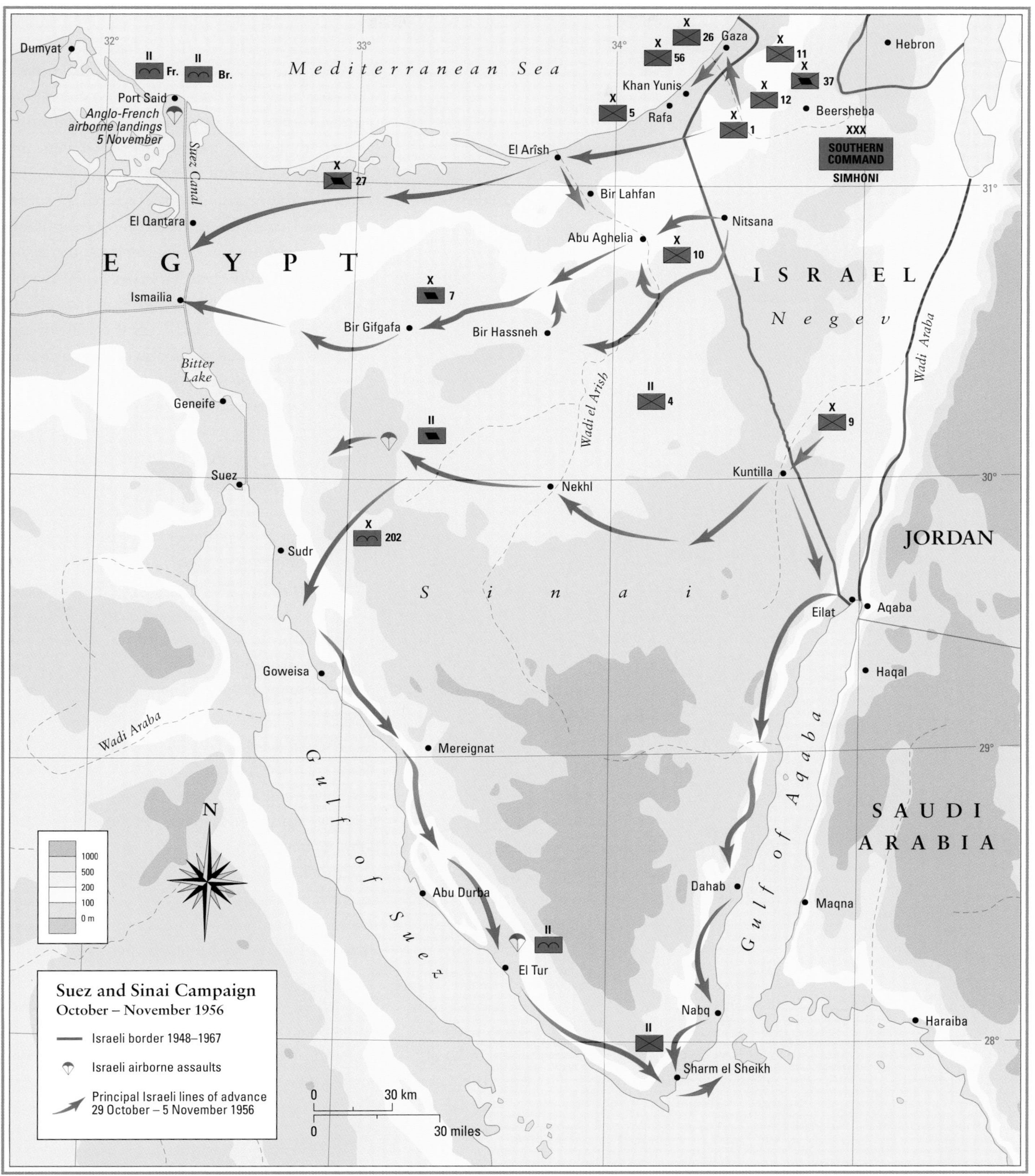
Suez and Sinai Campaign
October – November 1956
Israeli border 1948–1967
Israeli airborne assaults
Principal Israeli lines of advance 29 October – 5 November 1956
Mediterranean Sea
EGYPT
ISRAEL
Negev
JORDAN
SAUDI ARABIA
Sinai
Gulf of Suez
Gulf of Aqaba
Suez Canal
Bitter Lake
Wadi el Arish
Wadi Araba
Dumyat
Port Said
Anglo-French airborne landings 5 November
El Qantara
Ismailia
Geneife
Suez
Sudr
Goweisa
Mereignat
Abu Durba
El Tur
Sharm el Sheikh
Nabq
Dahab
Eilat
Aqaba
Haqal
Maqna
Haraiba
Kuntilla
Nekhl
Bir Gifgafa
Bir Hassneh
Abu Aghelia
Nitsana
Bir Lahfan
El Arîsh
Rafa
Khan Yunis
Gaza
Beersheba
Hebron
SOUTHERN COMMAND
SIMHONI
Fr.
Br.
1000
500
200
100
0 m
N
0
30 km
30 miles
32°
33°
34°
31°
30°
29°
28°

trying to get re-elected while the Soviet Union was preparing to crush liberal reforms in Hungary and prevent it from quitting the Warsaw Pact, the Soviet defensive alliance.

Israel was suffering guerrilla attacks along its borders and responded with reprisal operations against Jordan and the Gaza Strip. Given Anglo-French and Israeli concerns about Nasser, it is not surprising that secret meetings were held between the three countries at a private villa at Sèvres in France and a plan to attack Egypt was agreed. Despite British politicians denying collusion, Israeli Chief-of-Staff Moshe Dayan clearly confirmed in his book, *Diary of the Sinai Campaign*, that it did take place. Israel was to attack Egypt through the Sinai Desert using airborne assaults and armor to reach the Suez Canal while some units were to fight their way down the Sinai Peninsula to Sharm-el-Sheikh to break the Egyptian blockade, which prevented ships sailing up the Gulf of Aqaba to the Israeli port of Eilat. France would send paratroops from Algeria and Britain would send a large naval force from Malta and Cyprus to invade the Nile Delta and seize the Mediterranean end of the Suez Canal The dream was to restore the Canal to its former owners and end Nasser's rule in Egypt. Such thinking ignored the fact that Britain's military assets were outdated. Landing craft that had been used as pleasure boats since 1945 had to be requisitioned to carry troops.

On 29 October 1956, Israel began Operation Kadesh in a campaign across Sinai. Israeli air force planes attacked major communication centers that were then captured by ground forces and the blockade of Israeli shipping was lifted at Sharm-el-Sheikh. By the 4th November, the Israelis had taken their objectives but suffered 231 dead and 899 wounded. Egyptian casualties are estimated at some 2,000 dead and 4,000 wounded. Elsewhere, the British and French sent an ultimatum to Israel and Egypt to leave the Canal Zone or face an invasion. This ploy would in fact allow the Israelis to advance nearly to the Canal. The threat was ignored and on 31 October British and French planes bombed Egypt using British bases on Malta and Cyprus as a first stage of the invasion, named Operation Musketeer. Britain also deployed five aircraft carriers in the action and since nighttime bombing proved ineffective, carrier-based planes raided Egyptian targets and 200 aircraft by the end of 1 November.

Before the invasion force reached Egypt, the French persuaded the British to carry out a paratrooper assault on the Canal Zone. Accordingly, advance units of the 3rd Battalion of the British Parachute Regiment dropped on El Gamil airfield, which was captured with the bulk of the battalion flown in by helicopter. The French 2nd Colonial Parachute Regiment dropped on bridges at al-Raswa and then stormed Port Said, capturing its water works before storming Port Fuad and routing its Egyptian garrison. On 6 November, British commandos landed in Egypt, entered Port Said and commenced clearing fortified positions and houses that were used by snipers. Paratroopers were landed as were tanks and the British fought to link up with the French. However, hostilities rapidly ended with the United Nations demanding a ceasefire. British and French troops were withdrawn by 22 December and armistice lines were policed by a United Nations Emergency Force based on Egyptian soil, with its first elements landing on 15 November. British casualties were sixteen dead and 96 wounded. Egyptian losses are estimated at 650 dead and 900 wounded, along with around 1,000 civilian deaths.

Britain's quick acceptance of the UN-brokered ceasefire can be explained by numerous factors. There was strong opposition in the armed forces and the 20,000 reservists called up were not enthusiastic. The First Sea Lord Admiral Mountbatten had wanted the invasion called off before landing troops because Britain was suffering from world opprobrium. The country was split with angry scenes in the House of Commons. With even the conservative party divided, Prime Minister Anthony Eden was effectively forced to resign. American opposition was decisive in bringing financial pressure to bear on Britain. At the same time threats against Britain and France by the new Soviet leader Nikita Khrushchev greatly enhanced the prestige of the USSR in the Arab and non-aligned countries, diverting attention from the ruthlessness with which he suppressed the Hungarian uprising, with Soviet tanks in the streets of Budapest. Britain and France had suffered a massive loss of prestige and Arab nationalism had become increasingly strident, leading to growing support for independence movements in Aden, the Trucial States and Oman.

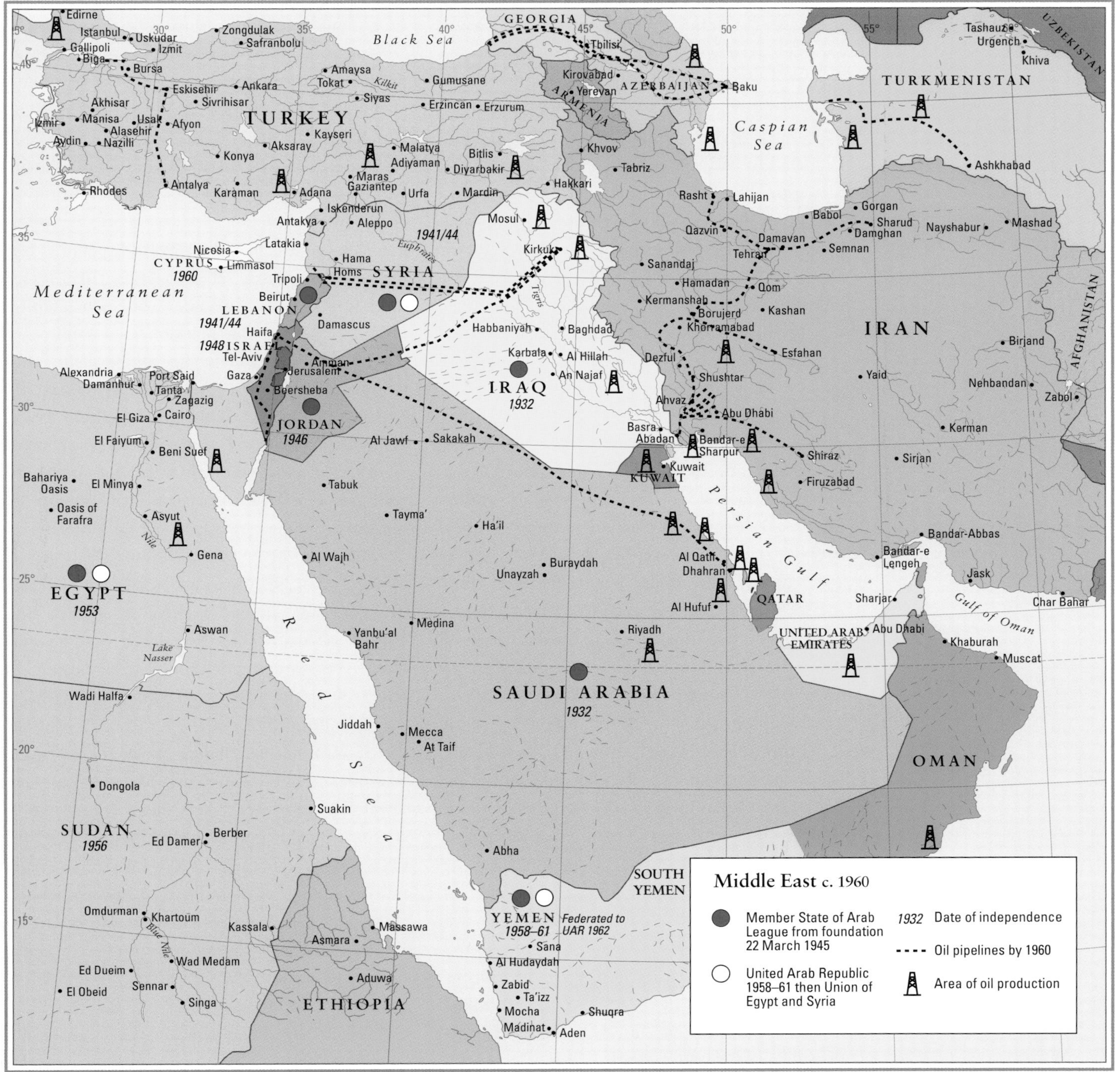

Six-Day War—Israel and the Arabs 1967

Many events led to the outbreak of the Six-Day War. Ever since the end of the 1956 Suez Crisis the Arab states had raided Israeli territory and met with counter-raids. Syrian shelling of Israeli settlements from the Golan Heights, in response to Israeli farming in the contested Demilitarized Zone, was a serious cause for concern. The Soviets misinformed Egyptian President Gamal Abd al-Nasser that the Israelis were massing troops and tanks on the Syrian border, and he responded by closing the Straits of Tiran, which would prevent shipping reaching Eilat, Israel's sole port on the Gulf of Aqaba, and by requesting U Thant, the UN Secretary-General, to withdraw UN troops guarding the Straits and Egyptian-Israeli frontier. This was followed by the deployment of large numbers of Egyptian troops in Sinai next to the Israeli border.

While international negotiations sought to defuse the situation Nasser's rhetoric grew ever more strident and the Israelis realized that the longer they waited for events to unroll the more organized Arab armies would become, so they decided upon a pre-emptive strike. On 5 June 1967 the Israeli air force, having flown in from the Mediterranean, assaulted Egyptian airfields, bombing and strafing planes and runways using delayed-action bombs. Israeli ground crews were so well trained that each plane could manage four or more sorties a day and the Egyptian air force was virtually wiped out, giving the Israelis vital air superiority over Sinai, the West Bank, and Golan Heights. The Syrians lost two thirds of their aircraft and their surviving planes retreated to the east of the country in order to survive. By the day's end 416 Arab aircraft had been destroyed while Israel lost 26. El Al, the Israeli commercial airline, was used to ferry Israeli students studying in foreign countries back to Israel where, as reservists, they could be placed in their units within 48 hours of the outbreak of war.

At the outbreak of hostilities, the Arabs possessed more soldiers, armor, aircraft, and population than Israel, which only had an army of 264,000, including reservists. However, Israeli intelligence and a penchant for a mobile style of war was to prove superior to the more conservative approach of Arabs, who built bunkers and fortified positions which could be encircled or bypassed. Israel was also forced to plan for a short war because the economy needed the reservists to make it work. The airborne successes of the first day were not without losses. Israeli armor attacked a major Egyptian defensive system at Abu Agheila-Kusseima, but had to constantly change its plans as an unknown Egyptian formation was protected by a complex minefield. Nevertheless, a four-day slugging match saw the Egyptians technically beaten. When the Egyptian Minister of Defence, Field Marshal Abdel Hakim Amer, ordered his troops to retreat, many of them were cut off when the Mitla and Gidi passes in the Sinai were captured by Israeli blocking units which had dashed forward. The Egyptians were now defeated and Sharm El-Sheikh was seized by the Israeli Navy and helicopter troops after a short engagement, thereby re-opening the Gulf of Aqaba to international trade. The conquest of Sinai was completed by the capture of Ras Sedr on the western coast of Sinai.

On 6 June, the Israelis attacked Jordanian forces, moving into Jerusalem and marching on Ramallah. A Jordanian brigade moving from Jericho to Jerusalem was defeated and a tank encounter took place east of Jenin. The Old City of Jerusalem was entered and a fierce battle took place with many casualties on both sides, but Jordanian resistance crumbled. The West Bank was captured and occupied, and the Jordan River reached, where the Israelis blew up the Abdullah and Hussein bridges. The campaign had been characterized by severe fighting, often hand-to-hand, but the

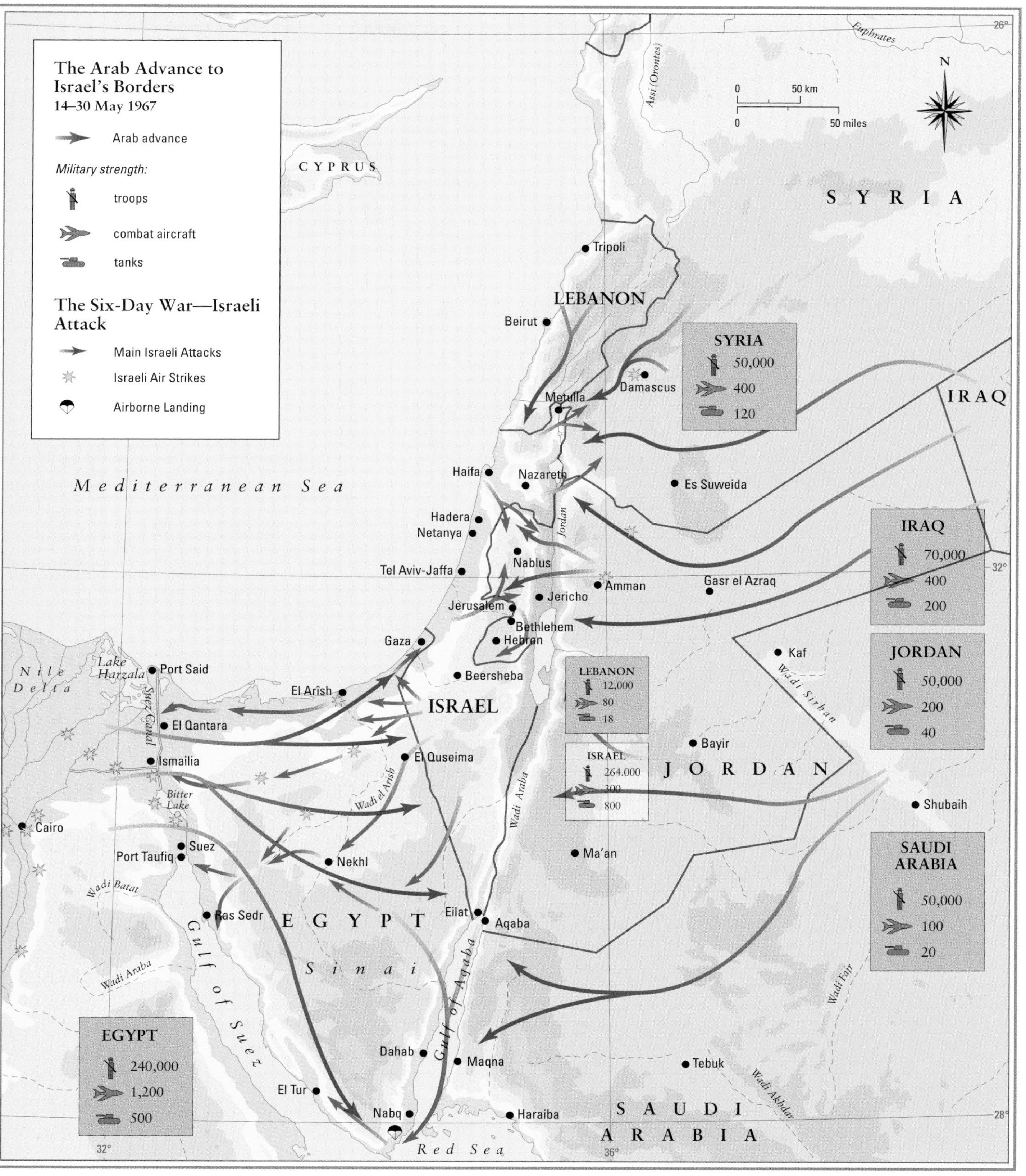
The Arab Advance to Israel's Borders
14–30 May 1967
Arab advance
Military strength:
troops
combat aircraft
tanks
The Six-Day War—Israeli Attack
Main Israeli Attacks
Israeli Air Strikes
Airborne Landing
SYRIA
50,000
400
120
IRAQ
70,000
400
200
JORDAN
50,000
200
40
SAUDI ARABIA
50,000
100
20
LEBANON
12,000
80
18
ISRAEL
264,000
300
800
EGYPT
240,000
1,200
500
Mediterranean Sea
CYPRUS
LEBANON
ISRAEL
EGYPT
Sinai
JORDAN
SAUDI ARABIA
Red Sea
Gulf of Suez
Gulf of Aqaba
Nile Delta
Tripoli
Beirut
Damascus
Metulla
Haifa
Nazareth
Es Suweida
Hadera
Netanya
Nablus
Tel Aviv-Jaffa
Amman
Gasr el Azraq
Jerusalem
Jericho
Bethlehem
Hebron
Gaza
Kaf
Port Said
Lake Harzala
Suez Canal
El Arîsh
Beersheba
El Qantara
Bayir
Ismailia
El Quseima
Bitter Lake
Shubaih
Cairo
Suez
Port Taufiq
Nekhl
Ma'an
Eilat
Aqaba
Ras Sedr
Dahab
Maqna
Tebuk
El Tur
Nabq
Haraiba
Wadi Sirhan
Wadi el Arish
Wadi Araba
Wadi Batat
Wadi Fajr
Wadi Akhdar
Jordan
Assi (Orontes)
Euphrates
N
0 50 km
0 50 miles
26°
32°
28°
36°

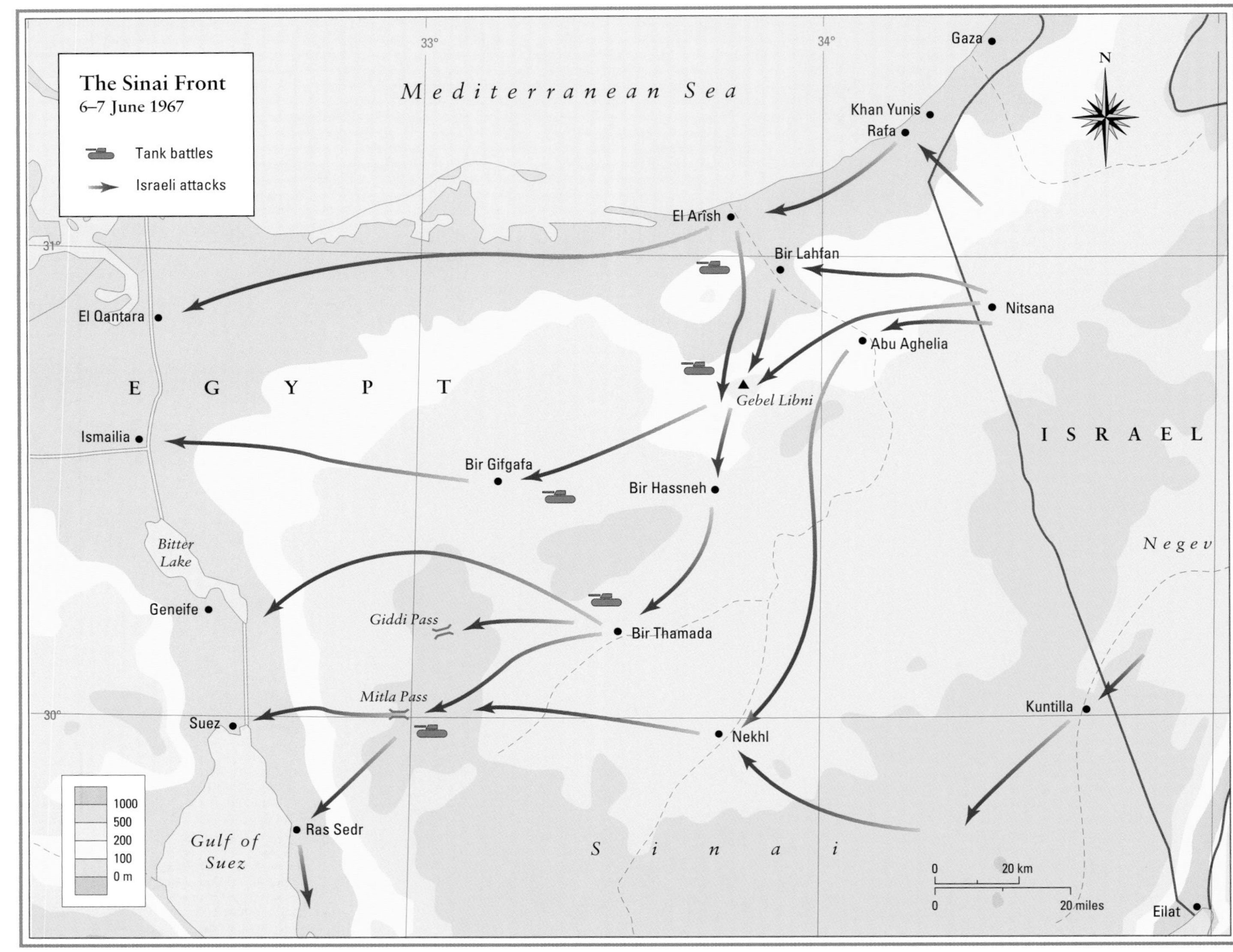

Jordanians succumbed to Israeli air superiority and suffered some 6,000 of its soldiers killed and missing. During the combat 600 Egyptian commandos, stationed on the West Bank, had sought to infiltrate Israel to attack airfields but they were detected and driven off, leaving 450 dead behind them.

Elsewhere, the Syrian air force was destroyed while Israeli towns in the Hula Valley were shelled by Syrian artillery based on the Golan Heights. The Israelis attacked the hills against determined resistance in established fortifications. Israeli aircraft attacked the defenses but could not destroy the bunkers, which had to be cleared by close-quarter combat. It was difficult to maneuver armor, forcing the tanks to engage at close quarters. A pincer movement caused the Syrians to lose the first day of conflict, but both sides inflicted serious losses on each other. The Israelis broke through to the plateau on top of the Heights and continued their advance next day, finally establishing strong positions on what became the Purple Line at ceasefire. Syrian resistance crumbled, with retreating soldiers abandoning tanks in full working order and Israeli soldiers were astonished to find some Syrians troops chained to their guns while their officers had fled. This

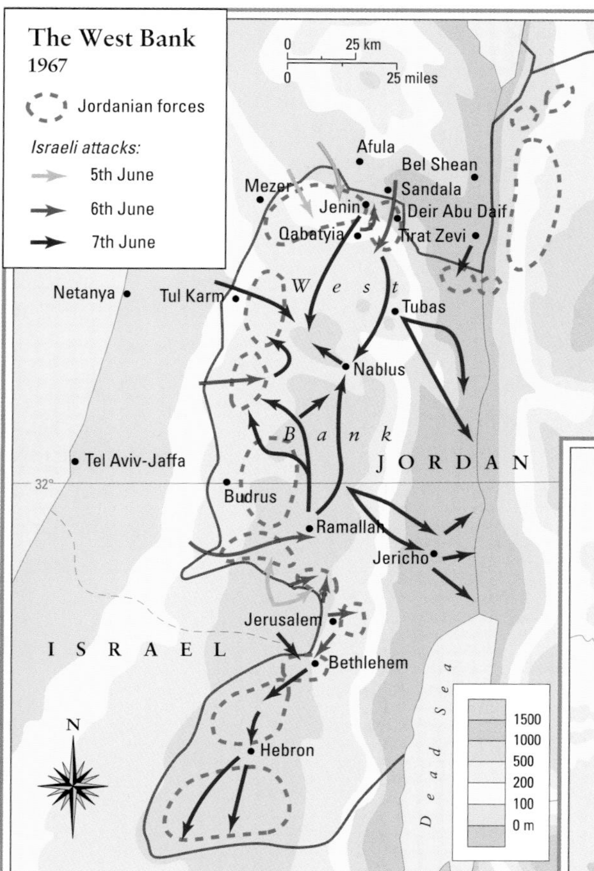

shocked the Israelis since they believed that officers should lead from the front, while tank commanders tended to advance with their heads exposed, the better to see. Kibbutz-born commanders were particularly impulsive and suffered higher casualties than others.

Israel had now acquired Sinai, Gaza, the West Bank, and Golan, and a huge Arab population on the West Bank. Many Palestinians fled the West Bank into Jordan, exacerbating the refugee problem while some 70,000 Syrians fled the Golan Heights during the fighting and these remained refugees. The Fatah faction of the Palestinian Liberation Organization, under Yasser Arafat, raided Israel from 1968, leading to the Battle of Karameh between the Israeli army and PLO/Jordanian forces in March 1968, which destroyed most of the Karameh refugee camp. The conquest of the Golan Heights meant that Israel's northern towns and settlements were freed from Syrian rocket attacks. Several Israeli settlements were built on Golan, bringing heavily irrigated agriculture to the region. The Gaza Strip became a base for Arab guerrilla fighters who attacked neighboring Israeli villages, which caused the Israelis to seal off the Strip with security fences. Fatah guerrillas attacked Israel from Jordan, with financial and political support from Syria and Egypt.

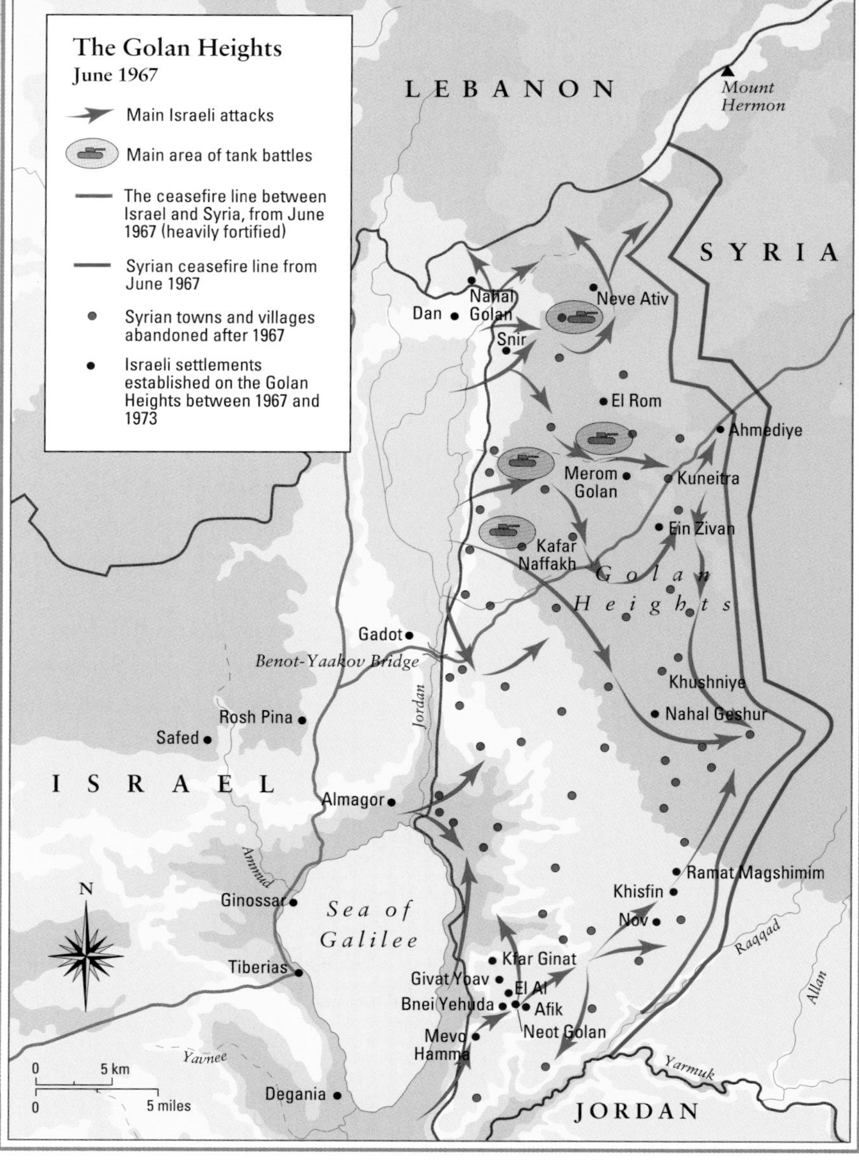

Oil Power

Oil can provide immense benefits to oil-producing states by generating the means to modernize societies, diversify the economy, and provide educational and health-care systems to citizens. Oil is also a key energy source allowing countries all over the world to function; indeed, it induces dependency which can be exploited. A major problem with oil-producing countries in the Middle East has been the web of patronage and relative lack of democracy. Ruling families can control all aspects of society, including the import of external influences, and rely on foreign workers and technicians for the smooth running of their states, while the security apparatus is run by the ruling family. The worst example of the misuse and abuse of power was that exercised in Iraq by Saddam Hussein and his sons, Uday and Qusay.

In 1973, oil became a weapon in the Arab-Israeli October War. When Egypt and Syria assaulted Israel in order to regain Sinai and the Golan Heights, lost in the 1967 Six-Day War, the US decided to re-supply Israel with weapons and munitions. In response, members of the Organization of Arab Petroleum Exporting Countries, comprising Iran, Iraq, Kuwait, Libya, Qatar, Saudi Arabia, and the United Arab Emirates, together with Egypt, Syria, and Tunisia, proclaimed an oil embargo on the United States, the United Kingdom, Japan, and the Netherlands. The Arab states hoped that pressure would be placed on the US to persuade Israel to withdraw from Sinai and the Golan Heights. Oil supplies to America's allies were disrupted and oil prices rose: then quadrupled by 1974. The embargo caused dissention in NATO. The Western countries faced a possible recession and economic slowdown, especially as the embargo of the Netherlands starved the oil refineries of Rotterdam, which supplied many countries in Europe. US Secretary of State Henry Kissinger engaged in shuttle diplomacy, visiting the states concerned and Israel in an attempt to negotiate an Israeli withdrawal from the occupied territories. This difficult task was impeded by Japan and some European states, who chose to ignore the US and support the Arabs. In January 1974 Kissinger was promised an Israeli retreat from parts of Sinai and an agreement to negotiate with Syria over the Golan Heights. By March 1974, the embargo was lifted.

The price rise in oil meant increased wealth for OAPEC states and Saudi Arabia, and Iran used the extra resources to engage in

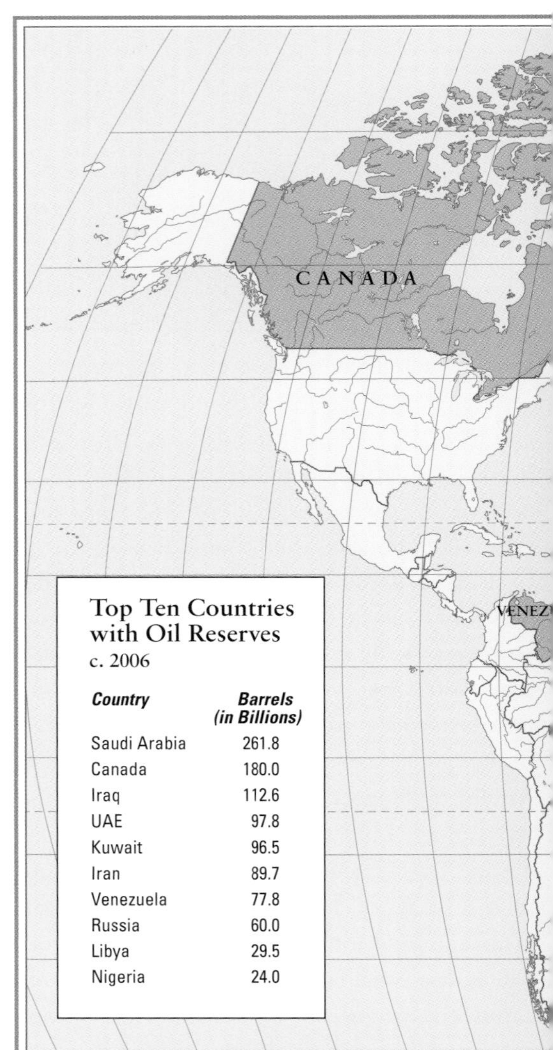

Top Ten Countries with Oil Reserves
c. 2006

Country	Barrels (in Billions)
Saudi Arabia	261.8
Canada	180.0
Iraq	112.6
UAE	97.8
Kuwait	96.5
Iran	89.7
Venezuela	77.8
Russia	60.0
Libya	29.5
Nigeria	24.0

an arms race in a competition to gain hegemony in the Persian Gulf. The US supplied arms to these American allies, while the Soviet Union sold weaponry to Iraq, causing a spiraling sense of insecurity. The Saudi army was acquiring five times the arms that Israel had, causing some consternation. The Shah of Iran used his wealth to implement a White Revolution, which failed and backfired as far as land reform was concerned. He incurred the enmity of the landed elites and the middle class, who were driven into the arms of Ayatollah Khomeini. He lost support in the country and the Ayatollah led the 1979 Revolution, which overthrew the Shah and lost the US one of its key allies.

If Iran implemented Shi'ite militancy, then the Saudis, too, faced an internal threat which their new arms could crush. In 1979, Wahabbi extremists, led by Juhayman al-Otaybi, seized the Grand Mosque in Mecca and proclaimed his brother, Muhammad Abdullah al-Qahtani, as the Mahdi. The subsequent siege of the mosque led to hundreds of casualties and a Shi'ite rebellion in al-Hasa was crushed. In reaction, the religious life of Saudi Arabia became more fundamentalist and fears of Shi'ite Iran increased. Then, the Iraq-Iran War began and the Middle East became even more unstable and volatile.

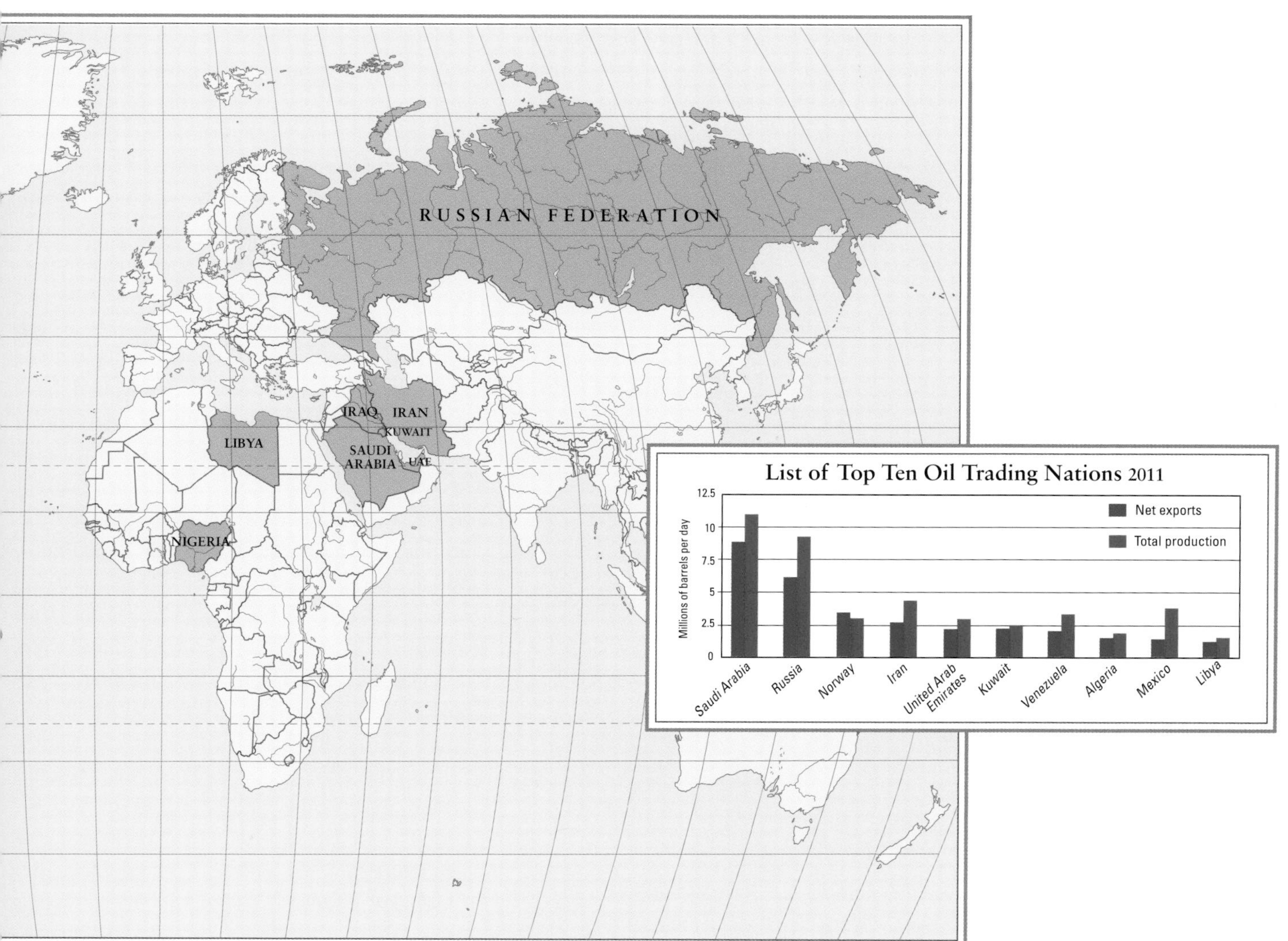

The October War 1973

When Egypt's President Nasser died in 1970 , he was succeeded by Anwar Sadat, who was determined to regain the territories lost in the Six-Day War. Sadat knew that tough reforms were necessary to restore the economy after the liabilities incurred by Nasser's socialist policies. A military success would engender the popular support he required for the reforms. Both Nasser and Sadat had begged for improved weapons systems from the Soviet Union, but the Soviet leader Leonid Brezhnev was reluctant to encourage a military adventure, as he was engaging in détente with the United States. In particular the Soviet Union was against any Egyptian crossing of the Suez Canal, believing that the Israeli Bar Lev Line along its banks would cause immense Egyptian losses, and consequent loss of face for the Soviets.

Frustrated, in July 1972, Sadat expelled almost all of the 20,000 Soviet military advisers in the country with a view to reorienting his foreign policy toward the West, and liberalizing the Egyptian economy. He persuaded Syria to join in with Egyptian war plans but was uncertain about Iraqi or Jordanian intentions.

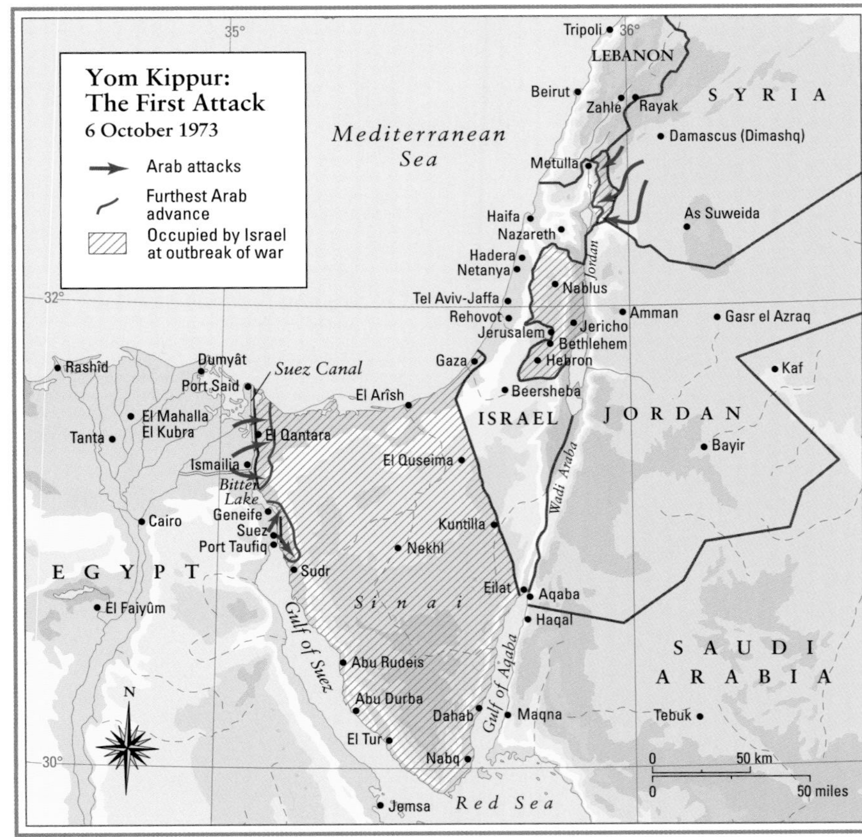

On 6 October 1973, during Ramadan and on the Jewish Day of Atonement, the Arabs launched attacks against Israel with Egyptian soldiers crossing the Suez Canal using high-pressure hoses to breach the sandbanks of the Bar Lev line and capturing all but one of its forts. Egypt's initial success was due to poor Israeli intelligence which had considered Egyptian maneuvers to be exercises and regarded the Bar Lev Line as impregnable. The Egyptians did not advance far, keeping their armor under the protection of SAM missile systems, stationed on the west side of the Canal. Israeli attempts to disrupt the Egyptians failed for several days until reserves were mobilized. Much armor was lost to portable anti-tank weapons and support by the Israeli Air Force was impossible due to the SAM shield. While the Egyptians were stationary, the Israelis built up their forces and concentrated their efforts in the Golan Heights, which were much closer to Israeli centers of population.

In the Heights, 180 Israeli tanks faced 1,300 Syrian, while the Syrians dropped commandos from helicopters to capture the important Israeli strongpoint on Mount Hermon. Syrian armor crossed the ceasefire line, puncturing Israeli fortifications, and advanced almost to the Benot-Yakov Bridge over the River Jordan. The Israeli 7th Armored Brigade held the northern front while suffering severe casualties, and was reduced to six tanks at the end of three days' fighting. Israeli mechanics repaired damaged tanks so rapidly that fifteen were quickly returned to the fray, denting the morale of the Syrian soldiers. Israeli reserves arrived, pushing the Syrians back to the ceasefire line. The Israelis moved toward Damascus, but were stopped when an Iraqi expeditionary force attacked the southern flank of the advancing Israeli salient. A Jordanian force joined the Syrians

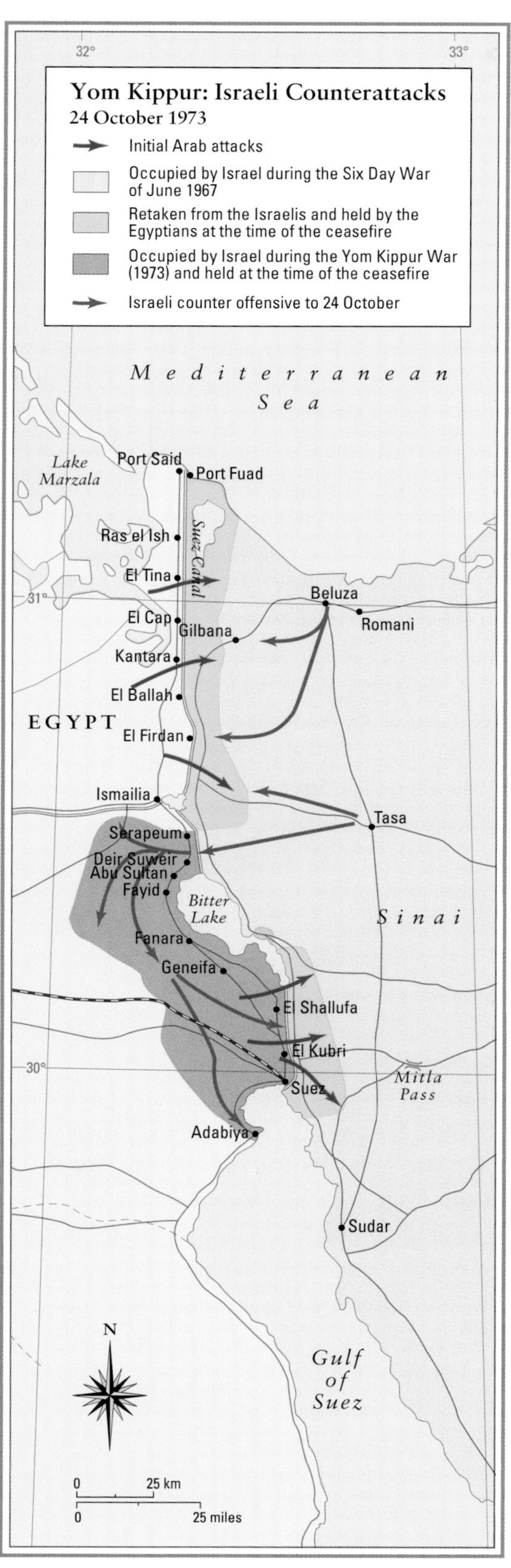

but avoided the fighting, only being there as a gesture toward Arab solidarity. Each side reorganized itself and a planned Syrian assault was only prevented by a United Nations imposed ceasefire.

In Sinai, the Israelis counterattacked in Operation Gazelle and managed to punch a hole through the Egyptian lines at the juncture of its 2nd and 3rd Armies. Crossing the Canal north of the Bitter Lake, Israeli armor poured south to the Gulf of Suez encircling the 3rd Army. At sea, the Israeli Navy sank Syrian missile boats at Latakia, and Egyptian vessels at Marsa Talamat and Baltim. Diplomatic maneuvers by US Secretary of State Henry Kissinger led to Israel and Egypt negotiating a disengagement agreement and eventually the Camp David peace treaty of March 1979, following Sadat's epoch-making visit to Jerusalem in November 1977. By April 1982 the Israelis had finally withdrawn from Sinai.

Israel in Lebanon and Gaza 1982–2012

The Palestinian issue spawned several resistance movements grouped under the Palestine Liberation Organization (founded in 1964), including the largest group al-Fatah, established by Yasser Arafat and others in 1959. The PLO operated from within Jordanian territory until it was expelled by the army in September 1970, causing it to move into southern Lebanon right by Israel's northern border. It used this new base to mount rocket attacks and raids into Israel upon cities like Kiryat Shemona in Upper Galilee.

On 6 June 1982 the Israeli Government, under Prime Minister Menahem Begin, decided to invade Lebanon in order to eradicate the PLO by destroying its fighters and infrastructure, to drive Syrian forces from the Beqaa Valley, and to bolster Christian Maronite forces whom the Israelis regarded as allies. The Israeli onslaught pushed the PLO back to Beirut, where a multinational force from the US, UK, France, and Italy helped evacuate PLO and Fatah fighters to other countries, with a new PLO headquarters created in Tunisia. By September Israeli forces were in West Beirut. Following the assassination of Lebanese President Bashir Gemayel, with whom they hoped to sign a peace treaty, the Israeli Defense Force allowed troops from the Lebanese Christian Phalangists Militia to enter the Sabra and Chatila refugee camps to find an alleged 2,000 remaining PLO members. Israeli troops surrounded the camps and used flares to assist the Phalangists while they massacred at least 800 civilians including women and children in the camp. Israeli Minister of Defense Ariel Sharon was deemed responsible and forced to resign. The Syrians were also pushed out of the Beqaa. In time, however, PLO fighters were replaced by militants of the Shi'ite Hezbollah movement.

A second Lebanese War began on 12 June 2006 when Israel invaded Lebanon in response to numerous Hezbollah rocket and mortar attacks on border towns. The IDF encountered entrenched positions and fierce resistance from Hezbollah soldiers. The guerrillas used tunnels for movement with fighters able to fire anti-tank missiles before disappearing from view. Fifty-two Israeli Merkava battle tanks were damaged and missiles were also used to collapse buildings sheltering troops. The IDF failed to dislodge Hezbollah from Lebanon but managed to inflict allegedly heavy casualties although sustaining many itself. The United Nations managed to broker a ceasefire and Hezbollah was expected to evacuate southern Lebanon, to be replaced by 15,000 Lebanese Government soldiers and by an enlarged United Nations Interim Force in Lebanon (UNIFIL). On 1 October 2006, most Israeli troops pulled out of Lebanon. A stalemate persists, with renewed Hezbollah rocket attacks and Israeli retaliation by military raiding and air strikes. Hezbollah receives supplies from Syria and Iran and has regained its strategic

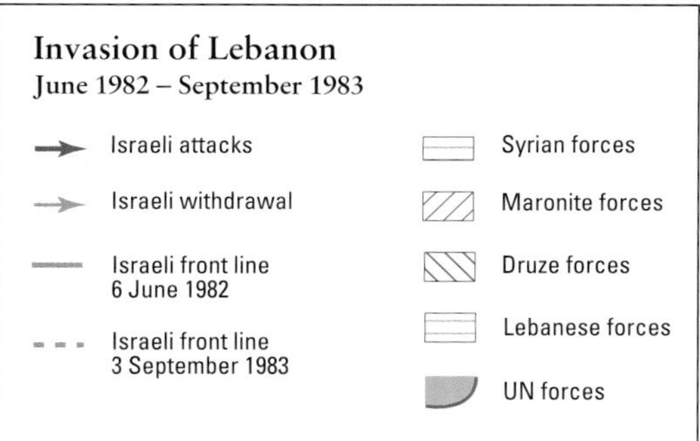

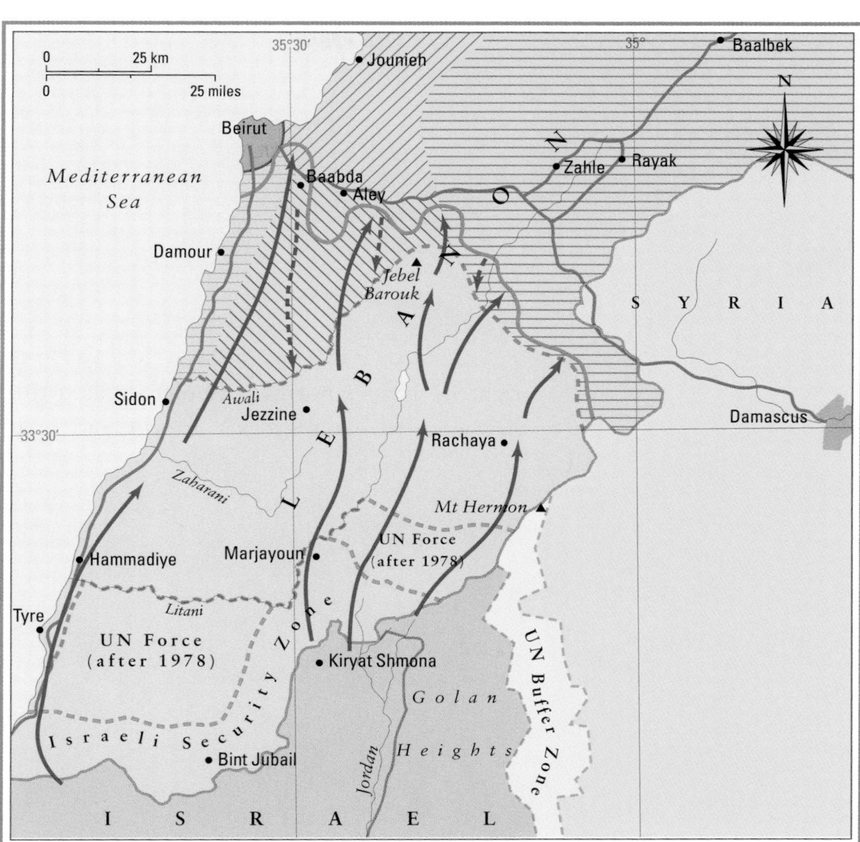

position in Lebanon and re-armed.

Another danger facing Israel was the rocket attacks begun by Hamas—the militant Islamist movement—from the Gaza Strip, from which Israel withdrew, dismantling the Jewish settlements, in 2005. Israel responded with air strikes, beginning on 27 December 2008 with jets and attack-helicopters hitting one hundred Hamas targets and buildings while an unmanned aerial vehicle or 'drone' exploded into Gaza police headquarters. The entire campaign saw a succession of air attacks with special bombs used to destroy tunnels on the Gaza-Sinai border. The IDF invaded Gaza on 3 January 2009. Targets included police stations, roadblocks, bunkers, rocket launching sites, and weapons stores. The IDF penetrated deeply into Gaza, Khan Yunis, and Rafah, these being major centers of population. Hamas fighters were winkled out in urban warfare but rocket and mortar attacks continued on southern Israeli settlements, with some rockets reaching as far as Beersheba and Ashdod. Faced with a growing chorus of international criticism, Israel announced a unilateral ceasefire on 18 January with a complete withdrawal by 21 January 2009.

The conflict resulted in somewhere between 1,160 and 1,400 Palestinian and thirteen Israeli deaths (four from friendly fire). The Israelis succeeded in disrupting Hamas activity and eliminated several of its leaders through targeted killings. Weapons were seized and smuggling tunnels destroyed. Hamas did not fight as well as Hezbollah had done in Lebanon and it suffered a drop in confidence and morale.

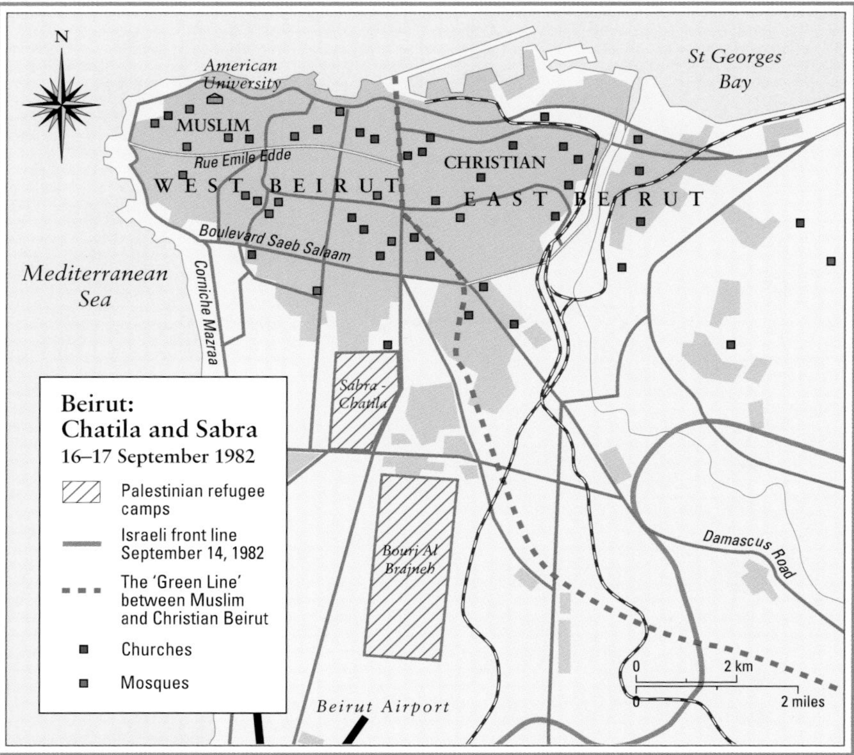

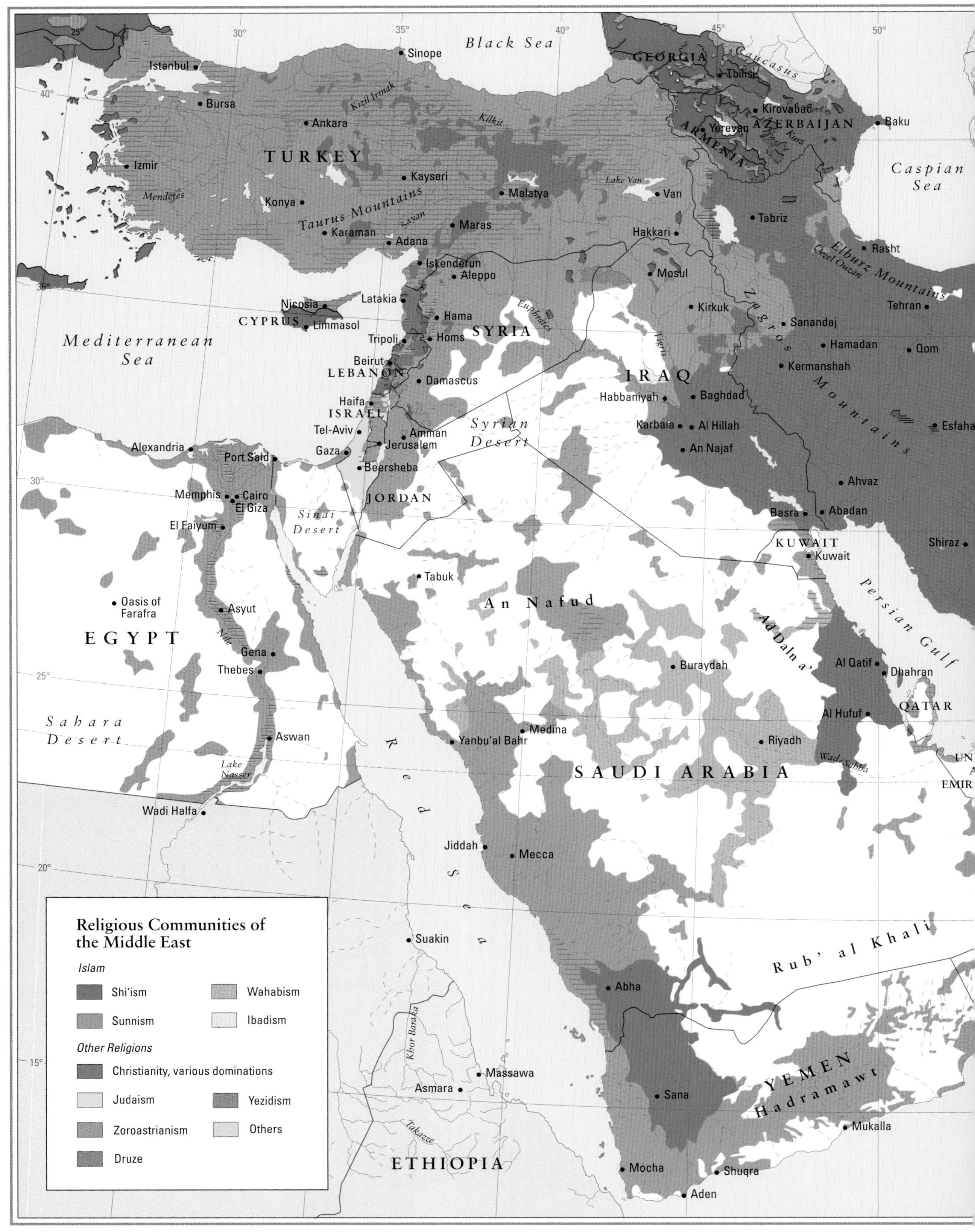
Religious Communities of the Middle East
Islam
Shi'ism
Wahabism
Sunnism
Ibadism
Other Religions
Christianity, various dominations
Judaism
Yezidism
Zoroastrianism
Others
Druze
Black Sea
Mediterranean Sea
Caspian Sea
Persian Gulf
Red Sea
TURKEY
GEORGIA
ARMENIA
AZERBAIJAN
CYPRUS
SYRIA
LEBANON
ISRAEL
JORDAN
IRAQ
KUWAIT
QATAR
EGYPT
SAUDI ARABIA
YEMEN
ETHIOPIA
Caucasus
Taurus Mountains
Zagros Mountains
Elburz Mountains
Syrian Desert
Sinai Desert
Sahara Desert
An Nafud
Ad Dahna'
Rub' al Khali
Hadramawt
Kizil Irmak
Kilkit
Menderes
Sayan
Lake Van
Euphrates
Tigris
Kura
Qezel Ouzan
Nile
Lake Nasser
Wadi Sabba
Kbor Baraka
Takazze
Istanbul
Bursa
Ankara
Izmir
Konya
Kayseri
Malatya
Karaman
Adana
Maras
Sinope
Van
Hakkari
Tbilisi
Kirovabad
Yerevan
Baku
Tabriz
Rasht
Tehran
Qom
Hamadan
Sanandaj
Kermanshah
Esfahan
Ahvaz
Abadan
Shiraz
Iskenderun
Aleppo
Latakia
Hama
Homs
Tripoli
Beirut
Damascus
Nicosia
Limmasol
Haifa
Tel-Aviv
Amman
Jerusalem
Gaza
Beersheba
Mosul
Kirkuk
Habbaniyah
Baghdad
Karbala
Al Hillah
An Najaf
Basra
Kuwait
Alexandria
Port Said
Memphis
Cairo
El Giza
El Faiyum
Oasis of Farafra
Asyut
Gena
Thebes
Aswan
Wadi Halfa
Tabuk
Buraydah
Al Qatif
Dhahran
Al Hufuf
Riyadh
Medina
Yanbu'al Bahr
Jiddah
Mecca
Suakin
Abha
Massawa
Asmara
Sana
Mukalla
Mocha
Shuqra
Aden
25°
30°
35°
40°
45°
50°
20°
15°

Regional Fault Lines

The regional conflicts in the Middle East—between Iran and Saudi Arabia, and between Israel and the Arab states—are bedeviled by the ethnic and religious fault lines that divide communities locally. Even Israel shares this problem, with disagreements and sometimes bitter feuds between Ashkenazim of mainly European descent, Sephardis from the Middle East and North Africa, Falashas from Ethopia, and the various Hasidic groups. But for the most part in Israel these groups are able to express their views and identities through the democratic process—one that is conspicuous by its absence in most of the surrounding states.

Egypt, for example, has yet to find a way of resolving questions about the position of Islam vis-à-vis the state, the relationships between Islamic and secular laws, and the role of its ancient community of Christian Copts (at least six million people or 7 percent of the population) whose presence long predated the coming of Islam. Following the uprising of January 2011, including the brief presidency of the Muslim Brotherhood's Muhammad Morsi (June 2012–July 2013) churches have been burned, and clergy and lay persons slain. Attacks on Copts have been blamed on partisans of the Muslim Brotherhood, founded in 1928 but suppressed under successive regimes, as well as on other Islamist groups. Sectarian attacks, however, continued after the military coup that deposed President Morsi, which led to the deaths of some 1,000 Brotherhood protestors.

A more enduring picture of pluralism is offered by Lebanon, whose various communities of Sunni and Shi'ite Muslims, Druzes, Maronites, and other Christians including Greek Orthodox, Greek Catholic and Armenian, developed a rough-and-ready power sharing arrangement through the unofficial national pact. According to this arrangement, which dates from 1943, the President is always a Maronite, the Prime Minister always a Sunni, the President of the

National Assembly always Shi'a and the military chief a Druze. While the national pact failed to prevent the eruption of the 1975–90 civil war, caused in part by the presence of Palestinians who upset the balance of forces, the pact is still observed, though with modifications following the 1990 Taif agreement. The radicalization of rural Shi'ites produced the militant Hezbollah organization that consistently resisted Israeli occupation of the south. Aided by Iran, Hezbollah has proved a formidable foe of Israel, regularly firing rockets into northern Galilee. Often regarded as a 'state within the state' Hezbollah is also a major political force in Lebanon with a dozen seats in parliament and a minister with strong cabinet influence.

The Syrian civil war, in which Hezbollah fighters sided with government troops against Sunni-backed rebels, produced tensions with the Muslim Brotherhood affiliated Hamas in Gaza with which it had previously been allied. The two organizations 'agreed to disagree' over Syria while continuing to collaborate in opposition to Israel. Syrian conflict, however, continues to raise sectarian tensions, reflecting the wider struggle between the Sunni opposition, backed by Turkey along with Saudi Arabia and Qatar, and the Asad regime supported by Iran. The latter is dominated by the Alawite minority from which President Bashar al-Asad hails, but enjoys support from the country's Christian minorities, as well as some leading Sunni families.

Like Syria, Iraq is divided along sectarian and ethnic lines, with two-thirds of Muslims being Shi'ite; the remainder, including the Kurds, are mostly Sunni. The Saddam Hussein regime was dominated by Sunni families based in the city of Tikrit. The aftermath of the Gulf War saw a Shi'ite rebellion brutally crushed, while the Marsh Arabs, who are Shi'ite, had their lands drained and environment ruined. In the aftermath of the Second Gulf War it is Sunni Muslims who now feel marginalized under a Shi'ite-dominated government. The Kurds, however, who mainly reside in the Kirkuk and Mosul regions, and comprise some 17 percent of the population, have reasserted themselves since the persecution they suffered under Saddam Hussein. They have their own autonomous region based on Suleymaniya (Sulemani). Tensions persist between the Shi'ite-dominated central government and the Kurdish region over oil royalties and the division of power, and Turkey is anxious about the threat that a revived Kurdistan may pose for its own Kurdish population, estimated at around 20 percent.

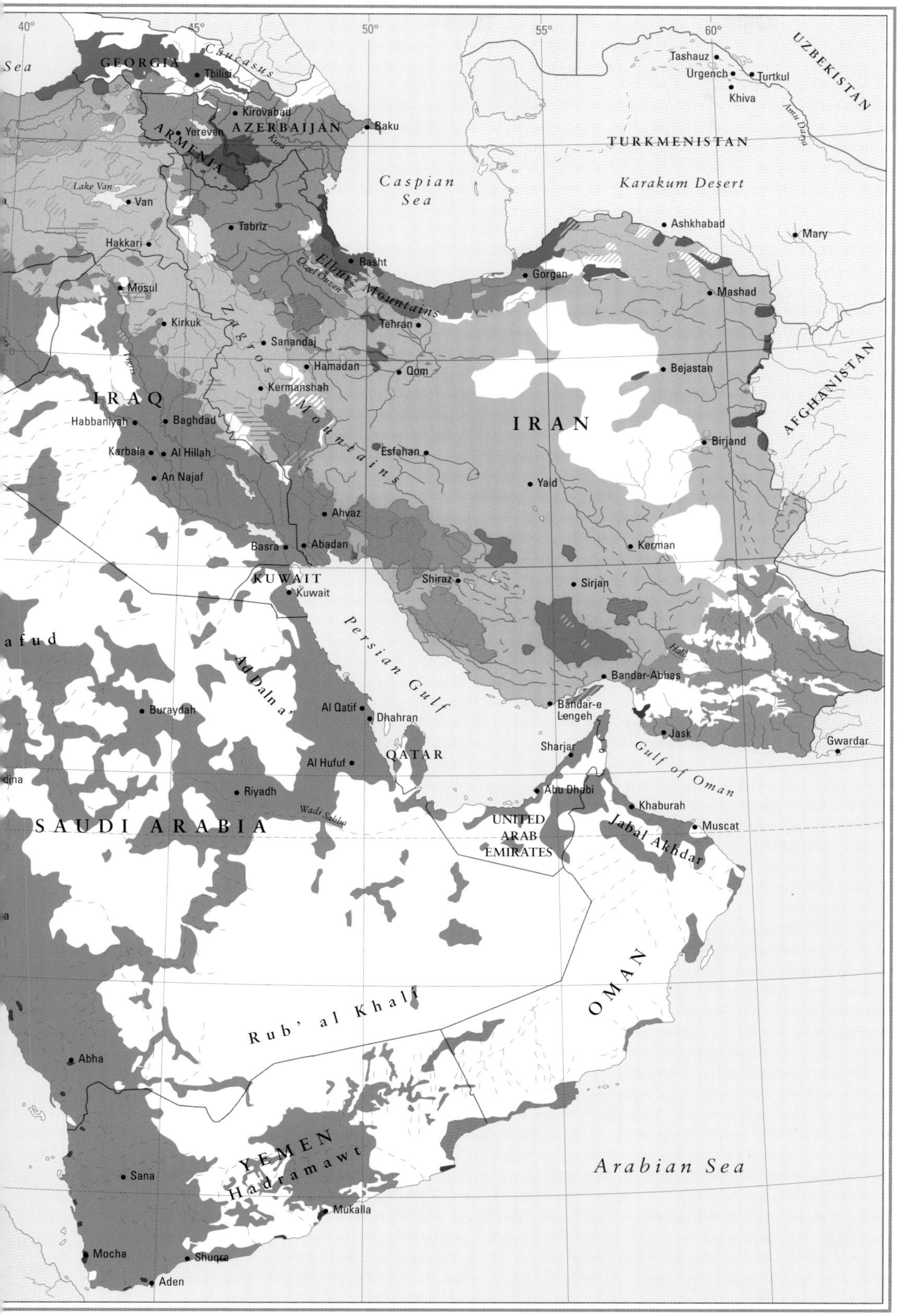

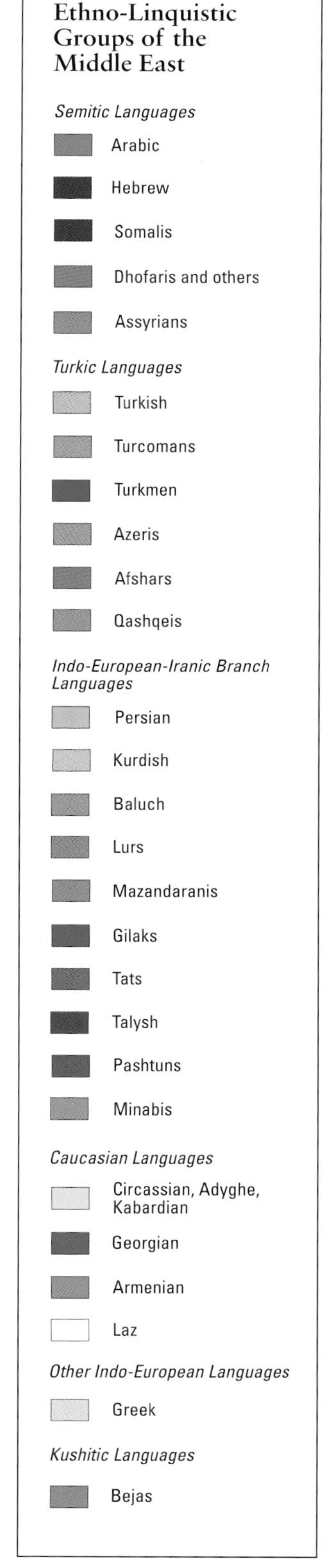

Ethno-Linquistic Groups of the Middle East
Semitic Languages
Arabic
Hebrew
Somalis
Dhofaris and others
Assyrians
Turkic Languages
Turkish
Turcomans
Turkmen
Azeris
Afshars
Qashqeis
Indo-European-Iranic Branch Languages
Persian
Kurdish
Baluch
Lurs
Mazandaranis
Gilaks
Tats
Talysh
Pashtuns
Minabis
Caucasian Languages
Circassian, Adyghe, Kabardian
Georgian
Armenian
Laz
Other Indo-European Languages
Greek
Kushitic Languages
Bejas
40°
45°
50°
55°
60°
GEORGIA
Tbilisi
Caucasus
ARMENIA
Yerevan
AZERBAIJAN
Kirovabad
Baku
Caspian Sea
TURKMENISTAN
Karakum Desert
Tashauz
Urgench
Turtkul
Khiva
UZBEKISTAN
Amu Darya
Ashkhabad
Mary
Lake Van
Van
Tabriz
Hakkari
Rasht
Elburz Mountains
Gorgan
Mashad
Mosul
Kirkuk
Sanandaj
Tehran
Zagros Mountains
Hamadan
Qom
Kermanshah
Bejastan
AFGHANISTAN
IRAQ
Habbaniyah
Baghdad
IRAN
Karbala
Al Hillah
An Najaf
Esfahan
Birjand
Yazd
Ahvaz
Basra
Abadan
Kerman
KUWAIT
Kuwait
Shiraz
Sirjan
Persian Gulf
Ad Dahna'
Bandar-Abbas
Buraydah
Al Qatif
Dhahran
Bandar-e Lengeh
Jask
Gwardar
QATAR
Sharjah
Al Hufuf
Gulf of Oman
Riyadh
Abu Dhabi
Khaburah
Muscat
SAUDI ARABIA
Wadi Sahba
UNITED ARAB EMIRATES
Jabal Akhdar
OMAN
Rub' al Khali
Abha
YEMEN
Hadramawt
Arabian Sea
Sana
Mukalla
Mocha
Shuqra
Aden

Iran-Iraq War 1980–88

A cluster of issues lie behind the 1980–88 war between Iraq and Iran, one of the twentieth-century's longest conventional conflicts, one that cost at least a million Iranian and up to half a million Iraqi lives. The Iraqi leader Saddam Hussein feared that the Iranian revolution would inspire Iraq's Shi'ites to rebel against his Sunni-dominated Baathist regime. He also sought to take advantage of the revolutionary chaos in Iran by attacking the oil-producing province of Khuzistan, whose Arabic-speaking populations had staged a series of Iraqi-inspired revolts, based on claims that the Ottomans had given Arab territory to Persia. Saddam also hoped to redress the 1975 Algiers agreement he had signed with the Shah. In exchange for Iran abandoning its support for Iraqi Kurdish separatists, the agreement established the Iran-Iraq border along the Thalweg Line running through the center of the Shatt al-Arab waterway, instead of along the eastern bank as previously claimed by Iraq. Saddam regarded the agreement as a national humiliation. Restoring the status quo would restore his control of shipping from the port of Basra.

In 1980 Saddam thought it would be a good time to attack. The Ayatollahs had purged the officer corps and had more than halved military expenditure from 15 percent to 7.3 percent of GNP. Moreover, following the occupation of the US Embassy in Tehran, the US had ended arms and spare parts shipments, weakening Iran's military machine, with the Iranian regime reliant on paramilitary formations consisting of the Revolutionary Guards, the Pasdaran, and the boys and older men of the Basij. In the course of the war Saddam received loans from the Sunni Gulf monarchies, who were worried about Iranian activity among their Shi'ite populations, and discreet support from the west, with the US providing satellite intelligence on Iranian deployments and European countries supplying armaments and raw materials for gas and chemical weapons.

Iraq launched its assault on Iran on 22 September 1980. Hussein began with a pre-emptive attack on Iranian air fields but this was not very successful; the Iranian air force was only weakened by lack of spare parts and went on the defensive while combat planes were cannibalized.

The Iraqi Army drove into Iraq but, by 1982, the invaders were driven back to the frontier nearly everywhere. The Iraqi military had failed dismally and were demoralized, having lost tens of thousands in casualties and some 30,000 prisoners. Many of the Generals who had failed were executed. Saddam sued for peace but the mullahs stated that they would fight until Saddam's regime was toppled.

The Iranians blocked Basra, ensuring that Iraq could only export oil by pipeline and goods had to be brought in by road. Iraq's finances dwindled and it was kept on track by subsidies from Kuwait and Saudi Arabia. In order to break Iraqi defensive positions the mullahs devised the 'human sea' tactic by which wave after wave of men and children were sent forward with promises of martyrdom, often fulfilled when they were shot to pieces. By 1986, these tactics allowed the Iranians to cross the Shatt near its mouth, capturing al-Faw. Iraqi counterattacks failed to dislodge the Iranians and a stalemate developed there.

The importance of the region was demonstrated firmly to the world when Iraq launched attacks on Kharg Island, seeking to destroy Iran's main oil terminal, spreading the war into the Gulf. Iran responded by attacking ships using Kuwaiti ports, which cut the oil exports of Iraq. In 1987, the US sent in warships to escort tankers and the British, French, and others sent in minesweepers. Soon 75 warships patrolled the Gulf, including Soviet vessels. Iran then threatened to close the Gulf by deploying missiles to fire at shipping near the Strait of Hormuz but demurred after an international response. In 1988, to Iraq's relief, the UN secured a ceasefire.

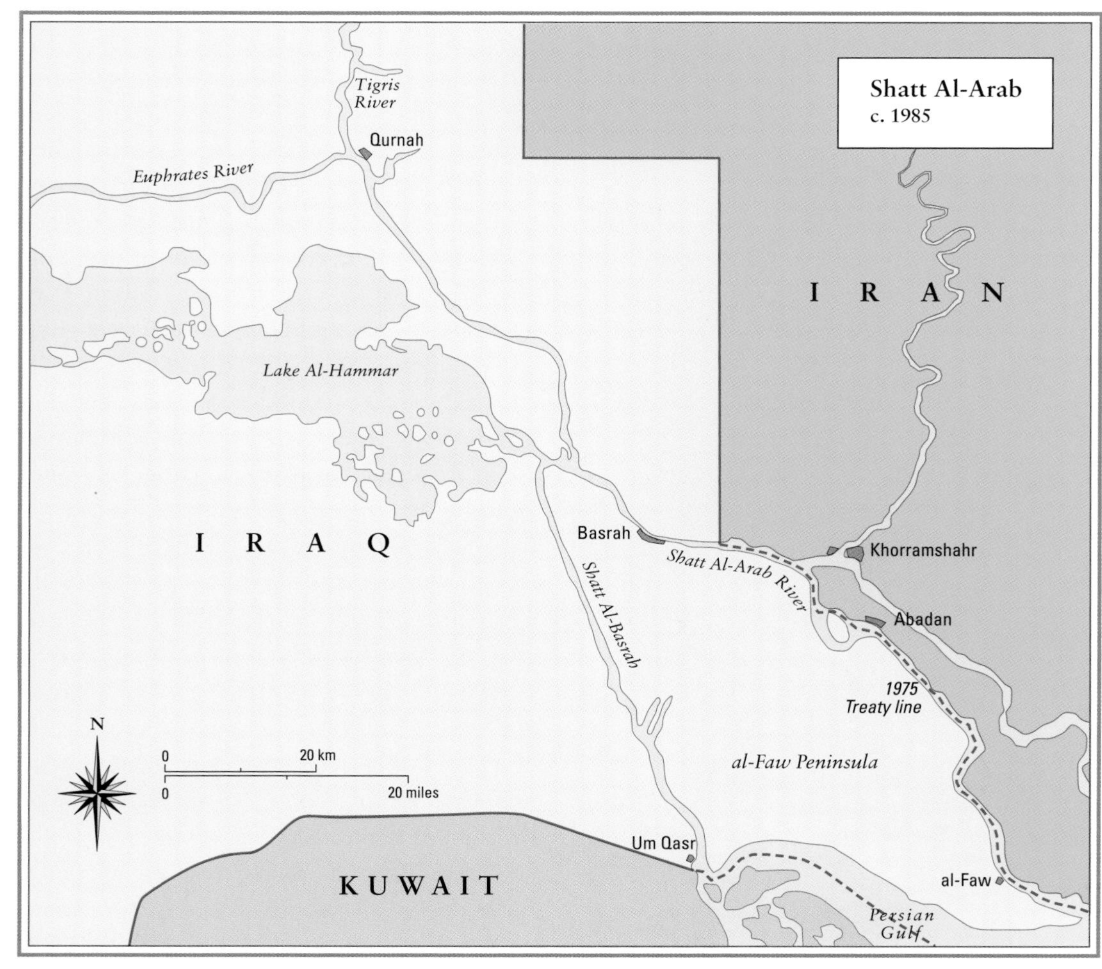

Gulf War 1990–91 (Operation Desert Storm)

Oil wells on fire in the aftermath of Desert Storm. The wells were set on fire by retreating Iraqi forces.

The 1980–88 Iran-Iraq War bankrupted Iraq, leaving the latter with a foreign debt of $380 billion and the cost of reconstructing border regions where combat had devastated the land. Saddam Hussein asked Kuwait for funds, claiming that the emirate owed an installment of $10 billion to offset the costs of the war, which had served to restrict the influence of Iranian revolution in the Gulf. Saddam also asked Kuwait to stop drilling for oil in the Rumaila field, claimed by Iraq, which straddled the Iraq- Kuwait border. Kuwait refused and, on 2 August 1990, Iraq invaded the emirate, annexing it as Iraq's nineteenth province and seizing its wealth. The United Nations passed Resolution 660 demanding that Iraq withdraw its forces. The US and other western countries had vital economic interests in Kuwait and also feared Saddam Hussein might have designs on the Saudi oilfields.

Saddam Hussein dismissed the Resolution believing that the UN would be unable to unite and muster a force against him; he was also loath to quit Kuwait since this would cause loss of face and probable domestic political dissent.

Contrary to Saddam's expectations, US President George H. W. Bush—a former UN Ambassador and head of the CIA—acted decisively, creating a UN coalition of 34 nations, including Egypt, Saudi Arabia, Syria, and Pakistan. When King Fahd of Saudi Arabia requested aid (allegedly under US pressure) the US poured in troops and aircraft in Operation Desert Shield. They were joined by large contingents from the UK and France while Germany and Japan partially financed the operation; the USA provided 73 percent of the personnel involved. Saddam was given an ultimatum (15 January 1991) to leave Kuwait, which he ignored.

On 16 January 1991, the coalition launched a month-long campaign of air strikes against Iraqi targets. Aircraft and cruise missiles and the forces of six carrier battle groups pounded radar installations and communication systems, and then airfields and aircraft. The Iraqi air force was destroyed or took refuge in Iran, allowing the coalition complete air superiority and the ability to attack armored formations and the national infrastructure. On 24 February, US forces crossed the border into Kuwait. Arab forces that were part of the coalition were tasked with clearing Kuwait City while US, British, and French armor were given a sweeping role. Some US forces cleared Kuwait while others swung through the desert, making a right hook to cut off Iraqi forces while the 101st Airborne Division established a roadblock on the main highway from Kuwait to Baghdad. The French 6th Light Division covered the left flank of the advance while Challenger tanks of the UK 1st Armoured Division hooked right through Iraqi armor aiming to reach the sea north of Kuwait City. It outflanked the Iraqi force and destroyed 300 vehicles in the process. Two Egyptian divisions, one armored and one mechanized, fought to the right of the British.

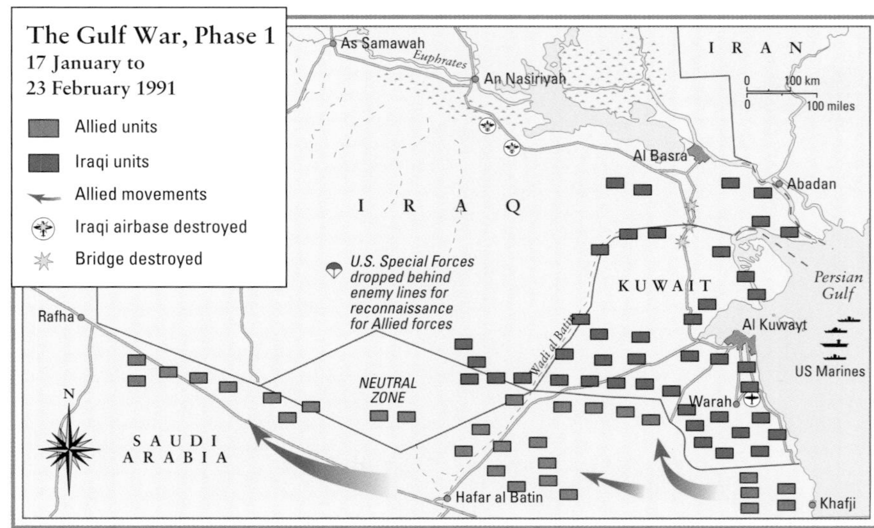

The emirate was swiftly recaptured with the Iraqis losing around 100,000 men, dead and wounded, against the coalition's 650. Escaping

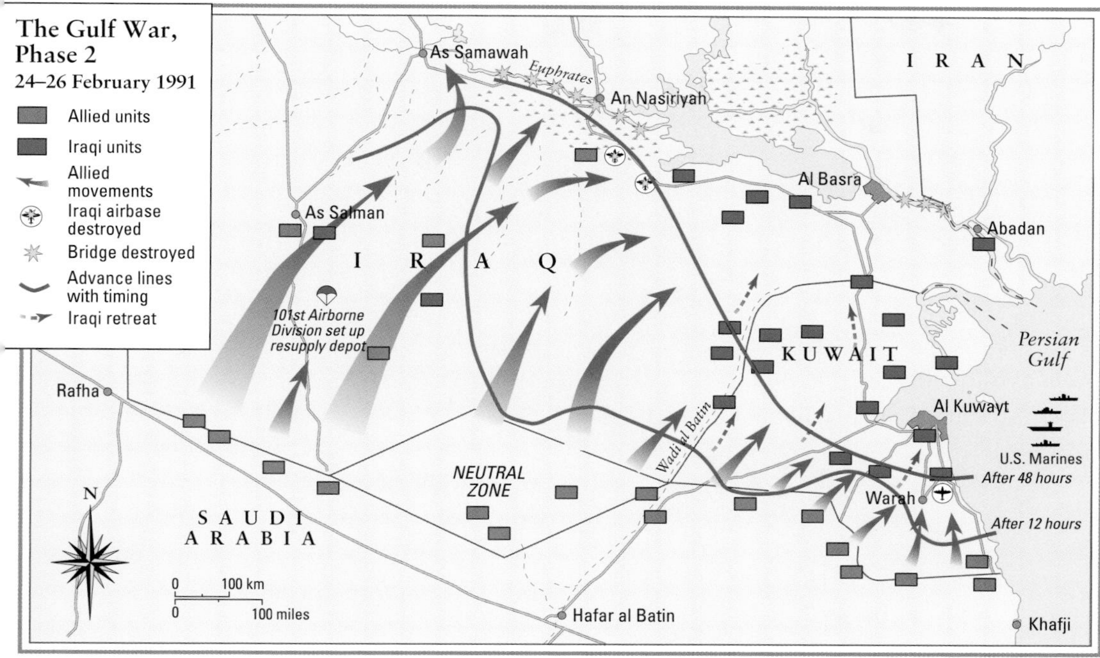

Iraqi vehicles on the Kuwait-Iraq highway were attacked from the air and the road became known as the Highway of Death. After approximately 100 hours of fighting on the ground President Bush, strictly adhering to the UN resolution, ordered a ceasefire and pulled his troops out of Iraq. Retreating Iraqis set 737 Kuwait oil wells ablaze, causing economic damage and pollution. The cost of damage caused by coalition aircraft ran to some $170 billion.

The war ended with the defeat of Iraq but Saddam Hussein remained in power, though humiliated with much of his industry and infrastructure destroyed.

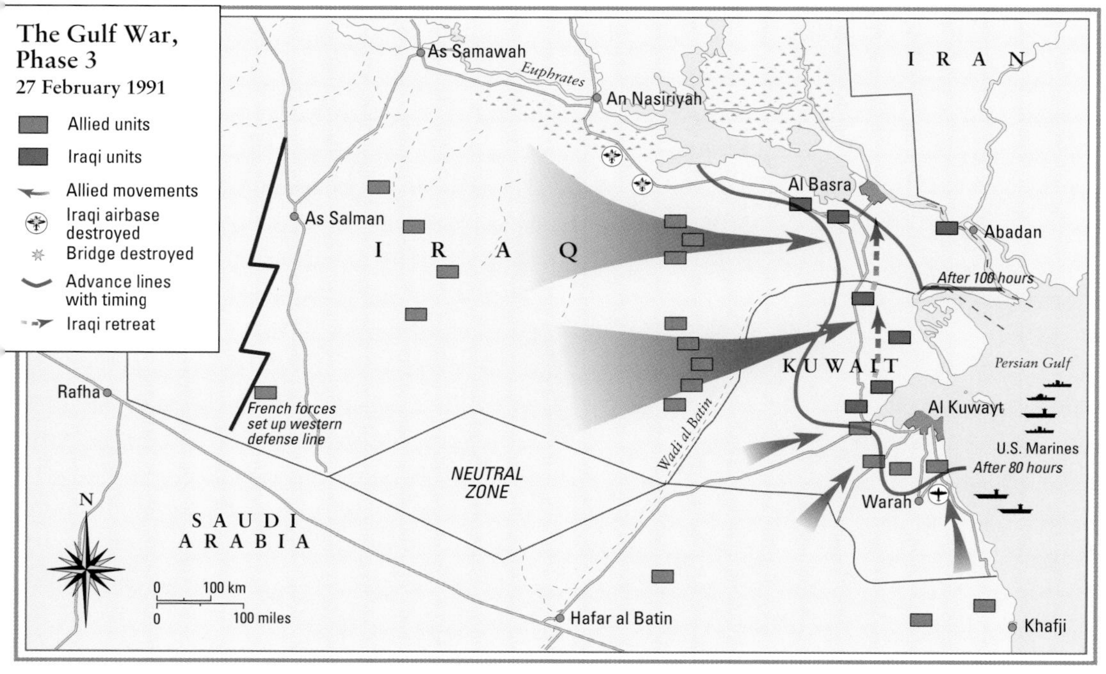

Second Gulf War 2003–11

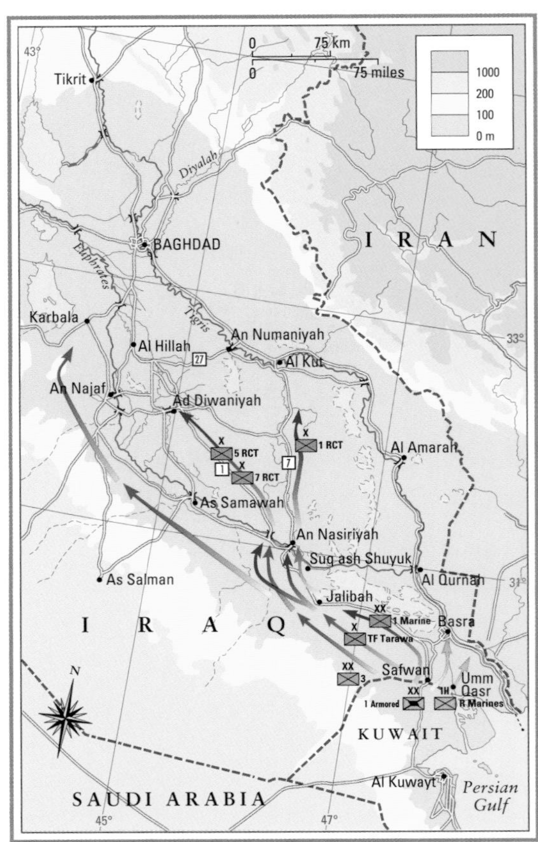

On 19 March 2003, the USA and Britain invaded Iraq. These allies claimed they were implementing UN resolutions that the UN itself had failed to implement, but these excuses were widely contested. Unlike the First Gulf War, the world generally believed that military action was a fundamental breach of the UN Charter's outlawing of aggressive war. Neither Mexico nor Canada joined in the campaign even though as signatories of the North American Free Trade Agreement they were economically dependent on the USA.

France believed that the UN should be directly involved, as in 1991, and condemned US President George W. Bush and Prime Minister Tony Blair, who led the campaign for action. Following the attacks on New York and Washington on 11 September 2001, neoconservatives behind the Bush administration convinced themselves that Iraq was harboring weapons of mass destruction (WMDs), including nuclear, biological, and chemical weapons, with Iraqi Scud missiles capable of hitting Israel, America's principal ally. However, claims that Saddam had been implicated in the 9/11 attacks were never proven and nor were his alleged deposits of WMDs ever found.

US troops were deployed in Kuwait and, alongside British, Australian, and Polish forces, invaded Iraq after a massive air attack on Iraq and its capital. A three-pronged advance to Baghdad began on 19 March 2003 without any declaration of war. The initial combat troops were: 248,000 US soldiers; 45,000 British; 2,000 Australian; and 194 Polish personnel from GROM, a Special Forces unit. Forty other countries provided troops, equipment, and support, especially in the aftermath of victory. There was also cooperation with Kurdish Peshmerga militias in north Iraq, who mustered some 70,000 fighters. Here, special operations units from the CIA and US army had been training the Kurds, turning them into an effective combat force.

The Al-Faw oilfields were secured by an air and amphibious assault, as were ports by US marines, while British commandos and Polish GROM took Umm Qasr and the southern Iraqi oil fields. Offshore oil platforms were seized by

Battle for Basra
March and April 2003

- British front line c. 30 March
- (1) Baath Party headquarters
- (2) Railway station
- (3) Governor's headquarters
- Airport
- Direction of British attack
- Areas of resistance
- 1 Royal Regiment of Fusiliers
- 2 3rd Battalion Parachute Regiment
- 3 Black Watch and 1st Royal Tank Regiment
- 4 Royal Scots Dragoon Guards
- 5 3rd Commando Royal Marines

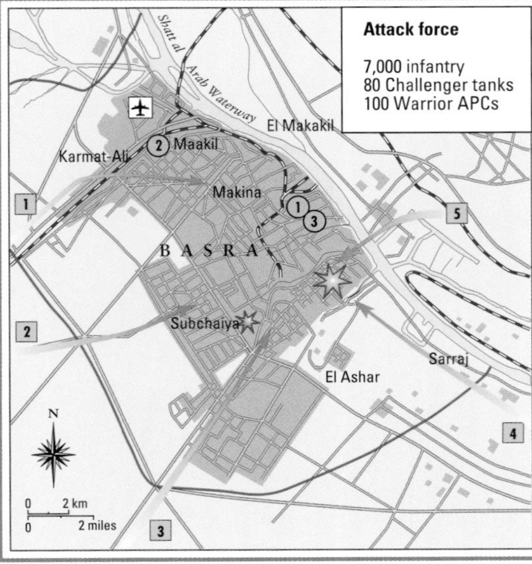

Polish commandos. US armor and infantry advanced north and then west through the desert toward Baghdad, while US marines traveled along Highway 1, through the middle of the country, reaching Nasiriyah. This city was a major road junction, with bridges over the Euphrates, and was near to Talil airfield. American marines secured the city and beat off attacks from Kut. The aftermath of this battle saw occasional flare-ups, though guerrilla activity ended by April. American forces then advanced and captured Najaf.

The British 1st Armoured Division moved through the marshlands to surround and then enter Basra. The Desert Rats, the 7th Armoured Brigade, fought fierce resistance and lost eleven men to the enemies' approximately 500. After Basra was secured, British forces advanced to meet the Americans at Al Amarah. US troops reached Karbala, occasionally meeting determined resistance that melted away, with the Americans winning every military engagement. Baghdad was surrounded, bridges across the Euphrates seized and the capital taken, with Saddam's regime falling on 9 April.

Forces loyal to Saddam had stockpiled weapons and explosives and, after the formal war was over, fought an insurgency against coalition troops. Guerrilla attacks ensued, with sniping, car bombs, suicide attacks, mortars, missiles, and improvised explosive devices. Most of these occurred in the Sunni triangle but soon religious insurgents joined in with Shi'ite attacks on the occupiers.

A Coalition Provisional Authority was established, two of Saddam's sons were killed and Saddam himself captured in December 2003, followed by his trial and execution at the hands of a new Iraqi government. Coalition forces were subjected to occasional attacks and these became worse in 2004 when four American civilian contractors were killed, leading to the Second Battle of Fallujah, where some 1,500 insurgents died with the same number being captured. In 2004 there were some 26,500 attacks and these increased to over 34,000 in 2005. However, a new Iraqi government was elected, a constitution written, and a new Iraqi army constructed with the help of foreign technical advisors. In 2009, British and Australian troops withdrew from combat, with US forces leaving in 2011. However, Iraqi democracy is very fragile under a new Shi'ite-dominated government, and insurgencies persist in a more fragmented society than under the Baathist regime.

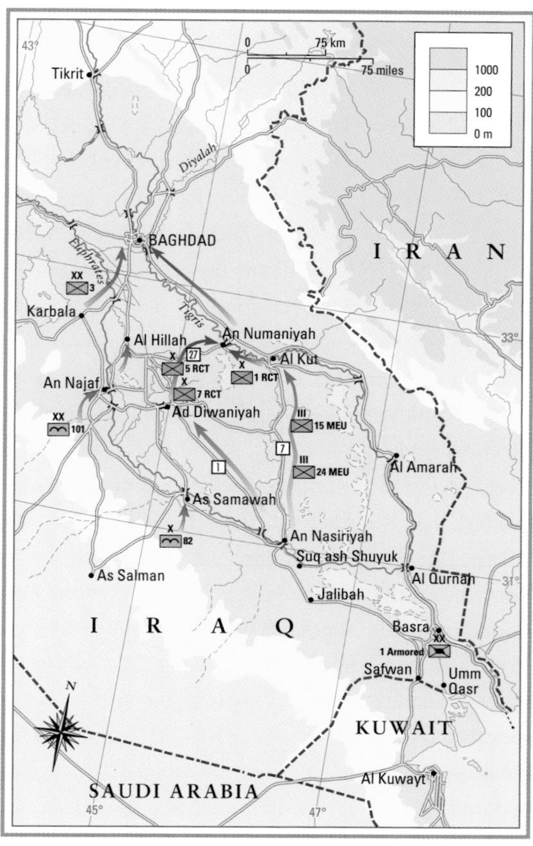

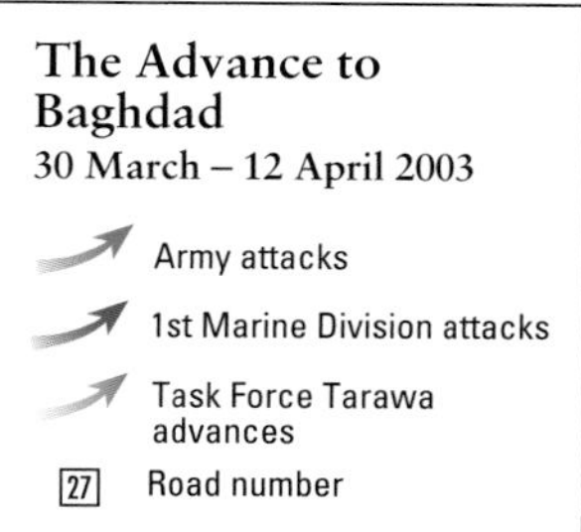

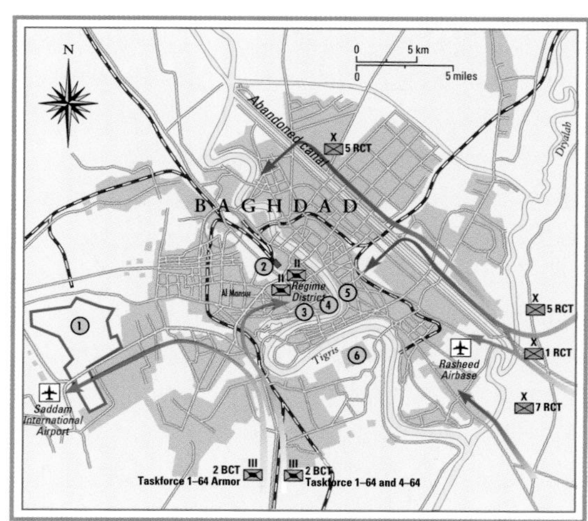

Battle for Baghdad
April 2003

Direction of main US attacks

- 5 April, First Thunder Run
- 7 April, Second Thunder Run
- 8 April, 1st Marine Division

1. Radwaniyah Presidential Palace and compound
2. Central train station
3. Baath Party headquarters
4. Republican Guard barracks
5. Saddam statue, pulled down on 9 April
6. Al Dawrah oil refinery

Airport

Arab Spring

The wave of protests and insurgencies known as the Arab Spring began in Sidi Bouzid, Tunisia, in December 2010 when Muhamed Bouazizi, a street seller, set himself on fire as a protest against police corruption and ill treatment. His action was a catalyst, sparking off Tunisia-wide protests that caused President Zine El Abidine Ben Ali to flee to Saudi Arabia after the army refused to intervene. Like a pebble dropped in a pool, ripples of unrest spread throughout the Arab world to Algeria, Jordan, Egypt, and Yemen, and other countries. By December 2013, leaders had been forced from power in Tunisia, Libya, Yemen, and Egypt, with NATO forces providing air cover for the rebels in Libya who ended by killing the Arab world's longest serving President, Muammar al-Qadhafy. There were also uprisings in Bahrain and Syria, the first being crushed by force with help from Saudi Arabia and the United Arab Emirates, while the second soon developed into a full, and bloody, civil war, causing at least 150,000 deaths and a massive refugee problem in the surrounding states. Major demonstrations also occurred in Algeria, Iraq, Jordan, Kuwait, Morocco, and Sudan with smaller protests in Mauritania, Oman, Saudi Arabia, Djibouti, Western Sahara, and the Palestine Authority.

The unrest had many causes. The demographic structure was changing with ever growing numbers of youths needing jobs in economically stagnant countries like Egypt. There was a widespread disgust with corruption, a widening gap between rich and poor, and sudden rises in food prices. Many Arab regimes had been corrupt and authoritarian, run by tribal or business coteries who had previously controlled the flow of information to ensure conformity. The appearance—from 1996—of the Qatari-owned al-Jazeera 24-hour news channel, followed by the ruler's announcement abolishing official censorship, lifted taboos on the public criticism of governments (with the obvious exception of Qatar's since the channel receives funding from the Qatari state.) Social media added rage to the recipe, by networking samples of police brutality or industrial protests, including strikes by Tunisian miners and Egyptian textile workers. Those possessing mobile telephones could use social media to pass information and pictures, bypassing governments and their possible disinformation.

In Egypt, protests commenced in January 2011, leading to the resignation of President Hosni Mubarak, and the military dissolved the Egyptian Parliament and suspended the Constitution. Presidential elections were held and Mohamed Morsi of the Muslim Brotherhood's Peace and Justice Party elected President. However, Morsi's failure to address economic issues and his attempts to pass an Islamist constitution without mechanisms for protecting politically vulnerable constituencies, such as Christians, women, and journalists, led to grow-

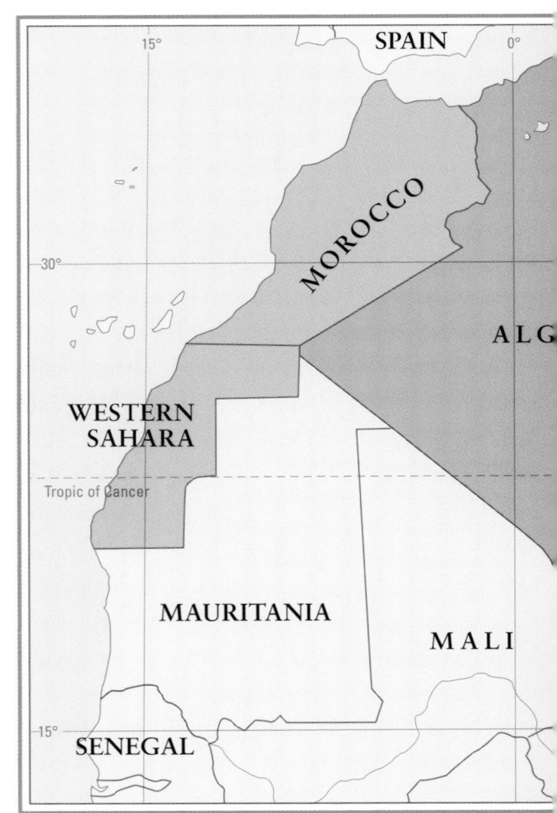

ing protests against his rule with fighting between supporters and proponents of the Brotherhood. In June 2013, the military toppled Morsi in a coup masterminded by the Defense Minister General Abd al-Fatah al-Sisi and installed an interim government to prepare Sisi's bid for the presidency. Around 1,000 Brotherhood supporters were killed in the aftermath, with the organization banned as terrorist.

Inspired by events in Tunisia and Egypt, human rights protests occurred in Bahrain where the Shiʻite majority was ruled by a Sunni monarch. With demonstrations involving more than 100,000 people, there were clashes with the police, and several deaths. Tensions mounted when the Bahraini military opened fire on the crowds and the King requested aid from the Saudi government and Gulf Cooperation Council, with member states contributing forces that entered and pacified Bahrain. An extremely harsh crackdown on the Shiʻa followed and a virtual proxy war ensued with Saudi Arabia backing the Sunni King while Iran allegedly backed the Shiʻites, though protesters insisted they were demanding equal rights, rather than acting for Iran.

Saudi Arabia has since become a center of counter-revolution, backing the Egyptian crackdown for fear that the Muslim Brotherhood would challenge the hegemony of its own tribal oligarchy.

Syria has also seen a proxy war with the Alawite Shiʻite regime which, at the time of writing, is being supported by Iran and Hezbollah sending Shiʻite fighters from Lebanon. The insurgents are supported by Qatar, Saudi Arabia, the United Arab Emirates, Turkey, and Jordan. Confusion reigns in Syria, with the Turkish-backed Free Syrian Army originally confronting President Assad. However a range of insurgents are now in the field, with Islamist groups, such as Jabhat al-Nusra and the Islamic State of Iraq and the Levant (ISIS) confronting the forces of the Russian and Iranian backed Assad regime. The battle continues.

BIBLIOGRAPHY

INTRODUCTION

Breasted, James Henry; *Ancient Times, A History of the Early World: an Introduction to the Study of Ancient History and the Career of Early Man*, Ginn & Co., Boston, MA, 1943 (2nd ed)

Fisher, W. B.; *The Middle East. A Physical, Social and Regional Geography*, Routledge, Abingdon, 2013

Gates, Charles; *Ancient Cities. The Archaeology of Urban Life in the Ancient Near East, Egypt, Greece, and Rome*, Routledge, Abingdon, 2003

ANCIENT TIMES

Bar-Kochva, Belalel; *The Seleucid Army: Organisation and Tactics in the Great Campaigns*, Cambridge University Press, Cambridge, 2012

Berlin, Andrea M. & Overman, J. Andrew; *The First Jewish Revolt*, Routledge, Abingdon, 2002

Boardman, John, Edwards, I. E. S., Sollberger, E., & Hammond, N. G. L.; *The Cambridge Ancient History, Vol. 3, Part 2: The Assyrian and Babylonian Empires from the Eighth to the Sixth Centuries* BC, Cambridge University Press, Cambridge, 1991

Bowden, Hugh (ed); *The Times Ancient Civilizations*, Times Books, HarperCollins, London, 2002

Braudel, Fernand & Reynolds, Sian; *The Mediterranean in the Ancient World*, Penguin, London, 2002

Breasted, James Henry; *The Battle of Kadesh: A Study in the Earliest Known Military Strategy*, University of Chicago, Chicago, IL, 1903

Brewer, Douglas J.; *The Archaeology of Ancient Egypt. Beyond Pharaohs*, Cambridge University Press, Cambridge, 2012

Bryce, Trevor; *The World of the Neo-Hittite Kingdoms: A Political and Military History*, Oxford University Press, Oxford, 2012

Campbell, Brian; *Warfare and Society in Imperial Rome, c. 31* BC–AD *280*, Routledge, Abingdon, 2002

Casson, Lionel; *The Ancient Mariners: Seafarers and Sea Fighters of the Mediterranean in Ancient Times*, Princeton University Press, Princeton, NJ, 1991

Crawford, Harriet E. W.; *Dilmun and its Gulf Neighbours*, Cambridge University Press, Cambridge, 1998

Crawford, Harriet; *Regime Change in the Ancient Near East and Egypt. From Sargon of Agade to Saddam Hussein*, Oxford University Press, Oxford, 2007

Crawford, Harriet; *Sumer and the Sumerians*, Cambridge University Press, Cambridge, 2004

Dawson, Doyne; *The First Armies*, Cassel & Co., London, 2001

Dodson, Aidan; *Afterglow of Empire: Egypt from the Fall of the New Kingdom to the Saite Renaissance*, The American University in Cairo, Cairo, 2012

Dothan, Trude & Dothan, Moshe; *People of the Sea: Search for the Philistines*, Prentice Hall & IBD, Upper Saddle River, NJ, 1992

English, Stephen; *Mercenaries in the Classical World*, Pen & Sword, Barnsley, 2012

Farrokh, Kaveh; *Sasanian Elite Cavalry* AD *224–642*, Osprey Publishing, Oxford, 2005

Farrokh, Kaveh; *Shadows in the Desert. Ancient Persia at War*, Osprey Publishing, Oxford, 2009

Fields, Nic; *Pompey*, Osprey Publishing, Oxford, 2012

Fisher, Greg; *Between Empires: Arabs, Romans, and Sasanians in Late Antiquity*, Oxford University Press, Oxford, 2013

Foster, B. R. & Foster, K. P.; *Civilization of Ancient Iraq*, Princeton University Press, Princeton, NJ, 2011

Freeman, Philip; *Alexander the Great*, Simon & Schuster Paperbacks, New York, NY, 2011

Fuller, John F. C.; *The Generalship of Alexander the Great*, Wordsworth Editions Ltd., Ware, Hertfordshire, 1998

Graft, David A.; *The Eurasian Way of War. Military Practice in Seventh Century China and Byzantium*, Routledge, Abingdon, 2014

Grainger, John D.; *Roman Conquests: Egypt and Judaea*, Pen & Sword, Barnsley, 2013

Hamblin, William J.; *Warfare in the Ancient Near East to 1600* BC. *Holy Warriors at the Dawn of History*, Routledge, Abingdon, 2000

Hamilton, Colin; *The Campaigns of Alexander*, Penguin, London, 2003

Hanson, Victor Davis; *Hoplites: The Classical Greek Battle Experience*, Routledge, Abingdon, 1993

Hazzard, Bill; *Hittite Fortification c. 1650–700* BC, Osprey Publishing, Oxford 2012

Healy, Mark; *New Kingdom Egypt*, Osprey Publishing, Oxford, 1992

Healy, Mark; *Qadesh 1300* BC: *Clash of the Warriors*, Osprey Publishing, Oxford, 1993

Healy, Mark; *The Ancient Assyrians*, Osprey Publishing, Oxford, 1992

Jones, Waldemar Heckel Ryan; *Macedonian Warrior. Alexander's Elite Infantryman*, Osprey Publishing, Oxford, 2006

Josephus, Flavius; *The Jewish War*, Penguin, London, 2003

Kelle, Brad; *Ancient Israel at War 853–586 BC*, Osprey Publishing, Oxford, 2007

Kriwaczer; *Babylon: Mesopotamia and the Birth of Civilization*, Atlantic Books, London, 2012

Leach, John; *Pompey the Great*, Routledge, Abingdon, 2013

Le Bohec, Yann; *The Imperial Roman Army*, Routledge, Abingdon, 1994

Leick, Gwendolyn; *Mesopotamia: The Invention of the City*, Penguin, London 2002

Leick, Gwendolyn; *The Babylonians: An Introduction*, Routledge, Abingdon, 2002

Nossov, Konstantin; *Hittite Fortifications, c 1650–750 BC*, Osprey Publishing, Oxford, 2008

Potts, D. T.; *The Archaeology of Elam. Formation and Transformation of an Ancient Iranian State*, Cambridge University Press, Cambridge, 2005

Rea, Cam; *The Rise of Parthia in the East: From the Seleucid Empire to the Arrival of Rome*, CreateSpace Independent Publishing Platform, Seattle, WA, 2013

Rice, Rob S., Anglim, Simon, Jestice, Phyllis, Rusch, Scott; *Fighting Techniques of the Ancient World 3000 BC–AD 500*, Amber Books, London, 2005

Robbins, Manuel; *Collapse of the Bronze Ages. The Story of Greece, Troy, Israel, Egypt, and the Peoples of the Sea*, iUniverse.com, Bloomington, IN, 2001

Rocca, Samuel; *The Fortifications of Ancient Israel and Judah 1200–586 BC*, Osprey Publishing, Oxford, 2010

Rocca, Samuel; *The Forts of Judaea 168 BC–AD 73*, Osprey Publishing, Oxford, 2008

Roux, Georges; *Ancient Iraq*, Penguin, London, 2012

Sayce, Archibald Henry; *The Hittites: The Story of a Forgotten Empire*, Forgotten Books, London, 2012

Sekunda, Nicholas; *The Persian Army 560–330 BC*, Osprey Publishing, Oxford, 1992

Shepherd, Si; *The Jewish Revolt, AD 66–74*, Osprey Publishing, Oxford, 2013

Sidebottom, Harry; *Ancient Warfare: A Very Short Introduction*, Oxford University Press, Oxford, 2004

Soggin, J. Alberto; *History of Israel from the Beginning to the Bar Kochba Revolt*, SCM-Canterbury Press Ltd., London, 1984

Spalinger, Anthony J.; *War in Ancient Egypt: The New Kingdom*, Wiley-Blackwell, Hoboken, NJ, 2005

Stoneman, Richard; *Palmyra and its Empire: Zenobia's Revolt against Rome*, The University of Michigan Press, Ann Arbor, MI, 1995

Tyldesley, Joyce; *Ramesses. Egypt's Greatest Pharaoh*, Penguin, London, 2001

Van De Mierop, Marc; *A History of the Ancient Near East ca 3000–323 BC*, Wiley-Blackwell, Hoboken, NJ, 2006

Van De Mierop, Marc; *King Hammurabi of Babylon*, Blackwell Publishing, Oxford, 2004

Vogel, Carola; *The Fortifications of Ancient Egypt 3000–1780 BC*, Osprey Publishing, Oxford, 2010

Waterfield, Robin; *Dividing the Spoils: The War for Alexander the Great's Empire*, Oxford University Press, Oxford, 2012

Waterfield, Robin; *Xenophon's Retreat: Greece, Persia, and the End of the Golden Age*, Faber & Faber, London, 2007

Watkins, Jack; *Encyclopedia of Classic Warfare 3000–1815 BC*, Amber Books, London, 2011

Wilkinson, Toby; *The Rise and Fall of Ancient Egypt*, Bloomsbury Paperbacks, London, 2011

Winsbury, Rex; *Zenobia of Palmyra: History, Myth and the Neo-Classical Imagination*, Gerald Duckworth & Co, Ltd., London, 2010

Wise, Terence; *Ancient Armies of the Middle East*, Osprey Publishing, Oxford, 1981

Xenophon, Cawkwell, George & Warner, Rex; *The Persian Expedition*, Penguin, London, 2004

Yasar-Landau, Assaf; *The Philistines and Aegean Migration at the End of the Late Bronze Age*, Cambridge University Press, Cambridge, 2010

Biblical Interlude

Bar-Kochva, Belalel; *Judas Maccabaeus: The Jewish Struggle against the Seleucids*, Cambridge University Press, Cambridge, 2002

Barnes, Ian; *The Historical Atlas of the Bible*, Cartographica Press, London, 2006

Barnes, Ian & Bacon, Josephine; *The Historical Atlas of Judaism*, Chartwell Books. Inc., Edison, NJ. 2009

Brettler. Marc Zvi; *The Book of Judges*, Routledge, Abingdon, 2001

Dougherty, Martin, Haskew E. Jestie, Phyllis, & Rice, Bob S.; *Battles of the Bible, 1400 BC to AD 73*, Amber Books, London, 2008

Finkelstein, Israel & Silberman, Neil Asher; *The Bible Unearthed. Archaeology's New Vision of Ancient Israel and the Origin of its Scared Texts*, Simon & Schuster, New York, NY, 2002

Gelb, Norman; *Herod the Great: Statesman, Visionary,*

Tyrant, Rowman & Littlefield Publishers, Lanham, MD, 2013

Golden, Jonathan M.; *Ancient Canaan and Israel*, Oxford University Press, New York, 2009

Hayes, John H. & Mandell, Sara R.; *The Jewish People in Classical Antiquity from Alexander to Bar Kochba*, Westminster John Knox Press, Louisville, KY, 1998

Kent, Charles Foster; *A History of the Hebrew People from the Settlement in Canaan to the Division of the Kingdom*, Kessinger Publishing LLC, Whitefish, MT, 2004

Killebrew, Anne E.; *Biblical Peoples and Ethnicity. An Archaeological Study of Egyptians, Canaanites and Early Israel 1300–100 BC*, Brill, Leiden, The Netherlands, 2006

Le Glay, Marcel, Voisin Jean-Louis, & Le Bohec, Yann; *A History of Rome*, Blackwell Publishing, Oxford, 1996

McKenzie, Steven L.; *King David: A Biography*, Oxford University Press, Oxford, 2000

Redford, Donald B.; *Egypt, Canaan, and Israel in Ancient Times*, Princeton University Press, Princeton, NJ, 1993

Sandara, N.; *The Sea Peoples. Warriors of the Eastern Mediterranean*, Thames & Hudson, London, 1985

Shanks, Hershel (ed); *Ancient Israel. A Short History from Abraham to the Roman Destruction of the Temple*, SPCK, London, 1989

Stevens, Joseph; *The Hasmoneans and their Supporters from Mattathias to the Death of John Hyrcanus I*, Scholars Press, Cambridge, 1990

Sweeney, Marvin A.; *King Josiah of Judah*, Oxford University Press, Oxford, 2001

Yadin, Yigael; *Masada. Herod's Fortress and the Zealots' Last Stand*, Weidenfeld & Nicholson, London, 1966

Clash of Faiths

Al-Rasheed, Madawi; *A History of Saudi Arabia*, Cambridge University Library, Cambridge, 2010

Amitai-Preiss, Reuven; *Mongols and Mamluks. The Mamluk-Ilkhanid War, 1260–1281*, Cambridge University Press, Cambridge, 2005

Ashbridge, Thomas; *The Crusades: The War for the Holy Land*, Simon & Schuster UK Ltd., London, 2012

Barber, Malcolm; *The Crusader States*, Yale University Press, New Haven, CT, 2012

Barnes, Ian; *The Historical Atlas of Knights and Castles*, Chartwell Books, Inc., Edison, NJ, 2007

Barnes, Ian; *World Religions*, Cartographica Press, London, 2007,

Bengie, Ofra & Litvak., Meir; *The Sunna and Shi'a in History*, Palgrave Macmillan, Basingstoke, 2011

Bennison, Amira K.; *The Great Caliphs: The Golden Age of the 'Abbasid Empire*, I B Tauris, London, 2011

Blow, David; *Shah Abbas: The Ruthless King Who Became an Iranian Legend; Emperor of Persia and Restorer of Iran*, I. B. Tauris & Co. Ltd., London, 2009

Burdett, Anita; *The Expansion of Wahabbi Power in Arabia, 1798–1932*, Cambridge University Press, Cambridge, 2013

Cagman, Filiz; *Turks: A Journey of a Thousand Years, 600-1600*, Royal Academy of Arts, London, 2005

Crowley; *Empires of the Sea: The Siege of Malta, the Battle of Lepanto and the Contest for the Center of the World*, Faber & Faber, London, 2009

Darlow, Michael & Bray, Barbara; *Ibn Saud: The Desert Warrior and his Legacy*, Quartet Books, Charlottesville, VA, 2010

De Vries, Kelly, Dickie, Iain, Dougherty, Martin J., Jestice, Phyllis; *Battles of the Crusades 1097–1444. From Dorylaueum to Varna*, Amber Books, London, 2007

Edwards, Sean J. A.; *Swarming on the Battle Field: Past, Present, and Future*, RAND, Santa Monica, CA, 2000

Faroqhi, Saraiya; *The Ottoman Empire. A Short History*, Markus Wiener Publishing Inc., Princeton, NJ, 1979

Fletcher, Richard; *The Cross and the Crescent. The Dramatic Story of the Earliest Encounter between Christians and Muslims*, Penguin, London, 2004

Gillingham, John; *Richard I*, Yale University Press, New Haven, CT, 2002

Haldon, John; *The Palgrave Atlas of Byzantine History*, Palgrave Macmillan, Basingstoke, 2010

Hansen, Valerie; *The Silk Road: A New History*, Oxford University Press, New York, 2012

Heath, Ian; *Byzantine Armies 886–1118*, Osprey Publishing, Oxford, 1979

Hindley, Geoffrey; *Saladin: Hero of Islam*, Pen & Sword, Barnsley, 2010

Hourani, Albert; *A History of the Arab Peoples*, Faber & Faber, London, 2005

Ibrahim, Raymond; *The Battle of Yarmuk: An Assessment of the Immediate Factors Behind the Islamic Conquests*, Lambert Academic Publishing, Saarbrücken, 2010

Kennedy, Hugh; *The Great Arab Conquests: How the Spread of Islam Changed the World We Live In*, Da Capo Press, Cambridge, MA, 2007

Kurkjian, Vahan M.; *A History of Armenia*, IndoEuropean Publishing.com, Bel Air, CA, 2014

Kinross, Patrick Balfour; *The Ottoman Centuries. The Rise and Fall of the Turkish Empire*, William Morrow, New York, 1979

Lock, Peter; *The Routledge Companion to the Crusades*, Routledge, Abingdon, 2006

Maalouf, Amin; *The Crusades Through Arab Eyes*, Saqi Books, London, 1984

Marozzi, Tamerlane; *Sword of Islam, Conqueror of the World*, Harper Perennial, London, 2005

Marshall, Christopher; *Warfare in the Latin East, 1192–1291*, Cambridge University Press, Cambridge, 1994

Marsot, Afaf Lurfi Al-Sayyid; *A History of Egypt: From the Arab Conquest to the Present*, Cambridge University Press, Cambridge, 2007

Masters, Bruce; *The Arabs of the Ottoman Empire, 1516–1918*, Cambridge University Press, Cambridge, 2013

May, Timothy; *The Mongol Conquest in World History*, Reaktion Books Ltd., London, 2012

Morgan, D.; *Medieval Persia, 1040-1797*, Routledge, Abingdon, 1988

Nicolle, David; *Armies of the Caliphates 862–1098*, Osprey Publishing, Oxford 1998

Nicolle, David; *Armies of the Muslim Conquest*, Osprey Publishing, Oxford, 1993

Nicolle, David; *Crusader Castles in the Holy Land, 1097–1192*, Osprey Publishing, Oxford, 2004

Nicolle, David; *Manzikert 1071: The Breaking of Byzantium*, Osprey Publishing, Oxford, 2013

Nicolle David; *The Age of Tamerlane*, Osprey Publishing, Oxford, 1990

Nicolle, David; *The Mamluks*, Osprey Publishing, Oxford, 1993

Nicolle, David; *Yarmuk* AD *636*, Osprey Publishing, Oxford, 1994

Norwich, John. J.; *A Short History of Byzantium*, Penguin, London, 2013

Palmer, Alan; *The Decline and Fall of the Ottoman Empire*, Faber & Faber, London, 2011

Philipp, Thomas & Haarmann, Ulrich; *The Mamluks in Egyptian Politics and Society*, Cambridge University Press, Cambridge, 2007

Pourshariati, Parvaneh; *Decline and Fall of the Sasanian Empire: The Sasanian-Parthian Confederacy and the Arab Conquest of Iran*, I. B. Tauris, New York, 2009

Raphael, Kate; *Muslim Fortresses in the Levant. Between Crusaders and Mongols*, Routledge, Abingdon, 2010

Riley-Smith, Jonathan; *The Atlas of the Crusades*, Facts on File Inc., New York, NY, 1990

Riley-Smith, Jonathan (ed); *The Oxford History of the Crusades*, Oxford University Press, Oxford, 2002

Rogan, Eugene; *The Arabs. A History*, Penguin, London, 2012

Rose, Jenny; *Zoroastrianisn: An Introduction*, I B Tauris, London, 2011

Sahin, Kaya; *Empire and Power in the Reign of Süleyman. Narrating the Sixteenth Century Ottoman World*, Cambridge University Press, Cambridge, 2013

Savory, Roger; *Iran Under the Safavids*, Cambridge University Press, Cambridge, 2007

Turnbull, S. R.; *The Ottoman Empire 1326–1699*, Osprey Publishing, Oxford, 2003

Tyerman, Christophe, (ed); *Chronicles of the First Crusade*, Penguin, London, 2011

Tyerman, Christophe; *God's War. A New History of the Crusades*, Penguin, London, 2007

Waterson, James; *The Knights of Islam. The Wars of the Mamluks*, Greenhill Books, London, 2007

EUROPEAN INTERVENTION

Aksakai, Mustafa; *The Ottoman Road to War in 1914*, Blackwell Publishing, Oxford, 2010

Allawi, Ali A.; *Faisal I of Iraq*, Yale University Press, New Haven, CT, 2014

Arielli, Nir; *Fascist Italy and the Middle East, 1933–1940*, Palgrave Macmillan, Basingstoke, 2012

Barr, James; *A Line in the Sand: Britain, France, and the Struggle for the Mastery of the Middle East*, Simon & Schuster, London, 2011

Barr, James; *Setting the Desert on Fire: T. E. Lawrence and Britain's Secret War in Arabia, 1916–1918*, Bloomsbury Publishing PLC, London, 2007

Brown, Malcolm; *T. E. Lawrence*, The British Library Publishing Division, London, 2003

Cole, Juan; *Colonialism and Revolution in the Middle East. Social and Cultural Origins of Egypt's Urabi Movement*, Princeton University Press, Princeton, NJ, 1993

Cole, Juan; *Napoleon's Egypt. Invading the Middle East*, Palgrave Macmillan, Basingstoke, 2007

Cronin, Vincent; *Napoleon*, HarperCollins Publishers, New York, NY, 1994

Elon, Amos; *Herzl*, Holt, Rinehart, and Winston, Boston, MA, 1975

Dunn, John P.; *Khedive Ismail's Army*, Routledge, Abingdon, 2013

Engle, Anita; *The Nili Spies*, Routledge, Abingdon, 1997

Fahmy, Khaled; *All the Pasha's Men: Mehmed Ali, His Army, and the Making of Modern Egypt*, Cambridge University Press, Cambridge, 1997

Featherstone Donald; *Tel el Kebir: Wolseley's Conquest of Egypt, 1882*, Osprey Publishing, Oxford, 1993

Fremont-Barnes, Gregory & Gerrard, Howard; *Nile 1798: Nelson's First Great Victory*, Osprey Publishing, Oxford, 2011

Fromkin, David; *A Peace to End All Peace. Creating the Modern Middle East*, Henry Holt & Co., New York, 1989

Hughes, Matthew; *Allenby and British Strategy in the Middle East, 1917–1919*, Routledge, London, 1999

Hughes, Matthew; *Allenby in Palestine*, The History Press Ltd., Stroud, Gloucestershire, 2004

James, Barrie G.; *Hitler's Gulf War. The Fight for Iraq 1941.* Pen & Sword, Barnsley, 2009

Kinross, Patrick; *Ataturk: The Rebirth of a Nation*, Phoenix, Blaine, WA, 2001

Knight, Paul; *The British Army in Mesopotamia 1914–1918*, Blackwell Publishing, Oxford, 2012

Lawrence, Thomas Edward; *Seven Pillars of Wisdom*, Penguin, London, 2000

Laqueur, Walter; *The History of Zionism*, Tauris Parke Paperbacks, London, 2003

Mango, Andrew; *Ataturk*, John Murray Publishers Ltd., London, 2004

Neep, Daniel; *Occupying Syria under the French Mandate. Insurgency, Space, and State Formation*, Cambridge University Press, Cambridge, 2012

Paris, Timothy J.; *Britain, the Hashemites and Arab Rule. The Sherefian Solution*, Routledge, Abingdon, 2003

Marsot, Afaf, Lutfi Al-Sayyid; *Egypt in the Reign of Muhammad Ali*, Cambridge University Press, Cambridge, 1984

Mohs, Polly; *Military Intelligence and the Arab Revolt. The First Modern Intelligence War*, Routledge, Abingdon, 2008

Mortlock, Michael J.; *The Egyptian Expeditionary Force, World War I: A History of the British-led Campaign in Egypt, Palestine, and Syria*, McFarland & Co., Jefferson, NC, 2010

Murphy, David; *The Arab Revolt*, Osprey Publishing, Oxford, 2008

Netanyahu, B.; *Founding Fathers of Zionism*, Gefen Publishing House, Jerusalem, 2012

Nicolle, David; *Lawrence and the Arab Revolt*, Osprey Publishing, Oxford, 1989

Perrett, Bryan; *Megiddo 1918: Lawrence, Allenby and the March on Damascus*, Praeger, New York, NY, 2004

Perret, Bryan, Chandler, David, & Dovey, Ed.; *Megiddo, 1918: The Last Great Cavalry Victory*, Osprey Publishing, Oxford, 1999

Strathern, Paul; *Napoleon in Egypt: "The Greatest Glory"*, Vintage, Vancouver, WA, 2008

Street, Ninian (ed); *The Royal Navy and the Palestine Patrol*, Routledge, Abingdon, 2002

Sugden, John; *Nelson: Sword of Albion*, Random House, London, 2012

Townsend, Charles; *When God Made Hell: The British Invasion of Mesopotamia and the Creation of Iraq, 1914–1921*, Faber & Faber, London, 2011

Ufford, Letitia W.; *The Pasha: How Mehmet Ali Defied the West, 1839–1841*, McFarland & Co. Inc., Jefferson, NC, 2007

Wilson, Derek; *Rothschild: A Story of Wealth and Power*, André Deutsch, London, 1988

Wilson, Mary Christina; *King Abdullah, Britain, and the Making of Jordan*, Cambridge University Press, Cambridge, 1996

Ulrichsen, Kristian Coates; *The First World War in the Middle East*, C. Hurst & Co. Publishers Ltd., London, 2014

Wilcox, Ron; *Battles on the Tigris: The Mesopotamian Campaign*, Pen & Sword, Barnsley, 2006

Zeidel, Ronen, Baram, Amatzia & Rohde, Achim; *Iraq between Occupations. Perspectives from 1920 to the Present*, Palgrave Macmillan, Basingstoke, 2011

Age of Technology

Ahmed, Mohammed M. A.; *Iraqi Kurds and Nation Building*, Palgrave Macmillan, Basingstoke, 2012

Allison, William T.; *The Gulf War, 1990–91*, Palgrave Macmillan, Basingstoke, 2012

Aly, Abdel Moriem Said, Feldman, Shai Shikake, Khalil; *Arabs and Israelis. Conflict and Peacemaking in the Middle East*, Palgrave Macmillan, Basingstoke, 2013

Azuri, Naseer; *Palestinian Refugees: The Right of Return*, Pluto Press, London, 2001

Cooper, Andrew Scott; *The Oil Kings. How the US, Iran and Saudi Arabia Changed the Balance of Power in the Middle East*, Random House, New York, NY, (Audio Book), 2011

Bobbit, Philip; *Terror and Consent. The War for the Twenty-first Century*, Penguin, London, 2009

Bregman Ahron; *The Fifty Years' War. Israel and the Arabs*, Penguin: BBC, London, 1998

Butler, L. J.; *Britain and Empire: Adjusting to a Post-Imperial World*, I. B. Tauris, London, 2002

Burke, Jason; *Al-Qaeda. The True Story of Radical Islam*, Penguin, London, 2007

Dayan, Moshe; *Diary of the Sinai Campaign*, Sphere Books, London, 1967

Demant, Peter R.; *Islam v Islamism: The Dilemma of the Muslim World*, Praeger Publishers Inc., Westport, CT

Dimbleby, Jonathan; *Destiny in the Desert: the Road to El Alamein-the Battle That Turned the Tide*, Profile Books, London, 2013

Donovan, Jerome; *The Iran-Iraq War. Antecedents and Conflict Escalation*, Routledge , Abingdon, 2011

Dunstan, Simon; *The Yom Kippur War: The Arab-Israeli War of 1973*, Osprey Publishing, Oxford, 2007

Elon, Amos; *The Israelis. Founders and Sons*, Penguin, Harmondsworth, 1983

Fawcett, Louise; *The International Relations of the Middle East*, Oxford University Press, Oxford, 2005

Fawn, Rick & Hinnebusch, Raymond A.; *The Iraq War: Causes and Consequences*, Lynne Riener Publishers Inc., Boulder, CO, 2005

Froman, Colin; *Right of Return: A History of Modern Israel*, CreateSpace Independent Publishing Platform, Seattle, WA, 2013

Gerges, Fawaz A.; *The Rise and Fall of Al-Qaeda*, Oxford University Press, Oxford, 2014

Gilbert, Martin; *The Routledge Atlas of the Arab-Israeli Conflict*, Routledge, Abingdon, 2012

Hamilton, Nigel; *Monty: Master of the Battlefield, 1942–44*, Hamish Hamilton, London, 1983

Hammond, Bryan; *El Alamein. The Battle That Turned the Tide of the Second World War*, Osprey Publishing, Oxford, 2012

Hayhurst, Chris; *Israel's War of Independence*, Rosen Publishing Group, New York, NY, 2003

Herzog, Chaim & Gazit, Schlomo; *The Arab-Israeli Wars: War and Peace in the Middle East from the War of Independence to the Present*, Greenhill Books, Barnsley, 2004

James, Barrie G.; *Hitler's Gulf War: The Fight for Iraq, 1941*, Pen & Sword, Barnsley, 2009

La Guardia, Anton; *Holy Land, Unholy War. Israel and the Palestinians*, Penguin, London, 2007

Levran, Aharon; *Israeli Strategy after Desert Storm. Lessons of the Second Gulf War*, Routledge, Abingdon, 1997

Lyman, Robert, & Gerrard, Howard; *Iraq 1941. The Battles of Basra, Habbaniya, Fallujah, and Baghdad*, Osprey Publishing, Oxford, 2006

Lynch, Marc; *The Arab Uprising: The Unfinished Revolutions of the New Middle East*, Public Affairs, New York, NY, 2013

McNamara, Robert; *Britain, Nasser, and the Balance of Power in the Middle East, 1952–1977. From the Egyptian Revolution to the Six Day War*, Routledge, Abingdon, 2003

Mills, Dan; *Sniper One. The Blistering True Story of a British Battle Group under Siege*, Penguin, London, 2008

Morris, Benny; *The Birth of the Palestinian Refugee Problem Revisited*, Cambridge University Press, Cambridge, 2004

Murray, Williamson & Woods, Kevin; *The Iran-Iraq War*, Cambridge University Press, Cambridge, 2014

Olsen, John A.; *Strategic Air Power in Desert Storm*, Routledge, Abingdon, 2003

Oren, Michael B.; *Six Days of War: June 1967 and the Making of the Modern Middle East*, Penguin, London, 2003

Ovendale, Ritchie; *The Origins of the Arab-Israeli Wars*, Routledge, Abingdon, 2004

Pearson, William; *Tornado Down*, Penguin, London, 2002

Peleg, Ilan, & Waxman, Dov; *Israel's Palestinians. The Conflict Within*, Cambridge University Press, Cambridge, 2011

Ramadan, Tariq; *The Arab Awakening. Islam and the New Middle East*, Allen Lane, London, 2012

Ross, M.; *The Oil Curse: How Petroleum Wealth Shapes the Development of Nations*, Princeton University Press, Princeton, NJ

Sassoon, Joseph; *Saddam Hussein's Ba'th Party. Inside an Authoritarian State*, Cambridge University Press, Cambridge, 2012

Sayigh, Yezid & Schlaim, Avi; *The Cold War and the Middle East*, Oxford University Press, Oxford, 1997

Schanzer, Jonathan; *Hamas v Fatah. The Struggle for Palestine*, Palgrave Macmillan, Basingstoke, 2008

Schlaim, Avi; *The Iron Wall: Israel and the Arab World*, Penguin, London, 2000

Smith, Colin; *England's Last War against France: Fighting Vichy 1940–42*, Phoenix, Blaine, WA, 2009

Smith, Colin; *Great Battles: The Battle of Alamein, North Africa, 1942*, Penguin, London, 2011

Taylor, Alan R.; *The Superpowers and the Middle East*, Syracuse University Press, Syracuse, NY, 1992

Varble, Derek; *The Suez Crisis, 1956*, Osprey Publishing, Oxford, 2003

Von Bismarck, Helene; *British Policy in the Persian Gulf, 1961–1968*, Palgrave Macmillan, Basingstoke, 2013

GLOSSARY

Ahrar al-Sham — Levantine coalition of militant Sunni fighters operating several units in the Syrian Civil War. Established in late 2011.

Al-Qaeda — Worldwide militant Islamicist organization founded by Osama bin Laden. Responsible for the 11 September 2001 attacks in the US.

Amorite — Ancient Semitic-speaking people inhabiting Syria and parts of Mesopotamia from the 21st century BCE.

Atabeg — Originally a Saljuq Turkish title of nobility given to the governor of a nation or province.

ANZAC — Australian and New Zealand Army Corps

Cataphractari — A heavily armored cavalryman covered from head to toe in scale armor riding a horse protected likewise. Important to the Medes and Persians.

Cimmerians — Ancient Indo-European people, probably Iranian-speaking, inhabiting a region north of the Caucasus and Sea of Azov. They attacked Urartu and entered Lydia.

Composite Bow — A recurve bow made from sinew, wood, and horn, generally used by steppe peoples.

Corselet — Defensive body armor, comprising a breast and back plate.

Corvus — Roman spiked boarding device used in naval warfare.

Crossbow — Medieval projectile weapon with a bow mounted horizontally on a stock firing a bolt or quarrel.

Cuneiform — Writing system using a reed to impress wedge-shaped marks on clay tablets. Originated in Sumer during the Uruk period.

Dardana — A tribe of the Sea Peoples identified with either the Greek Achaeans or a tribe from Adana in Anatolian Cilicia.

Falashas — Beta Israel or Ethiopian Jews immigrating to Israel in the late 20th century.

Fatah — Originally was the largest political faction in the Palestinian Liberation Organization. Lost its parliamentary majority to Hamas in the 2006 election.

Fedayeen — Soldiers prepared to sacrifice their lives for Islam. Now a term used for guerrilla fighters.

Feigned Retreat — Tactic used by steppe cavalry. An apparent retreat would be used to make an enemy lose formation in a chase. Once strung out, those in retreat would turn back and attack the pursuers.

Haganah — Jewish paramilitary formation in the British Mandate of Palestine.

Hamas — Sunni Islamic organization founded in 1987 to liberate Palestine from Israeli occupation. Has beaten Fatah in elections.

Harpax — In Roman naval warfare: a catapult hurling a grapnel into enemy rigging to winch the enemy close for boarding.

Hezbollah — Shiite Muslim militant group and political party in Lebanon. Represented in Lebanese Parliament. Fought Israel in 2006.

Hieroglyphics — Ancient Egyptian writing system based on pictures.

Holocaust — Systematic mass murder or genocide of some 6 million Jews by Nazi Germany and its allies.

Hoplite — Heavy infantry of ancient Greek city states. Formed from free citizens wearing body armor, helmet and grieves and armed with shield, spear, and sword.

GROM — Polish Special Forces: Operational Mobile Response Group.

Imam — Leader of a Muslim community.

Ikhwan — 'Brothers': warriors of Abd al-Aziz, founder of the Saudi dynasty and devout Wahabbites.

Irgun Zvai Leumi — Zionist militant organization. An offshoot of Haganah, believing in the use of armed force to establish a Jewish state.

Jihad — War against unbelievers in accordance with law of Islam. An internal process to reduce base instincts.

Kibbutz — Originally, an agricultural collective community in Israel combining socialism and Zionism.

Lamellar armor — Armor made from overlapping rectangular leather or metal plates laced together in rows.

Legion — A Roman legion normally comprised 5,400 heavy infantry subdivided into ten cohorts of 540 each. The cohorts were divided into six centuries of eighty men. Each soldier was armed with helmet, shield, body armor, a short sword (gladius) and heavy javelin (pilum). An auxiliary cavalry unit would be attached to a legion comprising horsemen who were not citizens or levied from subjugated peoples.

Lehi — (*see* Stern Gang)

Liwa al-Tawhid — Element of Syrian Islamic Liberation Front in Syrian Civil War operating in and around Aleppo. Active from 2012.

Lukka — One of the Sea Peoples, probably originating in Lycia.

Machalnik — Jewish and non-Jewish volunteers from outside Israel who fought for Israel in the War of Independence in 1948, especially in the air force.

Madrassah — "College", especially for religious studies.

Mahdi — Muhammad Ahmed (1845–85), a Sudanese Sufi Sheikh who defeated Turko-Egyptian troops and captured Khartoum.

Mamluk — Military caste ruling in medieval Egypt who were raised from Kipchak slave soldiers.

Mandate — League of Nations mandates establishing quasi-colonies ruled mainly by France and Britain, especially in the Middle East.

Merkava	Main battle tank of the Israeli Defence Forces produced in Israel.
Mishnah	Redaction of Jewish oral traditions.
Moshav	A type of Zionist agricultural community in the Yishuv where land is owned individually but equally.
NATO	North Atlantic Treaty Organization.
OAPEC	Organization of Arab Petroleum Exporting Countries.
Palmach	The elite strike force of the Haganah.
Parthian Shot	The act of shooting a bow over the rump of a horse at pursing enemies.
Phalanx	A mass of heavily armed infantry in ancient Greece in close deep ranks and files. The Macedonians carried particularly long pikes.
Pharisees	They were, at various times, a political group and social movement, later a school of religious thought. After the destruction of the Second Temple in Jerusalem in 70 BCE, their beliefs formed the ritual basis for a Rabbinic Judaism.
PLO	Palestinian Liberation Organization
Pogrom	A riot or violence against a specific ethnic or religious group intending massacre.
Sadducees	This sect was formed from the echelons of the Judaean population. They performed religious, social, and political roles in society.
Sanhedrin	An assembly of 20–25 men, usually appointed in every city of Biblical Israel.
Scythians	A group of Iranic-speaking tribes inhabiting the steppes of central Eurasia, noted for their horsemanship.
Shardana	(Sherden) were a tribe of Sea People wearing horned helmets, possibly coming from Sardinia.
Sheba	Thought to be the Kingdom of Saba in the Yemen in southern Arabia.
Shekelesh	A tribe of Sea People often identified with the Siculi of Sicily.
Shi'ites	Party of Ali; supporters of the rights of Ali and his descendants to lead the community of all Muslims.
Stele	Normally a stone slab carved with laws or lists of exploits.
Stern Gang	An extreme militant Zionist organization which used terror against British troops in mandate Palestine.
Suqur al-Sham	Rebel organization fighting the Syrian government in the Syrian Civil War; part of the Islamic Front.
Sunni	People who uphold the customs based on the authority of Muhammad and his Companions.
Talmud	The Talmud contains the Mishnah and the Gemara, an elucidation of the Mishnah. Central to Rabbinic Judaism.
Tel	An archaeological mound made by the ruins and detritus of historic occupiers; an example is Tel Megiddo.
Teresh	A Sea People identified variously with Etruscans or Thracians.
Tetrarch	A ruler of part of Herod's lands after his death.
Trucial States	A British protectorate on the coasts of North Arabia comprising Abu Dhabi, Dubai, Sharjah, Ajman, Umm al-Quwain, Ras al-Khaimah, Dibba, Hamriyah, Fujairah, Kalba, and Heera. Became the United Arab Emirates in 1971.
Urartu	A region comprising the plateau between Asia Minor, Mesopotamia, and the Caucasus; corresponds to the Kingdom of Van.
Vichy	Vichy France was the France ruled by Marshall Pétain after the defeat by Nazi Germany. It controlled a large portion of the French Empire.
Wahabbi	Ultra-conservative expression of Sunni Islam.
Washesh	One of the Sea Peoples.
Zealot	A political movement in Judaea which fought against Roman rule.
Zoroastrians	An ancient Iranian religion and philosophy. A major community are the Parsees in India.

Key to Military Maps: on pages 146, 149, 157, 158, 167, 174–175, 176–177, 187, 206–207, 208–208

Military Units – Types

- Infantry
- Cavalry
- Armored
- Airborne
- Parachute
- Artillery

Military Movements

- Attack
- Retreat
- Aircraft
- Explosion
- Airfield

Military Units – Size

- XXXXX Army Group
- XXXX Army
- XXX Corps
- XX Division
- X Brigade
- III Regiment
- II Battalion
- I Company

INDEX

A
Abbas I, Safavid Shah of Persia 139
Abbasid Caliphate 134
Abraham, Prophet 80
Abarshahr 72
Abd al-Aziz bin Saud 142
Abd al-Hamid II, Ottoman Sultan 152
Abdul-Illah, Emir of Iraq 174
Aboukir Bay, Battle of 148
Aboukir (town), Battle of 149
Abu Bakr, Caliph 112, 126
Achaeans (Ahhiyawa), people 32
Achish, King of Gath 86
Acre 31, 124
Actium, Battle of 57
Adad-nirari, King of Assyria 43
Adasi, King of Assyria 43
Adiabene 66, 72
Aelia Capitolina 64, 70
Ahab, King 94
Ahhiyawa 16,
Ahmed Urabi, (Arabi Pasha) Khedive 152
Ahmose I, Pharoah 34
Ahaz, King of Judah 96
Akiba ben Joseph, Rabbi 70
Akkad 24
Akkadian Empire 25
  fall of 42
Alexander Eschate (Khojend) 54
Alexander the Great (Alexander of Macedon) 18, 52, 56, 79
Alexandria 74, 110, 149
  Anglo-French attack 152
  British landing 152
Aldhemar, Bishop 119
Ali, Muhammad, Governor of Egypt 150, 151
'Ali, Muhammad, Ottoman commander (later Viceroy) 149
al-Jazeera, TV news channel 210
Aliyah (ascent) 180
Allenby, Sir Edmund, British General 17, 158, 166
Al-Mas'udi, historian 134
Alp-Arslan, Saljuq leader 114, 118
Amalekites, people 84
Amarna Letters 34, 36
Amenhotep IV, Pharoah 34
Ammon 84
Amon, temple of 90
Amorites 25, 28
Anatolia 25
An-Nasr, Caliph 115
Anshan 40
Antigomus I, Diadochi ruler 56
  murder of 56
Antiochus IV, Seleucid King 98
Antiochus V, Seleucid King 98
Antonig Fortress, Jerusalem 102
ANZAC 156
Appollonius. Syrian Governor of Samaria 98
Aqaba, Gulf of 34, 88, 190
Arabia 108, 164
Arabian Peninsula 88
Arabistan 72
Aramaeans, people 43, 46, 87
Archelaus, tetrarch 102
Ardashir I, Sassanian King 72
Aria 72
Armenia 106, 128
Artabanus V, King of Parthia 67
Artasvades, King of Armenia 60
Arsuf, Battle of 124
Aruna Pass 38
Arvad 96
Arzawa 16, 32
Ashdod 16, 31, 90
Ashkelon 16
  capture of 46
Ashur 28, 29
Ashurbanipal, King of Assyria 45
Assur 42
Assyrian Empire 42
Assryia 96
Assyrians 29, 34
Asuristan 72
Athens 50
Australian, Light Horse, cavalry 159
Avarayr, Battle of 106, 107
Ayatollah Khomeini 194
Ayn Jalut, Battle of 129
Azariah, King of Judah 96
B
Baathist, political party 204,
Bactria 52,
Badakhshan 26
Baghavard, Battle of 139
Baghdad 108
Baha' Al-Din Yusuf ibn Shaddad, writer 124
Baibars, Mamluk leader 129, 130
Baldwin of Boulogne 119
Balfour Declaration 172
Baqaa Valley 198
Bar Lev Line 196
Basil II, Byzantine Emeror 114
Bedouin, tribesmen 148, 185
Beersheba 17, 159
Belaharusur (Belshazzar), ruler of Babylon 47
Ben-Gurion, David, Israeli leader 184
Ben-hadad, King of Aram 92
Benjamins, tribe 82
Bethlehem 71
Bilu Movement 155
Bithynia 58
Blue Nile, river 15
Bohemond, Prince of Antioch 119
Book of Joshua 80
Bouazizi, Muhamed, street seller 210
Bush, George H., US President 206, 208
Byblos 31, 45, 96
C
Cairo 148, 149
Caligula, Roman Emperor 102
Cambyses, King of Persia 48
Canaan 26, 84
  invasion of 80
Canaanites, people 16, 78
Cappadocia 43, 58
Carchemish 32,
Carchemish, Battle of 46
Carden, Sackville, British Admiral 156
Carmel, Mount 86
Carrhae, Battle of 60
Cataphracts, armored cavalry 112
Cave of Horrors 70
Cave of Letters 70
Caesar, Julius, Roman General 58
Cedars of Lebanon 26,
Chaldaeans, people 46
Charax 66, 74, 77
Choga Mami, irrigation 24
Christianity 106, 108
Christian, Monophysite 108
Chronicles of Ancient Kings 24
Churchill, Winston, First Lord of the Admiralty 156
  British Prime Minister 174
Cilicia 43, 89, 115
  French occupation 168
Circassians, people 120
Clearchos, Spartan General 50, 51
Cleopatra, Ruler of Egypt 57
Code of Ur-nammu 28
Commagene, people 43
Companion Cavalry, Alexander's 19
Conrad III, Holy Roman Emperor 119
Constaninople Agreement 162
  Allied military administration 168
  capture of 136, 156
Convention of London 151
Copts, Christian 201
Corupedium, Battle of 56
Crassus, Markus Licinius, Roman General and triumvir 60, 66
Cresson, Spring of 122
Ctesiphon, Parthian capital, 66
Cuneiform script, Akkadian 28
Cyaxares, King of Media 46
Cyrus II, King of Anshan 47
D
d'Aigalliers, Brueys, French Admiral 148,
Damascus 16, 17, 89, 92, 132
Dandanqan, Battle of 114
Dardanelles, naval attack on 156
Darius, King of Persia 48, 52
David, King of Israel 86
Dead Sea 15
de Bailleul, Roussel, Norman leader 116
Decapolis, the 100
Degania, Kibbutz 155

Deir Yassin, Arab village 184
Denyen (Danuna), people 36
Der'a, rail junction 164, 166
Der Judenstaat, plans for a Jewish state 154
Dhu Nuwas, Himyarite King 108
Diadochi 56
Diaspora, Jewish 180
Dilmun 77
Dion 100
Diwan, council of notables 149
Doukas, Andronikos, General 116
Dulles, John Foster, US Secretary of State 186,
E
Ebers Papyrus, medical manuscript 76
Edessa, Battle of, 68, 72
Edessa, Christian state 119
Edom 84, 90
Egypt 20, 36, 40, 89
British Protectorate of 162
Egyptian Expeditionary Force (EEF) 158, 164, 166
Egypt, Kingdom of 34
Ehud, Judge 82
Eibshutz, Yehonathan, Rabbi 154
Ekron 90
El Alamein, Battle of 176, 177
Elam 40
Elamite Empire 40
Enshakushanna of Uruk, King 24
Epic of Gilgamesh 20
Eqwesh (Achaeans), people 36
Eriba-Adad I, King of Assyria 43
Eridu 24
Erishum I, King of Assyria 43
Esarhaddon, King of Assyria 45
Eshnunna 28
Ethiopia 15, 89
Euphrates, river 16, 18, 20
Ezion-geber 89, 94
F
First Arab-Israeli War (War of Independence) 182
First Crusade 118
Fortifications, in Mesopotamia and the Levant 22
G
Gadera 100
Galillee 86
Gamal Abd al-Nasser, President of Egypt 186, 190
Gath 86
Gaugamela, Battle of 52
Gaza 16, 52, 90
Strip 188, 193, 199
Gemayel, Beshir, Lebanese President 198
Georgia 128
Gezer 90
Ghassanids, tribe 108
Ghaznavids, dynasty 114
Ghengis Khan 128
Gideon, of Manasseh 82
Gilboa, Mount 86
Gilgal 84
Girsu 24
Golan Heights 190, 193
Golden Horde, Mongol tribes 128
Goliath, warrior 86
Gorgan 72
Gorgias, Seleucid General 98
Granicus, Battle of 52
Gregory VIII, Pope 123
Guaeus Pompeius Magnus (*also see* Pompey the Great) 58
Gulf War, Operation Desert Storm 206
Gutians, tribe 27
H
Hadhramaut 88
Hadrian, Roman Emperor 66
Haganah, Jewish Paramilitary Organization 172, 180, 182, 183, 184
Haifa 149
Hamath 45, 46, 89, 94
Hamilton, Sir Ian, British General 156
Hammurabi, King 28, 43
Hammurabi, the Stele of 40
Hanging Gardens of Babylon 46
Harappan Civilization 26
Hashemite Sharifs of Mecca 142
Hatshepsut, Queen of Egypt 34
Hattusas, Hittite capital 30, 32
Hattusili, Hittite King 31
Hazor 16, 80, 90, 92, 96
Hebrews, tribe 16, 78, 80, 82
elders 84
Hebrew University 155
Hejaz 150
railway 164, 166
Heliopolis, Battle of 110
Hellespont, Bridge of Boats 49, 52,
Heraclius, Byzantine Emperor 112
Herodium 70
Herod I, the Great 79, 102
Herod Antipas, tetrarch 102
Herodium, fortress 102
Herod's Palace 64, 102
Hezbollah, Shia movement 198, 202
Hindu Kush 52, 72
Hippos 100
Hiram, King of Tyre 87, 88
Hirsch, Rafael, Rabbi 154
Hittite Empire 30, 36, 78
Hittites 27, 34
Hogarth Message 162
Holy Lance, discovery of 119
Hoplites, Greek soldiers 50
Hormizdagan, Battle of 67
Horns of Hattin, Battle of 122, 123
Hospitaller Knights 122
crossbowmen 124
Hosni Mubarak, Egyptian President 210
Hulla Valley 192
Hurrians 27, 31
Husein, King of Jordan 186
Hyksos 34
Hyrcania 66
Hyrcanus, John 100
I
Ibadism 127
Ibn Battuta, Arab geographer 135
Ibn Muljam, Phariji leader 127
IDF 198, 199
Ikhwan (Bretheren) 142
Imbala, Battle of 147
Iran-Iraq War 204
Irgun 184
Irgun Zvi Leumi 180
Irrigation, systems of 20, 24
Isfahan, punishment of 132
Isin 28
Islam 126
Islam, spread of 110
Israeli Defence Forces (IDF) 184, 185
Issus, Battle of 52
J
Jaffa 124
Janneus, Alexander 100
Jaxartes, river 54
Jereboam, King of Israel 90, 94
Jericho 20
Jerusalem 17, 46, 58, 79, 80, 90, 98, 119, 120, 124, 184
Crusader Kingdom of 119, 120
restored 102
siege of 64
Jewish Revolt, First 62
Jewish Revolt, Second (Bar Kokhba Revolt) 70
Jews, Hellenized 98
Jezebel, Ahab's wife 92
Jezreel Valley 89, 90
Joash, King of Judah 94
John of Gischala 64
Jordan Valley 20
Jospehus, Jewish historian 64
Judah 98
Judaism 108
Judges, Biblical 82
K
Kadesh, Battle of 32, 34, 39
Kadesh, King of 38
Kafr-el-Dawwar, Battle of 152
Kaleb, King of Axum 108
Kandahar, Siege of 139
Kara Mustafa, Ottoman Grand Vizier 140
President of Turkish Republic 170
Karmak 90
Kashka, tribe 32
Kazallu 25
Kemal, Mustafa, Ottoman General 156
President of Turkish Republic 170
Kerma 40
Khalid ibn al-Walid, General 112, 113
Kharg Island 205
Kharijis, Seceders 127
Khazars, people 72
Khrushchev, Nikita, Soviet leader 189
Khuzistan 72, 204
King David Hotel, bombing of 180
King's Highway 17
Kipchaks, tribesmen 120

Kish 24
Kissinger, Henry Alfred, US Secretary of State 194
Kitos War 64
Knights Templar 120, 122
Konya 114
Kôse Dagh, Battle of 128
Kosovo, Battle of 136
Kudurmabuk, King of Elam 28
Kunduzche, Battle of 132
Kushans, people 72
Kushan Empire 77
Kushanshahr 72
Kush, Kingdom of 15, 40
Kut, surrender at 160
Kutuz, Mamluk Sultan 128
Kuwait 206, 208
L
Labarna, Hittite King 31
Lachish 80
siege of, 701 BCE 19
Lade, Battle of 49
Lagash 24
Lakhmids, tribe 108
Lamentations over the Destruction of Ur 40
Larsa 28
Lawrence, T. E., British Intelligence officer 164
Lehi (stern gang) 180
Libu, people 34, 36
Lipit-Ishtar, King of Isin 28,
Louis VII, King of France 119
Louis IX, King of France 119
Lugal-Anne-Mundu of Adab, King 24
Lukka 16, 36
Lukka, mercentaries 32
Lusignan, Guy, King of Jerusalem 122
Lysimachos, Diadochi ruler 56
M
Maccabean Revolt 79, 98
Maccabee, Jonathan 98
Maccabee, Simon 100
Magan (Oman) 25
Magnesia, Battle of 57
Mahdi, the expected savior 153
Maishan 72
Makran 72
Malik-Shah, Saljuq leader 114
Mamluks 120, 129, 130, 146
cavalry 148
Manishtushu, King 26
Manzikert, Battle of 116
Marathon, Battle of, 19, 49
Mari, Kingdom of 28, 43
Mark Antony, Roman Governor 57
Maronite, Christians 198
Masada 62, 63, 102
Mecca 110, 126
Medina 108, 110
surrender of 164
Medmet Habu 36
Megiddo 90, 96
Megiddo, Battle of 38, 164
Megiddo Pass 89
Mehmet II, Ottoman Sultan 136
Memphis 15
Merenpah, Pharoah 36
Meroë 40
Merv 72
Meshwesh, people 34
Meskana 122
Mesopotamia 16, 20, 22, 24, 26, 88
Miltiades, Athenian General 49
Military service 24
Mitanni 34
destruction of 43
Mitanni, Kingdom of 32
Mizpah 98
Moab 84
Moabites, people 46
Mohacs, Battle of 136
Mohammed VI, Ottoman Sultan 140
Mongols 128, 129
Morsi, Mohamed 210
Mosul, seized 160, 162
Mount Hermon 17
Mount Tabor, Battle of 149
Muawiya, first Umayyad Caliph 127
Muhammad VI, Ottoman Sultan 168
Muhammad, Prophet 110
Muhammad, 'Seal' of the Prophets 126
Murad, Ottoman Sultan 136
Mursilis I, Hittite King 31
Muslim Brotherhood 182, 201, 202, 210
Muwatallis, Hittite King 32
Myonnesus, Battle of 57
N
Nabataea 108
Nabonidus, King of Babylon 46
Nabopolassar, King of Babylon 46
Nadab, King of northern Israel 92
Nahash, Ammonite leader 84
Nahrawan, Battle of 127
Napata 34, 40
Napoleon Bonaparte, General 146, 147, 149
Naram-Sin, King 26
Navarino, Battle of 150
Nazareth, massacre of garrison 122
Nebuchadnezzer I, King of Babylon 40, 46
Nebuchadnezzer II, King of Babylon 46
Necho II, Pharoah 46
Negev 90
Nelson, Horatio, British Admiral 148
Nero, Emperor of Rome 62
Nicanor, Seleucid General 98
Nile, river 15, 18, 20, 34
Nile Valley 22
Nineveh 43, 46
Nippur 24
North Atlantic Treaty Organization (NATO) 210
Northern Arab Army (NAA) 164
Nubia 34
Nvarsak, Treaty of 107
O
OAPEC 194
October War 196
Oghuz Turkmen, people 114
Oil Production, export 194
Oman 72
Omdurman, Battle of 153
Omri, King 92
Operation Gazelle 197
Operation Kadesh 188
Operation Muskateer 188
Ophir 88
Opis, Battle of 47
Orkhan, Ottoman Sultan 136
Ormuz 77
Orodes II, King of Parthia 60
Orodes III, King of Parthia 66
Ottoman Empire 156, 160
growth of 136
P
Palestine 15, 16, 154
in rebellion 34
Jews arriving into 155
Palestinian Liberation Organization (PLO) 193, 198
Palmyra 68, 74
Palmyrene Empire 72
Parthians, people 66
Patishkhwagar 72
Peace of Apameia 57
Peace of God 118
Peel Commission 172
Peleset, people 36
Pella 100
Pergamon 58
Periplus Malis Erethryaei, navigational manual 77
Peroz I, Shah 107
Persian Empire 48, 138
Petra 108
Phalangist Militia, Christian 198
Phalanx, Infantry formation 18, 52
Phebes 15
Phoenicians, people 88
Philadelphia 100
Philistia 84, 86, 90
Phillistines, people 16, 78, 82, 86
Philip I, tetrarch 102
Philip II, of Macedon 52
Phoenicia 32
Phraates III, King of Parthia 66
Phrygians, people 32
Pianky (Piy), Pharoah 40
Picot, François Georges, French Government official 162
Pilgrimages, Christian 118
Piy, Pharoah 45
Pompey the Great 58
Pontus 58
Porus, Kingdom of 52
Psammuthis, Pharoah 40
Ptolemy, Diadochi ruler 56
Ptolemy Keraunos, King of Macedonia 56
Ptolemy, Seleucid General 98
Puabi, Queen, death of 21

Punt, land of 17, 31
Pusarma, Hittite King 31
Q
Qarqur, Battle of 92, 96
Queen of Sheba 88
Quintus Tineius Rufus, Roman Governor 70
R
Ramesses II, Pharaoh 19, 32, 34, 39, 76
Ramesses III, Pharaoh 34, 36, 37
Rashid al-Kilani, Iraqi General 174
Raynald of Châtillon, Lord of Oultrejordan 120, 122
Reza Pahlavi, Shah of Persia 175
Rezon, King of Damascus 89
Richard I, King of England 119, 120, 124
Rim-sin, King of Larsa 28
Rimush, son of Sargon the Great 26
Riyadh 142
Robert, Duke of Normandy 118
Romani, Battle of 158
Romanos IV, Byzantine Emperor 116
Russo-Turkish War 140
S
Saddam Hussein 194, 204, 205, 206, 209
Saddle of Benjamin 84
Safavid Dynasty, of Persia 138
Sahara Desert 15
Sakarya, Battle of 170
Saladin (Salah al-din Yusuf ibn Ayub) 119, 123, 120, 122, 124
Saljuq Empire 120
Saljuq Turks 114, 116
SAM (surface-to-air) missile system 196
Samaria 100, 102
Samuel, Prophet 84
Sargon the Great 24, 25, 26
Sassanian Empire 72, 73
Saul, King of Israel 84
Scud Missiles 208
Scythians, people 55
Sea of Marmara 156
Sea Peoples 16, 36
Second Crusade 119
Second Gulf War 208
Seitan 72
Seleucid Empire 56, 57
Seleukos, Diadochi ruler 56
Selim III, Ottoman Sultan 147
Septimus Odaenathus, King of Palmyra 75
Septimus Severus, Roman Emperor 66, 68
Seron, Governor of Coele-Syria 98
Seti I, Pharoah 34
Shalamaneser I, King of Assyria 43
Shalamaneser III, King of Assyria 92
Shalamaneser V, King of Assyria 45, 96
Shapur I, Sassanid King 68
Shapur III, Sassanid King 68
Sharif Hussein, Hashemite Arab leader 164
Sharm-el-Sheikh 188
Sharon, Ariel, Israeli Minister of Defense 198
Sharqat, Battle of 160
Sheba, Queen of 88
Shechem 90
Sherden, mercentaries 32, 36
Shoshenk I (Shishak I), Pharoah 78, 90
Sidon 31, 96
Siege craft 19
Silk Road 76, 134
Simon bar Giora 64
Simeon ben Gamaliel III, Rabbi 71
Sinai Desert 158 , 188, 193
Six-Day War 190
Smyrna 168
Sofala 88
Sogdiana 52, 57
Solomon, King 88
Solomon's fleet 88
  temple 90
Somalia 89
Soviet Union 188
Sparta 50
State of Israel, Declaration of 182
Subartu 42
Sudan 40
  incorporated in Egypt 150
Suez Canal 152, 153
  attack on 158
  Gulf of 197
Sultanate of Rûm 115, 130
Sumuabum, Amonite King 28
Suppiliuma II, Hittite King 19
Suppilulinmas I, Hittite King 32
Susa 40
Sûleymen I, Ottoman Sultan 136
Sykes-Picot Agreement 162, 163
Sykes, Sir Mark, British Government offical 162
Syria 16
  under 'Vichy' control 174
Syria Palaestina (Judaea) 64
T
Tafukah, Battle of 164
Takash, Shah of Khwarezm Empire 115
Talas, Battle of 134
Tale of Wen-amon 36
Tamerlane 132
Tang Dynasty, of China 134
Tarchaneiotes, Joseph, General 116
Taurus Mountains 26
Tel Aviv, foundation of 155
Teresh 36
Terrot tactics, deployment of 18
The Jewish War 62
Theodosius I, Emperor 68
Third Crusade 119, 123, 124
Thutmose I, Pharoah 34
Thutmose III, Pharoah 34, 38
Tiglath-Pileser III, King of Assyria 40, 44, 45, 96
Tigris, river 18, 20
Timur the Lame (Tamerlane) 132
Tiridates III, King of Armenia 102
Tirzah 92
Titus Flavius, Roman General 64
Tjekker, people 36
Toran, Plain of 122
Trajan, Roman Emperor 66, 70, 79
Treaty of Lausanne 170
Treaty of Sèvres 168
Treaty of St. Jean de Mauríenne 162
Tripoli, Crusader country of 119
Trojan War 32
Truce of God 118
Tudiya, King of Assyria 42
Tudkhaliyas I, Hittite King 31
Turkish Nationalists 170
Turkey, Republic of 163
Turan 72
Tyre 31, 45, 46, 52, 96, 149
U
Ugarit 31
Umar, Caliph 110, 112
United Nations (UN) 188, 190, 205, 206, 208
  Interim Force in Lebanon (UNIFIL) 198
Ur 24, 27, 28
Urban II, Pope 118
Urban settlements, early 20
Uruk 24, 46
Ushpia, King of Assyria 42
Uzbes, tribe 139
Uzziah, King of Judah 94
V
Varangian Guard 116
Vespasian, Roman General 62
  Emperor of Rome 63
Vologases IV 66
W
Wadi al-Khanzander, Battle of 130
Wahabi, creed 142
Warsaw Pact 188
Way of the Sea 90
Weapons of Mass Destruction (WMDs) 208
West Bank 192, 193
White Huns, tribe 72
Wilderness of Judah 92
Wilderness of Ziph 86
Wolsey, Garnet, British General 152
Woodhead Commission 172
X
Xerxes, King of Persia 49
Xois, Battle of 36
Y
Yarmuk, Battle of 112, 113
Yasser Arafat 198
Yazdegerd III, Sassanian King 72
Yemen 88
Yenbu, port 164
Yishuv, Jewish population in Palestine 172
Z
Zagros Mountains 16, 24, 43, 72
Zengi, Saljuq Governor 120
Zealots, Jewish 64
Zenobia, Queen of Palmyra 75
Zenophon 51
Zimri, chariot commander 92
Zionist, aspriations 154
Zobah 84, 87
Zoroastrisnism 106, 108

ACKNOWLEDGEMENTS

The publishers would like to thank the following picture libraries for their kind permission to use their pictures and illustrations:

RLPPMA Ltd 24, 34, 36, 46, 48, 66, 84, 90, 148, 150
Getty Archive 26, 102, 114, 186
Metropolitan Museum of Art 30
British Museum 43, 45, 96
Peter Newark's Historical Pictures 51, 52
University of Texas Libraries 58
Fabien Dany 72
Noura Raslan 112
Historial de Vendée 124
Bibliothèque Nationale Paris 128
Kunsthistorisches Museum, Vienna 136
Library of Congress 140, 152, 170, 172
Imperial War Museum, London 159, 166
Daily Telegraph 164
Public Domain 180, 184
US Department of Defense 206

For Red Lion Media:
Illustration: Alexander Swanston
Cartography: Jeanne Radford, Alexander Swanston and Malcolm Swanston
Typesetting: Jeanne Radford
Picture Research: Malcolm Swanston
Editor: Elizabeth Wyse
Additional contribution by Professor Ben Fortna